PUBLIC ADMINISTRATION IN ACTION

READINGS, PROFILES, AND CASES

Brooks/Cole Series in Public Administration

PUBLIC ADMINISTRATION IN ACTION

READINGS, PROFILES, AND CASES

Robert B. Denhardt
University of Central Florida

Barry R. Hammond
Slippery Rock University

BROOKS/COLE PUBLISHING COMPANY
PACIFIC GROVE, CALIFORNIA

Brooks/Cole Publishing Company
A Division of Wadsworth, Inc.

Printed in the United States of America

10   9   8   7   6   5   4   3   2   1

Library of Congress Cataloging-in-Publication Data

Public administration in action : readings, profiles, and cases /
  Robert B. Denhardt, Barry R. Hammond.
      p.   cm.
    Includes bibliographical references and index.
    ISBN 0-534-15960-5
    1. Public administration.   2. Public administration—Case studies.
  I. Denhardt, Robert B.   II. Hammond, Barry R.
  JF1351.P8175 1991
  350—dc20   91-25592
                                                     CIP

Sponsoring Editor: *Cynthia C. Stormer*
Editorial Associate: *Cathleen S. Collins*
Production Editor: *Penelope Sky*
Manuscript Editor: *Barbara Kimmel*
Permissions Editor: *Marie DuBois*
Interior and Cover Design: *Lisa Berman*
Cover Photo: *Howard Grey, Tony Stone Worldwide*
Art Coordinator: *Cloyce J. Wall*
Interior Illustration: *Cloyce J. Wall*
Typesetting: *ExecuStaff*
Cover Printing: *Phoenix Color Corporation*
Printing and Binding: *Arcata Graphics*
Credits continue on page 411.

Robert B. Denhardt is chair of the Department of Public Administration at the University of Central Florida, a recent past president of the American Society for Public Administration, and founder of ASPA's National Campaign for Public Service. Dr. Denhardt is the author of several books, including *Public Administration: An Action Orientation* and *Theories of Public Organization*, (both published by Brooks/Cole), and more than fifty articles in professional journals.

Barry R. Hammond is associate professor and chair of the Public Administration Department at Slippery Rock University, where he has received the President's Award for Outstanding Service. He is editor of *Dialogue*, the journal of the PA Theory Network. Dr. Hammond has served on a variety of committees for the American Society for Public Administration, and he is the principal representative for Slippery Rock to the National Association of Schools of Public Affairs and Administration.

The field of public administration offers many exciting opportunities to students considering careers in government: working on behalf of major social programs or those that benefit the environment; the chance to be involved in projects in the forefront of technology; the prospect of making a difference in the way important services are delivered to the public—all of these and many other possibilities have great appeal. But the study of public administration is not just for those who are considering careers in public organizations. Indeed, because so many areas of life are affected by government activity it is imperative that businesspeople and private citizens understand the operations of public agencies and how those operations can be affected.

Public administration requires an ability to *act*, effectively and responsibly, in real-world situations. This capacity is central to *Public Administration in Action*. We have brought together some of the most important contemporary thinking about public administration, and we have provided material that will help readers feel what it is actually like to work in public organizations. Intellectual *and* experiential understanding are an essential prelude to action.

Features
Each chapter includes both major conceptual articles that offer an overview of current thinking in the field, and shorter, action-oriented readings that provide topical commentaries, describe recent developments in the practice of public administration, or contain specific advice for future administrators. These articles are contemporary classics in the field.

The readings in each chapter are followed by a profile of an actual public manager, showing how the many different aspects of public administration come together in real life. Each chapter concludes with action-oriented cases (written specifically for this book) that illustrate the consequences of particular approaches to work in public organizations. The cases pose action choices: not merely, "What do you think about this case?" but rather, "What would you do in this situation?" They can be used as the basis for discussion, and for role-playing activities that let readers test and refine their administrative skills. A careful integration of readings, profiles, and cases will produce a more comprehensive view of the field than could otherwise be achieved.

We have selected materials that reveal the broad diversity of public administration. For example, some readings are about federal agencies, and others focus on state or local government or nonprofit organizations. Similarly, the profiles and cases are about administrators at all levels of government in a variety of fields. Everything we have included is relevant to the real-world experience of public administrators, and should inspire sound and informed action.

Acknowledgments

We have been aided by many people in our work on this project. It would have been impossible to produce the book without the patience and forebearance of our wives, Kathy and Deborah. Fortunately, both are also faculty members, and they understand the moods and frustrations that are part of the writing process. Michael Denhardt provided valuable help as a special research assistant.

Our students during the past twenty years have contributed significantly by sharpening our ability to make connections between the ideas of public administration and the actions of daily public service. Their questions and responses have made us bring the world of academic analysis closer to the world of practical concerns. Our graduate students in particular, many of whom are now in mid-career, always remind us that there is no index or table of contents in the real world.

We also acknowledge our reviewers: Betty Hecker, Boise State University; Landis Jones, University of Louisville; Steven Koven, Iowa State University; and Michael Vasu, North Carolina State University.

Robert B. Denhardt
Barry R. Hammond

C O N T E N T S

CHAPTER 1
THE FIELD OF PUBLIC ADMINISTRATION   1

CHAPTER 2
PUBLIC ADMINISTRATORS IN
THE POLICY PROCESS   46

CHAPTER 5
BUDGETING AND FINANCIAL MANAGEMENT   206

CHAPTER 6
PERSONNEL AND HUMAN RESOURCES   257

READINGS

PROFILE

CASES

CHAPTER 7
MANAGEMENT SKILLS FOR PUBLIC ADMINISTRATORS   308

READINGS

PROFILE

CASES

CHAPTER 8
PUBLIC ADMINISTRATION AND THE FUTURE   364

READINGS

PROFILE

CASES

PUBLIC ADMINISTRATION IN ACTION

READINGS, PROFILES, AND CASES

THE FIELD OF PUBLIC ADMINISTRATION

—

As someone interested in the public service, either as a possible career or just in terms of being able to influence public policy, you should recognize first the tremendous diversity of opportunities within the field of public administration. People in this field work at all levels of government—federal, state, and local—and in nonprofit organizations of all types. Some hold managerial positions in either line or staff agencies, whereas others are in analyst positions (policy analyst, budget analyst, and so on). The range of substantive areas in which public administrators work is incredible, spanning fields as diverse as forestry, transportation, and space exploration. In this section, we will examine the boundaries and characteristics of public administration, as well as some of the perspectives managers and analysts might bring to their work.

We can say generally that public administration is concerned with the management of public programs. As an administrator, you might find yourself working to establish or to carry out a particular public policy and, in doing so, you might well interact not only with citizens but with executive, legislative, and judicial officials at many different levels of government. In these interactions, you would need to be sensitive to some important values associated with democratic governance, values such as freedom, equality, and justice. You would certainly find yourself struggling with the values that guide the public service, values such as equity and accountability. And you would most certainly find yourself constantly searching for a better understanding of the public interest.

But beyond trying to sort out these many political considerations, you would find yourself enmeshed in a world characterized by managerial complexity. You would need to be able to bring your skills and abilities to bear on questions ranging from power and authority to communications and motivation to group dynamics and organizational change. You would need to know something about the tools and techniques available to modern managers, from budgeting and personnel management to strategic management and productivity improvement. And you would need the personal and interpersonal skills to make things happen in your organizations.

Throughout your work, you would need to balance the political and the managerial aspects of your work, abiding by democratic norms and values, while at the same time getting things done in a timely and expeditious fashion. You would find that public organizations sometimes have ambiguous service objectives, quite unlike the single "bottom line" you may encounter in business; you would also find that public policies are affected by many different people and groups and that there are many different decision points in the development and implementation of public policy; and you would find that you are working in an arena in which your actions will be highly visible and open to public scrutiny. Knowing something about the scope

1

and values that come into play in the conduct of public organizations will provide you with a context for successfully sorting through these difficult problems.

David H. Rosenbloom opens our discussion by pointing out three different approaches to expressing the role of the administrator—a managerial approach that emphasizes the efficient accomplishment of one's objectives through sound, "businesslike" management practices, a political approach that concerns itself more with issues of responsiveness and accountability, and a legal approach that emphasizes due process, the rights of citizens, and equity. In a sense, argues Rosenbloom, these three approaches reflect the separation of powers that is essential to American democracy and, consequently, all three must be a part of the administrator's self-understanding. As you read this article, try to think about how these three approaches affect the daily work of a public manager. When are they complementary and when are they in conflict?

In the next selection, Donald F. Kettl examines various recent approaches to understanding public organizations—the implementation approach, the public management approach, and the rationalist approach. Kettl argues that public administration in the future will be aided by the recognition of public agencies as political actors, alike in many respects, but also vastly different in others. Again, although this article is mostly directed to the study of public administration, think how the perspectives described here are reflected in practice. Also, be sure to apply the material near the end to an analysis of the work of administrators in different types of agencies. How is public administration different in different kinds of programs?

Robert B. Denhardt concludes this section by reviewing three central issues in public administration theory—the relationship between politics and administration, the interplay of bureaucracy and democracy, and several approaches to organization and management that have been used in the public sector. Throughout this discussion, there is the implication that public administration is different from business administration, primarily because public managers work in pursuit of the public interest. You should note the implications of this fact in terms of the way several important concerns in organization theory—from structure to behavior—are molded to meet the opportunities and constraints that the public sector presents. You might note also Denhardt's concluding comment, which suggests that in many ways the work of public managers provides an important model for managers elsewhere.

Our first profile features Stephen E. Reynolds, chief engineer for the State of New Mexico. Reynolds, as you will see, is nearing the end of a long career in the public service, a career that has seen him assume great importance in the "politics of water." The Reynolds profile is especially interesting as it describes Reynolds' role in developing public policy and explains something of his relationship with the New Mexico legislature. After reading the profile, you might try to analyze this article in light of the readings that precede it.

The cases in this chapter illustrate the complexity and uniqueness of public administration. In "The Death and Life of an Agency," you will explore the question of how the changing conditions in society can lead to modifications in an agency's mission, even before legislative action is taken. This will raise the troubling question of how far public administrators should go in devising new policies that may significantly change the agency's impact on its clientele. Finally, the case presents you with a positive explanation for the apparent deathlessness of public agencies. Too often the long life of public agencies is attributed to inertia rather than to a desire and capacity to change to serve new purposes.

The second case highlights the unique character of public management. " 'Don't Tell Them— Show Them' " illustrates two of the problems of transferring private management skills to the public or not-for-profit sector. One problem you will notice is the primary concentration on monetary concerns in the private sector. That concentration is often inappropriate in public-service organizations. A second problem is the difference in "ownership" perspectives in the nonprofit sector. Boards of directors in the nonprofit sector are more likely to represent a variety of stakeholders rather than shareowners, as is usually true in the private sector. The variety of stakeholders are often organizationally quite different. As a result, you will find they have distinct and sometimes divergent purposes for being involved in policy direction.

PUBLIC ADMINISTRATIVE THEORY AND THE SEPARATION OF POWERS

David H. Rosenbloom

. . . The contention of this essay is that the central problem of contemporary public administrative theory is that it is derived from three disparate approaches to the basic question of what public administration is. Each of these approaches has a respected intellectual tradition, emphasizes different values, promotes different types of organizational structure, and views individuals in markedly distinct terms. These approaches are conveniently labeled "managerial," "political," and "legal." They have influenced one another over the years, and at some points they overlap. Yet, their primary influence on public administration has been to pull it in three separate directions. Furthermore, these directions tend to follow the pattern of the separation of powers established by the Constitution. Consequently, it is unlikely that the three approaches can be synthesized without violating values deeply ingrained in the United States political culture.[1] . . .

THE MANAGERIAL APPROACH TO PUBLIC ADMINISTRATION

ORIGIN AND VALUES

In the United States the managerial approach to public administration grew largely out of the civil service reform movement of the late 19th century. In the reformers' words, "What civil service reform demand[ed], [was] that the business part of the government shall be carried on in a sound businesslike manner."[2] The idea of "businesslike" public administration was most self-consciously and influentially discussed by Woodrow Wilson in his essay on "The Study of Administration."[3] There, Wilson considered public administration to be "a field of business" and consequently largely a managerial endeavor. He also set forth the three core values of the managerial approach to public administration: "It is the object of administrative study to discover, first, what government can properly and successfully do, and, secondly, how it can do these proper things with the utmost possible efficiency and at the least possible cost either of money or of energy."[4] Thus, public administration was to be geared toward the maximization of effectiveness, efficiency, and economy.

The managerial approach was strengthened by Frederick Taylor and the scientific management movement.[5] Taylorism sought to enshrine the values of efficiency and economy in a world view that promised to achieve harmony and affluence among mankind. Later, Leonard White's influential *Introduction to the Study of Public Administration*[6] asserted that "the study of administration should start from the base of management rather than the foundation of law, and is, therefore, more absorbed in the affairs of the American Management Association than in the decisions of the courts." When the managerial approach to public administration was at the pinnacle of its influence in the 1930s, it was widely held, along with Luther Gulick, that "efficiency" was "axiom number one in the value scale of administration" and that politics could not enter "the structure of administration without producing inefficiency."[7]

The essence of the managerial approach's values was captured by Simmons and Dvorin in the following terms: "The 'goodness' or 'badness' of a particular organizational pattern was a mathematical relationship of 'inputs' to 'outputs.' Where the latter was maximized and the former minimized, a moral 'good' resulted. Virtue or 'goodness' was therefore equated with the relationship of these two factors, that is, 'efficiency,' or 'inefficiency.' Mathematics was transformed into ethics."[8]

ORGANIZATIONAL STRUCTURE

The managerial approach to public administration promotes organization essentially along the lines of Max Weber's ideal-type bureaucracy.[9] It stresses the importance of functional specialization for efficiency. Hierarchy is then relied upon for effective coordination.[10] Programs and functions are to be clearly assigned to organizational units. Overlaps are to be minimized. Positions are to be classified into a rational scheme and pay scales are to be systematically derived in the interests of economy and motivating employees to be efficient. Selection of public administrators is to be made strictly on the basis of merit. They are to be politically neutral in their competence. Relationships among public administrators and public agencies are to be formalized in writing and, in all events, the public's business is to be administered in a smooth, orderly fashion.[11]

VIEW OF THE INDIVIDUAL

The managerial approach to public administration promotes an impersonal view of individuals. This is true whether the individuals in question are the employees, clients, or the "victims"[12] of public administrative agencies. One need not go so far as Max Weber in considering "dehumanization" to be the "special virtue" of bureaucracy or to view the bureaucrat as a "cog" in an organizational machine over which he/she has virtually no control.[13] Yet there can be no doubt that a strong tendency of scientific management was to turn the individual worker into an appendage to a mechanized means of production. By 1920, this view of the employee was clearly embodied in the principles of position classification in the public sector: "The individual characteristics of an employee occupying a position should have no bearing on the classification of the position."[14] Indeed, the strong "position-orientation" of the managerial approach to public administration continues to diminish the importance of the individual employee to the overall organization.

Clients, too, have been "depersonalized" and turned into "cases" in an effort to promote the managerial values of efficiency, economy, and effectiveness. Ralph Hummel explains,

At the intake level of the bureaucracy, individual personalities are converted into cases. Only if a person can qualify as a case, is he or she allowed treatment by the bureaucracy. More accurately, a bureaucracy is never set up to treat or deal with persons: it "processes" only "cases."[15]

"Victims" may be depersonalized to such an extent that they are considered sub-human, especially where physical force or coercion is employed as in mental health facilities and police functions.[16]

The human relations approach to organization theory and some contemporary views argue that reliance on impersonality tends to be counterproductive because it generates "bureaupathologies."[17] Nevertheless, the managerial approach's impersonal view of individuals is deeply ingrained and considered essential to the maximization of efficiency, economy, and effectiveness.

THE POLITICAL APPROACH TO PUBLIC ADMINISTRATION

ORIGINS AND VALUES

The political approach to public administration was perhaps most forcefully and succinctly stated by Wallace Sayre:

Public administration is ultimately a problem in political theory: the fundamental problem in a democracy is responsibility to popular control; the responsibility and responsiveness of the administrative agencies and the bureaucracies to the elected officials (the chief executives, the legislators) is of central importance in a government based increasingly on the exercise of discretionary power by the agencies of administration.[18]

This approach grew out of the observation of some, such as Paul Appleby, that public administration during the New Deal and World War II was anything but devoid of politics.[19] Thus, unlike the origin of the managerial approach, which stressed what public administration ought to be, the political approach developed from an analysis of apparent empirical reality.

Once public administration is considered a political endeavor, emphasis is inevitably placed on a different set of values than those promoted by the managerial approach. "Efficiency," in particular, becomes highly suspect, as Justice Brandeis pointed out in dissent in *Myers v. United States* (1926):

The doctrine of the separation of powers was adopted by the Convention of 1787, not to promote efficiency but to preclude the exercise of arbitrary power. The purpose was, not to avoid friction, but, by means of the inevitable friction incident to the distribution of governmental powers among three departments, to save the people from autocracy.[20]

Rather, the political approach to public administration stresses the values of representativeness, political responsiveness, and accountability through elected officials to the citizenry. These are viewed as crucial to the maintenance of constitutional democracy, especially in view of the rise of the contemporary administrative state, which may be likened unto "bureaucratic government."[21]

One can find many examples of governmental reforms aimed at maximizing the political values of representativeness, responsiveness, and accountability within public administration. . . . The quest for responsiveness has also blended into attempts to promote the accountability of public administrators to political officials through a variety of measures including greater use of the General Accounting Office,[22] the creation of the federal Senior Executive Service, and structural changes such as the establishment of the Office of Management and Budget, the Office of Personnel Management, and the Congressional Budget Office. "Sunshine" provisions such as the Freedom of Information Act and "sunset" requirements are also examples of the attempt to promote political accountability. There is also a growing academic literature on the need to promote representativeness, responsiveness, and accountability in the modern administrative state.[23]

It is important to note that the values sought by the political approach to public administration are frequently in tension with those of the managerial approach. For instance, efficiency in the managerial sense is not necessarily served through sunshine regulations which can dissuade public administrators from taking some courses of action, though they may be the most efficient, and can divert time and resources from program implementation to the deliverance of information to outsiders. Consultation with advisory committees and "citizen participants" can be time consuming and costly. A socially representative public service may not be the most efficient one.[24] Nor is the intended shuffling of Senior Executive Servants from agency

to agency likely to enhance efficiency in the managerial sense. Rather it is thought that by providing this cadre of top public administrators a wider variety of experience, they may come to define the public interest in more comprehensive terms and therefore become more responsive to the nation's overall political interests. Moreover, while various budgeting strategies and sunset provisions can promote economy in one sense, the amount of paperwork they generate and the extent to which they may require agencies to justify and argue on behalf of their programs and expenditures can become quite costly. Indeed, a quarter century ago, Marver Bernstein reported that "many officials complain that they must spend so much time preparing for appearing at Congressional hearings and in presenting their programs before the Bureau of the Budget and other bodies that it often leaves little time for directing the operations of their agencies."[25] Managerial effectiveness is difficult to gauge, of course, but federal managers have long complained that their effectiveness is hampered by the large congressional role in public administration and the need to consult continually with a variety of parties having a legitimate concern with their agencies' operations.[26]

ORGANIZATIONAL STRUCTURE

Public administration organized around the political values of representativeness, responsiveness, and accountability also tends to be at odds with the managerial approach to organization. Rather than emphasizing clear lines of functional specialization, hierarchy, unity, and recruitment based on politically neutral administrative competence, the political approach stresses the extent and advantages of political pluralism within public administration. Thus, Harold Seidman argues that, "Executive branch structure is in fact a microcosm of our society. Inevitably it reflects the values, conflicts, and competing forces to be found in a pluralistic society. The ideal of a neatly symmetrical, frictionless organization structure is a dangerous illusion."[27] Norton Long makes a similar point: "Agencies and bureaus more or less perforce are in the business of building, maintaining, and increasing their political support. They lead and in large part are led by the diverse groups whose influence sustains them. Frequently they lead and are themselves led in conflicting directions."[28] Roger Davidson finds a political virtue where those imbued with the managerial approach might see disorder: "In many respects, the civil service represents the American people more comprehensively than does Congress."[29]

The basic concept behind pluralism within public administration is that since the administrative branch is a policy-making center of government, it must be structured to enable faction to counteract faction by providing political representation to a comprehensive variety of the organized political, economic, and social interests that are found in the society at large. To the extent that the political approach's organizational scheme is achieved, the structure comes to resemble a political party platform that promises something to almost everyone without establishing clear priorities for resolving conflicts among them. Agency becomes adversary of agency and the resolution of conflict is shifted to the legislature, the office of the chief executive, interagency committees, or the courts. Moreover, the number of bureaus and agencies tends to grow over time, partly in response to the political demands of organized interests for representation. This approach to administrative organization has been widely denounced as making government "unmanageable," "costly," and "inefficient,"[30] but, as Seidman argues, it persists because administrative organization is frequently viewed as a political question that heavily emphasizes political values.

VIEW OF THE INDIVIDUAL

The political approach to public administration tends to view the individual as part of an aggregate group. It does not depersonalize the individual by turning him or her into a "case," as does the managerial approach, but rather identifies the individual's interests as being similar or identical to those of others considered to be within the same group or category. For example, affirmative action within the government service is aimed at specific social groups such as blacks and women without inquiry as to the particular circumstances of any individual member of these broad and diverse groups. Similarly, farmers growing the same crops and/or located in the same national geopolitical subdivisions are considered alike, despite individual differences among them. The same is true in any number of areas of public administration where public policies dealing with people are implemented. This is a tendency, of course, that fits the political culture well—politicians tend to think in terms of groups, e.g., the "black" vote, the "farm" vote, labor, and so forth. Indeed, this approach is so strong that some, such as David Truman,[31] consider it the main feature of government in the United States. Theodore Lowi argues that a central tenent of the contemporary American "public philosophy" is that "organized interests are homogeneous and easy to define, sometimes monolithic. Any 'duly elected' spokesman for any interest is taken as speaking in close approximation for each and every member."[32] In this view of the individual, then, personality exists, but it is conceptualized in collective terms.

THE LEGAL APPROACH TO PUBLIC ADMINISTRATION

ORIGIN AND VALUES

In the United States, the legal approach to public administration has historically been eclipsed by the other approaches, especially the managerial. Nevertheless, it has a venerable tradition and has recently emerged as a full-fledged vehicle for defining public administration. It is derived primarily from three inter-related sources. First is administrative law. As early as 1905, Frank Goodnow, a leading contributor to the development of public administrative theory generally, published a book entitled *The Principles of the Administrative Law of the United States*.[33] There he defined administrative law as "that part of the law which fixes the organization and determines the competence of the authorities which execute the law, and indicates to the individual remedies for the violation of his rights."[34] Others have found this broad conception of administrative law adequate for defining much of the work of public administrators and the nature of public agencies. For instance, Marshall Dimock writes:

To the public administrator, law is something very positive and concrete. It is his authority. The term he customarily uses to describe it is "my mandate." It is "his" law, something he feels a proprietary interest in. It does three things: tells him what the legislature expects him to accomplish, fixes limits to his authority, and sets forth the substantive and procedural rights of the individual and group. Having a positive view of his mandate, the administrator considers himself both an interpreter and a builder. He is a builder because every time he applies old law to new situations he builds the law. Therefore law, like administration, is government in action.[35]

Taking a related view, Kenneth Davis argues that public agencies are best defined in terms of law: "An administrative agency is a governmental authority, other than a court and other than a legislative body, which affects the rights of private parties through either adjudication, rule-making, investigating, prosecuting, negotiating, settling, or informally acting."[36]

A second source of the legal approach has been the movement toward the "judicialization"[37] of public administration. Judicialization falls within the purview of Goodnow's definition of administrative law, but tends to concentrate heavily upon the establishment of procedures designed to safeguard individual rights. . . . Thus, judicialization brings not only law but legal procedure as well to bear upon administrative decision making. Agencies begin to function more like courts and consequently legal values come to play a greater role in their activities.

Constitutional law provides a third source of the contemporary legal approach to public administration. Since the 1950s, the federal judiciary has virtually redefined the procedural, equal protection, and substantive rights and liberties of the citizenry *vis-à-vis* public administrators.[38] The old distinction between rights and privileges, which had largely made the Constitution irrelevant to individuals' claims with regard to the receipt of governmental benefits, met its demise. Concomitantly, there was a vast expansion in the requirement that public administrators afford constitutional procedural due process to the individuals upon whom they specifically acted. A new stringency was read into the Eighth Amendment's prohibition of cruel and unusual punishment. Wholly new rights, such as the right to treatment and habilitation, were created, if not fully ratified by the Supreme Court, for those confined to

public mental health facilities. The right to equal protection was vastly strengthened and applied in a variety of administrative matters ranging from public personnel merit examinations to the operation of public schools and prisons. . . .

The legal approach to public administration embodies three central values. One is procedural due process. It has long been recognized that this value cannot be confined to any single set of requirements or standards.[39] Rather, the term stands for the value of fundamental fairness and is viewed as requiring procedures designed to protect individuals from malicious, arbitrary, capricious, or unconstitutional harm at the hands of the government. A second value concerns individual substantive rights as embodied in evolving interpretations of the Bill of Rights and the Fourteenth Amendment. In general, the judiciary views the maximization of individual rights and liberties as a positive good and necessary feature of the United States political system. Breaches of these rights may be tolerated by the courts when, on balance, some essential governmental function requires their abridgment. However, the usual presumption is against the government in such circumstances and, consequently, judicial doctrines place a heavy burden on official administrative action that infringes upon the substantive constitutional rights of individuals.[40] Third, the judiciary values equity, a concept that like due process is subject to varying interpretation. However, in terms of public administration in general, equity stands for the value of fairness in the result of conflicts between private parties and the government. It militates against arbitrary or invidious treatment of individuals, encompasses much of the constitutional requirement of equal protection, and enables the courts to fashion relief for individuals whose constitutional rights have been violated by administrative action.

One of the major features of the values of the legal approach to public administration is the downgrading of the cost/benefit reasoning associated with the managerial approach. The judiciary is not oblivious to the costs of its decisions, but its central focus tends to be on the nature of the individual's rights, rather than on the costs to society of securing those rights. This is especially evident in cases involving the reform of public institutions. As one court said, "inadequate resources can never be an adequate justification for the state's depriving any person of his constitutional rights."[41]

ORGANIZATIONAL STRUCTURE

As suggested in the discussion of judicialization, the preferred structure of the legal approach to public administration is one that will maximize the use of adversary procedure. The full-fledged judicial trial is the archetypical model of this structure. In terms of public administration, however, it is generally modified to allow greater flexibility in the discovery of facts. Juries are not used and hearing examiners often play a more active role in bringing out relevant information. Although this structure is often associated with regulatory commissions, its general presence within public administration should not be underestimated. For example, it is heavily relied upon in contemporary public personnel management, especially in the areas of adverse actions, equal employment opportunity, and labor relations.[42] It is also common in instances where governmental benefits, such as welfare or public school education, are being withheld or withdrawn from individuals.[43] The precise structure varies from context to context, but the common element running through it is the independence and impartiality of the hearing examiner.[43] . . . To a considerable extent, therefore, this model is at odds with all the values embodied in the other two approaches: It militates against efficiency, economy, managerial effectiveness, representativeness, responsiveness, and political accountability. It is intended, rather, to afford maximum protection of the rights of private parties against illegal, unconstitutional, or invidious administrative action.

VIEW OF THE INDIVIDUAL

The legal approach's emphasis on procedural due process, substantive rights, and equity leads it to consider the individual as a unique person in a unique set of circumstances. The notion that every person is entitled to a "day in court" is appropriate here. The adversary procedure is designed to enable an individual to explain his or her unique and particular circumstances, thinking, motivations, and so forth to the governmental decision maker. Moreover, a decision may turn precisely upon such considerations, which become part of the "merits" of the case. There are some outstanding examples of this in the realm of public administration. For instance, in *Cleveland Board of Education v. LaFleur* (1974)[44] the Supreme Court ruled that before a mandatory maternity leave could be imposed upon a pregnant public school teacher, she was entitled to an individualized medical determination of her fitness to continue on the job. In *Wyatt v. Stickney* (1971),[45] a federal district court required that an individual treatment plan be developed for each person involuntarily confined to Alabama's public mental health facilities. Emphasis on the individual *qua* individual does not, of course, preclude the aggregation of individuals into broader groups, as in the case of class action suits. However, while such a suit may be desirable to obtain widespread change, it does not diminish the legal approach's concern with the rights of specific individuals.

THE SEPARATION OF POWERS

Reflection upon these opposing approaches to public administration suggests that they cannot be synthesized for the simple reason that they are an integral part of a political culture that emphasizes the separation of powers rather than integrated political action. Thus, it is largely true that each of these approaches is associated with the values embodied in a different branch of government. The managerial approach is most closely associated with the executive. The presidency has taken on a vast number of roles and functions, but a major feature of its constitutional power is to make sure that the laws are faithfully executed. This is largely the role of implementation, which is the focus of the managerial approach's definition of public administration. The political approach, by contrast, is more closely associated with legislative concerns. It views public administrators as supplementary law makers and policy makers generally. Hence its emphasis on representativeness, responsiveness, and accountability. The legal approach is very closely related to the judiciary in its concern with individual rights, adversary procedure, and equity.

As Justice Brandeis pointed out, the founders' purpose in creating the constitutional branches was not simply to facilitate efficiency, coordination, and a smooth functioning of government generally. The purpose was also to create a system that would give each branch a motive and a means for preventing abuses or misguided action by another. This would prevent the "accumulation of all powers, legislative, executive, and judiciary, in the same hands," which, as Madison wrote in *Federalist #47*, the founders considered to be "the very definition of tyranny.". . .

In a very real fashion, however, a system of checks and balances has devolved to the administrative branch along with the three governmental functions. Thus, as has been argued in this essay, the values associated with each function have been transmuted into distinctive theoretical approaches toward public administration. These approaches have different origins, stress different values and structural arrangements, and view individuals in remarkably different ways. This is precisely because each stresses a different function of public administration. Consequently, although there may be room for greater synthesis of these approaches, seeking to unify theory by allowing one approach to drive out the others would promote public bureaucracy in the most invidious sense of the term. Rather, the task is to develop a distinctive theoretical core suitable to the political culture by building around the need to maintain values, organizational structures, and perspectives on the individual that tend to check and balance each other.

Precisely how such theory may be derived is, of course, not immediately evident or predictable. However, a few ideas come to mind. First, public administrative theorists must recognize the validity and utility of each of the approaches discussed here. Perhaps others can be added in the future, but the legitimacy of each of these is beyond question. Consequently, a definition of the field of public administration must include a consideration of managerial, political, and legal approaches. Second, it is necessary to recognize that each approach may be more or less relevant to different agencies, administrative functions, and policy areas. For example, regulation stresses adjudication and, consequently, probably should not be organized primarily according to the managerial or political approaches. Likewise, overhead operations most clearly fall within the purview of the managerial approach. Distributive policy *may* be best organized according to the political approach. Much more thought and research must be devoted to these matters before any firm conclusions can be reached. But clearly it is an administrative fallacy to try to treat all agencies and programs under a universal standard. This is one reason why the much vaunted "rational" budgeting techniques of PPBS and ZBB failed.[46] Third, as heretical as it will sound to some, public administrative theory must make greater use of political theory. As is argued here, the separation of powers goes well beyond the issues of legislative delegation and agency subdelegation—it reaches to the core of the leading theories of public administration. Finally, attention must be paid to the practical wisdom of the public administrative practitioners whose action is circumscribed by internal considerations of checks, balances, and administrative and political pressures generally. Individual public administrators are often called upon to integrate the three approaches to public administration and much can be learned from their experience.

NOTES

1. See Gabriel Almond and Sidney Verba, *The Civic Culture* (Boston: Little, Brown, 1965), whose findings provide a useful outline of the values forming the core of the U.S. political culture.
2. Carl Schurz, *The Necessity of Progress of Civil Service Reform* (Washington, D.C.: Good Government, 1894), p. 3.
3. Woodrow Wilson, "The Study of Administration," *Political Science Quarterly*, Vol. 56 (December 1941), pp. 481–506 (originally copyrighted in 1887).
4. *Ibid.*, p. 481.
5. Frederick Taylor, *The Principles of Scientific Management* (New York: Harper and Bros., 1917).
6. Leonard D. White, *Introduction to the Study of Public Administration* (New York: Macmillan, 1926), pp. vii–viii. See also Herbert J. Storing, "Leonard D. White and the Study of Public Administration," *Public Administration Review*, Vol. 25 (March 1965), pp. 38–51.
7. *Papers on the Science of Administration*, ed. by Luther Gulick and L. Urwick (New York: Institute of Public Administration, 1937), pp. 192, 10.
8. Robert Simmons and Eugene Dvorin, *Public Administration* (Port Washington, N.Y.: Alfred Publishing, 1977), p. 217.
9. Max Weber, *From Max Weber: Essays in Sociology*, translated and ed. by H. H. Gerth and C. W. Mills

(New York: Oxford University Press, 1958), pp. 196–244.

10. Peter Blau and Marshall Meyer, *Bureaucracy in Modern Society*, second ed. (New York: Random House, 1971), esp. p. 8. See also Victor Thompson, *Modern Organization* (New York: Knopf, 1961), pp. 58–80.

11. See Harold Seidman, *Politics, Position, and Power* (New York: Oxford University Press, 1970), chapter 1.

12. See Eugene Lewis, *American Politics in a Bureaucratic Age: Citizens, Constituents, Clients, and Victims* (Cambridge, Mass.: Winthrop, 1977).

13. Weber, *Essays in Sociology*, p. 228.

14. Jay Shafritz, et al., *Personnel Management in Government* (New York: Marcel Dekker, 1978), p. 94.

15. Ralph Hummel, *The Bureaucratic Experience* (New York: St. Martin's, 1977), pp. 24–25.

16. See Erving Goffman, *Asylums* (Garden City, N.Y.: Doubleday, 1961), esp. pp. 1–24; *Halderman v. Pennhurst State School*, 244 F. Supp. 1295 (1977); *Holt v. Sarver*, 304 F. Supp. 362 (1970); John Hersey, *The Algiers Motel Incident* (New York: Knopf, 1968).

17. See Amitai Etzioni, *Modern Organizations* (Englewood Cliffs, N.J.: Prentice-Hall, 1964), chapter 4, for a brief, cogent description of the human relations approach. Victor Thompson, *Modern Organization*, discusses bureaupathology at pp. 152–177.

18. Wallace Sayre, "Premises of Public Administration: Past and Emerging," in Jay Shafritz and Albert Hyde, eds., *Classics of Public Administration* (Oak Park, Ill.: Moore, 1978), p. 201. Dwight Waldo, *The Administrative State* (New York: Ronald Press, 1948), demonstrates how the basic value choices of managerial public administration are ultimately statements of political preference.

19. Paul Appleby, *Policy and Administration* (University, Ala.: University of Alabama Press, 1949); see also Theodore Lowi, *The End of Liberalism* (New York: W.W. Norton, 1969).

20. *Myers v. U.S.*, 272 U.S. 52, 293 (1926).

21. David Nachmias and David H. Rosenbloom, *Bureaucratic Government, U.S.A.* (New York: St. Martin's, 1980).

22. See William Keefe and Morris Ogul, *The American Legislative Process*, fourth ed. (Englewood Cliffs, N.J.: Prentice-Hall, 1977), p. 407.

23. See Frederick Mosher, *Democracy and the Public Service* (New York: Oxford University Press, 1968); Ralph Hummel, *The Bureaucratic Experience*; Morris Janowitz, Deil Wright, and William Delany, *Public Administration and the Public* (Westport, Conn.: Greenwood, 1977); Lowi, *End of Liberalism*; William Morrow, *Public Administration* (New York: Random House, 1975); and Bruce Smith and James D. Carroll, eds., *Improving the Accountability and Performance of Government* (Washington, D.C.: Brookings, 1982).

24. This was an implicit assumption of the 19th-century civil service reformers, who argued that "as the functions of government grow in extent, importance and complexity, the necessity grows of their being administered not only with honesty, but also with trained ability and knowledge," Carl Schurz, *Congress and the Spoils System* (New York: George Peck, 1895), p. 4. See Harry Kranz, *The Participatory Bureaucracy* (Lexington, Mass.: Lexington Books, 1976); and Samuel Krislov, *Representative Bureaucracy* (Englewood Cliffs, N.J.: Prentice-Hall, 1974) for discussions of social representativeness and efficiency.

25. Marver Bernstein, *The Job of the Federal Executive* (Washington, D.C.: Brookings, 1958), p. 30.

26. *Ibid.*, pp. 26–37. See also Herbert Kaufman, *The Administrative Behavior of Federal Bureau Chiefs* (Washington, D.C.: Brookings, 1981), esp. chapter 2.

27. Seidman, *Politic, Position, and Power*, p. 13.

28. Norton Long, "Power and Administration," in Francis Rourke, ed., *Bureaucratic Power in National Politics* (Boston: Little, Brown, 1965), p. 18.

29. Roger Davidson, "Congress and the Executive: The Race for Representation," in A. DeGrazia, ed., *Congress: The First Branch of Government* (New York: Anchor, 1967), p. 383.

30. See Seidman, *Politics, Position, and Power*, chapter 1.

31. David Truman, *The Governmental Process* (New York: Knopf, 1951); see also Arthur Bentley, *The Process of Government* (Chicago: University of Chicago, 1908).

32. Lowi, *End of Liberalism*, p. 71. See also Grant McConnell, *Private Power and American Democracy* (New York: Knopf, 1966), chapters 4 and 5.

33. Frank Goodnow, *The Principles of the Administrative Law of the United States* (New York: G.P. Putnam's Sons, 1905).

34. *Ibid.*, p. 17.

35. Marshall Dimock, *Law and Dynamic Administration* (New York: Praeger, 1980), p. 31.

36. Kenneth Davis, *Administrative Law and Government* (St. Paul: West, 1975), p. 6.

37. Dimock, *Law and Dynamic Administration*, chapter 10.

38. The case law and literature are too voluminous to cite. See David H. Rosenbloom, *Public Administration and Law: Bench v. Bureau in the United States* (New York: Marcel Dekker, 1983).

39. *Hannah v. Larche*, 363 U.S. 420 (1960).

40. See for instance, *Branti v. Finkel*, 445 U.S. 507, 518 (1980), which requires the public employer to "demonstrate that party affiliation is an appropriate requirement for the effective performance of the public office involved" when making a patronage dismissal.

41. *Hamilton v. Love*, 328 F. Supp. 1182, 1194 (1971).

42. See Robert Vaughn, *The Spoiled System* (New York: Charterhouse, 1975); Richard A. Merrill, "Procedure

for Adverse Actions Against Federal Employees," *Virginia Law Review*, Vol. 59 (1973), pp. 196–287.

43. *Goldberg v. Kelly*, 397 U.S. 254 (1970); *Goss v. Lopez*, 419 U.S. 565 (1975).

44. 414 U.S. 632 (1974). Argued and decided with *Cohen v. Chesterfield Co. School Board*.

45. *Wyatt v. Stickney*, 325 F. Supp. 781 (1971); 334 F. Supp. 387 (1972).

46. Allen Schick, "A Death in the Bureaucracy," *Public Administration Review*, Vol. 33 (March/April 1973), pp. 146–156; "Budgeting Expert Calls Carter Plan 'Disaster,'" *Houston Post*, April 8, 1977, p. 14A, quotes Peter Phyrr, originator of zero based budgeting, as calling the federal effort to institute ZBB all-at-once "absolute folly."

THE PERILS—
AND PROSPECTS—
OF PUBLIC
ADMINISTRATION

Donald F. Kettl

Every discipline periodically goes through a period of sometimes wrenching reassessment. For public administration, this reassessment has been nearly constant. Americans have always been distrustful of government power and, especially, administrative power. They have long believed that public administration is more inefficient and corrupt than private administration. Woodrow Wilson's memorable call to study the importance of running a constitution shows how, even in its earliest days, the modern study of American public administration has struggled for acceptance.

Public administration marked its high point of public and political acceptance with the New Deal. The Brownlow Committee's recommendations in 1938 that "the president needs help" from assistants with a "passion for anonymity" shaped the modern presidency and ushered public administration scholars onto center stage in national politics.[1] Then, during World War II, an entire generation of the field's key figures staged their own invasion of Washington and, from one end of town to the other, they managed key positions in the war effort. At the same time, institutes of government and bureaus of municipal research provided important service to state and local governments. Government searched for a strong and positive role, pursued with economy and efficiency. Public administration stood eager to help, and its assistance was eagerly received.[2]

Almost immediately after World War II, however, public administration's prominence slipped precipitously. The growth of the modern social sciences, especially more behaviorally oriented political science and a more statistically oriented economics, weakened public administration's hold on the study and practice of government. Leading scholars argued that public administration's prewar proverbs had borne little fruit and that public administration was unlikely to become a science.[3] Political science and much—but certainly not all—of the public administration community began a prolonged but never completely consummated divorce. Meanwhile, the emerging policy sciences challenged public administration's claim to prescriptions for effective management.

Social and political changes coupled with old problems to undermine the discipline further. The perception of governmental failure that plagued the late 1960s and early 1970s undermined the nation's belief that government could play a positive role. These perceptions, coupled with bureaucrat bashing by top politicians during the 1970s and 1980s, caused the public image of public administration to sink to a new low.[4] More subtle intellectual currents also weakened public administration's intellectual claims. New professions, from engineering and accounting to medicine and law, developed a cult of specialization, while the social sciences pressed toward "scientific" explanations of phenomena. Public administration's traditional focus on generalism stirred little enthusiasm and much outright hostility.[5] Public administration was certainly no longer queen of the social sciences. Indeed, it had trouble winning a place at court.

Throughout the 1960s and 1970s, public administration found itself under attack by other approaches to understanding governmental performance. These perils—especially challenges from the implementation, public-management, and rationalist perspectives—wounded the field's self-confidence and its self-awareness. Each of the attacks contributed important insights into administrative practice. After two decades of criticisms, though, public administration as a field retains important insights and good prospects. To realize those prospects, however, public administration must take two steps. First, it must rediscover the central questions of the discipline. Second, it must develop new answers to those questions that fit the changing realities of public programs. Let me first explore the perils that public administration has suffered and then examine the prospects the field offers.

THE PERILS OF PUBLIC ADMINISTRATION

In the decades after World War II, public administration faced three especially important intellectual challenges: the implementation challenge, from those trying to explain why agencies so often seemed to perform so badly; the public-management challenge, from those seeking to develop practical guides for top-level government officials; and the rationalist challenge, from those venturing a positivist/minimalist theory of bureaucratic behavior.

THE IMPLEMENTATION CHALLENGE

Many political scientists in the 1960s were struck by the failure of the Great Society to win the war (or even major skirmishes) on poverty. They developed a new field—implementation—to provide the "missing link" in public policy analysis between decision making and program evaluation.[6] Most of the implementation literature, however, quickly moved to the analysis of failure. In one early book, Pressman and Wildavsky describe their investigation into one Oakland, California, federal grant program with a famous subtitle: "How Great Expectations in Washington Are Dashed in Oakland; Or, Why It's Amazing That Federal Programs Work At All."[7] Students of implementation concentrated on why so often government programs failed to achieve the goals that Congress set for them.[8]

They rejected, at least implicitly, the nearly 100-year tradition of public administration as useless. "There is (or there must be) a large literature about implementation in the social sciences," Pressman and Wildavsky wrote in 1974. "It must be there; it should be there; but in fact it is not."[9] Pressman and Wildavsky began from the proposition that public administration had little to offer anyone studying program performance. That statement struck many public administration scholars by surprise because, even though they did not work under that label, most of them believed that the entire field was devoted to precisely that question. Implementation was different, however. Unlike public administration, which focuses on the behavior of agencies and of their employees, implementation focuses on the outcomes of public programs. Goals and resources are

put into the system, peopled principally by bureaucrats, and results—often at variance with intentions—result. Thus, instead of being the central focus of the school, the agency and its employees are instruments.

For students of implementation, failure was centrally defined as the inability of a program to achieve its legislative goals. (Later research examined problems in decision making and the design of public policy as well,[10] but the failure to achieve goals was the central and initial focus of implementation.) The causes of failure were legion, rooted especially in fundamental pathologies of public bureaucracy.[11] The problem most often was one of control: the inability of policy makers at the top to regulate the behavior of others in the policy process. They saw the environment of public policy implementation as very complex, however, and the many participants played endless games that distorted and delayed implementation.[12] The odds thus were stacked heavily against successful implementation. Nearly everything along the line from top policy makers to lower-level managers had to work perfectly if a program was not to become bogged down. In a process requiring 70 separate agreements, even if the chances of a successful agreement at each step were 99 percent, the odds of program success were less than 50-50.[13]

In the implementation school, public agencies are instruments toward the goals set by policy makers like members of Congress and the president. Members of these agencies have many personal goals and political cross pressures that frequently distort their behavior away from legislative goals and consequently produce failures. Problems persist because bureaucrats delay, obstruct, create red tape, vacillate, and hesitate. Agencies ideally should be self-evaluating and skilled at adapting new behavior to prevent old mistakes. The need of organizations for political support, however, makes them more cautious and conservative.[14] They get caught up in their own routines and ruling orthodoxies and become blinded to new signs and signals. Bureaucracy demonstrates "a preference for procedure over purpose."[15]

Of all the impediments to success, students of implementation rate bureaucracy the worst. "No one is clearly in charge of implementation," Ripley and Franklin conclude. Therefore, "Domestic programs virtually never achieve all that is expected of them."[16] The result is a depressing forecast of the prospects for learning and achievement. The implementation school thus provides a well-accepted explanation for learning failures and the frequent problems of performance that plague government agencies.

Two important weaknesses characterize the implementation approach, however. First, implementation looks especially bleak because of the negative cases its students have chosen to study. The implementation literature is based in failure; its scholars have rarely studied program successes, which are legion. Failures, of course, are often more intriguing, but they are not always more important. Stories such as "Mail Delivered Yet Again Today," "Social Security Checks Arrive on Time," or "Air-Traffic Control System Safely Guides Thousands of Planes" never make the papers and rarely attract scholars' attention. Because success stories have only rarely been studied, implementation scholars have not systematically compared successes and failures. Nor have they carefully differentiated the forces that produce failures instead of successes (or vice versa). It is, therefore, almost impossible to understand fully why failures occur, how frequently they happen, or what could have been done to prevent them.

Second, "success" and "failure" are far more elusive terms than the implementation literature suggests. The ultimate benchmark for most studies is the law as enacted by Congress and Congress's intent. The fuzziness of congressional goals, however, is legendary. Defining and redefining those goals as programs evolve is inevitable. So, too, is adapting broad national goals to the vast variety of local conditions. In many intergovernmental programs, in fact, adapting national goals to local needs was the central focus. The programs delegated substantial policy-making authority to state and local officials. Observations of "success" and "failure" therefore often varied greatly depending on who was conducting the observations. One would scarcely expect that every observer would draw the same conclusions about a program's results, especially when the very process of developing its goals was a complex affair. A "success" to a local official might seem a "failure" to a federal official. Moreover, judgments can change radically over time as well. Programs delayed sometimes become eventual successes, and

some early successes turn sour. Even a program brought to a standstill, such as construction of a new highway, may well be a "success" for an interest which did not want it finished.

Judgments of success and failure thus are most elusive. The implementation literature has produced a lively set of case studies and some intriguing explanations of governmental behavior. It has not, however, developed a systematic explanation of why some programs succeed while others fail, how implementation might vary among different program strategies (such as regulation on contracting or transfer programs), or even an acceptable definition of what constitutes "success" and "failure."

THE PUBLIC MANAGEMENT CHALLENGE

On the heels of the implementation movement came a new public-management school. Public administration focuses on agencies and their employees, and implementation concentrates on programs and their outcomes. The more-recent public management movement, by contrast, is based on the role of top administrative leaders, typically political appointees such as cabinet secretaries and agency administrators, and the strategies they set. In fact, the movement has its foundation on writing *about* such top officials *by* former officials.[17] (Public management, to some degree, has become a popular catchword for many different approaches to administration. Among many others, the public management net snares the bureaucratic politics and more-generic administrative science approaches. The discussion here focuses on the approach, circulated through case studies, that has seized the high ground at many policy schools.)

According to these studies, the strategies of public managers have three objects. First, they must develop strategies for efficiently and effectively overseeing their agency's programs. Second, since there usually are competing strategies that could be adopted, they must build political support, both inside and outside the agency, for their own views of their agencies' directions. Finally, they must maintain their agencies' health—its organizational capacity and credibility—and obtain needed resources—especially funding, personnel, legislation, and favorable constituencies.[18]

Management problems, according to this school, are especially likely to come from an organization's environment, and the public manager must devote considerable time to learning about, coping with, adapting to, and sometimes trying to shape that environment. Such adaptation, however, is limited by the constraints that public managers face: from the political environment, which sometimes can be hostile; from their own organizations, which sometimes resist managerial strategies; and from their own personalities and cognitive styles, which may limit the managers' vision and ability to persuade. The public-management movement thus has developed along three fronts. In looking to the outside world, the movement has examined relations between top executives and other political forces, especially the president, Congress, and interest groups.[19] In looking within the agency, the movement has adopted the patho-logical approach of implementation to chart the games that bureaucrats play in frustrating the strategies of top officials.[20] Finally, in looking at public managers' own styles, the movement has developed personality studies on the behavior of individual public managers.[21]

The public-management school is largely case-based. It is dominated by the personal reflections of individuals who have served in top adminis-trative positions and by case studies of individual public managers.[22] Indeed, Lynn contends that "there is no intellectual alternative to regarding the experience of each public executive as a unique case." Every manager finds himself or herself in a different situation, and broad generalizations are impossible.[23] The public-management school's approach to the problems of administering public programs is to present broad propositions about the need to adapt (and about the problems that can hinder adaptation); to add rich case studies about public managers who have been perceived as successful and unsuccessful; and to ground it all in Neustadt's dictum that executive power is the power to persuade.[24]

The public-management school has made useful contributions to the study of public policy and administration. Far more than implementa-tion, it celebrates the art of the possible. Far more than traditional public administration, it focuses on the unique role played by top-level adminis-trators and on the special problems they face.[25]

However, the problems of public management include much more than the behavior of people at the top of government agencies. Decision making is the very essence of administrative behavior, and it permeates bureaucracy from top to bottom. In fact, it is the central administrative act.[26] By giving short shrift to management at any but the agency's top levels, the public-management school blinds itself to important questions.

Top NASA managers, for example, never had the chance to decide whether the cold made launching the *Challenger* too risky on that fateful January 1986 morning because mid-level NASA administrators did not pass crucial information on to them. Top NASA managers did receive signals months before the explosion that the O-rings performed badly in cold weather, but the signals did not come in a form that demanded attention and strategy setting. The heavy concern in the public-management literature with building political support does not address why such problems come about or what public managers should do about them. The public-management school gives few clues about how to deal with other levels of the bureaucracy, or how those levels behave (except, perhaps, as an impediment to executive action). The public-management school thus gives few clues about how administration works—and why sometimes it does not.

THE RATIONALIST CHALLENGE

Economists, and political scientists following basic economic constructs, have developed a different approach. They have sought to develop a formal theory of bureaucratic behavior from the foundation of only a few assumptions, principally that bureau-crats (like all individuals) seek to maximize their utility, or satisfaction. The approach then asks how utility-maximizing individuals, when placed within an agency, are likely to respond.[27] It builds a framework on the assumption of rationally self-interested behavior that leads to a deductive theory of bureaucratic behavior.[28]

In one of the leading elements of the rationalist school, an agency can be considered a market in which employers seek to purchase the skills of employees. The employer can be considered the principal actor, who hires the employee as an agent to perform the organization's tasks. (More broadly, an organization, such as a government agency, can hire other organizations, such as contractors, for similar purposes. The agency then becomes the principal, the contractor the agent.) This structure allows the application of economic theories to bureaucratic behavior.

This principal-agent theory, as it is known, argues that principals must solve two basic tasks in choosing their agents. Principals must select the best agents, whether employees or contractors (or, for that matter, other third parties who serve as agents), and create inducements for them to behave as desired. Principals must also monitor the behaviors of their agents to ensure that they are performing their tasks well. Economists' elaboration of principal-agent theory is extremely mathematical, with individual behaviors modeled in complex algorithms. The theory can, however, be reduced to two basic problems.

First, the principal can never know everything about an agent. A supervisor can examine a potential employee's education, skills, personality, and background, but he or she can never be sure of selecting the best person for the job. Potential employees will know more about their own qualifications than potential employers can ever learn. Thus, the theory contends, employers tend to hire lower-quality applicants than desired. Principal-agent theorists have christened this the "adverse-selection" problem. Second, the principal can never be sure of knowing the full details of the agent's performance. There are always signals about an employee's performance, such as reports, complaints, direct observation, and work habits, but the employer can never know the full story. Principals are thus typically at an information disadvantage with respect to their agents, and agents therefore have an incentive to work to less than their capacity, since they know that performance inadequacies may not be detected. Principal-agent theorists call this the "moral hazard" problem.[29] Put together, the problems explain why control by managers of organizations is difficult.[30]

Principal-agent theory offers insight into problems, such as why the Department of Energy has had such difficulty in managing the contractors that manufacture the nation's nuclear weapons. It is difficult to choose good contractors (adverse selection). It is also hard to know what the contractor is doing, and whether its performance

matches the department's goals (moral hazard). Furthermore, principal-agent theory identifies the flow of information as the critical problem. Principals can improve their selection of agents if they can learn more about them before hiring them. Principals can reduce moral hazard by altering their agents' incentives and by improving the monitoring of their agents' behaviors.

As with implementation and public-management theories, however, principal-agent theory does not explain several important administrative issues. While the market approach produces interesting insights, market metaphors in the public sector often produce distortions because the "markets" themselves have imperfections. On the supply side, government often has relatively few choices in purchasing services. From mass-transit buses and subway cars to submarines and airliners, government rarely can call on more than a few suppliers. These suppliers enjoy a near-monopoly in the market, and as purchaser the government must solve all of the problems that exist in monopoly markets. Even in such mundane services as garbage collection, the number of potential contractors is often deceptively small.

The market is further distorted on the demand side because, for some items, government is often the only purchaser. The Department of Energy's contractors are not allowed to sell plutonium triggers for nuclear weapons to anyone but the government. The Newport News shipyard does not build aircraft carriers for anyone but the U.S. Navy, and many urban planning firms have few clients other than local governments and their redevelopment agencies. Economists call a high concentration of buyers a "monopsony," and in such conditions the flexibility of the government as buyer is often limited. Does the Navy dare, for both strategic and economic reasons, to allow one of the two manufacturers of nuclear submarines to go out of business?

Principal-agent theory, moreover, does not recognize well the role that power plays in organizational (or, more broadly, in political) life.[31] Because it is based on market behavior, it assumes relationships among equals, with principals and agents each seeking to develop an acceptable exchange. It thus neglects what Parsons calls "the central phenomenon of organizations."[32] It also neglects the considerable complexity in the environment of agencies and the many cross-cutting political pressures on administrators. The mathematical models could theoretically capture these additional complexities, but it is unrealistic to think that the full range of power relationships facing public administrators could be modeled in equations.

Furthermore, organizational goals are far more dynamic and evolutionary than the relatively static principal-agent models tend to capture.[33] Members of Congress frequently change their minds about which goals administrators should emphasize, and administrators themselves must set priorities among the many competing demands on their time and expertise. Goals, moreover, often evolve in collaboration between principals and agents. Defense contracts, for example, frequently are modified as Pentagon officials and contractors learn more about what works and what does not in a new weapons system. In intergovernmental grant programs, moreover, it is often difficult to recognize who is the principal and who is the agent. Different levels of government take different responsibilities for different pieces of the same program. The relationship here is less one of exchange than of constitutional collaboration. While dynamic goals theoretically are possible to model, they move far beyond the static models of principal-agent theory and enter into a realm of enormous complexity.

Market models offer important insights into the problems that government must solve. They focus attention on information flows in the relationship between principal and agent. Looking at public services in terms of the nature of the principal-agent relationship can also produce valuable insights about constraints on government's control of its agents. Market-based models, however, tend to be far better at asking questions than in answering them.

THE PROSPECTS OF PUBLIC ADMINISTRATION

Since World War II, the field of public administration has taken its lumps from many different directions. None of the competing theories, however, has succeeded in supplanting the more-traditional study of public administration. While each one has its important attractions, each one leaves critical questions unanswered. And these unanswered questions lead back to public administration's doorstep.

The prospects of public administration lie in rediscovering the fundamental issues on which the discipline is based. This in turn requires two steps. First, it requires recognizing and redefining the importance of agencies as actors within the political process.[34] Second, it requires understanding how the behaviors of agencies as actors vary and how to map that variance.

AGENCIES AS ACTORS

Agencies need to be understood as more than instruments that produce (or distort) policy outcomes, as stressed in the implementation school; as shaped by more than the decisions of political appointees, as discussed by the public-management school; and as more than the accumulation of individual transactions between employers and employees, as analyzed by the principal-agent school. Agencies, as agencies, need to be considered as important participants in their own right. One of the most important arguments of the early public-administration school was, quite simply, that organization matters, and that different organizational structures are likely to produce different outcomes.[35]

Between these early works and the perils of public administration came the important observation of open-systems theorists: the agencies must adapt to changes in their environment to be effective.[36] The political forces and technical problems with which bureaucracies must deal constantly change. Agencies shape and are shaped by the environment.

This leads to two important implications. First, agencies frequently are creatures of their past. Rules, standard operating procedures, and norms all are products of accumulated experience. They, in fact, often acquire lives independent of the forces that produced them. Members of bureaucracies may have long ago forgotten why rules were adopted or why they follow the norms that they do. Regulations, procedures, and standards often are products of the bureaucracy's adaptation to previous situations, and they take on lives independent of the forces that created them.[37] Agencies often therefore tend to be backward looking.

Second, the major challenge facing agencies as actors is to adapt to future problems from their backward-looking views. Behavior conditioned by the past provides a useful administrative shortcut, since every new problem does not require a new solution. Such behavior does not always produce the best answers to new problems, however. Organizations must therefore develop approaches to learning from mistakes and adapting to the future.[38]

This "new institutionalist" approach borrows heavily from the other schools. Like implementation, it self-consciously focuses attention on the relationship between the bureaucracy's behavior and its results, past and future. Like public management, it pays heed to both internal problems, such as communication, and external problems, such as political support. Like principal-agent theory, it recognizes the critical importance of information asymmetries. But unlike any of these other approaches, it focuses centrally on the importance of the agencies as independent actors. The burden of the argument is that agencies develop behaviors separate from the behaviors of those who happen to populate them at any one moment. The first step to understanding the prospects of public administration therefore is to develop better knowledge about how such behaviors are shaped, how behaviors shape bureaucratic outcomes, and what bureau leaders can do to improve those outcomes.[39]

VARYING BEHAVIOR

Not all bureaucratic behavior is the same, of course. One of the principal arguments of public administration's post-World War II critics was that the generalized principles of administrative theory did not answer questions then asked by theorists. To an important extent, the first century of American public administration was devoted to understanding basic forces and processes at work within agencies of all kinds and at all levels of government. When the search for generalizable common features ran dry, competing schools sprang up. Bureaucratic institutions have self-evidently evolved into large numbers and remarkable variety. American public administration must now be devoted to understanding better how administrative practice varies.

Can the variety be systematically mapped? The answer is "yes," but the answer depends on understanding the problems that government agencies must solve in adapting to their environments. Consider two federal bureaus, for example. In the Federal Aviation Administration (FAA), some employees provide a direct service for the flying public. They guide, with great skill and rare failure, thousands of airplanes to their destination every day. Other FAA employees, however, regulate and inspect the airline industry to ensure the safe maintenance and operation of their fleets. These jobs are distinctively different. The FAA's controllers work with willing clients who want nothing more than to be separated safely from nearby traffic. The controllers' radar, meanwhile, enables them to observe precisely what is happening in the skies they are supervising. That role is very different from that of the FAA's safety inspectors who often deal with airlines seeking to minimize expense and down time and who can only indirectly, at best, observe the effects of their activities. The administration of these programs, even though they exist within the same agency, is very different.

In the U.S. Department of Health and Human Services, officials know how much money is being spent on different medical services through the Medicare program because they know to whom they are writing checks and in which categories. Beyond the mailing of checks by HHS and cashing those checks by recipients, there needs to be little coordination. That is not the case with the administrative services that the many contractors working for HHS on the Medicare program provide. The very process of negotiating the contract ensures high agreement on goals; if agreement on aims is not reached, there is no contract. On the other hand, because contractors work at arm's length from HHS, simply determining what the contractors are actually doing is problematic.[40]

Can systematic differences be discerned among these programs and among the many other governmental programs that challenge administrators? Two concepts are useful for that purpose.

First, the agencies' behavior depends importantly on information. Information flow is most "sticky" —most threatened by distortions, losses, filtering, and condensation—at bureaucratic boundaries.[41] For air-traffic control and the distribution of Medicare checks, information flow is relatively clear. Air-traffic controllers look down at the radar screens in front of them, while HHS employees who process Medicare checks work from claim forms showing the services performed. In Medicare contracting and air-safety regulation, however, information about performance is only indirect and typically costly to obtain. That clearly makes a difference in the way agencies behave.[42]

Second, the agencies' behaviors depend also on the congruence between their goals and the goals of those with whom they deal outside the agency. While no airline wants to fly an unsafe plane, there is constant disagreement on just how much maintenance, to which standards, is enough. Disagreement on just how much medical care is enough and about how much the government should pay is common in Medicare benefits as well. In contrast, goal congruence in the air-traffic control system is absolute—everyone wants safe procedures. The contracting process between Medicare and its contractors at least assures basic agreement on goals. These differences also make a difference in how agencies behave.

In short, public administration is likely to be different in different kinds of governmental programs. In particular, public administration is likely to differ when the relative costs of obtaining information about an agency's outputs are relatively high or low. It is also likely to differ when the

congruence between an agency's goals and the goals of those outside the agency's boundaries are relatively high or low. As Figure 1 shows, four major governmental policy strategies can be sorted among these categories. Programs administered through grants and contracts (such as supplementary Medicare services) are likely to have relatively high information costs but relatively high goal congruence. Regulatory programs (such as the FAA's air-safety regulations) are likely to have relatively high information costs but relatively low goal congruence. Directly administered programs (such as the FAA's air-traffic control) are likely to have relatively low information costs and relatively high goal congruence. Finally, transfer programs (such as Medicare's benefits program) are likely to have relatively low goal congruence and relatively low information costs.

Public administration is likely to vary accordingly. This scheme suggests that directly administered programs, in general, will be the least problematic because goal congruence is relatively high and information costs are relatively low.[43]

Indirectly administered programs, such as grants and contracts, must seek a negotiated agreement on goals and struggle to acquire good feedback on performance. Administrators of transfer programs, such as Medicare and welfare, must

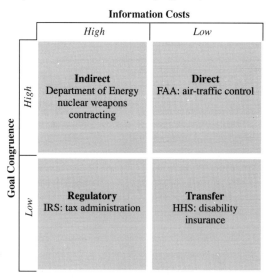

FIGURE 1
Variance of Programs by Information and Goals

worry about getting the checks into the hands of recipients and then about whether the recipients spend the money according to the government's goals. Regulatory administrators face the difficult challenge of trying to enforce changes in behaviors (and thus in goals) while having relatively poor information on whether they are successful.

RESCUING PUBLIC ADMINISTRATION

While its critics would not unanimously agree that public administration needs or deserves rescuing, several decades of alternative approaches to the field's basic problems have not supplanted it. The alternatives have been interesting, in part because of the weaknesses in more-traditional public administration to which they have pointed and in part because of the different questions they have asked. These weaknesses and questions, however, lead public administration back to basic questions: the importance of understanding agencies as actors, in their own right, in the political process; and the relationship between those agencies and the political environments in which they act.

Rescuing public administration, however, will require more than simply reestablishing the importance of agencies as actors in the political process. Its critics rejected public administration after World War II because it attempted to offer universal principles when a sophisticated, differentiated vision was needed. That requires recognizing not only what ties public administration together—such as a sense of the agency and its officials as political actors—but also how it varies. Different forms of the administrative process present different kinds of political and managerial problems. Rescuing public administration means recognizing and understanding these differences as well as the similarities. Perhaps the most important differences revolve around the costs of obtaining information and the difficulties in obtaining congruence on goals.

Finally, rescuing public administration means being alert to its changing forms and emerging issues. If understanding the variation in public administration replaces the search for principles, it will be easier to spot the shifting forms of administrative action. The administrative issues

surrounding the emergence of contracting for high-technology projects, the spread of transfer and regulatory programs, and the invention of new governmental forms such as government-sponsored enterprises and government corporations (in all their hybrid patterns) will be more apparent to students alert to both similarities and differences. Comprehending such forms of administrative life, and the different problems they bring to the public service, is key to bringing public administration home and restoring its life and vision.

NOTES

1. President's Committee on Administrative Management, *Report of the President's Committee, Administrative Management in the Government of the United States* (Washington: U.S. Government Printing Office, 1937).
2. An excellent self-examination of public administration's role is Frederick C. Mosher, ed., *American Public Administration: Past, Present, Future* (University: University of Alabama Press, 1975).
3. Herbert Simon, "The Proverbs of Administration," *Public Administration Review*, vol. 6 (Winter 1946), pp. 53–67; and Robert A. Dahl, "The Science of Public Administration: Three Problems," *Public Administration Review*, vol. 7 (Winter 1947), pp. 1–11.
4. National Commission on the Public Service (Volcker Commission), *Leadership for America: Rebuilding the Public Service* (Lexington, MA: Lexington Books, 1989), esp. pp. 53–61.
5. See Frederick C. Mosher, "Introduction: The American Setting," in Mosher, ed., *American Public Administration*, pp. 6–7.
6. Erwin C. Hargrove, *The Missing Link: The Study of the Implementation of Social Policy* (Washington: The Urban Institute, 1975).
7. Jeffrey L. Pressman and Aaron B. Wildavsky, *Implementation* (Berkeley: University of California Press, 1973).
8. See, for example, Martha Derthick, *New Towns In-Town* (Washington: Urban Institute, 1972); Eugene Bardach, *The Implementation Game: What Happens After a Bill Becomes a Law* (Berkeley: University of California Press, 1977); Paul Berman, "The Study of Macro- and Micro-Implementation," *Public Policy*, vol. 26 (Spring 1978), pp. 157–84; Richard F. Elmore, "Organizational Models of Social Program Implementation," *Public Policy*, vol. 26 (Spring 1978), pp. 185–228; Carl E. Van Horn, *Policy Implementation in the Federal System: National Goals and Local Implementors* (Lexington, MA: Heath, 1979);

D.A. Mazmanian and P.A. Sabatier, *Implementation and Public Policy* (Glenview, IL: Scott, Foresman, 1983); and Randall B. Ripley and Grace A. Franklin, *Policy Implementation and Bureaucracy*, 2d ed. (Chicago: Dorsey Press. 1986).

9. Pressman and Wildavsky, *Implementation, supra*, p. 166. In fact, a handful of studies on implementation had already been published, including Stephen K. Bailey and Edith K. Mosher, *ESEA: The Office of Education Administers A Law* (Syracuse, NY: Syracuse University Press, 1968); and Jerome T. Murphy, "Title I of ESEA: The Politics of Implementing Federal Educational Reform," *Harvard Educational Review*, vol. 41 (February 1971), pp. 35–63.

10. For a survey of these approaches, see Charles O. Jones, *An Introduction to the Study of Public Policy*, 3d ed. (Pacific Grove, CA: Brooks/Cole, 1984).

11. Brian W. Hogwood and B. Guy Peters, *The Pathology of Public Policy* (Oxford: Oxford University Press, 1985).

12. See Bardach, *The Implementation Game, supra*.

13. A notably more positive view is Malcolm L. Goggin, Ann O'M. Bowman, James P. Lester, and Laurence J. O'Toole, Jr., *Implementation Theory and Practice: Toward A Third Generation* (Glenview, IL: Scott, Foresman, 1990).

14. Aaron Wildavsky, "The Self-Evaluating Organization," *Public Administration Review*, vol. 32 (September/October 1972), pp. 509–520.

15. Pressman and Wildavsky, *supra*, p. 133.

16. Ripley and Franklin, *Policy Implementation and Bureaucracy, supra*, p. 12.

17. Richard R. Elmore, "Graduate Education in Public Management: Working the Seams of Government," *Journal of Policy Analysis and Management*, vol. 6 (Fall 1986), pp. 69–83. Excluded from this discussion are more-traditional approaches to public administration that have been re-christened "public management."

18. Laurence E. Lynn, Jr., *Managing the Public's Business: The Job of the Government Executive* (New York: Basic Books, 1981) and *Managing Public Policy* (Boston: Little, Brown, 1987). See also Elmore, "Graduate Education in Public Management"; and Philip B. Heymann, *The Politics of Public Management* (New Haven: Yale University Press, 1987). An excellent summary of public management literature is Hal G. Rainey, "Public Management: Recent Developments and Current Prospects" in *Public Administration: The State of the Discipline*, Naomi B. Lynn, Aaron Wildavsky (Chatham, NJ: Chatham House Publishers, 1990), pp. 157–184.

    The public-management movement builds self-consciously on the foundation of bureaucratic politics established by Graham T. Allison in "Conceptual Models and the Cuban Missile Crisis," *American Political Science Review*, vol. 63 (September 1969), pp. 689–718; and *Essence of Decision: Explaining the Cuban Missile Crisis* (Boston: Little, Brown, 1971). See also Morton H. Halperin with Priscilla Clapp and Arnold Kanter, *Bureaucratic Politics and Foreign Policy* (Washington: Brookings Institution, 1974).

19. See Heyman, *The Politics of Public Management, supra*; and Hugh Heclo, *A Government of Strangers: Executive Politics in Washington* (Washington: Brookings Institution, 1977).

20. See Lynn, *Managing Public Policy, supra*.

21. See Jameson W. Doig and Erwin C. Hargrove, eds., *Leadership and Innovation: A Biographical Perspective on Entrepreneurs in Government* (Baltimore: Johns Hopkins University Press, 1987).

22. Case studies prepared a Harvard's Kennedy School of Government are a special example of this approach. See, for example, Robert Reich, *Public Management in a Democratic Society* (Englewood Cliffs, NJ: Prentice-Hall, 1990).

23. Lynn, *Managing Public Policy, supra*, p. 5.

24. Richard E. Neustadt, *Presidential Power: The Politics of Leadership* (New York: John Wiley and Sons, 1960).

25. This problem, however, has scarcely been ignored in the public administration literature. See, for example, James W. Fesler, "Politics, Policy, and Bureaucracy at the Top," *Annals of the Academy of Political and Social Science*, vol. 466 (March 1983), pp. 23–41.

26. Herbert A. Simon, *Administrative Behavior: A Study of Decision-Making Processes in Administrative Organization*, 3d ed. (New York: Free Press, 1976).

27. See, for example, William A. Niskanen, Jr., *Bureaucracy and Representative Government* (Chicago: Aldine, Atherton, 1971).

28. For a summary of principal-agent theory, see Kenneth J. Arrow, "The Economics of Agency," in John W. Pratt and Richard J. Zeckhauser, eds., *Principals and Agents: The Structure of Business* (Boston: Harvard Business School Press, 1985), pp. 37–51. Terry M. Moe examines the potential of principal-agent theory for public agencies in "The New Economics of Organization," *American Journal of Political Science*, vol. 20 (November 1984), pp. 739–777.

29. The term comes from the insurance literature. Those who buy insurance know they are covered in case of harm and therefore do not have as strong an incentive to protect themselves from potential losses. They also know that the risks of a serious problem are relatively small, so their incentives for self-protection may further decrease. The insurance company, which must pay for any losses, cannot know how policy holders are behaving and finds it difficult to evaluate the safety habits of individual policy holders. This mismatch exposes the insurance

company to greater risks and points to fundamental uncertainties in its operations.

30. See, for example, Harrison C. White, "Agency as Control," in *Prinicpals and Agents: The Structure of Business*, John W. Pratt and Richard J. Zeckhauser, eds. (Boston: Harvard Business School Press, 1985), p. 188.

31. Charles Perrow, *Complex Organizations: A Critical Essay*, 3d ed. (New York: Random House, 1986), pp. 230–231.

32. Talcott Parsons, *Structure and Process in Modern Societies* (New York: The Free Press, 1960), p. 41

33. James G. March and Johan P. Olsen, *Rediscovering Institutions: The Organizational Basis of Politics* (New York: Free Press, 1989), p. 66.

34. This, in turn, means placing public administration within the new institutionalist school. See March and Olsen, *Rediscovering Institutions*; Stephen Skowronek, *Building a New Adminstrative State: The Expansion of National Administrative Capacities, 1887–1920* (Cambridge: Cambridge University Press, 1982); James G. March and Johan P. Olsen, "The New Institutionalism: Organizational Factors in Political Life," *American Political Science Review*, vol. 78 (September 1984), pp. 734–749.

35. See, in addition to the Brownlow Committee report, Luther Gulick and Lyndall Urwick, eds., *Papers on the Science of Administration* (New York: Institute of Public Administration, 1937), especially Gulick's paper, "Notes on the Theory of Organization," pp. 1–45.

36. See Daniel Katz and Robert L. Kahn, *The Social Psychology of Organizations* (New York: John Wiley and Sons, 1966); and James D. Thompson, *Organizations in Action* (New York: McGraw Hill, 1967).

37. March and Olsen, *Rediscovering Institutions*, *supra*, p. 38.

38. See, for example, Chris Argyris and Donald A. Schon, *Organizational Learning: A Theory of Action Perspective* (Reading, MA: Addison-Wesley, 1978); Richard L. Daft and George P. Huber, "How Organizations Learn: A Communication Framework," *Research in the Sociology of Organizations*, vol. 5 (1987), pp. 1–36.

39. Several public-administration scholars have made important contributions to these issues. See, for example, Frederick C. Mosher, *Democracy and the Public Service*, 2d ed. (New York: Oxford University Press, 1978), on personnel policy; Irene S. Rubin, *The Politics of Public Budgeting* (Chatham, NJ: Chatham House Publishers, 1990), on budgeting; and Barbara S. Romzek and Melvin J. Dubnick, "Accountability in the Public Sector: Lessons from the Challenger Tragedy," *Public Administration Review*, vol. 47 (May/June 1987), pp. 227–38, on organization theory.

40. See U.S. Comptroller General, *Medicare: Contractor Services to Beneficiaries and Providers* (Washington: U.S. Government Printing Office, 1988).

41. Parsons, *Structure and Process in Modern Societies*, *supra*, p. 18; Michael L. Tushman, "Special Boundary Roles in the Innovation Process," *Administrative Science Quarterly*, vol. 22 (December 1977), pp. 587–605; and Michael L. Tushman and Ralph Katz, "External Communication and Project Performance: An Investigation into the Role of Gatekeepers," *Management Science*, vol. 26 (November 1980), pp. 1071–1085.

42. Information flow at the "seams of government" is an important part of some public-management approaches as well. See Elmore, "Graduate Education in Public Management," *supra*, p. 77.

43. Critics from the privatization movement, of course, have suggested that such high goal congruence also produces ineffecent administration that other strategies, such as contracting out, can solve.

ISSUES IN PUBLIC ADMINISTRATION THEORY

Robert B. Denhardt

Public administration theorists have included scholars and practitioners with many different viewpoints and objectives. Most have drawn important material from the more general field of organization theory, though political theory has made important contributions as well.

Our concern here, however, will be to examine those developments in the field of organization theory that have been of most relevance to the study of public administration. My approach here will be to identify issues largely drawn from organization theory that have proven to be of interest to a wide variety of theorists and practitioners, issues that have been sources of continued controversy within the field of public administration, and issues that remain largely unresolved even today.

I. POLITICS AND ADMINISTRATION

Though the dichotomy between politics and administration is unquestionably one of the oldest issues in the field of public administration, the relationship between politics and administration remains one of the most contemporary. Woodrow Wilson's (1887) essay is taken by most commentators as the first major work in public administration. In that essay, Wilson laid the groundwork for the self-conscious study of public administration by pointing out the increasing difficulties faced by public agencies, saying, "It is getting harder to run a constitution than to frame one" (Wilson, 1887:200).

His solution was to operate the agencies of government on a businesslike basis, following accepted principles of management in the private sector and seeking the utmost in efficiency. But

in Wilson's view, this could never be accomplished as long as public agencies were subject to the corrupting influence of politics. For this reason, Wilson made a distinction between politics and administration: in the political realm, issues of public policy were to be formulated; in the administrative realm, they were to be implemented. Wilson's dictum was clear: "Administration lies outside the proper sphere of politics. Administrative questions are not political questions. Although politics sets the tasks for administration, it should not be suffered to manipulate its offices" (Wilson, 1887:210).

Two important concerns are raised by Wilson's argument, one the empirical question of whether politics and administration are (or can be) separated, the other the normative question of how to maintain the accountability of administrative agencies. The first of these questions was addressed just at the turn of the century by Frank Goodnow (1900), whose book *Policy and Administration* was (and is) taken by many to be a defense of the Wilsonian distinction between politics and administration. In fact, Goodnow's book argues that the formalistic separation of legislative and executive functions is often violated in practice. Though Goodnow holds that it is analytically possible to distinguish between the "expression" and the "execution" of the will of the state, he argues that these two functions cannot be clearly assigned to one branch of government or the other.

Similar arguments were developed by other writers, including W. F. Willoughby (1936), Luther Gulick (1933), Leonard White (1936), and Paul Appleby (1949). All acknowledge the difficulty of separating politics (or policy) and administration, with both Gulick and White providing specific illustrations of the role of civil servants in developing policy, either through their exercise of discretion in carrying out policy or through their advice to policy makers. For example, Gulick (1933:561) describes the work of the public employee as involving "a seamless web of discretion and action." Similarly, White (1936) notes the increasing "executive initiative in public policy," even arguing at one point that those who staff the bureaucracy may be in the best position to make recommendations free of political influence. In these ways, the dichotomy of politics and administration, if it had ever existed in either theory or practice, was quickly eroded. Indeed, by the time of Appleby's writing, it had apparently disappeared. He said simply, "public administration is policy-making" (Appleby, 1949:170).

One reason scholars began to assert more straightforwardly the involvement of bureaucrats in policy making was that bureaucrats were becoming involved in more policy making (Dunn, 1981; Peters, 1984; Ripley and Franklin, 1982; Seidman and Gilmour, 1986; Wildavsky, 1979). Certainly Wilson's work itself was encouraged by the fact that those staffing public agencies were no longer merely clerks, but were increasingly technicians and professionals from a variety of substantive backgrounds. That trend has continued as government in this country has grown and has become more and more complex. Those in public agencies are a source of expertise with respect to public policy matters and consequently are called on to present their ideas. Moreover, the scope and complexity of government today make it more difficult for the legislative branch to specify every detail of newly enacted policies. Consequently, there is increasing dependence on administrators throughout public agencies to exercise their discretion and to shape public policies as they see fit.

The increasing role of the bureaucracy in public policy, however, does not make the question of politics and administration less difficult. If the bureaucracy is in policy making to stay, how can we make sure that the policies arrived at are responsive to the public interest? How can we assure democratic accountability? Wilson's answer and the answer of most early theorists in the emerging field of public administration was that managers in public agencies should ultimately be accountable to the legislature, which is in turn accountable to the people, thus satisfying the requirements of democracy. In this hierarchical view of accountability, the separation of politics and administration is essential—the political neutrality of officials must be preserved.

Many recent studies have indicated the difficulties with such a position (see Thompson, 1983:245). Bureaucrats not only exercise discretion and provide advice, they shape public opinion through the information they provide, they mobilize support for their issues (and their agencies), and they bargain with numerous groups both within

and outside government to achieve their objectives. Under such circumstances, it is obviously difficult to speak of an adequate measure of accountability lying solely within the hierarchical relationship between the agency and the legislature (Lynn, 1981; Thompson, 1980, 1985).

For this reason, more contemporary discussions of responsiveness have cast the relationship between politics and administration in a new light: by what measures might we supplement hierarchical accountability so as to assure a "correspondence between the decisions of bureaucrats and the preferences of the community" (Rourke, 1969:3)? In general, the answers have taken two forms, the first seeking to instill a sense of subjective responsibility in those who staff public agencies, the second seeking formal or objective mechanisms to assure responsibility.

Hoping to develop a strong sense of responsibility on the part of civil servants, especially administrators, numerous writers through the decades have commented on those qualities they found desirable. Marshall Dimock (1936:132) hoped for "loyalty, as well as honesty, enthusiasm, humility, and all the other attributes of character and conduct which contribute to effectual and satisfying service." Appleby (1945:4) spoke of "a special attitude of public responsibility," while Stephen Bailey (1966:24) sought moral qualities of "l) optimism, 2) courage, and 3) fairness tempered by charity."

Several efforts have been made to bring these rather abstract qualities into existence. One stream of thought, associated primarily with Carl Friedrich (reprinted 1972) and Frederick Mosher (1968), argues that the emergence of professionalism within the bureaucracy should aid in the establishment of a proper set of values among bureaucrats. Friedrich felt that professionals, whatever their technical area, were likely to be more attuned to questions of administrative responsibility. Mosher focused more on those preparing specifically for administrative careers in government. As a part of their professional training, he argued, future administrators should be imbued with a sense of democratic responsibility. In Mosher's words, "the universities offer the best hope of making the professions safe for democracy" (Mosher, 1968:219).

Another stream of thought focuses on the kinds of commitments or oaths that are required of public servants. Many professional associations, including the American Society for Public Administration, have developed codes of ethics to which their members subscribe. Some, like the International City Management Association, have developed mechanisms for punishing violators of the code. Indeed, as John Rohr (1978) points out, all public employees take an oath to uphold the Constitution and, in his view, are therefore bound to support the values of the regime. These, according to Rohr, can best be determined through a careful review of the interpretations given the Constitution by the Supreme Court (see also Rohr, 1986).

Others have found dependence on the ethical commitment of the individual administrator insufficient as a device to assure responsiveness. Among these, Herman Finer (1972) and Theodore Lowi (1969) have both argued for greater legislative detail and increased supervision of administrative activities as means of limiting the choices bureaucrats might find it possible to make. Finer (1972:238) stated his position in this way: "Are the servants of the public to decide their own course, or is their course of action to be decided by a body outside themselves?" Feeling that bureaucrats holding a minority opinion might force their view on an unsuspecting public, Finer argued for the latter, specifically, that the legislature should engage in detailed consideration of its intent in formulating public policy and that it should exercise detailed supervision of the agencies of government.

Lowi (1969) argued from a quite different perspective but came to a similar conclusion. His concern was the fact that certain agencies of government seemed to develop a special relationship with certain private interests, often the very interests they were designed to regulate. In such cases, the bureaucracy may exercise discretion to favor certain private interests to the neglect of the larger public interest. Lowi's solution, "juridical democracy," envisions more detailed legislative action combined with more complete administrative rule making, both designed to eliminate discretion through the codification of as many relationships between agencies and their constituents as possible.

In addition to more specific legislation and greater legislative review of administrative actions, other suggestions designed to increase responsiveness have been proposed. Cooper (1982), for example, has discussed the numerous roles, obligations, and objective responsibilities that provide boundaries for administrative action; Gawthrop (1984) has explored the use of systems theory as a basis for redesigning organizational structures so as to fully incorporate ethical concerns.

Others have described various structural mechanisms that might be employed to assure responsiveness on the part of administrators. Among these are devices such as sunshine-and-sunset laws, surveys of citizen opinion, administrative hearings, and ombudsman programs; however, the two proposals most widely discussed are "representative bureaucracy" and "public participation" in administrative decision making. Proponents of representative bureaucracy argue that bureaucratic decisions are more likely to represent the general will of the people if government agencies are staffed in such a way as to reflect significant characteristics of the population. In its earliest applications, the notion of representative bureaucracy meant representation of various geographical constituencies (primarily the states) or, in its English version, the representation of social classes (Kingsley, 1944). In more contemporary times, representative bureaucracy is more likely to refer to representation based on race or sex (Krislov, 1974). Unfortunately, studies have shown mixed results in terms of responsiveness (Meier, 1979:169ff).

Public participation, employed as a device to ensure correspondence between the actions of civil servants and the wishes of the people, has an equally long, if not longer, history; however, it was given special emphasis in the 1960s and 1970s. Especially in what was called the "New Public Administration" (Bellone, 1980; Fredrickson, 1971, 1980; Marini, 1971; Waldo, 1971), the notion of public involvement was heralded. Through the creation of forums for citizen input ranging from open hearings to advisory boards to elected or appointed commissions, more information was sought from those likely to be affected by the decisions of the agency. In many cases, however, what appeared to be participation was better described as cooptation—"the process of absorbing new elements into the leadership or policy-determining structure or existence" (Selznick, 1949:13).

Why has the issue of politics versus administration continued to play a prominent role in discussions of public administration even today? At least three reasons come to mind. First, although the early writers on public administration did not argue for as strict a dichotomy of politics and administration as many people think, they did soon come to define their own subject matter in terms that seemed to imply such a distinction. By defining public administration as the work of government agencies (Willoughby, 1927), these writers quickly abandoned the notion of public administration as a function occurring throughout government and pursued instead an institutional view of public administration occurring within a certain setting, the agency. The implication, of course, was that such a study could be developed independent of studies of legislative processes and that a distinction could be made between legislation and implementation, between politics and administration.

Second, the urging of Wilson and others for government agencies to pursue the kind of efficiency modeled in private industry required some distinction between politics and administration. In order for agencies to be efficient, they could not be contaminated by either the corruption and dishonesty that often crept into the political process or the concern for responsiveness which, it was felt, was the prerogative of the legislature.

Finally, questions about the proper relationship (not dichotomy) between politics and administration have continued simply because defining that relationship goes to the heart of what public administration is all about. If the governance and management of public organizations differ from others in society, that difference must lie in the proper role of such organizations in defining and responding to the public interest. It is indeed the resulting tension, perhaps the inevitable tension between efficiency and responsiveness, that best characterizes work in public organizations.

II. BUREAUCRACY AND DEMOCRACY

As we have seen, the question of how to reconcile a concern for efficiency with a concern for responsiveness was treated by many early writers simply in terms of legislative control. The logic seemed to be that once the responsiveness of the agency to legislative mandate was assured, the agency should concentrate on operating in the most efficient manner possible. It was natural, therefore, that scholars and practitioners would be drawn to the best contemporary model for achieving organizational efficiency, the industrial or bureaucratic model. So, despite the fact that this model had certain autocratic features considerably at odds with democratic theory, it became the standard for administrative management in the public sector.

Such a position, however, skirts the question of whether an administrative body organized on nondemocratic lines is consistent with the notion of a democratic society. Certainly there were many who felt there was little problem here. For example, Frederick Cleveland (1920:15) would write: "The difference between an autocracy and a democracy lies not in the administrative organization but in the absence or presence of a controlling electorate or representative body outside of the administration with power to determine the will of the membership and to enforce its will on the administration." On the other hand, there were many who argued that "a democratic state must be not only based on democratic principles but also democratically administered, the democratic philosophy permeating its administrative machinery" (Levitan, 1943:359). These opposing arguments typify continuing discussions about the relationship between bureaucracy and democracy.

Just as discussion of politics and administration inevitably begins with the work of Woodrow Wilson, analysis of the concept of bureaucracy inevitably begins with the German sociologist Max Weber. In his classic examination of the concept of authority, Weber noted the importance of bureaucratic administration in supporting legal authority (as opposed to traditional or charismatic). The concept of bureaucracy, which is applied as easily to industrial and religious organizations as to those in government, contains several elements, among them the following: "1) [Officials] are personally free and are subject to authority only with respect to their impersonal official obligations, 2) they are organized in a clearly defined hierarchy of offices, 3) each office has a clearly defined sphere of competence . . . , 4) officials work entirely separated from ownership of the means of administration . . . , 5) they are subject to strict and systematic discipline and control in the conduct of the office" (Weber, 1947:328). In slightly more modern language, bureaucracy is characterized by hierarchical patterns of authority, a division of labor and specialization of tasks, and an impersonal arrangement of offices.

To Weber, and to many later writers, bureaucracy permits the greatest degree of efficiency in the conduct of human affairs and is therefore the most "rational" mode of social organization. Again Weber writes, "Experience tends universally to show that the purely bureaucratic type of administration . . . is, from a purely technical point of view, capable of attaining the highest degree of efficiency and is in this sense formally the most rational known means of carrying out imperative control over human beings" (Weber, 1947:333–334). Or, in another passage, "Bureaucratic administration is, other things being equal, always, from a formal technical point of view, the most rational type (Weber, 1947:337).

For those early students of public administration seeking the greatest possible efficiency in government agencies, the bureaucratic model, already becoming entrenched in industry, proved an attractive model. Fayol's (1949) scalar principle, for example, depicted the levels of authority in an organization as links forming a pattern of communication. (We might note, however, that Fayol did not argue for rigid adherence to hierarchical communications.)

Similarly, Willoughby (1927:37) sought to make the executive branch into a "single, integrated piece of administrative machinery," while Gulick (1937:44) praised the principles of hierarchical organization as the "bootstraps by which mankind lifts itself in the process of civilization." However, it was in the work of Herbert Simon that rationality in the field of administration received its most extensive treatment.

Simon began his analysis by noting the limits of human rationality, that human beings make decisions not on the basis of pure reason, as the classic model of economic man posits, but with the constraints of "bounded rationality." Indeed, it is because human beings are limited in their capacities that they join together in complex organizations. "The rational individual," according to Simon, "is, and must be, an organized and institutionalized individual" (Simon, 1957:102).

It is through joining together in organizations that people can attain the kind of rationality—read "efficiency"—that escapes them elsewhere.

As members of complex organizations, however, persons tend to behave in response to their own needs and interests. For example, Simon's discussion of why people respond to organizational authority is based on an "inducements-contributions" formula—a calculus in which certain inducements are offered individuals so that they contribute the desired actions. In making such decisions to contribute, individuals may not fully "maximize" their interests, but rather they "satisfice," they select what they consider a satisfactory alternative (Simon, 1957:xxvi). While "administrative man" is not fully rational, he does the best he can.

In contrast to the position that bureaucratic organization is the most rational form of social organization, others have argued that equating rationality and efficiency is not only theoretically incorrect, but also leads to structures and behaviors antithetical to important norms of a democratic society (Fischer and Sirianni, 1984; Hummel, 1982). Several critiques of bureaucratic life have appeared over the years (Whyte, 1956; Scott and Hart, 1979; Thayer, 1973; but see also Goodsell, 1983). Recently, three books written by theorists in the field of public administration have specified the major difficulties that seem to accompany bureaucratic organization.

In *The New Science of Organizations* (1981), Alberto Guerreiro Ramos argues that a market-centered society, a fairly recent historical development, has engendered a particular pattern of organization, which he terms the "economizing" organization. This pattern, based on the idea of instrumental rationality, the coordination of means to given ends, has come to dominate the way we think about organizing to the exclusion of other possibilities. This development is harmful in two ways: first, it has led to adoption of a particular social character in which man is stripped of the opportunity for personal growth and transformed into a mere constituent of the productive process; and second, it has permitted the growth of organized systems insensitive to ecological and psychological externalities. In contrast, Ramos argues for a new science of organizations that would enable us to envision alternative organizational designs, leading in turn to a "multicentric" or "reticular" society, in which differing forms of organization would be applied to different purposes.

The dehumanizing aspect of modern bureaucratic thought is further examined in Robert B. Denhardt's *In the Shadow of Organization* (1981). Denhardt agrees that the growth of complex organizations has led to a new and encompassing ethic of organization, a new way of seeing the world, a new metaphor for living, but one bound by the constraints of instrumental thinking. In contrast, he suggests a radical reordering of priorities, so as to give primacy to the growth of the individual rather than to the efficiency of the productive process, something that would require an alternative, personalist approach to life in an organizational society. Only through the development of a practical philosophy of life in an organizational society can concerns of individuation and emancipation be brought together. "The satisfaction of certain needs may be supported by the ethic of organization, but the needs of the spirit cannot. Organizations simply cannot bear the moral quest of the individual" (Denhardt, 1981:132).

Finally, Michael Harmon's *Action Theory for Public Administration* (1981), while equally critical of the influence of instrumental rationality in structuring our understanding of organizational life, focuses more on ways of achieving responsible human action in organizational settings. In contrast to the instrumental concept of the individual that is a part of bureaucratic thought, Harmon sees the individual as an intentional being, acting so as to bestow meaning on human action. Such a viewpoint suggests that we distinguish between directed behavior and intentional action, giving primacy to the latter, that is, to the everyday meanings that individuals attach to their own actions and to the actions of others. As this theme is developed, Harmon describes the resulting "proactive" administrator, one committed to disaggregated decisions and to concerns for equity and responsibility. The proactive administrator institutionalizes and facilitates consensual decision making both within the organization and with the clientele or public served (Harmon, 1981:155–161).

These general critiques apply with even greater force when one considers the valuational context of *public* administration. Whereas Willoughby (1927), White (1936), and Gulick (1937) held efficiency to be the primary objective of the study of public administration, Marshall Dimock challenged the mechanical application of the criterion of efficiency in public organizations, holding that efficiency alone is "coldly calculating and inhuman," whereas "successful administration is warm and vibrant. It is human" (Dimock, 1936:120).

Others pointed out that efficiency was only one of many criteria by which the work of public organizations might be evaluated, especially in a democratic society. For example, Robert Dahl (1947), in an important debate with Simon, suggested that public administration in a democratic society is almost by definition committed to values such as responsiveness, compassion, and concern. Efficiency may indeed be important, but it is often less important than the concerns of democracy. How would we evaluate the German prison camps of World War II, organizations that were marked by their efficiency?

A similar theme was developed by Emmett Redford in his book, *Democracy in the Administrative State*. Redford (1969:8) suggests that democracy rests on the concepts of individuality, equality, and participation, the latter including "1) access to information . . . , 2) access, direct or indirect, to forums of decision, 3) ability to open any issue to public discussion, 4) ability to assert one's claims without fear of coercive retaliation, and 5) consideration of all claims asserted." However, when one examines the way in which government agencies operate, one finds a far different set of assumptions in operation. The goals of the individual are subordinated to those of the organization, authority is distributed in a vastly uneven fashion, and there is relatively little opportunity for the participation of either those lower in the organization or clients of the organization in its decision processes. Redford concludes that attainment of the democratic ideal in the field of administration depends on the representation of many and diverse interests among decision makers.

The classic treatment of these issues, however, remains Dwight Waldo's book *The Administrative State* (1948). In this work and in other materials (Waldo, 1952,1980), Waldo pursues the notion that, without conscious intent, those who developed various approaches to organizational design and conduct were engaging in the creation of political theory. That is, the materials they developed for use in organization circles had direct implications for the political values of the society. Specifically, Waldo argued that the selection of efficiency as the primary value of public administration led to the development of bureaucratic structures and practices inconsistent with the normal standards of democracy. Indeed, it appeared that the earlier writers were arguing that " 'Autocracy' at work is the unavoidable price for 'Democracy' after hours" (Waldo, 1948:75).

The message of Waldo's work seemed clear: that an uncritical acceptance of the bureaucratic outlook constitutes a rejection of democratic theory. In contrast, Waldo called for a more democratic mode of organization, one consistent with the ideals of a democratic society. Such an alternative, he suggested, would necessarily involve a "substantial abandonment of the authority-submission, superordinate-subordinate thought patterns which tend to dominate our administrative theory" (Waldo, 1952:103). The mode of organization consistent with principles of democracy would necessarily be "postbureaucratic."

One final variant of the bureaucracy-democracy question asks whether democratic principles should be extended through many organizations in our society, not merely those in government. Certainly major aspects of public policy are being decided today by organizations that have traditionally been privately run. Moreover, there is no question that such organizations have a tremendous impact on the lives of individuals throughout the society. Under such conditions, one might well ask whether all organizations, not just those in the public sector, should be evaluated by the degree of their publicness, the degree to which they are responsive to the needs and interests of an informed citizenry. "In such an effort," writes Denhardt (1984:182), "public administration theory, especially theories of democratic administration, might come to be a model for organization theory generally."

III. ORGANIZATION AND MANAGEMENT

Our discussion of both politics and administration and bureaucracy versus democracy has emphasized the moral and political basis of work in public organizations. But what of the way in which public administration theorists have approached questions of organization and management? Have those theories and approaches that have been most influential in the field of public administration been distinctive in any way? Specifically, have they emphasized the values and concerns one would associate with democratic morality?

As we see, for the most part, the answer to these questions has been "no." Theorists and practitioners in public administration have largely depended on the same approaches to organization and management as those in the private sector. However, there is some support for the view that those in public administration have historically been more interested in humanizing relationships, both internal and external, and have been far more responsive to client needs and interests than their counterparts in business. Interestingly enough, these are just the features that are being heralded in modern studies of business practice.

Certainly, as we have seen, the early writers in the field of public administration were encouraged to follow the industrial or bureaucratic model of organization. Indeed, what came to be called the "administrative management" movement in public administration followed quite closely the recommendations of those in business that managers give priority in thought and action to structural concerns such as hierarchical authority, unity of command, span of control, line-staff relations, and the division of labor. Gulick's well-known essay "Notes on the Theory of Organization" (1937) exemplified the administrative management orientation. Gulick described the problems of management as those of creating an appropriate division of labor, then imposing on that division of labor mechanisms for coordination and control. He suggested four steps: (1) to define the job to be carried out, (2) to select a director, (3) to determine the nature and number of units required, and (4) to establish a structure of authority through which coordination and control can be achieved (Gulick, 1937:7).

An even more direct merging of public and private management occurred with the development of a generic orientation toward the study of management and organization. One major figure in this development was the public administrationist

Herbert A. Simon, who joined others in pursuing a "scientific" study of administrative behavior. In pursuing regularities in human behavior in complex organization, these "generic" theorists came to argue that such regularities were largely independent of their context, that, for example, the exercise of power and the capacity to motivate or delegate are much the same whether one is describing a family, an industrial organization, or a government agency. From this viewpoint, there emerged a new social science, organizational analysis, one drawing on work in business and public administration as well as sociology, psychology, and other disciplines.

This approach is well illustrated in Simon's own analysis of decision-making processes. As a generic phenomenon, Simon contends, decision making consists of intelligence (finding opportunities for decision making), design (developing alternatives), and choice (choosing from among these). Again, consistent with Simon's interpretation of human rationality, the decision maker hopes to maximize outcomes but is typically found to suffice.

Despite the appeal of the generic approach and its apparently closed system of decision making, public administration theorists were quick to point out certain limitations. For example, Charles Lindblom (1959) suggested that in actual practice Simon's model of decision making was rarely used. Instead, administrators typically chose an incremental approach, setting limited objectives and making limited comparisons based on experience and personal values. Similarly, Graham Allison (1971) argued that major policy decisions, such as those involved in the Cuban missile crisis of the Kennedy administration, do not follow either the classical rational actor model nor that contained in theories of organization. Rather, he argued, decisions result from a political process of bargaining and negotiation played out in a rapidly changing environment.

Other scholars pursued the idea of environmental uncertainty, noting that open systems of organization cannot be guided by strict notions of efficiency in pursuit of their objectives, simply because environmental shifts mean things are always changing. Philip Selznick's study of TVA (1949) examined the policy of decentralization and involvement of local groups that was employed by that agency in its early days. He pointed out

that the key criterion for evaluating organizations in fluctuating environments is not necessarily their efficiency, but their adaptability and their capacity to remain stable in the face of environmental changes. Similarly, Herbert Kaufman (1960) examined the environmental influences on rangers in the U.S. Forest Service, highlighting the efforts designed to maintain the loyalty and consistency of forest rangers in spite of the various environmental pressures placed on them at the local level.

More recently, Rainey and Milward (1983) have discussed policy networks that cut across various specific organizations in the delivery of public programs. This work, which draws in part from Aldrich and Whetten's (1981) work on inter-organizational networks, suggests that programs cut across agencies based on the kinds of organized interests that are involved. "Since programs are usually the focus for networks, program networks are the most important type of network for policymaking. These are networks that form among groups, individuals, and organizations on the basis of their interest in a particular program" (Rainey and Milward, 1983:143).

A concern for the influence of environmental factors on agency performance has also marked the work of those interested in implementation issues. Pressman and Wildavsky examined the failure of a particular economic development project, concluding that "what seemed to be a simple program turned out to be a very complex one, involving many participants, a host of different perspectives, and a long and tortuous path of decision points that had to be cleared" (Pressman and Wildavsky, 1973:94). In part, their recommendation was for legislative bodies to pay greater attention to creating organizational mechanisms for effective implementation as a part of policy formation; in part, it was a recommendation to scholars to consider more carefully the way in which implementation efforts affect or even determine policy outcomes (see also Wildavsky, 1979; Wholey et al., 1986).

Bardach (1977) pursued the latter theme as he tried to identify implementation games, patterns of bargaining and negotiation that occurred in the process of implementation, while more recently, George Edwards (1980) described the implementation process as involving communications, resources, dispositions and attitudes of the implementers, and bureaucratic structures. His recommendations with respect to organizational management focus on dealing with the problem of fragmentation and sound quite familiar: he proposes exactly what the administrative management theorists had proposed 50 years earlier—a center of executive power exercised through a hierarchical chain of command.

A more interesting and advanced interpretation of the work of public agencies is contained in Wamsley and Zald's *The Political Economy of Public Organizations* (1973). Wamsley and Zald propose a framework for analyzing administrative bodies by focusing on the juxtaposition of political factors and economic factors, in each case both those internal to the organization and those external to the group. Political factors are those involving power and interests, and economic factors are those affecting the market and its exchange of goods and services. It is the interaction of these various factors that establishes the capacity of the organization, including its organizational power structure (Downs, 1967).

Wamsley and Zald's emphasis on exchange mechanisms seems clearly related to Vincent Ostrom's important work on public choice. Ostrom's work is based on the assumption that rational individuals exercise their rationality with respect to public goods as well as private goods and that an analysis of public choices from this perspective will lead to important lessons for the design of public organizations. In this view, "Public agencies are not viewed simply as bureaucratic units which perform those services which someone at the top instructs them to perform. Rather, public agencies are viewed as means for allocating decision-making capabilities in order to provide public goods and services responsive to the preferences of individuals in different social contexts" (Ostrom and Ostrom, 1971:207). Ostrom pursues the logic of public choice to the point of identifying cases in which public enterprises can be operated within specific domains, thus opening the possibility for greater decentralization of power and authority. Ultimately, his proposal is for a form of democratic administration, based on multiorganizational relationships and intentional fragmentation, something the logic of public choice would see not only as more responsive, but also more efficient (Ostrom, 1974). (We should note that Ostrom's work has been criticized by

Golembiewski [1977], who indicates that individuals may seek to maximize values that do not necessarily enhance a democratic society and may even corrupt it. See also Ostrom's [1977] response.)

Unlike other writers with a primary interest in policy development (Edwards, 1980; Kingdon, 1984; Nagel, 1980), Ostrom puts policy analysis to work in the critique rather than the justification of bureaucratic structures, thus connecting him to an otherwise quite distinct group of theorists interested in organizational humanism. The work of this group is usually traced back to the well-known Hawthorne experiments in the 1920s and 1930s. These experiments, basically begun as efforts to examine how favorable working conditions might influence worker productivity, resulted in documentation of the importance of social and psychological factors in the productivity of American workers. Specifically, the research team found that in addition to creating goods or services, organizations also serve the purpose of "creating and distributing satisfactions among the individual members of the organization" (Roethlisberger and Dickson, 1940:562).

The Hawthorne conclusions were reaffirmed in the work of Chester Barnard, who, based on his career of executive service, wrote eloquently of the informal or social aspect of organizational work. To achieve cooperation, Barnard wrote, one must take into account the many and often contradictory forces operating on the individual organizational member. "Cooperation and organization as they are observed and experienced are concrete syntheses of opposed facts and of opposed thought and emotions of human beings. It is precisely the function of the executive to facilitate the synthesis in concrete action of contradictory forces, to reconcile conflicting forces, instincts, interests, conditions, positions, and ideals" (Barnard, 1938:21).

Similarly, theorists such as Douglas McGregor (1960) and Robert Blake and Jane Mouton (1981) argued for a more humanistic approach to management, the latter writing that a combination of high concern for productivity combined with a high concern for people is "positively associated with success, productivity, and profitability in comparison with any other theory" (Blake and Mouton, 1981:128). Most noteworthy, however, was the work of Chris Argyris, whose *Personality and Organization* (1957) was highly influential. Argyris noted that contemporary management practices, which tended to emphasize highly directive, control-oriented behavior on the part of managers, was actually counterproductive, for it was at odds with the basic strivings of the adult personality. Argyris emphasized instead a style of management that stressed the manager's understanding and facilitating human development within the organizations and eventually led to a strong concern for combining personal learning and organization development.

Among students of public administration, these various themes have been advanced most ably by Robert Golembiewski (Golembiewski, 1972, 1985). Golembiewski's work is most important for its infusion of moral considerations into discussions of organizational development and change. Golembiewski's early work makes an important connection between humanistic approaches to management and questions of morality, holding that "moral sensitivity can be associated with satisfactory output and employee satisfaction" (1967:53). His later efforts explored organizational development as an approach to understanding and improving the work of complex organizations. Yet, even here, his concern for morality was evident. For example, he describes five "metavalues" that guide the laboratory approach to organizational change and development: (1) mutual accessibility and open communications, (2) willingness to experiment with new behaviors, (3) a collaborative concept of authority, (4) establishing mutual helping relationships, and (5) developing authenticity in interpersonal relationships (1972:60–66).

The humanistic tendencies of modern students of public administration were emphasized in the "New Public Administration," a series of papers brought together at a conference at Syracuse University (Marini, 1971). These papers, although hardly uniform in content or perspective, did tend to emphasize a more active role for public administrators in the development of public policy and a more equitable and participative approach to the management of public organizations. Perhaps most notable in the latter area were the articles of Larry Kirkhart (1971) and Orion White (1971), both of whom emphasized open communications, greater equality of power, and the importance of consensus building in organizations. . . .

From this brief summary, it is clear that those in public administration have relied heavily on private sector work in their approach to organization and management. But one also gets a sense, especially in the work of Golembiewski, Ostrom, the new public administrationists . . . that humanistic considerations are not simply "useful," but in fact morally correct. It should not be surprising that such a feeling would prevail in public administration, marked as it is by concern for the public service. Interestingly, while several recent books in management for the private sector have espoused a service orientation and a participative approach to shared power in organizations, exactly such tendencies have marked public administration theory for the past several decades. In its approach to organization and management, public administration may well provide some important lessons for those in the private sector. . . .

REFERENCES

ALDRICH, H., and WHETTEN, D. A. (1981). Organization sets, action sets, and networks: Making the most of simplicity. In *Handbook of Organization Design*, Vol. 1 (P. C. Nystrom and W. H. Starbuck, eds.), Oxford University Press, Oxford.

ALLISON, G. T. (1971). *Essence of Decision: Explaining the Cuban Missile Crisis*. Little, Brown, Boston.

APPLEBY, P. (1945). *Big Democracy*. Alfred A. Knopf, New York.

——— (1949). *Policy and Administration*. University of Alabama Press, University, Alabama.

ARGYRIS, C. (1957). *Personality and Organization*. Harper & Row, New York.

BAILEY, S. (1966). Ethics and the public service. In *Public Administration: Readings in Institutions, Processes, Behavior* (R. T. Golembiewski, F. Gibson, and G. Cornog, eds.), Rand McNally, Chicago, pp. 22–31.

BARDACH, E. (1977). *The Implementation Game*. M.I.T. Press, Cambridge, Massachusetts.

BARNARD, C. (1938). *The Functions of the Executive*. Harvard University Press, Cambridge, Massachusetts.

BELLONE, C. (ed.) (1980). *Organization Theory and the New Public Administration*. Allyn and Bacon, Boston.

BLAKE, R., and MOUTON, J. (1981). *The Academic Administrator Grid*. Jossey-Bass, San Francisco.

CLEVELAND, F. A. (1920). *The Budget and Responsible Government*. Macmillan, New York.

COOPER, T. L. (1982). *The Responsible Administrator: An Approach to Ethics for the Administrative Role*. Kennikat Press, New York.

DAHL, R. A. (1947). The Science of Public Administration, *Public Administration Review, 7:* 1–11.

DENHARDT, R. B. (1981). *In the Shadow of Organization.* Regents Press of Kansas, Lawrence.

——— (1984). *Theories of Public Organization.* Brooks/Cole, Pacific Grove, California.

DIMOCK, M. E. (1936). Criteria and objectives of public administration. In *The Frontiers of Public Administration* (J. M. Gaus, L. D. White, and M. E. Dimock, eds.), University of Chicago Press, Chicago, pp. 116–132.

DOWNS, A. (1967). *Inside Bureaucracy.* Little, Brown, Boston.

DUNN, W. N. (1981). *Public Policy Analysis.* Prentice-Hall, Englewood Cliffs, New Jersey.

EDWARDS, G. C. (1980). *Implementing Public Policy.* Congressional Quarterly Press, Washington, DC.

FAYOL, H. (1949). *General and Industrial Management,* translated by C. Storrs. Pittman, London.

FINER, H. (1972). Administrative responsibility in democratic government. In *Bureaucratic Power in National Politics* (F. Rourke, ed.), Little, Brown, Boston, pp. 326–337.

FISCHER, F., and SIRIANNI, C. (1984). *Critical Studies in Organization and Bureaucracy.* Temple University Press, Philadelphia.

FREDERICKSON, H. G. (1971). Toward a new public administration. In *Toward a New Public Administration* (F. Marini, ed.). Chandler, San Francisco, pp. 309–331.

——— (1980). *New Public Administration.* University of Alabama Press, University, Alabama.

FRIEDRICH, C. J. (1972). Public policy and the nature of administrative responsibility. In *Bureaucratic Power in National Politics* (F. Rourke, ed.), Little, Brown, Boston, pp. 165–175.

GAWTHROP, L. C. (1984). *Public Sector Management Systems and Ethics.* Indiana University Press, Bloomington.

GOLEMBIEWSKI, R. T. (1967). *Men, Management, and Morality.* McGraw-Hill, New York.

——— (1972). *Renewing Organizations.* Peacock, Ithaca, Illinois.

——— (1977). A critique of "Democratic Administration" and its supporting ideation, *American Political Science Review, 71:* 1488–1507.

——— (1985). *Humanizing Public Organizations.* McGraw-Hill, New York.

GOODNOW, F. (1900). *Policy and Administration.* Macmillan, New York.

GOODSELL, C. T. (1983). *The Case for Bureaucracy: A Public Administration Polemic.* Chatham House, Chatham, New Jersey.

GULICK, L. (1933). Politics, administration, and the New Deal, *Annals of the American Academy of Political and Social Science, 169:* 545–566.

——— (1937). Notes on the theory of organization. In *Papers on the Science of Administration* (L. Gulick and

L. Urwick, eds.), Institute of Public Administration, New York, pp. 1–46.

HARMON, M. M. (1981). *Action Theory for Public Administration.* Longman, New York.

HUMMEL, R. (1982). *The Bureaucratic Experience,* 2nd ed. St. Martin's Press, New York.

KAUFMAN, H. (1960). *The Forest Ranger.* Johns Hopkins University Press, Baltimore, Maryland.

KINGDON, J. W. (1984). *Agendas, Alternatives, and Public Policies.* Little, Brown, Boston/Toronto.

KINGSLEY, D. (1944). *Representative Bureaucracy: An Interpretation of the British Civil Service.* Antioch University Press, Yellow Springs, Ohio.

KIRKHART, L. (1971). Toward a theory of public administration. In *Toward A New Public Administration* (F. Marini, ed.). Chandler, San Francisco, pp. 127–164.

KRISLOV, S. (1974). *Representative Bureaucracy.* Prentice-Hall, Englewood Cliffs, New Jersey.

LEVITAN, D. M. (1943). Political ends and administrative means, *Public Administration Review, 3:* 353–359.

LINDBLOM, C. E (1959). The science of muddling through, *Public Administration Review, 19:* 79–88.

LOWI, T. (1969). *The End of Liberalism.* Norton, New York.

LYNN, L. E., JR. (1981). *Managing the Public's Business.* Basic Books, New York.

MARINI, F. (ed.) (1971). *Toward a New Public Administration: The Minnowbrook Perspective.* Chandler, San Francisco.

MCGREGOR, D. (1960). *The Human Side of Enterprise.* McGraw-Hill, New York.

MEIER, K. J. (1979). *Politics and the Bureaucracy: Policymaking in the Fourth Branch of Government.* Duxbury Press, Massachusetts.

MOSHER, F. (1968). *Democracy and the Public Service.* Oxford University Press, New York.

NAGEL, S. (ed.) (1980). *Improving Policy Analysis.* Sage Publications, Newbury Park, California, pp. 15–33.

OSTROM, V. (1974). *The Intellectual Crisis in American Public Administration.* University of Alabama Press, University, Alabama.

———, and OSTROM, E. (1971). Public choice: A different approach to the study of public administration, *Public Administration Review, 31:* 203–216.

PETERS, B. G. (1984). *The Politics of Bureaucracy.* Longman, New York.

PRESSMAN, J., and WILDAVSKY, A. (1973). *Implementation: How Great Expectations in Washington Are Dashed in Oakland; Or, Why It's Amazing that Federal Programs Work at All.* University of California Press, Berkeley.

RAINEY, H. G., and MILWARD, H. B. (1983). Public organizations: Policy networks and environments. In *Organizational Theory and Public Policy* (R. H. Hall and R. E. Quinn, eds.), Sage Publications, Newbury Park, California.

RAMOS, A. G. (1981). *The New Science of Organizations.* University of Toronto Press, Toronto.

REDFORD, E. S. (1969). *Democracy in the Administrative State.* Oxford University Press, New York.

RIPLEY, R. B., and FRANKLIN, G. A. (1982). *Bureaucracy and Policy Implementation.* Dorsey Press, Homewood, Illinois.

ROETHLISBERGER, F., and DICKSON, W. (1940). *Management and the Worker.* Harvard University Press, Cambridge, Massachusetts.

ROHR, J. A. (1978). *Ethics for Bureaucrats.* Marcel Dekker, New York.

—— (1986). *To Run a Constitution.* University Press of Kansas, Lawrence, Kansas.

ROURKE, F. E. (1969). *Bureaucracy, Politics, and Public Policy.* Little, Brown, Boston.

SCOTT, W. G., and HART, D. K. (1979). *Organizational America.* Houghton-Mifflin, Boston.

SEIDMAN, H., and GILMOUR, R. (eds.) (1986). *Politics, Position, and Power: From the Positive to the Regulatory State,* 4th ed. Oxford University Press, New York.

SELZNICK, P. (1949). *TVA and the Grass Roots.* Harper & Row, New York.

SIMON, H. A. (1957). *Administrative Behavior: A Study of Decision-Making Process in Administrative Organization,* 2nd ed. Free Press, New York.

THAYER, F. E. (1973). *An End to Hierarchy! An End to Competition!* New Viewpoints, New York.

THOMPSON, D. F. (1980). Moral responsibility of public officials: The problem of many hands, *The American Political Science Review,* 74: 905–916.

—— (1983). Bureaucracy and democracy. In *Democratic Theory and Practice* (G. Duncan, ed.). Cambridge University Press, Cambridge, Massachusetts.

—— (1985). The possibility of administrative ethics, *Public Administration Review,* 45: 555–562.

WALDO, D. (1948). *The Administrative State.* Ronald Press, New York.

—— (1952). The development of a theory of public administration, *American Political Science Review,* 46: 81–103.

—— (ed.) (1971). *Public Administration in a Time of Turbulence.* Chandler, San Francisco.

—— (1980). *The Enterprise of Public Administration.* Chandler & Sharp, Novato, California.

WAMSLEY, G., and ZALD, M. (1973). The Political Economy of Public Organizations. Lexington Books, Lexington, Massachusetts.

WEBER, M. (1947). *The Theory of Social and Economic Organization.* Oxford University Press, New York.

WHITE, L. D. (1936). The meaning of principles in public administration. In *The Frontiers of Public Administration* (J. M. Gaus, L. D. White, and M. E. Dimock, eds.). University of Chicago Press, Chicago, pp. 13–25.

WHITE, O. F., JR. (1971). Administrative adaptation in a changing society. In *Toward a New Public Administration: The Minnowbrook Perspective* (F. Marini, ed.), Chandler, San Francisco, pp. 59–62.

WHOLEY, J. S., ABRAMSON, M. A., and BELLAVITA, C. (1986). *Performance and Credibility: Developing Excellence in Public and Nonprofit Organizations.* D. C. Heath, Lexington, Massachusetts.

WHYTE, W. H., JR. (1956). *The Organization Man.* Simon and Schuster, New York.

WILDAVSKY, A. (1979). *Speaking Truth to Power: The Art and Craft of Policy Analysis.* Little, Brown, Boston.

WILLOUGHBY, W. F. (1927). *Principles of Public Administration.* Johns Hopkins Press, Baltimore, Maryland.

WILSON, W. (1887). The study of administration, *Political Sci. Q.,* 2: 197–232.

STEPHEN E. REYNOLDS: TIME IS RUNNING OUT FOR ONE OF THE LAST OF THE GREAT "WATER BUFFALOS"

Tom Arrandale

Steve Reynolds is embarrassed. It's past 9 o'clock on a brisk Santa Fe night, and he's stolen into the press gallery for a smoke. Below, the New Mexico Senate is preparing to vote on a measure to protect the state's high mountain streams against any more dams or irrigation ditches.

Minority Leader Les Houston catches Reynolds' eye, lifts a forearm, fist closed with the thumb pointed up, asking for guidance. Reynolds is flustered, but returns the thumbs-up signal; Houston votes for the legislation. The bill passes, 26-14, and Houston, a combative Democrat-turned-Republican from Albuquerque, takes the floor to explain that he voted affirmatively "because the state engineer says it's all right."

"Next time, I think I'd better hide," Reynolds chuckles the next day. At the age of 72, Reynolds has just broken his own career-long rule against taking a stand on bills before the state legislature.

If Reynolds had turned thumbs down on the bill, "I'd have voted no," Houston explains later, licking an Eskimo Pie outside the chamber. "I've got that much confidence in his relationship to the water laws of the state of New Mexico. Not that many people can do that to me."

For 34 years, Stephen E. Reynolds has held a prosaic title as New Mexico state engineer. But as water boss in a desert state, Reynolds ranks among the most powerful public officials in the Rocky Mountain region.

He controls who gets water—and where and how they can use it—in a land where rainfall averages 15 inches a year. Ten New Mexico governors have been elected, and nine have left office, since Reynolds took the job in 1955. He has turned a two-year term into a lifetime appointment by mastering the intricate law and high-stakes politics that distribute scarce water in the arid West.

"Steve Reynolds is a classic," says Christopher Meyer, a National Wildlife Federation water resource attorney from Colorado. "He's the last of the great 'water buffalos,'" a holdover from a time when state engineers, influential lawyers, farmers and land developers joined with Western congressional delegations and federal bureaucrats to dam the West's rivers, divide their flows among fiercely competing states, and pump life-giving water across deserts and through mountain passes to supply crops and homes and factories.

Fifty years have gone by since Reynolds, a rawboned 6-foot-2-inch end, captained the 1938 University of New Mexico football team. Now he walks with a painful limp and gives himself an insulin shot each day for diabetes. But Reynolds retains a sharp-edged mind and a matchless command of the law and language of water resources.

"There's a saying in politics that he or she who has knowledge has power," says New Mexico's Republican governor, Garrey E. Carruthers, an economist who served four years as President Reagan's assistant interior secretary for water resources. "There are few lawyers who are better equipped to argue and debate the principles of water law than Steve Reynolds is, and he's not a lawyer."

"You damn sure if you're going to be state engineer you had better read and understand the law," Reynolds declares in a low-pitched voice as gravelly as the roar of a mountain stream.

Trained as a mechanical engineer, Reynolds serves as a judge when he makes economically crucial determinations to permit or disapprove requests to develop New Mexico's water. Two years ago, in what some regard as his finest hour, the state engineer conducted nine grueling months of fact-finding proceedings, then turned down thirsty El Paso, Texas, in its quest for the right to cross the state line and tap New Mexico's limited groundwater aquifers. . . .

"There is no other Steve Reynolds," says Steven J. Shupe, a former Colorado assistant attorney general who consults on regional water issues. "He is by far the most powerful individual dealing with water in the West."

New Mexico, like most Western states, makes scarce water available on a first-come, first-served basis. Following a doctrine of "prior appropriation" that evolved in California mining camps, Western state governments grant primary water-use rights to the first farmer, miner or city to dam a stream. To maintain water rights, those holding them generally must physically divert water every year for "beneficial use" in irrigation, industry or households. Water in New Mexico technically belongs to the state, but rights to use it are treated as private property that can be bought and sold, and the water can be piped miles away to new locations. As Reynolds is fond of saying, "Water will flow uphill to money."

State law gives the state engineer authority to regulate water use to keep limited supplies from being depleted. Reynolds must grant permits before water users can build new dams, shift the place where a stream is diverted from one point to another, or transfer water from irrigation to other uses. He can assert similar controls over pumping from groundwater basins by declaring that they are threatened by overdevelopment.

Reared on the green Illinois prairies, Reynolds came to the desert Southwest in the 1930s to study engineering. When New Mexico Governor John F. Simms, a college acquaintance, offered him the vacant state engineer's position, he moved to Santa Fe, boned up on water law and proceeded to apply it in forceful, often innovative ways.

In 1959, Reynolds went by the book and canceled two well permits held by then-Governor John Burroughs, who had failed to put them to use. He also took on Albuquerque, the state's largest city, by ordering the city government to acquire water rights on the Rio Grande to offset pumping from groundwater deposits that mingled with the river system. Reynolds' action, upheld by the New Mexico Supreme Court, pioneered coordinated strategies that other states later emulated for managing surface streams and interrelated groundwater deposits.

Allied with Clinton P. Anderson, then a powerful U.S. senator from New Mexico, in the 1960s Reynolds led Rocky Mountain states in their fight with California and Arizona over development of the Colorado River.

"He's been a magnificent administrator," says University of New Mexico law Professor Em Hall, at one time an attorney on Reynolds' staff. When disputes arise, Reynolds conducts quasi-judicial proceedings to gather hydrologic data and hear legal testimony, then decides whether to approve or turn down the water-use permits.

"He's the best trial judge I've worked before," Hall adds. "He's fair, he's sensitive, and he takes a real active role." The state engineer's decisions can be appealed to the courts, but Reynolds has usually won.

Over the years, Reynolds has angered farmers and ranchers on New Mexico's eastern plains by starting to regulate the groundwater pumping. He took on Indian pueblos and tribes that are pressing lawsuits to quantify potentially huge claims to water for reservations. He pressed legal "adjudications" to sort out convoluted water-rights claims along northern New Mexico streams, stirring resentment in narrow mountain valleys where Hispanic families have relied on community irrigation ditches, called acequias, since the 17th century. He drew environmentalists' ire when he supported the damming of the Gila River, the last free-flowing river in the state, and suggested cutting water-sucking cottonwoods down along the length of the Rio Grande to leave more water for fields and factories.

"He's survived in an impossible political world," says Hall. "I don't know how he's done it." . . .

While Colorado and other Western states hire "ditch riders" to tell irrigators when to open and close their water gates, Reynolds lets farmers work out water-sharing arrangements among themselves on most streams.

This hands-off approach also spares Reynolds from trying to identify a single public interest in a state where Indian tribes, Hispanic towns, Anglo ranchers and city-bred environmentalists hold different views of proper water management. "In this state, there is no one public interest," Hall says. "To determine the public interest is to take sides, and that would be political suicide."

"I'm no fool," Reynolds responds. "I wouldn't try to do that."

Reynolds has cultivated unquestioning support in New Mexico's part-time legislature. When the legislature is in town and water issues are on the agenda, Reynolds banishes his employees from the capitol and walks across the street himself. During committee proceedings, he sits near the back of cramped capitol meeting rooms with lobbyists and reporters. But chairmen always call on the state engineer for guidance.

His reputation is such that he often kills measures simply by raising doubts. For several years, environmental groups have pushed legislation to recognize water flowing downstream as a beneficial use protected by state law. But Reynolds cautions legislators that managing water left in the stream would force farmers to bear the cost of measuring daily flows to make sure in-stream rights were honored. Two years ago, Reynolds posed last-minute questions that killed a House-passed bill. This year the Senate passed a bill, crafted to Reynolds' specifications, restricting protection to mountain streams where development would be unlikely anyway. The House buried it.

Reynolds strengthened his political standing two years ago by heading off El Paso's efforts to acquire New Mexico water. Forced by U.S. Supreme Court decisions to consider El Paso's request, Reynolds, at the age of 70, handled the case himself. After nine months of hearings, he ruled that El Paso had not proved it would need the water within 40 years—the same standard he requires New Mexico's cities to meet. "He sat down there for months, in the middle of an explosive situation, and kept the proceedings moving," Hall says. "The decision he made was a brilliant judicial stroke, narrow, tight, short. He didn't say anything more than he had to." El Paso is challenging Reynolds' decision in court. . . .

THE DEATH AND LIFE OF AN AGENCY

It was an unmitigated disaster! The hearing had gone so badly that Caleb Kasper didn't even want to go home. What he really wanted to do was slink away to some isolated mountain retreat and spend the rest of his life fishing. When the state legislature passed the agency review statute, he had been a supporter. As part of the effort to improve government, a reform-minded governor and state legislature had passed a "sunset" law, which required all non-cabinet-level agencies and departments to be reauthorized every ten years. The initial list of agencies to be reviewed had included the Industrial Development Agency that Caleb had headed for the past six years.

The opportunity to be among the first agencies to be reauthorized under the new law had stimulated Caleb and his staff to a frenzy of activity. Months of preparation had gone into the careful crafting of an impressive set of internal review reports. The original mission of the Industrial Development Agency (IDA) was to stimulate the industrial development of the state. The original director had been recruited from one of the largest corporations in the state. His idea had been to have the IDA serve as a clearinghouse for starting industrial parks throughout the state. The agency quickly hired and trained staff to prepare grant applications for federal grants to do the site preparation in urban areas. The IDA had provided technical assistance to local governments in rural areas, where there was a possibility of starting an industrial park on entirely new land.

This part of the agency's past was well documented, and even the most hostile legislators at the hearing had praised the former director's efforts. When Caleb was appointed to head the agency, change had been inevitable. The federal programs that had allowed IDA to receive grants for industrial redevelopment in urban areas were being scaled back and in some cases eliminated. Most of the choice sites in the rural areas had been identified and industrial parks had been started. Caleb had called a week-long planning retreat for top administrators, during which they took stock of where the agency should be headed in the future.

At the retreat, two issues had been identified as the most pressing problems for the IDA. Under many of the grants from the federal government, the IDA was obligated to ensure that all applicable federal regulations were being observed in the redevelopment projects. The IDA had included the stipulation in the contracts it had signed with the developers, but very little checking had been done on whether the regulations were actually being followed. Caleb and his administrative group had decided to form an enforcement and investigations group, which they called the Compliance Review Bureau.

The second issue to emerge from the discussion of the agency's future was the growing number of bankruptcies among the developers. During the initial spurt of development, only a very small percentage of the projects were in financial difficulty. The original director had managed to get the legislature to authorize a modest bond issue, which provided funds to keep these projects going. Over the past two years, the rate of insolvency among the developers had grown. Caleb, whose background had been in banking, suggested that the IDA set up a refinance group to help those developers secure additional funding from private sources. They decided to call this division the Bureau of Refinance.

The two new bureaus experienced the usual problems. The contractors were not very happy about the Compliance Review Bureau's investigations of their projects. Two of the industrial parks were required to completely redo their waste-water management facilities because they didn't meet federal standards. One developer was discovered to have denied an occupancy application to a minority-owned business without justification. Rather than comply with the nondiscrimination requirements, the developer had sold his interest to another company. The Bureau of Refinance was quite successful. In fact, it was so good at finding private funding for distressed developers that some of the residential building companies began to complain that the IDA was making it hard for them to get money to build large residential developments.

With these new directions going so well, Caleb had anticipated no problem with the Government Operations Committee during the review. He could not have been more wrong. The first hint Caleb had came in the list of parties wishing to give testimony before the committee. Along with the usual groups were several that he had not anticipated. The Home Builders Association was on the list. The Industrial Resources Council was on the list. The Save Our Forests group was on the list. The Citizens for Taxpayer Justice was on the list. Because the list had been released only two weeks before the hearing, Caleb had only sketchy information about what these groups were going to say.

The hearing had started with an opening statement by the committee chairperson, who reviewed the reasons for the hearing and reminded the committee members that the vote on reauthorization would be taken immediately after the hearing. As one group after another testified that it thought the Industrial Development Agency had served its purpose in the past but ought to be abolished, Caleb got a sinking feeling in his stomach. Even the Industrial Resources Council offered only lukewarm support. By the time the Economy League testified that industrial parks were no longer an appropriate development technique because of environmental hazards associated with concentrations of industry, Caleb was beginning to panic.

Caleb's prepared testimony carefully reviewed the history of the agency and pointed to the success of the two new bureaus as indication that the work of the agency was not yet done. As he concluded his remarks, he asked permission to comment on the previous testimony. The chairperson consulted with the other committee members and agreed—with an admonishment to be brief.

Caleb looked around the room at the unsmiling faces and began in a low voice: "What you have heard today reflects on the changing role of the agency in state government. When the agency began its work, there was agreement between the developers and the agency officials. We all wanted to establish new industrial parks—and we did. The agency served to channel funds from the federal government to developers. Over the years, however, our role has changed. We are now required to regulate the development in order to ensure compliance with federal rules. That means that the agency officials and developers are often in conflict over the interpretation of the regulations." Caleb took a deep breath and went on. "In addition, we are now serving as a transfer agent to facilitate the flow of capital from the private sector to public sponsored projects. This has not made everyone happy. The agency recognizes that it must be responsive to the people it interacts with, but the agency also recognizes that it must serve the public at large, as well as its individual clients. We believe that we are doing a good job and deserve to be reauthorized for another ten years. Thank you very much for this opportunity to testify."

DISCUSSION QUESTIONS

1. Explain how you would vote on the question of reauthorization if you were a member of the Government Operations Committee.
2. What other arguments would you have used, if you were Caleb, to justify the reauthorization?
3. Did the administrators in the Industrial Development Agency do anything inappropriate when they redefined their mission at the planning conference?

"DON'T TELL THEM—SHOW THEM"

Christopher James Cromwell smiled at the modest group of people who were milling about the room. His sense of a new beginning was slowly growing as the meeting was about to begin. After his early retirement from the insurance industry, he had become increasingly frustrated and bored with the sameness of his day-to-day activities. The chance to become active in a community service organization promised to give him a whole new series of challenges.

Christopher had agreed to lead a newly formed group of community activists, called Literacy Liberators. Several of the churches in the community had picked adult illiteracy as the social problem most in need of remedy in the region. Money had been raised to start the organization, and the board was composed of members of the local school board and the participating churches. The Department of Community Services had agreed to provide a small grant of "in kind" administrative services, consisting of office space, telephone service, and a part-time secretary in the state office building.

As he tapped his glass to call the meeting to order, Christopher thought back to the interview with the board about his role as executive director. During the interview, Christopher had emphasized his experience with budgets and finance. He had told the board that most new organizations failed because there wasn't enough money to sustain the day-to-day operations. The board had been impressed with his knowledge of business practices and was relieved when he told them that, because he was retired, he would only accept a nominal salary.

"Welcome to the first organizational meeting of Literacy Liberators. My name is Christopher James Cromwell and I have been appointed executive director by the board. I have prepared an agenda for the meeting, which will take about an hour to complete, so unless there are any questions, I'd like to get started." The room gradually quieted as Christopher began to explain how the volunteers would be organized into groups and how the central office would coordinate their activities. By the time Christopher got to the fourth item—reimbursement of travel expenses—he noticed that several people were collecting their hats and coats to leave. "There are only a few more items," he said somewhat loudly, "and then we can open the floor for discussion." A young woman turned at the door and spoke quietly, "By the time you are finished telling us what you have decided, there won't be much left to discuss."

Around the room many of the people smiled and nodded their heads. They had come to the meeting to talk about the need to get people excited about how learning to read could change their lives. Some of them wanted to share their own experiences with a friend or relative who had learned to read and was now a "new person." Most of them were aware that the operation of the new organization would require some rules and procedures, but they didn't see that as the important part of this meeting.

Marjorie Supler, long-time director of the local charity organization, raised her hand. "Mr. Cromwell, why don't we just have you write up a handbook for the volunteers and have it ready for the next meeting? I think we ought to break up into small groups and come up with some ideas about how to identify the people who need the program." Christopher looked down at his papers and frowned. "I guess I got a little carried away. That's a great idea. Let's take about twenty minutes in groups and then have one person from each group give a report."

As the groups began to form and the buzz of conversation grew louder, Christopher reflected that he would constantly have to remind himself that these were volunteers and not employees. It was equally, if not more, important that people feel involved and that the meetings run according to plans. He made a note to sit down with Marjorie and get some advice about how to run the next meeting. He hoped that the volunteers would eventually appreciate the businesslike atmosphere of his meetings.

Six months later Christopher met with the board for his first report. He distributed the handbook for volunteers and the summary of expenses for the first year. One of the board members, Luke Jamison from the school board, asked if the figures for travel expenses were correct. "Yes and no," quipped Christopher. "Most of the volunteers don't turn in any expense vouchers. When I asked them about it, they said that it was more trouble to fill out the forms than it was worth. As a result, our expenses for travel are only about 20 percent of what I projected." "Won't that make it difficult to formulate our budget for next year?" Luke responded. "Probably," said Christopher, "but I'm learning that you have to be more flexible in voluntary organizations, like Literary Liberators. I will ask you to move the excess travel money to the supplies budget at the end of the year so that we can buy more reading materials. That will have to do until we can get some discipline instilled in the workers."

The board members asked several more questions about operations, and then Jacob Jackson rapped his gavel. "The next item of business for the board is the appointment of new members. Because this is our first year, some of us were appointed for one-year terms and others for two-year terms. According to our bylaws, we nominate new members at this meeting and vote on them at the next meeting." Christopher raised his hand. "If I may make a suggestion, I think the board ought to put a notice in the newspaper asking for people to volunteer to serve. That way we will get a broader cross section of the community." "I'm opposed to that idea," said Jacob. "I think we ought to renominate everyone now on the board. We just got started and we can't afford to lose the experience we have gained."

"Hold on a minute," said Luke. "My appointment comes from the school district. This board doesn't nominate me, the school board nominates one of its members to this board." Patti Smitzer chimed in, "I can't serve again because I'm moving out of the city and board members have to be city residents." Jacob looked frustrated and turned to Christopher. "Okay, put a notice in the paper, and I'll appoint a committee to screen the nominations. We've got to get better organized for next time, or we'll never make it." Christopher shook his head in wonder. It's upside down, he thought. You have to plan the agenda for the board and not plan the agenda for the volunteers. Maybe, he mused, that's because the volunteers are doing it for the sense of purpose and the board members do it from a sense of duty. Whatever their motives, Christopher thought the whole organization was too loosely constructed to last very long.

Christopher worked hard over the next month to explain to the volunteers why they needed to provide detailed reports on their activities. During one staff meeting, he pointed out that planning for the coming year would be impossible if the volunteers were not willing to indicate that they would be available for at least six months. One volunteer quietly said: "I'm not willing to treat this like a job. I got into this to help people, not build an empire for some report-oriented manager." "That's not what I'm asking," snapped Christopher. "Maybe not," said the volunteer, "but that's what it will end up being if you try to run this operation like a business."

The new board took office on the second Tuesday of January. Christopher told the new board that they would need to find a new executive director as their first item of business. "When you revise the job advertisement, be sure that you include a preference for previous experience in not-for-profit organizations. I have tried to get the organization off to a good start, but most of the volunteers don't seem to accept the need for sound management." The board accepted Christopher's resignation with relief. The volunteers had begun to resent his insistence on formal procedures and detailed records. Some of the volunteers had stopped offering to help. The next executive director would have to work hard to recapture the initial enthusiasm of the community.

As he drove home, Luke Jamison, the new chairperson of the board, thought the organization would survive this change of leadership. The money to operate the programs was not a problem. Luke was familiar with the difficulty of changing perspectives from private to public as a result of his service on the school board. "The people skills are more important than the financial know-how if your basic raw material is volunteers and the product is a service," he muttered out loud to himself.

DISCUSSION QUESTIONS

1. What other differences do you think Christopher encountered in his first year as executive director?
2. How would you have voted on whether to reappoint the old members of the board or seek new members by advertising?
3. Do you agree that volunteer organizations require more flexibility and fewer rules than other organizations?

PUBLIC ADMINISTRATORS
IN THE POLICY PROCESS

—

We have become quite accustomed to discussions of public policy. A new land use policy is developed at the local level, a revised highway and transportation policy is created at the state level, a new policy on arms sales to the Middle East is conceived at the federal level. In all of these cases, and thousands of others like them, people working in public organizations both affect and are affected by public policies. If you work in a public organization, you will inevitably play a role in the development and execution of public policy. Similarly, as a citizen, you are affected by many different types of public decisions and, in turn, you may wish to affect policy deliberations. In either case, knowing something about the process by which policies are made and implemented will be of great value.

We can say that policies are statements of goals and intentions with respect to a particular problem or set of problems; public policies are those formulated by legitimate governmental actors to deal with specific public problems. Those problems may be highly visible public problems, such as drugs and law enforcement, or they may be much less visible internal issues, such as the way travel vouchers are to be processed. Major public policies are arrived at through an often long and arduous process of debate and deliberation. Many people may be involved, among them policy activists interested in a particular issue, members of the executive branch or the legislature, and citizens in general.

Whereas once it was felt that administrators should not be a part of the process of policy development, today we recognize that public managers clearly play important roles not only in the implementation of public policy but also in its formulation. Working in a public organization, you may be directed to come up with a new policy proposal in your area of expertise. Or you may be called upon to prepare an analysis of the alternatives available with respect to a particular issue. Or you may be asked to testify before the legislature, presenting your agency's position on the issue.

Similarly, after the legislature has passed a particular policy, you may be required to implement that policy. In doing so, you may find that the legislation was intentionally vague on certain issues, allowing you a degree of discretion in interpreting the policy. You may also find that establishing a workable way of implementing the policy may be difficult without altering the intent of the policy. In either case, and in others, you may find that you are making policy.

Just as we recognize that administrators are deeply involved in the process of making public policy, we must also recognize that they must be guided by democratic principles as they do so. Unlike the chief executive or members of the legislature, most members of public organizations are not elected. Consequently, they are not directly responsible to the people. They certainly may be held accountable by elected officials, but their linkage to the citizenry is far less clear than is the case for elected officials. For this reason, those in public organizations always have to make sure that they are acting in the public interest.

It is this difficult issue that opens our discussion. In the first article in this section, Michael M. Harmon examines various approaches that administrators can take with respect to policy development. Using the concept of the public interest, Harmon suggests that a more proactive style, one in which the administrator continually tests his or her own policy preferences against those of constituent groups, holds the best possibility for improving advocacy and responsiveness. Try to think of specific administrators you know and how they approach their role in the policy process. Consider, for example, the role of a city manager (or other comparable official) in developing policy for your city.

In the development of policy, it may be necessary to review a variety of alternatives and weigh the costs and benefits of each. In the next article, J. Fred Springer draws on his experiences in working with a large public agency to examine both the technical and the personal dimensions of analyzing public policies. Importantly, Springer points out that policy analysis is not a purely rational process (as it is sometimes depicted), but one that takes place within an organizational context that is often chaotic and unpredictable. You may be especially interested in Springer's discussion of the "garbage can model" of organization, a model that may well describe organizations you are familiar with. In any case, both Harmon and Springer suggest the difficult personal choices that have to be made by public administrators as they engage in the public policy process.

After public policies are formulated, they must be implemented, a process examined here by Patricia W. Ingraham. Ingraham uses an interesting case study to demonstrate that the implementation process is a difficult one, but it is one for which administrators can be adequately trained, thus improving the prospects for effective and responsible public service. You may wish to employ Ingraham's framework in analyzing the implementation of a particular public policy (comparable to the Urban Cultural Park program) in your area.

Quite often the implementation of public policy requires working with many different groups, some of which are governmental and some of which are not. Indeed, Lester M. Salamon argues that the involvement of "third parties" in the delivery of public services is an increasing trend. Specifically, he describes the rise of "third-party government" by noting the increasing reliance on third parties—banks, industrial corporations, nonprofit organizations, and the like—for the delivery of public services. Under these circumstances, Salamon argues that we need to rethink our concept of public service, perhaps by thinking of government more as a "wholesaler" than as a "retailer" of public programs. Again, look for examples of "third party" service delivery in your area. Examples are most likely at the local or county level in the social services.

Our profile for this section features Anthony R. Kane, a senior manager in the Federal Highway Administration. The article focuses on Kane's involvement in developing a national transportation policy. In addition to noting the difficulties of developing major public policies (and the rewards of doing so), be sure to reflect upon the relationship between the career administrator involved in developing policy and the political appointees for whom it is developed.

The design of public policy is often a response to problems experienced in the implementation of programs. "Paramedical Services at the Scene of an Accident" illustrates the difficulties of policy design when several organizations are involved. Usually the definition of the problem is made more difficult because competing values are involved. This case gives you an example of the mutually conflicting demands of two fundamental values—justice and compassion.

The second case, "The Hospital Expansion Project," explores one of the most difficult problems of policy making. When two political jurisdictions pursue different goals, you will find that private parties are often caught in the middle. Innovative solutions are required to find a compromise that will accommodate the interests of all the actors. This case presents the vital role of cooperation in resolving policy disputes.

The third case, "How Many or How Big: Copy Machines as Technology," examines the impetus of technology in driving policy decisions. This case focuses your attention on a perennial problem of most organizations—should technology drive the organization of work, or should work be organized according to other priorities? The revolution in communications technology continues to create operational policy dilemmas for managers.

ADMINISTRATIVE POLICY FORMULATION AND THE PUBLIC INTEREST

Michael M. Harmon

Among students of public administration the concept of "public interest" has occasioned considerable debate, yet little consensus. Ironically, the lack of consensus in the academic community seems equalled only by the certainty with which official pronouncements are uttered in the name of public interest, a circumstance leading many scholars to abandon the concept altogether. While it is tempting to follow suit, such a collective quietude will in the long haul relegate the public interest to an innocuous position in the conventional wisdom shared by The Essential Brotherhood of Man and The American Way. In the hope that it is still a viable concept, an operational definition derived from a fundamental assumption about democracy will be offered, followed by a consideration within that context of styles of administrative behavior in formulating public policy.

While unanimous agreement on the matter is not anticipated, the argument is advanced that the fundamental premise underlying democracy is that the ethical or moral "correctness" of political and social values, and of resultant policy, is not subject to proof.[1] Freedom to propose change, or indeed to defend the status quo, is simply assumed because the legitimate limitation of such activity requires proof of an alternative position. Freedom's traditional democratic counterpart, equality, is justified on similar grounds. We need not contend that "all men are created equal"; rather, since no one can prove that his values or policy preferences are correct (unequal), the assumption of equality is all that remains. The burden of proof rests with the advocate of elitism. Since inequality cannot be proved, preferences are presumed to be of equal validity until subjected to appropriate tests of disproof.

This position, which defines democracy as essentially a null hypothesis, admittedly has little rhetorical appeal; but it is useful as a point of departure for redefining public interest and for addressing some normative issues relating to the role of administrators in formulating public policy.

SOME DIMENSIONS OF PUBLIC INTEREST THEORY

Academic discourse on the public interest reveals some dimensions under which conflicting views about the concept may be usefully summarized. The public interest is asserted to be either: (1) unitary or individualistic, (2) prescriptive or descriptive, (3) substantive or procedural, and (4) ultimate (static) or dynamic.

UNITARY VERSUS INDIVIDUALISTIC CONCEPTIONS OF THE PUBLIC INTEREST

A *unitary* conception of the public interest, as described by Meyerson and Banfield, is one in which "the 'whole' may be conceived as a single set of ends which pertain equally to all members of the public. . . . The plurality is an entity or body politic which entertains ends in a corporate capacity; these may be different from those entertained by any of the individuals who comprise the public."[2] Individualistic conceptions, according to these authors, assume that:

> . . . the ends of the plurality do not comprise a single system, either one which pertains to the plurality as an entity or one which is common to individuals. The relevant ends are those of individuals, whether shared or unshared. The ends of the plurality "as a whole" are simply the aggregate of ends entertained by individuals, and that decision is in the public interest which is consistent with as large a part of the "whole" as possible.[3]

An eloquent proponent of a unitary public interest is Walter Lippmann, who differentiated public from private interests.

Living adults share, we must believe, the same public interest. For them, however, the public interest is mixed with, and is often at odds with, their private and special interests. Put this way, we can say, I suggest, that the public interest may be presumed to be what men would choose if they saw clearly, thought rationally, acted disinterestedly and benevolently.[4]

The difficulty with Lippmann's view is that he assumes that the "correctness" of public policies, and of the values on which they are based, is in some way knowable. The only clue to aid in the enunciation of policies in the public interest is his admonition that men should act disinterestedly and benevolently. Disinterest, however, is at best a rare commodity in politics; and given even the purest of motives, there is no certainty that one can act in such a manner. Moreover, the curious array of political activities undertaken in the name of benevolence marks Lippmann's unitary version of the public interest as one of dubious utility. Possessing neither guarantees of disinterest and benevolence, nor (more importantly) objective "proofs" for making judgments about policy, a unitary public interest is rendered untenable. An individualistic public interest (based on the axiom of self-interest), on the other hand, is not bound by the constraints inherent in unitary versions. Specifically, proof becomes an issue when an advocate of a law or policy assumes the exclusive prerogative of making judgments for others. Since self-interest makes no necessary claim about the appropriateness of individual preferences for others, it does not violate the premise of unprovability. Choices made and preferences stated in this context are existential; proof is not an issue.

PRESCRIPTIVE VERSUS DESCRIPTIVE CONCEPTIONS

Our inability to prove the correctness of substantive goals and policies places additional constraints on what may be considered an appropriate definition of the public interest. While judgments may be made about what the public interest should be in regard to political issues, the absence of "ultimate" criteria for verifying such claims forces us to reject prescriptive interpretations. Since prescriptions about its substance are inherently tentative and uncertain, the public interest may be viewed more usefully as a descriptive concept. That is, it describes the result of political activity, rather than prescribing what that result ought to be. A descriptive interpretation does not, certainly, preclude advocacy of change as a legitimate political or administrative act. It is simply a reminder of the tentativeness with which policy proposals must be advanced in a democratic system.

SUBSTANTIVE VERSUS PROCEDURAL CONCEPTIONS

If we accept the position that the public interest is a descriptive concept, we may regard attention to the policy *process* as being an equally legitimate responsibility as our traditional concern with its *substance*. The former, in fact, is really the prior issue. In evaluating policy, emphasis must initially, at least, be shifted from its substance to the process by which it is created. Because of the tentativeness of criteria for evaluating substantive policies, attention is focused on the degree to which arbitrary constraints exist in political systems which tend to deny articulation of policy preferences and expenditure of political resources. It is the elimination of such constraints which allows (fully, in theory) latent values and resources to become manifest, permitting a more accurate identification or description of the public interest. The accuracy of its identification depends on the degree to which latent values, interests, and policy preferences are not prohibited from becoming manifest. It is in this sense that the elementary proposition that democracy is a process rather than a philosophy has meaning.

In supporting a procedural view of the public interest we are unable to infer a definitive blueprint of appropriate political and administrative machinery. From our initial premise that the correctness of policy preferences is ultimately unprovable we can infer only that procedures which limit the articulation of such preferences are unacceptable.

STATIC VERSUS DYNAMIC CONCEPTIONS

Since the public mood is in a continual state of flux, it is axiomatic that the public interest must be viewed as changing also, rather than static or constant. And if the public interest changes, the development of a political system which can respond effectively to those changes is imperative. Students of large-scale organizations have lamented that traditional criteria for evaluating organizational performance (such as production and profits) are inadequte because they are static indicators and do not account for changes in organizational goals. Warren Bennis[5] has argued that a "healthy" organization is, in part, one which can successfully respond on a continuing basis to changing demands from its environment. There appears to be a logical corollary here between the concept of "organizational health," at one level, and a procedurally based definition of the public interest, at the political level. Each idea in effect suggests that political and organizational systems are effective to the degree they are responsive to environmental demands. A healthy organization is a democratic one; a democratic political system is "healthy."

THE PUBLIC INTEREST REDEFINED

To summarize, the public interest, to be consistent with our initial premise, must be viewed as (1) individualistic rather than unitary, (2) descriptive rather than prescriptive, (3) procedural rather than substantive, and (4) dynamic rather than static. Put another way, *the public interest is the continually changing outcome of political activity among individuals and groups within a democratic political system*.[6] By stressing process rather than substance, this definition has important implications regarding the appropriateness of styles of administration in the formulation of policy in public organizations.

THE POLICY FORMULATION GRID

While administrators may possess little conscious knowledge of public interest theory, the manner in which they conduct their activities as advocates and/or implementors of policy reflects certain assumptions about the concept. A high degree of certainty about the correctness of a given policy, for example, may indicate an administrator's

implicit commitment to a fundamentally substantive and prescriptive view of the public interest. Static interpretations of the concept are evident in administrators having a consuming concern with the value of efficiency.

In an attempt to relate the public interest concept to the ways in which administrators perform their functions in the policy arena, a typology of administrative styles is depicted on a two-dimensional grid similar to the Managerial Grid [Figure 1] of Robert Blake.[7] *The Policy Formulation Grid* describes styles of administration relating to policy formulation in public organizations. *Responsiveness*, a central issue deriving from the foregoing discussion of the pubic interest, is depicted on the vertical axis of the grid; the horizontal axis indicates the extent of policy *advocacy* of administrators. The number 1 depicts minimal activity, while 9 indicates maximum activity. In the lower-left corner, the 1,1 style describes administrative activity which is both nonadvocative and unresponsive. The upper-left corner describes the 1,9 style in which the administrator is highly responsive, but minimally advocative. The 9,1 style in the lower-right corner depicts a high degree of policy advocacy accompanied by low responsiveness to political system demands. The 5,5 style, at the midpoint, is a compromise between responsiveness and advocative behavior, which are assumed by the administrator to be antithetical. A maximization of both of the grid's dimensions (i.e., high advocative *and* responsive behavior) is described by the 9,9 style in the upper-right corner. The terms *responsive* and *advocative* are intentionally defined broadly to accommodate their varying interpretations implicit in the five styles shown on the grid. While specific assumptions are made about their meaning in each of the styles, suffice it to say generally that *responsive behavior* is that which is accountable in some way to the democratic process, whether by voting, mutual adjustment, or some other method by which public demands are, or might be, legitimately translated into policy. *Advocative behavior* is defined as the active support by administrators for the adoption of policies.

SURVIVAL STYLE (1,1)

In his discussion of metropolitan special districts, John Bollens has argued that the limited scope of

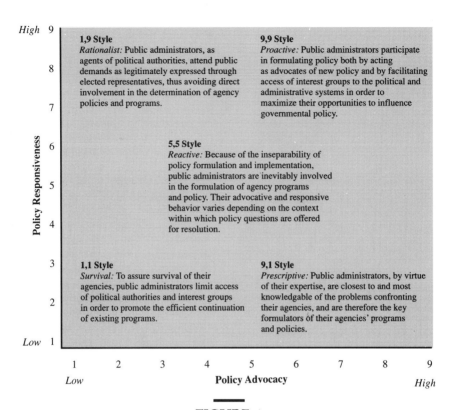

FIGURE 1
Policy Formulation Grid

such agencies has often resulted in their becoming isolated from agencies and problems related to their special purpose. While in some cases they are barred by district laws and political pressure from expanding and coordinating their functions with other levels of government, ". . . districts of limited purpose have shown little inclination to seek authorization for additional services."[8] A case in point has been described by Edward T. Chase, who criticized the Port of New York Authority for ignoring problems of mass transit in order to promote the "efficiency" of its own operations. While the PA's revenues rose steadily and impressively over the years, the problem of traffic congestion continually worsened.

> . . . on it own terms the PA is doing a grand job. But those terms, today, are cockeyed. The world has changed but the PA stubbornly refuses to cope with the new problems.

It cheerfully reports one achievement after another. Yet at the same time, mass transportation serving New York is faltering and the city is foundering under the weight and pollution of traffic.[9]

Because the Port Authority had established a reputation as an efficient agency providing vital services to the New York–New Jersey metropolitan area, its ultimate survival was seldom questioned. Yet, at the writing of the Chase article, the PA reflected essentially a style of administrative survival (1,1). Given almost unlimited discretion to formulate policy to promote "the improvement of transportation and terminal facilities," the PA chose to interpret its mandate narrowly. In the context of the Policy Formulation Grid, its advocative activity was minimal in that little effort was made to effect major policy changes. Effectiveness was seen in terms of the efficiency with which the Port Authority could execute existing policies. Further, by its refusal to respond to public demands to expand its responsibilities into the area of mass transit, its responsiveness was negligible.

RATIONALIST STYLE (1,9)

The rationalist style is in a broad sense a restatement of rationalist public interest theory described by Glendon Schubert.[10] Its primary assumptions have been stated by Norton Long.

> The legitimacy of the will, like the concept of sovereignty, provides the basis for a logical deductive system moving from the first principle—be it the will of the people via Congress, or the will of the people via Congress through President, or the will of the people via President. In any event, the prime problem of administration is to give effect to this will.[11]

Thus provided a presumably value-free premise for public administration, Herbert Simon, the leading modern advocate of administrative rationalism, concludes that problems of administration are reducible to problems of engineering. His statement provides an illustration of the 1,9 position on the grid.

> The theory of administation is concerned with how an organization should be constructed and operated in order to accomplish its work efficiently. A fundamental principle of administration, which follows almost immediately from the rational character of "good" administration, is that among several alternatives involving the same expenditure the one should always be selected which leads to the greatest accomplishment of administrative objectives; and among several alternatives that lead to the same accomplishment the one should be selected which involves the least expenditure.[12]

In attacking the utility of rationalist theory, Long presents a two-fold critique:

> The view of administration as sheerly instrumental, or even largely instrumental, must be rejected as empirically untenable and ethically unwarranted. The rejection will entail abandonment, on the one hand, of Herbert Simon's quest for a value-free administration and, on the other, of the over-simplified dogma of an overloaded legislative supremacy of his logical comrade in arms, Charles Hyneman. These two views fit like hand in glove. Legislative supremacy provides Simon with value premises, which can then permit a value-free science of administration the esthetic delight of unique and verifiably determinate problem solutions through the application of the value premises to the fact premises. . . . But, alas, we know this institutional divorce, however requisite for a value-free science of administration, does not exist.[13]

Not only do the rationlists err in assuming that policy formulation and implementation are separable, but they also assume that all legitimate values relevant to policy formulation are expressed through voting or elected representatives. Since most issues facing public administrators relate only to limited segments of the total population, the formal processes of voting and legislative representation are incapable of coping with demands of individuals and interest groups on a day-to-day basis. Administrators, therefore, are left with the responsibility not only of implementing policy handed down from their political superiors, but they must also confront the prior problem of constructing and maintaining a system through which demands can initially be articulated. The rationalists' failure to deal effectively with this issue renders their behavior as responsive only in a passive and highly formal sense. Regarding the dimension of advocacy, it goes almost without saying that the doctrine of legislative supremacy which the rationalists accept precludes them from advocating substantive policy.

Because total avoidance of policy advocacy and formulation is unlikely, the rationalist style in its purest sense is not descriptive of the dominant behavior of many administrators. Nonetheless, it has had considerable importance as an administrative ethic as illustrated by the consolidation in 1964 of the Los Angeles City and County health departments.[14] After more than 50 years of debate of the question, the City of Los Angeles decided to abolish its health function by taking advantage of state enabling legislation which allowed cities operating independent health departments to transfer, at no cost to them, that function to the county. In terms of money spent on public health services and numbers of people affected by the move, the city's action was the largest of its kind in the nation's history. Its incentive to transfer the health function was a legitimate one—to alleviate tax inequities suffered by city residents who paid taxes to support two health departments, the city's and the county's, while receiving direct benefits only from the city health department.

Because of City Council apathy about public health policy, City and County Health Department administrators were given almost total discretion in defining the future policies of the newly consolidated county department. Interestingly, during the dispute administrators and health officials voiced strong commitment to the ethical neutrality of administration in policy matters, a commitment due largely to the professionalization of Los Angeles governmental bureaucracies. The ethic of administrative neutrality conflicted sharply, however, with the finding that administrators were deeply involved in making important policy decisions regarding the transfer of the City Health Department to the county. This is not to say that the administrators were hypocritical; rather, their perceptions of what constituted policy decisions, as opposed to purely technical ones, were weighted heavily toward the latter. These perceptions were reinforced by their political superiors who delegated highly important decisions to the chief administrative officers and health department officials on the assumption that those decisions were mainly technical.

At the same time that public health policy relating to the consolidation was being made, professional and community action groups in the City of Los Angeles, which were generally vehemently opposed to the move, were given in most instances only pro forma consideration of their demands. Their limited avenues of real influence illustrate some of the pitfalls for responsiveness when the rationalist style is assumed to be descriptive of administrative activity when there are questions of policy formulation.

PRESCRIPTIVE STYLE (9,1)

Although rationalist and prescriptive styles appear at opposite corners of the grid, a distinction between the two in practice is frequently difficult to discern.

As already noted, perceptions of what constitute policy questions, as opposed to technical questions, vary among government officials. To the extent that generally accepted criteria for making such distinctions are lacking, distinguishing between rationalist and prescriptive administrators becomes complicated.

The prescriptive style of administration predominates institutions either where wide latitude for statutory interpretation by administrators is allowed or where the technical complexity of issues requires expertise peculiar to a very limited number of personnel within a agency. In the latter case, whether administrative neutrality exists in matters of substantive policy is often open to serious question. Administrative strategy reflecting elements of both 1, 9 and 9,1 styles is evident in what Sayre and Kaufman call the "doctrine of neutral competence."[15] Their argument is that administrators, to further their discretion over issues of substantive policy, make what are essentially policy decisions under the guise of technical expertise, i.e., they exhibit 9,1 behavior in the guise of a 1,9 style. In the Los Angeles health dispute, however, administrators decided important questions of policy, not because they were intent on increasing their discretion in such matters, but because the responsibility for making such decisions was delegated to them by their political superiors.

The subtle distinctions between the conclusions of Sayre and Kaufman and the health consolidation study illustrate the complexities surrounding the question of what determines administrative style in policy formulation. While personality and professional values undoubtedly are key determinants, administrative style is affected by a broad range of factors. A partial list of these would include: role expectations of superiors, subordinates, and peers; the political volatility of the agency; the number and diversity of client groups served by the agency; the specificity of the agency's statutory mandate; the apparent effectiveness of current operations; and the nature of agency-legislative relationships.

REACTIVE STYLE (5,5)

The difficulty in drawing clear distinctions between policy formulation and implementation requires administrative reactivists to operate in both areas, although they regard separation of the two as an ethically desirable yet unattainable norm. Lepawsky has described their dilemma:

> Perhaps the most promising way of continuing a healthy separation between politics and administration, while entertaining a growing concern about the need for tying them together, is to refine the relation of the administrator or managerial expert to policies or political questions. Administrators at all levels of responsibility are being constantly thrown into the area of decision-making, and their decisions inevitably add up to major policies in the subsequent course of events. . . .
>
> As a matter of governmental evolution, therefore, the administrator cannot avoid some policy making responsibility. However, he can more accurately define his role with relation to policy. Specifically, administrators should (1) constantly gather facts and prepare findings that may lead to changes in policy or to policy decisions; (2) inform their chief, and with his approval inform the policy-making body or (3) recommend and initiate policies but advocate them only with superior consent.[16]

The conclusion one is forced to draw from this statement is that without the most stringent prescription of the administrator's role, responsive and advocative behavior are inevitably compromised. The complications generated by Lepawsky's advice force the reactive administrator ultimately to conclude that to the extent he is advocative, he is unresponsive; conversely, responsive behavior is nonadvocative. Despite the good intent of Lepawsky and others in attempting to specify the appropriate limits of administrative advocacy, their suggestions frequently seem remote from the "real world" of the administrator. In a state of ethical confusion and with few clear guides for behavior, the reactivist relies primarily on the hard lessons of experience. An awareness of where power is located and how it is used provides him with little control *over* his environment, but enables him generally to cope successfully *within* it. His ability to anticipate the potential exercise of influence by others often makes him an effective tactician of the type described in Edward Banfield's case studies of Chicago politics.[17] Since the nature and amount of responsive and advocative

behavior in the reactive style are governed by context rather than conscience, personal risk taking is minimized and policy changes are, at most, incremental.

A common thread running through the prescriptive, rationalist, and reactive styles is the assumption that the freedom of administrators to advocate policy and their requirement to be responsive to public demands are popular norms. The issue is least troublesome to prescriptive administrators whose monopoly of technical knowledge justifies to their satisfaction their exclusive privilege not only of advocating policy, but of having the final say in its determination. Their Weberian and Taylorian heritage frees them from the uncertainties clouding normative controversies external to their immediate areas of concern. When pressed on the matter of responsiveness they may, often legitimately, reply that their policies are implicitly responsive. A conscious effort to test such assumptions, however, is not generally evident.

Rationalist administrators, whose historical antecedents can be traced to the American era of reform, confront the issue more directly, yet are left convinced of the essential polarity of responsiveness and advocacy. Accepting unequivocally the doctrine of legislative supremacy, they are certain of the rightness of their ethic, but are unsure of its workability under conditions of uncertainty and flux.

In achieving a balance between the conflicting norms of the rationalist and prescriptive styles, administrative reactivists avoid confronting the ethical problem directly by allowing the outcome of issues to be governed by the situation. Lacking a coherent philosophy of administration, they rationalize their position by arguing that they are at the mercy of forces over which they have only minimal control.

PROACTIVE STYLE (9,9)[18]

The dispute over whether advocacy and responsiveness are ultimately incompatible can be confronted more directly when reduced to a more basic level. To assume their incompatibility is fundamentally to make the commonly held assumption that individual freedom and social responsibility are incompatible. Robert P. Biller has argued that to assume this is to draw an unwarranted inference.

"Since we 'know' the meaning of each in only proximate ways, data about their apparent present or past incompatibility is useful only in determining the degree of confidence with which we would undertake risks involved in their fusion."[19] By initially remaining neutral on the issue, it is possible to gather data about conditions under which fusion or incompatibility may be predicted.

The literature of humanistic psychology leaves room for considerable optimism about the potentiality of their fusion. Abraham Maslow, whose discussion of *synergy* is somewhat representative of the humanistic or existential psychologists' views on the freedom-responsibility issue, contends that mentally healthy people, more often than less healthy people, make choices which are essentially synergistic, i.e., choices which satisfy selfish needs and at the same time satisfy those of others.[20] Becoming free involves making choices and taking risks to achieve one's potential, for which a high degree of self-awareness is a precondition. Acting responsibly entails a recognition of situational elements which either constrain behavior or make apparent new choices or directions. In this sense freedom and responsibility are congruent for the healthy person. The prime test of mental health occurs in the making of choices and taking of risks which force confrontation between "selfish" and environmental needs.

In the formulation of policy, the proactive administrator is responsible only secondarily in a political sense; primarily he is a responsible person and citizen. His sense of responsibility is derived not from prescriptions external to his life experience (as implied by strict adherence to the doctrine of legislative supremacy), but is mainly a function of his high degree of mental health. . . .

In contrast to rationalist administration, responsiveness in the proactive style is highly active. While recognizing legitimate legislative and legal constraints on his agency and himself, the proactive administrator is actively involved both in removing arbitrary barriers to interest articulation and in facilitating access of client groups (actual and potential) to the decision process. Responsible free choice is characterized by his advocacy of policies which are always subject to negotiation with his environment. In determining policy, proactive behavior implies reciprocal influence between the administrator and those to whom he is responsible, rather than passive acceptance and implementation only of those policies directed to him by his superiors.

Although situations will exist when the policies he advocates will be at odds with the demands of his constituents, the proactive administrator is less often forced into the position of making a clear choice between the two alternatives. By continually testing his own policy preferences against those of his clientele he is more likely to emerge with what Mary Parker Follett called a "creative synthesis"[21] than with the often dramatic but initially unpopular decisions of the type described by President Kennedy in his *Profiles of Courage*.[22] Although the fusion of advocacy and responsiveness cannot be guaranteed in every instance, the proactive style at least increases its probability.

CONCLUSION

No theory of public interest can realistically offer clear answers to the hard choices with which administrators and political leaders are confronted; nor does the theory presented here presume to do so. In fairness, all that can be reasonably demanded of such a theory is that it provide a framework within which administratative behavior may be tentatively, but productively, evaluated. In each of the styles on the Policy Formulation Grid are assumptions about the public interest, some of which are simply illogical and others destructive of democratic values. In behaving consistently with the theory of public interest offered here the proactive administrator is not assured correct answers. Perhaps it is not too presumptuous to suggest, however, that he will be aided in asking more of the right questions.

NOTES

1. Thomas Landon Thorson, *The Logic of Democracy* (New York: Holt, Rinehart, & Winston, 1962), pp. 138–139.
2. Martin Meyerson and Edward C. Banfield, *Politics, Planning and the Public Interest* (New York: The Free Press of Glencoe, 1955), p. 323.
3. *Ibid.*, p. 324.
4. Walter Lippmann, *The Public Philosophy* (Boston: Little, Brown and Company, 1955), pp. 41–42.
5. Warren G. Bennis, *Changing Organizations* (New York: McGraw-Hill, 1966).

6. While important normative questions about policy are clearly left unanswered by this definition, it avoids what might be labeled the General Bullmoose Syndrome of public interest theory characteristic of unitary and prescriptive interpretations.

7. Robert R. Blake and Jane S. Mouton, *The Managerial Grid* (Houston: Gulf Publishing Company, 1964).

8. John C. Bollens, *Special District Governments in the United States* (Berkeley: University of California Press, 1957), p. 91.

9. Edward T. Chase, "How to Rescue New York from Its Port Authority," *Harper's Magazine*, June 1960, p. 58.

10. Glendon Schubert, *The Public Interest* (Glencoe, Ill.: The Free Press of Glencoe, 1960).

11. Norton Long, "Power and Administration," *Public Administration Review*, Vol. IX (1949), pp. 24–25.

12. Herbert A. Simon, *Administrative Behavior* (New York: Macmillan, 1947), p. 38.

13. Long, *op. cit.*, p. 23.

14. Frank P. Sherwood, Michael M. Harmon, and Alexander Cloner, "The Inherited Decision: Health Consolidation in Metropolitan Los Angeles" (School of Public Administration, University of Southern California, October 1966), mimeographed.

15. Wallace Sayre and Herbert Kaufman, *Governing New York City* (New York: Russell Sage Foundation, 1960), p. 404.

16. Albert Lepawsky, *Administration* (New York: Alfred A. Knopf, 1949).

17. Edward C. Banfield, *Political Influence* (New York: The Free Press of Glencoe, 1961).

18. My first exposure to the word "proactive" was in an article by Hubert Bonner entitled "The Proactive Personality," in J. F. T. Bugental (ed.), *Challenges of Humanistic Psychology* (New York: McGraw-Hill, 1968), pp. 61–66. Some interesting insights into the psychology of proactive administration can be inferred from the essay. For an earlier and more comprehensive reference, see Bonner, *On Being Mindful of Man: Essay Toward a Proactive Psychology* (Boston: Houghton Mifflin, 1965).

19. Robert P. Biller, "Some Implications of Adaptation Capacity for Organizational and Political Development," paper prepared for the Minnowbrook Conference on the New Public Administration, Syracuse University, Syracuse, New York, September 1968, p. 22. The Biller paper also includes some insightful comments on the null hypothesis interpretation of democracy mentioned earlier.

20. Abraham Maslow, *Eupsychian Management* (New York: Dorsey, 1966).

21. Henry C. Metcalf and L. Urwick (eds.), *Dynamic Administration, The Collected Papers of Mary Parker Follett* (New York: Harper & Bros., 1942).

22. John F. Kennedy, *Profiles in Courage* (New York: Harper, 1956).

POLICY ANALYSIS AND ORGANIZATIONAL DECISIONS

Toward a Conceptual Revision

J. Fred Springer

Last summer, deep within the air-conditioned maze housing California's sprawling Health and Welfare Agency, I spent a lot of time talking to "bureaucrats." I was conducting preliminary field interviews on community-based "independent living centers" (ILCs) that were springing up to meet the needs of severely disabled persons around the state.[1] I knew that these centers had, somewhat reluctantly, accepted state support from the Department of Rehabilitation in 1976, and I was curious to see how the "activist" centers— where medical labeling of persons by disabling condition (such as MR and MS) was taboo, and disabled persons were never referred to as "clients"—could coexist with the highly routinized and traditionally professional vocational rehabilitation bureaucracy.

My first stop in the Agency's sections and units was at Field Services. A management auditing team had just returned from one of the state-supported centers, and I had an appointment with the team leader. He was bubbling with enthusiasm. Last year when they had conducted compliance audits in the centers, I learned, they had found record-keeping and fiscal procedures in shambles. Inexperienced staff and a personalized service orientation had minimized the attention directed toward standardized records, full job descriptions for each funded position, and other requirements for federal "pass through" funding. This year, he exulted, things were much improved. The Department had

found a way to use the compliance audits to tutor employees at the centers. Rather than taking action for noncompliance, last year's teams had explained the problems, and noted the deficiency so that action could be taken if the problems were not corrected in the following audit session. It had worked. Compliance monitoring had become management education!

Throughout the summer I crisscrossed Sacramento's K Street mall, moving between the stately old restored brownstones of the administrative sections and the stark modern offices of the research and planning section. In the Program Evaluation and Statistics Section I sipped coffee with the newly assigned program analyst who was charged with developing service measures and a case-load reporting system for ILCs that would receive continued state support. The problem was difficult, she explained. The center's philosophy of peer counseling was based on the importance of identification with the counselor and the strengthening of self-image. These are "squishy" concepts; it's hard to develop a tangible unit of service. If the centers wanted to "vendorize" these services to the state, however, they had to have a tangible basis for demonstrating performance and receiving funds. She was sure they would work it out.

Across the hall, in the Research Section, I chatted with an animated young intern from the local state university. She felt very lucky to have been assigned to the Independent Living Research Study that was being conducted with Health, Education and Welfare (HEW) funds. I flipped through the fat volume of tables and charts she handed me. It reported the method and results of a sophisticated three-wave application of the "client gains scale" developed and validated by the section. As I read the creative and rigorous scaling items in the report, she informed me of an unexpected benefit of the study. People involved in training had found the gains scale very useful for orienting rehabilitation counselors to the service philosophy and activities of the centers.

On my way to my appointment with the head of Planning and Program Development, I stopped and commiserated with a comprehensive services specialist who was laboring over a report entitled "The Feasibility of Requiring a Non-State Match from Independent Centers Receiving State Support." The report had been requested by the Joint Legislative Budget Committee. She was nearing completion of the demanding task, and was looking for someone who could appreciate the effort involved in several weeks of telephoning around the state and digging through reams of budget figures. She was also seeking empathy for the hours upon hours of uncompensated overtime the project had required. The committee knew that, politically, it would like to encourage local and private support of ILCs by requiring a nonstate match, she explained, but the key is how you define the match. As well as she could tell from existing support patterns, many of the smaller centers could not survive any match requirement in their first three years. Even after the "shakedown period," viability of matching would be complicated by the drastically differing levels of community support the centers have been able to attract.

Finally, I wound my way to the section manager's cluttered desk through the brightly colored room partitions. The big thing in program planning for the ILCs, he informed me, was Assembly Bill 2687. In the last session the California Legislature had mandated that the Department plan and implement five pilot projects that would fund successful ILC applicants to operate as experimental "comprehensive service centers" for the severely disabled. Planning the implementation was a challenge, the manager explained, partly because the Department had to be sure they could meet the detailed evaluation requirements mandated by the legislature. In assessing applications, the Department needed assurances that the intended services would be provided in a manner that was accountable through evaluation. Many of the centers would have to alter their service mix and internal procedures to meet requirements for the pilot program. In parting, the section manager suggested that it would be fascinating to research the policy changes local centers made in "grooming" for the grant applications.

SO THIS IS POLICY ANALYSIS

Over several weeks following my field interviews, I devised myriad approaches to make sense of the pastiche of bureaucratic activity I had encountered.

Although I had not sought it, I had been surrounded by individuals—in a variety of organizational units—involved in satiating the voracious appetite of decision-makers (or decision processes) for information. As Arnold Meltsner (1976:1) notes, "Getting information for policy decisions is nothing new. As certain as the winter solstice occurs each year, public bureaucracies continue to seek out information." The activities I observed did not contradict his view—monitoring data, questionnaires, public reports, budget documents, and computer printouts were all being consumed in quantity.

It seemed just clear that this pervasive information gathering was highly technical, and exacted substantial demands for technical competence from those who produced it. Staff of the Independent Living Research Study talked easily of "coefficients of reliability" for discrete subscales within the client gains measure; the Program Planning manager worried about contamination of the experimental pilot program through technical assistance activities, and so on. If we accept an inclusive definition of policy analysis as research carried out to facilitate policy decisions by providing relevant technical information (paraphrased from Mayer and Greenwood, 1980: 5),[2] my interviewees appeared to be "living" the process of policy analysis.

Although it seemed that I had been talking to practicing policy analysts, many of the impressions I took away did not sit easily with discussions of the role of policy analysis that typify scholarly literature on the subject. I was surprised by the degree to which information gathering and analysis permeated the activities of the agency. Much of the literature on policy analysis and policy decisions focuses on the distance between research and decisions in public organizations. Indeed, perception of this gap is a major impetus to the burgeoning interest in research utilization, which "may be conceived of as involving movement across the space between producers of knowledge (researchers) and users of knowledge (appliers)" (Rothman, 1980: 19). The controlling work in this area is the study by Caplan (1977) suggesting that policy analysts and decision-makers occupy two separate and somewhat alien communities with significantly different world views. My observations did not contradict this view specifically, but they did raise unsettling questions. If technical information is so alien to organizational decision-makers, why were the procedures and personnel I encountered so thoroughly steeped in the technology of policy analysis?

A second set of puzzling observations concerned the analysts themselves. It has become conventional to acknowledge that policy analysts are not the android caricatures that peopled early discussions of the "objective" role of the applied researcher. It has been well argued that analysts not only do, but sometimes should, adopt explicitly "political" roles (Meltsner, 1976; Benveniste, 1977). This politicized position certainly rang true for many of the individuals I interviewed. Their sympathies for the independent living movement were not hidden. What did seem out of sorts with the usual view of the analyst was a relatively low level of concern about whether their findings would influence decisions. To some extent, this may have reflected the supportive atmosphere in the department. However, it also was a by-product of the fact that attention and concern were focused elsewhere. For one thing, the range of uses for the analysts' efforts was much greater than a few critical decision points. Use of their findings simply would not rest on a few major policy decisions, and they knew it. There was plenty of opportunity for "creative" utilization. Second, many of the analysts were motivated by the process of analysis itself—gaining skills, solving puzzles, being "in the know." They were having fun!

Third, I was struck by the ambiguity of the "product" for which these analysts were responsible. The traditional definition of the product of analysis is "information" or, more specifically, a written report. In their recent study of research utilization in federal agencies, for example, Weiss and Bucuvalas (1980: 28) focus on "the border between the research and decision making spheres. *Studies* are produced by the research system, and *once completed*, they can influence the decision making system" (emphasis added). The transition "product" was not that clear in the Department of Rehabilitation. When I inquired about the destination and purpose of the client gains study report, I was met with a pained silence (in sharp contrast to the enthusiastic discussion of the study itself). Reference to the usefulness of the findings for training new counselors was offered as a

response, but it was clearly not a prior intent of the study. In some cases the use of findings was consciously diverted from a prior decision-making intent (the educational use of audit results). The pilot project "experiment" would eventually produce an explicitly requested evaluation report, but in the interim years the design of the experiment would produce new services, augmented budgets, jobs; and new categories of clients. Decisions about what programs and mixes of services should be funded would be influenced by analysts who were participating in the implementation of the experiment.

Finally, I was nagged by the disturbing feeling that in some instances the decision-making process that I had observed was "running backward" (Weik, 1969). The conventional view is that policy analysis contributes to rational decisions that proceed from predetermined preferences, to specification of alternative policies for achieving those preferences, and finally to applying rational techniques for comparing and choosing between those alternatives. The swirl of policy analysis surrounding the ILCs seemed to follow a different pattern. A political commitment had been made to the ILCs as institutions, and the techniques and processes of analysis were being used to justify and aid their success. The deed (commitment to ILCs) was father to the technical rationale. Similarly, the task of the monitoring project was to create measures that could capture the kinds of service that had emerged in the ideological context of the local centers; it was not primarily concerned with measuring the activities of the centers against a predetermined policy standard.

None of these observations is new. Somewhere in the growing literature on policy analysis and its various subfields (such as program evaluation, policy planning, and operations research), each of my complaints with the conventional image of policy analysis has been noted. What is missing, however, is a conceptualization of the policy process—and the role of policy analysis within it— that provides a framework congenial to the varied specifics of our "malaise." Without this framework I found myself thinking, "So *this* is policy analysis," and not quite knowing what *this* was.

The "rational problem-solving" model in some form remains the dominant overarching conceptual guide to understanding the relation between technical activities of analysts and decision processes of public organizations. In the remainder of this essay, I will attempt to suggest an alternative direction, one that places decision processes more clearly in an organizational as opposed to a logical context. The next section presents a brief review of some current themes of revision in thinking about policy analysis. The subsequent section presents a conceptual approach that accommodates and helps integrate these revisions, and suggests selected research implications of the approach.

STEPS TOWARD REVISION: A REVIEW OF CRITICAL THEMES

Policy analysis is one of the contemporary generation of academic subdisciplines that attempts to develop theoretical understanding in an area that is simultaneously adapting and growing as an applied profession. Within the range of interest generated by this coexistence, scholarly development of the field often has been of an uncomfortable nature. This discomfort can be traced partly to contradictory intellectual foci. Some scholars have displayed a centripetal tendency to search for the logical essence of policy analysis, and to assert its limitations. Others have displayed a centrifugal tendency to focus on the pragmatic obstacles confronting the policy analyst in the application of his or her craft. This tension can be demonstrated clearly in the critical response of those concerned with application to the preoccupation with the definition and explication of "rational decision logic" that dominated much of the early scholarly attention to policy analysis.

The reaction is epitomized in Robert Mowitz's observations regarding Lindblom's (1959) comparison of the method of "successive limited comparisons" with the "rational comprehensive" method ascribed to the proponents of applied policy analysis.[3] Mowitz (1980: 4), who has "emphasized the pragmatic" (Novick, in Mowitz, 1980: vii) in his decision theory, argues that

Lindblom may not have intended to legitimize ad hoc, rule-of-thumb decision making, but his article did provide intellectual support for those public administrators intent on protecting the status quo and on resisting any change in

existing decision mechanisms. . . . In essence, his argument is quite simple. He defines the systems approach as requiring absolute and total information, then proceeds to point out, quite obviously, that this cannot be achieved.

Like Mowitz, many practitioners and researchers who toiled in the fields of policy analysis grew weary of what they considered to be "straw man" arguments that could not be won.

In response, a sprawling literature has grown that treats policy analysis without attempting to resolve fundamental issues regarding the applicability of rational thinking to policy problems. Some, like Mowitz (1980: 14), explicitly state a beginning assumption that using rational analysis in public decisions is "possible" and "desirable"; from this point, one can get on with the question of how to do so, Meltsner (1976: 1) begins his study of analysis in the federal bureaucracy with the presupposition that "nobody can live in America without experts" and goes on to explicate the behavior of one subtype of expert—the policy analyst. Others have explicitly relaxed any assumptions regarding the desirability of rational analysis, and have restricted themselves to empirically explaining current patterns of research use in public decision-making. Weiss and Bucuvalas (1980: 1), for instance, assert that "research can have many consequences, good and bad" and restrict themselves to understanding "when and how research has an influence." Still others (Nelson, 1977) have been highly critical of current applications of rational analysis, yet maintain a belief in its value. The distinguishing characteristic of the literature reviewed here, however, is its focus on the various manifestations of policy analysis as *they are now practiced and utilized*, with respect to public decisions. In this section, I briefly review three themes that can be identified in this literature, each directing our understanding of policy analysis in a different way. . . .

Some observers have identified policy analysis as primarily a problem in organizational design. The principal concerns are (a) to devise formal organizational arrangements that provide the personnel and resources necessary for rational policy analysis, and (b) to design decision and communication systems that ensure that policy analysis will have access to decision points. In both forms, the perspective focuses on the location of personnel and resources in public organizations, the communication of analytic information to key decision points, and the institutionalization of these processes—rather than on the logical characteristics of the analytic process.

. . . Accordingly, improvements in the relevance and utilization of policy research may rest on the recruitment and placement of pertinent actors, or on the improvement of interpersonal skills for influencing the attitudes and behaviors of pertinent actors. In either case, the assumption is that policy will be as rational as the personal and informal processes that produce policy decisions. . . .

A third theme that has emerged in the study of policy analysis may be the most pervasive of all. As noted by Nachmias (1980: 1168), "The early evaluation literature separated utilization from politics and evaluation from policymaking." This resulted in the tendency to define the use of policy research in a formalized way that did not adequately recognize the complex, politicized settings in which both analysis and utilization take place. The imagery of effective use envisioned the

> direct and immediate application of the results of a research study to a particular decision. The expectation is that specific findings point to a specific answer and that responsible policymakers proceed to implement the answer in policy or practice [Weiss with Bucuvalas, 1980: 10].

The assumptions of this imagery—that decision points are clear, that findings are specific and unambiguous, and that decision-makers are in control of policy and implementation—doom it to failure. . . .

The current picture of the uses of policy analysis has been shaped by these themes. Policy analysis is but one of many considerations that decision-makers legitimately weigh in setting policy. Policy analysis has multiple uses in the decision process, including some that are political, unintended, or symbolic; and policy analysis enters decisions in subtle and indirect ways, having effects that are not always positive. The result is that policy analysis cannot realistically be considered a "guide" that directs decision-makers to better decisions. It is a resource that may be used well or poorly in setting and implementing

public policy. Nachmias (1980: 1167) provides the following succinctly relevant discussion of the utilization of research:

> [Utilization] means relevance to a great number of actors in a complex and fragmented policy process. From the point of view of policymakers, . . . research . . . can help them carry out their roles and achieve goals *they* . . . consider important. From the [researcher's] perspective, this means his or her findings are evaluated within the framework of an adversary political process in which policy decisions are reached through bargaining, compromise, and tradeoffs. In this process . . . information has to compete with a host of nonscientific factors that policymakers consider relevant.

In this view, rational analysis will be relevant to the extent that a variety of fragmented influences in a complex system reinforce its use.

A REVISED VIEW OF DECISION PROCESSES

The three themes presented above depict a rich and complex role for policy analysis in the making of public decisions. The richness and diversity of these broad brush strokes does help make sense of some of the behavior I observed last summer in California's Health Agency. I can recognize the importance of the formal creation of a variety of research and analysis units within the state bureaucracy; I can see the influence of the state's relatively generous legislative research capability in "experimental" legislation; and the influence of budgetary scrutiny is evidenced in the degree of effort put into "backing up" fiscal requests. Similarly, I can see that skillful actors have used information to support ILCs, and are careful to generate information that will be useful for that purpose. I can also recognize the variety of orientations that individuals carry toward policy analysis—from "technicians" in the Independent Living Study Group to the "entrepreneurial" orientations of departmental actors responsible for implementing the five-site pilot program. As I sift back through my observations one by one, I can usually find an insightful explanation somewhere in the three themes.

Although this literature makes me more comfortable interpreting some specifics in the behavior of analysts, I remain uncomfortable in my understanding of the interconnections between the perspectives I bring to bear. There are a lot of good ideas here, and they certainly apply to what policy analysts do in the settings I observed, but I can distill no overall understanding of how these aspects of policy analysis add up to policy decisions. At its core, our understanding of policy analysis must relate to "the tradition of viewing organizational participants as problem-solvers and decision-makers" (March and Olsen, 1979: 21); the concept of analysis cannot be divorced from these concerns. Yet, in the literature reviewed above, the relation of analysis and organizational decision-making becomes blurred. We can understand that analysts need resources and access, that they must involve themselves in the interpersonal dynamics of organizations, and that they must compete with other political influences; the ultimate, and cumulative, impact on policy decisions is less clear.

I suspect that clarity concerning the links between analysis and decisions is one of the major underlying appeals of the "rational problem-solving" model of decisions, which "is concerned with selecting the best course of action when the decisionmaker . . . has a clear goal to be achieved, can identify the various alternatives that can be used to achieve the goal, and is able to assign probabilities to the various possible outcomes for each alternative" (Palumbo and Wright, 1980: 1171). In this view of decision processes, the role of the analyst is to help the decision-maker optimize selections between alternatives. Despite continuous criticism of both its descriptive and prescriptive value, the rational problem-solving model remains a touchstone for proponents of rational analysis. This may be partly because it "seems an eminently sensible way to make decisions" (Hartle and Halpern, 1980: 127), but it is also because no clear alternative model of decision-making provides a better understanding of the contribution of analysis.[4]

Current thinking about decision-making surely admits that organizational design, personal attitudes, and the swirl of competing values and goals in political settings all affect policy choice, but "it sees these as limitations on an otherwise purposive and rational process" (Perrow, 1981: 296). It seems to me that a basic requirement for ordering the welter of current views on improving the contributions of policy analysis to public decisions is to reexamine our understanding of decisions themselves.

DECISIONS: THE POINT OF DEPARTURE

The point of access for studies of policy analysis under traditional rational models is clear. Analysis is useful at the point of decision—the point at which the decision-maker may use the analyst's information to optimize choice among alternatives. Decisions in this model are identifiable points along a sequence of events that has clear antecedents (setting of goals and formulation of alternatives) and clear consequences (implementation and impacts on the environment). One does not have to look far in the literature to find dissatisfaction with this formulation, and its incongruity with empirical reality is manifest to anyone who has participated in decisions. But if this is not an adequate concept of decision, what is?

Although there is little in the current literature that directly attempts to explicate a revised model of decision-making linked to policy analysis, several contributory themes emerge in the literature reviewed above. First, there is a recognition that decisions are not finite, one-time events that take place at easily identifiable points in time. According to Palumbo and Wright (1980: 1170), "Decisions are not discrete events; they are part of a process that extends over time." Carol Weiss (1980) argues that decisions "accrete" in uncoordinated steps by "staffs who have little awareness of the policy direction that is being promoted or the alternatives that are being foreclosed." Indeed, decisions may be so buried in the activities of organization members that decision-makers themselves are not aware that they are making them. Weiss and Bucuvalas (1980: 38) interviewed officials selected for their decision-making responsibilities, and found "a fairly general reluctance to admit making decisions of any substance." They conclude the following:

Of course, individuals holding the positions we sampled do in fact set policy and program direction. But many of them lack the sense of discretionary latitude and authority that the word "decision" implies [Weiss with Bucuvalas, 1980: 38].

The implication is curious: decision-makers make decisions while they think they are doing something else.

A related observation is that researchers "tend to 'reify' the concept 'decision' when, in fact, it is often hard to delineate specific points when decisions are made" (Rocheleau and MacKesey, 1980: 1213). In an insightful critique, Rein and White (1977:263) argue that the "problem-solving image" of policy research

appears to anthropomorphize the government, assuming that many individuals . . . think as one. . . . But governments do not think. Nor do individuals wired together in a table of organization think in unison.

They go on to argue that bureaucratic coordination of the actions of dispersed individuals is "at best loose." In this setting, "policy research can almost never dictate in so many words just what decision each [actor] will make" (Rein and White, 1977: 263).

Several more ideas have grown from the recognition that decisions are a continuous, disjointed process. One is that policy decisions may "drift" in ways that are not purposive but simply reflect the "buffeting" of a melange of disconnected influences (Kress et al., 1980). A related proposition is that decisions proceed through a process of "redefinition" and "reinvention" as time goes on. In applying this concept to the utilization of research, Palumbo and Wright (1981: 2) argue that "what is finally utilized will be considerably different from the original findings because these findings must be filtered through a number of individuals, groups, and existing structures in an organization before they will be used." A further insight that has emerged from observing decisions over periods of time is that decision sequences are often haphazard, so that fragmented components of a policy decision occur in ways that make the exact nature of the outcomes somewhat accidental (Dunsire, 1978).

The picture emerging from current discussion of the decision processes shows decisions to be complex, multifaceted, and often haphazard.

Probably the most important attempt to conceptualize this emerging picture of decisions is the imaginative, if sometimes bewildering, work of James March and Johan Olsen (1979). . . .

A basic insight of March and Olsen's ["garbage can model"] is that organizational decisions are not exclusively exercises in purpose and control. Rather, decisions are highly "context-dependent" —outcomes, depend on

how [the] situation (and the participant in it) fit into a mosaic of simultaneous performances involving other individuals, other places, other concerns, and the phasing of other events. What happens is often the almost fortuitous result of the intermeshing of loosely-coupled processes [March and Olsen, 1979: 261].

The imagery conjures up the "garbage can" label—decision situations are receptacles into which many issues and actors are dumped, often unceremoniously. This view of decisions appears compatible with much that we have culled from the revisionist policy analysis literature. Decisions are understood through the intermixing of people and events in organizations rather than through problem-solving logic.

The garbage can model provides a conceptualization of organizational decisions that encompasses many insights and innovations suggested by current literature on policy analysis. As such, this revision in thinking about decisions serves some useful functions. First, it outlines parameters regarding our expectations of what rational analysis can accomplish in complex, human decision processes. March and Olsen (1979:21) do not eschew rationality, they "assume organizational participants will try to understand what is going on, to activate themselves and their resources in order to solve their problems and move the world in desired directions." However, they also assume that decision-makers "are placed in a world over which they often have only modest control." Failures to resolve problems in a decision situation do not stem simply from inadequate solutions, but from a variety of personal, organizational, and environmental factors.

Second, the garbage can model begins to develop an overarching conceptual coherence to the fragmented revisionist literature on organizational decisions. In March and Olsen's view, "decisionmaking is not seen as an event" (Perrow, 1981: 296); rather "a decision is an outcome or an interpretation of several relatively, independent streams within an organization" (March and Olsen, 1979: 26). The identification of four such streams forms a beginning point for organizing and interrelating the factors that constrain organizational decisions.

The first stream consists of choice opportunities—occasions when an organization *expects* that decisions will occur: Budgets must be prepared, weekly staff meetings must occur, and "sunset" hearings loom on the horizon. Second, decisions involve streams of *participants*, those persons who have access to choice situations. Third, decisions involve streams of *problems* that take a variety of forms. They may be formal organizational requirements, such as replacing staff; exceptional events, such as a legislative mandate to initiate a program; or personal concerns, such as one's own career advancement. The major points are that all of these may get dumped into a choice situation together, and that problems are independent of choices—"they may not be resolved when choices are made" (March and Olsen, 1979: 26). Finally, decisions involve streams of *solutions*. Solutions are answers looking for questions—from the efficiency expert, the computer programmer, the organizational development consultant. It is fascinating that solutions often invoke problems; the ability to computerize creates questions that previously went unnoticed because they were unanswerable. As March and Olsen (1979: 27) phrase it, "Despite the dictum that you cannot find the answer until you have formulated the question, you often do not know the question in organizational problem solving until you know the answer."

A fundamental premise of the garbage can model is that each of these streams is relatively independent in the day-to-day activities of organizations—the streams can be "decoupled" readily. The load and timing of problems arising in an organization, for instance, may vary greatly without affecting the nature or timing of choice opportunities. Choice opportunities can arise while the attention of many participants is drawn elsewhere by unrelated demands: The result can be that decisions are made by those who had nothing else to do. Decisions occur at confluences of the streams, and the independent flow within each

stream means that the forces impinging on any choice opportunity will be highly context specific.

The picture of decisions as emerging from the confluence of four relatively independent streams in organizations provides a framework for organizing some of the emphases that emerged in the literature review. For instance, writers who emphasize organization design are fundamentally concerned with the definition and timing of choice opportunities, and with "extending invitations" to these choice opportunities to specific categories of participants, problems, and solutions. The focus makes sense. As March and Olsen (1979: 27) note:

> The streams . . . are channeled by organizational and social structure. Elements of structure influence outcomes of a garbage can decision process (a) by affecting the time pattern of the arrival of problems, choices, solutions, or decisionmakers, (b) by determining the allocation of energy by potential participants in the decision, and (c) by establishing linkages between the various streams.

This is exactly the intent of the proponents of "institutionalized" program evaluation, for example. They seek to tie certain solutions (causal analysis), problems (accomplishment of program goals), and participants (evaluators and legislators) together in a specific choice situation (budget decisions). Formally structuring choice situations as one relatively independent stream of decision processes is a sensible—but not determinative—strategy for accomplishing this linkage.

In another example, the literature treating policy analysis as a decision resource recognizes the "decoupling" of problems and solutions in organizations. Technical information is not simply relevant for optimizing the choices of decision-makers according to specified criteria. Information may be used to address a variety of political, organizational, or personal problems. A major evaluation, for instance, may be used to demonstrate the importance of a program or activity, to reaffirm a manager's commitment to "accountability," or simply to meet the obligation of a formal mandate. Writers within the theme also recognize that the "solution" may sometimes become the problem. Program managers, for instance, may expend considerable decision-making effort developing strategies to "demonstrate" effective program performance in an upcoming evaluation.

The ideas presented in this section sketch the beginnings of an understanding of decision processes that may help integrate our fragmented understandings of policy analysis and organizational decisions. At least they provide movement toward a conceptual alternative to the problem-solving view of decision-making, and that alternative is more compatible with the growing literature concerning the ways in which policy analysis is actually produced and used in organizations. . . .

NOTES

1. For a comprehensive discussion of independent living centers and the independent living movement, see the special issue of *American Rehabilitation* (July/August 1978). For discussion of the developing California program, see Stoddard and Brown (1980) and B. M. Brown (1978).

2. An extended discussion of the exact meaning of the term "policy analysis" is beyond the intent of this essay. The term is being used in an inclusive sense, with no attempt to distinguish policy from other techniques of rational analysis. Policy analysis, as used here, includes evaluation, planning, programming, optimization, systems analysis, forecasting, cost-benefit analysis, program budgeting, monitoring, management information and control, and other systematic, information-based techniques to aid in decision-making.

3. Lindblom's (1959) work forms one of the major contributions to "incrementalist" objections concerning "rational comprehensive" approaches. The objection is twofold: (1) that decision-making is primarily political rather than intellectual and therefore must restrict its scope to politically feasible (i.e., incremental) changes, and (2) that the cognitive/computational requirements of rational approaches exceed the capability of decision-makers. What is less clear is the interdependence of these two objections. If "scope" is lessened, are the cognitive/rational techniques of analysis attainable and helpful to the decision-maker? The failure to address the latter issue is part of the reason that incrementalist objections appear to some as a "straw man" strategy.

4. A number of authors have proposed variations that relax the requirements of the rational model (Dror, 1968; Etzioni, 1967; Rivlin, 1972). However, these approaches combine the elements of the rational model with other decision styles, rather than address the fundamentals of the model itself.

REFERENCES

BENVENISTE, G. (1977) The Politics of Expertise. San Francisco: Boyd Fraser. (Originally published in 1972.)

BROWN, B. M. (1978) "Second generation West Coast." Amer. Rehabilitation (July/August): 23–30.

CAPLAN, N. (1977) "A minimal set of conditions necessary for the utilization of social science knowledge in policy formulation at the national level," pp. 183–197 in C. H. Weiss (ed.) Using Research in Public Policy Making. Lexington, MA: D.C. Heath.

DROR, Y. (1968) Public Policy Making Re-Examined. San Francisco: Chandler.

DUNSIRE, A. (1978) Implementation in a Bureaucracy. New York: St. Martin's. Administration Rev. 27, 5: 385–392.

ETZIONI, A. (1967) "Mixed-scanning: a third approach to decision making." Public Administration Rev. 27, 5: 385–392.

HARTLE, T. W. and M. J. HALPERN (1980) "Rational and incremental decision making: an exposition and critique with illustrations," pp. 125–144 in M. J. White et al. (eds.) Managing Public Systems: Analytic Techniques for Public Administration. Belmont, CA: Wadsworth.

KRESS, G., G. KOEHLER, and J. F. SPRINGER (1980) "Policy drift: an evaluation of the California business enterprise program." Policy Studies J. 8, 7: 1101–1108.

——— and J. F. SPRINGER (1982) "Consulting environments in the public sector: implications for research utilization." Presented at the annual meeting of the Western Political Science Association, San Diego.

LINDBLOM, C. E. (1959) "The science of muddling through." Public Administration Rev. 19: 79–99.

MARCH, J. G. and J. P. OLSEN, with S. CHRISTENSEN, M. COHEN, H. ENDERUD, K. DREINER, P. ROMELAER, K. ROMMETVEIT, P. STAVA, and S. WEINER (1979) Ambiguity and Choice in Organizations. Bergen, Norway: Universitesforlaget.

MAYER, R. R. and E. GREENWOOD (1980) The Design of Policy Research. Englewood Cliffs, NJ: Prentice-Hall.

MELTSNER, A. (1976) Policy Analysts in the Bureaucracy. Berkeley: Univ. of California Press.

MOWITZ, R. J. (1980) The Design of Public Decision Systems. Baltimore: University Park Press.

NACHMIAS, D. (1980) "The role of evaluation in public policy." Policy Studies J. 8, 7: 1163–1169.

NELSON, R. R. (1977) The Moon and the Ghetto: An Essay on Public Policy Analysis. New York: Norton.

PALUMBO, D. J. and P. WRIGHT (1981) "Standing the utilization question on its head: utilization of evaluation research and the decision making process." Presented at the meeting of the Midwest Political Science Association, Cincinnati.

—— (1980) "Decision making and evaluation research." Policy Studies J. 8, 7: 1170–1177.

PERROW, C. (1981) "Ambiguity and choice in organizations (review)." Contemporary Sociology 14: 294–298.

REIN, M. and S. S. WHITE (1977) "Policy research: belief and doubt." Policy Analysis 4: 239–271.

RIVLIN, A. M. (1972) Systematic Thinking for Social Action. New York: Bookings Institution.

ROCHELEAU, B. and T. MacKESEY (1980) "Utilization-focused evaluation: a case study from the human services area." Policy Studies J. 8, 7: 1212–1221.

ROTHMAN, J. (1980) Using Research in Organizations. Newbury Park, CA: Sage.

WEIK, K. E. (1969) The Social Psychology of Organizing. Reading, MA: Addison-Wesley.

WEISS, C. H. (1980) "Knowledge creep and decision accretion." Knowledge: Creation, Diffusion, Utilization 1, 3: 381–404.

—— with M. J. BUCUVALAS (1980) Social Science Research and Decision Making. New York: Columbia Univ. Press.

WEISS, J. A. (1980) "Dilemmas of evaluating a balancing act: policies for prevention of child abuse." Policy Studies J. 8, 7: 1222–1228.

POLICY IMPLEMENTATION AND THE PUBLIC SERVICE

Patricia W. Ingraham

Aaron Wildavsky has noted that the study of policy implementation is " . . . the analytical equivalent of original sin; there is no escape from implementation and its attendant responsibilities." (Wildavsky, 1973, p. 194) Many analysts have taken Wildavsky at his word; in the past ten years the literature related to policy implementation has burgeoned. Pressman and Wildavsky's description of the implementation of economic development programs in Oakland, however, remains the landmark. Part of the subtitle, "How Great Expectations in Washington are Dashed in Oakland; Or Why It's Amazing that Federal Programs Work at All . . . ", clearly explains the tone that analysis set for future studies. Indeed, virtually every major study of implementation has described its problematic nature. (See, for example Bardach, 1977; Nakamura and Smallwood, 1980; Sabatier and Mazmanian, 1980.)

From this implementation literature two central themes emerge. The first is that public policies are inevitably altered as they move through the implementation process. These alterations are sometimes dramatic and sometimes change policy in ways apparently not intended by legislators and other public officials. A second, closely related theme is this: Because implementation is primarily an administrative process, problems with implementation are problems with administration and administrators. Such an interpretation often places responsibility for policy shortcomings—or even failure—upon the shoulders of public servants. Berman, for example, cites the resistance of bureaucracies to change as one reason for major policy alteration and problems during implementation. (Berman, 1980)

The general concerns noted in the first theme are worthy of additional analysis. The very limited utility of the second set of concerns is aptly summarized by Robert Denhardt: " . . . in other ways, the study of policy implementation represents a regression in the study of public organizations: the distinction between policy making and policy implementation exactly parallels the old politics-administration dichotomy; and the uncritical acceptance of such a distinction by many students of the policy process neither recognizes the role of the bureaucracy in framing public values nor addresses the issues of democratic accountability raised by activity." (Denhardt, 1984, p. 133)

In this paper, I wish to examine the problematics of policy implementation and their relation to the nature of, and demands on, the public service. To do so, it is necessary to examine characteristics of both the public policy process and the public bureaucracy, but also to examine some of the assumptions underlying many analyses of policy implementation. Specifically, I wish to focus on the nature of problem definition and policy formulation in a democratic system; i.e., on the problem of clarity. In addition, I wish to examine the relationship between implementation activities and administrative responsibility. Finally, I wish to consider the impact of implementation responsibilities on the public service.

POLICY IMPLEMENTATION IN THE POLICY PROCESS

The American public policy system is most accurately defined as a diffuse, evolutionary process. (Jones, 1977) Though we often speak of "stages," or "levels of development" for analytical purposes, in reality those distinctions are difficult to discern. With the exception of legislative adoption of a policy, or its creation by executive fiat, there are few points in policy evolution at which one can say, "that part is finished; let's move on to the next."

Participation in policy processes is likewise diffuse and somewhat undefined. Though a tidy definition would have fairly widespread participation only in policy initiation and definition, we know that participation by both the public and elected officials extends throughout the life of a policy or program. That participation may be sporadic, rather than continuous, but its influence on all points of the policy process is undeniable.

Nakamura and Smallwood note the continuing impact of this participation on implementation and describe the process this way: " . . . a series of circular linkages (exists) between the three environments of policy formation, implementation, and evaluation. The challenge of forging these linkages into a coherent whole falls upon the political actors who occupy leadership positions, particularly the policy makers, who must coordinate activities in all three spheres if they are to achieve their goals." (Nakamura and Smallwood, 1980, p. 163)

The problem is, of course, that these disparate spheres are not necessarily forged into a cohesive whole by elected officials. If they are not, the continuing task of problem solving falls to the public bureaucracy. Thus, the nature of the policy system—its openness, its diffusion, the value it places on participation and compromise—creates one important set of implementation problems.

To some extent, that set of problems is exacerbated by the fit between policy system weaknesses and bureaucratic strengths. There are certain characteristics of public bureaucracies that provide them unique opportunities in a diffuse and unspecific policy process. For example, bureaucracies are stable. The structures, and the career civil servants who inhabit them, remain essentially unchanged through many shifts of political actors. A policy or program direction, once established, generates internal momentum and support that is difficult to alter. Further, given the fact that public bureaucracies are open structures with well established lines of communication to interested external groups and organizations, policy momentum may be generated in the larger environment as well.

Some analyses of implementation, most notably Eugene Bardach's *The Implementation Game*, argue that this bureaucratic strength must be countered by continued political intrusion into bureaucratic definition activities during implementation. Significant political involvement in implementation processes, however, is double-edged. Though new political guidance during this activity may produce politically desirable policy alternations and changes, it is necessary to remember that initial lack of clarity in political direction is what caused the new intrusion. One outcome, therefore, may be to further muddy the waters. Another will be that the relationship between the implementor and political policy makers may shift in such circumstances; the locus of control will move more clearly to the elected officials or their staffs. Inevitably, however, it must return to the implementors. The "circularity of the linkages," as Nakamura and Smallwood and others describe this relationship between formal policy makers and bureaucratic implementors, creates uncertainty, and additional lack of clarity, in the implementation process. As Nakamura and Smallwood note, "If these linkages are not constructed carefully, the results can be chaotic." (Nakamura and Smallwood, 1980, p. 48)

The nature of the policy process, then, is a critical variable in exploring or understanding policy implementation. The level of participation, the key participants, the structure for participation, are all important considerations in an adequate analysis of implementation. Alone, however, such considerations, even when coupled with an awareness of policy system diffusion, do not fully explain why policy implementors encounter problems. They do suggest the utility of further examining specific activities within policy processes which will shape the nature of implementation activities. I suggest that an obvious starting point in this regard is that set of activities variously referred to as "problem definition," "policy formulation," or "policy design."

PROBLEM DEFINITION, POLICY DESIGN, AND IMPLEMENTATION

Though attention to policy implementation has greatly increased in recent years, attention to the related problem of design has been minimal. Three points about policy design are of major importance to implementation. The first is that if the problem to be addressed is not properly identified and if problem and solution are not appropriately linked in design, the gap—or failure—will become clear in implementation and will become an "implementation problem." The second is that, as Lerner and Wanat point out, "fuzzy" design and "fuzzy" mandates may lead to implementation procedures and guidelines that are equally undefined (Lerner and Wanat, 1983). A third and closely related point is that the American policy system is not necessarily self correcting, and identification of a problem at the level of implementation may not lead to clarification or redesign. It may only lead to the continued implementation —and institutionalization—of a policy that does not work. Whatever our obvious concerns about implementation, therefore, they must extend to problem definition and design.

Though problem definition and policy design are not extensively discussed in policy literature, they are complex activities, involving many levels of choice and decision making. Design can, and perhaps should, be a highly theoretical activity, linking theories of causality with problem definition and specification of desired outcomes. Ingram and Mann, describing why public policies are often perceived to fail, write: "Successful policy must be based upon an accurate theory about the causes of policy problems and the results that will occur if particular policy strategies are pursued. Policies may fail because linkages in the physical or social system are not well understood. Attempts at improving the scientific, technical, and analytic basis of policymaking are not likely to make much headway unless these reforms themselves are based on accurate theories regarding causation of political behavior." (Ingram and Mann, 1980, pp. 22–23)

One of the most insightful, yet concise, descriptions of problem definition and policy formulation is provided by Charles Jones (1977, Chapters 1 and 2). He notes that problem identification is a political activity, that problem definition is often the product of compromise, and that problem definition may not accurately describe the perceived or observed problem. This discontinuity was comprehensively documented for the first time in the late 1960s as political leaders and analysts alike pondered some of the obstacles encountered by Great Society programs. According to many observers, the problems were caused, at least in part, by failure to correctly or adequately define problems, as well as by failure to devise appropriate solutions. (See Moynihan, 1969; Donovan, 1967.) In retrospect, there are serious questions about the

extent to which elected officials and policy makers understood the complexity of the social and economic conditions toward which many of the poverty programs were directed. Further, though many of the solutions proposed, such as the Neighborhood Youth Corps, the Headstart Program and the Neighborhood Centers created by Community Action Agencies had technically been tried before, they had not be tested or evaluated in various settings and with different target groups. Neither had the implications of large scale governmental involvement in such activities been considered.

This set of policies and programs also identified the extent to which problems may be defined differently by different groups. In the case of poverty programs, policy makers perceived and identified one set of problems; for example, unemployment and lack of training. Implementation caused it to be very clear that the program recipients—the target groups—perceived the problem in different terms; racial prejudice, discrimination and generalized inequality. The enduring quality of this disparity, among scholars as well as practitioners, is evidenced by the continuing analytical debate surrounding the intent and purpose of public welfare programs. (See Piven and Cloward, 1979; Albritton, 1979; and Jennings, 1980.)

Even if problem definition is accurate and generally accepted, however, a mismatch may occur between that problem and the policy tool selected to lead to its solution. This mismatch may be a function of inadequate information, of imperfect understanding of the problem, or of the belief among policy makers that the perfect solution will be unacceptable to political decision makers or the larger public. In addition, the most common patterns for policy design in the United States are what Jones refers to as "routine" or "analogous." The first refers to the practice of essentially, " . . . reformulating similar proposals within an issue area that has a well established place on the agenda of government." (Jones, 1977, p. 56) The second is, " . . . treating a new problem by relying on what was done in developing proposals for similar problems in the past. . . . " (Jones, 1977, p. 56) Thus, we see agencies turning to similar agencies for problem solution ideas, states looking to other states, and nations turning to similar nations for solutions to what are perceived to be comparable problems. Though it is trite to observe that what works in one setting may not work in another, this simple fact may be overlooked in the transfer process. Again, the lack of "perfect fit" is discovered during implementation activities. The common failure to rigorously evaluate program success or failure prior to transference or expansion of a policy solution permits tremendous potential for dissatisfaction with actual performance.

As this discussion suggests, implementation may accurately be viewed as an exercise in continuous problem solving. Because those charged with policy implementation respond to different problems, to different actors, and to frequently changing circumstances, problem solutions are rarely, if ever, final.

Further, if we view implementation in these terms, the role of public bureaucracy and civil servants in implementation necessarily is one of actively shaping public policy. This is not to suggest that because bureaucratic policy making and problem solving during implementation is inevitable, it is also "good" or necessarily in the public interest. It is only to reiterate a point made earlier in this paper: If there is lack of clarity and direction in problem definition and policy formulation, implementation activities are undirected as well. Definition and direction may be clarified and enhanced during implementation; implementation may also, however, only exacerbate already confusing directions. Though most policy problems of this nature are not initially caused by administrators—though some may be—they will be solved, alleviated, or further aggravated by administrative action. To this extent, and to return to the second theme presented earlier in the paper, problems of implementation are problems of administration.

In a much larger sense, however, they are problems of the political system and of public policy processes. Their solution becomes another dimension of the responsibility of modern administrators.

THE URBAN CULTURAL PARK PROGRAM: A CASE STUDY

The problems caused by lack of clarity in formulation and design, and the complexity of implementation is well illustrated by the example of a program being implemented in New York State.

The Urban Cultural Park program was initiated by the New York State Legislature in 1977 when, at the urging of then Governor Hugh Carey and several of his appointees (most notably those at the New York State Office of Parks and Recreation) it mandated the Office of Parks and Recreation to prepare a plan for a statewide system of Urban Cultural Parks (UCPs). Though the New York program was to be the first statewide system of UCPs in the nation, the park concept was drawn from a program operating in Lowell, Massachusetts. The Lowell program was considered by New York policy makers to be an innovative and appealing approach to some of the problems of older cities, but the mandate to create a statewide plan was heavily influenced by the potential availability of federal funding for a demonstration program.

The apparent design of the Urban Cultural Park program was to be multipurpose and comprehensive. In transmitting the Summary Plan to the State Legislature in 1981, the Commissioner of Parks and Recreation defined the program in these terms: "The plan recommends the creation of an innovative state program which will help communities to make better use of resources they already have. These resources often lie within declining historic buildings and districts in the heart of our cities. Through the framework of an Urban Cultural Park System, these areas can serve to interpret the heritage of New York State, while becoming regional centers for economic and cultural development through a well defined and realistic revitalization process." (New York State Office of Parks and Recreation, 1981)

The lack of clarity in program design and purpose is evident in the name of the program as well. The Urban Cultural Park program does not create parks, in the sense in which the term is most commonly used. It does not create urban green spaces or areas for recreation. Nor is it cultural in the sense that term is most often used in public programs. The UCP program does not support symphonies, dance companies, or the visual arts. It is urban only in the loosest sense of the term. In Broome County, for example, a village and a small town are included with the City of Binghamton (population 50,000) to form the Susquehanna Urban Cultural Park. What then, is the Urban Cultural Park Program? The answer to that is evolving as the program is implemented, and the history of implementation has seen some dramatic shifts. A brief summary is useful.

The program was formally adopted by the State Legislature in July, 1982. The law created a statewide UCP system, designated thirteen initial Urban Cultural Parks and established procedures for creating a "management plan" for each of the parks. It also provided for future additions to the system and contained a small amount of State funding to serve as a catalyst for local action. The state support was limited to a period of eight years, and was to be supplemented by local and private investments.

The New York State Office of Parks and Recreation, now renamed the New York Office of Parks, Recreation and Historic Preservation, remained the program's bureaucratic home. That office was to work with the thirteen UCPs to determine the specific parameters of each local management plan. Primary responsibility for implementation, however, now shifted to the local Urban Cultural Parks.

Activity at the local level had actually been underway since 1977 when fifteen communities throughout the state (three of which were multi-jurisdictional) had begun work on feasibility studies and preliminary work programs. The generally positive outcome of these feasibility studies was one basis for the decision to move ahead with the 1982 legislation. The level of cooperation of these communities with the State Office of Parks and Recreation was also a factor in the decision of the American Planning Association to bestow its 1981 national "Outstanding Planning Program Award" to the OPR for its work on the UCP program. The groundwork for further local activity in implementation, therefore, had been established.

At this point in the program history, two political events assumed major significance. After Ronald Reagan's election in 1980 and his subsequent budget cutting activities, the potential federal funding, upon which so much of UCP formulation was based, was essentially eliminated. In New York State, Mario Cuomo was elected governor after Hugh Carey chose not to seek re-election. Cuomo did not initially support the Urban Cultural Park system and, in fact, has given it very low priority. In 1984, Governor Cuomo vetoed a bill which would have increased state contributions to the program, and state funding has remained constant at two and one-half million

dollars. Further evidence of lack of gubernatorial support is provided by Cuomo's failure to name the legislatively mandated thirteen member Commission whose purpose it is to provide guidance and direction to the UCP program. Except for the initial state funds which provided limited support for the local management plans, therefore, no state UCP funds have been appropriated or expended.

Another factor which has been significant is the manner in which the nature and purpose of the UCP program evolved as local governments began to structure their management plans. Most localities have interpreted program intent in terms of tourism, economic development, and historic preservation. This interpretation has clear implications for the New York State Office of Parks, Recreation and Historic Preservation which, of course, has no expertise in economic development and, until two years ago, had little in historic preservation. The state office has, nonetheless, a strong interest in retaining control of the UCP program and has argued that the name of the program not be changed to more accurately reflect its current direction. A program with the word "park" in its name, the office argues, clearly belongs in the Office of Parks and Recreation.

The current situation of the program, then, is this: the thirteen local governments are moving ahead with the development of their management plans, which have been partially funded by the State. Most local UCPs have hired outside consultants to assist them and all have obtained some local matching funds to permit staff support for plan development. Local government officials have become involved with the program, but not all understand its purpose. Largely at the instigation of state and local staff, a contingent of local officials lobbied in Albany for greater support of the program. The New York State Office of Parks, Recreation, and Historic Preservation, uncertain about how to proceed with an economic development program, has been slow to provide guidelines and regulations for plan development and has continued to emphasize that each program will, of necessity, be different. No coordination among local UCPs has occurred and communication among them occurs only at the initiative of the local staffs. The deadline for submission of the local management plan to Albany is June 30, 1985. The local UCPs are working toward meeting that date. State direction is minimal, continued state support is questionable, and federal support is not likely. Nonetheless, the program is being implemented.

Why do local staff and elected officials persist with implementation activities? There are several possible explanations. The first is that an inexorable momentum has been created: the local government staff who initiated program activities are still involved; local elected officials have incorporated the Urban Cultural Park into their set of community plans; the management plan consultants are continuing to emphasize the economic development potential of the UCP Program. Further, state staff continues to assume that, as local management plans are completed, new incentives for increased state activity will be created.

Another explanation is that the planning and coordination activities triggered by UCP demands have stimulated an exercise in local agenda setting which has utility even without funding. The discussions surrounding the delineation of Urban Cultural Park boundaries, for example, have forced local communities into thinking about what really is important in terms of historic preservation. The discussions have also caused local staff and officials to think about reasonable expectations for progress and about better use of existing local resources.

Still another explanation is that the economic development analysts and consultants have given those UCPs which include downtown areas in their boundaries new hope for downtown revitalization. The analyses of retail and commercial trade patterns produced by UCP studies are clearly valuable to planners and elected officials struggling to design revitalization strategies.

Finally, in some cases it appears that implementing UCP has become another exercise in creative grantsmanship; i.e., if UCP money isn't available, what is? Together, these considerations provide the necessary motivation for continued implementation. Despite the almost constant frustration, implementation proceeds.

IMPLEMENTATION, ADMINISTRATIVE RESPONSIBILITY, AND PUBLIC SERVICE

As the preceding discussion and case study suggest, problems of implementation are far reaching. They may extend beyond both the institutional boundaries and the expertise of administrators charged with implementation responsibilities. The issues involved are not only—or even primarily—technical; the questions and problems posed by implementing the Urban Cultural Park program cannot be answered and solved by new and better administrative techniques. The implementation conundrum for the public service is this: the solution to many conflicts and problems lies beyond their control. The complexity of the task pushes technical expertise and competence to and beyond its limits. Implementation activities, however, are an administrative function. Successful service delivery brings few kudos; public frustration with problematic implementation falls upon the public service. Further, the extensive policy making and redefinition activities which lack of legislative and political clarity force upon implementors raise many questions about administrative responsibility. Are public bureaucrats acting in the public interest as they define their legislative mandate in terms that permit bureaucratic action? Or, as we transfer policy definition and formulation to the bureaucratic arena, do we lose sight of the public interest?

Administrative responsibility is certainly not a new topic; theorists have addressed the issue for years. Carl Friedrich, for example, summarized the subject's major issues in 1940: " . . . A modern administrator is, in many cases, dealing with problems so novel and complex that they call for the highest creative ability. The need for creative solutions effectively focuses attention upon the need for action. The pious formulas about the will of the people are all very well, but when it comes to these issues of social maladjustment the popular will has little content, except the desire to see such maladjustments removed. A solution which fails in this regard, or which causes new and perhaps greater maladjustments is bad; we have a right to call such policy irresponsible if it can be shown that it was adopted without proper regard to the existing sum of human knowledge concerning the technical issues involved; we also have a right to call it irresponsible if it can be shown that it was adapted without proper regard for existing preferences in the community and, more particularly, its prevailing majority. Consequently, the responsible administrator is one who is responsive to these two dominant factors: technical knowledge and public sentiment." (Friedrich, in Rourke, 1978, p. 403)

Friedrich could well be describing the dilemma for administrative responsibility posed by the policy making implications of implementation activities. At what point in the continuous problem solving is the career civil servant—operating in the confines of a bureaucratic, rather than political, institution, with values that emphasize bureaucratic procedures and norms—likely to sit back and ask: Is this solution in the public interest? Indeed, is such an individual capable of discerning what the public interest might be for a specific policy question? Further, if policy solutions are too complex or too controversial to be adequately defined in the political arena, perhaps we would do well to admit that bureaucratic solutions will be tentative as well.

We demand that administrators act more responsibly than any other actors in the policy systems. We criticize them heartily when they do not. We do not always recognize, however, the unique contributions administrators and administrative responsibility can make to creating and maintaining a process which serves the public interest. Gary Wamsley, et al. summarize the components of that process this way: " . . . the 'public interest' refers to taking on several habits of mind in making decisions and making policy: i.e., attempting to deal with the multiple ramifications of an issue rather than a select few; seeking to incorporate the long range view into deliberations, to balance a natural tendency toward excessive concern with short term results; considering competing demands and requirements of affected individuals and groups, not one position; proceeding equipped with more knowledge and information, rather than less; and recognizing that to admit the 'public interest' problematic is not to say it is meaningless." (Wamsley, et al., 1984, p. 26)

The benefits of this process approach to administrative activity and administrative responsibility in relation to implementation are twofold. First, we move the discussion from handwringing about problems to consideration of constructive, long term concerns. We also move from the model of public servant as problem to a more appropriate model of public servant as problem solver. This is important not only because it will assist in altering the negative perception of the public service

which is often cited by citizens, elected officials, and sometimes bureaucrats themselves. A redefinition of the policy role—especially the implementation role—of career civil servants will also permit them to receive recognition and support for the very difficult nature of their job.

Recognizing the real nature of the administrative task and the real contribution of the public service will not revitalize the public service, however. The complete agenda for improvement must include other items, most of which deal with educating and training for the public service.

For example, we clearly know more about the nature of administrative problem solving as it relates to implementation than the literature would suggest. Lessons have been learned; we know which programs encountered which problems. We often know why. We have not catalogued that information in a systematic way. If we were to do so, it is likely that a recurrent set of concerns would emerge for implementation, just as they have emerged for policy evaluation or for studying motivation in the public sector. To translate much of this historical information about implementation problem solving into lessons which have utility for the classroom and the future public servant requires close collaboration between practitioners and theorists. There are obstacles to such collaboration on both sides. Nonetheless, a joint effort which would enhance our ability to illustrate the parameters of the problem and to teach problem solving in a concrete way would be of great benefit.

In addition, it is necessary that we not "regress," to use Denhardt's term, by substituting narrow technical expertise for problem solving ability. Many of the problems faced by career civil servants who implement public policies cannot be solved by better techniques. Techniques can help to understand the problems and perhaps to recommend solutions. In isolation, however, they will be inadequate for the task. To fully understand the complexity of modern administration, civil servants must not only know technical skills, but must also understand the constraints that the public policy environment places upon the utility of those skills. Education for the public service cannot, in short, fall back upon the outdated politics-administration dichotomy, or the principles of scientific management. We know better;

we must incorporate our experience and our insight into preparing others for public service careers.

REFERENCES

ALBRITTON, ROBERT. "Social Amelioration Through Mass Insurgency? A Re-examination of the Piven and Cloward Thesis," *American Political Science Review*, vol. 73, 1979, pp. 1003–1111; and "Reply to Piven and Cloward," pp. 1020–1023.

BARDACH, EUGENE. *The Implementation Game* (Cambridge, MA: MIT Press, 1977).

BERMAN, PAUL. "Thinking About Programmed and Adaptive Implementation: Matching Strategies to Situations," in Helen Ingram and Dean Mann, eds., *Why Policies Succeed or Fail* (Newbury Park, CA: Sage Publications, 1980), pp. 205–227.

DENHARDT, ROBERT. *Theories of Public Organization* (Pacific Grove, CA: Brooks/Cole, 1984).

DONOVAN, JOHN C. The Politics of Poverty (New York: Pegasus, 1967).

FRIEDRICH, CARL J. "Public Policy and the Nature of Administrative Responsibility," reprinted in Francis E. Rourke, *Bureaucratic Power in National Politics*, 3rd ed. (Boston, MA: Little, Brown, 1978), pp. 399–409.

INGRAM, HELEN, and MANN, DEAN. "Policy Failure: An Issue Deserving Analysis," in Helen Ingram and Dean Mann, eds., *Why Policies Succeed or Fail* (Newbury Park, CA: Sage Publications, 1980), pp. 11–32.

JENNINGS, EDWARD. "Urban Riots and Welfare Policy Change: A Test of the Piven-Cloward Theory," in Helen Ingram and Dean Mann, eds., *Why Policies Succeed or Fail* (Newbury Park, CA: Sage Publications, 1980).

JONES, CHARLES O. *An Introduction to the Study of Public Policy*, 2nd ed. (North Scituate, MA: Duxbury Press, 1977).

LERNER, ALLAN and WANAT, JOHN. "Fuzziness and Bureaucracy," *Public Administration Review*, Vol. 43, 1983, pp. 500–509.

LYNN, LAWRENCE E., JR. *Designing Public Policy* (Santa Monica, CA: Goodyear Publishing, 1980).

MOYNIHAN, DANIEL. *Maximum Feasible Misunderstanding* (New York: Free Press, 1969).

NAKAMURA, ROBERT T. and SMALLWOOD, FRANK. *The Politics of Implementation* (New York: St. Martin's Press, 1980).

PIVEN, FRANCIS F. and CLOWARD, RICHARD. "Comment on Albritton," *American Political Science Review*, Vol. 73, 1979, pp. 1012–1019.

PRESSMAN, JEFFREY and WILDAVSKY, AARON. *Implementation*, 2nd ed. (Berkeley, CA: University of California Press, 1979).

SABATIER, PAUL and MAZMANIAN, DANIEL. "The Implementation of Public Policy: A Framework of Analysis," *Policy Studies Review*, Vol. 8, 1980, pp. 538–560.

WAMSLEY, GARY; GOODSELL, CHARLES; ROHR, JOHN; WHITE, ORION; and WOLF, JAMES. "The Public Administration and the Governance Process: Refocusing the American Dialogue," paper presented at the Annual Meeting of the American Society for Public Administration, Denver, Colorado, April 6–10, 1984.

DOCUMENTS

Summary Plan: New York Urban Cultural Park System (Albany, NY: New York State Office of Parks and Recreation, April, 1981).

RISE OF THIRD-PARTY GOVERNMENT

Lester M. Salamon

In a paper I delivered at the American Political Science Association convention in 1980, I argued that a major rethinking was needed in the field of public management (Salamon, 1980a). Despite some significant progress, however, the basic message of that paper continues to apply today.

THREAT OF OBSOLESCENCE

Very simply, that message is this: that the field of public administration, and the concepts of public management, have grown increasingly out of touch with the actual operation of the public sector. Our field is not simply facing what Professor Vincent Ostrom in 1972 termed the "Intellectual Crisis of American Public Administration (Ostrom, 1972)." Rather, as Ira Sharkansky has noted, public administration, and indeed much of American political science, "teeters on the brink of obsolescence (Sharkansky, 1979:160)."

What is threatening public administration with obsolescence is not that the task of governing has become any easier or less intractable. To the contrary, what Woodrow Wilson wrote 100 years ago on the occasion of the centennial anniversary of the Constitution applies with even greater force today as we approach the bicentennial anniversary: "It is harder to run a constitution than to frame one (Wilson, 1887:197)."

The real reason that public management and public administration are in such difficulty is that our concepts and mindset have not kept pace with the changes that have occurred in the character of the public sector. In fact, the concepts and paradigms we are using do not even focus our attention on the right units of analysis.

SCOPE OF GOVERNMENT ACTION

Much of the attention in the public administration field continues to focus, for example, on the internal operation of government agencies, on the strengths and weaknesses of particular programs, and on the content of public policy in particular fields. Much is made of the massive expansion that has taken place over the past several decades in the scope of government action, for example:

- the seven-fold increase in the size of the federal budget between 1955 and 1979; and
- the extension of federal activity into new areas such as environmental protection, equal employment, energy, health, education, product safety, regional development, and others.

What has attracted far less attention, however has been a second, and far more fundamental change. This second type of change involves not the *scope* of government action, but the *form*.

TOOLS OF GOVERNMENT ACTION

The central point here is this: a technological revolution has occurred over the past several decades in the tools of government action, in the implements or mechanisms that the public sector uses to carry out public purposes. This transformation in the tools of government action is every bit as important as the growth in government's scope; and it is every bit as ingenious as the parallel breakthroughs in the scientific world or in engineering. But it is far less well recognized or understood. Indeed, it has been actively resisted at times by students of public administration because of the challenge it poses to a number of very cherished beliefs and concepts.

The message of this article is that such resistance is fruitless and that serious students of public management and serious public managers must begin to come to terms with the new challenges that these changes imply. To make this point, I want to highlight what I mean by the "changing forms of public action" and call attention to an important feature of some of the newer instruments of public action—their tendency to operate indirectly, by proxy or remote control, and involve an array of nonfederal or nonpublic third parties in the operation of public programs. I have therefore referred to this change as "the rise of third-party government (Salamon, 1980a; 1980b)."

CHANGING TECHNOLOGY OF PUBLIC ACTION

The starting point for this discussion must be the basic scope and character of the change I believe has occurred in the technology of public action. Exactly what is this change and how widespread is it? Indeed, what are tools or technologies of public action?

The major point I want to make here is that federal programs and activities, and increasingly state and local programs and activities, now come in more varieties than Heinz' pickles.

What is at issue here is not the number of federal programs, which has of course mushroomed well into the thousands. Rather, what is really at issue is the number of different types or forms of activity these programs embody, the different "mechanisms" these programs use. While most of us carry around in our minds a rather straightforward image of how the typical government program operates, in fact the various government programs really embody a variety of different forms of action, different means or mechanisms for carrying out public purposes.

The different instruments used by the federal government include project grants, formula grants, interest subsidies, loan guarantees, social regulation, economic regulation, and many more. It is my argument that these tools are quite different from each other but that these differences have never been systematically explored. By shifting the focus of attention away from individual programs or agencies, or broad fields of policy, and focusing instead on these different tools or instruments, therefore, a whole new dimension of government operation comes into view.

POLITICAL ECONOMIES OF ALTERNATIVE TOOLS

What makes the existence of different tools so important, in my view, is that each instrument has its own characteristics, its own procedures, its own network of organizational relationships, its own skill requirements—in a word, its own "political economy." Loan guarantee programs, for example, involve credit judgments, estimates of payback potentials, foreclosure procedures, and linkages with commercial banks. They therefore tend to attract personnel with backgrounds in finance and to rely on institutions with deep-seated aversions to risk.

Regulations, by contrast, involve a set of rules prescribing responsible behavior; enforcement agents to monitor performance and deter deviation; and penalties and a procedure for imposing them. Such programs tend to rely on personnel with legal backgrounds or technical expertise in the fields being regulated, and economic considerations tend to take a back seat.

In other words each of these tools is really a complex system of action and actors. Each has its own personality, and its own internal and external pressures.

SCALE

Since many of these tools of government action do not appear in the federal budget, they have escaped much attention. Yet their scale is often immense, and in some cases growing.

Take, for example, federal loan and loan guarantee programs.

- As recently as 1975, such activity amounted to $55 billion a year in new commitments.
- In 1985 alone it involved new commitments of $149 billion, up 270 percent over the 1975 figure.
- As of 1985, federally supported credit outstanding amounted to $669.5 billion.

Or take what have come to be called "tax expenditures," i.e., "exceptions to the 'normal structure' of the individual or corporate income taxes that reduce tax liabilities for particular groups of taxpayers to encourage certain economic activities or in recognition of special circumstances (OMB, 1981, Special Analysis, 204)." Tax expenditures are one means by which the federal government pursues public policy objectives and, as OMB points out, "in most cases can be viewed as alternatives to budget outlays, credit assistance or other policy instruments (OMB, 1981, Special Analysis, 202)."

Tax expenditures have become an increasingly favored means of action in a wide variety of areas.

While caution is in order in adding tax expenditures together because of unexamined interactive effects, it is clear that this device has grown rapidly—from an estimated $40 billion in 1976 to $157 billion by 1979. And while the tax bill seems likely to reduce such "tax expenditures," it has hardly eliminated them altogether.

Loan programs and tax expenditures are just two examples of massive tools of government action that are largely invisible from public view. Other new devices fall into the same category, e.g., regulatory activities, government-sponsored enterprises, insurance. In short, beyond the numerous forms of assistance reflected in the regular budget lies a whole "hidden budget" of activities that is every bit as large, and every bit as complex.

DISTRIBUTION OF TOOLS

The proliferation and growth of so many tools of government action means that each substantive area—education, housing, heath, etc.—is not only populated by a host of programs but also by a host of different forms of assistance. Take the business and commerce and health areas for example. The *Catalogue of Federal Domestic Assistance* records over 200 business assistance programs. These programs embody 14 different forms of action, and the catalogue does not even cover a number of types of federal activity, such as regulations and government corporations. In the health area, the catalogue records over 300 programs embodying 13 different tools of action.

Similar developments have also occurred at the state and local level.

- Special authorities at the local level now borrow more than state and local governments for capital construction.
- A recent survey found city governments contracting out for at least 66 different services, ranging from refuse collection to planning and subdivision control (Savas, 1982: 66).
- Vouchers for day care and other services are in increasingly widespread use.

In short, a veritable explosion has been under way in the technology of public action—a widespread, often ingenious surge of innovation in the way public objectives are pursued.

RISE OF THIRD-PARTY GOVERNMENT

Not only have the forms of government action become more numerous, but an important transformation has occurred in the way government operates in the domestic sphere. In particular, many of the newer or most rapidly growing tools of government action share a common characteristic: they are *indirect*, they rely upon a variety of nonfederal "third parties"—states, cities, banks, industrial corporations, hospitals, nonprofit organizations, etc.—for their operation.

This point is clearly evident from recent trends in federal spending and employment. . . . [F]ederal expenditures increased 12-fold in actual dollars, and four-fold in real dollars, between 1950 and 1978.

What has made this miracle possible is that the federal government is increasingly operating by proxy or "remote control." It does very little itself. Most of what it does, at least domestically, it does through others. The federal government is thus coming to resemble the picture that Harvey Mansfield painted some years ago of the American states when he wrote that they perform "some part of almost everything and the whole of very little. (Mansfield, 1967:116)." In short, we have created a complex system of third-party government (Salamon, 1980a) in which the federal government turns to other institutions to deliver the services it funds.

GRANTS-IN-AID: THE CLASSIC CASE

Grants-in-aid are perhaps the classic example of this phenomenon of third-party government. Grants-in-aid have grown massively over the past several decades, jumping almost 30-fold between 1955 and 1980 while total federal spending increased only 8-fold. Grants, in a sense, became the principal vehicle for pursuing federal domestic objectives. The grant system has also undergone important changes, as cities, counties, special districts, nonprofit organizations, and others have established direct relationships with the federal government.

What is most important for our purposes here is that grants-in-aid represent a system of action that makes the pursuit of federal purposes dependent on the "good offices" of state and local officials. It is state and local officials who determine whether federal programs will proceed and how well they will run.

If grants-in-aid are the classic instrument of third-party government, however, they have now been overshadowed by a variety of other vehicles as well. In *loan guarantee programs*, for example, it is the local banker who makes the loans and administers the federal program. In *regulatory programs* a major part of the compliance ultimately depends on the behavior of those being regulated. In Medicare, the federal government reimburses private hospitals that deliver the services, and even the reimbursement is handled by a third party.

SCOPE

This phenomenon of third-party government is so widespread that it is sometimes difficult to figure out who is doing what. The Urban Institute Non-profit Sector Project traced the flow of funds and the delivery of human services in 16 local areas across the country in 1982. This study reveals that most of the services government pays for are delivered not by government agencies but by private nonprofit and for-profit organizations.

In particular, as shown in the table, government agencies delivered only 39 percent of the publicly financed services that were provided in these sites. By contrast, nonprofit organizations delivered 42 percent and for-profit 19 percent (Salamon, 1986:7).

KEY DISTINCTION: SHARING OF AUTHORITY

What is distinctive about what I have termed "third-party government" is that it involves not simply the contracting out of clearly specified activities or the purchase of designated goods and services from outside suppliers. These are time-honored, traditional forms of government action.

What is distinctive about third-party government is that it involves the sharing of a far more basic governmental function: the exercise of discretion over the use of public aurthority and the spending of public funds.

The central reality of much of federal domestic activity today is that a major share—perhaps even the lion's share—of the discretionary authority is exercised not by federal officials but by one or another nonfederal, often nonpublic, implementer. In loan guarantee programs, for example, the availability of benefits is dependent on the decisions of local bankers to participate and on how they interpret the loan criteria or implement the work-out procedures.

In regulatory programs, enforcement efforts are frequently understaffed, forcing agencies to rely on strategies that give substantial leeway to the regulated industry. In state and local grant programs, too, despite the complaints of federal intrusion, most studies have come to the same conclusion that V. O. Key reached in the 1950s: federal grant

Share of Government-Funded Human Services Delivered by Nonprofit, For-Profit, and Government Agencies in Sixteen Communities, 1982 (Weighted Average)

| Field | *Percent of Services Delivered by* | | | |
	Nonprofits	*For-Profits*	*Gov't*	*Total*
Social services	56	4	40	100
Employment/training	48	8	43	100
Housing/community development	5	7	88	100
Health	44	23	33	100
Arts/culture	51	*	49	100
Total	42	19	39	100

SOURCE: The Urban Institute Nonprofit Sector Project.
Figures are weighted by the scale of government spending in the sites.
Percentages shown are computed by dividing the total amount of government support received by each type of provider in each field in all sites by the total amount of government spending in that field in all sites.
* Less than 0.5 percent

programs do as much to "liberate" states as to restrict them (Key, 1956:4).

What this suggests is that the challenge a public manager faces in maintaining the power to act is even harder than Norton Long taught us in his classic essay, "Power and Administration," four decades ago. What Long pointed out is that power in the American administrative state does not flow down from the top along the chain of command. Rather it flows "in from the sides" from an agency's political environment (Long, 1949).

What the third-party government concept makes clear, however, is that while power is flowing "in from the sides," it is also pouring out through the bottom, as agencies surrender control to third-party actors. There is here, therefore, further confirmation of Theodore Lowi's point that the past generation or more of American politics can be characterized most aptly not as the "public expropriation of private property" but as "the private expropriation of public authority (Lowi, 1969)."

It is important to note here, however, that the term "third-party government" has a different meaning than the term "privatization," which has been used to depict this phenomenon in recent years. Privatization, at least in some of its forms, suggests the surrender of governmental functions or responsibilities to private, nongovernmental institutions. Third-party government, by contrast, suggests only the *sharing* of governmental responsibilities with other entities.

In other words, the term third-party government emphasizes that important governmental responsibilities—e.g., assuring accountability, preserving a degree of equity—remain even when governments make use of other institutions to help pursue their purposes. . . .

THE IMPLICATIONS

What, then, are the implications of this? At least five deserve mention.

PRODUCTIVITY

In the first place, the recent changes in the forms of government activity and the rise of third-party government seem to have brought immense gains in public productivity, at least at the federal level. Relative to the growth of federal spending and activities, federal employment has dropped significantly.

Leaving aside issues of public satisfaction, output per person hour in the federal sector has increased.

What this suggests more generally is that public sector productivity can be improved most rapidly through changes in public technology of the sort described here, rather than through application of some of the more traditional nostrums of the public administration field, such as reorganization and incentive pay. This is comparable to the situation in other sectors of society, where productivity gains often depend on changes in basic production technologies. Expanding our knowledge about public technologies may therefore be the best route to further productivity improvements.

LEVERAGING

Secondly, in the course of improving federal productivity, the changes in the forms of government action considered here have successfully mobilized the resources, energies, and skills of virtually all segments of the society to meet public needs. This leveraging has not been without its strains, of course, but it is consistent with a long tradition of voluntarism and private action in this country. In a sense, we have fashioned our own unique way of addressing public problems that is neither wholly public nor wholly private, neither wholly federal nor wholly local, but is rather a complex blend of the two that differs from tool to tool and area to area.

There is, moreover, much to recommend this pattern of third-party government.

- It places government in the role of a wholesaler of policy rather than a retailer, a role that fits its capabilities far better.
- It utilizes the public sector for what it does best—setting priorities for the use of societal resources through a democratic political process, guaranteeing equity, and generating resources, yet takes advantage of the strength of other institutions for what they do best—delivering services, dealing with the public.
- Far from harming the public service, it may liberate it to perform more of an intelligence function and less of a drone function.

MANAGEMENT

This distinctive blending of public and private, and federal, state, and local, roles has also generated immense management difficulties for which traditional public administration theories simply fail to prepare us. Traditional public administration draws sharp lines between the public and private spheres and among levels of government, and it emphasizes hierarchic patterns of authority.

The tools of government action we have been discussing, however, involve a blurring of lines and shared patterns of authority. It is no wonder, then, that these forms of government action should involve immense confusion and contradiction over who should perform what roles and in what fashion.

In a sense, through these tools the public management problem has spilled beyond the borders of the public agency: it no longer involves simply the running of a public agency and the management of public employees. It also involves the manipulation of a complex network of players and institutions over which the public manager has only imperfect control, yet on which he or she must depend to operate an agency's programs.

Public administration research and theory, with its stress on personnel management, agency budgeting, etc., has far too little to say about this. Indeed, even some of the newer public administration theories, which emphasize informal relationships in bureaucracies rather than formal ones, still take the public agency as the basic unit of analysis. They thus overlook the extent to which the public management problem has poured over the borders of the public agency to encompass the wide variety of other institutions involved in running public programs.

ACCOUNTABILITY AND COORDINATION

Closely related to these issues of management are the important issues of accountability raised by these various forms of government action. Quite clearly, the more the government relies on tools that give major shares of responsibility to largely independent third-party agents, the more questions arise about how to keep government responsive to broad public concerns and how to achieve accountability in the delivery of public services. With authority and responsibility widely dispersed, no one is clearly in charge, and no one can reasonably be held accountable.

Finally, the proliferation of tools of government action complicates problems of coordination.

Not only are there numerous programs, but each one involves a different set of actors and a different pattern of activity. Achieving coordination under these circumstances becomes difficult indeed.

CHALLENGE TO PUBLIC ADMINISTRATION THEORY

The changes in the operation of the public sector that I have been discussing pose a significant new challenge to public administration theory. How, then, should we think about these changes? How well do existing theories accommodate them and what changes in theory are needed? Broadly speaking, two basic bodies of thought are available in the literature, and neither does full justice to the "third-party government" phenomenon.

CLASSICAL PUBLIC ADMINISTRATION

The first body of thought is what might be termed "classical" public administration, and traces its lineage back to Woodrow Wilson and Max Weber. Classical public administration theory is generally hostile to the whole phenomenon of third-party government, viewing it as a fall from grace and an abrogation of the appropriate responsibilities of public officials. Classical public administration objects to third-party government principally because of the threat it poses to accountability.

Following Wilson, those who adhere to this school identify accountability with a sharp division between politics and administration and with the centralization of political power in elected political leaders who can exercise full control over administrative agents and thus be held accountable for what those agents do (Wilson, 1887; Ostrom; 1962: 123-29). The only hope for democratic accountability, according to this school, is to concentrate the functions of government in professional bureaucracies functioning under close political control.

Third-party government, by contrast, violates this principle at every turn.

- It fragments power.
- It obscures who is doing what.
- It severs lines of control.

As it is now widely acknowledged, however, the "classical" theory has long had serious problems.

In the first place, centralized bureaucracies have been far more difficult to manage than the classical theories acknowledged. This is so not only because of third-party government but also because of informal relationships that complicate hierarchic control (Seidman, 1970). What is more, such agencies are often inefficient and ponderous. Finally, the grand old "golden days" of administrative clarity portrayed in the classical theories probably never existed.

Third-party government is not as new a phenomenon as many believe. The first social service program enacted by the federal government, for example, was a grant-in-aid to a sectarian, private old-age home in Washington, enacted in 1874. Similarly, some of our premier private, nonprofit agencies—e.g., Harvard, Columbia, and Yale—owe their origins and early sustenance to public support (Salamon, 1986). Finally, the new forms of action are too enmeshed to be wished away. And they fit too well with American values, which are hostile to large-scale bureaucracy.

POLITICAL ECONOMY/PUBLIC CHOICE THEORIES

This brings us to the second body of theory, which owes its origins to the theories of James Madison and Alexis de Toqueville. Far from bewailing third-party government, these theories advocate it as a preferred mode of operation. These theories take the view that different institutional arrangements are appropriate to produce different public goods and that competition leads to efficiency. Instead of stressing the need to improve the *quality* of public management, this view stresses the desirability of reducing the *quantity* of management that is required.

Rather than centralizing administrative power, advocates of this view would disperse it to take advantage of the forces of competition. This can be done by moving from administered systems to self-activating ones—e.g., by creating financial incentives for compliance with regulations instead of relying on the control systems of federal inspectors. Charles Schultz has referred to this strategy as "the public use of private interest (Schultz, 1976)."

But this approach, too, has its problems. In the first place, it takes as given what might be called

the "royal guard of eunuchs view" of the characteristics of the third-party implementers of public programs, the view that, like royal eunuchs, these agents have "no distracting wants of their own to impede the execution of their assigned tasks." In fact, however, the third parties running public programs often have incentives and interests that run counter to the program objectives and that can be reconciled with these objectives only at great cost.

In the second place, the conditions that are supposed to justify the use of third-party arrangements frequently do not exist in reality. For example, much of the argument for contracting out the provision of public services to nonprofit providers hinges on the presence of three conditions:

• competition in the service environment, so that governments can have a choice;
• government decisionmaking geared principally to cost effectiveness; and
• effective oversight by government to ensure compliance.

In fact, however, much of the recent research suggests that these three conditions rarely obtain and that government arrangers of services must frequently content themselves with the services the existing agencies have available rather than the ones that the clients being served more need (DeHoog, 1985).

CONCLUSION: TOWARD A NEW PUBLIC ADMINISTRATION

"A government ill executed," Alexander Hamilton wrote in *Federalist* No. 70, "whatever it might be in theory, is in practice a poor government." The rise of third-party government has greatly complicated the task of avoiding poor government in this sense.

It seems clear, however, that this form of action is with us for the foreseeable future, and that it offers advantages that cannot be denied. What is needed, therefore, is some way to come to terms with its problems without sacrificing its strengths. This will require major changes in the teaching and practice of public administration.

- We will have to rethink our conception of public service, emphasizing the public sector's role as a wholesaler of policy rather than a retailer—a role for which the public sector is probably better suited.
- We will have to replace a public administration built around the concept of government as a producer or provider of services with one that can take account instead of government's role as an "arranger" of services produced by others.
- We must develop a far more coherent understanding of the underlying characteristics of the different instruments the public sector has available so that better choices can be made about which is best for what purpose.
- We must move from a preoccupation with internal agency operations to the far more important problem of interorganizational persuasion.

The discussion here has certainly not settled all of these issues. But I have no doubt that these are the issues that are truly critical for the future evolution of the field.

REFERENCES

DEHOOG, RUTH HOOGLAND, 1985, "Human Services Contracting: Environmental, Behavioral and Organizational Conditions," *Administration and Society*, 16:427–454.

GRODZINS, MORTON, 1963, "Centralization and Decentralization in the American Federal System," in Robert A. Goldwin, ed., *A Nation of States: Essays on the American Federal System*, Chicago, Rand McNally.

KEY, V. O., 1956, *American State Politics: An Introduction*, New York, Alfred A. Knopf.

LONG, NORTON, 1949, "Power and Administration," *Public Administration Review*, 9:257–64.

LOWI, THEODORE, 1969, *The End of Liberalism*, New York, W. W. Norton & Co.

MANSFIELD, HARVEY C., 1967, "Functions of State and Local Government," James W. Fesler, et al., *The Fifty States and their Local Governments*, New York, Alfred A. Knopf.

MOSHER, FREDERICK C., 1980, "The Changing Responsibilities and Tactics of the Federal Government," *Public Administration Review* (November/December 1980), pp. 541–548.

OSTROM, VINCENT, 1972, *The Intellectual Crisis in American Public Administration*, University of Alabama, The University of Alabama Press.

SALAMON, LESTER M., 1980a, "The Rise of Third-Party Government," *The Washington Post*, June 29, 1980.

SALAMON, LESTER M., 1980b, "Rethinking Implementation." (Paper prepared for delivery at the 1980 Annual Meeting of the American Political Science Association, Washington, D.C., August 18–21,1980). Published as "Rethinking Public Management: Third-Party Government and the Changing Forms of Public Action," *Public Policy*, 29:3 (Summer 1981).

SALAMON, LESTER M., 1986. "Government and the Voluntary Sector in an Era of Retrenchment: The American Experience," *Journal of Public Policy*, 6:1–20.

SAVAS, E. S., 1982, *Privatizing the Public Sector: How to Shrink Government*, Chatham, N.J., Chatham House.

SCHULTZ, CHARLES, 1976. *The Public Use of Private Interest*, Washington, The Brookings Institution.

SEIDMAN, HAROLD, 1970, *Politics, Position and Power: The Dynamics of Federal Organization*, New York, Oxford University Press.

SHARKANSKY, IRA, 1979, *Whither the State? Politics and Public Enterprise in Three Countries*, Chatham, N.J., Chatham House.

WILSON, WOODROW, 1887, "The Study of Administration," *Political Science Quarterly*, 2:197–220 (June 1887).

ANTHONY R. KANE: BEHIND NATIONAL TRANSPORTATION POLICY

Nancy M. Davis

In 1982, he proposed increasing the federal gas tax by a nickel a gallon. Now, he wants to hike airline ticket taxes 25 percent.

He is Anthony R. Kane, 44, a senior manager in the Federal Highway Administration (FHWA). Last June, he was chosen by Transportation Secretary Samuel Skinner to direct a team charged with writing—and creating interagency consensus for—a comprehensive transportation policy.

Released in February, the policy sets goals for the nation's highways, transit lines, air traffic system and railroads and recommends paying for improvements with increased user fees. Under the plan, taxes on airline tickets, for example, would rise from the current level of 8 percent to 10 percent of fares.

"It's a question of fairness," Kane says, explaining that the FHWA is entirely funded from motor fuel taxes collected in the highway trust fund, while only about 60 percent of the Federal Aviation Administration's $7 billion annual budget comes from the airport trust fund. "Secretary Skinner will be pushing aviation users to foot a greater share of their bill," including the cost of modernizing air traffic control equipment, Kane says.

The new policy also endorses reducing highway trust fund reserves, focusing FHWA's resources on maintaining the interstate highway system, giving states more flexibility in the way they use grants and standardizing state truck regulations.

The policy calls for permitting local airports to charge user fees, eliminating outmoded railroad labor laws, levying fees on boaters, improving Department of Transportation safety inspection programs, regulating transportation of hazardous materials and spending more on research for high-tech solutions to transportation problems. Highway congestion, for instance, can be alleviated by developing so-called "smart" highways and equipping cars with radio sensors and computers that identify traffic jams, Kane says.

This ambitious agenda will serve as framework for congressional reauthorization of the nation's major aviation, transit and highway programs during 1990-91. The three programs account for $23 billion of the department's $27 billion fiscal 1990 budget.

This isn't the first time Kane has directed research of this magnitude. In 1979, armed with degrees in civil engineering and a brand-new doctorate in business administration, he managed a $7 million study that ultimately justified President Reagan's endorsement of the whopping nickel gas tax hike, which became part of the Surface Transportation Act of 1982.

In promoting the tax, Kane was called upon to testify before Congress and negotiate with public interest groups for the first time. Showing how the highway system had deteriorated was easy, he says, but it was "time-consuming to convince the President" and the public that a non-defense program should grow.

"The frustrating part of working on such studies is that you always have to remember that your job is providing support. It is particularly difficult if you're convinced that every product should be accepted," says Kane, who is a member of the Senior Executive Service.

"Your job is to offer options—with good reasons—and not necessarily provide answers to political appointees who are responsible for making choices. It can also be frustrating when you think they make the wrong choices."

He says the gas tax debate kept him from leaving government after an 18-year career. Recruited in 1968 as a Transportation planner, Kane completed a series of training assignments—including stints with state and local governments—before serving as a commissioned officer in the U.S. Public Health Service. Returning to DOT in 1972, he provided technical support for grantees, designed a computer model for analyzing highway projects and became chief of two FHWA units. Richard Morgan, the recently retired FHWA executive director, was a mentor.

Despite these early successes, in the late 1970s Kane started thinking about joining the private sector. He was tired of bureaucratic decisionmaking, discouraged by the poor public opinion of civil servants and thought his salary way too low. "Then, I just kept getting new challenges," he admits, almost sheepishly. "And now that I've invested all these years, I've decided to stay in government." Although the salary level still rankles, some financial pressure has been alleviated as his wife, Jackie, has grown successful in her career. She is an executive for ICM, a Denver-based national mortgage company. The Bethesda, Md., couple has two children.

Kane says he has found non-financial rewards in his work: In forming his current policy team, for example, he was allowed to recruit from every DOT agency and had a $1 million budget and a free hand in the research. In contrast to the gas tax study—conducted by contractors—this policy was created by DOT officials themselves.

"The process was just as important to Secretary Skinner as the product," Kane reflects. "Every Transportation Department official, such as those in the Federal Aviation Administration and the Coast Guard, had their own views on what should be national policy. What we had to do, in a collegial way, was get opposing camps together.

"That's why the Secretary's own staff did not lead this research. Rather, it was conducted by representatives of diverse agencies. What our team did was continually draft position papers and get reactions. Then the political appointees in the agencies— with their staffs—put on public hearings that required *them* to work together."

As the policy team disbands and Congress begins to address these issues, however, Kane is being promoted to another job that will also test his interpersonal skills: He'll be supervising FHWA's often controversial grants to state and local governments.

So this time, he won't have direct responsibility for shepherding his research into law. He has no regrets; he's not so sure he would want to gain a reputation for having brought two tax hikes to America.

PARAMEDICAL SERVICES AT THE SCENE OF AN ACCIDENT

It wasn't a heavy rain, just the light drizzle that often causes the worst problems. Jason Evans, a twenty-year sergeant with the Northville police department, knew that he should finish his coffee and get back to his patrol car. The late afternoon rush hour was beginning, and soon the tired and harried commuters would be hurrying home from work. As he pulled out of the station and switched on his radio, he heard the dispatcher's calm voice announce a three-car accident on Route 17 south. The initial report indicated that a head-on collision had occurred with an additional car involved. Jason switched on his siren and sped toward the scene.

On the other side of the city, the Number 4 firehouse alarm rang and two vehicles shot out of the doors as they rolled up. The first vehicle was Rescue Truck #1, with a driver and a paramedic inside. Close behind was Pumper #3, with a crew of four. Marc Sanchez, the paramedic in the rescue truck, was on the radio trying to find out how many people were involved and whether the emergency room at the local hospital had been alerted. As the two trucks sped toward the accident, Marc was glad that there wouldn't be a repeat of the disaster that happened the month before.

About a month earlier a similar accident had caused a shouting match between Marc and Sergeant Evans. Marc had arrived at an accident several minutes before Evans and had proceeded to treat the victims. In the process, Marc had moved two people out of their cars onto the road surface and away from the vehicles. Because one of the cars had been burning, the firemen who had arrived with Marc were hosing down the car and directing traffic. When Evans pulled up in his patrol car, Marc had barely noticed.

When the ambulances arrived to transport the victims to the hospital, Evans had called Marc over and told him never again to move anyone before the police arrived. Evans explained that the positions of the victims would be part of the evidence in the case if the police decided to file charges. Marc had replied that he didn't report to the police and that in his opinion the treatment of the people came before the establishment of evidence. Evans, quite upset by that point, responded that the control of the scene of any traffic accident was the responsibility of the police—and that included control of *any* emergency personnel who showed up, regardless of their chain of command. Marc, also getting angry, had shot back that he wasn't going to stand around and watch people suffer or die waiting for the police to show up.

As Jason Evans rounded the last corner, he saw a horrible sight. Two vehicles were engulfed in flames and the fire truck was just getting set up to try to extinguish the blaze. Jason pulled his car across the road and turned off his siren. As he stepped out of the cruiser to begin directing traffic, one of the paramedics ran toward him.

"Sergeant Evans, we got all of the people out of the cars before the fire started. If you want to talk to any of them before we transport them to the hospital, I recommend you do it now. I'll take over the traffic control for you." Sergeant Evans recognized Marc Sanchez. Evans remembered their last encounter and was about to explain that traffic control was the responsibility of the police, when he paused to consider that Marc might be trying to help get the investigation going right away. "Thanks, I'll take you up on your offer," said Evans. "I also told the firemen not to pull the cars apart until after you had gotten some pictures. They understand how important the initial positions might be," said Marc, grinning through the soot and smoke, "We're learning how to cooperate."

Evans and Sanchez were both reflecting the results of a meeting that had been held a few days earlier. The chief of police, the fire chief, the mayor, and two members of city council had gotten together with the city manager to work out the protocol for managing the emergency personnel at the scene of an accident. The result was a compromise, establishing that the fire department was in command as long as there was an active fire or an obvious danger of fire. If no fire was in progress or if none was likely, the police department was in command.

The hardest question to resolve was to whom the paramedical personnel should report. Although they worked in the fire department where the rescue truck was based, they were often needed in situations in which there was no fire. Tobias Knopf, the city manager, had finally suggested a rule of thumb to follow; whenever possible the paramedics will operate independently and render assistance without waiting for orders. If necessary, the ranking fire officer was responsible for instructing the paramedics. After any fire was extinguished, the paramedics would report to the ranking police officer until the emergency was considered over. This had not made everyone happy, but it was better than having shouting matches at the scene of an accident.

When Marc Sanchez got back to the fire station after the accident, he sat down in front of his locker and pulled off his protective jacket. Fire Chief Horace Checker stopped on his way to the office. "That was quick thinking out there today, Marc. Sergeant Evans told me you did exactly the right thing. It seems he had a chance to get statements from all of the drivers before they were taken to the hospital and, as a result, he thinks the case can be cleaned up in a few weeks rather than months." As Marc stowed his equipment, he reflected on the fact that the various uniformed services were finally working together rather than fighting over who was in charge. He guessed that the paramedics' authority would always be a problem because not everyone agreed on the importance of first establishing blame.

In the city manager's office, the phone rang. When Tobias Knopf put down the phone he shook his head and sighed. His assistant raised an inquiring eyebrow. "That was the city solicitor; the city is probably going to be sued by one of the accident victims who claims that his medical treatment was delayed because the police held him at the scene for questioning." "Can he do that?" asked the assistant. Tobias replied, "He probably won't win, but he can stir up the question all over again."

DISCUSSION QUESTIONS

1. Explain whether you think giving medical treatment or gathering evidence should be given priority at the scene of a traffic accident.
2. How would you solve the problem of "who is in charge" at the scene of a traffic accident?
3. What impact, if any, would having a central "911" dispatcher have on this type of problem?

THE HOSPITAL EXPANSION PROJECT

Greenvault Memorial Hospital has served as the only hospital in Folkstown for the past eighty years. As the town grew, the hospital expanded and modernized. Three years ago, a new board chairperson started a capital campaign to raise money for a major addition. As the plans were drawn up, it became apparent that the only available space for expansion lay across the city line in the adjoining township. Although this was recognized as a problem, the decision was made to go ahead with the plan, as everyone assumed that the expansion would be in the interest of the residents of the township as well as of those in the city.

The entire hospital board spent three days at a local resort going over the architect's plans and suggesting revisions. The final plans were approved with only one dissenting vote. The newest member of the board voted against the project because he felt that the cost estimates were too high and that the design was unnecessarily fancy. With a great deal of publicity, the board announced that it was ready to approve construction project bids. When the bids were opened, only one bid was within 5 percent of the projected cost; all of the others were much higher. The board awarded the bid even though the contractor insisted that any delay in beginning the project would invoke a penalty clause that required the hospital to bear the additional costs.

One week after the bid was awarded the first problem became apparent. The application for a construction permit was routinely approved by the city, and a preliminary estimate of the tax on the new addition was provided by the city assessor. The assessor had included the entire cost of the addition. At the same time, the township commissioners had also granted a permit, and they had also included the full cost of the addition in their tax estimate. Wallace Becker, business manager for Greenvault Hospital, contacted the township and the city to request a meeting to work out the problem. During the conversation, Frank Pliance, the township regulations officer, casually remarked that this would be a good time to work out the parking problem. "What parking problem?" Wallace inquired. Frank replied, "Didn't you get my addendum to the building permit? Well, never mind, I'll bring it to the meeting."

At the meeting, Frank explained that the township had, indeed, made an error in the computation of the tax estimate. He commented that because the tax status of the hospital had only recently gone from nonprofit to profit, the township staff was unfamiliar with the process. Wallace was relieved and relaxed in his seat. Judy Rankin, assistant to the city manager, began to collect her papers in preparation for the conclusion of the meeting. "So the only problem remaining is the provision for an additional 430 parking spaces," said Frank. "Wait a minute," Wallace sputtered. "Four hundred and thirty—that's preposterous! Where did you get that figure?"

Frank slid a short document toward Wallace with a resigned look on his face. "This should have been attached to the building permit, but it's all in the township records." Wallace briefly scanned the document:

> Greenvault Hospital has recently changed from an all residential treatment facility to a combination outpatient, clinic, and residential facility. As a result, the hospital is now considered a mixed occupancy facility under the township zoning ordinance Section 6.01 E. The requirements for medical and dental clinics are one space for each fifty square feet of gross floor space. The computed square footage for "clinic" use (excluding administrative, record keeping, and waiting areas) is 41,943. This requires 838 parking spaces. The submitted plan provides only 400. In order for this permit to be valid, a revised plan must be submitted to accommodate the additional spaces.

Wallace looked up at Frank. "What's going on here?" "Actually," said Frank, "you ought to ask Judy." Wallace turned to Judy who was fidgeting in her seat. Slowly she turned to Wallace. "The problem has been getting worse over the past several years. The hospital sits on the edge of a residential neighborhood. As you have more and more outpatients, they park on the street and walk into the clinics. The residents have been complaining to the mayor to do something. We know that you don't have room to expand your parking lots in the portion of the hospital located in the city, so we asked the township to help us with the problem." Wallace was angry now. "So that's it. The city wants us to accommodate all of the traffic without any use of the city parking capacity. I thought when we were forced to start paying taxes we could expect some cooperation."

Judy flushed. "That's not fair." She rose from her seat and began to pace around the room. "We could have raised this question years ago, but we were sensitive to your limited options. Now that you are expanding, we thought it was reasonable to request the township to change the zoning category and ask for the additional spaces." Wallace leaned over the table and looked directly at Frank. "It's too late to change the plans. We have already awarded the construction bid and there isn't enough room to add the spaces. Besides, I don't think that you can require us to solve the city's problem using the township's zoning ordinance." Frank looked startled. "I wouldn't count on that," he replied. "The permit isn't valid unless you revise the plans. If you start construction we'll get a court order to make you stop."

Two weeks passed as the attorneys from the hospital and the township solicitor tried to work out some solution. Wallace became more and more concerned that the construction would be delayed by the dispute. Finally, he decided to offer his own compromise. Quickly he jotted down some figures and made a few phone calls. He called Judy and Frank and asked them to meet him at the township building the next day. He then invited the mayor and the chairperson of the township board of commissioners to join the meeting. When they were all assembled, Wallace explained what he had in mind. "I've arranged to lease a two-acre plot in the township about a mile from the hospital. We'll operate a shuttle bus from the site to the hospital and require nonmedical regular shift employees to park there. That should increase the available on-site parking by the required 400 spaces without necessitating a revision in the plans."

Judy and Frank looked pleased. The mayor had a few questions about how the hospital would prevent the employees from parking on city streets anyway, but was generally in favor. The chairperson of the township board of commissioners was delighted. He had become increasingly uneasy about whether the change in zoning could be sustained in court. "I think that we ought to have a long-term development plan for the hospital submitted to a joint planning meeting between the city and the township," he offered. "It's time we started cooperating rather than competing."

DISCUSSION QUESTIONS

1. Explain whether you think the township was correct in changing the zoning designation of the hospital.
2. Discuss the kind of intergovernmental agreement the city and the township could have made that would have solved this problem.
3. Was the city correct in waiting until the expansion plans were proposed to formally raise the parking problem?

HOW MANY OR HOW BIG: COPY MACHINES AS TECHNOLOGY

Just as the meeting was about to start, Ralph stuck his head into Ramon Dias's office and grimaced. "The copies of your latest report won't be ready for another half hour or so." Ralph saw the look on Ramon's face and quickly withdrew. Around the table several of the people smiled and shook their heads. They all knew that either the copy machine was broken down or there were people standing in line to use it. This delay in getting copies was becoming more than an inconvenience, now it was wasting valuable time. Suddenly Ramon decided to use the first part of the meeting to discuss the problem with the group.

"How often has this been a problem?" Ramon asked the group. Susan immediately volunteered. "This is always a problem. Most of the people who use the copy machine are only doing one or two pages of memos or forms. If I have a longer document that needs multiple copies, I have to stand in line and wait like everybody else. I think we ought to have a rule that those who need a lot of pages done get to go first."

"Nonsense," snorted Kevin. "If you have a long document and need to have multiple copies, you ought to send it out to one of the private copy companies overnight rather than tie up the copy machine for an hour at a time. Those shorter forms need to be copied immediately because we have to send the originals to other offices. If the big jobs get priority, the rest of the work in the office will be delayed. I think we ought to have a limit on the number of pages and the number of copies anyone can make on the machine."

"I still think that we ought to buy small personal copiers for each office so that the memos and forms can be done immediately," Sam suggested. "That way only the larger jobs would have to go to the central copy machine. I know that sounds expensive, but look at the time we already waste. Besides, that way if one of the little copy machines wasn't working, you could go use someone else's."

"Speaking of breakdowns," said Michael, "I think that a newer, faster, more reliable machine is the answer. If we had a machine that could do all but our largest jobs in ten minutes, we wouldn't have a problem at all. The real problem is that the current machine isn't working about one-third of the time, and all the little jobs pile up to the point where we run the machine constantly after it is fixed."

Ralph stuck his head back into the room. "The copy machine just quit working. I sent the report out to Quik Print, but they say it will be about an hour and will cost us 12 cents a page." Ralph paused, then added, "I told Bill to wait for it and bring it right in to the meeting."

"That does it," Ramon grumbled. "I want each of you to prepare a recommendation on solving our problem. Let's assume that our cost per page is 5 cents, including maintenance of the current machine. We'll also assume that the average length of a single job is five pages and currently takes about two minutes. Further, we'll assume that we have approximately twenty jobs every hour. Finally, we will assume that the copier is usually not available about one hour of each seven-hour working day. Given the cost of sending out reports of more than twenty pages at 12 cents a page, and assuming that we have only five of those a week requiring ten copies, what is your recommendation?"

"What about new equipment? " said Michael. "What about more machines?" said Sam. "OK, " Ramon responded. "A new large machine costs $6,000 and runs 30 percent faster with 50 percent fewer breakdowns. The small machines cost $800 each, but we have to buy three of them to get that price. At the end of their useful life, the large machines can be sold for $1, 500 and the small machines for $200." "How long should we assume the machines will be useful?" asked Sam. "The large machine might last three years, but I doubt that the small machines will be good for more than two years," Ramon responded.

Susan closed her folder with a snap. "As purchasing officer, I must remind you of a few ground rules. We have an agency contract with a vendor, so don't just recommend several different kinds of machines. Secondly, our maintenance agreement on all of the copiers in this office has three more years to go, so don't include that expense. Finally, think about the possibility that we will be joining the local area computer network in the next year or so. That might reduce the amount of paper memos that we receive in the mail." "If you are going to bring computers into it," added Ramon, "think about how much of our interoffice communications are being done on personal computers and printed in multiple copies on the laser printer."

The other members of the group were scribbling notes and arguing as they left the room. As Ramon left the meeting, he wondered which of the various recommendations made would also look at the larger ramifications of the problem. He expected that the reports would include more than merely the cost. After all, each of the options would have an effect on how the work was accomplished in the office. Beyond the question of who gets to use the copier first, there were questions of what type of work had higher priority. Ramon decided that whoever came up with the best proposal was going to get an excellent rating for this evaluation cycle.

DISCUSSION QUESTIONS

1. If you were writing a recommendation for Ramon's consideration, what factors beyond cost would you mention?
2. How important are technology questions, such as what to do about the copy machine, to the overall performance of a government office?
3. What benefits did Ramon expect by asking for recommendations instead of making the decision by himself?

PUBLIC ADMINISTRATORS AND ORGANIZATIONAL COMPLEXITY

—

If you work in a public organization, you will likely find that what your particular organization is able to accomplish is significantly affected by other people and by other organizations. Indeed, complexity seems to be a hallmark of life in public organizations today. If you are developing a program for aid to handicapped veterans, for example, you will likely be besieged by various constituent groups, you will probably find it necessary to clear your ideas with dozens of other government agencies and certainly with members of the legislature, and you may find it a good idea to involve private or nonprofit organizations in the final delivery of the services you propose. Touching all the bases will be complicated and certainly time-consuming, but it will be necessary for the program to have a chance of success.

You may find it helpful to think of these various relationships that are established among organizations as forming interorganizational networks. That is, just as you might contact many different groups and agencies interested in, let's say, veterans' affairs, so will those other groups and organizations contact you and contact one another. Soon a pattern or network of relationships among those interested in veterans' affairs will develop. In some cases, these networks will be so strong that they may be referred to as "subgovernments," especially strong coalitions of groups sharing a common concern.

Of course, many of the relationships that you will develop will simply derive from your position in the political system. You are likely to interact frequently with other political actors, such as an elected chief executive (a president, governor, or mayor), with members of a legislative body (Congress, a state legislature, a city council, or a nonprofit's board of directors), and with the judiciary. Obviously, these relationships will be of special importance in affecting your work, and we will consider these in detail in this section.

Finally, we should note that, especially if you work at the state or local level, you are likely to spend a great deal of your time interacting with officials at other levels of government. Whether you are working on a grant funded by another level of government, pursuing a joint project involving persons from various levels of government, or responding to mandates imposed on you from above, the intergovernmental relationships that you become involved in may be quite intense. Understanding the various patterns of intergovernmental activity will be of significant value. In this section, therefore, we will focus on the administrator's relationship with various other government officials, at your level of government and at other levels.

Ronald C. Moe of the Congressional Research Service begins with a consideration of the relationship between the president and the bureaucracy, a relationship that he argues has undergone significant change in the last several decades. Moe suggests several ways in which the managerial role of the presidency might be reasserted in this country. Moe's analysis of the presidency might be applied as well to the governor of your state or perhaps even to your local mayor. Consider the managerial role that these executives play with respect to state and local public organizations.

Frederick M. Kaiser focuses on another relationship of great importance, that involving the Congress and the executive branch, especially the presidency. Kaiser's analysis suggests that congressional oversight of executive branch activities has increased over the past several decades. As you read the article, note the specific tools that the Congress has at its disposal in overseeing the work of public agencies. Then think about the tools that are available to your state legislature, to your city council, or to the board of directors in a nonprofit organization in supervising the management of public programs.

Phillip J. Cooper complements the previous discussions of the administrators' relationships with the executive and legislative branches with a discussion of the relationship between administrators and the judiciary. Cooper notes that active judicial involvement in administrative activities makes it increasingly important for public administrators to understand the judicial system and to interact effectively with judges and other legal officers. Remember that the important point here is not the specific cases that are discussed but the lessons that are drawn about the relationship between administrators at all levels of government and the judiciary.

Next we turn to a consideration of the ties between different levels of government. Deil S. Wright discusses evolving relationships among those at the federal, state, and local levels, relationships that Wright feels are now being better characterized by the term "intergovernmental management" than by earlier concepts. Wright notes that three groups—elected politicians, generalist administrators, and program managers—are likely to shape the intergovernmental agenda in the future. Wright's article is important, not only as it analyzes the historical development of intergovernmental relations in this country, but also as it provides a context within which administrators now work. For example, note Wright's comments about the nonhierarchical nature of intergovernmental relations. Think about the implications of this situation for the managers involved—the necessity to operate in ambiguity and to be effective in interorganizational negotiations.

In the final article in this chapter, Hal G. Rainey and H. Brinton Milward discuss the way in which many different organizations—some from different levels of government, some from the public and private sectors—often come together to form "networks" within particular policy areas. For instance, a federal program in transportation or energy is likely to be administered through a complex set of agencies at many levels of government and from many sectors, all bound together by their interest in that policy area. Considering the operation of such interorganizational policy networks may often be more helpful than focusing on agencies alone.

In this chapter, we profile Camille Cates Barnett, city manager of Austin, Texas. This profile is particularly suited to the discussion of the relationship between the manager and elected officials, in this case, the mayor and the city council. Traditionally, city managers have been portrayed as staying out of the arena of policy development and concentrating on management issues. As this profile shows, contemporary city managers are asserting more of a public role in policy development. It is important to understand this shift, but you should also recognize the pitfalls and dangers that may be associated with a more political role.

The cases in this chapter explore the changing relationship between the federal government and the state governments. In "The Fifty-five Mile Speed Limit," you will see the effect of the movement from the use of direct mandates by the federal government to a more complex monitoring with incentives system. Increasingly, states are being left to select alternatives for meeting federal standards. In order to select alternatives, states must attempt to determine the policy objectives of the federal agency. With overlapping and sometimes inconsistent objectives included in agency missions, this process must be repeated at least with each new administration, if not with each new agency director.

Nowhere is the difficulty of intergovernmental cooperation more difficult than in the nuclear waste disposal problem. Federal standards, interstate agreements, and conflicts between state and local governments are portrayed for you in the case "Low-Level Nuclear Waste Disposal." The controversial and emotional issue of nuclear waste makes this policy area one in which the partisan political world cannot stand back waiting for a technical solution. You will find that elected officials play a key role in this case.

Finally, "The Dangerous Reptiles Case" presents a look at the balancing act between administrative discretion and the courts. Congress has frequently passed legislation to protect the health and safety of citizens. The administrative agencies charged with the enforcement of those laws are confronted with action choices similar to the choices presented to you in the case. Courts are often asked to decide, after the action, whether the steps taken were justified and within the legal authority of the agency. You can expect that the tension between judges and administrators will increase as agencies are asked to take *preventive* action rather than *remedial* action.

TRADITIONAL ORGANIZATIONAL PRINCIPLES AND THE MANAGERIAL PRESIDENCY: FROM PHOENIX TO ASHES

Ronald C. Moe

The public law elevating the Veterans Administration to departmental status, passed by Congress in October 1988, contained a little noticed provision.[1] Section 17 of the Act provided for the establishment of a National Commission on Executive Organization patterned in general outline after the first Hoover Commission of the late 1940s. This new Commission, however, could have been activated only by presidential initiative. If the President had transmitted written notification to Congress within 30 days after the effective operational date for the Veterans Department (15 March 1989) that such a Commission would serve "the national interest," then, and only then, would the Commission have been created.

Although President George Bush and the Director of the U.S. Office of Management and Budget, Richard Darman, were at the receiving end of lobbying to decide in favor of the Commission, the final date of 15 April 1989 came and went without so much as a telephone call from the President or his representative to Congress. In effect, the President opted to forego this opportunity to review comprehensively the organization of the executive branch generally and the Executive Office of the President in particular, thus ending before it began the most recent attempt to enhance the President's capacity to manage the executive branch through organizational means.

Few actions, or in this instance inactions, could have demonstrated more forcefully how much differently Presidents view their managerial role today than was the case 50 years ago. Also clearly indicated was the indifference, perhaps even disdain, in which traditional organizational principles are held by today's political leaders. Recent Presidents have not been persuaded that a comprehensive *organizational strategy* is necessary for achieving their political or policy objectives and indeed have rejected, along with many public administrationists, the tenets of what have come to be considered traditional, or orthodox, organizational principles.[2]

Consider the contrast between 1939 and 1989. In 1939, President Franklin D. Roosevelt, heeding the recommendations of the three public administrators who constituted the President's Committee on Administrative Management (Brownlow Committee), forwarded to Congress a Reorganization Plan to create an Executive Office of the President, a Plan accepted by Congress.[3] These same three public administrators, Louis Brownlow, Luther Gulick, and Charles E. Merriam, were also active in 1939 in the founding of the American Society for Public Administration, an organization they hoped would preserve and promote the Progressive philosophy of administrative management as represented in the Brownlow Committee Report and the related concept of the President as manager of the executive branch.

Yet, 50 years later, in 1989, President George Bush could divine no persuasive reason why he should initiate a study of either the executive branch or his Executive Office from an organizational perspective. Recent Presidents have tended to reject the view that they are responsible in any substantive way for the organizational management of the executive branch. Nor do they appear to believe that there are principles of organization which they can use and defend. Organizational management has come to be considered an instrumental value dependent upon and subordinate to near-term political and policy objectives.

In fairness, Presidents are hardly alone in believing that no qualitatively superior theoretical basis exists for organizing the executive branch. Pragmatism and "adhocism" appear to have become organizational principles in their own right. And if there are any rules that ought to be observed on how best to design and organize to achieve desired objectives, these rules are not likely to be found in the wisdom emanating from public administration or public law. Business administration is a more likely source for whatever organizational insight might permeate the corridors of the White House.

Until quite recently, the fortunes of the institutional presidency and the field of public administration were closely linked.[4] Both enjoyed periods of prosperity and influence as well as periods of adversity. What was initially a smooth and high road for both through the 1950s gradually became rocky and subject to abrupt detours. The end of the road with respect to matters of organizational management may have been reached in 1989 with the President's rejection of the Commission proposal. Today, the institutional presidency and the field of public administration have become estranged and both now follow separate agendas with respect to organizational and management issues although neither can be said to be guided by a discernible set of principles or common purposes.

What happened to produce this unhappy state of affairs? There are, of course, numerous plausible answers to this question, and insight may be found in many quarters. This article suggests that two intellectual trends can be assigned much of the credit for this estrangement. The first is the gradual abandonment by public administrationists and political leaders alike of traditional principles of organizational management. And the second involves the redefining of the basis of presidential power and responsibility away from public law and administrative management toward a highly personal and politicized definition of the institutional presidency. The success of these trends has contributed to the continuing institutional decline of the presidency and the transfer of key structural functions to others, notably Congress.

ORGANIZATIONAL PRINCIPLES AND PRESIDENTIAL COMMISSIONS

Traditional public administration rests on the premise that legal authorities and organizational structure are important variables in determining an organization's success or failure. There are "principles" or "guidelines" to be followed in organizing governmental activities, and those

arguing for deviation from these principles have a heavy burden of proof to overcome. In the American democratic context, the basic objective of organizational structure is to provide legal authority to officers and accountability by those officers to politically responsible officials. A hierarchical structure is emphasized as it tends to enhance performance and responsibility within the political system.

In the last half century or so, three major presidential commissions have issued reports proposing comprehensive executive branch reorganization schemes. The first was the Brownlow Committee Report (1937),[5] next was the first Hoover Commission Report (1949),[6] and finally there was the Ash Council Report (1970).[7] The reports of these three commissions accepted as their point of departure the essential validity of the traditional principles of organization, and, while they differed in emphases, each sought to enhance the managerial capacity of the President.

Three themes emerged from these reports: the disparate executive branch should be reaggregated into fewer, functionally based executive departments; the policy-making processes in the executive branch should be better coordinated and integrated; and the institutional interests of the President should be promoted by properly staffed central managerial agencies.

The thrust of the major commission reports, plus some lesser task force reports during the 1950s and 1960s, was to provide a conceptual and legal basis for the President exerting centripetal pressure against the natural centrifugal tendencies of the other actors in the political system.

A brief survey of the experience of the last presidential commission with a comprehensive mandate, the Ash Council, is instructive because it marked a critical turning point in the attitude of Presidents toward executive reorganization as a political strategy. The Ash Council (1970) had recommended to President Richard Nixon a "package approach" combining the various elements of the "New Federalism," e.g., revenue sharing, with executive branch reorganization. As to restructuring the executive branch, the objective was to move away from the rather narrow, constituency-oriented domestic departments towards broader, functional departments. It was a dramatic proposal, traditional in its foundation yet innovative in application. Policy direction and lines of accountability to the departmental secretaries would be strengthened while administrative functions, e.g., personnel, would be decentralized, often to standardized regional offices. In short, a comprehensive conceptual approach was embodied in the four pieces of legislation forwarded to Congress, yet Congress was unimpressed. Only one proposal, a lesser one to reorganize the Bureau of the Budget, was passed by Congress and that with misgivings.[8]

The important point to recognize, however, is that with the failure of President Nixon's comprehensive strategy to reorganize the executive branch according to traditional organizational principles, the commission and report approach to organizational management fell into disrepute. And in the years since 1970, no President has sought to promote a presidential commission with a comprehensive organizational mandate, nor have Presidents expressed support for traditional principles of organization.[9] . . .

REORGANIZING WITHOUT PRINCIPLES

Organizational principles may have been politically discredited, but executive reorganization as a process still retained political appeal to President Jimmy Carter when he moved to Washington in 1977. He pledged "to clean up the mess," a mess he believed to be rooted in an inadequate organizational structure.[10] Carter announced that he would reorganize the entire executive branch and reduce the number of federal agencies from 1,900 down to 200. A President's Reorganization Project (PRP) was created within the U.S. Office of Management and Budget (OMB), and ultimately nearly 300 persons were engaged, half OMB personnel and half agency detailees. They labored mightily but little was accomplished and less published. The immense staff wallowed in a mire of confusion for nearly two years, finally dissolving without ceremony and without publishing any substantive, comprehensive report.

The initial leader of the PRP was Bert Lance, Director of OMB, who openly referred to the earlier Brownlow, Hoover, and Ash commission efforts as simply "box-shuffling." He rejected the tenets of traditional organizational doctrine. In Lance's words describing the PRP's mission:

> [R]eorganizing is more than box-shuffling, its objective will be to make government more efficient. Previous reorganizations have stressed moving agencies among cabinet departments. Ours will take a bottom-up approach, looking first to a program and people's needs and reworking structure and procedures to meet those needs.[11]

In other words, the Carter people were saying that the earlier reorganization efforts had essentially failed to achieve their potential because they started from public administration "principles" of organization and then attempted to apply these principles without regard for the "facts." What the Carter people would do, they contended, would be to begin with the facts and from these facts would evolve the principles. Wisdom would come from the bottom-up, not the top-down.[12]

The problem, they soon discovered, is that facts do not speak for themselves. Facts only make sense when there is a conceptual framework for reference and where generalizations can be tested against experience. The Carter people, in initially rejecting many traditional principles, set themselves up for frustration and ultimately failure.[13] This failure was to have serious consequences for public administration as a field and community, giving organizational management and executive reorganization another black eye. Public administrators, although they played only a minor role in the Project, except for the reorganization of the civil service in 1978,[14] were perceived as being devoid of practical ideas and political finesse. Political appointees decided that organizational management was a political dead end. They wrongly concluded that since organizational management could not solve all the problems, it could solve none of the problems.

The Reagan Administration came into office with a definite policy agenda, and this agenda did not include comprehensive executive reorganization. They discerned that since Carter had followed the organizational route and failed, they would follow another course to maximize their political clout. The budget was viewed as the key to their overall objective, the reduction in the capacity of the government to intervene in the economic and social spheres of national life. Good management, therefore, was to be judged by its contribution toward the achievement of that end.

Although President Ronald Reagan and his aides were not generally in sympathy with the idea of another presidentially oriented commission to undertake a comprehensive review of the management of the executive branch, they were persuaded that an "outside" study would be useful. Thus, the President asked J. Peter Grace to chair a private commission of corporate executives (President's Private Sector Survey on Cost Control) to submit a report to him on how to make the government work better for less money. The results of this two-year effort was a massive study which appeared in a condensed version under the provocative title: *War on Waste*.[15]

Like the earlier Carter Project, the Grace Commission rejected the idea that any general principles of organizational management were unique to the public sector. Indeed, the Commission went further by rejecting the distinctiveness of the public sector altogether. One need only read the opening paragraph of the Grace Report to catch a flavor of the intellectual attitude of the Commission:

> Most reports of presidential commissions begin with a lengthy introduction detailing the origins, premises, and methodologies of their studies before focusing on the results of the study. We are omitting such matters because we do not want to risk losing even one reader who might be turned away by having to wade through such preliminary material.[16]

The Commission was immense, composed of 161 chief executive officers of corporations (although they never met and were not an active factor in the Commission's work). This Commission employed 36 task forces, was staffed by some 2,000 people generally on loan from their corporations, and cost the equivalent of nearly $75 million. This grand effort brought forth some 2,478 specific recommendations, a list that mixed apples and oranges, Brobdingnagians with Lilliputians. Few public administrators were consulted, so that the purity of the research and its conclusions would not be sullied. This report was viewed by its sponsors as corporate America's gift to the Nation. Peter Grace claimed that if Congress were only wise enough to adopt the Commission proposals

totally, the savings would be in the trillions of dollars in the 1990s.

The dominant theme was that the public and private sectors were alike in their essentials and should be judged by the same set of economic variables and managerial principles. Government should be organized and managed like a large American corporation, that is, with a structure permitting top-down control. Congress was viewed, at best, as a nuisance, an impediment to good management, and was to be ignored whenever possible.[17]

Insofar as there was a theory underlying the Commission Report, it was caught in the early line: "it is with private sector management tenets in mind that the Grace Commission findings have been developed."[18] The reception of the Grace Commission Report was a disappointment, even to its promoters, in large part because it told the reader more about American private corporate biases than it did about the distinctive legal, organizational, and political factors that characterize the activities of the federal government. . . .

THE MANAGERIAL PRESIDENCY: "AN UNTENABLE PROPOSITION"

The retreat from belief that the President can and should actively manage the executive branch and that traditional organizational principles can be a useful management tool has spread to much of the public administration community. Peri Arnold, an insightful historian of executive reorganizations in this century, believes that comprehensive executive reorganizations, particularly as recommended by commissions, are a flawed presidential strategy. He says that two fundamental American value systems are in conflict; one stresses order and efficiency and the other stresses separating and balancing of powers (synonymous in some minds with disorder and inefficiency).[19] It is the managerial task of Presidents to employ a reorganization strategy and rhetoric to bridge this gap between efficiency and dispersed power. When considered in this light, Arnold contends "that the managerial conception of the presidency is untenable."[20]

Arnold offers a variation on Neustadt's theme by arguing that it is "the president's functional responsibilities which ought to dictate his relationships to institutions."[21] Presidents should retain freedom to act within government so that their ideas can be transformed into policies. The President's job, in short, is to be a "choice-maker" in the political system.

Thus the president ought to be concerned with administration, not because he is a manager but because administration is part of the system through which his choices become policy. Therein is the premise for an alternative model of presidential-administrative relations to that of the managerial presidency. The president's political and policy concerns come first and lead him to administration. Policy matters of high priority will define those aspects of administration that the president must engage. In this view the president is not so much a manager of administration; he is a tactician using it.[22]

There is a seductiveness in the reasoning of Arnold's position. Yet, it is really a restatement of Neustadt's argument that an imperative of the presidency is to accumulate power and to enjoy using it, presumably for good ends. Presidential management is seen as a derivative of policy choices and has little intrinsic value apart from those choices. No organizational principles are worth pursuing apart from those that assist in the realization of a policy objective.

Organizational questions are subordinate to decisions regarding function. But functions are like facts—they mean little unless they are an integral element of a larger scheme of thought. And it is the thesis of this article that the larger scheme of thought surely involves public law and not simply power.

A primary responsibility of the President is to enforce and implement the laws of the United States, and organizational management is a critical element in the proper execution of that responsibility. To be sure, Presidents need to be conversant with the techniques of persuasion, and they are well served if their political skills are sophisticated, particularly in foreign affairs. The techniques and skills useful to the job should not be confused, however, with ends; as indeed is all too frequently the case. The pursuit of power, like the earlier pursuit of efficiency, is an amoral exercise; both power and efficiency are instrumental values

that have meaning only when tied to a particular end. Needless to say, not all ends are virtuous.[23]

CONCLUSION

When the first issue of the *Public Administration Review* (PAR) appeared some 50 years ago, there was a general consensus that the President could and should manage the executive branch. His premier tool for administering this vast bureaucracy was a well-designed structure based in large measure upon the traditional principles of organizational management. This consensus involving managerial principles has undergone erosion. Today, another viewpoint enjoys the status of a near consensus: the President cannot and should not try to manage the executive branch. The job is too complex, the institutions too varied, and the resources too limited, so today's conventional wisdom holds, to expect a President to take an active interest in managing the executive branch.

This article takes issue with the new consensus and argues instead that the earlier consensus advocating an administratively responsible presidency retains both its relevance and validity. The new consensus, in effect, encourages the transference of both presidential power and responsibility to Congress and private institutions, a transference that weakens the constitutional basis of the American polity.

The contemporary President is the manager of the executive branch and cannot escape judgment regarding that stewardship. His choice is not whether to be a manager, but whether to be an effective or ineffective manager. Unfortunately, most recent Presidents have chosen to be ineffective managers, and this ineffectiveness has proven cumulative. In no area has the presidential retreat from managerial responsibility been more complete than in the organizational aspects of management. In rejecting the tool of organizational management based on traditional principles, a debilitating relativism has become the "new orthodoxy." The President and OMB have come to view agency structure as simply one of the bargaining chips for use in public policy making. Departments and agencies can be dismantled, hybrid public-private personnel systems created, and budgetary sleight-of-hand countenanced, all if it helps to "seal the legislative deal."

A President, if he is to be a serious player in institutional politics, needs a comprehensive management strategy that includes an organizational component. The utility of tested administrative principles, properly interpreted by the President to meet today's needs, is as great as it was in 1939. A principle is a generalized normative statement based on experience and does not purport to the universality of a "theory" or "law."[24] Experience suggests, for instance, that in a democratic political system based on law, a hierarchical organization is most likely to promote political and legal accountability as a value. Accountability, however, is not the only value to be served in designing organizations. A generalization, while admitting of exception, is useful as a touchstone by which to test and measure alternative organizational proposals.

Similarly, a President can, cooperating with Congress, manage the executive branch through properly drafted generic management laws (e.g., the Government Corporation Control Act and the Federal Property and Administrative Services Act), which shift the focus of administration to the general rather than the exceptional.[25] The administration of these generic management acts (there are between 100 and 150 such laws depending on the definition used)[26] requires a properly organized, managed, and staffed central managerial agency which functions in direct support of the President's institutional interests. Recent Presidents, including the current incumbent, George Bush, have generally downplayed non-budgetary management issues. Insofar as management issues have attracted presidential interest, the attraction has been their relevance to increasing presidential control over policy fields, not increasing the capacity of executive agencies and their managers to perform their statutory functions.

In an era when the federal government is providing fewer services directly to the public, relying instead upon third parties,[27] the need to protect the public's interest increasingly is centered upon the wise drafting of public laws and administrative regulations.[28] One proposal, thus far rejected by President Bush and OMB Director Darman, is to separate the President's budgetary and management responsibilities between two agencies. Instead of a single Office of Management and Budget, there would be an Office of the Federal Budget (OFB) and an Office of Federal Management (OFM), both headed by Directors subject to the advice and consent of the Senate and reporting directly to the President. Advocates of this proposal, such as one panel of the National Academy of Public Administration, contend that budget priorities always tend to displace management priorities and that the latter will only receive the attention they deserve if they have their own organizational base.[29] . . .

Once, governmental institutions could look to public administration for the type of guidance and leadership provided by the likes of Brownlow, Gulick, and Merriam. But that was a long time ago. The challenge in the last decade of this century is to rebuild the intellectual capital of the field of public administration. The purpose of this rebuilding exercise should be to assist governmental institutions, including the institutional presidency, to maintain their fundamental public law character while encouraging adaptation to a rapidly changing political environment. In pursuit of this mission, public administration may well discover a new generation of leaders worthy of the mantle worn by the founders of the field.

NOTES

1. P.L. 100-527; 102 Stat. 2635, Sec. 17.

2. The standard formulation of what has become known as the traditional or orthodox, principles of organization is to be found in: Luther Gulick, "Notes on the Theory of Organization," in Luther Gulick and L. Urwick, eds., *Papers on the Science of Administration* (New York: Institute of Public Administration, 1937), pp. 1–45. Wallace Sayre referred to the *Report of the President's Committee on Administrative Management and the Papers* as "the high noon of orthodoxy in public administration theory in the United States." "Premises of Public Administration: Past and Emerging," *Public Administrative Review*, vol. 18 (Spring 1958), p. 103.

3. Reorganization Plan No. 1 of 1939. Executive Order 8248. Richard Polenberg, *Reorganizing Roosevelt's Government: The Controversy Over Executive Reorganization, 1936–1939* (Cambridge, MA: Harvard University Press, 1966).

4. "A strong, administrative presidency was a corollary of the theory of administrative organization that

sustained the growth of an American discipline of public administration." Peri Arnold, *Making the Managerial Presidency: Comprehensive Reorganization Planning, 1905–1980* (Princeton, NJ: Princeton University Press, 1986), p. 359.

5. U.S. President's Committee on Administrative Management, *Report with Special Studies* (Washington: U.S. Government Printing Office, 1937).

6. U.S. Commission on the Organization of the Executive Branch of Government, *The Hoover Commission Report* (New York: Macmillan Co., 1949).

7. The Ash Council submitted some 13 memorandums to the President, three of which were made public. Later, based on the Ash Council recommendations, the President submitted separate bills to create four domestic departments. See U.S. Office of Management and Budget, *Papers Relating to the President's Departmental Reorganization Program* (Washington: U.S. Government Printing Office, 1971).

8. Larry Berman, "The Office of Management and Budget That Almost Wasn't," *Political Science Quarterly*, vol. 92 (Summer 1977): pp. 281–303. U.S. Congress, House, Committee on Government Operations, *Disapproving Reorganization Plan No. 2 of 1970*, H. Rept. 1066, 91st Cong., 2d sess. (Washington: U.S. Government Printing Office, 1970).

9. There have been several relatively comprehensive studies of operations in the federal government since 1970, most notably President Carter's Reorganization Project. But the Project, discussed above, was not organized in the traditional commission format. The most recent study group to issue a report (1989) was the National Commission on the Public Service, known popularly as the Volcker Commission, after its Chairman, Paul Volcker. This Commission, however, was privately funded, and submitted its Report with recommendations simultaneously to the President, Congress, and the general public. See U.S. Congress, House, Committee on Post Office and Civil Service, *Report and Recommendations of the National Commission on the Public Service* (includes reports of the five task forces), Comm. Print 4, 101st Cong., 1st sess. (Washington: U.S. Government Printing Office, 1989).

10. For a discussion of executive reorganization during the Carter years, consult Ronald C. Moe, *The Carter Reorganization Effort: A Review and Assessment*, Rept. No. 80-172 (Washington: Congressional Research Service, Library of Congress, Rept. No. 80-172, September 1980).

11. U.S., Executive Office of the President, *President's Reorganization Project* revised, mimeographed (Washington: April 1977), p. 3.

12. Harrison Wellford, the chief reorganization planner after Bert Lance's departure, "forthrightly denied that any overall principles, theory, or view of organization, administration, or the governmental system guided the planning operation." Arnold, *Making the Managerial Presidency, supra*, p. 330.

13. There were some major reorganizations during the Carter Administration; the establishment of the Departments of Energy and Education and the civil service reform legislation for instance, but the PRP was only one group among many attempting to exert leadership in these areas. See, for example Beryl A. Radin and Willis D. Hawley, *The Politics of Federal Reorganization: Creating the U.S. Department of Education* (New York: Pergamon Press, 1988).

14. Civil Service Reform Act of 1978 (5 U.S.C. 1101). For a discussion of what was intended by the civil service promoters of the Act and their evaluations of the Act after ten years, consult U.S. General Accounting Office, *Civil Service Reform: Development of 1978 Civil Service Reform Proposals*, GGD-89-18 (Washington: U.S. General Accounting Office, 1988).

15. President's Private Sector Survey on Cost Control, *War on Waste* (New York: Macmillan Co., 1984).

16. *Ibid.*, p. 1.

17. A Task Force Report (VIII) on Congress was titled *The Cost of Congressional Encroachment* (1983). It was a highly provocative report which named Members and listed their alleged favors and pleadings for special interests. The Commission leadership decided to delete the names when the Report was made public.

18. *War on Waste, supra*, p. 3.

19. Arnold credits the idea of two fundamental American value systems in conflict to James G. March and Johan P. Olsen, "Organizing Political Life: What Administrative Reorganization Tells Us About Government," *American Political Science Review*, vol. 77 (June 1983), pp. 281–296.

20. Arnold, *Making the Managerial Presidency, supra*, p. 362.

21. *Idem.*

22. *Ibid.*, p. 363.

23. The proponents of what has been referred to here as the traditional principles of organizational management have been criticized for making "efficiency" the end of administration. Luther Gulick did say: "In the science of administration, whether public or private, the basic 'good' is efficiency" ("Science, Values and Public Administration," *Papers*, p. 192). Dwight Waldo correctly challenges this assertion by arguing that efficiency for efficiency's sake is meaningless. Efficiency is an instrumental value since one must always ask: efficiency for what purpose? "Surely it is impossible—or at least immoral—to posit the

desirability of accomplishing all purposes efficiently. For some purposes are execrable."

24. The best discussion of "principles" in the context of the intellectual development of public administration remains: Waldo, *The Administrative State,* ch. 9.

25. For further discussion of generic laws as a basic tool for managing the federal establishment, see Ronald C. Moe and Thomas H. Stanton, "Government-Sponsored Enterprises as Federal Instrumentalities: Reconciling Private Management with Public Accountability," *Public Administration Review,* vol. 49 (July/August 1989), pp. 321–329.

26. For an overview of the generic management laws and regulations administered by the U.S. Office of Management and Budget, consult U.S., Congress, Senate, Committee on Governmental Affairs, *Office of Management and Budget: Evolving Roles and Future Issues.* Prepared by the Congressional Research Service, S. Print 99-134, 99th Cong., 2d sess. (Washington: U.S. Government Printing Office, 1986), pp. 395–675.

27. Lester M. Salamon, "Rethinking Public Management: Third-Party Government and the Changing Forms of Government Action," *Public Policy,* vol. 29 (Summer 1981), pp. 255–275. E. S. Savas, *Privatization: The Key to Better Government* (Chatham, NJ: Chatham House, 1987). Donald F. Kettl, *Government by Proxy: (Mis?) Managing Federal Programs* (Washington: CQ Press, 1988).

28. National Academy of Public Administration, *Privatization: The Challenge to Public Management* (Washington: National Academy of Public Administration, 1989). Ronald C. Moe, "Exploring the Limits of Privatization," *Public Administration Review,* vol. 47 (November/December 1987), pp. 453–460.

29. National Academy of Public Administration, *Revitalizing Federal Management: Managers and Their Overburdened Systems* (Washington: National Academy of Public Administration, 1983), pp. 11–13.

CONGRESSIONAL OVERSIGHT OF THE PRESIDENCY

Frederick M. Kaiser

Some of the most dramatic confrontations between Congress and the presidency over the past two decades have involved oversight—that is, Congress's review, monitoring, and supervision of executive activity and behavior. The Senate Foreign Relations Committee's televised hearings in the late 1960s helped to legitimize and mobilize opposition to the Vietnam war; the Ervin committee's 1973 investigation of Watergate showed how White House officials illegally used their positions for partisan gain and political advantage; the House Judiciary Committee's impeachment proceedings against Richard Nixon, the following year, ended his presidency; and select committee inquiries in 1975-76 identified serious abuses by intelligence agencies and, in 1987, detailed a range of illegal or questionable activities surrounding the Iran-contra affair.

Oversight, however, is more than highly publicized investigations by short-term select committees specially created to look into suspected executive abuses or into major policy failures. Indeed, investigations by such temporary panels are infrequent and, to a degree, misleading; establishing them indicates that routine monitoring and supervision through other, more conventional channels were nonexistent or inadequate to the task.

Congress, in fact, has adopted a wide range of techniques, nurtured a variety of devices, and fostered a number of opportunities to oversee the executive in general and the presidency in particular. Even with the so-called legislative veto declared unconstitutional,[1] many other avenues are available. In addition to the most easily identifiable—select committee inquiries and specifically designated oversight hearings by standing committees—these are

- hearings on appropriations, authorizations, regular bills, and other measures, including joint, concurrent, and one-house resolutions, and committee vetoes, which are the remnants of the legislative veto;
- formal consultation with and required reports from the executive;
- Senate advice and consent for executive nominations and for treaties;
- House impeachment proceedings and subsequent Senate trial;
- House and Senate proceedings under the Twenty-Fifth Amendment confirming a vice-president and potentially determining an acting president;
- informal meetings between legislators or staff and executive officials;
- congressional membership on governmental commissions and advisory groups;
- legislators' ombudsman role of handling complaints and questions from constituents and clientele groups;
- studies, reviews, and analyses by the staff of a committee or a member's office, congressional support agencies, and outside consultants; and
- investigations by noncongressional governmental units, such as statutory offices of inspectors general and independent counsels, which can respond to congressional requests for investigations and are required to report to Congress.

This article looks at some of these techniques in action and offers reasons why oversight has undoubtedly increased over the recent past. First, though, the article examines the objectives of and obstacles to overseeing the presidency and the changing perception and meaning of oversight.

OBJECTIVES AND OBSTACLES

Congressional oversight applies not just to cabinet departments, executive agencies, or regulatory commissions operating under their own separate laws. Despite special obstacles facing it, oversight also applies to the presidency. In addition to the president, in whom "executive Power [is] vested" by the Constitution, the presidency encompasses a substantial institutional apparatus, a flexible organizational network, and a large number of

advisers and assistants. The complex includes the
vice-president, who operates under the president's
instructions and public law—for instance, he
chairs an antiterrorism task force and serves on
the National Security Council (NSC); advisers in
the Executive Office of the President (EOP); several
statutory institutions, particularly the Office of
Management and Budget (OMB) and the NSC and
its staff; various ad hoc organizational arrangements,
such as presidential councils or interagency
groupings that are directed by EOP officials; and
presidential commissions, such as the Grace
commission, and other similar advisory bodies.

OBJECTIVES AND RATIONALE

Congress has implied constitutional authority,
clear responsibility, and pragmatic, vested interests
that support oversight of the presidency.

Constitutional powers.   Although the Constitution grants no formal, express authority to
oversee or investigate the executive, oversight is
implied in Congress's authority to appropriate
funds, enact laws, raise and support armies,
provide for and maintain a navy, impeach and try
the president and U.S. officers, and advise and
consent on treaties and presidential nominations,
among other powers.[2] Congress could not carry
out these duties reasonably or responsibly without
knowing what the executive was doing; how
programs were being run, by whom, and at what
cost; and whether officials were obeying the law
and complying with statutory intent.

Also, the necessary-and-proper clause allows
Congress to pass laws that mandate oversight, grant
relevant authority to itself and its support agencies,
and impose specific obligations on the executive,
such as reporting or consultation requirements.[3] The
Supreme Court, moreover, has legitimated Congress's investigative power, subject to constitutional safeguards for individual liberties.[4]

Democratic principles.   The philosophical
underpinning for Congress's power to oversee the
presidency is the checks-and-balances system. As
James Madison described it in *Federalist* number
51, the system works

> by so contriving the interior structure of the
> government as that its several constituent parts

may, by their mutual relations, be the means
of keeping each other in their proper
places . . . [and] in all the subordinate
distributions of power, where the constant aim
is to divide and arrange the several offices in
such a manner as that each may be a check
on the other.[5]

Oversight, as a way of keeping the executive
in its proper place, translates into detecting and
preventing waste, fraud, and dishonesty; protecting
civil liberties and individual rights from executive
abuses; ensuring executive compliance with
statutory intent; gathering information for law-
making and educating the public; and evaluating
executive performance.

Allied with the checks-and-balances notion is
the constitutional preeminence of Congress, the
first branch of government: "In republican government," again according to Madison, "the
legislative authority necessarily predominates."[6]
In tandem, the two principles—checks and balances plus legislative supremacy—endorse strong
congressional oversight of the executive. This
effort is certainly applicable to the presidency, a
unitary office headed by an indirectly elected
official, because of the potential for it to be captured by a "faction," usurp authority from other
branches, abuse governmental power, and infringe
on the rights of citizens.[7]

Other defenders of representative democracy
have recognized the inherent value of oversight.
Woodrow Wilson, writing about congressional
government in 1885, counseled that "quite as
important as legislation is vigilant oversight of
administration"; noting the divergence between
the ideal and real worlds, however, the future
president concluded that "the means which Congress has of . . . exercising the searching oversight
at which it aims are limited and defective."[8]

Congressional interests.   Aside from its utility
for democratic ideals, oversight plays a pragmatic
role in protecting Congress's own institutional
interests and political power from executive
encroachment or abuse. An inability to monitor
executive activity can allow subordinates of the
president to undertake operations that the
legislature has opposed and to run roughshod over
Congress. The Iran-contra committees found, for

instance, that executive personnel had evaded statutory reporting obligations, deceived congressional panels, and destroyed public documents, which could have implicated others and further incriminated the perpetrators.[9] Also, failure to supervise executive conduct can allow the White House to use law enforcement and intelligence agencies or its own personnel illegally and unethically, for partisan advantage or to intimidate and sabotage legitimate political opposition. The 1973 Watergate committee discovered efforts along these lines directed against legislators, among others, who were placed on an "enemies list" for opposing President Nixon's policies.[10]

Oversight is expected to serve yet another pragmatic purpose in the contemporary era. It is to be a principal means for Congress to regain lost power from the executive. As Allen Schick has noted, however, "It is from this perspective that members of Congress find oversight wanting. They sit at more hearings, commission more audits and studies, have access to more data, but do not feel that they really control what happens downtown."[11]

Despite this frustration surrounding oversight, other alternatives for gaining control over policy and the executive have their own built-in limits. For instance, passing highly specific, detailed laws often encounters strong objections from the executive, upset with restraints on its discretion; in any event, such laws are difficult to enact because of the usual need for bargaining and compromise to build majority support for a bill.[12] Indeed, partially because of the limitations of other devices, more is expected of oversight.

OBSTACLES

Congressional oversight of the presidency can run into particular obstacles that make it more difficult—and more costly politically—to conduct than overseeing other executive establishments, such as a departmental bureau or a program office.

The president and, to a lesser degree, the institutional presidency are set apart from the rest of the executive branch through a number of formal and informal mechanisms. Among these are the president's express and implied constitutional powers, such as his position as commander in chief and his claims of executive privilege, respectively; the prestige and perquisites associated

with the office of president; a nationwide electoral constituency and unequaled public visibility; and unparalleled ability to influence public opinion, to mobilize public support, and to set the policy agenda; and leadership of his party.

Congress's oversight efforts that challenge the president's powers—or his perception of them—and institutional supports, let alone the survival of an administration, can be met by a phalanx of defenses. Many of these arose in the Watergate investigation and the subsequent impeachment proceedings.

THE CHANGING PERCEPTION AND MEANING OF OVERSIGHT

Over the past two decades, there has been a significant change in the way congressional oversight of the executive has been viewed. This change hinges on different understandings of what constitutes oversight, how much is actually conducted, and why it occurs. The transformation—from neglect to resurgence—is evident in oversight of the contemporary presidency.

FROM NEGLECT TO RESURGENCE

Oversight—a word that lends itself to puns and possibly hyperbole—was labeled "Congress' neglected function" in the late 1960s.[13] The label has been hard to remove. During the next decade, legislators and observers were in agreement about "the inadequate oversight being done" and that it remained "one of Congress' most glaring deficiencies."[14]

Any lingering impression of neglect, however, has been seriously challenged in the interim. One study, for example, discovered a "very rapid recent growth in oversight" in the 1970s; the same author later added that the "amount of oversight done by Congress has increased substantially."[15] Another analysis boldly concluded that the "widespread perception that Congress has neglected its oversight responsibility is a widespread mistake."[16] Still another found that both the House and the Senate evidenced a "heightened sensitivity to oversight" and that "the resurgence in oversight is reflected in Congress' assertiveness toward recent presidents."[17]

One of the reasons for the early, and lingering, impression of neglect is the high expectation associated with oversight, in terms of both philo-sophical principles and practical purposes. As noted earlier, oversight is expected to serve as a key to ensuring executive accountability and regaining lost legislative power. Frustrated with an inability to achieve such high expectations, legislators and observers may unfairly brand a less than perfect performance as neglect.

COMPETING DEFINITIONS AND THEIR MEANING

Changing definitions and understandings of over-sight also help to explain its changing appearance.

If oversight, "strictly speaking, refers to review after the fact," as Joseph Harris defined it in the mid-1960s, then it is mostly composed of "inquiries about policies that are or have been in effect, investigations of past administrative actions, and the calling of executive officers to account for their finan-cial transactions."[18] The minimalist school relegates oversight to a narrow range of purposeful activities and recognizes only a limited amount of oversight taking place.

This view is in decided contrast to more recent, broadly encompassing definitions, such as Morris Ogul's: "Legislative oversight is behavior by legislators and their staffs, individually or collec-tively, which results in an impact, intended or not, on bureaucratic behavior."[19] Based on this, oversight can be viewed as the review, monitor-ing, and supervision of past or ongoing executive activity and behavior, including plans for future operations or projects.[20]

This field of vision is substantially wider than simple review after the fact and takes in a larger amount of activity. It means that oversight is "polymorphic," as one author termed it; that is, it appears in different guises, forms, and varieties.[21] As demonstrated in recent studies,[22] the expansive understanding means the following:

1. Oversight can be manifest or latent, occur-ring by design, as in a focused investigation into mis-conduct by White House aides, or even when not specifically intended or recognized by legislators; the latter could occur during confirmation hearings that also look into the conduct of the presidency.

2. Oversight can occur in either official or unofficial settings, such as committee hearings or informal gatherings among legislators and presi-dential aides and sometimes the president himself.

3. Oversight can be direct or indirect, depend-ing upon the location of the real target of an over-sight inquiry. It is direct where the immediate sub-ject and the long-range target are the same. For example, direct oversight of the presidency occurred when the Iran-contra committees examined the activities of the president's national security adviser and the NSC staff. Oversight is indirect where the immediate subject of an inquiry and the target differ. For example, indirect over-sight of the presidency occurred when an appro-priations subcommittee looked into a plan by OMB to consolidate inspection operations of the Customs Service and the Immigration and Naturalization Service; the subcommittee used hearings on Customs appropriations to question OMB's assumptions and projected savings, OMB's authority to implement the plan, and the presi-dential commission that generated it. The over-sight target in this case was the absent presidency, not the present Customs Service.

4. Oversight can follow either a police-patrol or a fire-alarm approach. It can be a planned, active, and direct effort by congressional panels, searching out problem areas and information; or it can be an ad hoc, reactive, and indirect effort, waiting on charges in the press or com-plaints from parties adversely affected by admin-istration policies.

5. Oversight can be either adversarial or supportive. Although it is usually stimulated by various conflicts between legislators and executive officials, oversight can also bolster a program or agency against its administration critics.

6. Oversight can have different purposes, either evaluation or control. It can be used to review and evaluate operations, programs, and activities of the presidency, thereby helping to ensure its accountability, or to check, control, and provide leverage over its specific actions, agencies, or officials.

OVERSIGHT IN ACTION

The various dimensions and characteristics of oversight are apparent in several contemporary illustrations of Congress's attempts to keep the presidency in its proper place, to paraphrase

James Madison's view of the checks-and-balances system. On its oversight travels, which can include unforeseen detours and result in collisions, Congress can take:

- different vehicles, such as standing committees, temporary select committees, support agencies, and outside entities;
- different avenues or routes, such as hearings on appropriations and bills, investigations by select committees, informal contacts with executive personnel, and proceedings on nominations, treaties, and impeachments; and
- different directions, such as adversarial versus supportive, police-patrol versus fire-alarm approach, and evaluation versus control.

A couple of highly publicized investigations—of the intelligence community in the mid-1970s and the Iran-contra affair in 1987—demonstrate that oversight, when reinforced by other favorable conditions, can have a dramatic effect. It has helped to force officials out of office, change policies, and provide the catalyst for new statutory controls over the presidency and new oversight powers.

1975 INTELLIGENCE COMMUNITY INVESTIGATIONS

By the mid-1970s, the war in Vietnam, Watergate, and the reasons behind Richard Nixon's resignation had illustrated major failures and failings in the contemporary presidency. Further evidence of this condition, first disclosed in press accounts, was a range of long-standing illegal and unethical activities by intelligence agencies. Of particular concern were attempts by the Federal Bureau of Investigation (FBI) to "neutralize" civil rights leaders, infiltration by the Central Intelligence Agency (CIA) of dissident groups, planned assassinations of foreign leaders, and secret drug testing on unwitting subjects. In some cases, these problems were compounded by White House pressure to undertake the activities or capitalize on them; in other cases, they were compounded by negligence in the presidency, a failure to insist on accountability or to provide proper controls over the agencies.[23]

Examinations. In 1975, to investigate the charges, both the House and the Senate took the unusual step of setting up temporary select committees with nearly identical jurisdictions and mandates. Their efforts ran into barriers set up by the executive over access to classified information. Policy disputes arose between Congress and the presidency, between Republicans and Democrats, and among Democrats, especially in the House.

The use of temporary select committees revealed a weakness within Congress. They were necessary because the regular system of oversight, particularly for monitoring executive activities and behavior, had been ineffective, insufficient, or nonexistent. The Senate investigating committee recognized this; it concluded that "Congress, which has the authority to place restraints on domestic intelligence activities through legislation, appropriations, and oversight committees, has not effectively asserted its responsibilities until recently."[24]

Other congressional inquiries supplemented the select committees'. The House Judiciary Committee, with the assistance of the General Accounting Office, occasionally called "Congress's watchdog," reviewed the FBI's domestic intelligence operations; this represented the first independent congressional investigation in the FBI's history. The House Foreign Affairs Committee, after receiving new authority, was able to monitor CIA covert operations abroad for the first time.

Effects. Shortly afterward, the House and Senate established Committees on Intelligence to consolidate oversight, funding, and legislative authority for the entire intelligence community. Congress also added new laws to restrict and control certain intelligence activities, to improve its own oversight capabilities, and to provide leverage over the agencies and their activities. These new arrangements and power cut into the substantial discretion over the CIA that administrations had enjoyed for nearly thirty years and cut into the sometimes symbiotic relationship between FBI directors and the White House that had proven harmful to democratic rights and to Congress.

1987 IRAN-CONTRA INVESTIGATIONS

The Reagan administration has faced major congressional inquiries on secret arms sales to Iran and the diversion of arms profits to the contras in Nicaragua. These covert operations ignored or violated statutory prohibitions on funding the contras, and they avoided established channels of communication for notifying Congress as well as other executive officials, including members of the NSC and the Joint Chiefs of Staff. The operations were directed principally by the president's assistant for national security, personnel on the NSC staff, CIA operatives and officials, and private parties, both foreign and domestic.[25]

Congressional examinations. Oversight of this episode has been undertaken by a number of congressional panels looking into the affair itself, into proposed legislation to prevent similar occurrences, and into the president's nomination of a new director of central intelligence.

The Senate Intelligence Committee mounted a preliminary inquiry into the Iran-contra affair shortly after it broke in the press, in late 1986. The panel followed up on this effort when it examined the CIA deputy director's involvement in the whole affair, while it considered his nomination to become director of central intelligence, and when it held hearings on new legislation to correct some of the underlying problems exposed by the investigation. The House Intelligence Committee reviewed aspects of the affair when it held hearings on a major bill to change presidential reporting requirements on covert operations. Still other House and Senate subcommittees inquired into possible drug-trafficking aspects of the Iran-contra affair and the adverse impact of the hostage-freeing effort on other executive agencies. Finally, a House Government Operations subcommittee, in part because of Iran-contra disclosures, has delved further into problems surrounding national security decision directives. These usually secret directives, issued over the president's signature and put into effect by his national security adviser, have been used to guide executive efforts in certain sensitive, classified matters, often without Congress's awareness.

Because of the widespread ramifications of the Iran-contra affair and jurisdictional overlap among congressional committees, both the House and Senate set up temporary select committees to consolidate the inquiry. The two panels, in what was apparently an unprecedented action, joined forces to conduct the inquiry, share information, hold hearings—including televised ones—and issue a report under both of their names. In addition to hiring outside counsel and other staff from the private sector, the Iran-contra committees relied upon congressional support agencies for additional personnel, studies, and reviews.

Independent counsel investigation. Another element in the Iran-contra investigation is the independent counsel, established in this case in part because of the initiatives of a House Judiciary subcommittee. An independent counsel can help Congress's oversight directly and indirectly, particularly over the presidency.[26]

First of all, an independent counsel is required to report to Congress about its activities and to advise the House of any grounds for impeachment. Establishing an independent counsel also relieves Congress of the burden of trying to force an otherwise reluctant administration to conduct a criminal investigation of its own staff; Congress thus saves scarce political capital for other oversight investments.

Indirectly, an independent counsel's investigation lends credibility and legitimacy to Congress's separate endeavors. It may even help induce congressional testimony from recalcitrant witnesses. Eventually, the counsel's investigation could uncover other evidence and produce additional information that helps later oversight efforts. In addition, the independent counsel could bolster Congress's current—and future—oversight powers by prosecuting presidential staffers for deceiving Congress and destroying public documents.

In the short run, however, the existence of an independent counsel can impede congressional oversight inquiries. The Iran-contra panels, for instance, took precautions against exposing some findings and against granting limited immunity to witnesses prematurely, in order to avoid jeopardizing the counsel's potential prosecutions. Despite some assistance, moreover, the Iran-contra special counsel reportedly blocked congressional investigators' access to some Justice Department records that might be needed for eventual prosecutions.

Conflicts arise between an investigative committee and an independent counsel because differing perspectives, competing interests, and some incompatible goals guide the two. Success for a committee is measured in public exposure of executive wrongdoing—not necessarily criminal activity—and errors in policy judgments; in changes in administration personnel, procedures, and conduct of policy; and in legislative initiatives. Success for a counsel, by contrast, is measured in criminal indictments and, ultimately, convictions. . . .

NOTES

1. *Immigration and Naturalization Service* v. *Chadha*, 462 U.S. 919 (1983). For follow-up to the decision, see U.S., Congress, House, Committee on Rules, *Legislative Veto after Chadha*, 98th Cong., 1st and 2d sess., 1983 and 1984; Louis Fisher, *Constitutional Conflicts between Congress and the President* (Princeton, NJ: Princeton University Press, 1985), pp. 178–83; Frederick M. Kaiser, "Congressional Control of Executive Actions in the Aftermath of *Chadha*," *Administrative Law Review*, 36(3):239–75 (Summer 1984).
2. U.S. Const., art. I.
3. Ibid. For examples of reporting and consultation requirements, see Kaiser, "Congressional Control," pp. 263–65.
4. *McGrain* v. *Daughtery*, 273 U.S. 135, 176–89 (1927); *Watkins* v. *United States*, 354 U.S. 178, 187 (1957); *Barenblatt* v. *United States*, 360 U.S. 109, 111 (1959).
5. *Federalist* no. 51, in *The Federalist Papers* (New York: New American Library, 1961), pp. 320, 322.
6. Ibid., p. 322.
7. Ibid. See also Madison, *Federalist* nos. 47–50, in ibid., pp. 300–319; Alexander Hamilton, *Federalist* nos. 67–77, in ibid., pp. 407–63.
8. Woodrow Wilson, *Congressional Government* (New York: Houghton Mifflin, 1885), pp. 297, 270, respectively.
9. U.S., Congress, Senate, Select Committee on Secret Military Assistance to Iran and the Nicaraguan Opposition, and U.S., Congress, House Select Committee to Investigate Covert Arms Transactions with Iran (hereafter called Iran-Contra Committees), *Report of the Congressional Committees Investigating the Iran-Contra Affair*, 100th Cong., 1st sess., 1987, S. Rept. 100–216 and H. Rept. 100–433, pp. 9–22.
10. U.S. Congress, Senate, Select Committee on Presidential Campaign Activities, *Final Report*, 98th Cong., 2d sess., 1974, S. Rept. 98–981, pp. 3–22, 130–49.
11. Allen Schick, "Politics through Law: Congressional Limitations on Executive Discretion," in *Both Ends of the Avenue*, ed. Anthony King (Washington, DC: American Enterprise Institute, 1983), p. 166.
12. Ibid.; Kaiser, "Congressional Control," pp. 239–41, 247, 271.
13. John F. Bibby, "Congress' Neglected Function," in *Republican Papers*, ed. Melvin R. Laird (Garden City, NY: Doubleday, Anchor Books, 1968), p. 477.
14. U.S., Congress, House, Select Committee on Committees, *Committee Reform Amendments of 1974*, 93d Cong., 2d sess., 1974, H. Rept. 93-916, p. 63; Roger H. Davidson, "Representation and Congressional Committees," *The Annals* of the American Academy of Political and Social Science, 411:55 (Jan. 1974).
15. Joel D. Aberbach, "Changes in Congressional Oversight," *American Behavioral Scientist*, 22:511 (May-June 1979); idem, "Congress and the Agencies: Four Themes of Congressional Oversight of Policy and Administration," in *The United States Congress*, ed. Dennis Hale (New Brunswick, NJ: Transaction Books, 1983), p. 285. See also idem, "The Congressional Committee Intelligence System: Information, Oversight, and Change," *Congress and the Presidency*, 14:51-76 (Spring 1987).
16. Mathew D. McCubbins and Thomas Schwartz, "Congressional Oversight Overlooked: Police Patrols versus Fire Alarms," *American Journal of Political Science*, 28:176 (Feb. 1984).
17. Walter J. Oleszek, "Integration and Fragmentation: Key Themes of Congressional Change," *The Annals* of the American Academy of Political and Social Science, 466:200-201 (Mar. 1983).
18. Joseph P. Harris, *Congressional Control of Administration* (Washington, DC: Brookings Institution, 1964), p. 9.
19. Morris S. Ogul, *Congress Oversees the Bureaucracy: Studies in Legislative Supervision* (Pittsburgh, PA: University of Pittsburgh Press, 1976), p. 11.
20. Ibid., p. 7. See also Loch Johnson, "The U.S. Congress and the CIA: Monitoring the Dark Side of Government," *Legislative Studies Quarterly*, 4:477 (Nov. 1980); Frederick M. Kaiser, "Oversight of Foreign Policy: The U.S. House Committee on International Relations," ibid., 2:257 (Aug. 1977); Bert A. Rockman, "Legislative-Executive Relations and Legislative Oversight," ibid., 9:416-18 (Aug. 1984).
21. Rockman, "Executive-Legislative Relations," p. 387.
22. See studies cited in notes 15–17 and 19–20 of this article.
23. U.S. Congress, Senate, Select Committee to Study Governmental Operations with Respect to Intelligence Activities, *Final Report*, 95th Cong., 2d sess., 1976, S. Rept. 94-755, book 1, pp. 127–52, 384–420, and book 2, pp. 5–20. For related developments, see Kaiser, "Oversight of Foreign Policy"; Johnson, "Monitoring the Dark Side"; Cecil V. Crabb, Jr., and Pat M. Holt, *Invitation to Struggle* 2d ed.

(Washington, DC: CQ Press, 1984), pp. 161–87; Thomas M. Franck and Edward Weisband, *Foreign Policy by Congress* (New York: Oxford University Press, 1979), pp. 46–62, 115–34.

24. Select Committee to Study Governmental Operations with Respect to Intelligence Activities, *Final Report*, p. 277.

25. Iran-Contra Committees, *Report*, pp. 11–22.

26. Ibid., pp. 686–88, 690. See also Charles Tiefer, "The Constitutionality of Independent Officers as Checks on Abuses of Executive Power," *Boston University Law Review*, 63:59-103 (Jan. 1983). The legal authority for the independent counsel, which has been recently reauthorized, is at 28 U.S.C. 591 et seq. In the meantime, moreover, the Supreme Court, in a 7 to 1 ruling, held the special counsel law to be constitutional. *Morrison, Independent Counsel* v. *Olson et al.*, Civil Action No. 87-1279 (U.S. Supreme Court, 29 June 1988).

CONFLICT OR CONSTRUCTIVE TENSION: THE CHANGING RELATIONSHIP OF JUDGES AND ADMINISTRATORS

Phillip J. Cooper

Administrators these days often express frustration, resentment, and anxiety over judicial intervention into administrative operations. The indictment is familiar. Beginning in the late 1960s and early 1970s, the story goes, federal courts began a movement toward greater interference in administrative matters that has become progressively more intrusive. The trend, the argument runs, continues to this day.

It should not be at all surprising that administrators resent judicial rulings limiting their discretion and mandating procedural or substantive policy changes in agency operations. After all, one of the administrator's primary tasks is to anticipate and eliminate contingencies in the organizational environment.[1] Judicial rulings would seem to be just one more troublesome factor constraining administrative flexibility.

However, the courts perform a variety of essential functions required of them by the Constitution and statutes. They must ensure that administrators do not exceed their statutory authority, ignore basic procedural requisites, conduct themselves in a manner that is arbitrary and capricious or an abuse of discretion, make important policy determinations without some kind of reasoned decision based upon a record, or violate the provisions of the Constitution.[2] Neither these functions nor the courts designated to perform them are going to be eliminated.

The problem then is to develop an effective working relationship between judges and administrators. But before such an accommodation can be reached it will be necessary to assess the current relationship between these legal and administrative institutions. The starting point for such a reassessment must be a realization that the federal courts, led by the Supreme Court, have changed the law governing administrative agencies in ways more charitable to administrators. It is not true that there is a continuing trend toward greater interference in administration. Recent cases indicate an increasing judicial sensitivity to management problems and priorities.

This article examines the premises underlying current tensions between judges and administrators. It then turns to a consideration of the various counts in the indictment brought by administrators against the courts indicating the importance of recent federal court rulings. There is one new area of tension developing between courts and agencies, cases in which administrators refuse to act at all or engage in administrative deregulation. Judicial reactions to this problem are also assessed. Finally, the article suggests that law is a discretion-reinforcing agent, a fact that argues for improved judicial-administrative relations and against continued hostility.

LAW AND ADMINISTRATION: NATURAL ANIMOSITY OR CONSTRUCTIVE TENSION

Two premises are essential to any discussion about law and administration. First, discretion is an essential commodity in modern public administration. Problems are simply too diverse and specialized and the environment too dynamic for legislators to provide more than a moderate amount of guidance to those who must administer public programs. Beyond that, managers must have sufficient flexibility to adapt their organizations and practices to changing conditions in order to perform effectively and efficiently. A lack of discretion would stifle creativity and confine administrators to rigid behavior patterns producing a panoply of bureaucratic dysfunctions long feared by scholars of organizational theory.[3]

The second premise is that law is intended to, and does in fact, limit discretion. Internal checks acquired by careful recruitment and training of promising public servants and the external checks provided by executive supervision and legislative oversight have never been thought adequate substitutes for the opportunity to call an official into court to demonstrate the validity of his or her actions. "No man in this country," the Supreme Court has admonished us, "is so high that he is above the law. No officer of the law may set that law at defiance with impunity. All of the officers of government, from the highest to the lowest, are creatures of the law, and are bound to obey it."[4]

From these two premises it follows that there will inevitably be tension between judges and administrators. Adding to that conflict are the differing perspectives of legally trained professionals and management educated professional administrators.[5] The former tend to treat as core values the utility of law as a defense against government intervention in personal and business affairs, the commitment to due process of law, an insistence upon equal protection of the law, and a concern for substantial justice. The latter, on the other hand, are by degrees more concerned with the latitude necessary to apply expertise to complex problems, the need for flexibility in meeting new challenges, and the goal of efficiency—what Gulick referred to as "the basic good."[6]

However, the fact that some tension exists between judges and administrators is not necessarily destructive nor should it transform natural tension into animosity. Such a polarized view of the judicial-administrative relationship would be understandable only if managers could successfully argue that absolute discretion is absolutely good and necessary or if legalists could contend that all discretion is bad. Neither argument has merit. Discretion does not necessarily have a straight-line correlation with efficiency.[7] The relationship is more curvilinear. No discretion would paralyze management. On the other hand, complete discretion may undermine efficiency. Sofaer, for example, found in his study of an agency with extremely wide discretion that broad flexibility can lead to "inconsistency, arbitrariness, and inefficiency."[8] He concluded that "the evidence seemed to refute the hypothesis that discretion results in less costly, speedier administration. . . . The presence of

discretionary power seemed throughout the administrative process, disproportionately to attract political intervention."[9] Legalists have the same problem. The relationship between just decisions and discretion is again nothing so simple as a straight-line negative correlation. Absolute discretion would mean a high probability of arbitrary and inconsistent administrative judgments. On the other hand, no discretion would mean rule-bound administration without accommodation for equity or any other consideration of individualized justice.

The challenge, then, is to find useful mixes of discretion and checks on abuses of discretion not only to achieve just decisions and bolster accountability but also to protect necessary administrative flexibility so that managers can administer their organizations efficiently. The most useful approach to thinking about law and administration is not a juxtaposition of law against administration, but development of an understanding of the interaction of courts and agencies as a necessarily ongoing relationship.

Before progress can be made in improving the judicial-administrative relationship, administrators must be made aware of some of the important changes in the law. There are indications in a variety of recent rulings of increased judicial sensitivity to administrative concerns.

JUDGES NEITHER UNDERSTAND NOR CARE ABOUT ADMINISTRATIVE PROBLEMS: MYTHOLOGY AND REALITY IN RECENT LEGAL DEVELOPMENTS

A common misconception is that a straight-line progression of judicial assumption of authority has occurred, substituting legal judgment for administrative discretion. Examination of administrative law cases over the past decade, however, indicates that part of this management perception is based upon a number of myths or misunderstandings, which are not generally supported by the case law. True, there are important controversies, but the relationship is not as adversarial as it may seem.

The last decade or so has witnessed significant changes in direction within the Supreme Court and some lower courts on issues of importance to administrators. In several areas, judges have openly recognized the importance of administrative discretion and have moved to protect it. One way to understand the importance of these rulings is to consider the charges issued by administrators against the judiciary and the manner in which a federal judge might respond to them.

1. Courts do not care about costs.

There is substantial evidence to the contrary. Consider the development of standards for administrative due process, judicial acknowledgment of the need to avoid supplanting legislative budgeting, and the recognition of fiscal problems faced by administrators in institutional reform litigation.

Even before the important recent changes in the requirements of administrative due process, the Supreme Court acknowledged the need to permit a flexible approach to due process to accommodate administrative circumstances. In a 1976 ruling, *Mathews v. Eldridge*, the Court went even further.[10] In *Eldridge*, the Court found that Social Security disability recipients were not entitled to a hearing before the termination of their benefits, though they would have an opportunity to be heard at some point later in the process. The significance of this decision lies not in permitting administrators to deny claimants any due process, but in granting flexibility in assessing what process is due under varying administrative conditions. In *Eldridge*, the Supreme Court developed a balancing test for determining how much process is due someone before an administrative agency which specifically recognizes fiscal and administrative burden as a major element of the balance. In order to decide what process is due, the Court said, one must consider:

first, the private interest that will be affected by the official action; second, the risk of an erroneous deprivation of such interest through the procedure used, and the probable value, if any, of additional or substitute safeguards; and finally, *the Government's interest, including the function involved and the fiscal and administrative burdens that the additional or substitute procedural requirements would entail.*[11] (Emphasis added.)

The *Eldridge* balancing test has been the controlling due process standard since 1976.[12] The Court has consistently rejected calls for expanded

administrative due process since that time and has, in fact, relaxed some of the requirements imposed in earlier cases.[13]

This approach to due process overtly considers the problems of financial and administrative burden so important to administrators. There are other indications that judges at both the Supreme Court and lower court levels are increasingly aware that their rulings have substantial fiscal implications for public administration.[14]

The Sixth Circuit Court of Appeals recently made the point rather forcefully that courts should not supplant the budgetary process. The case resulted from a challenge by parents to the closing of an innovative day treatment facility, known as Jewel Manor, by the Kentucky Department of Human Resources. The reason for the elimination of the facility was budgetary pressure. Disappointed parents argued that the closing of Jewel Manor meant a change of placement for their children within the meaning of the Education for All Handicapped Children Act (EHCA). As such, they insisted, the state was precluded from closing the facility unless it could justify the change of placement or establish some other equally acceptable program. The court of appeals admonished the district judge to grant wide deference to state and local governments in matters of program modification.

> These [state] authorities do not, by electing to receive funds under the EHCA, abdicate their control of the fiscal decisions of their school systems. . . . Congress did not compel, as the price for federal participation in education for the handicapped, a wholesale transfer of authority over the allocation of educational resources [away] from the duly elected or appointed state and local boards. . . .[15]

The Supreme Court has extended that expression of concern about compulsion of state expenditures. The Third Circuit Court of Appeals affirmed a district court ruling ordering reform of Pennsylvania mental health programs in part on grounds that the Disabled Assistance and Bill of Rights Act of 1975 mandated minimum requirements for appropriate treatment in the least restrictive setting. The state received funds under that act and was therefore obligated to comply with the statute's standards. The Supreme Court reversed finding that the legislation "intended to encourage, rather than mandate, the provision of services to the developmentally disabled."[16] In reaching this conclusion, the Court observed:

> The fact that Congress granted to Pennsylvania only $1.6 million in 1976, a sum woefully inadequate to meet the enormous financial burden of providing "appropriate" treatment in the "least restrictive" setting, confirms that Congress must have had a limited purpose in enacting [this section of the law]. . . .

> Our conclusion is also buttressed by the rule of statutory construction established above, that Congress must establish clearly its intent to impose conditions on the grant of federal funds so that the States can knowingly decide whether or not to accept those funds.[17]

As the dissenters pointed out, the Court's reading of the statute was extremely generous to the states involved.

Thus, evidence shows that judges are aware of some of the fiscal implications of their judgments and are concerned about the need to minimize these burdens. That does not mean they are willing to accept a budgetary justification for violating constitutional rights, but neither are they oblivious to administrative problems.

Some question exists, however, as to whether administrators have tried in complex litigation to assist judges to understand relevant fiscal dimensions and to work out accommodations where necessary to minimize judicial-administrative tension. For example, in one northern school desegregation case, the state, when called upon by the judge to produce a proposed remedy, sent six plans, recommended none of them, and provided only one witness for the remedy hearing whose only role was to explain what was in the plans.[18] The state provided the judge no help whatsoever in understanding the administrative and fiscal problems involved in implementing any of the proposed remedies. In an Alabama case, state mental health officials were given six months to take action to remedy unconstitutional conditions at state mental health facilities, but they took no action at all. Moreover, the state refused offers of assistance from federal agencies. After indicating his understanding that state administrators may have lacked funds to implement reforms, the judge

asked just how that prevented the administrators from producing a plan that could be implemented when funds did become available.[19]

Administrators can improve their relationship with judges in such cases by making careful decisions about when to fight and when to negotiate. They can present detailed and understandable explanations of their concerns about financial and administrative feasibility. They can resist the temptation simply to ignore likely judicial action until it is forced upon them.

2. Courts are increasingly unwilling to defer to the expertise of administrators. Again, there have been a number of opinions, particularly Supreme Court rulings, demanding deference to administrative expertise. The Court has issued these admonitions in two types of cases, rule-making review and institutional reform litigation.

The Court's leading ruling on judicial review of administrative rulemaking was the unanimous opinion issued in *Vermont Yankee Nuclear Power Corp.* v. *United States Nuclear Regulatory Commission.*[20] *Vermont Yankee* warned lower courts against fashioning procedural requirements beyond those contained in the statutes administered by the agency involved. Lower courts are to examine the record prepared by the agency during rulemaking, and, if it is adequately supported and within the statutory authority of the agency, the action is to be affirmed.[21] While there has been disagreement among members of the Court as to precisely how much deference is due,[22] the prime forces expanding rulemaking procedural requirements in recent years have been legislation and executive orders, not judicial mandates.

The Court subsequently issued a number of rulings demanding lower court respect for and deference to administrative expertise at the state as well as the federal level. Two of the more forceful decisions concerned administration of programs for handicapped children and mental health treatment.

Amy Rowley's parents objected to the individual education plan (IEP) developed for their daughter by the Hendrick Hudson School District under the requirements of the Education for All Handicapped Children Act. While school officials had provided an FM microphone, training for teachers, tutorial assistance, and speech therapy for the hearing-impaired child, they refused the Rowley's request for a sign language interpreter in the classroom. Amy was acknowledged by all to be a bright child who read lips well enough to earn passing marks at least in her elementary grades in a regular classroom. But she did this in spite of the fact that she could only understand about half of the information conveyed. In sum, she was not able to perform up to anything like her potential without the additional assistance of a sign language interpreter. For that reason, they argued, Amy was denied the "free appropriate public education" required by the EHCA. The lower courts agreed, but the Supreme Court reversed.

The Court concluded that the act did not require the state to do more than ensure that "personalized instruction is being provided with sufficient support services to permit the child to benefit from instruction" plus meet the procedural requirements for parental participation in development of plans. If that was done, the child was by definition receiving a "free appropriate public education."[23] Perhaps of equal importance, however, was the Court's discussion of how judges are to decide whether the child is in fact receiving benefit from the plan. The Court insisted upon increased deference to administrative expertise.

> In assuring that the requirements of the Act have been met, courts must be careful to avoid imposing their view of preferable educational methods upon the States. The primary responsibility for formulating the education to be accorded a handicapped child, and for choosing the educational method most suitable to the child's needs was left by the Act to state and local educational agencies in cooperation with the parents or guardian of the child. . . .

> We previously have cautioned that courts lack the "specialized knowledge and experience" necessary to resolve "persistent and difficult questions of educational policy."[24]

But the Court's admonition to judges on the need for deference was not limited to this particular program. In the same term, the Court issued a decision in *Youngberg* v. *Romeo* which, though it recognized a constitutional claim for protection against abuse and a requirement for some mental health care for institutionalized retarded persons, carried a strong warning against judicial second-guesses of expert administrative judgment.[25] Justice Powell insisted that "courts must show deference to the judgment exercised by a qualified professional." He concluded:

> By so limiting judicial review of challenges to conditions in state institutions, interferences by the federal judiciary with the internal operations of these institutions should be minimized. Moreover, there certainly is no reason to think judges or juries are better qualified than appropriate professionals in making such decisions [about the kind of care and treatment needed by a patient]. . . . (Courts should not "second-guess the expert administrator on matters on which they are better informed.")[26]

This was a suit which asked, among other things, for damages against hospital and state officials for the lack of treatment. Pressing the need to protect administrative discretion and recognize fiscal difficulties, the Court wrote:

> [L]iability may be imposed only when the decision by the professional is such a substantial departure from accepted professional judgment, practice, or standards as to demonstrate that the person responsible actually did not base the decision on such a judgment. In an action for damages against a professional in his individual capacity, however, *the professional will not be liable if he was unable to satisfy his normal professional standards because of budgetary constraints.* . . .[27] (Emphasis added.)

In other cases, the Court has held that judges must "design procedures that protect the rights of the individual without unduly burdening the legitimate efforts of the states to deal with social problems"[28] and insisted that "courts cannot assume that state legislatures and prison officials are insensitive to the requirements of the Constitution or to perplexing sociological problems of how best to achieve the goals of the penal function in the criminal justice system. . . ."[29]

3. The Supreme Court is continually expanding the authority of federal district courts to issue complex remedial orders obstructing

administrative operations. There are two important factors to be considered in assessing the remedial decree cases. First, administrators have often welcomed suits against prisons and mental hospitals as means to pressure legislators for increased appropriations.[30] Thus, it is not always clear that the relationship of court to agency in these cases is primarily adversarial.

In fact, for a decade now the Supreme Court has been moving to make it harder for trial judges to justify issuance of a remedial order,[31] narrowing the scope of such orders,[32] and limiting the duration for which district judges may retain supervisory jurisdiction over administrative institutions.[33] In cases involving school desegregation, mental health, and prison conditions, the Court has admonished lower courts to avoid unnecessary orders, to carefully tailor those which are necessary to remedy constitutional violations without undue interference in agency operations, and to terminate control over those institutions as soon as possible.

4. The Supreme Court keeps expanding legal protections available to employees at the expense of managers' discretion. An expansion of employee rights did occur in the late 1960s and early 1970s. Once again, however, care must be exercised in judgments about judicial interference with administration. In the first place, many employee rights were created by statute or executive order and not judicial rulings.[34] It is, of course, true that federal courts added protections, particularly in the area of First Amendment free speech and association as well as due process requirements in adverse personnel actions. However, important changes have been made in recent Supreme Court decisions that define employee rights, particularly in the First Amendment and due process fields.

Using the *Eldridge* balancing formula, the Court has drawn back from what were some years ago expanding administrative due process requirements in employee terminations concerning which employees are entitled to a hearing[35] and the type and timing of any hearing that is required.[36] These cases have indicated that the Court will be reticent to require more elements of due process than are specified in statutes and regulations. Moreover, they have rejected claims by employees that civil servants are entitled to a hearing before they are removed from their jobs rather than some time later in the administrative process.

In the First Amendment field, the Court has shifted the burden and increased the level of proof required for the employee to prevail on complaints of unlawful termination in violation of First Amendment free speech protections.[37] The most direct statement of the Court's intention to leave managers free of unnecessary judicial involvement in personnel decisions came recently in *Connick v. Myers.*[38]

The *Connick* case arose when Myers, a deputy district attorney in Orleans Parish, Louisiana, got into a disagreement with her supervisor regarding a job transfer. She had been offered a transfer and promotion based upon her performance, but she resisted the step up because it would have required her to prosecute cases in the court of a judge with whom she had been working for some time on an offender diversion program. She saw the move as a conflict of interest. When her supervisor disagreed and insisted upon the move she charged that this was another example of his poor administration of the office. Her criticism alleged a range of administrative problems including attempts to coerce employees into participating in partisan political activities. The supervisor indicated her views were not widely shared within the office. At that, Myers went home and prepared a questionnaire which she circulated to other employees. Her supervisor summoned Myers who was summarily dismissed. The district court awarded damages on grounds that there was no question that she had been fired because of her First Amendment protected speech and there was no showing of significant impairment of organizational operations as defined by previous case law that justified the termination.[39]

The Supreme Court reversed, finding that Myers had not adequately demonstrated the public significance of her speech. In so doing, the Court added a new requirement to the existing burden an employee must carry in defending his or her speech against reprisal. It was not, however, merely the Court's change of this test regarding when an employee can be disciplined that made the case so important, but it was also Justice White's insistence upon deference to management discretion in such matters.

When employee expression cannot fairly be considered as relating to any matter of political, social, or other concern of the community, government officials should enjoy wide latitude in managing their officers, without intrusive oversight by the judiciary in the name of the First Amendment. Perhaps the government employer's dismissal of the worker may not be fair, but ordinary dismissals from government service which violate no fixed tenure or applicable statute or regulation are not subject to judicial review even if the reasons for the dismissal are alleged to be mistaken or unreasonable.[40]

We hold that where a public employee speaks not as a citizen upon matters of public concern, but instead as an employee upon matters only of personal interest, absent the most unusual circumstances, a federal court is not the appropriate forum in which to review the wisdom of a personnel decision taken by a public agency allegedly in reaction to the employee's behavior. . . .

When close working relationships are essential to fulfilling public responsibilities, a wide degree of deference to employers' judgment is appropriate. Furthermore, we do not see the necessity for an employer to allow events to unfold to the extent that the disruption of the office and the destruction of working relationships is manifest before taking action.[41]

The Court's language in *Connick* coupled with its cautions against extensive judicially imposed due process requirements indicates a significant shift toward deference to administrative interests.

5. The Supreme Court has consistently issued rulings that make it easier to bring suit in federal court.

It is true that in the late 1960s and early 1970s the Warren Court relaxed the rules governing who could bring a suit in federal court permitting a wider range of litigation. However, the Burger Court has issued a string of decisions placing significant limits on standing to sue and other procedural standards governing access to federal courts.[42] In fact, it is in the area of court access rules that the Burger Court has made some of the most dramatic changes from the Warren Court precedents.

The Burger Court has sent other signals indicating that groups interested in changing policy should look to arenas other than the federal courts. For example, it rejected the claim that public interest groups acting as private attorneys general could collect attorneys' fees when they sued successfully.[43] (Congress later reversed that ruling by statute.) The Court has also restricted the ability of private groups to claim a right to sue under statutes that do not specifically authorize private litigation, the so-called implied right of action.[44] Just because there may be a violation of law that government is unable or unwilling to prosecute, does not mean that a group of private individuals may step into the breach and demand court action. For several reasons, then, it simply is not true that the trend of the Warren Court years to open the doors of the federal courthouse to more lawsuits has been continued by the current Court.

6. Federal courts are constantly expanding the threat to administrators from tort liability judgments.

The controversy surrounding the vulnerability of officials and units of government to damage claims is considered elsewhere in this symposium. But since administrators' frustration and anxiety about tort lawsuits is an important part of the conflict between judges and managers, some caveats are worthy of brief mention here.

First, while the Supreme Court has permitted more types of suits for damages over the past decade, it has brought about a kind of trade-off for administrators. At the same time that it has been allowing a wider range of damage suits, it has been limiting broad remedial orders that interfere with ongoing administration.[45] The message to lower courts is to limit interference with current administrative operations, but to let claimants come into court after the fact and collect damages if they can make their case.

Second, recent liability rulings are not unrestricted invitations to sue public officials. Even in the decisions expanding the range of possible damage claims, the Supreme Court has created a series of immunities making it relatively difficult for a plaintiff to win a case.[46] More recently, the Court has recognized that its official liability decisions have placed added burdens upon public administrators discouraging initiative and producing time-consuming and costly litigation.[47] In *Harlow v. Fitzgerald*, the Court expanded the standard immunity afforded public officials in federal tort suits and instructed judges to guard against unnecessary pretrial discovery and other burdensome procedures.[48]

In sum, the rules and judicial trends affecting the judicial-administrative relationship are not part of a continuing judicial assault on public administration. In a variety of areas the federal courts have demonstrated a sensitivity to the problems administrators must face. That does not mean that they have been willing to serve as rubber stamps for administrative action, but it does give lie to some of the more extreme charges that the courts are about the business of undermining administrators.

ADMINISTRATIVE DEREGULATION AND REFUSAL TO ACT: A DEVELOPING JUDICIAL-ADMINISTRATIVE TENSION

In one area an increase has recently occurred in judicial-administrative tension. Historically, legal challenges to administrators have primarily concerned efforts to limit overzealous use of administrative discretion. In the administrative environment of the late 1970s and the 1980s, however, attention has shifted to situations in which administrators either refuse to act at all or withdraw from previously developed policies. Although the need to compel administrative action as well as guard against excessive administrative zeal is rarely discussed these days, it is an important issue that was stated by Carl Friedrich more than 40 years ago.

> Too often it is taken for granted that as long as we can keep government from doing wrong we have made it responsible. What is more important is to insure effective action of any sort. . . . An official should be as responsible for inaction as for wrong action; certainly the average voter will criticize the government as severely for one as for the other.[49]

The efforts of the Carter and Reagan administrations to deregulate and generally move administrative agencies to less proactive approaches to their work have been the focal point of controversy. It is important in any discussion of administration and law to consider not only limits on the discretion to act but also the legal forces compelling the exercise of discretion. The cases calling for mandatory use of administrative authority have been basically of four types: (1) those objecting to an administrative refusal to launch a fact-finding or policy-making process; (2) agency refusal to issue rules; (3) intentional delay in agency action; and (4) rescission of existing or proposed policies.

Controlling the agency agenda is an important element of administrative discretion. Deciding what problems to address and assigning priorities is often more than a question of efficient management. It may involve a strategic decision. Administrators would frankly prefer to avoid some problems. Take the case in which the involvement of the Food and Drug Administration (FDA) was demanded in the capital punishment controversy. Death row inmates petitioned the FDA to launch an investigation to determine whether the pharmaceuticals used for execution by lethal injection were safe and effective for the specific application to which they were put. Drugs could only meet that criteria if they brought about quick and painless death, but the inmates alleged there was substantial evidence that in improper dosage and administration the drugs currently used could "leave a prisoner conscious but paralyzed while dying, a sentient witness of his or her own slow lingering asphyxiation." FDA refused to investigate on grounds that it lacked jurisdiction to review state-sanctioned uses of drugs for these purposes. The agency did not argue that it lacked the capacity to inquire into this matter, but that it was without jurisdiction in the case. Moreover, the agency claimed that even if it had jurisdiction, it also had complete and unreviewable enforcement discretion concerning whether and when to take administrative action. The FDA refused to act on the basis of that discretion.

The D.C. Circuit Court of Appeals, however, found that the agency did have jurisdiction which it had previously asserted, for example, in drug experiments involving state prison inmates. The court rejected the claim to unreviewable enforcement discretion and found the FDA refusal to launch an investigation arbitrary and capricious. The court wrote:

In this case FDA is clearly refusing to exercise enforcement discretion because it does not wish to become embroiled in an issue so morally and emotionally troubling as the death penalty. Yet this action amounts to an abnegation of statutory responsibility by the very agency that Congress charged with the task of ensuring that our people do not suffer harm from misbranded drugs. . . . As a result of the FDA's inaction, appellants face the risk of cruel execution and are deprived of FDA's expert judgment as to the effectiveness of the drugs used for lethal injection. . . .[50]

While the court will not dictate the outcome or the particular administrative process to be employed, the simple assertion of absolute discretion will be challenged.

Another problem area is the refusal to make rules. The Eighth Circuit Court of Appeals, recently found that the secretary of agriculture had abused his discretion by refusing to issue rules under a statute governing farm loan foreclosure. A family charged that the Department of Agriculture had an obligation under the statute to promulgate rules and provide adequate notice to those affected concerning possible deferments of foreclosures. The government argued that the statute "merely created an additional power to be wielded at the discretion of the agency, or placed in the Secretary's back pocket for safekeeping."[51] The court found the refusal to make rules or institute any kind of process of reasoned decision making a "complete abdication" of responsibility.[52]

In some ways related to the refusal to make rules is the tactic of delaying for as long as possible the issuance of rules required by statute. Here again, courts seem willing to draw a line. Efforts by the Environmental Protection Agency (EPA) to delay implementation of rules required by the Resource Conservation and Recovery Act covering toxic wastes were successfully challenged in a number of lawsuits. Among the remedies sought by the plaintiffs in one of the cases was an award of attorney's fees under the Equal Access to Justice Act. The court awarded the fee finding that the intentional delaying tactics employed by the agency were "exactly the type of arbitrary governmental behavior that the EAJA was designed to deter."[53]

Finally, a number of challenges have been brought against efforts of administrators to deregulate by rescinding existing agency regulations or withdrawing pending rules. The Federal Communications Commission (FCC) efforts to reduce its regulatory control over broadcasting have prompted several such lawsuits. Another recent example is the withdrawal of mandatory automobile passive restraint rules by the Department of Transportation. In both cases, administrators claimed that the decision to reduce regulation administratively was not really policy making and was a purely discretionary matter not subject to judicial examination. The courts rejected that claim in both cases and insisted that a change in policy is a policy decision whether it results in promulgation of a new rule or abandonment of an old one. In fact, a panel of the D.C. Circuit Court of Appeals said, "such abrupt shifts in policy do constitute 'danger signals' that the Commission may be acting inconsistently with its statutory mandate. . . . We will require therefore that the Commission provide a reasoned analysis indicating that prior policies and standards are being deliberately changed, not casually ignored."[54] Having said that, however, the court upheld the FCC deregulation. It cautioned the commission that it was perilously close to violating its statutory responsibility but found enough evidence to say the FCC had met its requirements of reasoned analysis.

The Supreme Court did not find the necessary foundation for the rescission of the passive restraint rule and remanded the matter to the agency. It concluded that an "agency changing its course by rescinding a rule is obligated to supply a reasoned analysis for the change beyond that which may be required when the agency does not act in the first instance."[55] Since a rule was presumably adopted in the first instance on the basis of a careful reasoning process using the agency's expertise and available evidence, there is a presumption in favor of the rule. The Court concluded:

In so holding, we fully recognize that "regulatory agencies do not establish rules of conduct to last forever, . . . and that an agency must be given latitude to adapt their rules and policies to the demands of changing circumstances. . . ." But the forces of change do not always or necessarily point in the direction of deregulation. In the abstract, there is no more reason to presume that changing circumstances require the rescission of prior action, instead of a revision in or even the extension of current regulation. If Congress established a presumption from which judicial review should start, that presumption—contrary to petitioner's view—is not *against* safety regulation, but *against* changes in current policy that are not justified by the rulemaking record.[56] (Emphasis in original.)

There is one final problem of what might be termed negative discretion. Administrators often argue that judges should defer to their administrative expertise regardless of the type of policy under consideration. However, judges sometimes doubt that administrators are entitled to such deference when there does not appear to be a policy at all but rather a failure to make any policy or to enforce existing standards. Justice Brennan, for instance, observed that while judges ought to defer to the expertise of correctional administrators, the prison conditions frequently in dispute often arise not from a policy decision based upon administrative expertise but from sheer neglect. "There is no reason of comity, judicial restraint, or recognition of expertise for courts to defer to negligent omissions of officials who lack the resources or motivation to operate prisons within the limits of decency."[57]

Federal District Judge Bruce Jenkins of Utah came to a similar conclusion recently in a case involving claims made against the government by the families of alleged victims of nuclear testing. The court awarded damages to those who demonstrated that their illnesses stemmed from the testing. Jenkins rejected the notion that there should be a deference to administrative discretion in this sort of case. There was, he said, "no official policy of indifference to safety."[58] The "actions taken were negligently insufficient—not as a matter of discretion at all—as a matter of deliberate choice making—but as a matter of negligently failing to warn, to measure and to inform, at a level sufficient to meet the stated goals of the Congress, the executive branch and the Atomic Energy Commission."[59]

In sum, administrators may not assume absolute administrative discretion when they refuse to act as compared to cases where they are alleged to have acted too vigorously. The problem of relating administrative discretion and judicial obligations to ensure accountability is all the more difficult when there is no policy for a given action but an actual departure from stated policy or simple neglect. This concept of negative discretion is an aspect of the judicial-administrative relationship that is very much a developing matter and worthy of attention.

LAW AS A DISCRETION-REINFORCING AGENT

There are and always will be natural tensions between administrators and judges over the nature and boundaries of administrative authority. Yet there is a simultaneous positive aspect to this law-administration relationship. It is worthwhile to assess the reasons administrators ought to attempt to foster better working relations with judges, notwithstanding the difficulties such a prescription entails.

Knowledge of the legal elements of administration is an enabling force. Formal authority of administrators is derived from a statute or executive order. Care in using such authority supports effective administration. There is an admittedly rough but useful analogy to the budget process. An agency without adequate fiscal resources is in serious trouble. The amount of funds available is a significant factor in the agency's ability to perform. It is both an enabling force and, in a sense, a constraint. The fact that budgetary politics are complex and often disappointing does not indicate that a good manager ought to abandon concern for the subject or cease efforts to improve relationships with appropriations committees. The same is true of law and administration.

An understanding of legal developments is also important as a defensive matter. It can help to avoid liability judgments, prevent the loss of invested time and effort when agency decisions are reversed, avoid loss of control over one's agency to a complex remedial court order, and lead to savings of money as well as time from having to replicate and improve work rejected in judicial review.

Two other key functions are served by enhancing the relationship between administrators and judges. Understanding the relationship provides increased predictability which is critical to any manager. The first task is to understand judicial trends sufficiently to anticipate likely judicial responses to agency actions. An awareness of legal limits on administration provides an ability to predict not only what courts will do with respect to one's own but also to other agencies. Administrators thus informed can manage their operations with some expectation of how other agencies will be able to respond. Administration without attention to law would not mean more efficiency, it would mean chaos.

Finally, administrators need legal support for their claim to legitimacy within government and, perhaps more importantly, within the larger society. There is a certain irony in the fact that administrators busy challenging the legitimacy of judicial involvement in policy making are in danger of being convicted by their own arguments. Many of the charges made against judges can be made in only slightly modified form against administrators. They are not elected. Many cannot be removed from office except for cause. It is extremely difficult to keep them responsive and responsible. They frequently do precisely what the majority of the people do not wish them to do. The list goes on. Beyond that particular threat to legitimacy, however, is the need for assistance in establishing a legitimate place for administrators in the constitutional framework. Our constitutional authority is derivative. We obtain our authority by inference and indirectly.[60] We must always be able to trace our authority back through the chain of statutes and judicial rulings that support us.

CONCLUSION

This article has assessed common assumptions about the evolving relationship between federal courts and administrators. It has provided evidence that despite the natural tensions between administrators and judges, it is an overstatement to charge that federal judges neither understand nor care about the harm their rulings may cause to management. In fact, legal authorities and opinions, if properly understood, are enabling and protecting forces providing sources of administrative discretion and protecting its use.

Moreover, the federal judiciary, led by the Supreme Court, has in several respects drawn back from intervention in administration in open recognition of the need for managerial flexibility. That good reasons exist for not applauding some of those deferential rulings does not change the fact that they do support more discretion. One rapidly developing area of judicial-administrative challenge is likely to remain of importance in the near term at least: the refusal of administrators to use the discretion that they possess.

Good reasons exist for administrators to develop their relationship with courts, reasons of an extemely practical nature and others of wider import, including the need to have law as a support for the legitimacy of public administration. In the final analysis, administrative discretion does not exist for its own sake. Administrators are vested with particular authority to serve public purposes in a society predicated on a rule of law. Natural tension, yes, but necessary as well.

NOTES

1. Victor Thompson, *Bureaucracy and the Modern World* (Morristown, N.J.: General Learning Press, 1976), p. 10.
2. 5 U.S.C. §706.
3. See Robert K. Merton, "Bureaucratic Structure and Personality," in Merton et al. (eds.), *Reader in Bureaucracy* (New York: Free Press, 1952).
4. *United States* v. *Lee*, 106 U.S. 196, 220 (1882).
5. It is, of course, understood that many are administrators as a second profession and that a substantial proportion of those managers have not received advanced training in public administration. See Frederick Mosher, *Democracy and the Public Service* (New York: Oxford University Press, 1984).
6. Luther Gulick and L. Urwick (eds.), *Papers on the Science of Administration* (Fairfield, N.J.: A.M. Kelley, 1977), p. 192.
7. Phillip J. Cooper, *Public Law and Public Administration* (Palo Alto, Calif.: Mayfield, 1983), pp. 217–219.

8. Abraham Sofaer, "Judicial Control of Informal Discretionary Adjudication and Enforcement," *Columbia Law Review*, vol. 72 (December 1972), p. 1374.

9. *Ibid.*, pp. 1301–1302.

10. *Mathews v. Eldridge*, 424 U.S. 319 (1976).

11. *Ibid.*, p. 335.

12. Evidence for this is provided in my study on administrative due process since *Goldberg v. Kelly* which was reported in "Due Process, the Burger Court, and Public Administration," *Southern Review of Public Administration*, vol. 6 (Spring 1982), pp. 65–98.

13. See, e.g., *Parham v. J.R.*, 422 U.S. 584 (1979); *Bishop v. Wood*, 426 U.S. 341 (1976); *Paul v. Davis*, 424 U.S. 693 (1976); *Board of Curators v. Horowitz*, 435 U.S. 78 (1978); and *Ingraham v. Wright*, 430 U.S. 651 (1977). The court has spoken of the *Eldridge* balancing formula as "the familiar test prescribed in Mathews v. Eldridge." *Schweiker v. McClure*, 72 L. Ed 2d 1, 9-10 (1982).

14. One federal district judge put it this way: "Subject to constitutional limitations, Arkansas is a sovereign State. It has a right to make and enforce criminal laws, to imprison persons convicted of serious crimes, and to maintain order and discipline in its prisons. This Court has no intention of entering a decree herein that will disrupt the Penitentiary or leave Respondent and his subordinates helpless to deal with dangerous and unruly convicts.

"The Court has recognized heretofore the financial handicaps under which the Penitentiary system is laboring, and the Court knows that Respondent cannot make bricks without straw." *Holt v. Sarver*, 300 F. Supp. 825, 833 (E.D. Ark. 1969). See also Ralph Cavanagh and Austin Sarat, "Thinking About Courts: Toward and Beyond a Jurisprudence of Judicial Competence," *Law & Society Review*, vol. 14 (Winter 1980), p. 408.

15. *Tilton v. Jefferson County Bd. of Ed.*, 705 F.2d 800, 804-805 (6th Cir. 1983).

16. *Pennhurst State School v. Halderman*, 451 U.S. 1, 20 (1981).

17. *Ibid.*, p. 24.

18. See, generally, *Bradley v. Milliken*, 345 F. Supp. 914 (E.D. Mich. 1972).

19. *Wyatt v. Stickney*, 334 F. Supp. 1341, 1344 (M.D. Ala. 1971).

20. *Vermont Yankee Nuclear Power Corp. v. U.S. Nuclear Regulatory Commission*, 435 U.S. 519 (1978).

21. See, e.g., *Federal Communications Commission v. WNCN Listeners Guild*, 450 U.S. 582 (1981) and *Office of Communications of the United Church of Christ v. FCC*, 707 F.2d 1413 (D.C. Cir. 1983).

22. See, e.g., *Industrial Union Dept, AFL-CIO v. American Petroleum Institute*, 448 U.S. 607 (1980) and *American Textile Manufacturers Institute v. Donovan*, 452 U.S. 490 (1981).

23. *Hendrick Hudson Bd. of Ed. v. Rowley*, 458 U.S. 176, 189 (1982).

24. *Ibid.*, p. 208.

25. *Youngberg v. Romeo*, 457 U.S. 307 (1982).

26. *Ibid.*, pp. 322–323.

27. *Ibid.*

28. *Parham*, 422 U.S. at 608, n. 16. This case involved commitment of juveniles to state mental hospitals.

29. *Rhodes v. Chapman*, 452 U.S. 337, 352 (1981), a case challenging conditions at Ohio's principal maximum security prison. See also, *Bell v. Wolfish*, 441 U.S. 520, 539 (1979).

30. Stephen L. Wasby, "Arrogation of Power or Accountability: 'Judicial Imperialism Revisited,'" *Judicature*, vol. 65 (October 1981), p. 213. See also, Stonewall B. Stickney, "Problems in Implementing the Right to Treatment in Alabama: The Wyatt v. Stickney Case," *Hospital & Community Psychiatry*, vol. 25 (July 1974), pp. 454–455.

31. See, e.g., *San Antonio Independent School District v. Rodriquez*, 411 U.S. 1 (1973); *Washington v. Davis*, 426 U.S. 229 (1976); *Personnel Administrator v. Feeney*, 442 U.S. 256 (1979); *Rizzo v. Goode*, 423 U.S. 362 (1976); and *Rhodes v. Chapman, op. cit.*

32. See, e.g., *Milliken v. Bradley*, 418 U.S. 717 (1974); *Dayton Bd. of Ed. v. Brinkman*, 433 U.S. 406 (1977); *Columbus Bd. of Ed. v. Penick*, 443 U.S. 449 (1979); *Dayton Bd. of Ed. v. Brinkman*, 443 U.S. 526 (1979); and *Firefighters Local Union No. 1784 v. Stotts*, 81 L. Ed 2d 483 (1984).

33. *Pasadena Bd. of Education v. Spangler*, 427 U.S. 424 (1976).

34. Indeed one purpose of the Civil Service Reform Act of 1978 was to assemble and clarify the various statutory protections for civil servants provided by, among others, the Civil Rights Act of 1964 as amended, the Age Discrimination in Employment Act of 1967, the Fair Labor Standards Act, and the Rehabilitation Act of 1973. 5 U.S.C. §2302(b) (1978).

35. *Bishop*, 426 U.S. 341, and *Paul*, 424 U.S. 693.

36. *Arnett v. Kennedy*, 416 U.S. 134 (1974).

37. Consider the shift from *Pickering v. Bd. of Education*, 391 U.S. 563 (1968), to *Mt. Healthy Bd. of Ed. v. Doyle*, 429 U.S. 274 (1977), to *Givhan v. Western Line Consolidated School Dist.*, 439 U.S. 410 (1979).

38. *Connick v. Myers*, 75 L. Ed 2d 708 (1983).

39. *Myers v. Connick*, 507 F. Supp. 752 (ED La. 1981), aff'd 654 F.2d 719 (5th Cir. 1981).

40. *Connick*, 75 L. Ed 2d at 719-720.

41. *Ibid.*

42. See *Allen v. Wright*, 82 L. Ed 2d 556 (1984); *Valley Forge Christian College v. Americans United for Separation of Church and State*, 454 U.S. 464 (1982); *Duke*

Power Co. v. *Carolina Environmental Study Group,* 438 U.S. 59 (1978); *Simon* v. *Eastern Kentucky Welfare Rights Organization,* 426 U.S. 26 (1976); and *Warth* v. *Seldin,* 422 U.S. 490 (1975).

43. *Alyeska Pipeline* v. *Wilderness Society,* 421 U.S. 240 (1975).

44. *Middlesex County Sewerage Authority* v. *National Sea Clammers Assn.,* 453 U.S. 1 (1981); *California* v. *Sierra Club,* 451 U.S. 287 (1981); *Touche Ross & Co.* v. *Redington,* 442 U.S. 560 (1979); and *Cannon* v. *University of Chicago,* 441 U.S. 677 (1979).

45. See, *Rizzo,* 423 U.S. 362. See also, David Rosenbloom, "Public Administrators' Official Immunity: Developments During the Seventies," *Public Administration Review,* vol. 40 (March-April 1980), pp. 166–173.

46. See, e.g., *Butz* v. *Economou,* 438 U.S. 478 (1978).

47. 457 U.S. 800 (1982).

48. *Ibid.,* pp. 817-818.

49. Carl Friedrich, "Public Policy and the Nature of Aministrative Responsibility," in Friedrich and E. S. Mason (eds.), *Public Policy* (Cambridge, Mass.: Harvard University Press, 1940), p. 4.

50. *Chaney* v. *Heckler,* 718 F.2d 1174 (D.C. Cir. 1983).

51. *Allison* v. *Block,* 723 F.2d 631, 633 (8th Cir. 1983).

52. *Ibid.,* p. 638.

53. *Environmental Defense Fund* v. *EPA,* 716 F.2d 915, 921 (D.C. Cir. 1983). The other key case compelling production of rules was *Illinois* v. *Gorsuch,* 530 F. Supp. 340 (D.D.C. 1981).

54. *Office of Communications of the United Church of Christ,* 707 F.2d at 1425.

55. *Motor Vehicle Manufacturers' Assn.* v. *State Farm Mutual,* 77 L. Ed 2d 443, 457 (1983).

56. *Ibid.*

57. *Rhodes,* 452 U.S. at 362 (Brennan, J., concurring in part, dissenting in part).

58. *Irene Allen* v. *United States,* 588 F. Supp. 247, 337 (D. Utah 1984).

59. *Ibid.,* p. 338.

60. I am indebted for this idea, if not these precise words, to John Rohr.

FEDERALISM, INTERGOVERN- MENTAL RELATIONS, AND INTER- GOVERNMENTAL MANAGEMENT: HISTORICAL REFLECTIONS AND CONCEPTUAL COMPARISONS

Deil S. Wright

. . . To the extent that one overarching theme does encompass this study, it is best described as an effort to review and analyze the administrative complexities of multijurisdictional relationships in the U.S. political system. The nature of these relationships have evolved over successive eras, periods, or phases.[1] Hence, the historical invitation approaches an imperative. . . . While history can provide the needed root(s) for contemporary understanding, without analysis and interpretation history offers little or limited fruit. Therefore, the historical reflections provided in the first part of this article subsequently give way to a systematic comparative effort. The comparisons center on the conceptual trilogy incorporated in the title: (1) federalism (FED), (2) intergovernmental relations (IGR), and (3) intergovernmental management (IGM).

THE ROOTS OF FED, IGR, AND IGM

It is common and appropriate to trace the origins and character of federalism (FED) to the framers

Deil Wright is Alumni Distinguished Professor at the University of North Carolina at Chapel Hill.

at the Philadelphia Convention and especially to Madison and his collaborators in *The Federalist*.[2] An alternate and perhaps more appropriate origin point for an administratively oriented entry to the topic, however, is Woodrow Wilson's classic essay on administration.[3] The attention and significance that Wilson accorded FED in his oft-noted essay is regularly overlooked.[4] Two themes, (1) effectiveness and (2) administrative responsibility, were prominent in Wilson's analysis and are reflected in the following quotations.

> (1) Our duty is, to supply the best possible life to a *federal* organization, to systems within systems: To make town, city, county, state, and federal governments live with a like strength and an equally assured healthfulness, keeping each unquestionably its own master and yet making all interdependent and co-operative, combining independence with mutual helpfulness. The task is great and important enough to attract the best minds.[5]

> (2) This interlacing of local self-government with federal self-government is quite a modern conception. . . .

> The question for us is how shall our series of governments within governments be so administered that it shall always be to the interest of the public officer to serve not his superior alone but the community also with the best efforts of his talents and soberest service of his conscience?

> How shall this be done alike for the local part and for the national whole?[6]

The first passage conveys Wilson's vision of a strong and healthy set of interdependent "systems" of governance. It is remarkably contemporary and could be comfortably inserted into a recent presidential speech or a report of the U.S. Advisory Commission on Intergovernmental Relations (ACIR). His phraseology also suggests that Wilson perceived (perhaps dimly) what has, since the 1930s, been called *intergovernmental relations* (IGR).

In the second excerpt Wilson makes a direct link between FED and administration through the issue of administrative responsibility. For Wilson FED was clearly linked to the question: To whom and in what way are public administrators (officials) responsible? The administrator is, according to Wilson, subject not only to the claims of his or her hierarchical (or intergovernmental) superior, but also "the community" as well. It would not be an inaccurate or inappropriate reading to substitute "the public interest" for "the community" in Wilson's text, especially given the time and context of his 1887 article. Such a substitution calls to mind the exchange a half century later (1940–1941) between Friedrich and Finer over the nature of administrative responsibility and of how a public administrator could and should serve the public interest.[7]

The Friedrich-Finer debate occurred not only in close proximity to the "new federalism" of the New Deal.[8] It also coincided with a new concept that had a significant link with a major public administration issue. IGR was the conceptual innovation; the issue was the politics-administration dichotomy.

Writing in 1939–1940, coterminous with the beginnings of American Society for Public Administration (ASPA) and *Public Administration Review* (*PAR*), G. Homer Durham focused attention on "Politics and Administration in Intergovernmental Relations."[9] Durham explored how the new concept of IGR contributed to a revised theory of the politics-administration relationship. He noted that "the growing maze of relationships, legal and extralegal, within the federal system has radically altered any ancient bases-in-fact for such views as the separation of politics from administration."[10]

Durham's own words best convey his approach to blending politics and administration in an interjurisdictional context.

So what of politics and administration in intergovernmental relations? Their interlocking indicates the unreality of checks, balances, and divisions into politics *and* administration. As a guide to a "new theory of the division of powers," the idea of *administrative politics*, or the interrelations of public administrators in what appear to be increasingly more permanent offices with tenure, forms a more realistic concept. Too, with the importance of the Presidency emphasized, the political party emerges as an instrument of policy and consent in a new light. Questions of structure and function in the federal system preclude, under present boundaries and constitutional restrictions, the emergence of a more significant

factor than the party in clearly defining the policy-phase of a new "administrative politics."[11] (Italics in the original.)

The emphasis and the confidence reflected in this passage are representative of the period that Newland has called the "founding years" and the "golden era" of public administration.[12] Three factors undergird Newland's claim for the era in which Durham wrote: (1) the accepted primacy of the executive, especially the President, (2) the symbiotic relationship between politics and administration as essential in government, and (3) the presence of a cohesive public administration network that produced a strong sense of community. These elements also formed a firm foundation for an emerging consensus about the character and content of IGR.

The term that Durham suggested, *administrative politics*, did not prosper, but it was clearly indicative of the search for an alternative conceptual framework to capture and characterize the major changes occurring in political, policy, and administrative relationships. The much-discussed separation of administration from politics would soon be demolished. In its place something akin to a continuum of politics-in-administration would emerge.[13]

Durham was unquestionably accurate in viewing IGR, conceptually and operationally, as contributing to the demise of the dichotomy that others subsequently confirmed.[14] Furthermore, his critique of the dichotomy and its connection to FED and IGR should not be underestimated. Dwight Waldo, for example, later (1948) noted: "There is a close similarity between the rigid politics-administration viewpoint and that philosophy of federalism that pictured state and nation moving noiselessly and without friction each in its separate sphere."[15]

Although Durham moved with the intellectual flow in attacking the politics-administration dichotomy, his analysis was not as prescient nor as predictive concerning two other variables he explicitly identified: (1) political party, and (2) professionalism (permanent tenure). Durham anticipated and projected the "importance of the (political) party" as an instrument in producing "a decentralizing of . . . power."[16] In this respect he was a precursor of more extensive developments of the party-as-decentralizer thesis by David Truman,[17]

Morton Grodzins,[18] William Riker,[19] and William Buchanan.[20] Decline in party identification, party loyalty, and party efficacy are developments that have raised current questions about the relationship, if any, of the party system to centralizing and decentralizing forces. A 1986 ACIR report, calling for a strengthening and revival of political parties at the grass roots, serves as a reminder of the staying power and pertinence of the issue.[21]

Durham's oblique reference to professionalism touched on another variable whose effect he could, in the late 1930s, only partly perceive. The broad and strong centralizing effects of professionalism were not fully explored and confirmed until later. One subsequent and visible analytic exposition of the force of professionalism on interjurisdictional relations was presented by Beer in his presidential address to the American Political Science Association in 1977.[22] Beer's focus on "representational federalism," put the quietus, if one was needed, on the politics-administration dichotomy. Beer argued that new forms of influence had evolved in the United States, especially since the 1930s, and that the original federal arrangement accommodated them in a way consistent with its historical, flexible, and open-ended character.

Two contemporary structures of interest in Washington, according to Beer, are the "technocrats"[23] and the "topocrats." The former represent the "new professionalism" in national, state, and local governments. They constitute the "professional-bureaucratic complex" of functional program specialists, most easily understood as the vertical linkages forming "picket-fence federalism."[24] The "topocrats" consist of the associations of political and administrative generalists at the state and local levels—governors, state legislators, mayors, county executives, and city managers. They have mobilized on behalf of varied common concerns to make their presence and influence felt in the halls of Congress, the executive branch, and even the judiciary.

The presence of tensions between technocrats and topocrats is hardly new. It had surfaced even as Durham wrote in the late 1930s, but systematic investigation of the cleavages came later in a variety of forms and contexts.[25] The normative issue raised by the cleavage(s) should not be bypassed, however. What has been the effect of these new representational forms on other aspects of the democratic process? Have the technocrats and topocrats caused, as Beer fears, "dilutions of the popular will"? Despite corporate instead of personal representation, Beer concedes that the two entities have added significant strengths to the modern state. He wonders, however, whether "this may be at some cost to free government."[26]

The origin of IGR was closely associated with the demise of the politics-administration dichotomy. It was also connected with the rise of new forms of association and organization that have altered the channels of political representation, policy articulation, and program implementation within the American federal system. Generalist administrators, of the genre about which Harlan Cleveland has spoken so eloquently, have moved to center stage in virtually all aspects of the policy process.[27] Likewise, the managers of specific functional programs, most recently called "policy professionals," have assumed featured roles.[28]

We now turn from this historical review to the task of fitting the roles and functions of these clusters of administrative officials into a broader contextual and comparative framework. For that purpose it is useful to introduce the concept of *intergovernmental management* (IGM).

INTERGOVERNMENTAL MANAGEMENT (IGM)

The concept of federalism has two centuries of U.S. history, tradition, law, and practice behind it. The concept of IGR has a comparatively short half century of application to the American context, and it remains a term that falls somewhat short of either standardized or universal usage. By way of contrast, IGM appeared as a phrase on the public scene only recently—during the 1970s.[29] To date it seems ensconced in the esoteric vocabularies of small, specialized, and even self-interested segments of observer-practitioners of the U.S. governance processes. Among the purposes of this exposition of IGM is the aim to reduce if not remove the mist and mystery surrounding the term. A further intent is to advance the utility of the concept for both analytical and applied purposes.

Woodrow Wilson argued for and actively pursued strategic solutions to issues involving both

FED and administrative responsibility.[30] Wilson's confidence in finding clear and constructive solutions to those issues may or may not have been justified, even in his day. Today, however, the complexity, variety, and seemingly intractable nature of interjurisdictional problems appears biased against major, strategic, or dramatic changes in the roles and functions of different political jurisdictions. With some exceptions, many if not most of the intergovernmental system changes have been modest, gradual shifts that have occurred incrementally. It took near-herculean presidential political efforts in 1981–1982, for example, to produce a noteworthy impact on national-state-local relations.[31] Even then the central proposal of Ronald Reagan's New Federalism, the shifting and sorting out of functions, died aborning.[32]

The emergence of IGM as a concept was associated with three important developments. One was the management-related consequences of national-level policy activism occuring chiefly in the 1960s, but carrying over into the 1970s. A second and related factor was the difficulty in implementing numerous intergovernmental programs, a difficulty that focused prime attention on management problems. A third aspect highlighting IGM has been the gulf or gap between career personnel and political actors. These three developments, quite apart from the political and polarizing effects of "bureaucrat-bashing," have given public management and managers a deserved but not necessarily desired level of visibility.

The emergence of IGM seems indicative of the present modest, marginal, and moderate approach to the resolution of current interjurisdictional issues. Some might even argue that IGM is indicative of the minimalism and myopia prevalent in contemporary American politics, public policy, and public administration.[33] Essays and research under the IGM rubric have blossomed in the past decade, and three defining features have emerged which exemplify its limited (but noteworthy) focus. *Problem solving, coping capabilities,* and *networking* are the three most common terms used in defining IGM. Together they emphasize its implementation focus as well as the centrality of the roles of policy professionals.[34]

Robert Agranoff examined human service delivery programs in the early 1980s and defined IGM as "an emerging concept in the study of

affairs between governments, reflecting the increase in public officials who work at the margins between their governments."[35] The activities that constituted IGM in a metropolitan context, according to Agranoff, "in no way lead to fundamental changes in the social structure or resolve complex problems within the metropolitan areas."[36] More broadly, Agranoff argued that the kinds of problems that IGM addresses "are not the type of fundamental solutions that eliminate major social problems nor do they lead to any substantial realignment in the federal system."[37]

The problem-solving focus and implementation emphasis of IGM have been extensively illustrated in articles, essays, and monographs. The more controversial aspects of IGM, however, call for further comment. Only a brief clarification of selected issues can be attempted here.

IGM, with its strong emphasis on the word *management*, has gained modest usage but has also generated significant controversy. Controversy arises when its use suggests a clear hierarchical ordering in the relationships among American political jurisdictions.[38] Stephen Schechter addressed this issue early in the 1980s:

> The popular acceptance of intergovernmental management is not a historically discrete occurrence. The starting premise of this article is that "intergovernmental management" (as that term has developed since 1974) is best understood not as a president's pipe dream but as the completion of the twentieth century revolution in public administration first enunciated by Woodrow Wilson. For its adherents, "intergovernmental management" is more than merely compatible with federalism; it is both the natural extension and resuscitating element of the twin commitment to federalism and managerialism in a time of scarcity—both of resources and leadership.[39]

Schechter's concern was not the incompatibility of IGM with federalism "but simply that the *constitutional* relationship between the two has been largely ignored."[40] Elsewhere, Schechter sharply contrasted the different orientations of the terms:

> The basic difference between federalism and managerialism, and hence the tension between

them, has to do with ends and limits. The end of federalism, in the American system at least, is liberty; the end of managerialism is efficiency. In this sense, the challenge of *public* management consists largely in directing the "gospel of efficiency" to the constitutional ends of limited government.[41]

Sketched on a broader canvas, IGM might be construed as a major manifestation of two important and related organizational forces at work in U.S. political, economic, and social processes.

One of these forces has been called by a political theorist "the age of organization."[42] Major and immense social, political, and administrative organizations, with associated large powers, must be managed. These organizations, their subcomponents, and their members must be enticed, herded, or goaded into action toward some asserted goal.

A second force associated with IGM is the escalation of regulation. The rise in regulation has been traced to a dramatic decline in trust and legitimacy—diminished trust in and among public officials and plummeting legitimacy in the relations between citizens and administrative agencies. Increased litigiousness accompanies and compounds the "regulated society" and highlights the operational aspects of IGM.[43] Thousands of problems arise that must be solved by courts, by administrative appeals units and processes, or by mediation, negotiation, and bargained compromises emerging from specialized, boundary-spanning management skills.

With these issues and contexts as background, this article turns more directly to an exposition and clarification of IGM. It is a concept that captures and to some extent codifies an important dimension of contemporary policy-relevant and politically-significant administrative activity.

COMPARING FED, IGR, AND IGM

One approach to an understanding of IGM is comparative—to contrast it with the related concepts of FED and IGR. Comparisons are made on the basis of several political system features . . . : (1) units involved, (2) authority relationships, (3) means of conflict resolution, (4) values, (5) political quotient, and (6) leading actors/participants.

Space constraints limit the amount of attention that can be given to the descriptors. . . .

SYSTEM FEATURES

1. The types of entities or jurisdictions involved in boundary spanning interactions constitute the first system feature. For FED the primary historical focus has been on national-state relationships with considerably lesser attention devoted to interstate relations. A distinctive feature of IGR has been its extensive interjurisdictional focus. It has commonly included consideration of all possible combinations and permutations of interaction(s) among every type of U.S. political jurisdiction.[44] . . .

IGM encompasses all of the jurisdictional interactions included under IGR. Writers, researchers, and practitioners using the IGM concept, however, have employed the term to include two extrajurisdictional dimensions. One is the politics-in-administration continuum referenced earlier. This takes explicit account of the intrusion of politics into management and *vice versa*.[45]

A second dimension folded into the IGM concept is the mixture of public-private sector relationships. The delivery of public programs and services has increasingly involved third-party intermediaries from the nonprofit, independent, and for-profit sectors. "Contracting out" and "privatization" are two terms that capture some of the extraordinary changes in public administration activity that have been reflected in the concept of IGM.[46]

The addition of these two dimensions or continua to the formal governmental entities involved under FED and IGR adds significantly to system complexity. The added complexity reflects the reality of managing under conditions where there is no sharp demarcation of political versus administrative activities and roles. Furthermore, the involvement of private and nonprofit sector organizations in the conduct of public programs may be relevant, prominent, or even crucial for securing results. This produces a blurring or blending among the public, private, and nonprofit sectors in the conduct of public policy.

2. Authority relations constitute a second system feature. . . . The pattern of power distribution varies under the three different concepts. In the case of FED, while power may be fragmented

and variably clustered, it is ultimately lodged in last-resort cases in the hands of the *national* government. In IGR the power distribution pattern is posited as less hierarchical; asymmetric relations in terms of power are common, although there may be some persistence in perceived superior-subordinate relationships. Lovell has argued that it is not surprising to find IGR circumstances in which no one is "in charge." Coordination or concerted action may occur in a variety of ways, sometimes more by accident and by informal links than by force or by central direction.[47]

The nature of authority relations in IGM is preponderantly nonhierarchical. The presence and pervasiveness of networks create the presumption of widely if not evenly shared power distribution patterns. There may be varying dependency-autonomy power patterns among specific entities in a network, but across the complete network there is no prime, single, or central source of guidance. The intraorganizational pattern of matrix management is a precedent and analog for interjurisdictional relations.[48]

3. One proposition widely accepted in organization theory is Downs's assertion about interorganizational conflict. Downs argues that every organization operates in an environment in which it is in some degree of conflict with other organizations in that environment.[49] The extensiveness of conflict in political and organizational systems mandates consideration of the means by which conflict is resolved. . . .

The constitutional base of FED and the prominence of courts as decision units specifying enforceable rules of law are generally acknowledged. Hence the courts and statutes under FED arrangements are significant vehicles of conflict resolution. The popular election of nearly 500,000 public officials in the United States makes elections another important means of conflict resolution (as well as creation). Additionally, in many states and in most local governments, a variety of referenda elections are held to resolve specific issue conflicts.

Markets, games, and coalitions are three broad categories of structuring competition and resolving conflicts in an IGR context. The literature on IGR games is modest but noteworthy.[50] More extensively and rigorously developed in IGR is the concept of markets. Dating chiefly from the 1950s, the idea of governmental entities operating as firms in a market environment has assumed significant proportions.[51] One need not adopt one or another of the philosophical positions surrounding the public choice approach to make constructive use of a market perspective.[52] Anton has revised and extended the coalitional approach to IGR by relying on "benefits coalitions."[53]

The concepts and behavioral domains of bargaining and negotiation serve as hallmarks for IGM conflict resolution strategies. More specific mechanisms under these rubrics are mediation and dispute settlement processes. Literature on these mechanisms has expanded rapidly in the 1980s.[54]

The problem-solving thrust underlying IGM encourages, perhaps demands, movement toward agreements that involve continued or continuous subsequent interactions among parties to the conflict. This contrasts with court cases under FED which tend toward authoritative termination of interparty contacts. It also differs from markets, games, and coalitions under IGR where contacts may be distant or nonexistent and interparty relations may focus chiefly on assuring that all players abide by some set of prespecified rules.

4. The fourth system feature . . . is a values component. This feature references the scope, content, and intent the user has in mind when employing one of the three concepts. For FED the value or aim, as mentioned by Schechter, may be variously described as liberty, freedom, or constitutional rights. These broad but fundamental values of an ordered society are purposes fostered by FED when viewed as a set of constitutional arrangements. They were values the founding fathers sought and promoted through constitutional "rules of the game."

By way of contrast, IGM posits as an underlying value or end, the notion of achieving specific or concrete program results. Schechter referred to "efficiency" and "managerialism," not necessarily in a favorable light, as the ends or aims of IGM. Clearly, the problem-solving thrust used as one of the defining features of IGM gives the term a results-oriented bias.

For IGR, neither the specific, programmatic, results-focused bent of IGM nor the global, systemwide values of liberty and freedom of FED appear appropriate. Indeed, one reason IGR was coined in the 1930s was the lowered value content and reduced connotative character of the concept. IGR developed and appeared to gain greater usage because of its denotative nature. As a descriptive term, IGR emphasizes an understanding of the images, orientations, or perspectives of the various actors operating between and among political jurisdictions. This predominantly descriptive and analytic nature of IGR is inadequate to convey the results-focused emphasis of IGM.

5. A fifth system feature is indicated by the term "political quotient." The term is intended to convey the popular scope and public visibility of the issues covered under each concept.

The types of issues associated with FED tend to be ones that Bulpitt classified as "high politics" in the United Kingdom.[55] Illustrative of such issues in the United States are those connected with "new federalism" during the Nixon and Reagan Administrations, the "creative federalism" of the Johnson Administration, and similar broad-based, politically-charged policy initiatives. The level of partisanship linked to FED issues is substantial and the locus of decision making on these issues tends to be in Washington, D.C. Both the visibility level and the locus for action on these issues come from potent centripetal forces in the political (or social) system. These characteristics promote what might be called a "politics of the center."

If high- and centrally-based politics dominate FED issues, then low-level, implementation-oriented politics characterize IGM activities. Note that politics is not absent from problem-solving and implementation efforts. IGM issues, and the strategies associated with their resolution, simply contain notably lower visibility, more limited scope, and lesser political quotient(s).

IGR matters, on the other hand, are posited as having intermediate levels of politics and partisanship. Advocacy of substantive policy is present, but in a constrained and confined context. Coordination among different and multiple public policies is a valued political aim. Furthermore, IGR and IGM involve state and local (peripheral) entities in the policy process. The type of "politics" present in these arenas might be termed the politics of implementation, the politics of coordination, and the politics of central *and* peripheral participation. . . .

CONCLUDING OBSERVATIONS

All nations of any significant size and consequence confront one of the fundamental problems of governance. How should the competing claims of central and peripheral authority be resolved? The issue is more ancient than the kingly controversies among the 12 tribes of Israel. It is also as current as the latest round of U.S. Supreme Court decisions on state power(s) over abortion, flag burning, and school prayers.

Constitutionally, the issue is commonly framed in legal terms: Which jurisdiction has the authority to do what, with what degree of discretion or autonomy? Administratively, the "basic theoretical question" has been posed by Fesler as "How to relate area and function?"[56] Like the blending of politics and administration, the two questions overlap and are intertwined. The linkage between constitutional arrangements grounded in politics and organizational implementation matters centered around administration is a theme that permeates this article. . . .

NOTES

1. Daniel J. Elazar, "The Shaping of Intergovernmental Relations in the Twentieth Century," *The Annals*, vol. 359 (May 1965), pp. 10–22; David B. Walker, *Toward a Functioning Federalism* (Cambridge, MA: Winthrop, 1981); Deil S. Wright, "Intergovernmental Relations: An Analytic Overview," *The Annals*, vol. 416 (November 1974), pp. 1–16.

2. Alexander Hamilton, James Madison, John Jay, *The Federalist Papers* (New York: New American Library, 1961). See also Martha Derthick, "American Federalism: Madison's Middle Ground in the 1980s," *Public Administration Review*, vol. 47 (January/February 1987), pp. 66–74.

3. Woodrow Wilson, "The Study of Administration," *Political Science Quarterly*, vol. 2 (June 1887), pp. 197–222; reprinted in Jay M. Shafritz and Albert C. Hyde, eds., *Classics of Public Administration* (Chicago: The Dorsey Press, 1987), pp. 10–25. Subsequent citations are from the reprinted source.

4. Deil S. Wright, "A Century of the Intergovernmental Administrative State: Wilson's Federalism, New Deal Intergovernmental Relations, and Contemporary Intergovernmental Management," in Ralph C. Chandler, ed., *A Centennial History of the American Administrative State* (New York: Macmillan, 1987), pp. 219–260.

5. Wilson, "The Study of Administration," p. 18.

6. Ibid., p. 19.

7. Carl J. Friedrich, "Public Policy and the Nature of Administrative Responsibility," in Carl J. Friedrich and Edward S. Mason, eds., Public Policy: 1940 (Cambridge, MA: Harvard University Press, 1940), pp. 3–24; Herman Finer, "Administrative Responsibility in Democratic Government," Public Administration Review, vol. 1 (Autumn 1941), pp. 335–350.

8. Jane Perry Clark, The Rise of a New Federalism: Federal-State Cooperation in the United States (New York: Columbia University Press, 1938), 347 pp.

9. G. Homer Durham, "Politics and Administration in Intergovernmental Relations," The Annals, vol. 207 (January 1940), pp. 1–6.

10. Ibid., p. 1.

11. Ibid., p. 6.

12. Chester A. Newland, Public Administration and Community: Realism in the Practice of Ideals (McLean, VA: Public Administration Service, 1984), 45 pp.

13. Cheryl Miller Colbert, "An Empirical Analysis of Politics-in-Administration: State Agency and State Agency Head Participation in the Policy Process" (PhD dissertation, University of North Carolina at Chapel Hill, 1983), 270 pp. Colbert locates seven instances where the politics-in-administration continuum appears. See also, James H. Svara, "Dichotomy and Duality: Reconceptualizing the Relationship Between Policy and Administration in Council Manager Cities," Public Administration Review, vol. 45 (January/February 1985), pp. 221–232.

14. Four representative statements on the aridity and demise of the politics-administration dichotomy are: Paul H. Appleby, Policy and Administration (University: University of Alabama Press, 1949), 173 pp.; Norton Long, "Power and Administration," Public Administration Review, vol. 9 (Autumn 1949), pp. 257–264; Wallace Sayre, "Trends in a Decade of Administrative Values," Public Administration Review, vol. 11 (Winter 1951), pp. 1–9; Wallace Sayre, "The Premises of Public Administration: Past and Emerging," Public Administration Review, vol. 18 (Spring 1958), pp. 102–105.

15. Dwight Waldo, The Administrative State: A Study of the Political Theory of American Public Administration (New York: Ronald Press, 1948), p. 128.

16. Durham, "Politics and Administration in Intergovernmental Relations," p. 6.

17. David B. Truman, "Federalism and the Party System," in Arthur W. Macmahon, ed., Federalism Mature and Emergent (Garden City, NY: Doubleday, 1955), pp. 115–136.

18. Morton Grodzins, "American Political Parties and the American System," Western Political Quarterly, vol. 13 (December 1960), pp. 974–998.

19. William Riker, Federalism: Origin, Operation, Significance (Boston: Little, Brown, 1964), 169 pp.

20. William Buchanan, "Politics and Federalism: Party or Anti-Party?" The Annals, vol. 359 (May 1965), pp. 107–115.

21. U.S. Advisory Commission on Intergovernmental Relations, The Transformation in American Politics: Implications for Federalism (Washington: U.S. Government Printing Office, 1986), 382 pp. For highlights of the report, see U.S. Advisory Commission on Intergovernmental Relations, "New Relationships in a Changing System of Federalism and American Politics," National Civic Review, vol. 75 (November/December 1986), pp. 336–345.

22. Samuel H. Beer, "Federalism, Nationalism, and Democracy in America" American Political Science Review, vol. 72 (March 1978), pp. 9–21.

23. Ibid, p. 18.

24. Terry Sanford, Storm Over the States (New York: McGraw Hill, 1967), p. 80.

25. Edward W. Weidner, "Decision-Making in a Federal System," in Arthur W. Macmahon, ed., Federalism Mature and Emergent (Garden City, NY: Doubleday, 1955), pp. 363–383; Edward W. Weidner, Intergovernmental Relations as Seen by Public Officials (Minneapolis: University of Minnesota Press, 1960), 162 pp.

26. Beer, "Federalism," p. 20.

27. Harlan Cleveland, "Theses of a New Reformation: The Social Fallout of Science 300 Years After Newton," Public Administration Review, vol. 48 (May/June 1988), pp. 681–686. See also, Harlan Cleveland, The Future Executive (New York: Harper & Row, 1972), 140 pp.

28. The "policy professionals" category is discussed extensively and perceptively in Paul E. Peterson, Barry G. Rabe, and Kenneth K. Wong, When Federalism Works (Washington: Brookings Institution, 1986), 245 pp.

29. Ross Clayton, Patrick Conklin, and Raymond Shapek, eds., "Policy Management Assistance—A Developing Dialogue," Public Administration Review, vol. 35 (December 1975, special issue), pp. 693–818; see especially, Ann C. Macaluso, "Background and History of the Study Committee on Policy Management Assistance," pp. 695–700.

30. Wilson, "The Study of Administration."

31. One noteworthy source for an assessment of the Reagan presidency is John L. Palmer, ed., Perspectives on the Reagan Years (Washington: Urban Institute Press, 1986), 215 pp. Others include John L. Palmer and Elizabeth V. Sawhill, eds., The Reagan Experiment: An Examination of Economic and Social Policies under the Reagan Administration (Washington: Urban Institute Press, 1982), 530 pp.; John William

Ellwood, ed., *Reductions in U.S. Domestic Spending: How They Affect State and Local Governments* (New Brunswick, NJ: Transaction Books, 1982), 337 pp.; Richard P. Nathan and Fred C. Doolittle, *The Consequences of Cuts: The Effects of the Reagan Domestic Program on State and Local Governments* (Princeton, NJ: Princeton Urban and Regional Research Center, 1983), 221 pp.; Lester M. Salamon and Michael S. Lund, eds., *The Reagan Presidency and the Governing of America* (Washington: Urban Institute Press, 1984), 500 pp.; John E. Chubb and Paul E. Peterson, eds., *The New Direction in American Politics* (Washington: Brookings Institution, 1985), 409 pp.

32. Richard S. Williamson, "The 1982 New Federalism Negotiations," *Publius: The Journal of Federalism*, vol. 13 (Spring 1983), pp. 11–32; Timothy J. Conlan, "Federalism and Competing Values in the Reagan Administration," *Publius: The Journal of Federalism*, vol. 16 (Winter 1987), pp. 29–48; and Stephen B. Farber, "The 1982 New Federalism Negotiations: A View from the States," *Publius: The Journal of Federalism*, vol. 13 (Spring 1983), pp. 33–38.

33. Charles H. Levine, "Human Resource Erosion and the Uncertain Future of the U.S. Civil Service: From Policy Gridlock to Structural Fragmentation," *Governance: An International Journal of Policy and Administration*, vol. 1 (April 1988), pp. 115–134; Barbara Ferman, "Slouching Toward Anarchy: The Policy-making/Implementation Gap Revisited," *Governance: An International Journal of Policy and Administration*, vol. 2 (April 1989), pp. 198–212. For opposite (left and right) political stances on the rigidities and inertia in U.S. governmental system(s), see Robert Lekachman, *Visions and Nightmares: America After Reagan* (New York: Macmillian, 1987), 316 pp.; and Charles Murray, *Losing Ground: American Social Policy, 1950–1980* (New York: Basic Books, 1984), 323 pp.

34. Myrna Mandell, "Letters to the Editor: Intergovernmental Management," *Public Administration Times*, vol. 2 (15 December 1979), pp. 2, 6; Daniel J. Elazar, "Is Federalism Compatible with Prefectorial Administration?" *Publius: The Journal of Federalism*, vol. 11 (Spring 1981), pp. 3–22; Stephen L. Schechter, "On the Compatibility of Federalism and Intergovernmental Management," *Publius: The Journal of Federalism*, vol. 11 (Spring 1981), pp. 127–141; Deil S. Wright, "Managing the Intergovernmental Scene: The Changing Dramas of Federalism, Intergovernmental Relations, and Intergovernmental Management," in William B. Eddy, ed., *Handbook of Organizational Management* (New York: Marcel Dekker, 1983), pp. 417–454; Robert Agranoff and Valerie A. Lindsay, "Intergovernmental Management: Perspectives from Human Services Problem Solving at the Local Level," *Public Administration*

Review, vol. 43 (May/June 1983), pp. 227–237; Stephen R. Rosenthal, "New Directions for Evaluating Intergovernmental Programs, *Public Administration Review*, vol. 44 (November/December 1984), pp. 491–503; Robert Agranoff, *Intergovernmental Management: Human Services Problem Solving in Six Metropolitan Areas* (Albany: State University of New York Press, 1986), 199 pp.; Robert Agranoff, "Managing Intergovernmental Processes," in James L Perry, ed., *Handbook of Public Administration* (San Francisco: Jossey-Bass, 1989), pp. 131–147.

35. Agranoff, *Intergovernmental Management*, p. 1.

36. Idem.

37. Ibid., p. 2.

38. Elazar, "Is Federalism Compatible with Prefectorial Administration?"; Schechter, "On the Compatibility of Federalism and Intergovernmental Management."

39. Ibid., pp. 127–128.

40. Ibid., p. 129.

41. Ibid., p. 136.

42. Sheldon S. Wolin, *Politics and Vision: Continuity and Innovation in Western Political Thought* (Boston: Little, Brown, 1960), p. 260.

43. James D. Carroll, "The New Juridical Federalism and the Alienation of Public Policy and Administration," *American Journal of Public Administration*, vol. 16 (Spring 1982), pp. 89–106. See also: Michael D. Reagan, *Regulation: The Politics of Policy* (Boston: Little, Brown 1987), 241 pp.; U S. Advisory Commission on Intergovernmental Relations, *Regulatory Federalism: Policy, Process, Impact, and Reform* (Washington: U.S. Government Printing Office, 1984), 326 pp.; Christopher K. Leman and Robert H. Nelson, "The Rise of Managerial Federalism: An Assessment of Benefits and Costs, *Environmental Law*, vol. 12 (Spring 1982), pp. 981–1029; and Margaret Wrightson, "From Cooperative to Regulatory Federalism," *SIAM Intergovernmental News*, vol. 9 (Spring 1986), pp. 1, 5. In her concluding sentence Wrightson makes a telling point about present and future regulatory relationships: "Taken together and projected into the future these trends suggest that the residue of the grand (Reagan) experiment could be a federalism that looks decidedly more regulatory than cooperative" (p. 5).

44. Deil S. Wright, *Understanding Intergovernmental Relations*, 3d ed. (Pacific Grove, CA: Brooks/Cole, 1988), 511 pp.

45. James H. Svara, "Dichotomy and Duality."

46. Hugh Heclo's phrase for the use of intermediaries is "government by remote control." See Hugh Heclo, "Issue Networks and the Executive Establishment," in Anthony King, ed., *The New American Political System* (Washington: American Enterprise Institute, 1978), p. 92. An alternate term is "third-party government." See Lester Salamon, "The Rise of

Third-Party Government," *Washington Post*, 29 June 1980, p. C7, where it is noted that "the heart of this change is a shift from direct to indirect or 'third party' government, from an arrangement in which the federal government ran its own programs to one in which it relies primarily on others—states, cities, special districts, banks, non-profit corporations, hospitals, manufacturers, and others—to carry out its purposes instead." A more extensive development of this thesis is found in Lester M. Salamon, "Rethinking Public Management: Third-Party Government and the Changing Forms of Government Action," *Public Policy*, vol. 29 (Summer 1981), pp. 255–275. A similar but more long-term historical analysis is Frederick C. Mosher, "The Changing Responsibilities and Tactics of the Federal Government," *Public Administration Review*, vol. 40 (November/December 1980), pp. 541–548. The use of and controversy surrounding "third-party" participants have expanded considerably since the terms "privatization" and "contracting-out" gained recent prominence. E. S. Savas, *Privatizing the Public Sector: How to Shrink Government* (Chatham, NJ: Chatham House, 1982), 164 pp., and E. S. Savas, *Privatization: The Key to Better Government* (Chatham, NJ: Chatham House, 1987), 308 pp., are two examples of strong advocacy for privatization. Two reflective and more cautionary essays are: Ted Kolderie, "The Two Different Concepts of Privatization," *Public Administration Review*, vol. 46 (July/August 1986), pp. 285–291; and Ronald C. Moe, "Exploring the Limits of Privatization," *Public Administration Review*, vol. 47 (November/December 1987), pp. 453–460. The literature on contracting out is extensive. It has expanded recently as the phrase has become associated with the idea of privatization. See Ruth H. DeHoog, *Contracting Out for Human Services* (Albany: SUNY Albany Press, 1984), 186 pp. An essay that links management and privatization with selected aspects of IGR is James D. Carroll, "Public Administration in the Third Century of the Constitution: Supply-Side Management, Privatization, or Public Investment?" *Public Administration Review*, vol. 47 (January/February 1987), pp. 106–114. An exemplary case study of privatization, implementation, and intergovernmental problem solving in water pollution control efforts is Gerald W. Johnson and John G. Heilman, "Metapolicy Transition and Policy Implementation: New Federalism and Privatization," *Public Administration Review*, vol. 47 (November/December 1987), pp. 468–478.

47. Catherine H. Lovell, "Where We Are in Intergovernmental Relations and Some of the Implications," *Southern Review of Public Administration*, vol. 3 (June 1980), pp. 6–20; Catherine H. Lovell, "Coordinating Grants from Below," *Public Administration Review*, vol. 39 (September/October 1979), pp. 432-439.

48. Stanley M. Davis and Paul R. Lawrence, *Matrix* (Reading, MA: Addison-Wesley, 1977); James E. Webb, *Space Age Management* (New York: McGraw Hill, 1969), 173 pp.

49. Anthony Downs, *Inside Bureaucracy* (Boston: Little, Brown, 1967), 292 pp.; see especially chapter 17, "Bureau Territoriality," pp. 211–222.

50. Norton Long, "The Local Community as an Ecology of Games," in Norton Long, ed., *The Polity* (Chicago: Rand McNally, 1962), pp. 139–155; Eugene Bardach, *The Implementation Game: What Happens After a Bill Becomes a Law* (Cambridge, MA: MIT Press, 1977), 323 pp.; Deil S. Wright, "Intergovernmental Games: An Approach to Understanding Intergovernmental Relations," *Southern Review of Public Administration*, vol. 3 (March 1980), pp. 383–403.

51. Vincent Ostrom, Charles M. Tiebout, and Robert Warren, "The Organization of Government in Metropolitan Areas: A Theoretical Inquiry," *American Political Science Review*, vol. 55 (December 1961), pp. 831–842; Robert Warren, "A Municipal Services Market Model of Metropolitan Organization," *Journal of the American Institute of Planners*, vol. 30 (August 1964), pp. 193–203; Vincent Ostrom and Elinor Ostrom, "A Behavioral Approach to the Study of Intergovernmental Relations," *The Annals*, vol. 359 (May 1965), pp. 137–146.

52. Donald B. Rosenthal and James M. Hoefler, "Competing Approaches to the Study of American Federalism and Intergovernmental Relations," *Publius: The Journal of Federalism*, vol. 19 (Winter 1989), pp. 1–24.

53. Thomas J. Anton, *American Federalism and Public Policy: How the System Works* (New York: Random House, 1989), 244 pp.

54. Nancy A. Huelsberg and William F. Lincoln, eds., *Successful Negotiation in Local Government* (Washington: International City Management Association, 1985), 211 pp.; Roger Richman, Orion F. White, Jr., and Michaux Wilkinson, *Intergovernmental Mediation: Negotiations in Local Government Disputes* (Boulder, CO: Westview Press in cooperation with the National Institute of Dispute Resolution, 1986), 173 pp.

55. Jim Bulpitt, *Territory and Power in the United Kingdom: An Interpretation* (Manchester, U.K.: Manchester University Press, 1983), 246 pp.

56. James W. Fesler, "The Basic Theoretical Question: How to Relate Area and Function," in Leigh E. Grosenick, ed., *The Administration of the New Federalism: Objectives and Issues* (Washington: American Society for Public Administration, 1973), pp. 4–14. See also, James W. Fesler, *Area and Administration* (University: University of Alabama Press, 1949), 158 pp.

PUBLIC ORGANIZATIONS: POLICY NETWORKS AND ENVIRONMENTS

Hal G. Rainey and H. Brinton Milward

. . . Organizational analysts have increasingly been observing that the permeation of public organizations by elements in their environments makes it difficult to designate the boundaries of the organizations. This in turn creates difficulties in choosing the appropriate unit of analysis. Specifying organization boundaries is never easy, but public and social service organizations tend to be so closely interrelated with an array of other organizations and entities that it is often hard to say how the organizations should be separated for analysis or even whether they should be. "A system of very porous organizations may have more unit character than any one of them taken alone. . . . If the focal organization is found to be very permeable . . . environmental factors become internal characteristics of the set that now forms the real operative unit of analysis" (Freeman, 1978: 337).

Such observations stem in part from the accountability of most public organizations, particularly governmental departments, to other entities with high degrees of formal authority over them. Agencies are nested in larger governmental structures (Meyer, 1979: 32), and it is hard to say whether they should be regarded as organizations in their own right or parts of a larger organization (Hood and Dunsire, 1981; Kimberly, 1976: 591). For example, are legislative committees that "own" an agency part of the hierarchical structure of that agency or are they components of the agency's environment?

A related complication is the fragmented, pluralistic nature of the public policy process and of public service delivery systems in the United States. Political scientists have coined such terms as "iron triangle," "policy subsystem," "policy subgovernment," "issue network," and "policy community" to refer to the complex network of individuals, groups, and organizations at different levels of government, and in both public and private sectors, that act together in the formation and implementation of policy in particular policy areas. An agency will be inextricably linked with such a network, and different subunits of large agencies are usually involved in different networks. This adds to the difficulty of specifying agency boundaries and designating what is appropriately considered part of the environment.

THE PRIMACY OF PROGRAMS

The most important thing about these unit of analysis issues is that they represent a reality about the setting of public organizations in the United States that needs to be taken into account in analyzing them. In governmental processes in the United States, the most important focus of activity is frequently not a specific public organization but a complex network of organizations and other entities whose activities are often centered on a particular public "program." This is especially true in the delivery of client services and/or where funds for programs are granted across sectors and levels of government.

Funds granted from federal or state levels to lower levels, for a program in health, welfare, transportation, energy, or housing, will link together an enormous number of individual actors and organizations in Washington, the fifty states, and thousands of localities. In the development of the "contract state" over the last twenty years, federal agencies have more and more assumed the role of providing the money, rules, and guidelines for programs that are actually delivered by a host of organizations in state and local government and the private and quasi-private sectors.

The grant money goes to fund programs, not particular organizations. State and local agencies often use federal grant money to pay private organizations to help in provision of public services. In vocational education, for example, the Bureau of Adult and Occupational Education gives grants to state and local vocational institutes to provide training in occupational skills. These institutes, in turn, often pay private companies or nonprofit organizations such as Goodwill Industries to provide some of the training. The form of these arrangements may vary substantially in the fifty states and numerous localities.

These program-centered delivery systems are distinct as organizational forms because they are quite loosely linked (Weick, 1976). They connect literally hundreds of organizations, mainly through financial incentives and certain power relations, such as threats of federal takeover if services are not provided. The authority of higher levels is usually quite limited, however (Salamon, 1980). Dependence is reciprocal, and the organizations are linked mainly through bargaining, rather than hierarchy (Bish, 1971; Dahl and Lindblom, 1953).

ALTERNATIVE APPROACHES IN PUBLIC POLICY STUDIES

The complications are part of the reason for the divergence between the public bureaucracy literature and the organization theory research that the recent literature is beginning to address. A similar divergence exists between organization theory and public policy studies. Much of organization theory quite naturally has focused on organizations as focal units of analysis. The operation of the public bureaucracy, public policy processes, and the delivery of public services, however, involve complexes of organizations and entities. A given organization is only a part of the terrain that analysts of public policy must cover.

Researchers concentrating on implementation of public policy and delivery of public services have been developing approaches that incorporate the complex linkages we have described. In Europe, scholars at the International Institute of Management in Berlin have adopted the "implementation structure" as the unit of analysis in their studies of public policy (Hjern and Porter, 1981). In the United States, researchers associated with Vincent and Elinor Ostrom in the Workshop in Political Theory and Policy Analysis at Indiana University have developed the concept of the "public service industry" for analysis of public service delivery systems. These approaches are explicitly inter-organizational but also attempt to incorporate the

role of individual political actors, political coalitions, and multilevel bargaining that are involved in the public policy process. They also extend and clarify previous literature by emphasizing empirical measures.

Another approach has been suggested by Salamon (1980). He suggests that we reorient research on public management and public organizations away from a focus on the behavior of individuals, organizations, and institutions to an emphasis on the "tools" of government management. These include formal grants, categorical grants, regulations, loan guarantees, insurance, subsidies, tax incentives, and other techniques by which government seeks to achieve its purposes. Salamon feels that these "tools" can be used as the basic organizing concepts in public management research (1980: p. 264):

> The central premise . . . is that different tools of government action have their own distinctive dynamics, their own "political economies," that affect the content of government action. This is so for much the same reasons that particular agencies and bureaus are considered to have their own personalities and styles—because each instrument carries with it a substantial amount of "baggage" in the form of its own characteristic implementing institutions, standard operating procedures, types of expertise and professional cadre, products, degree of visibility, enactment and review processes, and relationships with other societal forces.

These alternatives have in common the treatment of public organizations, or parts of them, as components of more elaborate governmental structures. This approach may actually be preferable for analysis of public service delivery systems and broad mechanisms of government action. From the point of view of organizational analysis, however, there is the problem that organizations and their internal management may become lost or at least subsumed and treated as "black boxes" (Beyer et al., 1982) as they have been in policy research in the past. These approaches challenge researchers to confront the difficult question of how we account for these complexities in elaborating our conceptions of the environments. In spite of the complications, however, there are still very useful studies that have focused on governmental bureaus and departments as units of analysis (Kaufman, 1981; Hood and Dunsire, 1981; Meyer, 1979). It is clear that for many issues in research and management, such units have sufficient identity of analysis as focal units and need to be analyzed as such.

INTERORGANIZATIONAL POLICY NETWORKS

Clearly there is useful work to be done in clarifying the relations between public organizations and the complex of entities with which they are linked. The two major empirical studies of public bureaucracy that have recently been reported have underscored this need. As we noted, Meyer (1979) calls for further analyses of the networks and constituencies in which agency leaders operate. Hood and Dunsire (1981) have looked at program links with other departments and transactions with other organizations and individuals as major environmental variables, and elaboration of these variables would be valuable.

Since programs are usually the focus for networks, *program networks* are the most important type of network for policymaking. These are networks that form among groups, individuals, and organizations on the basis of their interest in the operation of a public program.

Their interest in the program can have many bases. For example, David Walker (1980-81: 1195-1196) has identified five different kinds of organized interests in the United States that relate to intergovernmental program delivery.

1. sociomoralistic (Right to Life groups, Creationists)
2. demographic (Black, Hispanic, Indian, Women's, Youth, and Senior Citizens)
3. economic (business, labor, farmers, doctors)
4. programmatic (highway officials, Chief State School Officers)
5. levels of government (National Association of Counties, National League of Cities, National Governors Association, National Council of State Legislatures, U.S. Congress of Mayors)

We would also add three additional organized interests that affect program delivery.

6. regional (sunbelt, frostbelt)
7. politicomoralistic (antinuclear groups, environmental and preservationist groups)
8. ideological (Marxists, social democrats, neoconservatives)

In any one policy area there may be program networks based on any one or more of these original interests. Thus program networks may be linked by multiple membership between groups with different organizational bases and interests in a particular program.

Such networks usually cross-cut federating, centralizing structures within government. Large agencies at various levels of government are often explicitly designed as "holding companies" for subunits that represent diverse programs. As noted earlier, governments at the federal, state, and local levels impose standard overarching structures for organizations within their jurisdiction and often at lower levels of government as well. From the point of view of the central management of such federating structures, the complex linkages to which we refer usually represent "centrifugal" forces (Lynn, 1981) that oppose the centralizing tendencies of executives.

More comprehensive analyses of these complex linkages between agencies and environmental components will be valuable in explaining internal structure, process, and behavior, as a number of examples illustrate. Surveys have found that state employees tend to identify more closely with their program counterparts at the federal level than with the state governments and agencies in which they are employed. Kaufman (1981) pictures the bureau chiefs whom he studied as much more responsive to particular congressional committees than to their departmental superiors. Such countervailing patterns of authority help to explain an apparent paradox in the literature we reviewed at the outset. It contains frequent claims that public bureaucracies have elaborate hierarchical control mechanisms but, at the same time, many observations that hierarchical control is weak (for example, Warwick, 1975; Gawthrop, 1969; Golembiewski, 1969). This is explainable if we conceive of public bureaucracies as cross-cut and fragmented by linkages between organizational subunits and various external polical and institutional entities—other agencies, legislative staffs, other levels of government, constituencies, and interest groups. As noted, Warwick (1975) argues that the elaborate hierarchical control mechanism—layers of clearance and review, rules and so on—proliferate in part because of superiors' efforts to exert control over the semiautonomous subunits below them. Moreover, there are numerous examples of changes in bureau structure and procedure that were made or not made because of political pressures by interest groups, legislative subcommittees, other agencies, or other levels of government or some complex of these and other components. Thus effective analysis of organizational identification, control, structure, change, and other major variables requires attention to the complex political and institutional networks in which public bureaucracies are involved.

In sum, a number of recent studies have emphasized the importance of the political and institutional environments of public organizations as influences on their internal management, structures, processes, and employee behaviors. They have provided general propositions and findings concerning these relations and exhortations to more elaborate analyses. The environmental processes are quite complex, however, because of the complexity of our political system and public policy process. It appears that approaches based on the interorganizational literature, research on networks, and analysis of "policy networks" will be particularly valuable in identifying the environmental components and analyzing their impacts on public organizations.

REFERENCES

BEYER, J. M., J. M. STEVENS, and H. M. TRICE (1982) "Exploring the black box in research on public policy: the implementing organization." Presented at the Albany Conference on Organization Theory and Public Policy, State University of New York at Albany, April 1-2.

BISH, R. L. (1971) The Public Economy of Metropolitan Areas. Chicago: Markham.

DAHL, R. A. and C. E. LINDBLOOM (1953) Politics, Economics and Welfare. New York: Harper & Row.

FREEMAN, J. H. (1978) "The unit of analysis in organizational research," in Meyer and Associates (eds.) Environments and Organizations. San Francisco: Jossey-Bass.

GAWTHROP, L. C. (1969) Bureacratic Behavior in the Executive Branch. New York: Free Press.

GOLEMBIEWSKI. R. T. (1969) "Organization development in public agencies: perspectives on theory and practice." Public Administration Review, 29 (July/August).

HECLO, H. (1977) A Government of Strangers. Washington, DC: Brookings Institution.

HJERN, B. and D. PORTER (1981) "Implementation structures: a new unit of administrative analysis." Presented at the International Conference on the Analysis of Intergovernmental and Interorganizational Arrangements in Public Administration. Indiana University, Bloomington, May 11-14.

HOOD C. and A. DUNSIRE (1981) Bureaumetrics. University: University of Alabama Press.

KAUFMAN, H. (1981) The Administrative Behavior of Federal Bureau Chiefs. Washington, DC: The Brookings Institution.

KIMBERLY, J. R. (1976) "Organizational size and the structuralist perspective." Administrative Science Quarterly 21, 4: 571-597.

LYNN, L. E., Jr. (1981) Managing the Public's Business. New York: Basic Books.

MEYER, M. (1979) Change in Public Bureaucracies. London: Cambridge University Press.

———and Associates (1978) Organizations and Environments. San Francisco: Jossey-Bass.

SALAMON, L. M. (1980) "Rethinking public management: third party government and the changing forms of government action." Public Policy 20 (Summer): 255-275.

WALKER, D. B. (1980-81) "Tackling dysfunctional federalism." Policy Studies Journal 9, (Special Issue No. 4).

WARWICK, D. P. (1975) A Theory of Public Bureaucracy. Cambridge, MA: Harvard University Press.

WEICK, K. E. (1976) "Educational organizations as loosely coupled systems." Administrative Science Quarterly 32, 2: 1-19.

CAMILLE CATES BARNETT: THE NEW CITY MANAGER IS: 1. INVISIBLE   2. ANONYMOUS 3. NON-POLITICAL 4. NONE OF THE ABOVE

Alan Ehrenhalt

A few minutes after 10 on a slow Wednesday morning in Austin, Texas, police dispatchers look up from their terminals and there is Camille Barnett, sweeping through headquarters, shaking hands, cracking jokes and greeting every employee who crosses her path: "How y'all doin'? Are you busy? Can I say hi to you? Just wanted to come by and see how things are goin'."

A couple of hours later, in the ballroom of the Hyatt hotel on the edge of downtown, the guests at the annual University YWCA luncheon look up from their plates and there is Camille Barnett again, hitting them with an unexpected rouser of a keynote address. "Isn't this great?," she exults, pronouncing the first word Texas-style, with the "s" sounding more like a "d." "Isn't this great? We're all dressed up, we're eating good food, and we're here to celebrate women!" Her voice rises at the end of the sentence, and the audience responds with a rousing cheer of its own.

These are performances that any governor, any mayor, any congressman would find it difficult to improve on. This woman is a natural campaigner. What she is not, or at least is scrupulous not to appear to be, is a politician. Camille Cates Barnett, M.P.A., Ph.D., holds the one job in American government whose very existence is supposed to represent the denial of politics. She is a city manager.

The city manager movement, launched in the second decade of this century, at the height of the Progressive reform era in this country, was based on a few very simple but powerful ideas. The most important one was that politics and government could be separated. Local governments could be freed from the tyranny and corruption of urban ward politics and made clean, efficient and rational.

As laid out by Richard Childs, the system's creator and, for half a century, its chief advocate, the model regime consists of a five-member city council, with all the members elected by the community at large, and with the mayoralty a merely ceremonial office rotated among the council members. The five-member "board of directors" hires a professional manager to administer the city.

The manager, so the theory goes, runs the city like a business. He (and it was always a he) does not make policy. He is ideologically neutral. He simply translates the wishes of the council into action, without concern for partisan or factional advantage. The council is his only constituency; he does not worry about the views or needs of the broader electorate unless the council tells him to. He is fair, courteous and diligent—and he is quiet. He is not a public figure. The closer he comes to anonymity among ordinary citizens, the better he is doing his job. . . .

The city manager system has worked. It just hasn't worked the way it was supposed to. Most obviously, the gulf between politics and management, between policy and administration, turned out to be a fiction. It was possible for managers to stay out of partisan bickering. It was possible for them to handle some of the community's routine administrative chores in a neutral way some of the time. But it wasn't possible for them to do their jobs without ever making policy choices or gauging the mood of the citizens or bargaining to knit together a majority on the council—"learning to count to three," as managers all over the country soon came to describe the way things really worked. . . .

From the birth of the movement up until the 1970s, city managers were taught the doctrine of invisibility in public administration school, and they showed up for their first jobs determined to avoid publicity at all costs. Most of them honored the doctrine, to the extent they could, every day of their careers. When Louis Brownlow, one of the pioneers in city management, wrote a book summing up his years in the profession, he called it *A Passion for Anonymity*.

The notion of inconspicuous power continued to turn up in much of the writing on the subject through the 1970s. "We may wear a non-political mask when we face the public," the city manager of Tacoma, Washington, William Donaldson, wrote in 1973, "but it is a mask that hides one of the best politicians in town—even if he is an anonymous one."

At the time those words were written, Dan Davidson was the city manager in Austin. He honored the principle of anonymity for nine years in that office, years in which the city began to grow enormously and fought bitterly over how big it wanted to become. Davidson was a powerful man, a policy maker and a skillful politician, a guiding force behind the pro-growth coalition.

It is not accurate to say Davidson remained unknown during his years as manager: By the end of his tenure in 1980, the anti-development activists were sporting "Dump Davidson" bumper stickers on their cars. What is fair to say is that every drop of publicity he got was a drop too much for him. He understood very well that he was a politician; he had no desire to be a public figure. . . .

It is a long way from Dan Davidson to Camille Barnett. A few months ago, *Austin Magazine* ran a cover story on Austin's first female city manager, complete with two full-page pictures, one smiling and the other baring her teeth in a pose of mock ferociousness. The cover story was called "The Real Camille." It described her childhood in Houston, her educational background and her governmental career. The cover itself did not even mention her last name. The presumption was that all the readers would know it. The writer of the story reported that "Barnett's frequent public appearances and vibrant personality have . . . added glamour and prestige to a job which, prior to her arrival, sometimes seemed like a behind-the-scenes administrative janitor position."

Dan Davidson, highly supportive of Barnett's performance, nonetheless concedes that she is doing her job in a way that he would have found impossible. "She is bound to become, and already has become," he says, "a celebrity."

Nobody has accused Camille Barnett of craving publicity for its own sake, or in competing for headlines with the elected officials. She very scrupulously avoids that. She likes being an administrator of a city—she has written two books about it. But at the age of 40, after a public administration career of nearly 20 years that has included stops in Dallas, Houston, Grand Rapids, Michigan, and Sunnyvale, California, she has come to believe that what she was taught in graduate school no longer applies: If she wants to do a good job of managing the city, she has to be visible.

In her first few months as Austin's city manager, in the summer of 1989, Barnett was averaging six speeches a week. They weren't speeches the elected officials had turned down; they were part of a careful strategy for establishing herself as a public figure in Austin. Nowadays, she is down to about three speeches a week. But she is also doing a radio call-in show once a month, and meeting on a regular basis with the editorial board of the *Austin American-Statesman*.

You could comb the 2,632 communities in America with city managers and not find many clones of Camille Barnett. It is hard to imagine many of them being equally adept, the way she is, at glad-handing city employees, delivering a stem-winder to the YWCA and maintaining managerial control over basic city services at the same time. But if few city managers have the temperament to do it exactly Camille Barnett's way, more of them are coming to something like her conclusion: The doctrine of invisibility is obsolete.

"If you view your job the way we used to do it," she says, "shuffling paper and having meetings, you miss the boat."

The changing role of the city manager over the past decade is a topic of endless discussion in the academic literature on public administration and at the regular gatherings of the managers themselves. In all those discussions, one word sticks out: "broker." The city manager of the 1990s is the broker-in-chief among all the competing interests that maneuver for power in the modern city. Camille Barnett doesn't like to use that word; she would rather call herself a "negotiator," or a "facilitator." But the concept is the same. The city manager isn't there so much to make decisions as to make deals.

Even the International City Management Association, the professional association and main cheerleader for city manager government, freely acknowledges that "brokerage" is not a dirty word. "Brokering and negotiating," an ICMA publication proclaimed several years ago, "may be the prime talents of the manager of tomorrow." Howard Tipton, the long-time city manager of Daytona Beach, Florida, traces the change a different way: "Administrative efficiency," he says, "is not as important as making the deals that build the vision of what the city wants to become."

Good city managers have always been negotiators, of course, even in the days before many of them admitted to being politicians. But in the early days of the movement, the days of Richard Childs and Louis Brownlow, there weren't very many players in the negotiating process. In a city whose affairs were dominated by its business community (which most city manager cities were; that was where the impetus for adopting the system nearly always came from), and whose city council members mirrored the preferences of the chamber of commerce, and whose city manager owed his job to the council, agreement wasn't very difficult to achieve. A natural consensus existed. It may have been one that ignored the views of the poorer and less articulate segments of the community, but it was there, and it made the system work. . . .

One would be hard pressed to claim that the changing role of the city manager has been the catalyst for changes in urban public policy. In general, the managers have been responding to the empowerment of new forces in the community, not creating it. Still, it would be fair to say that by acting as broker, the modern city manager provides one more point of access to the political system for those clamoring to be heard.

Some of the brokerage jobs a modern city manager has to perform are jobs the city council is determined to avoid. "We're always telling the manager to bring all the interest groups together in a room and work out something," says Smoot Carl-Mitchell. "We don't want to deal with it. And she gets them all in there and they come out holding hands.". . .

On other occasions, having a public constituency means forcing the elected officials to think a little harder about taking actions the city manager doesn't like. In mid-June, a majority of the council voted for a tax cut that would require a reduction of roughly $6 million in the 1991 city budget. Barnett was against it. She didn't denounce it in public—no city manager could afford to do that—but she did find some ways to use her role as a public figure to make her opinions known. She talked to the editorial board of the *American-Statesman* and explained what the consequences of a tax cut would be. She began slipping a line or two into her public speeches. "What makes a great city," she told her YWCA audience, "is not a low tax rate, but a high heart rate."

Those are small protests. They are unlikely to dissuade a city council majority from doing what it has made up its mind to do. But they add up to one more weapon in Camille Barnett's arsenal that the invisible city manager of the past did not possess. "It's a delicate balance," she says. "I think it's abdicating for a manager not to tell people what she thinks. But you don't ever want to upstage your council members. You don't ever want to assume the role of a politician. I make a big point of not confronting the council in public. If I use my visibility to attack the council, I'm in deep trouble."

THE FIFTY-FIVE MILE SPEED LIMIT

Foster Atwood had been asked by the newly elected governor of a large Middle Atlantic state to join the governor's policy planning staff. His specific assignment was to develop a plan that would revise the method of patrolling the state's highways. The problem stemmed from a report by the federal Department of Transportation that an independent sampling of traffic in the state indicated that far too many motorists were exceeding the federally mandated speed limit. The report went on to threaten a cutoff of all federal highway funds to the state if something were not done. Foster wasn't surprised; when he drove on the interstate at the legal speed limit, most of the cars and many of the trucks passed him quite easily. Perhaps of greater urgency, however, was Foster's awareness that the number of accidents per 1,000 miles driven was rising dramatically.

Foster was not the first person to study this problem. His predecessor, Sheila Williams, had already looked at the problem and gathered some of the information necessary. Her report provided him with a set of alternative strategies for patrolling the highways and with the associated costs and probable reductions in both accidents and speeders. Also included in the materials was a study of the revenue generated by the issuance of citations. Foster found a table that summarized the information. Attached to the table were the following explanatory notes.

The cost of servicing each accident that occurs during a patrol is 250 dollars. The likelihood of accidents, however, differs depending on the type of patrol being used. The stationary patrol results in a .50 probability of two (2) accidents per shift; the cruising patrol results in a .30 probability of two (2) accidents per shift; and the airplane patrol results in a .25 probability of two (2) accidents per shift. Finally, the number of citations issued per shift

	Stationary	Cruising Car	Airplane/Chase
Car cost per shift	$600	$800	$1,500
Revenue per shift	$600	$375	$225
Cost of each accident to state	$250	$250	$250
Likelihood of two (2) or more accidents per shift	.50	.30	.25

varies by type of patrol: stationary patrols issue 8 citations on average; cruising patrols issue 5 citations on average; and airplane patrols issue 3 citations on average.

Foster decided that he needed to meet with the Federal Department of Transportation people. A previous study indicated that accident rates of *less* than an average of one (1) per patrol were typical of states in which the Department of Transportation found acceptable levels of speeding. But the crucial question was whether an increase in the numbers of patrols would actually satisfy the requirement. From the information supplied by Ms. Williams, it appeared that changing the type of patrols would be more effective.

Serge Amisis had worked for the Department of Transportation for nine years. He had started as a policy analyst and still considered himself a pretty good researcher. Since his last promotion, however, he had spent less and less of his time with the data and more time negotiating agreements with state officials. His first appointment of the day was typical. He hoped that Foster Atwood would be reasonable. Serge poked the intercom button and told his secretary to send in Mr. Atwood.

Foster and Serge exchanged the usual greetings and settled down to the business at hand. "The dilemma as I see it," Foster started out, "is that we could spend a lot of money trying to reduce the average speed motorists travel on our highways and still not necessarily affect the number of accidents." Serge raised one eyebrow. "I assume that those two things are connected—don't you?" Foster nodded. "They are, but not directly. For example, if the weather is particularly bad in a given month and we have changed to airplane patrols, the planes won't be able to patrol and the bad weather may contribute to an increase in the number of accidents. What I really need to know is whether you people are more interested in reducing the number of accidents or in reducing the average speed at which people travel."

Serge regarded Foster with an appraising glance. "Your question is really about our methodology, isn't it? I'll tell you how we measure and you can decide what to do. We have a list of states in which the accident rate per thousand miles driven is one standard deviation above the mean or higher. Those states are examined to determine whether any peculiar physical explanation—lots of winding mountain roads, for example—can account for the rate of accidents. If no peculiar circumstances exist, we send out teams of DOT monitors to check the average rate at which people drive on the highways. When that data is analyzed, we inform the state that their federal highway funds are in jeopardy."

Foster thought about what Serge had said. "So, if our accident rate is around normal, it doesn't matter how fast our drivers are going, because you wouldn't be monitoring, right?" Serge frowned. "Not necessarily. We do some spot checking in the states with normal accident rates, but essentially we believe the single most important explanation for the accident rate is the speed of travel." Foster leaned forward. "But other factors do enter into it, don't they?" "Well, yes they do," Serge admitted. "We have adjustments, for example, for states that have no inspection of motor vehicles. We also adjust for the proportion of miles of limited access as opposed to regular access roads."

Foster jumped in quickly, "Let me guess—limited access roads have fewer accidents than regular access, right?" "On average that's correct," Serge replied. "So if my state would concentrate on building more limited access roads, we might reduce our average accident rate to the point where you only did spot checks," Foster offered. "Perhaps," said Serge, "but we have also found that the average speed is higher on the limited access roads. So it might not help you escape the penalty imposed for excessive speeding." "So," Foster mused out loud, "its really a question of whether we want to avoid your monitoring or try to get the motorists to slow down on the interstates."

Serge stood up to indicate that the meeting was over. "My advice to you is to concentrate on better enforcement of the speed limits. While it may cost you more money in the short run, it may enable you to build better highways in the long run. When we started this program, we were trying to save gasoline by getting people to travel at the most efficient speed. We've discovered that the reduction in accidents was pretty dramatic. With better crash protection technology in the newer cars, we expect even better results in the future." Foster left the meeting still worried about whether more or different enforcement would enable his state to escape the penalties. It might take quite a while for people to change their driving habits, and the political pressure from irate motorists would be fierce.

On the plane going home, Foster began to rough out a plan. First, he would recommend that the fines for speeding be increased dramatically. That would help with the cost of more airplane patrol enforcement. Then, he would recommend that the state begin a long-term plan for changing from regular to limited access on some major highways. Finally, he would suggest that the state department begin its own monitoring program to predict when the federal limits were being exceeded. As Foster put away his calculator and leaned back in his seat, his mind drifted back to something his first supervisor had told him: "Trying to affect the behavior of a large number of people is like trying to predict the weather. There are so many variables that it's more an art than a science."

DISCUSSION QUESTIONS

1. Do you think that Foster's recommendations will reduce the speed at which motorists travel in his state?
2. Do you think the methods used by Serge to decide how to monitor are reasonable and fair?
3. What other actions would you recommend that Foster suggest?

LOW-LEVEL NUCLEAR
WASTE DISPOSAL

Ever since the near disaster at Three Mile Island, Jim Bates had a particular sensitivity to the public reaction to radiation hazards. When he was appointed chief of staff of the governor's Commission on Low-Level Nuclear Waste Disposal, he was determined to keep a low profile. The previous year, Pennsylvania, New York, New Jersey, and West Virginia had signed an agreement to cooperate in building a low-level nuclear waste disposal site. The agreement had been reached only after intense pressure from the Nuclear Regulatory Commission in Washington, D.C. Now that the agreement was signed, it was Pennsylvania's responsibility to implement it. Jim's first six months on the job were mostly devoted to identifying the people who needed to be brought together to make the commission successful. The list was a long one, with some obviously difficult matchups.

At the top of the list were the federal officials from the Nuclear Regulatory Commission staff. The federal government was understandably very sensitive about the issue of nuclear waste. The debacle at Hanaford, Washington, was still a sore point with the staff. Jim met Yavette Collins at a conference and casually mentioned that he was planning to draft the multistate disposal plan required by the Hazardous Waste Disposal Act of 1985. Yavette, a twenty-year veteran of the NRC staff, offered to act as a liaison with the NRC but cautioned Jim that he must go slowly if he wanted to avoid the usual premature opposition from local officials. She suggested that he begin with a site survey before drafting the plan.

While Jim was pondering how to select a site, he was called to the governor's policy planning meeting. At the meeting, he was told to make arrangements to attend the governor's annual conference, where he would meet his counterparts in the three other states that would be sending low-level nuclear waste to Pennsylvania. "By the way," said Bill Olson, the governor's chief legislative assistant, "be sure that you brief Senator O'Connell when you get back. He was really angry that we agreed to build the site in our state. Even though we generate 60 percent of the waste in the three-state area, he felt that we could have agreed to pay 60 percent of the cost and shipped the waste to one of them."

At the governor's conference, the four key people had a brief meeting. The three other state representatives pressed Jim to move quickly to identify the site. They each would have to arrange for the transportation of the waste and needed to know exactly where it would be going. Marty Vieto from New York was particularly insistent that the site be selected within the next six months. "Look," he said, "we all know that there is going to be lots of local resistance, no matter where it is. The sooner we start the process, the sooner we can get over all of the road blocks and protests and court challenges." Paul Sands from New Jersey agreed that the preliminary geologic reports indicated that there were only four general areas in Pennsylvania that were suitable according to the NRC regulations, so those people wouldn't be surprised when the decision was announced.

Sandy Montwell wasn't so sure that speed was all that desirable. Her state, West Virginia, didn't plan to ship a large volume of waste, but she knew from experience that without extensive and gradual preparation, local officials and citizens could quickly mobilize significant political pressure against a project. Sandy suggested that Jim start discussions with the local officials in all four areas and try to discover which group was most amenable. Her final comment to Jim as the meeting broke up was based on hard won experience. "Jim," she said quietly, "look at the unemployment figures in each area and start with the argument that construction of the site will take several years and provide lots of jobs."

Soon after Jim returned to his office he called Senator O'Connell. They agreed to meet the following week to go over the planning process for the site. Senator O'Connell ended the conversation with a warning: "This project had better have some advantages for us or the whole thing will become a political time bomb. The governor sold us out last time and now he had better have some good things to announce." Jim wondered, as he replaced the phone, how to keep Senator O'Connell from turning the site selection into a major controversy. The conflicting advice he was getting about how much citizen involvement to solicit didn't help him decide what to do next.

Senator O'Connell arrived at the meeting with Jim in a sour mood. He had just come from a budget hearing and wasn't pleased that two of the projects he had suggested had been turned down. Jim began by discussing the geologists' reports and indicating that the low-level site would have to be in one of the four areas designated as geologically safe. The senator looked at the map and growled, "One of those areas is in my district!" "I know that," Jim replied, "and I have a proposal to make." Jim outlined his proposal to locate the site in Senator O'Connell's district. Part of the proposal was a massive local public-works project to build new roads, bridges, and dams to ensure the safe transportation of the waste. Jim pointed out that after the facility was completed, the area would have the best chance to attract new industry because of the excellent access provided by the improvements. Jim finished his proposal and looked directly at Senator O'Connell. "The problem, as you well know, is going to be getting the local communities to accept all this."

A shrewd look passed across Senator O'Connell's face. "So you want me to be the one to organize the local groups to support the project?" "That's right," said Jim. "You'll be able to help us to identify the right people to contact and the people who might cause trouble." "I'll think about it for a few days and get back to you," Senator O'Connell said slowly. "If we do this right, I might even get a big boost for my next campaign. On the other hand, it could all blow up in my face." "Isn't that the way it always is when you do something really important?" said Jim softly.

DISCUSSION QUESTIONS

1. If you were Senator O'Connell, would you help Jim organize the community groups?
2. What would you do next if you were Jim, and Senator O'Connell agreed to help?
3. If you lived in one of the communities where the waste disposal site was going to be located, what role would you see for yourself and others in the process?

THE DANGEROUS REPTILES CASE

Adventurous Pets, Inc., an animal importer incorporated in the state of Delaware and doing business in forty-six other states, had imported approximately two-hundred horned lizards from South America. Selling these lizards as "pets" through a chain of pet stores, the company advertised these animals as "safe for household pets." During the past six months, thirteen children have been hospitalized after playing with the lizards. All of the children exhibit a fever and a rash that resists antibiotics. No deaths have been reported. Investigators for local health authorities have been unable to establish the exact process by which the animals might have caused the condition.

Adventurous Pets maintains that the lizards were not involved and that the connection is purely coincidental. They are, however, willing to meet and discuss the situation. So far, Adventurous Pets has not agreed that the lizards fall under government regulation, and they have not submitted any data concerning the lizards. Approximately 130 lizards have been sold to date.

Under the authority of the lead investigator for the Bureau of Noxious Fauna and pursuant to the Dangerous Reptile Act of 1988, Shawn Archer was charged with determining what action if any would be taken in the case. The director called a meeting to draw up a plan of action that would cover all eventualities. The director was willing to go to the full extent of authorized agency action, if required. The following excerpts from the act were applicable:

> The Bureau of Noxious Fauna [herein after BNF] is authorized to investigate all cases of suspected animal-caused injury to humans and, after consideration of the information so gathered, to issue seizure orders, restraining orders, requirements of licensing for vendors and/or owners, impositions of special conditions of sale, requirements for chemical or surgical modifications of animals prior to sale or captivity, issuance of findings and publicity of same, and other actions as may be authorized by law.
>
> The BNF shall, upon receipt of three or more complaints of a serious nature concerning a single species, respond to such complaints within 10 days. Actions undertaken to investigate such complaints may encompass subpoena power and seizure of records, property, or other evidences. BNF shall be permitted, but not required, to use evidence, information, or other data collected by state and local authorities, but shall not rely solely upon such in final action.
>
> All sectors of the Administrative Procedures Act as amended shall apply to BNF unless otherwise superseded in the statute. Final agency action shall be reviewable as to substantial

evidence on the record. Procedures for the making of the record shall be promulgated by the agency. Emergency action by the agency shall be permitted to prevent serious and imminent danger to the health and/or safety of the public. Such action shall not be subject to injunctive relief by a court of law.

Definitions: "reptile" shall be any animal which reproduces by egg laying AND is cold blooded; "dangerous" shall mean likely to cause harm or suffering. . . .

Two other pieces of information were considered by Shawn before he began his investigation. First, one of the children in the hospital is the daughter of a powerful congressman whose staff has brought this situation to Shawn's attention. Second, the agency has been involved in two judicial reviews of former action. In one, the court upheld the destruction of a family of "pit vipers" brought back from India by a university and kept by a professor. In the other case, the court overturned an order requiring that "poisonous fish" be surgically altered before sale.

Shawn's recommendations were such that contingencies based on the possible actions of Adventurous Pets were explored and a time line was established for action. The results of Shawn Archer's recommendations led to the following court case.

ADVENTUROUS PETS, INC. V. THE BUREAU OF NOXIOUS FAUNA

Pursuant to its authority under the Dangerous Reptile Act of 1988, the Bureau of Noxious Fauna ordered Adventurous Pets, Inc., (an animal importer incorporated in the state of Delaware and doing business in forty-six other states) to destroy all remaining unsold South American lizards in its possession. Further, the bureau ordered Adventurous Pets to repurchase all of the lizards sold at the original purchase price from as many customers as could reasonably be found. Finally, the bureau subpoenaed the import records of Adventurous Pets, Inc. in order to determine whether any violations of import regulations had taken place.

Adventurous Pets, Inc. filed a motion in the District Court of Washington, D.C., seeking to quash the order to destroy the remaining lizards. The district court ruled that the Dangerous Reptiles Act of 1988 prevented injunctive relief and refused to grant the order. The reptiles were destroyed under the supervision of federal marshals. Adventurous Pets has filed a new motion to set aside the order to repurchase the previously sold lizards. Claiming that the agency had no substantial evidence on which to base the order, Adventurous Pets has refused to release its customer records. The district court determined (1) that the order exceeded the authority granted to the Bureau of Noxious Fauna and (2) that insufficient evidence existed on the record to warrant the seizure of records.

The Bureau of Noxious Fauna appealed to the Supreme Court on a writ of certiorari contending (1) that the emergency powers granted under the act were sufficient to justify the order and (2) that a public danger continues to exist unless the lizards are located and destroyed. Further, the bureau contends that no formal record is required under the emergency powers granted in the act and that therefore the district court erred in granting the stay of the order.

FACTS

The Bureau of Noxious Fauna convened a special meeting on June 22, 1990, at which no representative of Adventurous Pets was present. Adventurous Pets had submitted an affidavit of "harmlessness" drawn by its staff veterinarian, certifying that the lizards were completely safe. The bureau's reptile expert (Ph.D. in reptology) argued that too little was known about this species of reptile for anyone to be able to guarantee that no harm could be caused. She argued that further research was needed before the lizard should be allowed to be sold to the general public. The chief investigator, Shawn Archer, indicated that seven complaints had been filed and that eight days had passed since the receipt of the fourth complaint. The bureau lawyer suggested that the agency take action in order to prevent a lawsuit from an injured party claiming that the agency had violated the law by not acting. A member of the staff of a congressman was present at the meeting.

On June 23, 1990, the director of the bureau signed an order seizing the remaining lizards, ordering their destruction, and ordering Adventurous Pets to repurchase the original lizards and to surrender records indicating from whom the lizards had been purchased. Adventurous Pets refused to cooperate and tried to have the order quashed. Failing in its attempts, Adventurous Pets refused to cooperate with the bureau, failed to return phone calls, and denied the bureau's investigators access to its files. Federal marshals entered Adventurous Pets' stores and destroyed the lizards on June 28, 1990.

DISCUSSION QUESTIONS

1. Did the Bureau of Noxious Fauna exceed its authority under the Dangerous Reptiles Act when it: (a) ordered the destruction of the lizards? (b) ordered the seizure of business records? (c) ordered the repurchase of the lizards by Adventurous Pets?
2. Were the procedures used by the bureau adequate due process under the Fourteenth Amendment in terms of protection of property?
3. Was adequate notice given of the action to be taken by the bureau?
4. Was there sufficient evidence on the record to justify the action taken by the bureau?
5. Was the presence of a nonagency person at the meeting inappropriate as an ex parte contact?

THE ETHICS OF PUBLIC SERVICE

—

Over the past decade or two, both academicians and practitioners in the field of public administration have become more intensely interested in the ethics of public service. But the topic of ethics has proven to be an encompassing one. Certainly, as a public official, you should be concerned about such issues as fraud, waste, and abuse in the public sector. But you must also think carefully about your own role as a public manager in a democratic society. What are your obligations to elected officials, to administrative superiors, and to the public generally? And what happens when these obligations are in conflict with one another? How can you operate as efficiently as possible but at the same time stay in touch with your various constituencies?

All of these concerns derive from the fact that, even though you hold a managerial position, you are acting in a political context and must behave in a way consistent with democratic values. As we saw earlier, this situation may present you with difficult challenges. For example, if you are given wide discretion in implementing a program, how can members of the public be sure that you are operating in their best interest? There are several possible answers. Some might argue that professionals in the public service should be expected to have instilled in them, as professionals, public service values, and that these values should ensure behavior consistent with the public interest. Others, perhaps more cynically, might argue that there is no reason to assume that such values will prevail and, for that reason, legislators ought to strictly proscribe the work of administrators.

Of course, one way that you might seek to understand more clearly the public interest would be through frequent communications with those affected by the decisions you are making. For example, you might interview citizens in an affected area, you might hold a series of open hearings, or you might establish advisory committees to oversee your work. But, while these approaches may help you be more responsive, they are quite time-consuming and may mean that you won't be able to claim as much efficiency as you would like. Again, there is a dilemma.

These issues of democratic responsibility may present great difficulties, but you may also encounter more specific ethical problems in your work in public organizations. For example, how can you be sure that your approach to public decisions is fair and equitable? What do you do when you are told to do something you think is wrong? What do you do when you think those above you in the organization are doing something improper or even illegal? How can you establish and enforce a high moral tone within your agency? How can you develop mechanisms to encourage ethical behavior throughout the organization? How can you make sure that proper behavior is rewarded and not punished?

The readings in this chapter provide some initial answers to questions such as these. We start with some broad concerns about the role of public administrators in a democratic society, opening with a selection by Debra W. Stewart, who examines in more detail the question of accountability. She notes, as we have, that some scholars and practitioners have argued for strict legal controls on the behavior of public administrators, while others have suggested that professional norms can be counted upon to properly guide such behavior. Stewart herself suggests that an explicit analysis of the values that lie behind public decisions will help to bridge these two approaches. You may want to consider whether the open airing of values that Stewart proposes (and that William Coleman undertook in the Concorde case that Stewart discusses) will really work in most cases.

As mentioned above, one approach to assuring responsive behavior is through the extensive involvement of citizens in administrative decision making. John Clayton Thomas describes one city's experience in trying to be more responsive to citizen preferences by increasing citizen involvement in the administrative process. Generally speaking, Thomas finds the Cincinnati experience one that suggests optimism with respect to greater involvement. Used properly, greater citizen participation in administrative activities can improve the quality of public decisions and public actions. What instances of citizen involvement can you recall in your own community? How successful were they, both from the standpoint of public officials and from the standpoint of the local citizens?

H. George Fredrickson takes the discussion a step further by exploring the concept of social equity as a "third pillar" of public administration, alongside the oft-heard concerns for efficiency and effectiveness. Although the importance of equity as a criterion for public decision making has been disputed, Fredrickson contends that administrators can and should take equity into account in their work. Fredrickson's discussion is highly philosophical at points, but be sure to notice the way that the questions he discusses are played out in practice. Here is an example of theoretical differences having very important implications in the lives of individuals.

Following these articles that focus on the role of public administration in a democratic society, the final article discusses a somewhat more practical and immediate case of ethics in the public service. James S. Bowman discusses "whistle-blowers," those members of public (or other) organizations who disclose improper or even dangerous actions taken by their superiors. Bowman notes that although whistle-blowing involves risks for the individual, it plays an important role in maintaining high ethical standards and should be encouraged and protected. While reading this article, focus on the ways in which organizations might encourage whistle-blowing and protect whistle-blowers from improper retribution.

Our profile in this chapter is of Larry J. Brown, county manager of Hillsborough County, Florida. The profile illustrates not only some specific ethical questions but, more importantly, some important issues of democratic responsibility. Consider carefully the relationship between elected political leaders in a community and the appointed officials asked to manage their government. Think also about the ethical issues involved in changing a system in the way Brown is attempting to change Hillsborough County.

The cases developed for this chapter present a variety of moral dilemmas that typically confront public actors. The stark contrasts of illegal behavior or official corruption have not been portrayed, not because they do not exist, but because those are the "easy" issues in ethics. The first two cases, "To Tell the Truth—But the Whole Truth?" and "Office Space in Miami," explore the borderline of what is commonly known as whistle-blowing. In these cases, individuals become involved in organizational processes that they believe may be unethical. The cases offer you an opportunity to empathize with an individual who must take action to stop organizational activities when the issues are less than clear.

The third case, "Trusting Is a Two-Way Street," looks at the other side of the organization–individual problem. The question of whether organizational procedures are partly to blame for unethical actions is presented in this case. Can procedures that strike a balance between accountability and individual responsibility be adopted, or is human nature such that unethical behavior is the expected norm?

The last case, "You Can't 'Unknow' Something," explores the conflict-of-interest problem from the perspective of the individual caught in a delicate situation. You will notice that the emphasis in this case is on balancing intentions with actions. As society sets increasingly high standards for public servants both before and after public service, these ethical and moral dilemmas are bound to increase for public administrators.

PROFESSIONALISM VS. DEMOCRACY: FRIEDRICH VS. FINER REVISITED

Debra W. Stewart

As a professional field, public administration has yet to come to terms with tension reflected in the classic debate between Carl Friedrich and Herman Finer on the role of professionalism versus democratic accountability in guiding public administrative decision-making. (Friedrich, 1940; Finer, 1941) As public service claims position in the ranks of the other developed professions (law, medicine, etc.), it continues to be visited by the partisans of accountability and responsiveness who demand adherence to the popular will over the fellowship of the profession.

This article addresses the implications of strict adherence either to the principle of democratic accountability or the principle of professionalism as the sole principle informing administrative decision-making. The thesis developed is that, while each emphasis plays a role in ensuring bureaucratic accountability, neither is adequate to guide the manager through the ethical quandries he or she confronts. The debate between Friedrich and Finer assumed that the standards of judgment are external to the personal morality of the decision-maker. While it is true that certain external criteria impinge, the ultimate expression of administrative judgment is individual and personal. Hence, this article suggests that accommodation of these two perspectives within the professional field of public administration can only be reached within the context of the current thinking about management ethics in the public sector.

A review of Carl Friedrich's and Herman Finer's theses sets the framework for this analysis. Then current implications of these two paths to securing bureaucratic accountability are explored. Finally, the place of individual moral analysis and judgment in contemporary administrative decision-making is considered.

THE FRIEDRICH-FINER DEBATE

The debate between Carl Friedrich and Herman Finer in the 1930s and 1940s constitutes a classic public administration scholarly exchange. Confronting the reality of bureaucratic power and looking to the emerging technocratic culture foreshadowed in an America preparing for war, Carl Friedrich saw flaws in the strict interpretation of administrative responsibility. In Friedrich's view, administrative responsibility was much more comprehensive in scope than simply executing policies already formulated. "Public policy," he suggested, "is a continuous process, the formulation of which is inseparable from its execution." (Friedrich, 1940:225) Because the administrator in the complex organizational world emerging in the 1940s commanded a degree of technical knowledge not accessible to the general public, "responsibility" came to take on a new and different meaning. While responsible administrators must remain responsive to popular sentiment, it was the scrutiny of colleagues in the "fellowship of science" that gave force to the term "responsibility" as fellow professionals oversaw the implementation of technical knowledge.

Friedrich's thought resonates today in our discussion of public administration professionalism. The nature of a profession is to apply a specialized knowledge in the service of a designated clientele. (Goldman, 1980:33) Here the normative foundation of work derives from the requirements and the mandates of the profession.

In response to Friedrich's redefinition of administrative responsibility as responsibility to the "fellowship of science," Finer charged that such notions obscured the very meaning of responsibility in a political context. He argued, ". . . There is no responsibility unless there is an obligation to someone else; no one is interested in a question of responsibility as a relationship between man and a science, but as it involves a problem of duty—and the problem of duty is an interpersonal, not a personal, matter." (Finer, 1941:269) "Responsibility in the sense of an interpersonal, externally sanctioned duty is, then, the dominant consideration for public administration." (Ibid.) Finer argued that focus should be on ensuring that the mechanisms for securing continuing responsiveness of administrative professionals are in place and functioning.

This classic exchange resurfaces regularly in our literature, suggesting that neither position was sufficiently persuasive to settle the difference of opinion on how to control bureaucratic behavior. On balance, it is probably fair to say that most political scientists have found Friedrich's position more compatible with the reality they observe and with the requirements of the modern state. (Sigelman and Vanderbok, 1978:442) Broad theories about representative bureaucracy have been built on Friedrich's assumption. (Mosher, 1968; Long, 1952) Still, echoing the Finer tradition, emphatic demands to heightened accountability by curbing administrative discretion recur in the literature. (Lowi, 1969:7)

Some scholars claim the time has come to lay this debate to rest; that both professional (Friedrich) and institutional (Finer) controls must be present for administrative responsibility to be assured. (Meier, 1975:542) But this response, while reasonable and not untrue, is inadequate because it fails to indicate how each source of advice should be utilized. The argument to be presented here is that simply striking the right balance between professionalism and accountability is not enough. In some situations, neither gives adequate direction for administrative action. In the following paragraphs, the author analyzes each principle in terms of its implications when given emphasis in the current environment of administrative decision-making.

ACCOUNTABILITY THROUGH DEMOCRATIC INSTITUTIONS

Herman Finer saw two options available to the architects of administrative practice in the early 1940s: either public servants would decide their own course or their course of action would be decided by a body outside themselves. (Finer, 1941:249) He stood for the proposition that public

administrators should not decide their own course. Finer's perspective did not imply a dim view of the character of public administrators. He acknowledged that government might well be staffed with good people. But he warned that "we must beware of the too good men as the too bad, [for] each in his own way might give the public what it doesn't want." Finer advocated a world in which public officials would be responsible to the elected representatives of the public who would determine the course of action of the public servant to the most minute degree that is technically feasible. (Ibid.) Adherence to these details of the prescribed course of action would be secured through courts and disciplinary controls within agencies and through the authority exercised over officials by politically accountable ministries. (Finer, 1941) According to Finer, the challenge was simply to ensure that these controls worked by implementation strategies which would leave little room for managerial missteps.

Judged from a contemporary standpoint, the problem with Finer's blueprint for accountability is that it requires elaborate institutional controls to ensure that the various courses of action mandated by the public are uniformly implemented. However, in a pluralistic system the institutionalization of particular controls in the service of one set of goals often makes it impossible to achieve other equally important goals for which an agency is held accountable. Personnel practices in the public sector best illustrate this problem.

The merit system in public employment was developed as part of a reform movement which aimed to purify a government riddled by patronage and corruption by making merit selection the avenue for advancement. Current advocates for merit practices argue that "the merit method has no substitute in providing the conditions of competence and continuity that are essential to the operation of complex administrative machines of modern government." (Stahl, 1971:41) Today, our civil service systems with their emphases on a battery of competitive examinations and established vertical advancement practices represent an effort to institutionalize "merit" principles in selection for government employment and promotion.[1]

Certainly these strategies further attainment of the original objectives. As Mosher (1968:203-204) notes, merit systems achieve their purposes by eliminating many irrelevant considerations (family ties, party identification, etc.) in assessing an employee and by measuring the relative capability to perform a specific type of work. The whole Civil Service reform movement represents the development and implementation of strategies designed to ensure that elected officials can remain accountable for the programs and the policies they promise by employing a neutrally competent group of civil servants standing ready to carry out political mandates. The problem is that, in an effort to secure accountability on this front, we have developed a system for selection and promotion which sometimes inhibits achieving other goals for which the public sector CEO is also accountable.

Juxtaposing civil service systems with affirmative action plans best illustrates this point. In recent years public sector jurisdictions around the country have expressed a firm commitment to EEO as a basic tenet of government practice and increasingly are held accountable for making good on their commitment. Through the courts, through affirmative action committees and plans, and through the commitment of top administrators, the policy goal of gaining equal representation of women and minorities at all levels of government organization is advanced. Progress, however, is often inhibited by the institutional expression of the merit principle. The case of New York State best illustrates this point.

New York has made a strong commitment to achieving equal employment opportunity in public sector employment while at the same time preserving a highly institutionalized state civil service system. In New York State the typical promotion process involves four separate stages:

1. The establishment of a set of criteria for eligibility to compete for a promotion;
2. The competitive examination process;
3. The canvassing of candidates to determine if they want to be considered to fill an existing vacancy; and
4. The selection of an individual from the pool of the top three candidates who have expressed an interest in the job. (Steinberg, 1981:2-3)

This process is the institutional expression of merit selection. It is designed to curb managerial discretion to hire less competent persons and thus to ensure that top elected officials can be held accountable for enacting their programs through the competent efforts of neutral civil servants.

Adherence to this process, however, often prevents top elected officials from achieving their public commitment to equal employment opportunity. Ronnie Steinberg's (1981) careful study of the impact of the Civil Service system in New York found that both eligibility requirements and the rule of three constituted institutional barriers to the advancement of women and minorities in state government. Eligibility to compete for managerial jobs requires incumbency in job titles held by low numbers of women and minorities and restricting the hiring officials to consider only the top three candidates limit opportunity even further. This dilemma described in New York is echoed in public jurisdictions around the country where political leaders attempt to achieve EEO objectives through civil service procedures.

Ensuring democratic accountability in administrative practice by spelling out to a minute degree the way a goal is to be achieved works in a system where goals are rank-ordered and non-competitive. But in complex organizations, guided by multiple and conflicting goals, the logic of Finer's approach leads to developing parallel sets of institutional requirements to see that all goals are achieved. The purpose of one set of implementation strategies may be to combat the effects of another. Many affirmative action programs with reporting requirements for goals and time tables are designed with this logic in mind.

However, and this author (Stewart, 1984) has argued elsewhere, the effect of this approach, institutionalizing procedures to serve competing goals and exacting high accountability from managers in attempting these goals, turns managers into referees of process and often results in significant goal displacement from the point of view of the public policies at stake. While accountability is central in any democratic system, Finer's strategies for achieving it ultimately hold administrators accountable for monitoring processes rather than achieving ends. Since processes, driven by significant value thrusts, inevitably conflict, Finer's solution seems inadequate for a complex administrative system riddled with competing claims.

ACCOUNTABILITY THROUGH PROFESSIONALISM

But, if Finer fails us, what of Friedrich's notion of professionalism as a check on the arbitrary and irresponsible behavior of administrative officials? Does the standard Friedrich offers, insisting that individual officials act in a way consistent with the highest requirements of scientific work (Friedrich, 1940:245), provide a satisfactory solution?

The first task in answering the above questions is to decide if public servants are sufficiently "professionalized" for Friedrich's notion to be broadly applicable. Friedrich's (1940:233) rationale seemed to envisage a mature professionalism in which standards of conduct would be clearly articulated by the profession and deviation from these standards subjected to thorough scrutiny by fellow professionals. While many public service roles meet this standard, some clearly do not. Using Mosher's (1968:106) categories, the "general professions" (law, medicine, engineering) represented in public service as well as the "public service professions" (corrections officials, social workers, teachers) fully merit the "profession" label. In each case the professional officials follow the objectives of a professionally formed conscience, a conscience which is given shape by professionally defined frameworks for viewing, stating, and resolving problems.

In contrast, public management professions (personnel managers, budget officers, purchasing officers, etc.), termed by Mosher as "emergent," fall short of meeting all the requirements for membership in the professional club. Certainly these occupational groups are *becoming* established professions by systematizing the body of knowledge and theory in their field, by establishing professional journals, by requiring specialized higher education, by offering a lifetime career to its members, and by continuing efforts to establish rules of ethics. (Mosher, 1968:106; Kline, 1981:277) It seems just a matter of time until these groups reach a level of maturity that would confer the full rights to self-regulation enjoyed by the established professions.

But in order to create the best case for analysis of Friedrich's contribution to solving our problem of accountability in democracy, we consider only the established professions. The argument is that public accountability is achieved through professional public servants who, under strict scrutiny of peers, apply a specialized body of knowledge in the interests of their clientele. Even in this narrow context, does adherence to professionally defined guidelines solve our problems? Does it provide the kind of framework for administrative decision-making that will satisfy the demands for accountability in our political system?

There are two difficulties with turning to professionalism as the solution to the problem of bureaucratic accountability. First, the professional response cannot be assumed to be coterminous with the right response in all situations and, second, in some situations behavior called for by professionals is not congruent with that mandated by personal moral judgment. Two brief examples will illustrate these problems.

Recently, in a middle-sized southern city, the press clashed with medical professionals when a severely mentally disturbed child hung himself in a local detention center. The child's mother had tried to commit him several days earlier to the community mental hospital and had been turned away by the resident medical professionals because they were not staffed to handle such severe cases. The doctors in charge were striving to cure the patients currently in the hospital and felt that to add a severely disturbed child to this environment would diminish their ability to cure the less disturbed patients they already had. Their professional mores directed them to cure the sick but to do so had to deny admission to this particular child who was very sick indeed.

While this response might be professionally appropriate, it was, from the point of view of the mother and the press, cruel and irresponsible. After the child committed suicide in the detention center where he was placed, the press charged that unbridled professionalism invites such violations of the public interest. Critics alleged that, because doctors need successes, they often create programs which serve narrow and more easily treatable populations. They acknowledged that medical professionals need to succeed a reasonable percentage of the time both for their own self-image and because, when competing for funds within a public bureaucracy, they need to demonstrate accomplishment. But they charged that professional judgment in this context violated the public interest.

The second case describes a situation where a professional norm dictates action in conflict with the personal moral judgment of the professional. A man with a distinguished record in the corrections field became warden of a large state prison in the midwest. Moving from a non-capital punishment state to one where capital punishment was the law, the new warden inherited supervision of two women on death row. About six months into the warden's tenure, one of the death row inmates entered into the last stage of her appeal process. The warden had always been very professional and objective about the disposition of particular cases. He had always firmly supported enforcement of the law as enacted by the legislature and applied by the courts. In the abstract he had no problem with the death penalty; however, in this situation he became increasingly uneasy about being part of a system that would end the life of the woman he had come to know.

The woman was generally recognized as a mainstay of the social support system in the prison. She served as a counselor, even a mother figure for many young offenders. Though she seemed personally reconciled to her fate, she was making a significant contribution to enhancing the quality of prison life. She had become a new person in prison; execution of this person seemed unnecessary and wrong. Yet, the professional code of corrections administration offered the warden no help in sorting through the dilemma he faced. On the contrary, it denied the legitimacy of the moral qualms he was experiencing.

These two cases point out the two principal problems with relying on "professionalism" to secure bureaucratic accountability. First, the rules and standards which determine the validity of professional judgment are themselves subject to a kind of political determination and control. (Harmon, 1974:13) In the case of the director of medical services who turned away the mortally ill child, the line between professional judgment and personal and organizational requirements appears to have been blurred in this decision. Such blurring challenges Friedrich's belief that the professional bridle achieves bureaucratic accountability.

The second problem with finding solace in the concept of professionalism is philosophical in nature. Professional ethics, the appeal to special norms and principles to override normal moral judgment, is only acceptable if the effect on the character of the professional is not too detrimental. (Goldman, 1980) The effect would be too detrimental if a professional norm caused serious conscience problems for the morally sensitive professional or if it promoted a justified insensitivity to moral rights. Our case of the warden about to supervise the execution of an inmate convicted of a capital crime illustrates the first point. His own moral judgment surfaced to demand attention along with the dictates of his professional code. While adherence to the code seemed professionally right, he continued to be plagued by moral qualms. In contrast, the medical director example demonstrates how a professional norm might generalize to a global insensitivity to moral considerations. (Goldman, 1980:32) Taken together, it appears that the power of professionalism as the solution to the problem of bureaucratic accountability is eroded by the reality of organizational intrusion on professional norms and by the ethical quandaries entailed in displacing personal moral judgment of the professional.

MORAL ANALYSIS AND BUREAUCRATIC ACCOUNTABILITY

Carl Friedrich and Herman Finer joined issue over a problem with no simple solution. Resolution lies in abandoning the hope to find a conclusion in one position or the other, or even both. Frederick Mosher (1968), writing in the Friedrich tradition, is right in describing professionalism as the most significant characteristic of the public service today. This inevitably means professionally defined ways of viewing and solving problems. But to acknowledge this is not to minimize the chilling effect of bureaucratic autonomy on democracy. Theodore Lowi (1969:304), voicing the Finer perspective, may also be right in his critique that broad administrative discretion in pluralist political systems impairs the rational ordering of public policy and the routinization of practice. Pluralist politics might do a disservice to society by the extent to which it makes a politician out of a bureaucrat. Perhaps it would be better if we could force resolution of competing claims upward where dispute would be most susceptible to public scrutiny. (Ibid.) But from the point of view of the administrator on the front line, efforts to curb administrative discretion often result in institutionalizing procedures to serve the goals of competing interests. In this context the manager becomes merely a manager of process whose success is measured by his/her alacrity in monitoring processes rather than achieving ends. (Stewart, 1984:17) It is not only foolish to build a system which is increasingly staffed by professionals so that it rewards incapacity for judgment, it can also lead to significant goal displacement from the vantage point of the organized interest at stake. (Ibid.)

It seems that both autonomous public servants, constrained principally by their professional norms, and loyal bureaucrats, rigidly monitoring rules, fail to provide the answer to questions of accountability. But a promising answer is found in the recent work on management ethics. The present article proposes that the public interest is best served by a system of administration in which those with operational responsibility for making hard choices among competing claims are also charged with the value analysis that supports those choices. (Stewart, 1984:18) Casting the public administrator as a moral analyst may bring resolution to the Friedrich-Finer debate.

Douglas Yates (1982:17) suggests the context in which values analysis might be set. According to Yates, proper bureaucratic control can be achieved by requiring bureaucrats to provide an open, public accounting of the valuative basis of their decisions on significant policy issues. Yates cites the example of the Secretary of Transportation, William Coleman, who, at the time of the controversy over whether the Concorde could land at Kennedy Airport, provided the public with a careful analysis of the legal, environmental, and political values involved. By providing full accounting of this weighing of relevant values, Coleman provided the basis for a broader public debate about the competing claims inherent in the policy dispute. He also gave the citizens an opportunity to see what kinds of values were driving decisions of the policy-maker. (Yates, 1982)

Explicit analysis of values behind bureaucratic decisions is the bridge which would link Finer's requirement for bureaucratic accountability with Friedrich's claim for professional autonomy. Formal controls and sanctions as well as professional norms and codes are essential to ensure effective control of administrative decision-making. (Meier, 1975:542) But to gain full benefit as well as protect against limitations of each, a finely honed capacity for moral analysis and judgment must occupy the interstitial zone between Finer and Friedrich.

CONCLUSION

Public servants need an ethical framework for representing the values and norms of their professions as well as for responding to legitimate demands for democratic accountability. Elsewhere (Stewart, 1984) the author has proposed one ethical framework which calls for systematic analysis of stakeholder interests and sensitive reflection on injury done to some interests by active service to others. While detailed discussion of this framework is not fitting here, the author would argue that this or some other conceptual apparatus is essential to bridge the gap between the equally legitimate values of professionalism and democracy expressed in the Finer-Friedrich debate.

NOTE

1. The decentralization of the merit system triggered by the Civil Service Reform Act of 1978 in the federal sector has addressed only the level at which the merit system should be implemented, not the substance of the system itself.

REFERENCES

FINER, HERMAN (1941). "Administrative Responsibility in Democratic Government." *Public Administration Review* 1 4:335–350; reprinted in Peter Woll (ed.). *Public Administration and Public Policy.* New York: Harper Torch Books, 1966.

FRIEDRICH, CARL J. (1940). "The Nature of Administrative Responsibility." *Public Policy* 1:3–24; reprinted in Peter Woll (ed.). *Public Administration and Public Policy.* New York: Harper Torch Books, 1966.

GOLDMAN, ALAN H. (1980). *The Moral Foundations of Professional Ethics.* Totowa, N.J.: Rowman and Littlefield.

HARMON, MICHAEL (1974). "Motivation and Organizational Democracy." *Public Administration Review* 34 (January):11–18.

KLINE, ELLIOT H. (1981). "To Be a Professional." *Southern Review of Public Administration* 5, 3:258–281.

LONG, MORTON (1952). "Bureaucracy and Constitutionalism." *American Political Science Review* 46 (September):808–818.

LOWI, THEODORE J. (1969). *The End of Liberalism.* New York: W.W. Norton.

MEIER, KENNETH JOHN (1975). "Representative Democracy." *American Political Science Review* 69 (June):526–542.

MOSHER, FREDERICK C. (1968). *Democracy and the Public Service.* New York: Oxford University Press.

SIGELMAN, LEE and WILLIAM VANDERBOK (1978). "The Saving Grace? Bureaucratic Power and American Democracy." *Polity* 10:440–445.

STAHL, O. GLENN (1971). *Public Personnel Administration,* 6th ed. New York: Harper & Row.

STEINBERG, RONNIE (1981). "Barriers to Advancement." Paper presented for a conference on "Overcoming Barriers to Advancement for Women" at the University of Pittsburgh, September 19.

STEWART, DEBRA (1984). "Managing Competing Claims: An Ethical Framework for Human Resource Decision Making." *Public Administration Review* 44, 1:14–22.

YATES, DOUGLAS (1982). *Bureaucratic Democracy.* Cambridge: Harvard University Press.

CITIZEN INVOLVEMENT IN PUBLIC MANAGEMENT: LESSONS FROM MUNICIPAL ADMINISTRATION

John Clayton Thomas

When public administration scholars contemplated reform of the profession in the 1960s and 1970s, one of their principal recommendations was to increase citizen involvement in the administrative process.[1] Unfortunately, the involvement which grew in part from that recommendation is now widely perceived as more problem than solution. Public managers lament the burdens of the new citizen involvement—stressful confrontations with citizen groups, delays in decision making, etc;[2] supporters of citizen groups complain that public agencies have become no more responsive to those groups;[3] and many outside observers contend that the public interest is neglected because public managers and citizen groups have become preoccupied with minor parochial concerns.[4] In the end, the citizen involvement once thought to be essential for the vitality of the public service can appear instead to be a principal factor in its contemporary deterioration.

This essay argues the opposite point of view. Generalizing from the experiences of some municipal officials, this essay will contend that increased citizen involvement, rather than being inimical to the interests of the public service, may actually be capable of aiding in its revitalization. The effects of this involvement are unlikely to be all positive, but, with the appropriate planning, the benefits may far exceed the costs, in the process advancing the cause of the public service.

CITIZEN PARTICIPATION IN CINCINNATI

The evidence for this argument comes from Cincinnati, Ohio, where citizen involvement in municipal governance has greatly increased in recent decades. In Cincinnati, as in many American cities today, this involvement focuses principally on neighborhood participation. The city has many characteristics conducive to residents identifying with neighborhoods: (a) a large population of 384,000 according to the 1980 Census, (b) many hills which furnish natural boundaries for neighborhoods, and (c) population diversity with a 34 percent black proportion and a smaller, but sizable, Appalachian white proportion. By the late 1960s those characteristics had combined with some historical factors to produce an active neighborhood movement.[5] In 1980 the city had approximately fifty community councils, representing areas ranging in population from under a thousand to over 30,000. The rise of these groups in the 1960s was followed shortly by a wave of experiments with neighborhood involvement in municipal decision making.

DATA SOURCES

The research on this involvement relied on several types of information. The experiments themselves were defined on the basis of historical materials, including bureaucratic files at City Hall, newspaper articles, and library materials. Information also came from interviews of municipal and neighborhood leaders who had been party to the initial experiments.

To assess the effects of the experiments, in-depth and open-ended interviews were conducted in the summer of 1980 with City and neighborhood leaders who could speak to the contemporary nature of community involvement in the city. Separate interview formats were designed for (1) City department and division heads, (2) City Council members, and (3) community council (neighborhood organization) leaders. Most of the interviews were tape recorded (with the knowledge of the interviewees) and subsequently transcribed by the author.

The most important interviews for this paper's concern with the public service were with the City's administrators. These interviews covered the fifteen major service delivery areas of the City: Parks, Recreation, Development, Planning, Police, Fire, Buildings and Inspections (in particular, the Housing Division), Health, Public Works (including the divisions of Highway Maintenance, Engineering, Traffic Engineering, Waste Collection, and Municipal Facilities), Water Works, and Sewers. At least one official was interviewed in each area, with that official being either the department or division head or, with larger departments, the official primarily involved with community councils. In many departments more than one person was included in the interview or more than one interview was conducted.

The interviews with City Council members and neighborhood leaders, though of lesser importance here, provide helpful contrasting perspectives. City Council members provide a more political perspective and, because they are elected at large, more of a citywide perspective. Five Council members were interviewed, including two Democrats, two Republicans, and one Charterite (a reform party), a breakdown fairly representative of the actual partisan makeup of the Council in 1980. Neighborhood leaders, in turn, provide a grass roots perspective on how the new community involvement works. Fourteen neighborhood leaders were interviewed, including eight white males, four white females, and two black males. The fourteen were chosen as a roughly representative cross-section of the different types of city neighborhoods.

THE MECHANISMS FOR COMMUNITY INVOLVEMENT

Although the historical record shows that Cincinnati experimented with community involvement in the 1960s, no lasting changes went into effect until the 1970s. The first major change, in fact, may not have come until the beginning of the federal Community Development Block Grant (CDBG) program in 1975. The City chose then to make the basic CDBG spending decisions through a Community Development Advisory Council (CDAC), composed of twelve neighborhood representatives, twelve at-large representatives, and a chairperson (who has sometimes

been a neighborhood representative). The CDAC was to formulate an annual CDBG plan, in part on the basis of proposals solicited from the neighborhoods, for review and approval by City Council. The extensive neighborhood representation on the CDAC has assured a significant neighborhood component in that plan.[6]

Shortly thereafter in 1976, the City made a second major change by transforming its community planning program into four Community Assistance Teams (CATs), each assigned to one of four city quadrants (or approximately 10-15 neighborhood groups each). The CATs were asked to serve as a liaison between community groups and City Hall on any issues which might arise on either side. That included their traditional responsibility for planning with the neighborhoods, but it also included assisting in the implementation of community plans (i.e., working to assure that City departments were acting on the plans) and helping in a variety of other ways. The effect was to facilitate neighborhood involvement in municipal affairs.

In 1977, finally, the City instituted a formal system for channeling community proposals into the annual budget process. The City had experimented in this area since 1973 (an experimentation which helped to produce the CDAC process), but a system for community involvement in the budget process was not formalized until 1977. Under this system the first step in the budget process is for each community to formulate proposals for short-term projects, proposals which are then distributed to the appropriate departments to arrive concurrent with the department's tentative budget allocation. The department can then consider the neighborhood proposals as it decides how to divide its anticipated budget.

FROM POLITICS TO ADMINISTRATION

Judging from the various interviews, the mechanisms have transformed community involvement in municipal decision making. They have done so, first, by promoting a move from politics to administration, from an earlier community group emphasis on elective politicians to a current emphasis on appointive administrators.

Neighborhood groups in their early growth years of the 1960s favored the City Council and the Mayor in their dealings with City Hall, but that changed once the City's current community involvement mechanisms began to fall in place. After 1975, according to veteran Council members, neighborhood interactions with Council and the Mayor declined either in absolute numbers or as a proportion of all neighborhood contacts with City Hall.

This decline or leveling off occurred because the communities were increasingly working directly with the departments or, if working indirectly, then going through the CATs rather than through City Council. The structure of the community involvement mechanisms encouraged this direct neighborhood-department interaction, and most Cincinnati observers think the encouragement has been heeded. Department officials, in particular, see themselves increasingly involved with community groups. Officials in eight of the fifteen departments reported increased interaction with community groups over recent years, and *no* official reported a decline in that interaction. (Most of the other officials either were in departments with consistently low rates of community contacts, or had been with the City for too brief a time to comment on historical trends.) Most of the community leaders concurred. When asked whom they tended to contact most often—City Council, the departments, or the City Manager—eleven of fourteen neighborhood leaders said they usually start at the departmental level, which one community leader described as "the kosher way to do it."

FROM PETITION TO NEGOTIATION

The changing approaches to these interactions are at least as significant as their increasing volume. Interviews with departmental officials and community leaders suggested that the dominant approach has evolved from petition to negotiation, that is, from community groups approaching City Hall with occasional petitions for action to community groups negotiating on an ongoing basis with the departments over the nature of municipal activities in the neighborhoods.

Petitioning and public hearings represent the two traditional approaches to community involvement. With petitioning, involvement comes only at the instigation of the community. With public hearings the City at least invites involvement, but

the sincerity of the invitation can be questioned since citizens are often allowed only to react to proposals already formulated by government officials.

The trend in Cincinnati, however, has been toward negotiation, where departments contact community groups to seek their active involvement in program planning and execution *before* the department has formulated plans. Officials in a number of departments reported this type of contact, and community leaders corroborated those reports. In some cases the negotiation has evolved to what could be termed interdependence, where departmental administrators converse with community council leaders on a regular basis, often independent of particular programs. Their purpose is to maintain regular communication which might be of help either to the department or to the community. The most obvious efforts along these lines in 1980 were by the Police and Fire Divisions, both of which were sending a departmental representative, a police officer or firefighter to every community council meeting.

Neither all of the departments nor all of the community leaders were involved in negotiation or interdependence, but many in both groups were, and their numbers appeared in 1980 to be growing. A third to a half of the departments, for example, were involved in negotiations with neighborhood groups by that time. By any standards Cincinnati had experienced a significant transformation in how communities are involved in municipal governance.

ADMINISTRATIVE ADVANTAGES IN COMMUNITY INVOLVEMENT

Most of these changes in the governmental process might have been anticipated from the nature of the community involvement mechanisms adopted by Cincinnati. In particular, the central role of municipal administrators in the new community involvement was clearly inherent in the structure of the mechanisms.

What might not have been anticipated is how readily municipal administrators have taken to this involvement. Rather than balking at the growing involvement with communities, most administrators seem to have embraced it. Although the administrators as a group are only modestly more positive than negative in their evaluations of the involvement, officials in those departments with the most community involvement are almost unanimous in their favorable evaluations. The critical or mixed reviews came only from those departments with the least involvement.

The evaluations are positive because these administrators have found that community involvement has some administrative advantages. Specifically:

1. Better channels of communication: Many administrators reported that the community councils serve as useful contacts in the communities giving departments a source for information when they have questions about community opinions. As such, neighborhood groups provide a means for improving the quality of information on which municipal decisions are based. As a Waste Collection official commented, "I think it (community involvement) is for the better. At least we've got somebody as a contact in each of the communities." The councils can at the same time help the departments to satisfy formal requirements for community input on many programs, as another administrator noted: "Community councils eliminate the need for a public hearing because they hold it for you."

2. Improved program implementation: Several administrators argued that involving neighborhoods in departmental decisions facilitates implementation of those decisions in the neighborhoods. As a housing official put it, "They've made it easier for programs to function in neighborhoods because they participated in the decisions." Another report of this advantage came from the seemingly unlikely source of the City's Engineering Division. Engineering divisions are notorious for opposing community involvement, preferring to run highways through neighborhoods without regard for how residents are affected. The Cincinnati City Engineer acknowledged some historical truth to this reputation in Cincinnati, but contended that his division has changed its ways, partially in the hope of improving implementation:

As we have learned from our past mistakes— or let's say the way we operated in the past—it would be an exercise in futility to make plans for a new street or highway without involving the community.

So, where we are planning a new street, we try to bring them on board as soon as possible.

The discovery of this advantage is hardly surprising. Theories of decision making have long postulated that people who are involved in making decisions are more likely to cooperate in putting those decisions into operation. The Cincinnati findings suggest only that what is true of small groups can also apply to decisions made with larger publics.

3. More services for the dollar: Participative decision making is sometimes advertised as increasing organizational productivity. Community involvement can bring an analogous benefit, judging from what many Cincinnati administrators said, by enlisting neighborhoods as active participants in program execution and service delivery. Here neighborhoods go beyond simply accepting implementation to actually join in the implementing. The result can be more services for the same or lower cost.

This idea has been popularized recently as coproduction, defined as the joint efforts of community groups and local governments to deliver municipal services.[7] Most Cincinnati administrators did not use that term, but did cite numerous examples of community groups assisting in the delivery of their department's services. Some examples were relatively modest, as with the Highway Maintenance use of community groups to help in neighborhood street inspection. Others were of considerably greater magnitude, as with the cooperative efforts of the Recreation Department and one community council on a community center. The Department built the center, but lacked money for its operation, so the community council contracted with the City to handle that operation. This advantage does have its limitations, as explained below, but most departments with substantial community involvement did perceive dollar benefits from coproduction.

4. Protection from criticism: Participation in decision making can also reduce the likelihood of criticism once the decision is made because those involved in making the decision take ownership for the decision. The more actors who are involved

in making the decision, the fewer who may be left to criticize the decision later.

This advantage for administrators was suggested as often by the community council leaders as by the municipal administrators. Those community leaders who were most involved with the departments expressed reluctance to take conflicts beyond the departments. As one leader said, "No one wants to go to City Council with anything unless they have to." They seemed to feel that their relationships with departments could be damaged by appeals to higher authorities (except when the department supported the appeal). Thus, an experienced community council leader spoke disparagingly of those community councils which act as "squeaky wheels" by going to City Council. She argued that they "haven't done their homework," even if they are successful with Council.

This attitude has the obvious benefit for departmental administrators of sparing them from some City Council and City Manager interventions. As such, cooperation and negotiation with the communities may be a means by which departments can avoid the preoccupation with "brushfires" sometimes said to accompany increased community involvement in municipal affairs.[8]

5. Clout in the budget process: Just as community involvement can keep some complaints *against* departments from going to higher authorities, so it can also increase the amount of community support *for* departments which gets to those authorities. In particular, many Cincinnati administrators argued that community councils can be useful allies in the budgeting process. According to one department head, "If these people can convince City Council that they really need something, it's a good possibility that Council will give it to them."

Illustrative of this advantage, two municipal departments in Cincinnati are widely perceived as having minimized their budget cutbacks in the late 1970s by virtue of support from neighborhood groups. When budget cuts were threatened, officials from these departments appeared before City Council with their neighborhood supporters or with the tacit threat that those supporters would appear en masse if the cuts became a reality. An official from one of these departments was candid about the tactic: "We tell Council, 'We'll save you from the political dogs if you'll save us from the budgetary dogs.'" What this may reflect is that the organization which presents a united front to its funding base can be more successful in getting funds.

THE ADMINISTRATIVE DISADVANTAGES

This is not to say that community involvement proceeds without problems for Cincinnati's administrators. However, the disadvantages often attributed to citizen involvement have proved illusory or exaggerated in the context of the extensive Cincinnati community involvement, even as some new, but lesser, disadvantages emerged. Consider first, the putative disadvantages which were not much evident in Cincinnati.

1. Unpleasant antagonism? Observers sometimes argue that citizen participation is characterized by unpleasant antagonism. As Cupps notes: "A frequently voiced complaint is the overdramatization, hyperbole, and shrillness with which citizen groups sometimes present their case."[9] Memories of the 1960s suggest how unpleasant and unproductive this can be, and why administrators might wish to avoid it entirely.

Those memories also suggest, however, that this disadvantage could be overstated. The unpleasant confrontation politics of the 1960s has greatly moderated, in part because its high emotional level was difficult to maintain. As well, the Cincinnati experience indicates that unpleasantness is a likely casualty when citizen participation evolves into government-community negotiations. Thus, few Cincinnati administrators spoke of much unpleasantness in their dealings with the communities, except to note it as characteristic of an earlier era. As for the communities, some are now more protective than critical of favorite departments.

2. Interference with professional judgments? Administrators sometimes argue that they have been professionally trained to do their work, and community involvement interferes with their professional judgments.[10] That interference, assuming the professional judgments have validity, could distort policies and programs away from the public interest.

This is a difficult problem, but it goes beyond the arguments just presented. If the professional prefers one course of action and a neighborhood prefers another, it may not be readily evident whose judgment should prevail. The judgment derived from technical expertise is not necessarily superior to the less educated, but perhaps more representative, judgment of the community.

Cincinnati's administrators have had to face this problem. A Traffic Engineering spokesperson, for example, said that the division makes most decisions "from a traffic control standpoint" (i.e., professional criteria), with the result that, on citizen requests for new traffic signals, "we probably recommend against a traffic signal nine times for every one we recommend." Some community leaders argued that those decisions are wrong. Who is right?

As that example indicates, these conflicts have not disappeared in Cincinnati, but the evidence does suggest that they have diminished, in part because of changing professional values. Many municipal professions—in areas ranging from housing and development to police protection to highway engineering—now favor incorporation of community opinions into what had previously been exclusively professional decisions. These changing values were most obvious in Cincinnati among the planners with their strong community planning emphasis,[11] but the change could also be seen in an area such as police, where one official described community involvement as a "necessary adjunct to the patrol effort. The patrol effort can't go anywhere without it." Several other departments, including some with histories of domination by technicians, also appeared to be routinely incorporating community preferences into departmental decisions. As a result, complaints about neighborhood interference with professional judgments are less frequently heard from Cincinnati's administrators.

3. Increased dollar costs? Community involvement is also sometimes faulted for increasing dollar costs due to the program revisions necessary to satisfy communities. In the words of a Cincinnati administrator, "A problem we usually find is that their involvement costs the City quite a bit of money because they want embellishments that are far beyond the reasonable utility" of the City effort.

However, the only example of embellishments did not appear to support the contention. The

City planned to build a firehouse, and officials proposed a structure with concealed, barred windows and without any foliage around the building, thus to protect the firehouse in case of attack. The neighborhood asked for exposed windows and surrounding foliage to make the firehouse more esthetically pleasing, "embellishments" which did not appear to be that expensive. If they were expensive, it could have been because the City had *not* involved the community in the initial planning of the building. As a consequence, the community suggestions could be incorporated only as embellishments, rather than as integral parts of the initial building plan. Perhaps even more important, there is the question of whose design preferences made more sense: those of siege-oriented administrators, fearing attacks from the community, or those of a seemingly hospitable community seeking a structure not greatly at odds with the adjacent architecture.

4. Costly delays? There have also been frequent suggestions that community involvement produces costly delays in both decision making and implementation. Cupps, for example, argues that "citizen groups are using their growing political influence and administrative and legal leverage to create excessive delays—in some cases near paralysis—of the administrative and judicial processes."[12]

That complaint may be valid for some forms of citizen participation, but it does not appear to be valid for Cincinnati's community involvement. When asked, only two of the City's administrators—neither one from a department with extensive community involvement—reported any problems with community-induced delays. The reasons for that finding are not hard to guess. With truly participative decision making, the decision-making process may be slowed because more parties are involved, but the implementation process can be expedited, as already documented, because those parties are more likely to accept whatever decision is reached. The end result may be no more delays than in a traditional decision-making process.

Many of the supposed problems with community involvement, in other words, are greatest when decision making occurs *outside* of a participative mode. Problems of antagonism, interference with professional judgments, dollar costs, and delays are likely to diminish when administrators accommodate community involvement within a participative decision-making style. Unfortunately, some new problems then emerge to trouble administrators.

1. The long learning process: To begin with, most administrators must undergo a long and difficult process of learning how to cope with the new community involvement. The advantages to community involvement do not develop either quickly or easily, and probably outweigh the disadvantages only when this learning process is substantially completed.

The learning process is lengthy because there are many skills to be learned. Administrators need to learn, for one thing, how to assess who particular groups represent since neighborhood groups, like other groups, do not always represent whom they say they represent. Making these determinations, according to those Cincinnati officials who work closely with the neighborhoods, requires the use of a variety of techniques (e.g., asking for a membership list, viewing group turnout at public hearings, maintaining multiple contacts in each neighborhood) which could be learned only over time.

Perhaps more important, these administrators had to learn how to proceed differently in making decisions. Increased community involvement brings at least three new elements to the decision-making process. The first and most obvious is the increased number of decision makers and opinions. As one official said, "There are many more agendas on the table that you have to deal with." Second, the new agendas often differ greatly from the traditional agendas. Communities presumably wanted a role in municipal decision making because they did not like the direction many decisions had taken. Third, many communities initially brought distrustful attitudes to this decision making. As late as 1980, a Parks official could report, "There's a certain amount of mistrust in some of the communities because of how they've been dealt with" in the past. These new elements could be accommodated only if administrators learned to make decisions more slowly and with input from more sources.

2. Time costs: Community involvement takes a great deal of time, just as participative decision-making always takes more time. The time is necessary, for one thing, for the learning process. Few municipal administrators were so well schooled that they did not need to go through that rigorous and time-consuming process. Additional time continues to be necessary after that because there are, as one Cincinnati administrator said, "more bases to touch" and more negotiations to conduct. Even an administrator generally sympathetic to community involvement could rue this cost: "When you're up here in City Hall at seven o'clock at night trying to work something out, you may wish you didn't have it" (community involvement).

3. Personnel costs: The time costs sometimes translate into significant personnel costs. A number of administrators reported that they had been forced either to reassign existing personnel or to hire new personnel in order to accommodate the volume of interaction with community groups. (It is probably impossible to estimate whether these costs exceed the dollar savings which the departments get through community involvement.)

4. Unreliability: Neighborhood organizations have a reputation for unreliability. Rather than being stable and dependable, these organizations often fluctuate between feast and famine. That can become a disadvantage for the public administrator if it means that the neighborhood organization which was helpful last year is nowhere to be found this year. That possibility is especially troubling now that neighborhood organizations are assuming larger roles in service delivery. Cincinnati, for example, has seen at least one recreation center's existence threatened because a community council was unable to provide the promised staffing for the center's day-to-day operation. These problems are not insuperable, but they do demand that cities be cautious about sharing responsibilities with neighborhood groups.

DOES THE PUBLIC INTEREST SURVIVE?

This comparison of advantages and disadvantages explains why Cincinnati's administrators are mostly supportive of the new community involvement. The comparison does not yet, however, justify an endorsement of that involvement. There remains a nagging question about what has happened to the public interest as the many private interests of the neighborhoods, allied with some municipal departments, have assumed their new importance in City Hall. One might suspect that the public interest would suffer since attention to the interests of the parts could induce neglect of the interest of the whole.[13]

Municipal administrators are not the best people to speak to this issue because their circumscribed functional responsibilities limit the perspective possible on the citywide interest. A better judgment can come from such sources as (a) City Council members elected on the at-large basis which encourages a citywide perspective and (b) local newspapers which also usually favor a citywide perspective. Accordingly, Council members were asked, and newspaper accounts examined closely, for any evidence that the citywide interest had been slighted as a consequence of the new community involvement.

That evidence did not materialize. To the contrary, on almost every issue where a slighting of the public interest might have been anticipated, the public interest appears to have fared at least as well as it would have in the absence of community involvement. For example:

1. The governing process has not become more difficult as more parties have become involved. City Council members saw no signs of the chaos sometimes reported elsewhere.[14]
2. The municipal budget has not been forced upward beyond the City's means, as supposedly can happen when the many parts of government become too powerful.[15] Quite the opposite has happened as the City cut spending in the years when community involvement was increasing most rapidly.[16]
3. Community involvement has not even produced noticeable distortions within the budget ceiling, as has sometimes been suggested of other cities.[17] In fact, when a new City Manager wanted to concentrate CDBG spending in a particular neighborhood in the early 1980s, he had no trouble doing so.

In other words, contrary to what might have been expected, the public interest in Cincinnati has suffered hardly at all at the hands of the new community involvement.

That outcome cannot be explained by any lack of neighborhood power. That power has been demonstrated in Cincinnati in the allocation of CDBG funding, with almost 60 percent of the funds in the 1975-82 period going to residential neighborhoods. Moreover, the clout of the neighborhoods, not the preferences of City Hall, largely explained which neighborhoods got more and which got less of the funding.[18]

A CONSENSUS ON THE CITYWIDE INTEREST

Explaining the survival of the citywide interest must begin instead with the fact that the new community involvement has seldom resulted in the neighborhoods being opposed to what appears to be in the citywide interest. Cincinnati's community councils have usually agreed with others in the city on major public interest issues. With retrenchment, for example, the councils mostly concurred with City Hall on what had to be done. As one City official commented:

> There's a pretty widespread realization now that the City can't do everything, and that other resources are going to have to be tapped. That doesn't seem to be a sticking point. Communities seem to understand that. Nobody wants more taxes.

It is not the saintliness of the community groups which has produced this support of the public interest. It appears instead, almost paradoxically, to be the community involvement itself which has won the support. By having a role in defining the citywide interest, rather than being told by City officials what that interest is, the neighborhoods have apparently been persuaded of the wisdom of the resulting definition.

Three examples may make the point. First, by being involved in the budget process as retrenchment was occurring, the community councils became more aware and more accepting of the City's need to cut back. More than one community council leader indicated a willingness to go along with retrenchment, so long as they were involved in deciding how the cuts would be made. City officials for their part often mentioned the cooperation of the communities in the retrenchment process.

Second, through the involvement on the Community Development Advisory Council, neighborhood representatives were persuaded in the early 1980s of the citywide interest in concentrating large chunks of CDBG funding in a few neighborhoods, as the City Manager preferred. They were persuaded, though, only because (a) City officials took the time to explain why this targeting was in the citywide interest, and (b) the neighborhood representatives then had the opportunity to approve or even modify how that interest was put into operation.

Finally, the neighborhoods united behind a 1980 school tax levy after they were involved, as they had not been with previous unsuccessful levies, in deciding on the nature of the levy. The need for a levy was explained to the councils in a series of neighborhood meetings held *before* the size of the levy was specified, such that the eventual size could reflect neighborhood input. The neighborhoods then played a primary role in the levy campaign as School Board officials let the "neighborhoods run whatever kind of levy campaign they wanted."[19] The eventual outcome was victory by a 55 percent majority, a sharp contrast to a two-to-one ratio of defeat for a similar levy scarcely a year earlier, and on a budget of less than half that of the earlier campaign.

In short, increasing power to the parts of the city and the parts of its government, as is likely to accompany increased citizen involvement, need not produce neglect of the public interest, *if* those parts are given a role in defining that public interest. That role can make them more likely to accept and sometimes promote whatever interest emerges as the public interest, even when that interest is, as often in Cincinnati, more someone else's conception than their own.

IMPLICATIONS: CITIZEN INVOLVEMENT AND THE REVITALIZATION OF THE PUBLIC SERVICE

The Cincinnati experience provides grounds for optimism about the role of citizen involvement in the future of the public service. Rather than being a pernicious influence on the quality of the public service, citizen involvement may hold substantial promise for contributing to the much needed revitalization of the public service.

The contribution can come most directly from improvements in the quality of public decisions, a quality frequently questioned in the recent criticism of the public sector and the public service. Judging from the Cincinnati experience, citizen involvement can improve that quality in at least three ways. First, citizens and citizen groups can provide better information for making decisions. That information might prevent repetitions of the numerous ill-advised public decisions (e.g., high-rise public housing, the large-scale undirected displacements from urban renewal areas) which have undermined support of the public service.

Second, the involvement in making decisions can make citizen groups likely to accept, rather than impede, the implementation of those decisions. The well-documented problems in implementing public decisions have almost certainly undermined respect for the decisions themselves, eventually also affecting how the decision makers too are viewed.[20] Broader citizen involvement could reduce those problems by building the acceptance of decisions necessary for successful implementation.

Third, the promise of more services for the dollar through citizen involvement could improve the public service's now tarnished reputation for efficiency. Inefficiency has become perhaps the primary complaint levelled at the public service. More citizen involvement cannot be expected to silence the complaint, but it could mute the criticism.

Beyond these potential improvements which anyone would welcome, citizen involvement can also bring some changes which public administrators might welcome out of strictly selfish motives. Public administrators may not speak openly of desires for reducing outside criticism of their agencies and improving their competitiveness in the budgetary process, but those by-products of citizen involvement could hardly be viewed as unpleasant prospects.

SOME CONDITIONS FOR SUCCESS

The overall good of the public service requires, however, that these latter benefits not be allowed to dominate the process of citizen involvement. That involvement could conceivably produce enough departmental autonomy—through insulation from criticism and independent power in the budget process—to prove corrosive of the public interest and of the public service itself.

This problem may be minimized, judging from the Cincinnati experience, by finding ways to structure citizen involvement into defining the public interest. The dominant emphasis of citizen involvement has usually fallen on the role of citizen groups in defining private geographic or functional interests, rather than the broader public interest. However, the mechanisms for citizen involvement in Cincinnati have occasionally charged neighborhood representatives in partnership with other city leaders, with defining the broader public interest, too. That charge appears to have tempered the preoccupation of neighborhood representatives with their narrow geographic interests, and in a manner likely to redound to the benefit of the municipal public service.

The promise of citizen involvement is affected by a number of other conditions, too. In the first place, the advantages of citizen involvement are likely to predominate only when the involvement is real, that is, only when the administrator has surrendered some decision-making power to the citizen groups. Citizen involvement *without* some surrender of power actually invites many of the disadvantages commonly attributed to citizen and community participation. Citizens have distrusted government for too long to be safely asked now for their opinions unless those opinions are likely to affect decisions.

Second, not every administrator or every department may be suited to extensive community involvement. Decision-making theorists Vroom and Yetton argue that administrators should be flexible, changing their decision-making styles depending on the problem, but Fiedler may be closer to the truth when he contends that the individual's leadership style is usually not that malleable.[21] Community involvement may require that the individual be more "relationship motivated" than "task motivated" in order to cope with the many relationships required. It also requires skills at negotiation if decision makers are to accommodate both citizen and agency interests within a single decision. Not every administrator will have these skills or be interested in developing them. In cities, for example, professionals trained decades ago to make the best

technical decisions in the reform tradition may find it impossible to adjust to a new standard of group-negotiated decisions. In addition, in those departments where the nature of services makes interactions with citizen groups relatively infrequent, administrators may not find a net advantage in taking the time to adapt to extensive citizen involvement.

Third, new initiatives at citizen involvement probably should not be undertaken unless resources are sufficient to cover the accompanying costs. Community involvement in Cincinnati required more staff time, more spending to pay to hire additional staff, more time for making decisions, as well as a long process of learning how to work with the new involvement. An agency risks trouble if it begins such an involvement program without first knowing that the costs are affordable.

Unfortunately, this means that many public agencies could be unwise to initiate new citizen involvement programs in the current climate of fiscal austerity. The dollar costs of the involvement could exacerbate the basic fiscal problems, and the time costs could conflict with the need to make decisions quickly if revenues suddenly fall short of expectations.

On the other hand, citizen involvement can be useful in the retrenchment process if the involvement was established *before* the retrenchment began. Citizen involvement then adds no complications not already a part of agency decision making. The involvement can instead diffuse some of the responsibility for unpopular spending cuts to the citizen groups, thereby saving public officials from much of the political fallout which those cuts can bring. Citizen involvement complicates matters only if it is begun amid retrenchment. An agency in that position is essentially taking on two difficult tasks at once.

In the end, citizen involvement will inevitably be a part of the future of the public service. The growing numbers of citizen groups at all levels of government in recent decades make that involvement a foregone conclusion, regardless of the preferences of policy makers. The question is whether the involvement will be a negative force for inertia and chaos or a positive force for increasing the vitality of the public sector and the public service.

NOTES

1. See, for example, Frank Marini (ed.), *Toward a New Public Administration: The Minnowbrook Perspective* (Scranton, Pa.: Chandler Publishing, 1971).

2. These complaints are perhaps best documented in D. Stephen Cupps, "Emerging Problems of Citizen Participation," *Public Administration Review* 37 (September/October 1977), 478–87.

3. The skepticism about this responsiveness can be seen in Albert Hunter, "The Urban Neighborhood: Its Analytical and Social Contexts," *Urban Affairs Quarterly* 14 (March 1979), 267–88.

4. See, for example, Donald F. Kettl, "Can the Cities Be Trusted? The Community Development Experience," *Political Science Quarterly* 94 (Fall 1979), 437–51.

5. This history is detailed in John Clayton Thomas, *Between Citizen and City: Neighborhood Organizations and Urban Politics in Cincinnati* (book-length manuscript in preparation).

6. More than half of the CDBG funding over the 1975-82 period was allocated to the residential neighborhoods. See Thomas, *Between Citizen and City*.

7. See, for example, Gordon P. Whitaker, "Coproduction: Citizen Participation in Service Delivery," *Public Administration Review* 40 (May/June 1980), 240–46; or, Roger S. Ahlbrandt, Jr., and Howard Sumka, "Neighborhood Organizations and the Coproduction of Public Services," *Journal of Urban Affairs* 5 (Summer 1983), 211–20.

8. See Douglas Yates, *The Ungovernable City: The Politics of Urban Problems and Policy Making* (Cambridge, Mass.: The MIT Press, 1977).

9. See Cupps, "Emerging Problems of Citizen Participation," p. 482.

10. See Daniel M. Barber, *Citizen Participation in American Communities* (Dubuque, Iowa: Kendall/Hunt Publishing, 1981), p. ix.

11. The nature of this change in the planning profession is graphically described by Martin L. Needleman and Carolyn Emerson Needleman, *Guerrillas in the Bureaucracy: The Community Planning Experiment in the United States* (New York: John Wiley, 1974).

12. Cupps, "Emerging Problems of Citizen Participation," p. 482.

13. Kettl makes this very argument in "Can the Cities Be Trusted?"

14. Yates, *The Ungovernable City*.

15. The growth of the federal budget has sometimes been attributed to this kind of process. See Daniel Bell, "The Revolution of Rising Entitlements," *Fortune* 91 (April 1975), 98–103, 183, 185.

16. These spending trends are documented in Charles H. Levine, Irene S. Rubin, and, George C. Wolohojian, "Resource Scarcity and the Reform Model: The Management of Retrenchment in Cincinnati and Oakland," *Public Administration Review* 41 (November/December 1981), 619–28.

17. Kettl, "Can the Cities Be Trusted?"

18. As detailed in Thomas, *Between Citizen and City*.

19. See the campaign account in *Cincinnati Enquirer*, "He Rocked Boat, Set It on Course," June 8, 1980.

20. One of the first and still among the best descriptions of implementation problems is Jeffrey L. Pressman and Aaron B. Wildavsky, *Implementation* (Berkeley: University of California Press, 1973).

21. Victor Vroom and Philip Yetton, *Leadership and Decision Making* (Pittsburgh: University of Pittsburgh Press, 1973); Fred E. Fiedler, *A Theory of Leadership Effectiveness* (New York: McGraw-Hill, 1967).

PUBLIC ADMINISTRATION AND SOCIAL EQUALITY

H. George Frederickson

It was 1968. Inequality and injustice, especially based on race, was pervasive. A government built on a Constitution claiming the equal protection of the laws had failed in that promise. Public administrators, those who daily operate the government, were not without responsibility. Both in theory and practice public administration had, beginning in the 1940s, emphasized concepts of decision making, systems analysis, operations research or management science, and rationality. In running the government the administrator's job was to be efficient (getting the most service possible for available dollars) or economical (providing an agreed-upon level of services for the fewest possible dollars). It should be no surprise, therefore, that issues of inequity and injustice were not central to public servants or to public administration theorists.

To remedy what seemed a glaring inadequacy in both thought and practice, I developed a theory of social equity and put it forward as the "third pillar" for public administration, holding the same status as economy and efficiency as values or principles to which public administration should adhere. The initial reasoning went this way:

To say that a service may be well managed and that a service may be efficient and economical, still begs these questions: Well managed for whom? Efficient for whom? Economical for whom? We have generally assumed in public administration a convenient oneness with the public. We have not focused our attention or concern to the issue of variations in social and economic conditions. It is of great convenience, both theoretically and practically, to assume that citizen A is the same as citizen B and that they both receive public services in equal measure. This assumption may be convenient, but it is obviously both illogical and empirically inaccurate.[1]

Social equity began as a challenge to the adequacy of concepts of efficiency and economy as guides for public administration. In time social equity took on a broader meaning.

Social equity is a phrase that comprehends an array of value preferences, organizational design preferences, and management style preferences. Social equity emphasizes equality in government services. Social equity emphasizes responsibility for decisions and program implementation for public managers. Social equity emphasizes change in public management. Social equity emphasizes responsiveness to the needs of citizens rather than the needs of public organizations. Social equity emphasizes an approach to the study of and education for public administration that is interdisciplinary, applied, problem solving in character, and sound theoretically.[2]

The development of the concept of social equity was followed by a considerable literature both pro and con. Philosophically the views ranged from social equity as providing the proper normative basis for a new public administration on the one hand to social equity as an attempt by some to "steal popular sovereignty" on the other.[3] Researchers, especially in the public policy fields, began to analyze variations in the distribution of public service by income, race, and neighborhood, and eventually by gender. The concept of equity was included in the first adopted Principles for the American Society for Public Administration (ASPA), which later became the Code of Ethics. In 1981, the *ASPA Professional Standards and Ethics Workbook and Study Guide for Public Administrators*, in the section on professional ethics, listed as the first two Principles to be the pursuit of equality, which is to say citizen A being equal to citizen B, and equity, which is to say adjusting shares so that citizen A is made equal with citizen B.[4]

In the past 20 years the phrase social equity has taken its place as a descriptor for variables in the analytic constructs of researchers in the field, as a concept in the philosophy of public administration, and as a guide for ethical behavior for public servants. With the passage of 20 years and the attendant advantages of hindsight, some stock taking is called for, and the Golden Anniversary of the *Public Administration Review* is an appropriate occasion for this reflection.

This review of the place of social equity in public administration begins, as it should, with philosophical and theoretical developments. That is followed by a consideration of the especially important relationship between social equity and the law and what has transpired in the last generation. Following that, developments in analysis and research are reviewed.

PHILOSOPHICAL AND THEORETICAL DEVELOPMENTS

Public administration, it has been said, is the marriage of the arts and sciences of government to the arts and sciences of management.[5] Efficiency and economy are primarily theories of management while social equity is primarily a theory of government. In the early years of modern American public administration the marriage, particularly in the conceptions of Woodrow Wilson, was balanced.[6] Theories of business efficiency were routinely mixed with theories of democratic government, the argument being that a government can and should be efficient and fair. However, by the 1950s the marriage was dominated by management theories and issues, having begged questions of equity and fairness. Even though it was and is generally agreed that public administration is part of the political process, there was little interest in developing specifics regarding the ends to which politics and public administration could be put.

In the early years it was also the conventional wisdom that public administration was neutral and only marginally involved in policy making. Under those conditions it is possible to ignore social equity. Now the theology holds that public administration is a part or form of politics, that it often exercises leadership in the policy process, and that neutrality is next to impossible. If that is the case, then it is not logically possible to dismiss social equity as a suggested guide for administrative action, equal to economy and efficiency.

Initial attempts to return to the marriage questions of equity and fairness were simplistic and superficial. Willbern, in his splendid review of the early literature on social equity and the so-called new public administration, observed that critics were "not very precise in defining the goals or values toward which administration and knowledge must be arrived."[7] He concluded that:

> Those who wanted to challenge the "system" and the "establishment" on grounds of social equity have met with a good many rebuffs and even evidence of backlash. But it would probably be a great mistake to dismiss these essays as an expression of a passing mood, an articulation of the particular times in which they were written. On intellectual, analytical grounds, there is something of value and consequence here, a real addition to our faulty and inadequate understanding of human behavior in administrative situations.[8]

So the task was clear, social equity needed flesh on its bones if it was to be taken seriously as a third pillar for public administration. The process was begun with a symposium on "Social Equity and Public Administration," which appeared in the *Public Administration Review* in 1974. In an especially important way, that symposium is illustrative of theory building in public administration.

First, the subject is parsed, in this case, into considerations of social equity: (1) as the basis for a just, democratic society; (2) as influencing the behavior of organization man; (3) as the legal basis for distributing public services; (4) as the practical basis for distributing public services; (5) as operationalized in compound federalism; and (6) as a challenge for research and analysis.[9]

Second, the subject having been taken apart, good theory building suggests putting it back together. Looking back, it is now clear that considerable progress has been made in thinking about, understanding, and applying various parts of the subject. But it has yet to be put back together.

Third is the arduous task of definition. In this case, it was appropriate to turn to the theories of distributive justice for definition. The phrase social equity and the word equality were essentially without definition in the field. As Rae and his associates have said: "Equality is the simplest and most abstract of notions, yet the practices of the world are irremediably concrete and complex. How, imaginably, could the former govern the latter?"[10] Yet, social equity was advanced in the 1960s and 1970s as an essential third pillar of public administration.

When ideas such as social equity or the public interest or liberty are suggested as guides for public action, the most compelling definitions are often the most abstract. And so it was in this case. The initial attempts to define social equity as it applies to public administration were fastened to John Rawls' *A Theory of Justice*.[11] The Rawlsian construct as an ideal type addresses the distribution of rights, duties, and advantages in a just society. Justice, to Rawls, is fairness. To achieve fairness the first principle is that each person is guaranteed equal basic liberties consistent with an extensive system of liberty for all. The second principle calls for social and economic inequalities to be managed so that they are of greatest benefit to the least advantaged (the difference principle); it seeks to make offices and positions open to all under conditions of *fair* equality of opportunity.

For much of the last two decades perspectives on Rawlsian justice have occupied the intellectual high ground of concern for social equity. While philosophical and scholarly interest in Rawlsian theory has been strong, and certainly the objectives of fairness through justice are compatible with the social equity perspective on public administration, the theory has thus far been of limited use in the busy world of government.

This analysis turns, then, to a more descriptive theory for both greater definition and more likely applicability to the theories and practices of public administration. Following Douglas Rae and associates, a rudimentary language and a road map are set forth for the notion of equality, with attendant definitions and examples.[12] I label this the Compound Theory of Social Equity. This Compound Theory serves as the basis for later considerations of legal and research perspectives on social equity in public administration.

SIMPLE INDIVIDUAL EQUALITIES

Individual equality consists of one class of equals, and one relationship of equality holds among them. The best examples would be one person-one vote and the price mechanism of the market, which offers a Big Mac or a Whopper at a specific price to whomever wishes to buy. The Golden Rule or Immanuel Kant's Categorical Imperative are formulas for individual equalities.

SEGMENTED EQUALITY

Any complex society with a division of labor tends to practice segmented equality. Farmers have a different system of taxation than do business owners, and both differ from wage earners. In segmented equality, one assumes that equality exists within the category (e.g., farmers) and that inequality exists between the segments. All forms of hierarchy use the concept of segmented equality. All five-star generals are equal to each other as are all privates first-class. Equal pay for equal work is segmented equality. Segmented equality is, in fact, systematic or structured inequality. Segmented equality is critically important for public policy and administration because virtually every public service is delivered on a segmented basis and always by segmented hierarchies.

BLOCK EQUALITIES

Both simple individual and segmented equalities are in fact individual equalities. Block equalities, on the other hand, call for equality *between* groups or subclasses. The railroad accommodations for Blacks and whites could be separate, so long as they were equal in *Plessy v. Ferguson* (1889).[13] *Brown v. Board of Education* (1954)[14] later concluded that separation by race meant inequality; therefore, the U.S. Supreme Court required school services to be based upon simple individual equality rather than block equality, using race to define blocks. The claims for comparable worth systems of pay for women are, interestingly, block egalitarianism mixed with equal pay for equal work, which is segmented equality.

THE DOMAIN OF EQUALITY

How does one decide what is to be distributed equally? The domain of equality marks off the goods, services, or benefits being distributed. If schools and fire protection are to be provided, why not golf courses or recreational facilities? Domains of equality can be narrowly or broadly defined, and they can have to do with *allocations* based on a public agency's resources or they can be based on *claims*—claimants' demands for equality. Domains of equality constantly shift, aggregate, and disaggregate. Certain domains are largely controlled by the market such as jobs, wages, and investments, while others are controlled primarily by government. It is often the case that the governmental domain seeks equality to correct inequalities resulting from the market or from previous governmental policies. Unemployment compensation, Aid to Families with Dependent Children, college tuition grants, and food stamps are all kinds of governmental compensatory inequality to offset other inequalities outside of the governmental domain of allocation but within a broader domain of claims.

Domains can also be intergenerational, as in the determination of whether present taxpayers or their children pay for the federal debt built up by current deficits.

EQUALITIES OF OPPORTUNITY

Equalities of opportunity are divided into *prospect* and *means* opportunity. Two people have equal opportunity for a job if each has the same probability for attaining the job under conditions of prospect equality of opportunity. Two people have equal opportunity for a job if each has the same talents or qualifications for the job under conditions of means-equal opportunity. Examples of pure prospect equality of opportunity are few, but the draft lottery for the Vietnam War is very close. In means equality of opportunity, *equal rules*, such as Intelligence Quotient (I.Q.) tests, Standard Achievement Test (SAT) scores, equal starting and finishing points for footraces, and so forth define opportunity. "The purpose and effect of these equal means is not equal prospect of success, but legitimately unequal prospects of success."[15] Aristotle's notion that equals are to be treated equally would constitute means-based equality of opportunity.

In any given society not all talent can be equally developed. Following John Schaar: "Every society has a set of values, and these are arranged in a more or less tidy hierarchy. . . . The equality of opportunity formula must be revised to read:

equality of opportunity for all to develop those talents which are highly valued by a given people at a given time."[16] How else, for example, can one explain the status of rock musicians in popular culture?

THE VALUE OF EQUALITY

The value of equality begins with the concept of *lot equality* in which shares are identical (similar housing, one vote, etc.) or equal. The advantage of lot equality is that only the individual can judge what pleases or displeases him or her. Lots can also be easily measured and distributed, and they imply nothing about equal well-being. The problem, of course, is that lot equality is insensitive to significant variations in need. To remedy this, Rae and associates suggest a "person equality" in which there is nonarbitrary rule-based distribution of shares based on nonneutral judgments about individuals' needs. A threatened person may require more protection (and police officials may so decide) merely to make that person equal to the nonthreatened person. The same can be said for the crippled as against the healthy child, the mentally retarded as against the bright. Person-regarding equality is often practiced in public administration to "make the rules humane."

It is clear that any universal scope for equality is both impossible and undesirable. Rather than a simple piece of rhetoric or a slogan, the Compound Theory of Social Equity is a complex of definitions and concepts. Equality then changes from one thing to many things—equalities. If public administration is to be inclined toward social equity, at least this level of explication of the subject is required. In the policy process, any justification of policy choices claiming to enhance social equity needs to be analyzed in terms of such questions as: (1) Is this equality individual, segmented, or block? (2) Is this equality direct, or is it means-equal opportunity or prospect-equal opportunity? (3) What forms of social equity can be advanced so as to improve the lot of the least advantaged, yet sustain democratic government and a viable market economy? The Compound Theory of Social Equity would serve as the language of the framework for attempts in both theory building and practice, and it would serve to answer these questions.

SOCIAL EQUITY AND THE LAW

Marshall Dimock made this dicta famous: "public administration is the law in action." It should be no surprise, then, that the most significant developments in social equity have their genesis in the law. "Local, state and national legislators—and their counterparts in the executive branches—too often have ignored, abdicated or traded away their responsibilities. . . . By default, then, if for no other reason, the courts would often have the final say."[17] The courts are the last resort for those claiming unequal treatment in either the protection of the law or the provision of service. Elected officials—both legislators and executives—are naturally inclined to the views and interests of the majority. Appointed officials—the public administrators—have until recent years been primarily concerned with efficiency and economy, although effectiveness was also an early concern, as noted by Dwight Waldo in *The Administrative State*.[18]

EMPLOYMENT

The most important legal influences resulting in more equitable government are in the field of employment, both public and nonpublic. The legal (not to mention administrative) questions are: who ought to be entitled to a job, what are the criteria, and how ought they to be applied?

The Civil Rights Act of 1964 as amended and the Equal Employment Act of 1972 were designed to guarantee equal access to public and private employment. This was done by a combination of block equalities (whereby persons in different racial categories could be compared and, if found subject to different treatment, a finding of violation of law would be made) and a means-equal opportunities logic (whereby fair measurements of talent, skill, and ability would determine who gets jobs). The landmark case was *Griggs v. Duke Power*, in which the U.S. Supreme Court held that job qualifications that were not relevant to a specific job and that on their face favored whites over Blacks were a violation of the law.[19] The Court clearly rejected the idea of prospect equality, but because it upheld the idea of equality by blocks or, to use the words of the law, "protected groups," a strong social equity signal was sent.

Race-consciousness as an affirmative action was to be based upon equality between Blacks and whites both in the work cohort and between the work cohort and the labor market—a kind of double application of equality.

John Nalbandian, in a recent review of case law on affirmative action in employment, observed that cases subsequent to *Griggs* have systematically limited "affirmative action tightly within the scope of the problem it was supposed to solve." The case law has sought to limit negative effects, such as unwanted inequality befalling nonminorities as a result of these programs.[20] *The University of California Regents v. Bakke* was the most celebrated example of judicial support for block equality to bring Blacks up to an enrollment level equal to whites, while at the same time protecting a nonminority claimant who would likely have qualified for admissions in the absence of a protected class.[21]

The affirmative action laws, and the Court's interpretations of them, have had a significant effect on equalizing employment opportunities, first between minorities and nonminorities and more recently by gender.[22] Nalbandian predicts, however, that the values of social equity may decline in a shift toward a new balance in employment practices, giving greater emphasis to efficiency.[23]

CONTRACTING

In the 1977 Public Works Employment Act the national government established a minority-business-enterprise 10-percent set-aside, requiring that 10 percent of all public works contracts be reserved for firms owned by minorities. The 10-percent set-aside was tested and affirmed in *Fullilove v. Klutznik* (1980). U.S. Supreme Court Justice Thurgood Marshall, for the majority, said:

> It is indisputable that Congress' articulated purpose for enacting the set-aside provision was to remedy the present effects of past racial discrimination. . . .
>
> Today, by upholding this race-conscious remedy, the Court accords Congress the authority to undertake the task of moving our society toward a state of meaningful equality of opportunity, not an abstract version of equality in which the effects of past discrimination would be forever frozen into our social fabric.[24]

For the minority, Potter Stewart argued:

On its face, the minority business enterprise provision at issue in this case denies the equal protection of the law. . . . The fourteenth Amendment was adopted to ensure . . . that the law would honor no preference based on lineage.[25]

Clearly, in this case, Marshall and Stewart use different domains and diverge on the issue of what is to be equal. To Marshall, block equality is essential, while to Stewart individual equality is required. Finally, as to employment (in this case contracting) opportunities, Marshall prefers it to be prospect equality while Stewart wants it to be means equality.

In a 1989 affirmation of the 10-percent set-aside provisions of the 1977 Federal Public Works Employment Act, the U.S. Supreme Court struck down a 30-percent set-aside for minority construction firms on contracts with the city of Richmond, Virginia. This was immediately regarded as a significant setback for the affirmative action programs of 33 states and over 200 municipalities. The *Richmond* decision reasoned that the fourteenth Amendment was violated by the set-aside because it denied *whites* equal protection of the law.[26] No doubt the set-aside provision has enhanced social equity. It is clear, however, that the law has used inequality to achieve equality.

GOVERNMENT SERVICE

In 1968 Andrew Hawkins, a Black handyman living in a neighborhood called the Promised Land, an all-Black section of Shaw, Mississippi, gathered significant data to show that municipal services such as paved streets, sewers, and gutters were unequally distributed. Because these services were available in the white section of Shaw, Hawkins charged that he and his class were deprived of the fourteenth Amendment guarantee of equal protection of the law. The U.S. District Court disagreed, saying that such a distribution had to do with issues of "municipal administration" that were "resolved at the ballot box."[27] On appeal, the decision of the District Court was overturned by the U.S. Court of Appeals, in part based on this amicus curiae brief from the Harvard-MIT (Massachusetts Institute of Technology) Joint Center for Urban Studies:

. . . invidious discrimination in the qualitative and quantitative rendition of basic governmental services violates an unyielding principle . . . that a trial court may not permit a defendant local government to rebut substantial statistical evidence of discrimination on the basis of race by entering a general disclaimer of illicit motive or by a loose and undocumented plea of administrative convenience. No such defense can be accepted as an adequate rebuttal of a prima facie case established by uncontroverted statistical evidence of an overwhelming disparity in the level and kind of public services rendered to citizens who differ neither in terms of desire nor need, but only in the color of their skin.[28]

While the appellate court ruled in Hawkins' favor, it construed the issue of equal protection so narrowly as to all but preclude significant court intervention in service allocation decisions where *intent* to discriminate cannot be conclusively demonstrated.

Desegregation of public schools following *Brown* v. *Board of Education* has resulted in varied and creative ways to define and achieve equality. Busing is a means of achieving at least the appearance of block equality. Busing has, however, been primarily from the inner city out. Magnet schools are an attempt to equalize the racial mix via busing in the other direction. Building schools at the margins of primarily white and primarily Black (or Hispanic) neighborhoods preserves the concept of the neighborhood school while achieving integration. The major problem has been jurisdictional or to use the language of equality, domain. The familiar inner city, primarily nonwhite school district surrounded by suburban, primarily white school districts significantly limits the possible equalizing effects of *Brown* v. *Board of Education*. This is especially the case when wealth and tax base follow white movement to the suburbs. State courts have in many places interpreted the equality clauses of state constitutions to bring about greater equality. Beginning with *Serrano* v. *Priest* in California, state equalization formulas for school funding have in many states required the augmentation of funding in poor districts.[29] Ordinarily this is done on a dollar-per-student basis. This procedure broadens the domain of the issue to the state, and it is also a simple formula for individual equality. It does, of course, bring about this equality by race-based inequality.

From the point of view of competing concepts of equality, the Kansas City, Missouri, School District desegregation cases may be the most interesting. After *Brown* v. *Board of Education* determined that separate but equal schooling was in fact unequal and unconstitutional, two questions remained. Was it sufficient for school districts and state departments of education to stop segregating? Or, was it necessary to repair the damage done by a century of racially separate school systems? In *United States* v. *Jefferson City Board of Education* the Court of Appeals declared that school officials: "have an affirmative duty under the Fourteenth Amendment to bring about an integrated unitary school system in which there are no Negro schools and no white schools—just schools. . . . In fulfilling this duty it is not enough for school authorities to offer Negro children the opportunity to attend formerly all-white schools. The necessity of overcoming the effects of the dual school system in this circuit requires integration of faculties, facilities and activities as well as students."[30]

Later in *Swann* v. *Charlotte-Mecklenburg Board of Education* the U.S. Supreme Court stated that "the objective today remains to eliminate from the public schools all vestiges of state imposed segregation."[31]

Two conditions pertain in Kansas City, Missouri. First is a dual housing market resulting from an interaction between private and governmental parties in the real estate industry, resulting in racially segregated residential areas. This has resulted in racially segregated schools roughly mirroring the segregated neighborhoods. Originally segregated all-Black schools are now schools of mostly Black students and teachers. The 11 suburban school districts surrounding Kansas City have almost all white students and teachers.

In *Jenkins* v. *Missouri* in 1984 the trial court under Judge Clark found the Kansas City Missouri School District and the State of Missouri liable for the unconstitutional segregation of the public schools.[32] The problem, of course, was the remedy. It is one thing to identify inequality; it is another to achieve equality. The School District tried and failed to secure passage of tax levies and bond issues to comply with Judge Clark's order.

Following the *Liddell* and *Griffin* cases, Judge Clark ordered both tax increases and bond issuances to cover the remedies sought in 1986.[33] The court also held that 75 percent of the cost of the plan was allocated to the State of Missouri for funding. The appellate court sustained all of Judge Clark's remedies with the exception of a 1.5-percent surcharge on incomes earned in Kansas City by nonresidents and instructed the state and the district to proceed with the remedies.[34]

If the majority of the citizens had turned down bond issues and had refused higher taxation to enable the school district to meet its desegregation objectives, how could the judge justify imposing those taxes as a matter of law? He said,

> A majority has no right to deny others the constitutional guarantees to which they are entitled. This court, having found that vestiges of unconstitutional discrimination still exist in the KCMSD is not so callous as to accept the proposition that it is helpless to enforce a remedy to correct the past violations. . . . The court must weigh the constitutional rights of the taxpayers against the constitutional rights of the plaintiff students in this case. The court is of the opinion that the balance is clearly in favor of the students who are helpless without the aid of this court.[35]

From an equality point of view, there are several examples of competing views of fairness. *First*, with the individual definition of equality, each vote is equal to each other vote, and the majority wins in a representative democracy. The court here clearly said that a majority cannot vote away the constitutional rights of a minority to equal schooling. *Second* is the dimension of time or intergenerational equality. The century of inequality in schools for Black children was to be remedied by a period of inequality toward non-minorities to correct for the past. *Third* is the question of domain. To what extent should the issue be confined to one school district? Because schools are constitutionally established in the State of Missouri, Judge Clark concluded that the funding solutions for desegregation were ultimately the responsibility of the state. Indeed, Arthur A. Bensen II, an attorney for the plaintiff, argued persuasively that it was fully within the authority of Judge Clark not only to impose either state or areawide financing to solve school desegregation but also to reorganize the school districts to eliminate the vestiges of prior discrimination.[36] The judge chose not to go that far.

Many more examples of equality can be traced to the courts, including equalizing funding for male and female student athletes in schools and colleges.

An especially interesting and relevant interpretation of the relationship between social equity and law as they have to do with public administration is provided by Charles M. Harr and Daniel W. Fessler. They suggest that the basis for equality in the law is less likely to be found in the United States Constitution and federal statutes and more likely to be found in state constitutions and statutes. "Recognizing the growing practical difficulties in relying on the equal protection clause, we assert the existence—the convincing and determinative presence—of a common law doctrine, *the duty to serve*, as an avenue of appeal that predates the federal Constitution."[37] More than 700 years before the Constitution, judge-made law in the England of Henry III held "that, at a fundamental level of social organization, all persons similarly situated in terms of need have an enforceable claim of equal, adequate and nondiscriminatory access to essential services; in addition this doctrine makes such legal access largely a governmental responsibility."[38] All monopolies—states, districts, utilities—are in the common law "clothed with a public interest" and obligated to the "doctrine of equal service."[39] If Harr and Fessler are right and if the state-based school funding equalization cases are illustrative, social equity will emerge at the grass roots rather than be imposed by the federal courts. . . .

CONCLUSION

It is a great irony of these times that all of this has occurred during a period referred to as the "age of the new individualism" or the "age of narcissism."[40] The dominant political ethos of the last 12 years has been pro-business and anti-government, anti-tax, anti-welfare, and particularly anti-bureaucracy. This ideological consensus seems to indicate that the majority share this ethos. In addition, this has been a lengthy period of sustained economic growth.

Yet, under the surface of majoritarian consensus, one sees a significant adjustment of the workforce from primary production to information and service at net lower wages, a sharp increase in two-worker families, a profound discontinuity in income and ability to acquire housing, transportation, and food, an increase in homelessness, and an increase in poverty.[41] Thus, while social equity has undergone development as a theory—and while public administrators have, following a social equity ethic, ameliorated the effects of inequality—still inequality has increased as a fact.[42]

Most important in these conclusions is the research which indicates that public administration tends to practice social equity. This is no surprise to those who are in public management at the local level. Public administrators solve problems, ameliorate inequalities, exercise judgment in service allocation matters, and use discretion in the application of generalized policy. Fairness and equity have always been common-sense guides for action. Some are concerned that this seems to put bureaucracy in a political role.[43] No doubt exists that public administration is a form of politics. The issue is, what theories and beliefs guide public administrators' actions? As it has evolved in the last 20 years, social equity has served to order the understanding of public administration and to inform the judgment necessary to be both effective and fair.

NOTES

1. H. George Frederickson, *The New Public Administration* (University: The University of Alabama Press, 1980), p. 37.
2. *Ibid.*, p. 6.
3. George Berkeley, *The Administrative Revolution: Notes on the Passing of Organization Man* (Englewood Cliffs, NJ: Prentice-Hall, 1971); Victor Thompson, *Without Sympathy or Enthusiasm* (University: The University of Alabama Press, 1975).
4. Herman Mertins, Jr., and Patrick J. Hennigan, eds. *ASPA Professional Standards and Ethics Workbook and Study Guide for Public Administration* (Washington: The American Society for Public Administration, 1981), pp. 22–23.
5. Dwight Waldo, *The Administrative State* (San Francisco: The Ronald Press, 1948).
6. Woodrow Wilson, "The Study of Administration," *Political Science Quarterly*, vol. 56 (December 1941; originally copyrighted in 1887).

7. York Willbern, "Is the New Public Administration Still With Us?" *Public Administration Review*, vol. 33 (July/August 1973), p. 376.

8. *Ibid.*, p. 378.

9. David K. Hart, "Social Equity, Justice and the Equitable Administrator"; Michael M. Harmon, "Social Equity and Organization Man: Motivation and Organizational Democracy"; Eugene B. McGregor, Jr., "Social Equity and the Public Service"; Steven R. Chitwood, "Social Equity and Social Service Productivity"; David O. Porter and Teddie Wood Porter, "Social Equity and Fiscal Federalism"; Orion J. White, Jr., and Bruce L. Gates, "Statistical Theory and Equity in the Delivery of Social Services," vol. 34, *Public Administration Review* (January/February 1974), pp. 3–51.

10. Douglas Rae and Associates, *Equalities* (Cambridge, MA: Harvard University Press, 1981), p. 3.

11. John A. Rawls, *A Theory of Justice* (Cambridge, MA: Harvard University Press, 1971).

12. Much of what appears in the following page is taken from Rae and Associates, *Equalities* (Cambridge, MA: Harvard University Press, 1981).

13. *Plessy v. Ferguson*, 163 U.S. 537 (1896).

14. *Brown v. Board of Education of Topeka* (I) 3/4/47 U.S. 483 (1954).

15. Rae, *op. cit.*, p. 66.

16. John Scharr, "Equality of Opportunity and Beyond," in NOMOS IX: *Equality*, J. Rowland Pennock and John W. Chapman, eds. (New York: Atherton Press, 1967), p. 231. See also Scharr, "Some Ways of Thinking About Equality," *Journal of Politics*, vol. 26 (November 1964), pp. 867–895.

17. Charles M. Haar and Daniel W. Fessler, *Fairness and Justice: Law in the Service of Equality* (New York: Simon and Schuster, 1986), p. 18.

18. Waldo, *op. cit.*

19. *Griggs v. Duke Power Company*, 401 U.S. 424 (1971). The U.S. Supreme Court in 1989 stepped considerably back from the Duke Power requirement that employees must demonstrate that the hiring requirements do not discriminate. In *Wards Grove Packing v. Antonio*, in a five-to-four decision, the U.S. Supreme Court now requires a plaintiff to prove employment discrimination. See *New York Times* (June 7, 1989), pp. 1 and 11. *Wards Grove Packing v. Antonio*, Doc. No. 87-1387, 5 June 1989.

20. John Nalbandian, "The U.S. Supreme Court's 'Consensus' on Affirmative Action," vol. 49, *Public Administration Review* (January/February 1989), pp. 38–45.

21. *University of California Regents v. Bakke*, 438 U.S. 265 (1978).

22. Patricia W. Ingraham and David H. Rosenbloom, "The New Public Personnel and the New Public Service," vol. 49, *Public Administration Review* (March/April 1989), pp. 116–125.

23. Nalbandian, *op. cit.*, p. 44.

24. *Fullilove v. Klutznik*, 448 U.S. 448 (1980).

25. *Idem.*

26. From *The New York Times* (January 24, 1989), pp. 1 and 12. See *City of Richmond v. Crosan*, 98 LE2d 976, 108 SCt 1010 (1989).

27. *Hawkins v. Town of Shaw*, 303 F. Supp. 1162, 1171 (N.D. MISS. 1969).

28. Haar and Fessler, *op. cit.*, p. 14.

29. *John Serrano, Jr., et al. v. Ivy Baker Priest*, 5 Cal. 3d584. See also Richard Lehane, *The Quest for Justice: The Politics of School Finance Reform* (New York: Longman, 1978).

30. *Green v. School Board*, 391 U.S. 430, 437-38 (1968).

31. *Swann v. Charlotte-Mecklenburg Board of Education*, 402 U.S. 1 (1971).

32. *Jenkins v. Missouri*, 593 F. Supp. 1485 (W. D. MO 1984).

33. *Liddell v. State of Missouri*, 731 F. 2D 1294, 1323 (8 Cir. 1984) and *Griffin v. School Board of Prince Edward County*, 377 U.S. 218, 233, 84 S. Cp. 1226, 1234, 12 L. Ed. 2d256 (1964).

34. *Jenkins v. State of Missouri*. 855 Fed. R. 8th Circuit 1297-1319.

35. *Jenkins v. State of Missouri*, 672 F. Supp. 412.

36. Arthur A. Bensen II, "The Liability of Missouri Suburban School Districts for the Unconstitutional Segregation of Neighboring Urban School Districts," University of Missouri at Kansas *City Law Review*, vol. 53 (Spring 1985), pp. 349–375. Bensen's argument was counter to case law based on *Milliken v. Bradley*, 418 U.S. 717 (1974), in which the U.S. Supreme Court found that jurisdictional boundaries are not barriers to effective segregation, except desegregation under certain conditions. Bensen claims that the Kansas City case satisfies those conditions.

37. Haar and Fessler, *op. cit.*, p. 43.

38. *Ibid.*, p. 21.

39. *Idem.*

40. Christopher Lasch, *The Culture of Narcissism: American Life in an Age of Diminishing Expectations* (New York: Norton, 1978).

41. Frank Levy, *Dollars and Dreams: The Changing American Income Distribution* (New York: Russell Sage Foundation, 1987).

42. William Julius Wilson, *The Truly Disadvantaged: The Inner City, the Underclass, and Public Policy* (Chicago: The University of Chicago Press, 1987).

43. Rodney E. Hero, "The Urban Service Delivery Literature: Some Questions and Considerations," *Polity*, vol. 18 (Summer 1986), pp. 659–677.

ADMINISTRATIVE DISSENT: WHISTLE-BLOWING

James S. Bowman

THE EMERGENCE OF WHISTLE-BLOWING

The late 1960s and 1970s witnessed the initiation of the "age of the whistle-blower." It was the C-5A military transport, the New York City Police Department, the Vietnam War, Watergate, and the Kerr-McGee Oklahoma nuclear plant that dramatized whistle-blowing: Ernest A. Fitzgerald exposed defense contract overruns; Frank Serpico spoke out against corruption in city government; Daniel Ellsberg made the famous Pentagon Papers public; the mysterious Deep Throat was instrumental in uncovering the misdeeds of the Nixon administration; Karen Silkwood's death represented the danger in trying to reveal information to the public. Although not every conscientious employee becomes a national *cause célèbre*, such employees have been responsible for disclosing problems such as regulatory corruption, merit system abuses, dangers to public health, and conflict-of-interest irregularities. Indeed, had it not been for whistle-blowers, the public would never have learned about most of the scandals of the past decade.

Given pervasive group norms in organizations, whistle-blowing is, nonetheless, not a common occurrence. Yet neither is whistle-blowing merely the product of a series of isolated incidents. Instead, it may be indicative and symbolic of the problems frequently encountered in contemporary management. It is for this reason that the issue of professional dissent is an important one. There are no ethics without action. Ethics cannot survive unless people speak their conscience when it really matters, when the essence of training programs and ethics codes is applied in actual situations.

Responsible commentators now believe that corruption is ubiquitous and systemic in American life and cannot simply be dismissed as a part of "post-Watergate morality" (Caiden and Caiden, 1979:308; Comptroller General of the United States, 1980).[1]

Although dissent at the workplace is as old as humankind, it has only recently crystallized into a movement comparable in content, if not scope, to earlier civil rights and liberation movements. By the late 1970s, whistle-blowing began to be institutionalized by the activities of public interest groups, professional associations, and Congress. This suggests how far society has come in its quest for truth and justice in organizations.

The more sensational examples of official impropriety, in short, have brought into focus latent concerns about the freedom of expression in government. People today are more receptive to these concerns than ever before, perhaps because the liberties of the public employee are the liberties of a substantial percentage of the citizenry. Blowing the whistle will continue as government grows larger, as expectations of work rise, as more females, with fresh perspectives on work, enter the labor force, as America increasingly becomes a nation of employees, and as corruption persists in bureaucracy. Alan F. Westin (Westin and Salisbury, 1980:xi) writes that "many observers . . . believe . . . [that] . . . demands for new individual rights . . . will reach their mature status in the 1980's."[2]

Although it may be true that the public is becoming more sympathetic to whistle-blowers, many bureaucracies remain hostile to them.[3] Representative William Clay (D., Mo.) has noted that whistle-blowers are the "new niggers" in organizational society, following student antiwar protesters, civil rights activists, and communists (U.S. Congress, 1980a:196). Once attention is focused on the employee, the bureaucracy knows how to deal with the problem. Dissenters are regularly given meaningless assignments, transferred to remote locations, forced to undergo psychiatric examinations, ordered to do work for which they are not qualified, assigned to "turkey farms," fired from their jobs, and otherwise neutralized and retaliated against by having their careers destroyed. By abusing personnel procedures, bureaucracy can rid itself of abnormality. Certainly it is easier to deal with the dissenter than the object of dissent. Public officials rarely welcome challenges to their authority, as exemplified by the Nixon White House designation of John Dean as a "bottom-dwelling slug."

Yet the vast majority of these employees are not malcontents, misfits, neurotics, crusaders, nor radicals. Typically, a whistle-blower is a middle manager, a knowledgeable individual who can see policy problems, but who may not have a vested interest in ensuring that they are never made public. Most are ordinary Americans with no record of political activism or animosity toward government. Indeed, the act of whistle-blowing is likely to be conservative because it seeks to restore, not change, a preexisting condition (Weinstein, 1979b:7). Few are poor workers experiencing problems in doing their jobs. The issues they raise are not generally questions of broad policy nor abstract questions of management ethics, but instead involve violations of law or serious dangers to public safety. She or he naively expects problems to be solved when they are brought to the attention of those in positions of authority. When they are not and corruption goes unchallenged, the conscientious employee exposes the problem by blowing the whistle. It is not, however, a whistle of authority, but one of desperation (Westin, 1981:2).

Presidents, senators, professional associations, public interest groups, ethicists, and journalists all have attempted to define whistle-blowing. A useful definition was offered by Alan Campbell, Director of the Office of Personnel Management, during the 1980 congressional oversight hearings on the subject.

Quite simply, I view whistle-blowing as a popular shorthand label for any disclosure of a legal violation, mismanagement, a gross waste of funds, an abuse of authority, or a danger to public health or safety, whether the disclosure is made within or outside the chain of command (U.S. Congress, 1980a:196–197).

Thus, a whistle-blower is an employee who reveals information about illegal, inefficient, or wasteful government action that endangers the health, safety, or freedom of the American public.

The difficulties in judging whistle-blowers and the issues exposed are vividly suggested by comparing Judas Iscariot and Martin Luther. Weighing all the dilemmas in blowing the whistle, as Sissela Bok suggests, is not an easy task. The ideal case—where the cause is just, where all administrative appeals have been exhausted, where responsibility is openly accepted, and where the dissenting employee is above reproach—is unusual.

Given the indispensable services performed by so many whistle-blowers, strong public support is often merited. But the new climate of acceptance makes it easy to overlook the dangers of whistle-blowing: of uses in error or in malice; of work and reputations unjustly lost for those falsely accused; of privacy invaded and trust undermined (Bok, 1979:3).

Bok suggests that different instances of whistle-blowing can be distinguished by using the rare, clear-cut cases as benchmarks to analyze more complex actions. Attorney Peter Raven-Hansen (1980:34) advises that such cases may be characterized by a whistle-blower who focuses on the abuse itself, not personalities, uses appropriate administrative channels before "going public," anticipates and documents retaliation, and knows when to give up and move on. Norman Bowie (1982) posits six criteria to be met if an act of whistle-blowing can be justified: (1) if it is done with an appropriate moral motive; (2) if all internal channels of dissent have been exhausted; (3) if it is based on evidence that would persuade a reasonable person; (4) if an analysis has been made of the seriousness, immediacy and specificity of the problem; (5) if it is commensurate with one's responsibility; and (6) if it has some chance of success. Ultimately, the courts have maintained that a balance must be struck between the exercise of free speech and the authority of government to discharge employees for the good of the service. The difficulty in defining this balance is no excuse for permitting the kind of abuse discussed earlier. Dissent in organizations suggests that society questions the idea that management possesses superior ethical wisdom and desires a new balance between employee rights and management perogatives (see Ewing, 1983).

There are at least two significant societal issues related to whistle-blowing. The first is responsibility and accountability in a system of representative democracy. In light of pervasive citizen distrust in government, this is hardly an academic or philosophical problem. Ways need to be found to introduce democratic rights into bureaucracies. The second issue is that in order to assure responsibility and accountability, due process procedures are necessary to protect employees who care about the general interest. Effective methods need to be discovered to balance an individual's duty to his or her employer with his or her duty to the public. In fact, "many of the rights and privileges . . . so important to a free society that they are constitutionally protected . . . are vulnerable to abuse through an employer's power" (Blades, 1967:1407). Society has a right, in a word, to learn about significant problems in American politics without having those who expose them destroy their careers in the process.

It is critical, in short, that the "I win, you lose," zero-sum approach to dissent in organizations change. Responsible protest should be treated fairly to the benefit of both the employee and the employer. Directing corrective efforts to the dissenter him/herself instead of the policy issue in question will not alter the conditions that make whistle-blowing necessary. Disclosure of waste, illegal activity, and abuse of power should be seen as a commitment to make government more worthy of public trust. Open discussion strengthens, not weakens, democracy. Despite the attention that dissent in organizations has received in recent years, whistle-blowing alone will never establish standards of public accountability and credibility that the citizenry deserves and expects. If, however, the measures reviewed below were instituted, blowing the whistle would be less necessary than it is today.

PROTECTING DISSENTERS

If whistle-blowing has come of age, it does not automatically follow that effective plans of action are developed and implemented. Since the lack of internal procedures is frequently responsible for whistle-blowing (U.S. Congress, 1978:2), what changes might serve to protect the rights of dissenters while assuring effective management? Robert F. Allen (1980:37ff) identifies four elements of any successful, long-range change program.

First, in an effort to deal with the causes of behavior instead of its symptoms, administrators should ask themselves: "What did we contribute to this behavior?" Second, instead of relying on simple explanations for organizational problems, thorough understanding involves: (1) analysis of the organization's cultural setting, (2) introduction of the possibility of change and employee involvement, (3) implementation of new strategies, and (4) evaluation of change and development of a continuing renewal process. Third, by creating answers to such questions as "what behavior is rewarded and penalized by the institution?" a sound data base can be established. Finally, an audit of the organization's ethical and moral results, can point the way to constructive change. While this approach does not deemphasize individual responsibility nor ignore scandals, it does address the underlying weaknesses that produce them. Blaming the bearer of bad tidings, after all, is a way of freeing conforming employees and their organizations from complicity in what is happening around them.

Whistle-blowing would not be necessary if managerial indifference was not so pervasive and if effective procedures were used to incorporate dissent into decisionmaking. Thus, in the context of long-range change, the need to resort to whistle-blowing in the short run can be reduced by providing mechanisms to ensure that managers take criticism seriously.

Although it may be that some executives welcome criticism, communication techniques such as suggestion boxes and "open door" policies lack power to compel top management to examine criticisms they are reluctant to deal with, and can turn out to be a trap for the employee. Since she or he is objecting to management policy, it is not reasonable to expect an unbiased review of the dissent or the dissenter. More systematic procedures may not entirely deal with these problems, but they may have a significant deterrent effect if employers know that their actions will be subject to review. Both internal and external checks may be useful depending on the circumstances. The absence of such safeguards virtually guarantees that dissent will develop into confrontation between management and the employee.

One internal device is an "ethical audit." Used for years in business, the social audit is a methodical review of a corporation's activities in the area of social responsibility (e.g., environmental pollution, affirmative action, community relation). An expanded or refocused effort could include ethical concerns in all areas of decisionmaking beyond those normally included in a social audit. Since audits are usually done after the fact, an ongoing technique used in some organizations is the appointment of an ethical advisor comparable to a legal or financial advisor, as noted earlier. This person could act not only as a "devil's advocate" in policy decisions as mentioned in the last section, but also could formulate ethical statements, design an employee bill of rights, serve as an ombudsman or inspector general, provide space on standard forms for dissenting opinions, and/or serve on review boards.

A second possibility would be to formalize the decision-making process. Policy objectives could be clearly specified and criteria established for all decisionmakers so that the procedure and content of decisions would be made more visible and accountable. The organization's standards and how they are being implemented could be part of its major reports. Bureaucratic competition in the form of overlapping jurisdictions and rival organizations may also prevent concentrations of power and guard against corruption.

Since the personnel process is frequently used to harass and remove whistle-blowers, a third internal check would be to emphasize the importance of ethics and employee rights throughout the personnel system as discussed earlier, including agency-sponsored outplacement services for separated employees. Finally, Sissela Bok (1980:292) suggests that the organization should develop and state conditions, perhaps in a code of conduct, under which the whistle *must* be blown. This could lessen the risk and tension of whistle-blowing by reducing the burden of choice for the individual critic.

However helpful such internal mechanisms may be in improving management and protecting individual rights, their limitations must be recognized. Kenneth T. Bogen (1978:129) points out that "the true protection offered by . . . [any] . . . intra-organizational procedures depends upon the good will of management, the very lack of which often produces whistle-blowing."

External checks on administrative responsibility are, therefore, desirable. Employee unions, for example, can assist whistle-blowers. Historically

unions have been more interested in the material conditions of work life than in civil liberties. Nonetheless, as members become more sophisticated and educated, activities in this area should grow, as long as employees cannot protect themselves without the union. Many of the same comments also apply to professional societies, most of which have been reluctant to defend the independence of their members. Useful programs that might be undertaken would be to provide ethical consulting services, operate preferential reemployment networks for whistle-blowers, and publicize those organizations that violate professional standards.

The most popular current remedy for organizational abuse is statutory relief for whistle-blowers. Since action is ordinarily not taken against agency management, however, there is little reason not to retaliate against dissenters. Thus, a recent study of eight public laws that include employee protection sections found that such provisions have had limited success (Chalk and von Hippel, 1979:55). Perhaps the most innovative type of statutory relief would be to extend unlawful discrimination on the basis of race, color, religion, sex, national origin, age, and union membership to political, social, or economic views. Lawrence Blades (1967:1433) argues that it is anomalous that the courts provide relief to an employee discharged because of race or religion, but they do not provide protection for an employee discharged because of the exercise of free speech. Indeed, it has been pointed out that as long as federal law denies employees the right to engage in partisan political activities and the right to strike, their constitutional right to petition the government should be broadly construed. Failing that, statutory hiring preferences for abused employees could be enacted.

The most discussed form of statutory protection in recent years has been the Civil Service Reform Act of 1978. The act is an effort to strengthen the processes by which wrongdoing can be exposed and dealt with by establishing a channel for reporting fraud, waste, and abuse. In this way, the surfacing of allegations and evidence of government illegalities would no longer have to depend on random and sometimes bizarre events. Part of the act established the Merit Systems Protection Board and the Office of Special Counsel with the power to investigate prohibited personnel practices, including reprisals against whistle-blowers. Although it may be too early for definitive judgments, most indications are not reassuring (U.S. Congress, 1980a; Comptroller General of the United States, 1980; *Federal Times*, August 23, 1982).

Even though the Office of the Special Counsel is required to maintain the anonymity of the whistle-blower, agencies are permitted to investigate themselves. To date, such investigations have been less than satisfactory. If the Special Counsel determines that a prohibited personnel practice is involved, the case is referred to the Merit Systems Protection Board. In carrying out its function, the board has adopted more formal judicial procedures than had existed under the Civil Service Commission, which had been called a "whistle-blower's graveyard." The initial, precedent-setting cases before the board suggests a tendency for the rights of dissenters to be subordinated to the needs of efficiency. Equally significant is that in 1980 the Office of Special Counsel was subject to massive budget cuts, which reduced its staff by two-thirds and adversely affected all areas of operations, including the near total curtailment of statutory activities. In late 1982, the first Senate-confirmed Special Counsel (the three previous incumbents had been appointed on an acting basis) inherited an office plagued by budget problems and low staff morale, and threatened by Congress with extinction. It appears that only now are systematic arrangements being put in place to provide a regularized means to investigate wrongdoing.

As Rosemary Chalk and Frank von Hippel (1979:55) point out, whatever due process protections "are provided [they] will have little value unless they are embedded in a process which deals effectively with the substance of dissent." The situation of the whistle-blower, in other words, will only be marginally improved unless the issues she or he raises are dealt with. If internal checks are little more than window dressing and external checks are ignored or turned into management tools, little change can be expected and confidence in government can only be further undermined.

Indeed, congressional hearings on the implementation of the Civil Service Reform Act consisted largely of, in the words of the subcommittee chairwoman, "blowing the whistle on whistle-blowing protections" (U.S. Congress, 1980a:33). Most of the testimony claimed that the safeguards were a failure, and that reforms had been transformed to where there is no more protection now (perhaps less) than under the preexisting system. In a prescient observation, Deena Weinstein (1979a:134) stated that:

> All of the proposed reforms of bureaucratic abuses which work within the present system confront a basic dilemma. The ground of hierarchical administrative authority is that a specific group of officials should be held responsible for the conduct . . . of the organization. The presence of abuses . . . shows that officials cannot or will not behave responsibly. . . . Reform of abuses concentrates in making officials accountable to other agencies. Such accountability, however, weakens their autonomy or, in the case of cooption, allows them to be even more abusive. . . . Reform, then, diffuses responsibility and gives officials excuses for their failures.

Stated differently, intentionally developed devices for guaranteeing accountability are as likely as not to formalize techniques of evasion. Weinstein goes on to argue that the reason for this is that there are deep social conflicts over the purposes organizations should serve. "Without the consensual loyalty and trust of the citizenry," J. Patrick Dobel (1978:969) writes in a treatise on corruption, "reforms will simply be shams to rationalize the continuation of corrupt practices."

In short, whistle-blowing is a manifestation of serious problems concerning the legitimacy of American government. Both the long- and short-run methods discussed above to help protect dissenters may be quite useful in specific organizations and for individuals. Until more basic issues about the conduct of administration are addressed, however, such devices can never be truly effective in reducing the underlying need to blow the whistle, and whistle-blowing will remain a dangerous, if essential, task. The quest for more ethical government must ultimately permit public employees to fulfill their role as autonomous and responsible citizens in American democracy.

CONCLUSION

There is a compelling need for clearer guidance in identifying major sources of unethical conduct and for a clarification of significant problems to make public employees more sensitive to actual and potential problems that challenge government as a whole. Agencies should undertake a variety of steps to alert their officials to ethical dilemmas, among those discussed above:

1. Initiation of an imaginative training program
2. Development of an enforceable code of conduct
3. Establishment of channels and encouragement of professional dissent

Careful thought in advance about ethical problems will lead to a working consensus on what is acceptable conduct, and thereby avoid inappropriate behavior arising from ignorance. The administrative task is to prevent the necessity for whistle-blowing, enforce ethical codes, and provide training opportunities. When organizations employ professionals, in other words, they have the obligation to provide support structures for professional actions.

If an agency desires ethical conduct, the first thing it should do is to have a meeting of top management. The head of the department should explain that she or he does not want anyone in the organization to engage in unethical practices, and that training programs, codes of ethics, and professional dissent will be developed and supported. It should be affirmed that serving the public interest is a vocation requiring intellectual excellence and moral integrity. If top managers do not understand this, resignations should be requested (Hill, 1976:13). Such an initiative, albeit drastic, will bring about fundamental—not cosmetic—changes in the way business is done in the agency. Exemplary behavior on the part of senior managers plus the threefold program of action discussed in this analysis will keep moral discourse alive.

Examples of the failure of reform efforts are not hard to find, and cynics delight in recounting them. They fail when they are but window dressing from the outset meant to please or exhaust employees, or when they are turned into manipulative management tools (Bok, 1980:292; Feldman, 1980:477). A great deal of energy is expended in bewailing the impossibility of combatting waste, corruption, and mismanagement in government. Such energy would be put to better

use in employing the techniques discussed here. Ethics in government is a matter of social relations; substantial improvement can be expected only if organizations and their members act. The release or promotion of those whose conduct warrants it is a matter of vigorous personnel management.

Organizations must, in their own interest, come to grips with the complexity of their operations that seem to make it possible for questionable practices to flourish. The problem of administrative ethics is one of discretion in the pursuit of the public good. Agencies must plant and nourish a standard of ethical performance that takes into account the realities of everyday management. Ignoring the problem will not make it go away, and may well make it worse. Surely it is better for administrators to be aware of the complexities of important issues than to act on unexamined premises. The oath of office creates a moral community among government employees that demands an ethical commitment to the public trust. The challenge is to instill in the civil service a program of action that builds upon that oath. . . .

NOTES

1. Or, as Monypenny (1953a:428) stated it 30 years ago, . . . "corruption may be a part of the political system rather than an excrescence upon it."
2. This is not necessarily a concensus view. Gene G. James (1980:99, 104), for example, notes the rise in whistle-blowing incidents, but argues that unless there are major changes in laws and professional associations, whistle-blowing should not be expected to increase in the near future.

   Available evidence on the fate of whistle-blowers may be germane, but is also conflicting. In an in-depth analysis of ten cases, Westin (1981) found that just one person won reinstatement, two secured partial damages, whereas the other seven were unable to obtain vindication of their professional reputations. James (1980:103) cites a study of complaints filed under the Occupational Health and Safety Act, which found that of 60 cases, one was won, eight lost, and the rest were pending—hardly a record to encourage further dissent. Bok (1980:283) claims that most whistle-blowers "are destined to fail." Yet Waters (1978:28) states that nearly all whistle-blowers who have been punished for their views won their cases when they challenged their punishment in court.

3. The problem stems from the fact that bureaucracies resemble authoritarian states that do not permit legitimate opposition. Employees in hierarchical organizations cannot act politically except in disloyal opposition; dissent is a political phenomenon that occurs in organizations that are not supposed to be political systems (Weinstein, 1979a). The reason for this is that the prevailing, if long discredited, administrative myth is that bureaucracy is a rational, non-partisan, technical process, divorced from politics. Ethical action punctures the myth of value-free neutrality and social concensus in administration. It suggests that bureaucracy is a political system consisting of human beings as purposive actors with a sense of individual responsibility.

REFERENCES

BAILEY, S. K. (1960). Ethics and the Politican. Occasional paper, Center for the Study of Democratic Institutions, Santa Barbara, Calif.

BLADES, L. E. (1967). Employment at Will vs. Individual Freedom: On Limiting the Abusive Exercise of Employer Power. *Columbia Law Review* 67:1404–1435.

BOGEN, K. T. (1978). Whistle-blowing by Technical Experts. Unpublished Thesis, Princeton University, Princeton, N.J.

BOK, S. (1979). Whistleblowing and Professional Responsibility. *New York Education Quarterly* 11:2–10.

BOK, S. (1980). Whistleblowing and Professional Responsibilities. In *Teaching Ethics in Higher Education*, D. Callahan and S. Bok (eds.). New York: Plenum, pp. 277–295.

BOWIE, N. E. (1982). *Business Ethics*. Englewood Cliffs, N.J.: Prentice-Hall.

CAIDEN, G. (1978). Administrative Reform: A Prospectus. *International Review of Administrative Science* 44:106–120.

CAIDEN, G. (1980). Public Maladministration and Bureaucratic Corruption: A Comparative Perspective. Paper presented at the National Conference on Fraud, Waste, and Abuse, Pittsburgh, Pa.

CAIDEN, G., and CAIDEN, N. (1979). Coping with Administrative Corruption: An Academic Perspective. In *Dynamics of Development—An International Perspective*, S. K. Shama (ed.). New Delhi: Concept Publishing, pp. 478–494.

CHALK, R., and VON HIPPEL, F. (1979). Due Process for Dissenting "Whistle-Blowers." *Technology Review* 81:49–55.

COMPTROLLER GENERAL OF THE UNITED STATES (1978). *Federal Agencies Can, and Should Do More to Combat Fraud in Government Programs*. Washington, D.C.: General Accounting Office.

COMPTROLLER GENERAL OF THE UNITED STATES (1980). *The Office of the Special Counsel Can Improve Its Management of Whistleblower Cases*. Washington, D.C.: General Accounting Office.

DOBEL, J. P. (1978). The Corruption of the State. *American Political Science Review* 72:858–873.

EWING, D. (1983). *Do It My Way or You're Fired!* New York: Wiley.

FEDERAL TIMES, August 23, 1982.

FELDMAN, D. L. (1980). Combatting Waste in Government. *Policy Analysis* 6:467–477.

HILL, I. (1976). The Ethical Basis of Economic Freedom. Paper presented at National Leadership Conference of the American Medical Association, Chicago.

JAMES, G. G. (1980). Whistle Blowing: Its Nature and Justification. *Philosophy in Context* 10:99–117.

MONYPENNY, P. (1953a). A Code of Ethics for Public Administration. *George Washington Law Review* 21:423–444.

RAVEN-HANSEN, P. (1980). Do's and Don'ts for Whistleblowers: Planning for Trouble. *Technology Review* 82:34–44.

U.S. CONGRESS, HOUSE OF REPRESENTATIVES (1980a). *Civil Service Reform 1980—Whistleblowers*. Committee on Post Office and Civil Service Subcommittee on Civil Service, 96th Cong., 2d sess.

U.S. CONGRESS, SENATE, COMMITTEE ON GOVERNMENTAL AFFAIRS (1978). *The Whistleblowers: A Report on Federal Employees Who Disclose Acts of Government Waste, Abuse, and Corruption*. Washington, D.C.: U.S. Government Printing Office.

U.S. CONGRESS, SENATE, COMMITTEE ON GOVERNMENT OPERATIONS, SUBCOMMITTEE ON INTERGOVERNMENTAL RELATIONS (1973). *Confidence and Concern: Citizens View American Government*. Washington, D.C.: U.S. Government Printing Office.

U.S. CONGRESS, SENATE, COMMITTEE ON APPROPRIATIONS (1980b). *GAO Effects Related to the Problems of Fraud in the Government*. 96th Cong., 2d sess.

WATERS, J. S. (1987). Catch 20.5: Corporate Morality as an Organizational Phenomenon. *Organizational Dynamics* 6:3–19.

WEINSTEIN, D. (1979a). *Bureaucratic Oppositions*. New York: Pergamon.

WEINSTEIN, D., (1979b). Opposition to Abuse Within Organizations: Heroism and Legalism. *ALSA Forum* IV:5–21.

WESTIN, A. F. (1981). *Whistle-Blowing! Loyalty and Dissent in the Corporation*. New York: McGraw-Hill.

WESTIN, A.F., and SALISBURY, S. (1980). *Individual Rights in the Corporation*. New York: Pantheon.

LARRY J. BROWN: CULTURES CLASH AS OLD-TIME POLITICS CONFRONTS BUTTON-DOWN MANAGEMENT

Rob Gurwitt

A few years back, during one of the heavy Florida rains that settle in from time to time over Tampa Bay, residents living around one Hillsborough County lake called their county commissioner, asking for help to keep it from overflowing. He sent out a crew to start pumping.

A day later, despite the county workers' best efforts, the water level was still rising. After some investigation, it turned out that the commissioner from the neighboring district, responding to his own set of worried constituents, had also dispatched a crew with a pump. Unknown to the two crews, each was frantically draining water into the other's lake.

That story resurfaced not long ago as the lead to a full-page *Tampa Tribune* editorial lambasting the elected commissioners for taking such matters into their own hands. "That account," the newspaper growled, "is perhaps the ultimate horror story on the effects of county commissioners meddling in administrative affairs."

Editorial disgruntlement, however, did nothing to prevent commissioners from weighing in a week later with a series of gripes about the county administrator's handling of his job. They complained about his budgeting procedures, his hiring practices and his personnel policies. One went so far as to accuse the administrative staff of trying to orchestrate a media campaign against the commission. "I personally resent the utilization of high-priced county employees . . . to turn the tide of public sentiment in favor of the administrator," he wrote.

For close to two decades now, Hillsborough County's commissioners and its professional administrators have been exchanging such barbs. Their struggles have been spiced by two major corruption scandals, and have helped paralyze county government to the point where it has fallen dismally short in meeting some basic demands.

There is no mystery to what happened. During those 20 years, the portion of Hillsborough County that sits outside Tampa grew from a loose patchwork of staid, rural communities into a burgeoning metropolitan area. Its political institutions were left standing in the dust. . . .

. . . So two years ago, an almost desperate county commission imported Larry J. Brown to administer the county government. Brown, who had just spent five years overseeing urbanized Arlington County, Virginia, is regarded by his professional peers in the International City Management Association as one of the leaders in county government. He is a nationally prominent example of the direction county management everywhere is headed: technically proficient, managerially innovative, almost corporate in his outlook. And he has set out to reshape Hillsborough County government in his image.

It is not proving to be easy. Accusations of bad faith, sometimes overt, sometimes spoken quietly, are once again traveling up and down the short hallway between the administrator's and commissioners' offices. Brown has angered a vocal faction of the county staff and stirred doubts about his ability to navigate Hillsborough's treacherous political shoals.

In part, the problem is one of personalities. Brown, a 6-foot-4-inch piano-playing technocrat of serene self-confidence, is moving with considerable speed. "I don't wear well," he says. "People give me a job to do, and I do it. I just tell them, 'Get out of my way.' "

Getting out of the way is not a habit of Hillsborough County politicians, though, which leads to a more fundamental dilemma. Officials are discovering that fixing the county's service delivery machinery, which is Brown's responsibility, is not enough on its own to set the county back on course. The people who actually decide where the county should be headed—the politicians—are part of the equation as well. But as pressure has grown on them to cast off their old habits, to shift away from who-you-know informality in their dealings with the county machinery and their constituents, they have found themselves casting about with only marginal success for a new role.

"The county is in transition," Brown says. "Whether or not I survive is not as important as recognizing that it is in transition from that which used to be the established way of doing business to something else out there that people can't quite define." . . .

Just how far the county had to go on that score was borne home in 1983, when three of the five commissioners were convicted of taking bribes for votes on rezoning requests. County government, federal prosecutors charged, had become a "racketeering" enterprise.

The impact of the bribery scandal was severe. Never very high, public confidence in county government plunged. But the scandal also boosted efforts to pass a home rule charter expanding the commission from five to seven members and drawing a hard and fast line between the commissioners and the administrator. As William Reece Smith Jr., a prominent Tampa attorney and former head of the American Bar Association, politely puts it, "County commissioners, it was anticipated, would have less administrative responsibility and less involvement in county administration." It passed overwhelmingly.

Things didn't quite work out as planned. Despite changes in its membership, the board squared off in 1985 against Administrator Norman Hickey over its right to call meetings with county department heads—even when Hickey objected. They eventually compromised, but relations were permanently soured; Hickey quit the next year to go run San Diego County. That was when the board began looking around for someone of Larry Brown's caliber.

It really had no choice. By 1986, the county was in desperate straits, the results of a planning hiatus that had lasted for years while commissioners "were more interested in lining their own pockets than in benefiting the county," in the words of Tampa developer Edd McGrath.

The roads were a mess. Where bumper-to-bumper traffic had once been a rarity, it now stretched from one end of the county to the other. Even worse was the sewage treatment system. "There wasn't adequate financing, there was not adequate management to provide for planning and construction, and there was not adequate integration of land-use planning with facilities planning," says Jim Bourey, the assistant county administrator now responsible for overseeing planning efforts.

Leaks and overflows brought threatened lawsuits and thousands of dollars in fines against the county. The state ordered officials to keep developers from hooking up to most of the county's plants. Some developers sued the county for promising them connections and then denying them hookups to its facilities.

Finally, there was the county organization itself. Layers of bureaucracy muffled direction from the top before it reached workers on the line. Morale took repeated hits from the scandals, from mistakes and from tongue-lashings delivered by commissioners in the aftermath of those mistakes. There was little premium placed on performance. When Brown arrived, says Assistant County Administrator Ruth Ann Bramson, "the only awards program was for time in the system. . . . What kind of a message does that send about the organization's priorities?"

Small wonder, then, that Brown won his administrator's position on a unanimous vote. It was a rare mandate, the St. Petersburg Times noted wryly at the time, coming from commissioners "who normally won't even give each other the time of day, much less agree on it."

The commissioners were equally unified in what they wanted. "Almost to a person, in a variety of words, they said, 'We want change,'" Brown reports of his conversations with the commissioners at the time.

They got it. In a controversial early move, Brown knocked out entire layers of mid-level management, slicing the organization to five levels, from administrator to work crew.

"Hillsborough County government provides services," Brown explains. "We don't make widgets; we do things for people. If we want to improve the quality of that, then we have to concentrate our resources on the street folks who are actually delivering it and not on the overhead of the organization, which is basically put in place, over time, to filter information between decision makers."

The idea is to make it easier for information to get from the street to the top and back down, and to shift authority down to the employees who can use it to make decisions more efficiently and boldly than in the past. . . .

Inevitably, that attitude has brought political fallout from some longtime managers and, as a result, from the commissioners. "Morale of the employees has been at an all-time low since Mr. Brown began his reorganizations," Commissioner Rubin Padgett wrote at the end of January in his evaluation of Brown's job performance. "Employee morale has plummeted," echoed Pam Iorio. "Management by chaos," complained a third, James "Big Jim" Selvey.

It's not clear just how bad morale is. Bobby Smith, president of the county's American Federation of State, County and Municipal Employees local, says that within his own parks department, "people seem to have more pride and enthusiasm about doing their work now." Adds Keith Templeman, an administrative support manager in the public-utilities department who lost some areas of responsibility with the reorganizations, "Sure, it's a little bit of a kick in your ego. But if they give me a smaller job to do but give me more authority to do it with, maybe it wasn't that diminished."

Brown's attitude is simple. "Some people deserve to be nervous, because they've never been evaluated on performance," he says. "It's a very small number, but when there was a threat in the past, they'd call up their friend, who'd call a friend, and all of a sudden the threat was gone. It doesn't work like that anymore.". . .

Brown's strongest support for his vision of professional management may well come not from the board, which has to decide whether or not to renew his contract a year from now, but from Tampa's business elite.

"The business community has come increasingly to appreciate the vital importance of efficient and effective county government, and of good public servants," says attorney Reece Smith, who is a leading member of Tampa's old-line business elite. What that translates into is business support for a commission willing to give a professional administrator and his staff the room to work.

It is not only Tampa's older leadership that appreciates Brown's style. Change is coming to the executive suites of local banks, insurance companies and other businesses as a generation of leaders retires, companies are bought up, and management shifts occur. Some members of the new generation of leaders see Brown almost as one of them.

"Larry Brown is attempting to run the county like a business, which means trying to clean up the bureaucracy," says George Koehn, president and chief executive officer of SunBank in Tampa. "If he were left alone to run that thing, the results he'd get would be far superior to anything the county commission could come up with."

But business pressure on the board to come together may be offset by the very thing that makes a clear direction so important: Hillsborough's growth. New players are arriving every day, and once-weak voices, such as neighborhood associations and environmental groups, are learning how to turn up the volume when they want commissioners to listen. Busansky won her seat last year with civic group support, beating a Tampa city councilman who had an enormous campaign treasury funded by development interests. As the newer players struggle with developers over how the county will grow, the board may find itself pulled apart in ever more painful ways.

Still, Brown is convinced that, with time, Hillsborough County's politicians will see things his way simply because, as politicians, they can't afford not to. "From the civic association types, to the political power structure, to the behind-the-scenes movers and shakers, they all know the county has got to change in order to be relevant in the future," he says. "You keep county government the way it is, and it'll be ignored."

TO TELL THE TRUTH—BUT THE WHOLE TRUTH?

Senator McClain left the committee room and headed for the elevator that would take him to the underground train back to his office suite. As he stared idly at the closed doors of the elevator, he reminded himself that humility in victory was a virtue. The meeting of the Subcommittee on Investigations for the Committee on Overseas Trade had gone quite nicely. He had managed to obtain the appointment as chairman of the selection committee for foreign trade ambassador. Senator McClain knew that with all the other work the committee had to do before recess, this post put him in position to literally name the new trade ambassador. Yes, he would have to work with the people from the White House and, yes, he would have to listen to the majority leader's staff people, but in the final analysis he would be the one to present a name to the committee. He had a very good idea what that name would be.

While Senator McClain was riding the train back to his office, Jason Masters was winding up the morning staff meeting. Jason had served as Senator McClain's administrative assistant for the past two terms. Prior to that, he had been a legislative assistant in another senator's office. Jason Masters was an insider on Capitol Hill. "The last item for today is the probable appointment of the senator to head up the selection of the new trade ambassador. Sandy and Wendy, I want you to be on this project. The senator will probably be calling a meeting with the White House people for next week. Make sure that you leave your mornings flexible. That's all for now; let's remember that all calls from the media about this will be referred to me."

Wendy Sanko quickly went back to her desk and phoned her roommate. "Bad news," she began when her roommate answered. "I've got to work next week, so have fun at Atlantic City." Just as she put the phone down, Sandy Carpenter dropped into the chair next to her desk. His short, blond, curly hair, which explained his nickname, was already rumpled from his constant habit of running his hands through it. "So, what do you think old Mastermind Masters wants us to do with this one?" Sandy was the newest member of Senator McClain's staff and had not yet learned the innate caution practiced by the more experienced members. "Ask him yourself," Wendy solemnly murmured, "he's standing right behind you." "In my office—right now," growled Jason.

When a sheepish Sandy and a resigned Wendy had settled into the plush chairs around the small conference table in Jason's office, he let the silence stretch out for just a few moments longer than necessary. Finally, he leaned back and folded his hands over his stomach. "I picked you two for a reason. Sandy, despite your uncontrolled mouth, you're the best researcher in the office—at the moment. Wendy, I think you have talent and you're about ready to move up. If you handle this right, I may start mentioning you for one of the assistant positions coming vacant." Sandy and Wendy knew better than to make any comment at this point. Jason would ask them if they had questions at the end, and both knew he hated to be interrupted.

"Here is a list of names that I want you to start working on. Sandy, you'll be responsible for digging up all the financial data on them so that we won't be surprised in the hearings. Wendy, you start mentioning these names to the staff people of the other senators on the committee. Be sure to leave them with the impression that we don't need any more names. The current biographic descriptions are in these packets." Jason slid a bulky manila folder across the table to each of them. "Any questions?" Wendy paused, then said firmly, "Are these clear with the leadership?" "Good question," replied Jason. "You let me worry about the leadership. I'm having lunch with the majority leader's chief of staff today. By this afternoon, we'll have the clearance."

That's one smart lady, Jason thought as Wendy and Sandy left the office. I hope that she is smart enough to get the message I sent her. Jason turned to the pile of papers on his desk and began to skim them for content and possible controversy. The door opened and Senator McClain strode in with a jubilant look on his face. "It's in the bag, Jason," he beamed. "Call Toliver and tell him to get ready to go under the microscope." "He's already been warned, Senator," Jason replied. "I talked to his lawyer yesterday about the problem and was told they were fixing it." "Good," Senator McClain grinned, "I'm going over to the Trade Department this afternoon to lay the ground work with the secretary. I don't want him to feel like he isn't on the inside track on this one."

Two weeks later, Wendy and Sandy sat together in the senate cafeteria over coffee. Sandy was clearly upset. "I tell you that it doesn't make any sense. Why would Masters have me doing this research? It's so easy the summer intern could do it. Every time I call somebody, it's as if they expected the call and had the information on their desk. Not one person has said they'll get back to me." Wendy shrugged her shoulders. "So what? Most of these people have been trying to get an appointment for years. They probably have their background information updated monthly." Sandy frowned. "Perhaps that's true of their own people, but when was the last time a major bank didn't tell you that it would have to check with its client before it released financial data?" Wendy thought a moment then offered, "Maybe the FBI has already done the background security check so the figures were recently compiled." "Doubtful, but possible," said Sandy as he finished his coffee.

Wendy stopped Jason in the corridor later that day. "Jason, we've finished the background stuff on that list of names for trade ambassador. What do you want us to do with it?" "Put it on my conference table—including any notes you or Sandy made," Jason paused. "And by the way, nice job." Wendy was puzzled. Jason never complemented people for routine work. In fact, Jason rarely complimented people for extraordinary work. As Jason walked away, Wendy got the feeling she was missing something. Wendy didn't like that feeling, so she decided to do a little digging on her own.

By the end of the week, Wendy had put it all together. She asked for a meeting with Jason and was scheduled for early Monday morning. Wendy was strangely calm as she began the meeting. "I found out something very interesting about Wolford Toliver. Did you know that he declared bankruptcy in 1952? Moreover, did you know that he was subsequently involved in an insider trading scheme that the Security and Exchange Commission investigated?" Jason was perfectly still. "The thing that I'm sure you do know is that none of this is indicated on his financial disclosure forms," Wendy finished.

Jason steepled his fingers in front of his face and tapped them gently together. "I was wrong; you're the best researcher in this office, not Sandy." Jason got up from the table and walked over to look out the window. "Wendy, you may as well get used to this if you plan to go any further in your career. Wolford Toliver is far and away the best person for this appointment. Senator McClain has been trying to entice him into government service for a long time. Toliver has always objected by saying he couldn't stand the light of day. Six months ago, he finally told the senator about his early financial problems and the brush with the Security and Exchange Commission. We did some legal research and discovered that the bankruptcy court sealed the records and the SEC investigation resulted in no charges. His disclosure forms are technically correct."

When Jason swung around to face Wendy there was a look of determination on his face. "Most of the people who could do this job have a few skeletons in their closet. I'm asking—no, I'm telling you that what you have discovered isn't relevant to his appointment, and that you are going to forget you ever knew anything about this matter." "What about Sandy?" inquired Wendy. "If he suspects anything, he has sense enough to keep quiet about it," replied Jason. Wendy gathered her papers and started for the door. "I'll let you know what I have decided this afternoon."

DISCUSSION QUESTIONS

1. If you were Wendy, what would you do?
2. Do you think that the requirement for full and complete financial disclosure prevents many people from serving in government?
3. How helpful would the ASPA Code of Ethics be in resolving Wendy's problem?
4. Why is it important to understand the difference between something that is technically legal and something that is ethical or moral?

OFFICE SPACE IN MIAMI

Astrel Williams sat in the coffee shop across the street from her office. For several weeks, she had been wrestling with a problem. She hoped that this morning's meeting would help her to decide on a course of action. Astrel was waiting for Thomas Strada. Thomas had been her first supervisor fifteen years ago when Astrel first joined the Customs Service. They had formed a warm relationship, which had helped Astrel decide on a career in the federal service and had sustained her through two job changes in the last ten years. Thomas, on his part, had seemed to enjoy the role of "Dutch uncle" to Astrel. His own career in the federal service had ended five years ago when he retired to take a position as a consultant with the Dade County government.

The problem Astrel needed to discuss with Thomas this morning had begun when the regional director had called her to his office to announce that the entire regional office was moving to new space in Miami Beach. The director, Arnando Garcia, seemed highly pleased with the move. He had been appointed only recently, and this was to be his first major accomplishment. Astrel was cautiously enthusiastic. She knew that the move would set all her plans back at least three months. On the other hand, the old office building was deteriorating at an alarming rate. Astrel was running out of space to put her rapidly increasing staff, and she had recently resorted to storing records in the parking garage under the building.

Astrel and Arnando discussed the allocation of space in the new facilities based on a preliminary floor plan that Arnando had prepared. Astrel was impressed with the size of the office complex that the director had been able to lease. When she commented that he must have done something right to get all that room, Arnando's face clouded. "Doing right has nothing to do with getting it done!" he growled. Astrel thought that the reaction was much more intense than the comment deserved, but she quickly forgot about it in the press of preparations. When she finally got a chance a few days later to drive across the causeway to see the building, a sense of uneasiness made her remember the remark. The building was not only brand new but had private security guards and an elaborate electronic security system!

The next day, more out of curiosity than suspicion, Astrel had dropped in on the chief budget officer for the region. Lenny Como and Astrel had both started at about the same time, so she felt comfortable asking for some information. "Lenny, I just saw the new office space—wow, that must have doubled our rental expenses for the year." Lenny looked puzzled. "Actually the overall outlay for office space is about the same." Astrel was shocked, but said nothing. Her next stop was the Operations Office. She didn't know anyone there, so she resorted to a bit of subterfuge. "I need to schedule some events in our new office complex for next year," she told the clerk on duty. "I need to know who owns the building we're moving into so I can make arrangements for extra parking," she said with a straight face. The slip she was handed read Caribbean Import Consortium, Inc.

A week later she had concluded that something was definitely wrong. Caribbean Import Consortium was a company formed by sixteen importers for the sole purpose of constructing a building and providing upscale office space for each of the firms. The Chamber of Commerce had indicated that the entire building was occupied, but they estimated that the rentals for space in that area would be at the top of the scale for Southern Florida. Astrel concluded that Arnando had made a "sweetheart" deal to get space in the new building. In return, the import companies probably expected at least quick access to the Customs Service, if not outright special treatment for their shipments.

The monthly general planning meeting was totally devoted to the move. Astrel gave her report on the training schedule and how she planned to work around the interruption caused by the move. As regional training director, Astrel would have to reschedule many of the sessions she had planned. At the end of her report, she turned to Arnando and commented that she was a bit worried about the image that the new facility would convey to the field personnel coming in for training. "They may think we're living pretty high when they see the fancy space we have." Arnando looked annoyed. "It's time we changed our image from seedy to modern," he snorted. "Astrel, stop in my office after the meeting," Arnando said in a low voice as she sat down.

In the office after the meeting, Arnando closed the door and walked up close to Astrel. "I hear that you've been making the rounds of the offices investigating the arrangements for the new space. I'm telling you to drop it. Don't make waves you can't survive." Astrel left the office worried about her previous actions. She had sent an inquiry to the Inspector General's Office in Washington about the rules for leasing only yesterday. If Arnando heard about that, she would really be in trouble. She called Thomas Strada and set up the breakfast meeting that afternoon.

Thomas Strada entered the coffee shop exactly on time. His slim figure and white hair fit nicely with the cream colored linen suit and pale brown tie. Sliding into the booth next to Astrel, he grinned. "Are you working undercover operations now Astrel?" She flushed and quickly explained why she had asked to meet outside the office. Thomas' face turned from grave to grim as he listened to her story. "Has anyone else raised any questions?" Thomas asked immediately after she finished. "Not that I can tell," replied Astrel. "Most of them don't want to look a gift horse in the mouth." Thomas sighed, scratched his chin and began playing with his napkin. "You have two choices, and you need to make a decision in the next twenty-four hours. You can use the information supplied by the Inspector General's Office to begin a formal complaint, or you can go to the media with your information."

"What's the point of leaking this to the media?" Astrel asked in a shocked voice. "Very simple," said Thomas. "If you leak this to the media, you may just be able to remain anonymous. The reporters will dig up the information and the publicity may force the director to cancel the lease. While he may suspect that you tipped them off, he won't be able to move against you officially." "And if I file a formal complaint with the inspector general . . . ?" Astrel's voice trailed off. She could see her career coming to a rapid end. Even if she won and the inspector general forced the lease to be cancelled, her chances of being promoted were ended forever.

"There's one other option," Thomas said hesitantly. "I have a good contact in the Treasury Department in Washington, D.C. He might be willing to put some heat on the director, off the record. It's risky, because I don't know how Arnando got his appointment, so we'd be in water over our heads." Astrel considered what Thomas had offered. She knew that if the situation got out of hand, Thomas might end up being dismissed from his consultant position. It was nice to have a friend to talk to, but she wasn't sure she wanted Thomas to risk his retirement just to prove her point. "I'll call you this evening with my decision," Astrel said, as she paid for their breakfasts and left the coffee shop.

DISCUSSION QUESTIONS

1. What would you do if you were Astrel?
2. Was Thomas' analysis of the options realistic or too cynical?
3. Do you think Astrel is being fair to Arnando by not confronting him directly?

TRUSTING IS A TWO-WAY STREET

Eddie Rihn had never been told that he was likable. In fact, most people who talked to Eddie were glad when the conversation was over. It wasn't that Eddie was nasty; it was just that Eddie approached life with a simple philosophy. The facts speak for themselves, and facts were comprised of numbers on paper. Eddie had done very well in school and had risen steadily in the Accounting Department of Karblis, Talker, and Kline. When the senior partner asked Eddie to take on a special project, Eddie was cautiously enthusiastic. The project involved the reorganization of the state Highway Department. Previously, the Highway Department had been operated from the central office in the state capital. The new secretary of highways wanted to decentralize the department so that the four regional offices would essentially operate independently.

Among the many things that Eddie was asked to look into was a new system for travel vouchers. Under the centralized system used by the state, the rules were so complicated and the process so slow that many of the employees in the Highway Department had simply stopped submitting any vouchers at all. Equally as bad, the time and energy consumed by the accounting department in the central office checking those vouchers that were submitted was costing more than the amount of money reimbursed to the employees. When Eddie inquired about the lack of vouchers, one of the regular state auditors told him that many employees simply took time off from work as a kind of compensation for having to pay their own way. The managers of the various bureaus knew about the problem, Eddie was told, but were generally willing to look the other way rather than make a fuss.

Eddie decided to make the new travel voucher system for the regional offices one of his first and top priorities. While less money was involved than in the purchasing procedures, Eddie knew that the travel voucher problem was an issue that directly affected the morale of the employees. The kind of officially tolerated dishonesty that existed in the old system could very well lead to a general willingness to "wink" at much more important rules. Perhaps, Eddie mused as he sat at the small desk that had been provided in the eastern regional office, he ought to do a more thorough investigation of the attitudes of the bureau managers before he suggested any new rules.

The first manager Eddie interviewed was very reluctant to talk about the problem. After repeated assurances that nothing that was said would be written down, the manager began to explain his view of the problem. "Just between you and me," said

Mort Claxton, "the problem started a few years ago when we didn't adjust the amounts reimbursed with the vouchers. People began to grumble that even when they did submit them, they still had to pay part of the trip because it cost more than the system allowed." Mort paused, fiddled with a pen on the desk, and continued. "The absolute worst was about a year ago when people refused to attend conferences and optional training sessions. Some of the professional staff began to combine their vacations with the conferences, and gradually they simply didn't report all of the days as vacation. I knew it was happening, but at least they were going to the conferences again. Now I don't quite know what to do about it. I know it's wrong and I have warned people to be careful, but I don't want to reprimand anyone for doing what everyone else is also doing." Eddie looked at Mort for a moment and then sighed. "We'll have to do something entirely different from the old system. Something that the people will be willing to try just to see if it works."

The stories from the other bureau managers were about the same. Two of them insisted that there wasn't any cheating but did admit that there was only the absolute minimum amount of travel being done by their staffs. One manager was openly angry about the problem. When Eddie interviewed her, she became quite intense and serious. "The problem goes further than the travel vouchers. It has begun to affect other aspects of the office. I'll tell you a true story, and I don't care who else you tell it to, either. We recently computerized our bureau, and part of the package provided by the vendor was a discount on hardware and software for members of my staff." Lydia Dichte got up from her chair and began to pace around the office. "One day, I got a call from the salesman who sold us the package. He wanted to know if we were interested in an expanded software system due to our expansion in staff. I told him we weren't interested because we hadn't hired anyone recently. The salesman was stunned. His records showed that we had purchased twenty-five more computers than our original staff size would warrant. When I checked around the office I discovered that the staff was selling the discounted equipment to other employees at the list price and keeping the discounted difference." Lydia stopped pacing and stood in front of Eddie's desk. "When I confronted one of them, he told me to mind my own business and I'd go a lot further in my career."

Eddie began to draw up the new system right after Lydia left his office. Three major ideas were at the center of the system. First, the regional offices would no longer reimburse expenses for lodging; instead, each employee would tell a travel officer the place and number of nights and the travel officer would arrange a direct billing to the bureau from the hotel or motel. Second, a per diem would be paid for meals with no receipts required. Finally, mileage for auto travel and fares for airlines, trains, buses, and taxis would be paid immediately to the employee on presentation of receipts and an approved travel request. By reducing the amount of out-of-pocket money the employees were required to spend, Eddie was sure that people would cooperate.

As Eddie turned out the light in the office and closed the door for the day, he thought about the basic problem. People were likely to be trustworthy if the system treated them with respect. On the other hand, if the system were too simple and open to abuse, a few people would find a way to take advantage of it. Over the years, the system had become so complex in an attempt to close off all the possible abuses that people had simply resorted to going around the system. "I suppose," Eddie mused aloud, "this new system will have holes too, but maybe it will stop the spread of unethical conduct to other areas."

DISCUSSION QUESTIONS

1. Do you think that the new system will solve the problem, and if not, why not?
2. Was Eddie correct in his thinking that the problem would get worse and spread to other unethical practices in the offices?
3. How does one balance a respect for people's basic honesty with a desire to ensure that people don't cheat the system?

YOU CAN'T "UNKNOW" SOMETHING

Fastbyte Computer Systems opened for business in 1984. With only three employees and the founder, Stephen Tate, the company managed to make a name for itself in a highly specialized area. Fastbyte wrote computer programs that merged two or more databases to find matches according to complex instructions. By 1990, Fastbyte had thirty-six employees and had recently gone public. In the process of becoming a public company, Stephen Tate had recruited some people to serve on the board of directors who could really be helpful. One of those people was Sheila Clipper. Sheila was a lawyer and a former lobbyist in the state capital. Her contributions to the board were her contacts in government. She knew who to see and what to say to make things happen.

Stephen Tate knew that his company was ready for "the big time." No more little jobs for auto parts stores and mail order manufacturers—Stephen wanted some of the long-term contracts that would put his company into the news and into the black forever. Stephen and Sheila had lunch at the country club one afternoon, and Stephen told her of his plans. "What we need," Sheila drawled, "is a good consultant." "I don't need any more advice, I need some access," Stephen grouched. "We're talking about the same thing," Sheila replied lazily. "I'll suggest someone at the next board meeting, and you just be an enthusiastic supporter."

About a month later, the board heard Sheila propose that the company investigate the possibility of entering a new market. The market she had in mind was government information retrieval and analysis. "Over the past few years, the legislature has been demanding that government agencies come up with a way to ensure that they aren't getting ripped off. Many of those agencies have computerized databases of their clients, but no way to check whether their clients have provided the same information to other agencies. We could write that software and provide annual updates and revisions forever." Sheila looked around the table. "What we need is a consultant who can advise us on the various problems we might encounter in the governmental market." "Great idea," said Stephen. "If you have someone in mind, let's hear it."

"As it happens, I do have a name to suggest—William Arrow. He is currently the executive director for the Municipal Managers Association. He knows computer systems, and he has a ton of experience with state agencies," Sheila smiled. "He also owes me a favor." The board discussed the new venture for about an hour and authorized Stephen to hire William Arrow as a consultant at the prevailing rate for no more than five-hundred hours.

Bill Arrow was pleased when Sheila called. His work with the municipal managers had become routine lately, and he was eager for something different. At forty-two, Bill was afraid that the world might be moving beyond him. His reaction, however, was somewhat cautious. "What, exactly, do you want me to do?" he asked Sheila. "Two things really," Sheila responded. "First, we need a compilation of all the various types of databases used by state agencies. You know—the type of machines they use, whether the software is specially written or off the shelf—that kind of stuff. Second, we need to know who else has gotten a contract to do database merges for state agencies. Skip the details on terms and rates and concentrate on the process of getting the contract. Look into the specifications required and the service agreements. Find out whether it's a committee decision or a single person who finally decides."

Over the next three months, Bill used the contacts he had built up over the years to compile the report. Several times, he dropped in on Stephen Tate to discuss his findings. While he was at Fastbyte, Stephen took him around to introduce him to the programmers and trouble-shooters who worked for Fastbyte. Bill got some very good advice on the type of questions he should be asking the agency people. When the report was finally finished, Bill attended a board meeting to summarize the project. He told the board what they wanted to hear. First, he told them that there were only two other companies that had managed to secure contracts with state agencies; both were large companies from out of state. Second, he told them that typically the contracts were put up for bid with the final decision resting with the secretary of the department. "I won't be surprised, however, if the actual decision is made by the chief data analyst. The legal requirement that the secretary decide isn't realistic, given the technical nature of the service being purchased," Bill concluded.

Sheila walked with Bill to the parking lot after the meeting. "Great report and a very smooth presentation," she enthused. "In fact, the board has agreed to the full five-hundred hours it had originally authorized." "But it only took about two-hundred hours," Bill objected. "True, but it's worth more than that to the company. We'll simply raise your hourly rate and send you the whole amount. Give yourself a little credit—you're worth more than the standard amount. Besides, some day you can return the favor." Bill drove away feeling pretty good about himself and the work he had done.

The election for governor the following fall produced an upset victory for a political novice. One wintery afternoon, Bill Arrow's phone rang. "This is the governor's appointment secretary. The governor would like to meet with you to discuss a possible appointment in his administration. Would next Wednesday be convenient—say 2 P.M.?" Bill hurriedly agreed and wondered who had put his name in the hat. The appointment went well; the governor had stressed his determination to cut down on the waste and fraud in government and had asked Bill to consider joining the staff as coordinator of data analysis. "I've heard about the research you've done on databases, and I'm eager to do something across all of the agencies," the governor had said.

Bill accepted the appointment, and before the first year was completed, the governor had gotten a requirement in the budget bill that every agency must share its database with the Office of Budgetary Affairs. Bill was put in charge of writing the statewide specifications for computer hardware and software that every agency had to follow. When the specifications were published, Bill felt a real sense of accomplishment.

When his secretary told him the director of the budget was on the phone, Bill expected warm congratulations. What he got was a terse request to meet the following morning. At the meeting, the secretary of the budget and his chief of staff seemed embarrassed. "Frankly," said the secretary "we don't have anybody over here who can really tell whether these bids we are getting make sense. Would you be willing to take a look at them and make a recommendation?" "No problem," grinned Bill. "It might be fun to see how the vendors like some of the provisions I put into the specs." Bill was given a small room just down the hall and four enormous folders were set in front of him. The smile on his face faded as he looked at the label on the largest folder. In bold black printing it said FASTBYTE COMPUTER SYSTEMS. Several hours later, Bill put down the last folder and groaned. It was agonizing to realize that the proposal that seemed best was from Fastbyte—or did it seem best because Bill knew so much more about Fastbyte?

DISCUSSION QUESTIONS

1. What should Bill tell the budget secretary?
2. How important to his decision is the fact that Bill had accepted more money than his contract with Fastbyte had originally specified?
3. Does it make any difference that Bill would only be recommending rather than deciding who would get the contract?

V

BUDGETING AND FINANCIAL MANAGEMENT

—

A public budget is similar to your personal budget; the budget helps you keep track of where the money comes from and where it goes. And just as your personal budget is a record of what you consider most important, so a public budget represents a statement of the priorities of government. As a public manager or as a citizen hoping to influence public policy, your ability to compete for the scarce resources of government will be critical. And nowhere is that competition played out more fiercely than in the budget process.

There are several stages to the budget process. The budget must be formulated (typically by the chief executive), approved by the legislature, executed or administered by various agencies during what is called the "fiscal year," and then, usually, reviewed and audited following the fiscal year. At any stage in this process, decisions may be made that will affect the program you are particularly interested in. And because there are always many contenders for funding— recall the intense battles over the federal budget during the last several years—if you don't understand the process and if you are not adept at working through the process, you may well be left behind.

While it will be helpful to you to learn the technical language of budgeting and financial management, you may also want to be attentive to the politics of the budgetary process. There are several strategies you might employ to bolster your position, not the least of which is building support among groups and associations that benefit from your work. Similarly, building effective relationships with other governmental actors, especially building the confidence in you that the chief executive and members of the legislature have, will also be quite helpful. Finally, especially during times of fiscal stress, you may have to come up with creative proposals to attract support or to ease the problems associated with budget reductions.

Public officials recently have tried a number of measures to cope with limited revenues. One of the most widely used among these, especially during the Reagan years, was privatization—a strategy in which governmental services are performed by private agencies, often operating under a contract with the government. For example, trash collection in many communities is performed by a government agency, and in many others it is performed by private firms. As we will see, the privatization strategy offers some benefits, but it is not without problems.

In this chapter we examine some of the ways governments approach the question of budgeting scarce resources, beginning with some general discussions of how budgets should be developed and how financial accountability can be maintained. Following these discussions, we turn to more specific techniques used by public managers in their efforts to do "more with less."

Irene S. Rubin begins the discussion with a review of a variety of "theoretical" approaches to budgeting, some of them normative—giving advice—and others descriptive. Rubin argues that, for the most part, the advice of budget reformers has been sound and budget practices have improved—especially at the state and local levels. However, she argues that scholars still need to understand more clearly the actual behavior of those involved in budget preparation and review. In reading the Rubin article, focus on some of the practical ways in which budgets can be integrated into larger management systems. Budgets are used for financial control, for planning, and to help in managing an organization. How can these various functions be integrated?

Rubin's analysis is complemented by that of Charles A. Bowsher, comptroller general of the United States, who suggests that, in comparison with practices in many progressive state and local governments, the federal system of financial management is in need of improvement. Primarily, Bowsher argues for greater attention to systematic program planning and for the development of integrated systems of budgeting and financial management that would be able to provide the right information at the right time. You may want to note that both Rubin and Bowsher give substantial credit to state and local governments for their progressive approaches to budgeting and financial management. Why do you think integrated financial management systems at the federal level have been difficult to achieve?

As we have noted, many governments and many public agencies have found it necessary to cut back or reconfigure public services given limited or even reduced revenues. Charles H. Levine notes that most managers are interested in the growth and development of their agencies, but that many may find it necessary to cut back or to manage declining (rather than growing) organizations. Levine suggests several specific and practical strategies for dealing with reduced revenues and examines the implications of each. What may be necessary in the long term, according to Levine, is a new, even radical, view of the importance of growth in society and in public agencies. After reading this article, you might list the various strategies discussed and then try to find illustrations of these in the work of local agencies.

One aspect of cutback management that Levine introduces is the privatization of public services, a topic debated by John R. Miller and Christopher R. Tufts, who suggest that privatization is a means to "more with less," and Harry P. Hatry, who suggests that privatization is not a panacea and may even present unforseen problems. Following this debate, you might want to draw up a set of questions that should be asked of an agency considering a move to privatize a particular service. Don't forget to include the ethical questions that privatization raises.

We profile Robert L. Mandeville, state budget director in Illinois. Mandeville's tenure in office and the tremendous amount of power he holds are both of great interest. But you should also note the combination of technical skill and managerial (and political) skill that he brings to his job. You might also be interested in Mandeville's motivation for continuing in the public service—that the work is simply more interesting than elsewhere, primarily because what you do affects human lives.

Budgeting and financial management often seem to be the epitome of the technical side of public administration. The first case in this chapter, "Tomorrow's Bill Comes Due Today," demonstrates that the management of public finance is much more than a technical question. As public resources continue to shrink, problems of providing sound financial management will increase. This case raises for your consideration two of the most difficult questions confronting budget and financial managers in the public sector. How can long-term problems be solved within the requirements for annual budgets? How can we manage to provide the resources to serve growing communities without bankrupting the future? The discovery of "unfunded liabilities" at the local level will become a much more common occurrence in the future.

The second case, "Where Do We Park All Those Cars?" confronts the problem of funding capital improvements in an era of federal cutbacks and increased control of local finance by state governments. The case also exemplifies the difficulty of declining revenues and expanding problems by posing the problem of alternative solutions to a common policy predicament. When local governments face problems that are driven by forces beyond their local community, they are usually faced with additional restrictions designed to solve or ameliorate state and national problems.

The third case, "Contracting for Mandatory Recycling Services," is designed to provide a look at the issue of "privatization." From the perspective of the local government—and particularly local administrators—the privatization issue further complicates an already complex situation. In our case, privatization is presented as one alternative used to meet a state mandated service. In a fashion similar to the federal government's requiring states to find a way to meet national standards, many states are mandating services that must be delivered by local governments. Contracting with private vendors is often the only alternative, given the reluctance of local citizens to raise the tax revenues needed to provide the services.

BUDGET THEORY AND BUDGET PRACTICE: HOW GOOD THE FIT?

Irene S. Rubin

Theory in budgeting, like much of public administration, has been of two kinds, descriptive and normative. Descriptive theory is based on close observation or participation in public sector activities. Theorists describe trends, sequences of events, and infer causes, paying attention to local variations as well as uniformities across cases. Normative theory—advice—may be based on a much narrower range of observations than descriptive theory and its proposed solutions may be based on values rather than observations. If the explanatory power of the descriptive theory is too weak, or if the advice of normative theory is not adopted by public officials or is adopted and abandoned because it does not work, the gap between theory and practice may become unacceptably wide.

An examination of the gap between budget theory and practice requires separate examination of the success over time of normative and descriptive budget theory. This article is therefore divided into two parts, one on normative theory and one on descriptive theory. In each part, the past, present and likely future of the relationship between theory and practice is outlined. Where the analysis indicates deterioration of the relationship, suggestions are made on how the relationship might be improved.

THE CONTENT OF NORMATIVE BUDGET THEORY

Normative budget theory dates back at least to the turn of the century. Lively budgeting debates took up whole issues of journals in a variety of social science disciplines. The practical advice reformers gave about accounting and budget exhibits was supported by a theory of government and the way budgeting relates to the state. Individual theorists differed on particulars, but the executive budget reform proposals[1] were generally based on a federalist model of government. Reformers looked longingly back at Hamilton's financial authority and across at the political systems of England, Switzerland and Germany.[2] They wanted a stronger, more independent executive, more like the Prime Minister in a parliamentary form of government, and less role for parties and party caucuses; generally they sought a smaller role for legislators. Their concern for the growth of government spending often led them to recommend that the legislature in general, and Congress in particular, give up the option of increasing executive-branch recommendations of the executive. These proposals led to debate on the role of the budget process in a democracy.[3]

While many reformers were concerned to limit the growth of government and the access of special interests, it mattered to them how it was to be done. They looked at the evolution of line-item controls that legislative bodies had devised to control machines, especially in New York City, and they argued that although effective in achieving their purpose, they hamstrung the executive and created less efficient government.[4] It was not only spending control the reformers were after, but efficient government. They specifically rejected line item budgets and detailed appropriations in favor of lump sum appropriations that allowed better management.

The program for achieving the reformers' goals included not only the expansion of the power of the executive to formulate policy and review proposals but also new budget formats to convey decision-making information about programs to the legislature and the public for their review. Public accountability was an important theme in this reform literature, and it could only be achieved by improving the quality of budget information and publicizing that information. The public as well as the legislature should understand what the government was doing and how much it was spending to achieve particular goals.

These reformers did not argue that new services should not be included in the budget, only that the cost for doing so should be the lowest possible commensurate with the quality of services demanded. They therefore advocated cost accounting (with its program budgeting implications) and detailed performance budgets based on unit costs. The assumption was that when such information was made public, there would be an outcry if one city's park services cost much more than another's.[5]

The budget reformers at the turn of the century also emphasized the role of planning in the budget. They argued that budgets must contain a work plan and provide funding for future as well as current needs. Some of the reformers went further and argued that budget planning was a way of finding and responding to unmet needs in the community. Otho Cartwright, for example, argued that he would go further than his fellow budget advocates in arguing for a state law that would provide the means to ask the public what its needs were. He argued that members of the public should be allowed to present their case to the proper government authority. He envisioned civic societies that would advocate particular policies, such as more industrial safeguards or better sanitation in the schoolhouses.[6]

While there was considerable variation in the scope of planning advocated by the early reformers, they agreed that planning was inherent in budgeting. Some of the reformers explicitly linked city planning and budgeting, arguing that poor planning for growth and inadequate sewers, streets, and tunnels cost more money in the end and were inefficient. They implied that a vision of the future city, which would bring order out of chaos, had to be linked to the budget and plans for capital and service spending.[7]

Budget planning meant at the least choosing particular target levels of service by activity and figuring out in advance what it would cost in personnel and supplies to accomplish those specific goals. The reformers rejected a model of budgeting that allowed the departments to ask for what they wanted instead of requesting what they needed to accomplish particular tasks. They were convinced that there was much waste in government and that expenditures could be cut back without losing much in the way of services. They did not think that changes could be implemented only at the margins. They told stories of cutting departmental budgets in half while improving services.[8]

Paralleling these early budget reformers were the public economists, who advocated some of the same kinds of reforms, but from a different theoretical perspective. While the budget reformers emphasized both the need to run government like a business and the constitutional basis for their reforms, the public economists based their arguments on what they perceived as rational choices and optimization of decision making. Both groups emphasized the need to get the most from each dollar, but the public economists were less concerned with cost accounting and management and more concerned with choices between options, laying out the options carefully and choosing between them on carefully specified grounds.

Over the years, many specific budget reforms have been formulated and advocated, then adopted, rejected, or modified. Many of these reforms have the same goals or purposes as those of the reformers of the early 1900s. Program budgeting, for example, and its explanation of what government is trying to accomplish at what cost, addresses specific concerns raised by the early reformers; the linking of planning to programming in the Planning, Programming, Budgeting System (PPBS) was also foreshadowed many years earlier. Performance budgets, with their varied emphasis on measuring demands and workloads or efficiency and unit costs, also reflect earlier concerns. The idea of determining desired service levels, associating costs with each one, and budgeting for only desired levels of service is the heart of Zero-Based Budgeting (ZBB) and Target-Based Budgets, but it was also part of the early reformers' attempts to judge what was needed versus what was wanted and to get out of the budget waste that had accumulated over the years. Current models of budgeting for outcomes perfectly express the activist, efficiency, and accountability goals of the early reformers. Management by objectives links the specific annual goals of the city to work loads and the personnel evaluation system, an elaboration of the old reformers' goals.

NORMATIVE THEORY AND PRACTICE

How successful has this normative theory and its specific offspring been? Evaluations of budget reforms, both specifically and generically, have often been negative. The reformers urged wide public participation in budgeting, with open hearings, advertisements, public presentation of budget exhibits, and budgets that were explanatory to the average person. Such participation was either short lived or did not materialize. Calls for a consolidated budget that explained to the public the range of programs and types of spending have dimmed in the face of continuing fragmentation, multiyear budgets, off-budget accounts, and different types of spending. Specific reforms, such as Management by Objectives (MBO), PPB, and ZBB have been evaluated and declared to be failures.[9]

More generically, the incrementalists argued that many reforms required comprehensive evaluation of programs and specific delineation of spending for specific purposes, which would have negative effects. A great number of programs could not be compared at one time, and the effects of making spending clearer would undoubtedly be more conflict. They disapproved of the idea of bringing the public more into the budgeting process for fear of increased and conflicting demands. They argued that budgeting should not be reformed.[10]

A review of the literature suggests that budgeters have underestimated the success of normative theory for a variety of reasons. One reason is that once a reform has been widely adopted, people tend to forget the role of normative theory in bringing the changes about. The federal government, most of the states, and nearly all cities with over 10,000 population have adopted the executive-budget model. Other kinds of recommendations, such as keeping enterprise funds separate, setting rates for public enterprises so as not to make a profit, and using the modified accrual basis of accounting have become accepted budgetary practices. The distinction between the detailed budget presentation of the President to Congress and the lump sum appropriation of Congress in its approved budget was suggested by the budget reformers, and it has been the dominant pattern in the federal government for many years. The idea that budgets should be tools for public accountability, and therefore should be easy to read, has been widely accepted and often inventively implemented.[11]

Even more recent and controversial recommendations for budget reform like zero-based budgeting, program budgeting, management by objectives,

and performance budgeting have been far more successful than many people in public administration have thought. Some studies suggested that many budget reforms were fads that had few or no lasting effects; in some cases they changed the budget formats but not the decision making.[12]

Some of the most discouraging of the evaluations have been at the federal level. But there is only one federal government, it is highly complex and unusual, and it is not typical of the states or local governments or of public budgeting in general. Historically, state and local governments have often innovated first and successfully and then the innovation has spread to the federal government. That such innovation should be judged essentially by what happens in the federal government seems unjustifiable. Budget innovations have been much more widely adopted and implemented at state and local levels, especially in the past decade.

Other reasons that success with normative budgeting has been underestimated are that evaluators looked too quickly to find consequences and tried to find the innovation in the exact form in which it was introduced. "The absorptive character of government, gradually adapting and incrementally augmenting its activities, suggests that change may more easily be measured on a time scale congenial to a forester or a geologist than to a Congress or a White House in a hurry."[13] Many of the innovations were clumsy when introduced, so that public administrators adopted and then adapted them, piecing together parts of reforms that suited their environments. Consequently, if one looked right away for the impacts of a specific budget innovation, one was likely to see fumbling implementation or even evasion of key provisions, but if one looked a decade or more later, one was likely to see a blending of pieces of different reforms that were functioning well in some places.

The reforms were often oversold, leading to the inevitable claim that they could not deliver. "In order for major reform legislation to become law, exaggerated claims are made for its future performance."[14] If one claims that a budget reform will reduce the federal deficit and the federal deficit remains, the reform appears to have failed, even if a variety of more modest improvements were made. Evaluations that examine the evolution of goals over time and evaluate outcomes on a scale of achievement have found budget innovations moderately successful.[15]

NORMATIVE THEORY AND PRACTICE ON THE STATE AND LOCAL LEVELS

At the municipal level in the United States, many proposed budget reforms have been adopted in whole or in part and have been adapted to the needs and capacities of the local communities. Sometimes it has taken cities many years to implement the changes because they did not have the necessary information base, accounting system, or staff time. Sometimes the reform has been interrupted or delayed, or even lost, but budget changes can occur gradually. The direction of the change is obvious when looked at over the period of a decade or more.

One study of a national sample of cities compared a 1976 International City Management Association survey with a study using the same survey instrument in 1982 and 1983. Over that time period, the change in reported budget sophistication was dramatic. The use of program, zero base, or target budgeting had increased from 50 percent to 77 percent of the sample; the use of MBO increased from 41 percent to 59 percent; and performance monitoring was up from 28 percent to 68 percent. About two thirds of the sample reported they used program budgeting, while a third reported using either ZBB or Target-Based Budgeting, which is a form of ZBB. The number of cities reporting that they had tried and dropped these innovations was not negligible, but it was still quite low. Reports of effectiveness varied by specific technique, but the ones which reported the most widespread adoption, such as program budgeting, were considered effective by about 44 percent of the respondents. Only performance measurement among the widely adopted tools got generally low ratings for effectiveness.[16]

A more recent study looked at the same budget practices in 1987 and found little additional use of these techniques but considerable stability in the numbers of users. The authors concluded that these tools "have become staples rather than fads in public management."[17] All of these studies do not include very small cities and so exaggerate somewhat the overall rate of usage. Still for cities with over 25,000 in population, the use of these tools remains high and constant.

Cross-sectional studies on self-reported data are useful, especially when done at intervals with the same instrument, but they leave one wondering what those who reported them meant by ZBB or MBO. Did it mean that the city went through all the information gathering and analysis implied in the process or that a vague statement of goals was added to the budget before each program? Nor is it clear from these studies if cities are gradually adding to existing reforms in a logical way so that one builds on the next or if they are modifying existing practices to be less threatening or more effective. To answer some of these questions, a mini-panel study was designed, looking at the budgets of 15 cities across the country over approximately 10 years, from about 1977 to about 1987. The smallest of the cities was about 40,000 population.[18]

Briefly, the results confirm the cross-sectional data. In 1977 nine cities out of the 15 had relatively straightforward line-item budgets; ten years later, only five cities had straight line-item budgets. There was increasing use of some form of performance measures, although the definition and measures of performance were not stable either across departments or across time. The use of ZBB or Target-Based Budgeting was low but stable: two out of the fifteen used zero-based or target-based budgeting at the beginning and at the end of the period. The most dramatic change was in MBO. In 1977 none of the cities used this technique as part of the budget format, but by 1987, four of the 15 were using it. From the budgets themselves it appears that some of the cities were using the formats more seriously as part of their decision-making process than others. And some cities included a variety of formats not specifically named.

To get a sense of smaller cities and the most recent data, 12 municipal budgets from suburban Dupage County, Illinois were examined. Sizes ranged from 6,700 to 90,000 population. One had no real budget (which is legal under Illinois law), six had straight line-item budgets, the others had some combination of program budgets with goals and objectives statements, or program budgets with MBO and performance measures. Cities of 14,000 and smaller population were much more likely to have straight line-item budgets. This is not really surprising, as their municipal operations are likely to be much simpler, and staff and council are much more likely to know each other and the programs intimately without the help of management controls and informative budgets.

It is clear from reading these budgets that in most cases the budget process itself has changed, not only the format. For example, in Hanover Park, a village of about 32,000 population, the President and the Board of Trustees first set forth their goals for the year, and then the departments' objectives are set and supporting goals are established. The process lasts over six months. In the budgets, the departments and boards list their previous year's objectives, which ones they obtained on time and which ones are still ongoing, and then describe their objectives for the next budget year. In Bensenville, population about 16,000, the budget introduction lists the goals and objectives for the city for the upcoming year: these include both potential service expansions and possible mergers and reorganizations of service delivery. The year's tasks include an evaluation of a neighborhood survey of citizen satisfaction with services and redesign of the city's handling of complaints. Each department lists concrete and extensive objectives and goals in the budget.

The most dramatic of the budgets from Dupage County is that of Downers Grove, population about 43,000. That budget combines program budgeting, line-item controls, and an MBO system. The system was developed over more than a decade. It has been combined with a five-year financial plan to create what the manager calls "results budgeting." The five-year plan is an integrated long-range operating budget and capital improvement plan. It describes where the city is headed and what the financial requirements will be. Portions of the plan appear in the annual budget. The City Manager, Kurt Bressner, argues, "The importance of integrating the MBO system into the budget cannot be overstated. Through this step, the desired results are directly linked to the resources necessary to achieve them."[19] This is exactly what the budget reformers of the early 1900s were trying to achieve. Many cities have pieces of this integrated system, and they seem to be moving in this direction, even though they do not have it all assembled yet.

This is not to say that no simple line-item budgets exist out there. Commission cities, of

which only a few remain in the whole country, tend to budget in a line-item and highly decentralized fashion, but as an outdated and largely abandoned reform, commission cities are not typical of future trends. Small cities, counties, and some rural cities still budget with simple line items with no explanation, but they probably do not need much more sophistication.

The response of state governments has been similar to that of the cities. More than half the states make use of program budgets, performance reporting and monitoring, program analysis, program evaluation, and forward year projections of revenue and expenditure.[20] Seventy-four percent of the states report using program budgeting; 38 percent of the users report that it is highly effective, and 62 percent report that it is somewhat effective. ZBB is used by fewer states, 20 as opposed to 37 that use program budgeting, but the proportion of those reporting effectiveness is about the same. Performance monitoring is fairly widespread, but a lower percentage of states that report such monitoring consider it highly successful. Nevertheless, a high proportion consider it somewhat effective. Most of these budget innovations have been hybridized and adapted, using parts of some and parts of other reforms.[21]

What is equally interesting are the reforms that now seem to represent the state of the art. Increasingly, planning is merging with budgeting. The result is multiyear budgeting, which is not just a projection of budget numbers but a corporate plan which includes statements of policy, underlying assumptions, and goals for the community.[22] In drawing up the plans, consideration is given to unmet needs, changes in the community, anticipated growth, and changing technology. Perhaps more common in rapidly growing and changing communities, these plans are the local adaptations of PPBS, home grown, to fit the local need. Even when no corporate long-term plan exists, there is often a capital long-term plan with the explicit goal of creating a preapproved list of priorities in which the first year of the plan pops out as a section of the next year's budget.

The recent integration of MBO with the budget implies that goal setting, personnel evaluation, work loads, and budget are being integrated in some budgets. The program manager in essence promises to do so much work and gets so much budget to do it. When integrated with the budget, this work load data gives the citizen a good look at exactly what his or her money is doing. MBO has the advantage of linking the budget with the personnel evaluation system, and hence it is more than a plan or report.

What budget reform has not yet generally achieved at the local level is good cost accounting and good performance budgeting. Cost accounting has sometimes become political. When a particular service is sorted out for a cost analysis, councilmembers may view the service as too expensive and try to use cost accounting to make it politically vulnerable. Or a manager may try to make a program look less expensive through cost accounting to defend it from its detractors. Cost accounting does not have the appearance of a neutral skill that can help save money. With respect to performance measures, departments have resisted what appears to them to be unfair evaluations. The department heads often fear, with some justification, that low efficiency ratings will be blamed on them and the council will take away resources from them in a misguided effort to increase efficiency. Since departments seldom have complete control over what are viewed as departmental outcomes—such as dollar losses for fires—department heads fear that they will be blamed for such things as a rash of arson fires, regardless of the quality of their work. Nevertheless, some elements of performance budgeting have crept into municipal budgets, even if they are not yet working to everyone's satisfaction.

In short, contemporary budgeting at the state and local levels reflects many of the practices recommended by budget theory, and it continues to evolve. Public administration has clearly been successful in proposing reforms that are attractive to practitioners when those reforms have appeared to have the capacity to solve budgetary problems. The reforms have not always worked to everyone's satisfaction, but the relation between normative budget theory and budget practice has been close, especially at state and local levels.

NORMATIVE THEORY AND PRACTICE AT THE FEDERAL LEVEL

In recent years the record at the federal level has not been as strong. Budget reformers had a major

hand in designing the executive budget process in 1921, and reform ideas were evident in the redesign of congressional budgeting in 1974. But reform ideas played little role in the 1985 deficit reduction act known as Gramm-Rudman-Hollings.

The 1974 reform emphasized the role of professional budget staff to enable Congress to have sufficient information to make budget decisions. It also emphasized the importance of having overall budget targets and ways of setting and enforcing budget priorities. These were two persistent themes in the reform literature.

By contrast, the Gramm-Rudman-Hollings deficit reduction act set up a variety of across-the-board cuts—with many of the most popular entitlement programs exempted—that would automatically be invoked if the normal budget process could not achieve a specified target for deficit reduction. Where previous budget reforms had tried to include entitlement programs to bring them into budget scrutiny and to make them part of budget tradeoffs, Gramm-Rudman-Hollings exempted them; where previous budget reforms had striven to make thoughtful comparisons among competing programs, Gramm-Rudman-Hollings cut across the board.

The Gramm-Rudman-Hollings deficit reduction law was often referred to as a bad idea whose time had come.[23] The reported intent of the law was to make the mandatory cuts so distasteful to both Democrats and Republicans that they would join together to make a proper budget that would reduce the deficit below the trigger level for the automatic cuts. Instead, the law has worked to enhance the incentives to make deficits look smaller than they are (to get below the trigger level) by using "smoke and mirrors." Senator James Exon has argued, "Rather than force action, the Gramm-Rudman process fakes action. . . . After two years of operation, Gramm-Rudman has not worked."[24]

It was not just Gramm-Rudman-Hollings that suggested that normative theory was not working at the federal level; many other budget reform proposals of the past few decades have not worked well at the federal level. Part of the reason seems to be the size and complexity of the federal government. Putting together a citywide list of priorities coming from a half dozen or even a dozen city departments is a massive task but not an impossible undertaking. Putting together a priority list of programs in one department of the complexity of the federal Health and Human Services without an agreed upon set of criteria for such a ranking may well be impossible or so difficult as to overwhelm any advantage the process might have produced.

Another problem has been that reform proposals have not kept up well with the increased complexity of the federal budget over the years. Parts of the federal budget receive continuing appropriations that are semi-permanent and do not go through annual budget review. Many capital projects such as weapons systems are authorized for expenditure over a period of years, and the matter of what part has been spent or remains to be spent clouds the logic of an annual comprehensive review. Reformers' programs have included consolidated annual budgets with explicit comparison between major categories of spending, but the reality of federal budgeting today is multiple budgets, and parts of the budget are multiyear.[25] More important, some compelling reasons exist for the increased complexity, and it is not likely to go away any time soon. The result is that many old reform proposals no longer make much sense.

Other reform proposals have been taken as far as they usefully can be taken. For years, the reform proposal for assuring balanced budgets was increasingly to strengthen the power of the chief executive over the budget. In the states, for example, the governors have been given stronger and stronger budget vetoes. But the reform has probably already gone too far, contributing to an atrophy of legislatures, and the trend for the past 10 to 20 years has been back in the other direction, to give legislatures more balanced responsibilities over budget matters.[26] It has become increasingly clear that legislatures are not necessarily more profligate than governors and that Congress is not historically more likely to spend than the President.[27] Some executives are more prone to spending, and some legislatures are more prone to spending. A reform that purports to control spending by giving the executive more and legislatures less spending power seems wrong-headed.[28]

Part of the problem of the recent failure of budget reform at the federal level has been the focus on trying to reduce the size of the deficit through reforming budget processes or legislating discipline. A budget reform can help carry out the goals of politicians once they have made up their minds, but it cannot make up their minds. Public administration may have been asking budget reform to do the impossible.

Some of the increasing complexity of the budget that has made federal reforms so difficult has affected state and local levels as well. Capital projects may sprawl across years. Budgets at all levels are likely to contain a variety of resources, including loan guarantees, loans and revolving funds, contracts, insurance, grants, subsidies, and direct service delivery. The problems of exaggerated executive budget power are more extreme at the state and local level than they are at the national level. As a result, many traditional bits of reform advice are becoming less relevant at all levels of government.

IMPROVING THE RELATIONSHIP BETWEEN NORMATIVE THEORY AND PRACTICE

How can the relationship of normative budget theory and practice be improved in the coming years? First, a better understanding is needed of what the budget process and format can and cannot do so that reform proposals will be realistic. Greater clarity is required about the difference between being idealistic, asking for budgets to be completely transparent, for example, and suggesting budget reforms as solutions to broader problems that such reforms may influence only marginally. The former is an important part of public administration; the latter at best makes budget reform look impotent, and at worst, detracts attention from more likely solutions.

Second, reconsideration is needed to what accountability means and how to achieve it in budgets that allocate multiple resources on a multiple year basis. For example, what does "consolidated" mean in such a budget? One does not want to add tax expenditures to outlays—they are different kinds of numbers and they do not meaningfully add. One does not want to include the balances in trust funds to offset the deficit, as the United States government now does, when those funds can never be spent to reduce that deficit. So some parts of the budget should remain separate; full consolidation in the context of different types of expenditures and expenditure restrictions should not be a goal.

However, openness and clarity of presentation are more urgent in this context of multiyear and multisource budgets than they were when budgets were simpler. The completeness of the budget takes on increasing importance. Are the costs of tax breaks adequately represented? How are the costs of loans presented? Are various subsidies reported? How? What about the shifting of costs through regulation of the economy? How are unfunded liabilities being reported, where, and with what accuracy? In short, what is not in the budget that should be? This avenue of budget reform needs to be continued and applied more widely at state and local levels.

The appropriate level of budgetary secrecy must be reexamined. Openness of budget decision making to the public also opens the budget process to interest groups; is that an adequate argument for closing budget decisions? To what extent have procedures been created or endorsed to close deliberations to the public and press while still keeping them open to interest groups? One could argue, for example, that the federal black budget for security agencies is a secret only from the American public and not from foreign powers. Can budget processes be prescribed that buffer decision makers somewhat from interest groups and still keep them open and accountable to the public?

What level of secrecy is justified and at what potential and actual cost? The tendency has been to create budget systems that are closed on the executive side and open on the legislative side; as budget power has shifted overwhelmingly toward the executive branch, what has been the impact on public accountability and democratic government? Is the trend toward greater balance between the legislature and the executive gradually solving the problem of accountability, or is the legislature going to become more isolated or insulated as it regains more budget power?

Third, indicators are needed to give early warning when various processes or interests are getting out of balance, with potentially serious and unwanted consequences on the budget. Perhaps indicators need to flash a warning when the budget estimates have become too rosy. Governments need to avoid the extremes of centralization or decentralization, of executive or legislative dominance, of openness and secrecy. Perhaps a need exists to measure and monitor the swings, to give early warning of needed adjustments. It would also be useful to monitor the budget process itself for signs of excessive strain and potential future collapse. How much stress can the process take? How much delay is too much? What does failure of the budget process look like?

Fourth, balance needs to be struck between precontrols and postcontrols in budget implementation. How effective have various measures to evaluate programs been with respect to the budget? Are program audits or even financial audits used in the preparation of new budgets? Is there a way to make such audits more useful, more accessible to more people? Varied controls are at governments' disposal now, but how many are too many? Budget practice is alert to the possibility of giving agencies too much autonomy, but how should governments guard against the inefficiencies of giving them too little? This was a problem that bothered the early reformers, but normative budgeting has not yet worked out a good set of answers.

If ways can be recommended to improve accountability in complex budgets, the link between taxpayers and public decision makers can be strengthened. If ways can be recommended to public officials to explain what they are doing and how well they are doing it, perhaps the antigovernment flavor of tax revolts can be moderated. The match between theory and practice may also be improved if budgeters learn to give conditional rather than absolute advice. It is necessary to learn when particular reforms are likely to work and when they have outlived their usefulness. If reform can be reconceptualized, reaching for a new set of ideals beyond reducing the deficit and even beyond traditional goals of increased efficiency and fiscal control, budgeters will have a better chance of affecting the future of budget practice. . . .

NOTES

1. For a definition and well-known exposition of the arguments for an executive budget, see Frederick A. Cleveland, "The Evolution of the Budget Idea in

the United States," American Academic of Political and Social Sciences, *The Annals*, vol. 62 (November 1915), pp. 15–35.

2. For the theoretical underpinnings of this reform, see particularly Henry Ford Jones, "Budget Making and the Work of Government," American Academy of Political and Social Sciences, *The Annals*, vol. 62 (November 1915). pp. 1–14.

3. One elegant version of this argument appears in Edward A. Fitzpatrick's, *Budget Making in a Democracy* (New York: MacMillan, 1918). He opens his book with a quote from Gladstone, "Budgets are not merely affairs of arithmetic, but in a thousand ways go to the root of prosperity of individuals, the relation of classes and the strength of kingdoms" (p. vii).

4. The argument that New York City had overdone budget controls through excessively detailed line items is made by Henry Bruére, "The Budget as an Administrative Program," *The Annals*, vol. 62 (November 1915), pp. 176–191. Fitzpatrick emphasizes this failure in drawing up his proposals for a more reformed and effective legislature and better information in the budget format for legislators to review. See Fitzpatrick, chs. 5 and 6.

5. See, for example, Paul T. Beisser, "Unit Costs in Recreational Facilities," *The Annals*, vol. 62 (November 1915), pp. 140–147.

6. Otho Grandford Cartwright, "County Budgets and Their Construction," *The Annals*, vol. 62 (November 1915), pp. 229–230.

7. See, for example, J. Harold Braddock, "Some Suggestions for Preparing a Budget Exhibit," *The Annals*, vol. 62 (November 1915), p. 157. He waxes rhapsodic on the relationship between city planning and budgeting. "It means that the great distributive function of our economic life is to be articulated with the other great function, production, in agreement with the dominant principle of the day—efficiency."

8. For one such example, see Tilden Abramson, "The Preparation of Estimates and the Formulation of the Budget—The New York City Method," *The Annals*, vol. 62 (November 1915), p. 261.

9. Allen Schick, "A Death in the Bureaucracy: The Demise of Federal PPB," *Public Administration Review*, vol. 33 (March/April 1973), pp. 146–156, and Richard Rose, "Implementation and Evaporation: The Record of MBO," *Public Administration Review*, vol. 37 (January/February 1977), pp. 64–71. For a negative pronouncement on ZBB, see Allen Schick, "The Road from ZBB," *Public Administration Review*, vol. 38 (March/April 1978), pp. 177–180.

10. Arnold Meltsner and Aaron Wildavsky, "Leave City Budgeting Alone! A Survey, Case Study, and Recommendations for Reform," in John P. Crecine, ed., *Financing the Metropolis: Public Policy in Urban Economics*, vol. 4, Urban Affairs Annual Reviews, (Newbury Park, CA: Sage, 1970), pp. 311–358.

11. For example, Elgin, Illinois, lists each year all the interfund transfers, where they came from, where they went to, and for what reason. (This is an innovation I would recommend for many other cities.) Budget issues are described for each program before the numbers are presented. The Town of Windsor, Connecticut, has a budget that reports demand data, such as the number of fire incidents per year over a five-year period and the reported crime rate over a decade. This data outlines the basis on which a budget is formulated. Windsor's extremely clear program layout describes the functions of each program, describes any changes, and discusses key issues. Program narratives tell the reader what specific issues the program is dealing with each year and why.

12. Thomas Lauth in his article, "Zero-Based Budgeting in Georgia: The Myth and the Reality," *Public Administration Review*, vol. 38 (September/October 1978), pp. 420–430, argues that those who expected Zero Based Budgeting to eliminate programs were disappointed, that budgeting remained incremental, and that ZBB took place in that context. Allen Schick makes a similar point for the federal level in "The Road from ZBB," *Public Administration Review*, vol. 38 (March/April 1978), pp. 177–180.

13. Rose, *op. cit.*, *supra*, p. 64.

14. Howard Shuman, *Politics and the Budget* (Englewood Cliffs, NJ: Prentice-Hall, 1984), p. 276.

15. See, for example, David Sallack and David Allen, "From Impact to Output: Pennsylvania's Planning-Programming-Budgeting System in Transition," *Public Budgeting and Finance*, vol. 7 (Spring 1987), pp. 38–50. Another example of this type of analysis is in Shuman, *Politics and the Budget*, chapter 10. Rudolph Penner and Alan Abramson, *Broken Purse Strings: Congressional Budgeting, 1974–88* (Washington: The Urban Institute, 1988), evaluate the 1974 Budget Impoundment and Control Act over a 14-year period, with careful evaluation of what the original goals of the Act were for those who designed it, rather than some of the claims later made for it. They argue, as others have argued, that the reform was neutral in terms of aims to increase or decrease spending, and hence the law cannot reasonably be judged on failure to curtail spending. They claim some successes and some failures of the reform over time.

16. Theodore Poister and Robert P. McGowan, "The Use of Management Tools in Municipal Government: A National Survey," *Public Administration Review*, vol. 44 (May/June 1984), pp. 215–223.

17. Theodore Poister and Gregory Streib, "Management Tools in Municipal Government: Trends over the

Past Decade," *Public Administration Review*, vol. 49 (May/June 1989), p. 242.

18. The cities are New York City; Pittsburgh, Pennsylvania; Baltimore, Maryland; San Antonio, Texas; Durham, North Carolina; Cambridge, Massachusetts; Tucson, Arizona; Wichita, Kansas; South Bend, Indiana; Amarillo, Texas; Baton Rouge, Louisiana; Victoria, Texas; Oklahoma City, Oklahoma; Spokane, Washington; and Grand Forks, North Dakota. These cities were chosen on three criteria: range of size, distribution across the country, and the availability of sample budgets ten years apart. There may have been some bias in the sample, as cities with better budgets may have been more eager to send a sample to an archive.

19. The quotation is from Downers Grove's 1989-1990 budget introduction.

20. Stanley Botner, "The Use of Budgeting/Management Tools by State Governments," *Public Administration Review*, vol. 45 (September/October 1985), pp. 616–620.

21. Sixty percent of respondents in the 1987 Georgia State Survey said they had used strategic planning. Seventy percent reported using some form of financial trend monitoring, and 68 percent reported using multiyear revenue and expenditure forecasts. Poister and Streib, *op. cit., supra*, p. 242.

22. The author served as consultant to such a planning process in 1988-1989 for the city of Warrenville, population about 9,000. A fictionalized version of the process is described in a teaching case written by this author, "Dollars, Decisions, and Development," in *Managing Local Government*, James Banovetz, ed., the International City Management Association, 1990.

23. Lance LeLoup, Barbara Luck Graham, and Stacey Barwick, "Deficit Politics and Constitutional Government: The Impact of Gramm-Rudman-Hollings," *Public Budgeting and Finance*, vol. 7 (Spring 1987), pp. 100–101.

24. This quote is from Penner and Abramson, *op. cit. supra*, p. 76; they cite their source as Hedrick Smith, *The Power Game: How Washington Works*, (New York: Random House, 1988), p. 667.

25. For a good discussion of the level of complexity in recent federal budgeting and its implications for public budgeters, see Naomi Caiden, "Shaping Things to Come: Super-Budgeters as Heroes (and Heroines) in the Late-Twentieth Century," in Irene Rubin, ed., *New Directions in Budget Theory* (Albany: SUNY Press, 1988), pp. 43–58.

26. For a discussion of this historical trend and specific examples, see Irene Rubin, *The Politics of Public Budgeting: Getting and Spending, Borrowing and Balancing* (Chatham, NJ: Chatham House, 1990).

27. For a good summary of the evidence with respect to the federal level, see Norman Ornstein, "The Politics of the Deficit," in Phillip Cagan, *Essays in Contemporary Economic Problems: The Economy in Deficit, 1985* (Washington: The American Enterprise Institute, 1985) pp. 311–334. R. Douglas Arnold has been instrumental in debunking the argument that the tendency of a Member of Congress to support pork projects has increased and is causing increases in federal spending. Such spending has decreased as a proportion of the budget in recent years. "The Local Roots of Domestic Policy," in Thomas Mann and Norman Ornstein, eds., *The New Congress* (Washington: The American Enterprise Institute, 1981), pp. 250–287. For a summary of the argument that governors may be expansionist or tightfisted, see Aaron Wildavsky, *Budgeting, A Comparative Theory of Budgetary Processes*, 2d. ed. (New Brunswick, NJ: Transaction Press, 1986), pp. 229–236.

28. Evidence from the states is not supportive of the argument that more and more powerful executives mean less expenditure per capita. States without line-item vetoes for the governors do not spend more per capita than states that have such enhanced executive budget powers. Benjamin Zycher, "An Item Veto Won't Work," *Wall Street Journal*, 24 October 1984. Line-item and reduction vetoes often do not reduce expenditures, but rather substitute the governor's proposals and wishes for those of the legislature. See, for example, Calvin Bellamy, "Item Veto: Dangerous Constitutional Tinkering," *Public Administration Review*, vol. 49 (January/February 1989), pp. 46–51. See also Glenn Abney and Thomas Lauth, "The Line-Item Veto in the States: Instrument for Fiscal Restraint or an Instrument for Partisanship," *Public Administration Review*, vol. 45 (May/June 1985), pp. 372–377.

SOUND FINANCIAL MANAGEMENT: A FEDERAL MANAGER'S PERSPECTIVE

Charles A. Bowsher

The 1980s have been years of unprecedented growth in the nation's budget deficit. Current projections indicate that deficits will continue to increase if present policies are continued, and consensus is growing that this would create ever increasing risks for economic stability and growth. The response to this consensus will involve an enormous challenge to federal managers.

Revenue increases, spending cuts, or both, are the only available ways of correcting current and future imbalances in the nation's budget. Most reform proposals focus on the need to restructure our current program priorities and tax policy. They are often described as longer term measures. But I suspect that effects of the budget problem on federal managers will be much more immediate.

In civilian agencies, managers will face increasing pressures to cut programs and to reduce costs. In the Department of Defense, they will face equally great demands to assure that the rapid growth is managed effectively and that increased defense resources are translated into increased defense capability. Timely and reliable program and financial information are critical to successful management under these circumstances. However, our current financial management structure and supporting systems are not capable of coping with the demands which must be placed on them if managers are to meet their responsibilities. We must begin now to modernize the federal government's financial management structure and put the systems into place that will serve the needs of the public and the government.

FINANCIAL MANAGEMENT ISSUES

CONSISTENT AND RELIABLE FINANCIAL INFORMATION IS ESSENTIAL FOR GOOD MANAGEMENT

The activities of the federal government are massive in comparison to those of any other nation or industry. For example, over $2 billion is spent daily to keep the government operating. Controlling such an immense operation requires accurate and timely information so that difficult policy and management decisions are made before they are too late. However, today's financial reports do not provide a clear picture of government activities. In many cases they are so untimely or irrelevant (or both) that they are useless as a basis for managerial decision-making.

A clear example of this problem is the lack of consistency in the way the federal budget is prepared versus the way expenditures and revenues are accounted for and reported. Budgets are requested and justified in terms of programs and projects, such as infant health care or claims for flood control. Accounting and other financial reports, however, often focus on appropriations and categories of expense, such as travel or personnel, without relating them to the particular programs or projects for which the funding was requested and approved.

Managing the government efficiently also requires reliable and timely management reporting that compares expectations with actual performance. The current federal financial structure focuses management's attention on obligation and outlay reporting that seldom compares budgeted with actual financial data. While both obligations and outlays are important, neither is a consistently reliable measure of the actual resources consumed in carrying out government programs. Obligation-basis reporting is essential in monitoring the extent to which agencies are making commitments for future payments. Cash-basis reporting is essential in managing fiscal, debt, and credit policies. However, reporting that compares the resources actually consumed to provide an output with those budgeted to achieve the desired results would provide managers with a better basis for decision making.

Budgeting and accounting should be on the same basis and use the same reporting categories so that meaningful management reports can be produced, measuring actual results against plans. An integrated budgeting and accounting system that focuses on the resources used or consumed to achieve program results will help to assure that the costs of activities are consistently recorded across government. Such a system could compare and report the estimated and actual costs of operations, organizations, programs, and projects.

Among the benefits to the federal government of adopting such a system would be:

- The ability to compare planned with actual use of resources;
- Reliable project status reporting;
- If desired, the ability to establish user fees for government services that fully cover the cost of those services;
- The ability to compare activities of similar operations across the government;
- The ability to compare activities of similar operations across the government;
- More accurate budget estimates based on actual past program and project costs;
- The ability to measure the input of resources and the output of performance;
- Greater assurance that financial transactions are not artificially moved from one fiscal year to another; and
- Increased accountability for the management of public funds.

PROJECT REPORTING HELPS MANAGEMENT TO FOCUS ON SPECIFIC ACTIVITIES

Project reporting provides specialized reports to monitor and control specific activities, such as construction of capital assets or development of major weapons systems. This form of reporting is lacking or is not always complete or consistent with existing federal financial systems. The Department of Defense Selected Acquisition Reports (SARs), reporting on the status of major weapons systems, illustrate the need for improved project reporting. For example, in the December 1982 SARs:

- The $20.1 billion baseline SAR estimate for the B-1 bomber excluded more than $1 billion in

costs, such as flight simulators for pilot training, that were clearly part of the program.
- The estimate for the Army's Bradley Fighting Vehicle showed an illusory decrease of $679 million in ammunition cost. This amount was subtracted because SARs do not include ammunition costs unless the ammunition is unique to a specific weapon system. In this case, the Army had decided to buy the same ammunition for the Bradley and the Light Infantry Vehicle.
- Though they are built by the same contractor, two different inflation estimates were used for the Navy's Tomahawk Missile and the Air Force's Ground Launched Cruise Missile. Since the December SARs must tie to the president's budget, it is evident that the budget requests for these two systems were based on incompatible assumptions.

The SARs are provided to Congress quarterly. They were created by the Defense Department in 1969 because its management systems, which focused on obligations, did not provide needed information on costs, production rates, and technical performance. Though useful, the SARs have three major limitations. First, the SARs rely on contractor and other information that does not necessarily tie to the accounting systems of the Department of Defense and can be reconciled to the budget only in December.

Second, information on the same weapons systems may be reported differently from one year to the next, and the changes are not always clearly explained. The SAR of December 31, 1982, for example, reported the Trident II submarine as a new weapon system even though the only difference between it and the Trident I was the type of missile it would carry. This had the effect of disrupting the historical data on what is essentially the same weapon system.

Finally, the information in the SARs is not consistent with that in other budget documents provided to Congress. According to the Congressional Budget Office, cost estimates in the December 31, 1982, SAR for 13 systems excluded at least $40.8 billion in program costs reported elsewhere.

From this discussion, it should be obvious that the SARs have serious weaknesses as a project reporting system. Those deficiencies must be corrected if the current defense building is to be managed effectively and public support for that building is to be sustained. The problem, however, is not limited to the defense program. Many civilian agencies also undertake large projects, and the project reporting systems in many cases are just as inadequate or maybe worse than the SAR system.

Clear, summary project reports . . . would make it much easier for members of Congress and executive branch policy officials, as well as program managers, to quickly determine the status of projects—civilian or military—and explore further the causes of any increased cost estimates and schedule slippages. They would have information about a project's expected cost, how this compares to previous estimates, how much money has been spent, what it has been used for, and what has been accomplished.

PERFORMANCE INFORMATION CAN ASSIST PROGRAM AND BUDGET EVALUATION

A management system that measures only financial resources is incomplete. An effective system also measures what is produced using these resources. Assessing government accomplishments requires measuring employee and program performance. Though the size and complexity of the government make it difficult, developing effective performance measurement systems is clearly possible. Output measures are already in place for large parts of the government. Many of the measures need to be improved—and most of all they need to be used—but their existence demonstrates the feasibility of the approach.

A well-developed financial management structure should include performance information that can be used for both day-to-day management and policy and budgeting decisions. An effective system of measuring program performance requires:

- agreeing on objectives and relevant measures of accomplishment;
- systematically collecting reliable, consistent, and comparable information on costs and accomplishments; and
- supplying that information routinely for use in management, planning, programming, and budgeting.

Strong performance monitoring systems can answer many routine questions about program performance. Consider, for instance, a program whose goal is to immunize children against certain childhood diseases (e.g., mumps, polio). A reliable system of performance indicators would provide information on the level of resources and effort devoted to each program site, the number of eligible children being served, the number of immunizations administered, and the cost per immunization. The incidence of these diseases in children could also be monitored.

Even the best systems, however, cannot answer all important questions about program effects and policy alternatives. Therefore, a modern structure of financial management should include a systematic way to identify questions that warrant special analysis. In our example, we may notice that at several sites there is a precipitous drop in the number of children being immunized. But our indicators give little clue as to why this should be so. A study could be undertaken to determine the reason for the drop and the appropriate actions to take.

Such special studies can provide decision makers with important additional information about program performance. But it is equally important that these studies be designed so that their results can be integrated with the information produced by the regular performance and financial reports. The results can then be used to help identify both future resource and program needs and ways of improving the routine performance measures in use.

PLANNING FOR CAPITAL INVESTMENTS MUST BE STRENGTHENED

Federal capital investment activity is managed through numerous agencies, programs, and funding sources. No structured approach exists to make capital investment decisions, and no policy mechanism is in place to assess capital investment priorities for the government as a whole. The lack of visibility for investment decisions, coupled with a budget and accounting approach which treats capital spending as if it were the same as spending for current operations, creates what some consider to be a systematic bias against capital investment.

The needed visibility of capital budgeting within the unified budget could be achieved by displaying capital investment activities separately. Thus, each major functional category in the budget (e.g., national defense, energy, agriculture) might include an operating component and a capital investment component.

The capital component could include new investments in capital assets, whether acquired directly by the federal government or through loans and grants to state and local governments. The several capital components could be combined to represent the federal government's capital budget. The operating component would include salaries, utilities, contracted services, and other expenses not related to investment, as well as depreciation expenses if applicable.

This separation of capital and operating expenditures within the unified budget would:

- elevate the visibility of capital investment decisions;
- facilitate the development of replacement planning; and
- allow a comparison of the long-term costs and benefits of capital investments across budget functions.

Federal managers have long complained about a perceived bias against productivity enhancing capital investment. The approach suggested here could help to eliminate any such bias. It has many of the advantages of a separate capital budget. At the same time, it maintains the integrity of the unified budget, an essential defense against manipulating the definition of capital investment.

PLANNING AND PROGRAMMING CAN IMPROVE DECISION MAKING ON MAJOR POLICY ISSUES

Sound financial management requires a process that focuses attention on major policy issues and alternatives and their probable future consequences. To be effective, the process needs information on the actual costs and benefits of prior decisions. Increasingly, the major problems facing the nation defy short-term, narrowly focused solutions. With rising health care costs and an aging population, for example, managing the costs of Medicare requires both a long-term strategy and consideration of the interaction of Medicare with other health programs, such as Medicaid, and with private health insurance programs.

The federal government currently has few of the necessary pieces of such a process. Often, top management attention to policy or legislative issues is unstructured, divorced from actual experience, focused on individual programs, and concerned only with the next year or two. Budgeting remains the dominant financial management process and the focus of decision makers' attention. The budget process tends to operate as a separate system that ignores or "crowds out" information from both agency planning and program offices and the accounting system. Consequently, products developed in these two phases are not used well in the budgetary process. Yet sound budgeting and sound financial management depend both on the analysis of future trends and program needs (planning/programming) and on past performance (accounting). No single process should dominate.

A structured planning and programming process can help identify solutions to major long-term problems, such as financial health care. The cornerstone of this concept is the use of a formal, analytical process for considering the medium- and long-term implications of current decisions. To be successful, the planning and programming structure must be an integral part of financial management decision-making, as it is in the Defense Department. When the planning, programming, and budgeting system (PPBS) was tried by civilian agencies in the late 1960s, it failed in part because it was added to, and often competed with, existing systems and processes, rather than being built into the basic structure of financial management.

A well-developed, modern, government-wide structure of planning and programming would highlight the major policy and program options available to decision makers together with their likely benefits and costs. Making these decisions in a more systematic way would reduce some of the pressure on the budget process. It would also enable Congress, the president, and agency officials to focus their policy deliberations more systematically on the major issues facing the nation.

The inadequacies of the planning and programming elements of the decision process have serious, but often unrecognized, implications for managers. It is in these stages where program goals and strategies are examined and expectations are set. If these expectations are poorly conceived or incompatible, or if the budget process ignores them, it is the manager who must cope with the resulting ambiguity and explain the failure to achieve expected results. Thus, the manager has a very real stake in developing an effective planning and programming system.

FULL DISCLOSURE OF ALL COSTS AND LIABILITIES IS NECESSARY FOR ADEQUATE PLANNING AND BUDGETING

Congress and the executive branch must be fully aware of all the government's financial commitments to adequately manage and oversee its activities. Today the federal budget does not include all governmental activities, nor does it disclose all costs of those activities that do appear in the budget. In addition, financial reports do not fully disclose the government's financial commitments. For example, the government's liability for retirement benefits represents a major commitment of future federal resources. A recent report estimated the unfunded portion of retirement benefits to be several hundred billion dollars. But the budget only partially recognizes retirement benefits being earned by today's civilian employees, while those of military personnel were not recognized at all until Congress changed the law in the Department of Defense Authorization Act of 1984. The comprehensiveness of the budget will be further reduced if the current plan to move Social Security retirement and disability funds off the budget in 1993 is implemented.

The Federal Financing Bank had $106.9 billion in off-budget loans outstanding in 1983 and issued some $32 billion in new loans in 1982. In addition, costs of direct loans, such as loan write-offs and interest subsidies, are not routinely disclosed to decision makers. Anticipated write-offs, such as those for foreign military sales and many loan programs, are often not recognized in the budget or the accounting systems. The cost of interest subsidies is often buried as part of the interest on the public debt. Thus, decision makers may be misled into assuming that programs are less expensive than they are.

Loan guarantees are another case where the government's financial condition is not fully disclosed. Contingent liabilities should be accurately measured and incorporated into the government's financial reports.

To avoid the risk of inappropriately mortgaging the future, decision makers should recognize the long-term consequences of current benefit and loan programs. Budget documents, financial statements, and reports received by Congress and the executive branch should fully disclose the financial position of the government and reflect all costs of government activities.

In the short run, it is often tempting for program managers and policy officials to seek to hide the true costs of their programs. It may appear that doing so allows them to acquire greater resources in support of their objectives than would otherwise be possible. That temptation should be resisted for two reasons. First, the results will come back to haunt the manager and the program itself when the true costs are eventually disclosed, as they surely will be. Second, if this sort of distortion is allowed, other managers also will play the same game, with unpredictable results. Managers, as well as taxpayers, are better served if resource allocation decisions are made on a level playing field, where numbers mean what they appear to mean.

THE FEDERAL BUDGET PROCESS COULD BE STREAMLINED

Reliable, timely information is indispensable to an effective budget process. However, equally important is a budget process that focuses the attention of decision makers on available choices. The current budget processes of Congress and the executive branch are unduly detailed, repetitive, and work-intensive. These processes urgently need to be simplified and streamlined so that decision makers can more easily concentrate on the budget choices that confront them.

Over the years, both Congress and the executive branch have made changes designed to improve their budget processes. The Congressional Budget and Impoundment Control Act of 1974 created an essential framework for Congress to set national priorities. But the act did this by adding to the existing machinery for authorization, appropriation, and tax legislation. Though it devotes an ever greater proportion of its time to budget issues and the budget process, Congress in recent years has been unable to pass a budget and enact all appropriations laws before the beginning of the fiscal year.

Improvements tied in the executive branch—e.g., planning, programming, and budgeting; management by objective; zero-base budgeting—also have generally been added to existing systems and processes. As a result, both Congress and the executive branch are faced with burdensome processes marked by repetitious detail that obscures, rather than highlights, budget choices.

Budget execution, like budget preparation, has grown more detailed and complex. Managerial flexibility and efficiency is increasingly limited by the growing number of constraints on the uses of funds imposed by both Congress and executive branch officials. Recognition is growing that the federal budget process must be simplified. Proposals for improving the congressional budget process have come from both within Congress and such outside groups as the Committee for Economic Development. Those proposals include selected changes in congressional organization and procedures; a biennial budget for part or all of the federal government; and the adoption of a single, omnibus budget, appropriations and tax bill. All these proposals have the common goal of reducing the number of layers in the congressional budget process and/or reducing the number of budget decisions that Congress must make each year. Similar issues have been raised about the executive branch process, as indicated by the 1983 National Academy of Public Administration report, *Deregulation of Government Management* and by continuing reform efforts within the Office of Management and Budget.

Proposals for reform in both Congress and the executive branch should be judged against the overriding objective of making the process more manageable and understandable. Members of Congress and top executive branch officials must be less encumbered with unnecessary detail so they can give more attention to major policy issues, the long-term consequences of current budgetary decisions, and the oversight and management of government programs and agencies.

If these reform efforts succeed, the implications for managers will be substantial. Much of the burden of the present, inordinately complex budget formulation process falls on program managers, as does the task of managing programs for which the levels of funding keep changing from day to day or week to week as one continuing resolution succeeds another.

GOOD FINANCIAL INFORMATION REQUIRES STRONG ACCOUNTING, AUDITING, AND REPORTING

The importance of good financial information underscores the need for well-designed, integrated budgeting and accounting systems. Because current systems are not integrated, budgets are frequently developed without reliable information on what has occurred. This often leads to unrealistic budget planning and difficulty in controlling budget execution. Reforms are needed to strengthen how the government accounts for financial resources and to improve the financial information used by Congress and the executive branch. The consistent application of comprehensive accounting principles and standards by all agencies would ensure comparability of financial data throughout the government. Then, financial data would reflect differences in fact, rather than differences in the accounting treatment of the same facts.

Consistent, comparable data from integrated financial systems is essential for preparing government-wide financial statements. These statements can supplement budgeting and accounting information by giving an overall picture of the financial health of the government that is not available elsewhere. They could also disclose the cumulative financial effect of decisions on the nation's resources and provide early warning signals to policy makers. Many organizations, such as publicly owned corporations, are required to present comprehensive financial reports to the public. Just as shareholders expect management to report the financial position of their companies, so taxpayers should hear about the financial position of their government. Many state and local governments are moving toward this practice, partially influenced by federal reporting requirements for revenue sharing and other grant programs.

Auditing introduces discipline to the financial reporting process by confirming the accuracy and reliability of the information in financial statements. Financial auditing enhances the oversight of programs by providing a better basis for selecting areas for program audit and evaluation. Auditing is also essential to any program to strengthen internal controls. The Federal Manager's Financial Integrity Act of 1982 represents important progress. This act requires each executive agency to report annually on its compliance with internal control standards prescribed by the comptroller general and on its plans for correcting problems.

As with other elements of a strong financial management, structure federal managers have a stake in the quality of public financial reporting on their programs. Taxpayers have shown their skepticism about the efficiency and effectiveness with which their tax dollars are being spent. Publishing audited financial statements—accompanied by corrections of any deficiencies they reveal—can make a major contribution to restoring confidence in our governmental institutions.

MODERN FINANCIAL SYSTEMS ARE NEEDED TO MAKE IMPROVEMENTS

Federal decision makers are working with financial management systems that were designed for a bygone era. Many of the gaps, inconsistencies, inefficiencies, and wide disparities in quality previously discussed are the result of these antiquated systems. According to a recent presidential study commission, much of the government's data processing technology is out-of-date, and senior officials of the government have no practical means of collecting summarized management information on a government-wide basis.

Current financial management systems also are inefficient. For example, a recent GAO study revealed that the average cost to issue a federal payroll check varies from about $2 to $14, depending on what payroll system is used.

Agency efforts to update obsolete equipment for their financial management systems often do not take full advantage of improved technology. Frequently, agencies acquire new hardware without redesigning their systems to fully exploit the capabilities of the new equipment. Some agencies (such as the Air Force, the Department of Agriculture, the Department of Commerce, and the Veterans Administration) have tried to modernize and consolidate their systems. But accomplishments are limited by the need to interact with antiquated systems elsewhere.

Two basic approaches may be used to improve current systems. One is to redesign existing systems without altering the basic roles and missions of agencies involved in federal financial management. This approach will yield new systems and equipment. But it will not achieve the most efficient operations.

A second approach might be to revise the basic structure of financial management by locating a few (20 or so) processing centers in the cabinet departments and major agencies to handle both disbursements and financial accounting. Other federal agencies could share common systems for related activities, allowing substantial savings in development and operating costs. The result would be higher productivity in federal financial management operations and more timely, compatible, and reliable financial information.

Consistent, comparable information from the individual agency systems should flow into a central system that is capable of routinely summarizing, consolidating, and reporting relevant information to top policy makers in the executive branch, members of Congress, and the public on a timely basis.

PUTTING IN PLACE A MODERN FINANCIAL MANAGEMENT STRUCTURE

Recognition is growing that federal financial management must be modernized. Many efforts are now underway to improve financial management systems and reporting, including projects in the Departments of State, Treasury, and Commerce, as well as the government-wide initiatives of "Reform '88." Congress is considering several proposals for reform as well. The challenge is to integrate these efforts into a broader strategy for comprehensive overhaul of the structure. This can lead to the creation of a more modern, efficient, responsive, and reliable financial management structure to support decision making and management in both Congress and the executive branch.

Many of the benefits that could be achieved through a modern structure of financial management already exist in the integrated financial management systems of progressive state and local government. Such a structure can be built for the federal government, but it will not emerge by accident, nor can it be created through isolated efforts in a few agencies. Building the structure will require the design and installation of new systems over an extended period. Coordination of new and existing system development activities can yield major benefits at little additional cost. An equally important investment must be made in the people who implement and operate the system. They must be recruited more carefully, trained more thoroughly, and offered a more attractive career path.

Organizational realignments will be needed. Financial operations should be consolidated into more efficient units that use modern technology.

Responsibilities for interagency policy making should be clearly assigned. Finally, all actions must be coordinated to serve the needs of the government as a whole. Because developing a new system is likely to overlap several presidential administrations, it will require firm commitment, clearly identified leadership responsibility, and continuity of purpose. These key ingredients, however, can only exist if supported by a broad and stable bipartisan consensus—including Congress and the executive branch.

A modern structure for managing federal government finances will not cause the budget deficit to disappear, nor will it make difficult budget decisions easy. However, structural and systems improvements can help to ensure that policy makers, executive branch officials, and federal managers receive timely, viable, relevant, and consistent information with which to make those decisions.

ORGANIZATIONAL DECLINE AND CUTBACK MANAGEMENT

Charles H. Levine

Government organizations are neither immortal nor unshrinkable.[1] Like growth, organizational decline and death, by erosion or plan, is a form of organizational change; but all the problems of managing organizational change are compounded by a scarcity of slack resources.[2] This feature of declining organizations—the diminution of the cushion of spare resources necessary for coping with uncertainty, risking innovation, and rewarding loyalty and cooperation—presents for government a problem that simultaneously challenges the underlying premises and feasibility of both contemporary management systems and the institutions of pluralist liberal democracy.[3]

Growth and decline are issues of a grand scale usually tackled by only the most brave or foolhardy of macro social theorists. The division of scholarly labor between social theorists and students of management is now so complete that the link between the great questions of political economy and the more earthly problems of managing public organizations is rarely forged. This bifurcation is more understandable when one acknowledges that managers and organization analysts have for decades (at least since the Roosevelt Administration and the wide acceptance of Keynesian economics) been able to subsume their concern for societal level instability under broad assumptions of abundance and continuous and unlimited economic growth.[4] Indeed, almost all of our public management strategies are predicated on assumptions of the continuing enlargement of public revenues and expenditures. These expansionist assumptions are particularly prevalent in public financial management systems that anticipate

budgeting by incremental additions to a secure base.[5] Recent events and gloomy forecasts, however, have called into question the validity and generality of these assumptions, and have created a need to reopen inquiry into the effects of resource scarcity on public organizations and their management systems. These events and forecasts, ranging from taxpayer revolts like California's successful Proposition 13 campaign and financial crises like the near collapse into bankruptcy of New York City's government and the agonizing retrenchment of its bureaucracy, to the foreboding predictions of the "limits of growth" modelers, also relink issues of political economy of the most monumental significance to practices of public management.[6]

We know very little about the decline of public organizations and the management of cutbacks. This may be because even though some federal agencies like the Works Progress Administration, Economic Recovery Administration, Department of Defense, National Aeronautics and Space Administration, the Office of Economic Opportunity, and many state and local agencies have expanded and then contracted,[7] or even died, the public sector as a whole has expanded enormously over the last four decades. In this period of expansion and optimism among proponents of an active government, isolated incidents of zero growth and decline have been considered anomalous; and the difficulties faced by the management of declining agencies coping with retrenchment have been regarded as outside the mainstream of public management concerns. It is a sign of our times—labeled by Kenneth Boulding as the "Era of Slowdown"—that we are now reappraising cases of public organization decline and death as exemplars and forerunners in order to provide strategies for the design and management of *mainstream* public administration in a future dominated by resource scarcity.[8]

The decline and death of government organizations is a symptom, a problem, and a contingency. It is a symptom of resource scarcity at a societal, even global, level that is creating the necessity for governments to terminate some programs, lower the activity level of others, and confront tradeoffs between new demands and old programs rather than to expand whenever a new public problem arises. It is a problem for managers who must maintain organizational capacity by devising new managerial arrangements within prevailing structures that were designed under assumptions of growth. It is a contingency for public employees and clients; employees who must sustain their morale and productivity in the face of increasing control from above and shrinking opportunities for creativity and promotion while clients must find alternative sources for the services governments may no longer be able to provide. . . .

STRATEGIC CHOICES

Public organizations behave in response to a mix of motives—some aimed at serving national (or state or local) purposes, some aimed at goals for the *organization as a whole*, and others directed toward the particularistic goals of organizational subunits. Under conditions of growth, requests for more resources by subunits usually can be easily concerted with the goals of the organization as a whole and its larger social purposes. Under decline, however, subunits usually respond to requests to make cuts in terms of their particular long-term survival needs (usually defended in terms of the injury which cutbacks would inflict on a program with lofty purposes or on a dependent clientele) irrespective of impacts on the performance of government or the organization as a whole.

The presence of powerful survival instincts in organizational subunits helps to explain why the political leadership of public organizations can be trying to respond to legislative or executive directives to cut back while at the same time the career and program leadership of subunits will be taking action to resist cuts.[9] It also helps to explain why growth can have the appearance of a rational administrative process complete with a hierarchy of objectives and broad consensus, while decline takes on the *appearance* of what James G. March has called a "garbage can problem"—arational, polycentric, fragmented, and dynamic.[10] Finally, it allows us to understand why the official rhetoric about cutbacks—whether it be to "cut the fat," "tighten our belts," "preserve future options," or "engage in a process of orderly and programmed termination"—is often at wide variance with the

unofficial conduct of bureau chiefs who talk of "minimizing cutbacks to mitigate catastrophe," or "making token sacrifices until the heat's off."

Retrenchment politics dictate that organizations will respond to decrements with a mix of espoused and operative strategies that are not necessarily consistent.[11] When there is a wide divergence between the official pronouncements about the necessity for cuts and the actual occurrence of cuts, skepticism, cynicism, distrust, and noncompliance will dominate the retrenchment process and cutback management will be an adversarial process pitting top and middle management against one another. In most cases, however, conflict will not be rancorous, and strategies for dealing with decline will be a mixed bag of tactics intended either to *resist* or to *smooth* decline. The logic here is that no organization accedes to cuts with enthusiasm and will try to find a way to resist cuts; but resistance is risky. In addition to the possibility of being charged with nonfeasance, no responsible manager wants to be faced with the prospect of being unable to control where cuts will take place or confront quantum cuts with unpredictable consequences. Instead, managers will choose a less risky course and attempt to protect organizational capacity and procedures by smoothing decline and its effects on the organization.

An inventory of some of these cutback management tactics is presented in Figure 1. They are arrayed according to the type of decline problem which they can be employed to solve. This collection of tactics by no means exhausts the possible organizational responses to decline situations, nor are all the tactics exclusively directed toward meeting a single contingency. They are categorized in order to show that many familiar coping tactics correspond, even if only roughly, to an underlying logic. In this way a great deal of information about organizational responses to decline can be aggregated without explicating each tactic in great detail.[12]

The tactics intended to remove or alleviate the external political and economic causes of decline are reasonably straightforward means to revitalize eroded economic bases, reduce environmental uncertainty, protect niches, retain flexibility, or lessen dependence. The tactics for handling the internal causes of decline, however, tend to be more subtle means for strengthening organizations

	Tactics to Resist Decline	Tactics to Smooth Decline
	External	
Political	*Problem Depletion* 1. Diversify programs, clients and constituents 2. Improve legislative liaison 3. Educate the public about the agency's mission 4. Mobilize dependent clients 5. Become "captured" by a powerful interest group or legislator 6. Threaten to cut vital or popular programs 7. Cut a visible and widespread service a little to demonstrate client dependence	1. Make peace with competing agencies 2. Cut low prestige programs 3. Cut programs to politically weak clients 4. Sell and lend expertise to other agencies 5. Share problems with other agencies
Economic/ Technical	*Environmental Entropy* 1. Find a wider and richer revenue base (e.g., metropolitan reorganization) 2. Develop incentives to prevent disinvestment 3. Seek foundation support 4. Lure new public and private sector investment 5. Adopt user charges for services where possible	1. Improve targeting on problems 2. Plan with preservative objectives 3. Cut losses by distinguishing between capital investments and sunk costs 4. Yield concessions to taxpayers and employers to retain them
	Internal	
Political	*Political Vulnerability* 1. Issue symbolic responses like forming study commissions and task forces 2. "Circle the wagons," i.e., develop a seige mentality to retain esprit de corps 3. Strengthen expertise	1. Change leadership at each stage in the decline process 2. Reorganize at each stage 3. Cut programs run by weak subunits 4. Shift programs to another agency 5. Get temporary exemptions from personnel and budgetary regulations which limit discretion
Economic/ Technical	*Organizational Atrophy* 1. Increase hierarchical control 2. Improve productivity 3. Experiment with less costly service delivery systems 4. Automate 5. Stockpile and ration resources	1. Renegotiate long-term contracts to regain flexibility 2. Install rational choice techniques like zero-base budgeting and evaluation research 3. Mortgage the future by deferring maintenance and downscaling personnel quality 4. Ask employees to make voluntary sacrifices like taking early retirements and deferring raises 5. Improve forecasting capacity to anticipate further cuts 6. Reassign surplus facilities to other users 7. Sell surplus property, lease back when needed 8. Exploit the exploitable

FIGURE 1
Some Cutback Management Tactics

and managerial control. For instance, the management of decline *in the face of resistance* can be smoothed by changes in leadership. When hard unpopular decisions have to be made, new managers can be brought in to make the cuts, take the flak, and move on to another organization.

By rotating managers into and out of the declining organization, interpersonal loyalties built up over the years will not interfere with the cutback process. This is especially useful in implementing a higher level decision to terminate an organization where managers will make the necessary cuts knowing that their next assignments will not depend on their support in the organization to be terminated.

The "exploit the exploitable" tactic also calls for further explanation. Anyone familiar with the personnel practices of universities during the 1970's will recognize this tactic. It has been brought about by the glutted market for academic positions which has made many unlucky recent Ph.D's vulnerable and exploitable. This buyers' market has coincided neatly with the need of universities facing steady states and declining enrollments to avoid long-term tenure commitments to expensive faculties. The result is a marked increase in part-time and non-tenure track positions which are renewed on a semester-to-semester basis. So while retrenchment is smoothed and organization flexibility increased, it is attained at considerable cost to the careers and job security of the exploited teachers.

Cutback management is a two-crucible problem: besides selecting tactics for either resisting or smoothing decline, if necessary, management must also select who will be let go and what programs will be curtailed or terminated. Deciding where to make cuts is a test of managerial intelligence and courage because each choice involves tradeoffs and opportunity costs that cannot be erased through the generation of new resources accrued through growth.

As with most issues of public management involving the distribution of costs, the choice of decision rules to allocate cuts usually involves the tradeoff between equity and efficiency.[13] In this case, "equity" is meant to mean the distribution of cuts across the organization with an equal probability of hurting all units and employees irrespective of impacts on the long-term capacity of the organization. "Efficiency" is meant to mean the sorting, sifting, and assignment of cuts to those people and units in the organization so that for a given budget decrement, cuts are allocated to minimize the long-term loss in total benefits to the organization as a whole, irrespective of their distribution.

Making cuts on the basis of equity is easier for managers because it is socially acceptable, easier to justify, and involves few decision making costs. "Sharing the pain" is politically expedient because it appeals to common sense ideals of justice. Further, simple equity decision making avoids costs from sorting, selecting, and negotiating cuts.[14] In contrast, efficiency cuts involve costly triage analysis because the distribution of pain and inconvenience requires that the value of people and subunits to the organization have to be weighed in terms of their expected *future* contributions. In the public sector, of course, things are never quite this clear cut because a host of constraints like career status, veteran's preference, bumping rights, entitlements, and mandated programs limit managers from selecting optimal rules for making cuts. Nevertheless, the values of equity and efficiency are central to allocative decision making and provide useful criteria for judging the appropriateness of cutback rules. By applying these criteria to five of the most commonly used or proposed cutback methods— seniority, hiring freezes, even-percentage-cuts-across-the-board, productivity criteria, and zero base budgeting—we are able to make assessments of their efficacy as managerial tools.

Seniority is the most prevalent and most maligned of the five decision rules. Seniority guarantees have little to do with either equity or efficiency, *per se*. Instead, they are directed at another value of public administration; that is, the need to provide secure career-long employment to neutrally competent civil servants.[15] Because seniority is likely to be spread about the organization unevenly, using seniority criteria for making cuts forces managers to implicitly surrender control over the impact of cuts on services and the capacity of subunits. Furthermore, since seniority usually dictates a "last-in-first-out" retention system, personnel cuts using this decision rule tend to inflict the greatest harm to minorities and women who are recent entrants in most public agencies.

A *hiring freeze* is a convenient short-run strategy to buy time and preserve options. In the short run it hurts no one already employed by the organization because hiring freezes rely on "natural attrition" through resignations, retirements, and death to diminish the size of an organization's work force. In the long run, however, hiring freezes are hardly the most equitable or efficient way to scale down organizational size. First, even though natural and self selection relieves the stress on managers, it also takes control over the decision of whom and where to cut away from management and thereby reduces the possibility of intelligent long-range cutback planning. Second, hiring freezes are more likely to harm minorities and women who are more likely to be the next hired rather than the next retired. Third, attrition will likely occur at different rates among an organization's professional and technical specialities. Since resignations will most likely come from those employees with the most opportunities for employment elsewhere, during a long hiring freeze an organization may find itself short on some critically needed skills yet unable to hire people with these skills even though they may be available.

Even-percentage-cuts-across-the-board are expedient because they transfer decision-making costs lower in the organization, but they tend to be insensitive to the needs, production functions, and contributions of different units. The same percentage cut may call for hardly more than some mild belt tightening in some large unspecialized units but when translated into the elimination of one or two positions in a highly specialized, tightly integrated small unit, it may immobilize that unit.

Criticizing *productivity criteria* is more difficult but nevertheless appropriate, especially when the concept is applied to the practice of cutting low producing units and people based on their *marginal product* per increment of revenue. This method is insensitive to differences in clients served, unit capacity, effort, and need. A more appropriate criterion is one that cuts programs, organization units, and employees so that the *marginal utility* for a decrement of resources is equal across units, individuals, and programs thereby providing for *equal sacrifices* based on the *need* for resources. However, this criterion assumes organizations are fully rational actors, an assumption easily dismissed. More likely, cuts will be distributed by a mix of analysis and political bargaining.

Aggregating incompatible needs and preferences is a political problem and this is why *zero base budgeting* gets such high marks as a method for making decisions about resource allocation under conditions of decline. First, ZBB

is future directed; instead of relying on an "inviolate-base-plus-increment" calculus, it allows for the analysis of both existing and proposed new activities. Second, ZBB allows for tradeoffs between programs or units below their present funding levels. Third, ZBB allows a ranking of decision packages by political bargaining and negotiation so that attention is concentrated on those packages or activities most likely to be affected by cuts.[16] As a result, ZBB allows both analysis and politics to enter into cutback decision making and therefore can incorporate an expression of the *intensity of need* for resources by participating managers and clients while also accommodating estimates of how cuts will affect the *activity levels* of their units. Nevertheless, ZBB is not without problems. Its analytic component is likely to be expensive—especially so under conditions of austerity—and to be subject to all the limitations and pitfalls of cost-benefit analysis, while its political component is likely to be costly in political terms as units fight with each other and with central management over rankings, tradeoffs, and the assignment of decrements.[17]

These five decision rules illustrate how strategic choices about cutback management can be made with or without expediency, analysis, courage, consideration of the organization's long-term health, or the effect of cuts on the lives of employees and clients. Unfortunately, for some employees and clients, and the public interest, the choice will usually be made by managers to "go along" quietly with across-the-board cuts and exit as soon as possible. The alternative for those who would prefer more responsible and toughminded decision making *to facilitate long run organizational survival* is to develop in managers and employees strong feelings of organizational loyalty and loyalty to clients, to provide disincentives to easy exit, and to encourage participation so that dissenting views on the location of cuts could emerge from the ranks of middle management, lower level employees, and clients.[18]

PONDERABLES

The world of the future is uncertain, but scarcity and tradeoffs seem inevitable. Boulding has argued, "in a stationary society roughly half the society will be experiencing decline while the other half will be experiencing growth."[19] If we are entering an era of general slowdown, this means that the balance in the distribution between expanding and contracting sectors, regions, and organizations will be tipped toward decline. It means that we will need a governmental capacity for developing tradeoffs between growing and declining organizations and for intervening in regional and sectorial economies to avoid the potentially harmful effects of radical perturbations from unmanaged decline.

So far we have managed to get along without having to make conscious tradeoffs between sectors and regions. We have met declines on a "crisis-to-crisis" basis through emergency legislation and financial aid. This is a strategy that assumes declines are special cases of temporary disequilibrium, bounded in time and space, that are usually confined to a single organization, community, or region. A broad scale long-run *societal level* decline, however, is a problem of a different magnitude and to resolve it, patchwork solutions will not suffice.

There seem to be two possible directions in which to seek a way out of immobility. First is the authoritarian possibility; what Robert L. Heilbroner has called the rise of "iron governments" with civil liberties diminished and resources allocated throughout society from the central government without appeal.[20] This is a possibility abhorrent to the democratic tradition, but it comprises a possible future—if not for the United States in the near future, at least for some other less affluent nations. So far we have had little experience with cutting back on rights, entitlements, and privileges; but scarcity may dictate "decoupling" dependent and less powerful clients and overcoming resistance through violent autocratic implementation methods.

The other possible future direction involves new images and assumptions about the nature of man, the state and the ecosystem. It involves changes in values away from material consumption, a gradual withdrawal from our fascination with economic growth, and more efficient use of resources—especially raw materials. For this possibility to occur, we will have to have a confrontation with our propensity for wishful thinking that denies that some declines are permanent. Also required is a widespread acceptance of egalitarian norms and of anti-growth and

no growth ideologies which are now only nascent, and the development of a political movement to promote their incorporation into policy making.[21] By backing away from our obsession with growth, we will also be able to diminish the "load" placed on central governments and allow for greater decentralization and the devolvement of functions.[22] In this way, we may be able to preserve democratic rights and processes while meeting a future of diminished resources.

However, the preferable future might not be the most probable future. This prospect should trouble us deeply.

NOTES

1. The intellectual foundations of this essay are too numerous to list. Three essays in particular sparked my thinking: Herbert Kaufman's *The Limits of Organizational Change* (University, Alabama: The University of Alabama Press, 1971) and *Are Government Organizations Immortal?* (Washington, D.C.: The Brookings Institution, 1976) and Herbert J. Gans, "Planning for Declining and Poor Cities," *Journal of the American Institute of Planners* (September, 1975), pp. 305–307. The concept of "cutback planning" is introduced in the Gans article. My initial interest in this subject stemmed from my work with a panel of the National Academy of Public Administration on a NASA-sponsored project that produced *Report of the Ad Hoc Panel on Attracting New Staff and Retaining Capability During a Period of Declining Manpower Ceilings.*

2. For an explication of the concept of "organizational slack" see Richard M. Cyert and James G. March, *A Behavioral Theory of the Firm* (Englewood Cliffs, N.J.: Prentice-Hall, 1963), pp. 36–38. They argue that because of market imperfections between payments and demands "there is ordinarily a disparity between the resources available to the organization and the payments required to maintain the coalition. This difference between total resources and total necessary payments is what we have called *organizational slack.* Slack consists in payments to members of the coalition in excess of what is required to maintain the organization. . . . Many forms of slack typically exist: stockholders are paid dividends in excess of those required to keep stockholders (or banks) within the organization; prices are set lower than necessary to maintain adequate income from buyers; wages in excess of those required to maintain labor are paid; executives are provided with services and personal luxuries in excess of those required to keep

them; subunits are permitted to grow without real concern for the relation between additional payments and additional revenue; public services are provided in excess of those required. . . . Slack operates to stabilize the system in two ways: (1) by absorbing excess resources, it retards upward adjustment of aspirations during relatively good times; (2) by providing a pool of emergency resources, it permits aspirations to be maintained (and achieved) during relatively bad times."

3. See William G. Scott, "The Management of Decline," *The Conference Board RECORD* (June, 1976), pp. 56–59 and "Organization Theory: A Reassessment," *Academy of Management Journal* (June, 1974) pp. 242–253; also Rufus E. Miles, Jr., *Awakening from the American Dream: The Social and Political Limits to Growth* (New York: Universal Books, 1976).

4. See Daniel M. Fox, *The Discovery of Abundance: Simon N. Patten and the Transformation of Social Theory* (Ithaca, N.Y.: Cornell University Press, 1967).

5. See Andrew Glassberg's contribution to this symposium, "Organizational Responses to Municipal Budget Decreases," and Edward H. Potthoff, Jr., "Pre-planning for Budget Reductions," *Public Management* (March, 1975), pp. 13–14.

6. See Donella H. Meadows, Dennis L. Meadows, Jorgen Randers, and William W. Behrens III, *The Limits to Growth* (New York: Universe Books, 1972); also Robert L. Heilbroner, *An Inquiry into the Human Prospect* (New York: W.W. Norton, 1975) and *Business Civilization in Decline* (New York: W.W. Norton, 1976).

7. See Advisory Commission on Intergovernmental Relations, *City Financial Emergencies: The Intergovernmental Dimension* (Washington, D.C.: U.S. Government Printing Office, 1973).

8. Kenneth E. Boulding, "The Management of Decline," *Change* (June, 1975), pp. 8–9 and 64. For extensive analyses of cutback management in the same field that Boulding addresses, university administration, see: Frank M. Bowen and Lyman A. Glenny, *State Budgeting for Higher Education: State Fiscal Stringency and Public Higher Education* (Berkeley, Calif.: Center for Research and Development in Higher Education, 1976); Adam Yarmolinsky, "Institutional Paralysis," *Special Report on American Higher Education: Toward an Uncertain Future* 2 Vol, *Daedalus* 104 (Winter, 1975), pp. 61–67; Frederick E. Balderston, *Varieties of Financial Crisis*, (Berkeley, Calif.: Ford Foundation, 1972); The Carnegie Foundation for the Advancement of Teaching, *More Than Survival* (San Francisco: Jossey-Bass, 1975); Earl F. Cheit, *The New Depression in Higher Education* (New York: McGraw-Hill, 1975) and *The New Depression in Higher Education—Two Years Later* (Berkeley, Calif.: The Carnegie Commission on Higher Education, 1973); Lyman A. Glenny, "The Illusions of Steady States," *Change* 6 (December/January 1974–75), pp. 24–28; and John D. Millett, "What Is Economic Health?" *Change* 8 (September, 1976), p. 27.

9. For recent analyses of related phenomena see Joel D. Aberbach and Bert A. Rockman, "Clashing Beliefs Within the Executive Branch: The Nixon Administration Bureaucracy," *American Political Science Review* (June, 1976), pp. 456–468 and Hugh Heclo, *A Government of Strangers: Executive Politics in Washington* (Washington, D.C.: The Brookings Institution, 1977).

10. See James G. March and Johan P. Olsen, *Ambiguity and Choice in Organizations* (Bergen, Norway: Universitetsforlaget, 1976); and Michael D. Cohen, James G. March, and Johan P. Olsen, "A Garbage Can Model of Organizational Choice," *Administrative Science Quarterly* (March, 1972), pp. 1–25.

11. See Charles Perrow, *Organizational Analysis: A Sociological View* (Belmont, Calif.: Wadsworth Publishing Company, 1970) and Chris Argyris and Donald A. Schon, *Theory in Practice: Increasing Professional Effectiveness* (San Francisco, Calif.: Jossey-Bass, 1974) for discussions of the distinction between espoused and operative (i.e., "theory-in-use") strategies.

12. For extensive treatments of the tactics of bureaucrats, some of which are listed here, see Frances E. Rourke, *Bureaucracy, Politics, and Public Policy* (second edition, Boston: Little, Brown and Company, 1976); Aaron Wildavsky, *The Politics of the Budgetary Process* (second edition, Boston: Little, Brown and Company, 1974); Eugene Lewis, *American Politics in a Bureaucratic Age* (Cambridge, Mass.: Winthrop Publishers, 1977); and Simon, Smithburg and Thompson, *Public Administration*.

13. See Arthur M. Oken, *Equity and Efficiency: The Big Tradeoff* (Washington, D.C.: The Brookings Institution, 1975).

14. For a discussion of the costs of interactive decision making see Charles R. Adrian and Charles Press, "Decision Costs in Coalition Formation," *American Political Science Review* (June, 1968), pp. 556–563.

15. See Herbert Kaufman, "Emerging Conflicts in the Doctrine of Public Administration," *American Political Science Review* (December, 1956), pp. 1057–1073 and Frederick C. Mosher, *Democracy and the Public Service* (New York: Oxford University Press, 1968). Seniority criteria also have roots in the widespread belief that organizations ought to recognize people who invest heavily in them by protecting long time employees when layoffs become necessary.

16. See Peter A. Pyhrr, "The Zero-Base Approach to Government Budgeting," *Public Administration Review* (January/February, 1977), pp. 1–8; Graeme M. Taylor, "Introduction to Zero-base Budgeting," *The Bureaucrat* (Spring, 1977), pp. 33–55.

17. See Brewer, "Termination: Hard Choices—Harder Questions"; Allen Schick, "Zero-base Budgeting and Sunset: Redundancy or Symbiosis?" *The Bureaucrat* (Spring, 1977), pp. 12–32 and "The Road From ZBB" *Public Administration Review* (March/April, 1978), pp. 177–180; and Aaron Wildavsky, "The Political Economy of Efficiency," *Public Administration Review* (December, 1966), pp. 292–310.

18. See Hirschman, *Exit, Voice and Loyalty*, especially Ch. 7, "A Theory of Loyalty," pp. 76–105. Despite the attractiveness of "responsible and toughminded decision making" the constraints on managerial discretion in contraction decisions should not be underestimated. At the local level, for example, managers often have little influence on what federally funded programs will be cut back or terminated. They are often informed after funding cuts have been made in Washington and they are expected to make appropriate adjustments in their local work forces. These downward adjustments often are also outside of a manager's control because in many cities with merit systems, veteran's preference, and strong unions, elaborate rules dictate who will be dismissed and the timing of dismissals.

19. Boulding, "The Management of Decline," p. 8.

20. See Heilbroner, *An Inquiry into the Human Prospect*; also Michael Harrington, *The Twilight of Capitalism* (New York: Simon & Schuster, 1976).

21. For a discussion of anti-growth politics see Harvey Molotch, "The City as a Growth Machine," *American Journal of Sociology* (September, 1976), pp. 309–332.

22. Richard Rose has made a penetrating argument about the potential of governments to become "overloaded" in "Comment: What Can Ungovernability Mean?" *Futures* (April, 1977), pp. 92–94. For a more detailed presentation, see his "On the Priorities of Government: A Developmental Analysis of Public Policies," *European Journal of Political Research* (September, 1976), pp. 247–290. This theme is also developed by Rose in collaboration with B. Guy Peters in *Can Governments Go Bankrupt?* (New York: Basic Books, forthcoming 1978).

PRIVATIZATION IS A MEANS TO "MORE WITH LESS"

John R. Miller and Christopher R. Tufts

America's industrial leaders have come to realize that to be competitive in the global economy they must demonstrate to the buying public that their products represent the best value. Such mode of economics-based decision making is now being applied by taxpayers to the goods and services produced by government. Taxpayers and consumers alike are demanding the best quality and value for their hard-earned dollars.

Companies realize that in order to win in the marketplace and make a profit, they must "accomplish more with less"—fewer people, less money, less time, less space and fewer resources in general. To be competitive and profitable, many companies are adopting "downsizing" business strategies. Key components of downsizing include: productivity and quality improvement programs; mergers, streamlining operations; and divestiture of businesses in which they are not competitive. These strategies must be balanced by more creative management.

Government has a comparable challenge. Faced with public demand for increased or improved services in a period of diminishing resources and a changing pattern of accountability, government officials must also develop innovative solutions to win public confidence. This article discusses the concept of downsizing government and specifically focuses on privatization of service delivery as one alternative.

DOWNSIZING

Government downsizing is the selective application of a broad range of management and cost reduction techniques to streamline operations and eliminate unnecessary costs. These same techniques can be applied to the development or expansion of government service, as well as to maintaining service levels, improving quality, and reducing existing government service cost. In all cases the objective is the same: Identify practical solutions and implementation plans that best serve the public through more effective management and delivery of government services, while saving or avoiding unnecessary costs.

Downsizing alternatives can be grouped into five major categories:

- Productivity and quality improvement programs;
- Consolidation (intra- and inter-government cooperation);
- Privatization;
- Program reduction;
- Program abandonment.

The objective of "accomplishing more for less" is most frequently achieved by exercising a combination of downsizing alternatives. For example, a government may initiate a productivity and quality improvement program in its health services; consolidate, through a multijurisdictional agreement, to provide shock trauma medical treatment; contract with the private sector to provide drug prevention programs; attempt to reduce the demand for service through the imposition of user fees for ambulance service; and eliminate minor injury treatment services at government hospitals. Each potential opportunity for downsizing must be approached creatively to ensure the public still receives the best service at the lowest possible cost.

PRIVATIZATION AS A DOWNSIZING CHOICE

As many corporate leaders are retrenching to do better what they do best, so too must government be willing to do the same. Peter Drucker, in his book *The Age of Discontinuity*, called for "reprivatization" of many government functions, saying "The purpose of government is to make fundamental decisions and to make them effectively. The purpose of government is to focus the political energies of society. It is to dramatize issues. It is to present fundamental choices. The purpose of government, in other words, is to govern. This, as we have learned in other institutions is incompatible with 'doing.' Any attempt to combine governing with 'doing' on a large scale paralyzes government's decision-making capacity."

One downsizing alternative for government to consider is to competitively engage the private sector to produce goods and services that are readily available from many commercial sources. Although the current impetus for privatization is largely pragmatic, the guiding political philosophy behind it is as old as the nation itself. Americans have long alternated between the Jeffersonian and Hamiltonian philosophies of government. However, the new momentum for privatization transcends political and ideological boundaries, and is rooted in the determination of creative government managers to develop innovative solutions to serve the public interest.

Today a broad and growing consensus recognizes that privatization, properly implemented, is a viable and legitimate response to a wide range of philosophical and practical concerns. Experience is showing that the private sector can indeed provide many services rendered by government with equal or greater effectiveness, and at lower cost. Consequently, privatization is likely to exert a powerful influence over the shape of political and economic institutions in coming years.

WHAT IS PRIVATIZATION?

George W. Wilson, Distinguished Professor of Business and Economics at the Indiana University School of Business, defines privatization on a philosophical plane. He writes, "The broader and more relevant meaning of privatization must refer to nothing more or less than greater reliance upon market forces to generate production of particular goods and services."

In practical terms, privatization is a process by which government engages the private sector to provide capital or otherwise finance government programs, purchase government assets, and/or operate government programs through various types of contractual arrangements.

As privatization usually occurs in combination with other downsizing initiatives, so too do many privatization transactions involve a combination of methods. For example, private sector capital financing, using such vehicles as leveraged leasing, lease purchases, and turnkey contracts, is frequently accompanied by operation of government programs through one of four types of arrangements: franchises, grants, vouchers, or contracts.

Privatization is nothing new. It can be traced to the first Bank of the United States which served as the Federal government's fiscal agency and principal depository of the Treasury and was owned by private shareholders. When the Federal government wanted to deliver mail to its citizens west of the Mississippi, it contracted with 80 horseback riders and spawned the Pony Express. The Homestead Act gave settlers government-owned land for a small fee if they would cultivate soil for a fixed period.

In the last decade, privatization has expanded from capital construction and professional service contracts to traditionally in-house administrative and public service programs. The majority of governments now contract for at least some legal, medical, engineering, technical and other professional services. Indeed, state and local government spending for public services performed by the private sector rose from $27.4 billion in 1975 to well over $100 billion in 1985. The trend toward privatization will continue to grow even though the growth rate for state and local governments appears to be slowing.

State governments, though less active than local governments with privatization, are experimenting in many areas. The state of California alone in 1985 wrote 7,000 contracts, worth over $2 billion, to carry out administrative or public service functions, including mental health, corrections, and a full range of administrative services.

OBJECTIVES OF PRIVATIZATION

What are the primary objectives of privatization? They are:

- To improve the use of scarce resources by reducing the costs of providing public services, particularly where private enterprise is strong and government is assured of more effective services at lower costs;

- To modify the role of government from that of a primary producer of goods and services to that of governing;
- To enable government to meet responsibilities that might otherwise be abandoned because they are too costly;
- To reduce the debt burden;
- To limit tax rates.

Privatization of government services should be considered:

- When government's operations are unrelated to the central function of governance. Examples of governance are legislative, judicial, and certain financial activities (e.g., rate setting, debt issuance, revenue policy);
- When current government service is in direct competition with services operated by the private sector;
- When the cost of an existing government-provided service exceeds the available or projected resources;
- When current government operations are inefficient and/or service is of poor quality and all remedial actions have resulted in insufficient improvement.

PRIVATIZATION SUCCESSES

As already noted, privatization transactions cover a wide range of services. The following are examples of applications of various types of privatization.

Fire protection: Rural/Metro Fire Department Corporation, a privately owned company, serves half a million people in Arizona (one-fifth of the state's population), and 100,000 more in Tennessee. Rural/Metro Corp.'s $4.3 million contract with Scottsdale, Arizona for 1987-88 averages out to $36 per capita per year, compared with an average of $50 for public fire departments in similar cities. Scottsdale's fire insurance rates are average.

Ambulance service: Newton, Massachusetts, estimates saving nearly $500,000 by privatizing its ambulance service while at the same time increasing ambulance availability and coverage.

Street light maintenance: The City of New York is divided into eight service areas for the provision of street light maintenance. All eight are competitively bid. No single company can "win" more than two service areas.

Legal: In Los Angeles County, Rolling Hills Estates broke off a contract it had with the County Prosecutor to handle all its cases, mostly involving violations of building and other town codes. Rolling Hills Estates now pays a private law firm to act as Town Prosecutor.

Grounds maintenance: The school district of Rye, New York, recently contracted for grounds maintenance with a private company at an estimated savings of $34,000.

Prisons: The Dade County Jail is run by the Corrections Corp. of America, which runs several correction facilities throughout the United States, including two for the United States Immigration and Naturalization Service in Texas. Some interesting questions arise in privatizing corrections. Who chases escapees? Who is liable for the prisoners and their actions? Is prisoner rehabilitation compatible with profit? (Court decisions so far indicate that *both* the government and private contractor are liable for the actions of private guards.)

Fleet maintenance: The city of Philadelphia contracts for the repair, maintenance and replacement of its motor vehicle fleet at an estimated savings of more than $4 million over the past four years.

Health care: In Corsicana, Texas, the Navarro County Hospital was old, losing money, and about to lose its accreditation. To put it in shape, $12 million was needed. The county turned it over to the Hospital Corporation of America, which built a new hospital right next to the old one. The former hospital cost taxpayers $50,000 a year to operate. The new one is paying taxes of over $300,000 a year. In a similar vein, in 1983 the city of Louisville, Kentucky, turned over the operation of a teaching hospital at the University of Louisville to the Humana Corporation. This hospital now benefits from the advantages of mass purchasing, gained by being part of Humana's 85-hospital chain.

Public defender services: Shasta County, California, reported a $100,000 per year savings in indigent-defense court costs by contracting its entire public defender program to a private firm run by a former member of the district attorney's staff in association with six full-time lawyers, three secretaries and a part-time investigator. The switchover was prompted by a study that showed Shasta's in-house Public Defender's Office was about one-third more costly than contract services would be.

Data processing: Orange County, California, whose population has doubled to over two million since 1973, estimates that it has saved more than $3 million over the past 12 years by hiring a private firm to run its computer center. "Without automation and the professional know-how to use the computers efficiently," said Howard Dix, manager of the center's operations, "the county would have faced an explosive growth in costs for personnel and facilities."

PRIVATIZATION FAILURES

Let us now look at some failures in privatization, and the pitfalls they illustrate.

Two towns in Ohio hired a private security firm to provide police protection. The equipment provided was totally unacceptable. Both towns fired the private company and hired the guards to be public police officers.

In another case, a city contracted for trash pickup at one cent per household per month less than the city could provide the service. The company could not work that cheaply. Within months, the company was raising cash by selling equipment given it by the city. At Thanksgiving and Christmas, garbage piled up faster than the company could collect it. A new company took over the contract. Said the mayor of the city, this "case makes me a lot more cautious. It was false economy to take a bid that was low by one cent per household per month."

New York City's Parking Violations Bureau scandal is a sore reminder of what can happen in contracting for services. Several public officials and businesspeople pled guilty to, or were convicted of, serious crimes involving contract corruption. Two contracting corporations, without admitting any guilt concerning the alleged bribes, reached an out-of-court settlement with the city wherein the companies paid $600,000 in damages.

In a New Jersey city, private trash haulers bill residents directly. As local landfills close, the haulers' costs rise dramatically, and they in turn raise the rates they charge. Complaints to the haulers have been unavailing, and the reaction of some residents is to cancel service and dump their own garbage illegally in any open space. This has precipitated a limited health emergency. City officials are now considering eliminating use of the franchised haulers and instituting municipal trash collection, even though it will require raising property taxes.

HOW TO ACCOMPLISH PRIVATIZATION TRANSACTIONS

To avoid the pitfalls of the failure examples, a careful process should be followed. The process should begin with analysis of privatization alternatives (franchises, grants, vouchers, and contracts) relative to the current delivery methods practiced. This analysis should examine implementation feasibility, technical performance, and costs. Its objectives are to determine which services may be privatized, select the most appropriate privatization method, and develop a scheduled work plan for implementation of the privatization transaction.

In order to meet these objectives, a multi-disciplined team approach should be followed. At minimum, this team should consist of personnel with technical experience in the function under review; legal, personnel, fiscal, and contracts staff; and political advisory and independent review support. The team approach provides the appropriate balance of expertise to ensure that all issues are identified and practical solutions are formulated. In addition, the use of political and independent review advisory support will assist in building the necessary consensus and commitment to change among all constituent groups. Most important, the team approach provides appropriate balance between program, fiscal, and political considerations.

IMPLEMENTATION FEASIBILITY ANALYSIS

Implementation feasibility analysis is the study of the political, legal, market, government operations, and other factors of each privatization option relative to the status quo, to anticipate the difficulties in accomplishing each option. The team approach provides the appropriate expertise to identify issues and barriers and develop solutions to minimize the impact of the issues and eliminate the barriers. The objective of the implementation feasibility study is to develop action plans identifying the specific objectives, scope, process, responsibilities, and timing for implementation of each service delivery option. The implementation feasibility study must address:

Political barriers: Are the current coalitions of beneficiaries, near beneficiaries, service providers, government administrators, officials, political activists, unions and general populace amenable to change? How do you build the coalitions necessary to support the change process?

Legal issues: What are the statutory, regulatory and tax law barriers, incentives, and/or requirements for privatization? What modifications to union agreements or ongoing contracts are required? What is the impact on liability?

Market: Is the private sector market mature or developing? Has the private sector shown interest through unsolicited proposals, industry studies, or research by industry experts? How capable is the private sector of providing quality goods or services? Is there a sufficient number of qualified bidders to ensure competition and provide the government a favorable risk/reward ratio? Does the private sector perceive a favorable risk/reward ratio? What is the private sector track record in government contract performance?

Government operations: Will privatizing selected functions disrupt continuity of operations? How will the affected employee be treated? What effect will privatization have on accountability? Who will monitor the private sector? How, and with what frequency will the private sector be monitored? What performance measures will be used to determine whether performance standards have been met? How will the government control the quality, timing and cost of delivery of services to be privatized? What are appropriate penalties (or incentives) to ensure compliance with performance standards and service requirements?

Other factors: Who will have control over the staff, equipment, and facilities? Are the resources available to do the necessary analysis, conduct the planning, preparation, and execution of privatization transactions?

TECHNICAL PERFORMANCE ANALYSIS

Once a government has examined the implementation feasibility of the privatization options, it needs to compare the overall implementation difficulties anticipated against the total benefits to be derived. Each option must be evaluated in terms of technical performance criteria including, but not necessarily limited to: availability, quality and effectiveness, risks, and program impacts. Through review of historic experience within and outside the jurisdiction, demographic and geographic studies, and/or the performance of pilot programs, analysis can be performed to evaluate each option. Criteria should be weighted and each alternative scored to determine the optimal anticipated technical performance option. At a minimum the criteria should include:

Availability and costs to citizens: Will individual consumers obtain improved choices of supply and service levels? Will all consumers including disadvantaged groups or geographically remote regions be served? If user fees are charged, will disadvantaged users be able to afford the level of service they need? Will the service cost to all consumers be fairly distributed? Will the overall cost to citizens increase?

Quality and effectiveness: Will government objectives be achieved more effectively? Will the quality of service improve?

Risks: Will service disruptions be more likely? What contingencies will be required? A risk analysis that quantifies the technical, implementation, and cost risks associated with each of the alternative delivery options provides a comprehensive and disciplined approach towards reducing uncertainty and focuses the attention of the team on the most critical issues.

Program impacts: What synergies or benefits will be derived? Will the government benefit from new technology? What impact will there be on the operations of other departments, especially if the program or service is for internal government use?

COST ANALYSIS

Since privatization is heavily influenced by cost, a thorough costing, economic, and pricing analysis must be performed for each option. The purpose of this analysis is to estimate potential savings, assess the economic impact, determine specific costs, and establish pricing requirements. The three types of studies most frequently performed are:

Financial feasibility studies: A determination of the current and future gross and net costs or savings of the planned privatization transaction in relation to the costs of the current method of operation.

Cost benefit analyses: A determination of the costs of new methods of providing services or doing business, compared against the benefits of the alternatives, to identify the methods that are the most cost-responsive.

Cost and pricing studies: An identification and examination of the direct, indirect, fixed, variable, opportunity, and oversight costs associated with a privatization transaction for different levels of service; a definition of what will happen to total costs as the service levels change; and the recommendation of pricing strategies and/or prices to achieve desired utilizations, cash throw-offs, and/or rates of return.

For each study the first step should be to determine what constitutes cost, where the data should be obtained, how costs should be calculated, and how costs should be projected for future years. For a cost comparison between government service performance and a service contract between government and a private vendor, the major cost elements to examine include:

GOVERNMENT PERFORMANCE COSTS

- Personnel costs: basic pay (salaries or wages), other entitlements (e.g., night differential, hazardous duty differential), fringe benefits (e.g., FICA, pension, workers' compensation), other (e.g., overtime, uniform and meal allowances);

- Materials and supplies costs: costs of raw materials, replacement parts, repairs, office supplies, and equipment, necessary to provide a product or perform a service;
- Overhead costs: operations overhead (e.g., supervision) and general administrative overhead (e.g., personnel, data processing, legal);
- Other specifically attributable costs, such as rent, utilities, maintenance and repairs, insurance, depreciation or use charges, travel;
- Additional costs, unusual or specific circumstances that occur only under government operation or don't fit other categories.

CONTRACTOR PERFORMANCE COST

- *Realistic* contract price: the contractor must be able to deliver the service at the quantity and quality desired at the bid price, and still make a reasonable profit, for a contract price to be realistic;
- Start-up costs (e.g., learning curve);
- Contract administration costs, including execution of quality assurance monitoring, payment processing, negotiation of change orders, and contract close-up;
- Conversion costs (e.g., disposing of expendable items, retraining, severance pay, lease termination penalties, conducting the privatization transaction);
- Additional costs (e.g., lost volume discounts).

COST ADVANTAGE BASED ON THE ABOVE COSTS

The cost advantage is defined as the difference between the total government performance cost and the total contractor performance cost, adjusted for additional or lost tax revenues. Because of the risks involved in implementing such a change, public managers should generally look for a major cost advantage before shifting to new modes of service delivery, to avoid being caught short like the city that changed to contracted trash pickup for only a one cent per household cost differential.

SELECTION AND IMPLEMENTATION

Having completed implementation feasibility, technical performance, and cost analyses, a government manager can select the preferred method of service delivery. Privatization can be one of several downsizing alternatives available to government managers. It is not a panacea for challenges facing government managers. If analysis shows that government provides a service more efficiently and effectively than the private sector, it should continue to do so. Privatization offers an opportunity to introduce the cost-saving, creative, service-generating aspect of competition into the public arena. It is important that public managers retain both decision-making and ultimate responsibility for public services. It is they who must decide what services will be privatized and who will provide them.

Not all methods of privatizing will benefit all parties or work in all situations. The concept works best when public managers carefully examine public assets and services to determine which could be replaced by private functions, thoroughly evaluate private sector competition, assemble representatives from all affected parties to agree on alternatives and solutions, and analyze the combination of tactics to satisfy a broad range of constituents. The key is to develop a workable mix of program and fiscal alternatives.

Privatization is an appealing concept because it offers governments flexibility in meeting their public responsibilities and, at the same time, presents entrepreneurs with a new set of challenges. Entrepreneurs, as George Gilder notes in his book *The Spirit of Enterprise*, are "engineers of change." The challenge to public managers today is to identify and manage change.

PRIVATIZATION PRESENTS PROBLEMS

Harry P. Hatry

Admittedly, public officials should periodically consider options for greater use of the private sector for delivering their services. This is good public policy and good public management.

But public officials should also examine existing instances of private sector delivery and consider the option of switching *back to public employee delivery*. This is also good public policy. For a number of reasons, private delivery can become inefficient or have quality problems.

THE BEST OF TIMES, THE WORST OF TIMES— TO CONTRACT

Our work at The Urban Institute indicates that the appropriateness and success of using a particular privatization option is *highly situational*. Success depends on many factors that are individual to the particular public agency, in the particular location and at the particular time. Success of a privatization approach depends on:

• The current level of performance of the current delivery system. A government agency may indeed be delivering the service quite efficiently and with good quality—leaving little room for improvement. (As hard as some people find it to believe, often public employee delivery *does* work very well.) In other situations, the service may be inefficient or of poor quality. This is the situation that provides the major opportunity for successful change.

• The way the option is implemented. Without good implementation even the best ideas will go awry. For example, in a switch to contracting, the quality of the request-for-proposal process is key to assuring that a capable contractor is selected.

And a sound, sustained contract administration and monitoring process is essential to assuring that contractor performance remains up to par.

THREAT OF PRIVATIZATION IS OFTEN ENOUGH

I believe that the major advantage of the privatization movement is not that the private sector can reduce costs or improve service to a great extent, but that consideration of privatization encourages public officials and public employees to innovate and to break down obstacles to improving public employee efficiency.

Increasingly, examples occur where employees and their unions agree to changes, such as reductions in the size of garbage collection crews, when faced with a city council threat to contract the service.

Other governments have introduced procedures that involve direct competition between public and private agencies. In the "Phoenix Model," public agencies such as the City of Phoenix Public Works Department submit proposals that compete directly with bids received from private firms for services such as garbage collection and street sweeping. (The City Administrative Services codified this in January 1985 as "Management Procedure: Procedure for Preparing Cost Estimate City Services Under Consideration to be Performed by Private Industry on a Contractual Basis.")

In a third approach, Kansas City, Phoenix and other cities have split their work, such as garbage collection, into districts, some of which are served by private contractors (if they win) and some by public employees. The city reports on comparative costs, encouraging competition between public and private service providers.

PRIVATE ISN'T NECESSARILY CHEAPER

Lower cost with improved efficiency is the most frequently given reason for contracting. I am not convinced, as some others are, based on the evidence thus far available, that privatization lowers costs in most instances. Hospital care is one of the few areas that has been extensively studied in recent years. A University of California study of contracting the management of public hospitals in a number of counties in California did not find evidence that the contractors had achieved cost savings. The study did find evidence that the private firms were better at securing revenue.[1] Last year's National Academy of Sciences study of private versus public hospital care found that "studies of hospital costs that control for size (and in some cases for case mix and other factors) show for-profit hospitals to have slightly *higher* expenses than not-for-profit public and private institutions."[2]

The Urban Institute recently worked with two states (Delaware and Maryland). In three of the four programs that the states considered for a change to contracting, we found that state employees were likely to achieve costs similar to or lower than the private sector. In one, food service for inmates of Delaware's prisons, we surveyed ten other states that had contracted for inmate food service. Six reported higher costs with contracting, three lower, and one reported about the same costs. Delaware's own current costs appeared to be similar to those expected if the service were contracted. The department is still considering contracting, its motivation being the difficulty in hiring prison kitchen supervisors and, secondarily, the desire of some prison administrators to reduce the administrative headaches in arranging for meals.

Columbia University's classic 1970's analysis of solid waste collection costs found higher *average* unit costs for public employee delivery than for contractor-delivered service.[3] But it also found that the most expensive delivery method was delivery by franchised firms—firms that dealt directly with households and not through a government. The more recent Ecodata study of Los Angeles County also showed that private vendors were, on average, cheaper. In all these comparisons, however, averages hide the fact that in some cities the unit costs were lower for public employee delivery than in some contracted cities.

Vouchers, while often an excellent way to give consumers more choice, do not necessarily involve lower costs. It depends on how the government sets the value of the vouchers. Hennepin County (Minnesota) in its trial of day care vouchers found that total costs increased when it switched to vouchers.

It is dangerous to generalize as to the success of privatization options. There will be situations where a switch will be worthwhile and cases where it won't be.

THREE IMPORTANT POTENTIAL PROBLEMS WITH PRIVATIZATION

Three major potential problems in privatization are almost always raised by public employee unions. While these problems are acknowledged by advocates of privatization, they are often treated too casually, as if they were easy to overcome, only minor inconveniences. These three problems are: 1. potential for corruption; 2. possibility of reduced quality of service; and 3. possibility of reduced access of disadvantaged citizens to services.

Corruption. High financial stakes introduce great temptations to individuals to engage in illegal action. We have frequent examples—New York City's Parking Violations Bureau; recently, in the District of Columbia, in all sorts of contract awards; and, over the years, the City of Chicago has had its share of problems. The American Federation of State, County and Municipal Employees (AFSCME) has taken great pains to document numerous instances of hanky-panky in public sector contracting.[4] The possibility of corruption can be reduced by establishing sound procurement procedures, and in the case of divestiture, by installing appropriate regulations. Nevertheless, the threat remains.

Possible Reductions in Service Quality. Again, when substantial payments are involved, a natural temptation is to do whatever is necessary to maximize profitability and skimp on quality to save dollars, particularly in for-profit organizations. This temptation becomes even greater when a firm gets into financial difficulties. This sometimes happens even with private nonprofit organizations. The principal protections against poor quality are performance contracting and adequate performance monitoring. The need for these protections has been noted by both proponents and opponents of privatization. A classic example of this problem is recent shoddy aircraft maintenance in deregulated airlines facing major financial problems. Some airlines have been assessed large fines for inadequate maintenance.

However, it is much easier to say that monitoring is needed than to provide it. Most government contracts I have seen in recent years have very weak or non-existent performance requirements. To make matters worse, performance monitoring of contracts is very sparse.

Possible Reduced Access to Services for Disadvantaged. The incentives to private firms—particularly for-profit firms—are to avoid clients for whom securing payment for services is likely to be difficult, and to avoid clients who may be particularly difficult and expensive to help, such as disadvantaged clients.

This problem has become particularly acute in the delivery of medical services. Persons without medical insurance or other funds have reportedly been turned away from private hospitals and even from emergency room care. The National Academy of Sciences study cited earlier concluded that access is a major national concern. The study found that for-profit hospitals served fewer uninsured patients and had a smaller proportion of uncompensated care than non-profit hospitals. The researchers felt that although the percentage differences were small among the types of providers, they could nonetheless "translate into large numbers of patients: Data from four of five states demonstrate that not-for-profit hospitals provide two or three times as much uncompensated care, on average, than for-profit hospitals. (Both types provided less uncompensated care than public hospitals.)"[5] Debate continues about what laws and regulations should be introduced to encourage or require private hospitals to admit patients regardless of their ability to pay, particularly emergency-care patients.

This problem can be alleviated through contractual and statutory requirements and the provision of subsidies. Alleviating the problem, however, will often reduce the benefits of privatization.

CONCLUSION

Privatization should be viewed as neither panacea nor poison. It is simply one tool available to public officials. Before they attempt to apply it universally, there are points they should remember:

- The success of privatization is highly situational, dependent on local circumstances and how well the new approach is implemented.
- Periodically consider options that involve greater use of the private sector.
- Periodically consider switching *back* from *private* delivery to *public* delivery.
- Give serious attention to the three potential problems of privatization-corruption, reduced service quality, and reduced access of the disadvantaged to services.

Perhaps the main virtue of the privatization movement is that it encourages public employees to improve their own productivity in order to help ensure their own competitiveness in the face of privatization. Increasingly, the message to the public sector is that if a service has problems in efficiency or quality, the agency needs to "shape up or be shipped out." The net result should be less costly and higher quality services for all the public.

NOTES

1. William Shonick and Ruth Roemer, *Public Hospitals Under Private Management: The California Experience*, Institute of Governmental Studies, University of California, Berkeley, 1983, Chapter 5.
2. Bradford H. Gray, Editor, *For-Profit Enterprise in Health Care*, National Academy Press, Washington, D.C., 1986, p. 93.
3. Barbara J. Stevens and E. S. Savas, "The Cost of Residential Refuse Collection and the Effect of Service Arrangement," Graduate School of Business, Columbia University, September 1976.
4. See, for example, John D. Hanrahan, *Government For Sale*, American Federation of State, County and Municipal Employees, Washington D.C., 1977.
5. *Ibid.*, p. 116.

ROBERT L. MANDEVILLE: THE FINANCIAL WIZARDRY (OR SLEIGHT OF HAND) OF A FISCAL SPIN DOCTOR

John M. Dowling

On Saturday nights, almost without fail, a middle-aged, mildly retarded man with a six-pack of beer in hand trudges about a block down Glenwood Avenue in Springfield, Illinois, a cobblestone side street lined with comfortable homes and shaded by a canopy of oaks and maples.

Reaching a certain two-story brick house, he knocks at the door and enters, his boots leaving a trail of snow across the living room in wintertime. He parks his beer in the refrigerator and parks himself on a family-room couch to watch television with the man who lives in the house—not a relative, not even a neighbor, really.

"He comes to our house because we will open the door," Robert L. Mandeville says. "We've never said no. It doesn't really cost me anything other than an hour and a half of watching TV. But if there is not that community support, there's no way someone like this man can remain on his own. He'd be in an institution."

Then, in a different way, he would still be part of Robert Mandeville's life, a digit on a computer printout, the object of a few more thousands of the $20-odd billion channeled each year through Mandeville's domain, the Illinois Bureau of the Budget—arguably the single most powerful agency of the state's government. It is a measure of Mandeville's skill and flexibility that he has held the job of director for 12 years, from the first to the latest day of the longest-running administration in Illinois' history, longer than any other chief state fiscal officer now on the job in the United States.

And it is a measure of Mandeville that he believes that much of what is done with the billions of dollars he oversees would, in a more perfect world, be better done by individuals, often in gestures simple enough to be accomplished in one's family room on a Saturday night.

"If you really stop to think about what state government does, no one else is going to do it. You and I as individuals aren't going to run a mental health system or a corrections system. So government has to do it, or it doesn't get done.

"But I personally believe that myself and others as individuals have to do more. I'm willing to do it, but I'm not sure others are. I'm willing to take in runaways, and I've done that before. I'm willing to help people individually, I've done that before, but I don't think enough people are."

From his manner and appearance, the 57-year-old Mandeville seems more plausible as a low-profile good Samaritan than as a high-stakes player in a sophisticated, intensely political state government. To picture him, bring to mind your favorite high school math teacher, sometimes rumpled but never quite disheveled, poised at the blackboard to explain patiently just one more time the lesson that still puzzles his class. Give him an unruly shock of wavy, graying hair, a penchant for homely analogies to a family budget and a tendency to stretch his vowels so that Washington comes out "Warshington" and short is something near "shahrt." It's a folksy image that might have disarmed a legislator or an agency director once upon a time. But after Mandeville's nearly 20 years in state government, the word on him is definitely out.

"He's probably the single most influential behind-the-scenes character in the whole state," says Douglas L. Whitley, president of the Taxpayers Federation of Illinois, a respected watchdog group that focuses on revenue and spending issues. "His role is the overall role. He sees all the agency budgets, oversees all the bond offerings, signs off on major contract proposals and the major public works projects. He estimates the revenue, controls the cash flow, builds the budget, argues for the budget and knows the day-to-day operations inside out."

"He's had the advantage of watching the other states over the last 12 years and learning from their mistakes and their successes," observes four-term Governor James R. Thompson, a Republican, who asked Mandeville to join his administration on the day after he was elected. "He's not a rigid ideologue, but he blends the right amount of fiscal toughness, and the ability to say no to budget requests, with compassion and a very human and inquiring side. He brings a very nice balance to the job."

Mandeville's power flows from the status of his bureau as an arm of the governor's office. Legally, it is the governor who is charged with responsibility for presenting a balanced budget to the General Assembly each year. And when lawmakers have had their way with the governor's plan, it is his to reshape again with perhaps the most extensive array of veto powers of any governor in the nation, a remarkable combination of meat ax and scalpel that allows him to veto a bill outright; reduce or eliminate any line or lines within an appropriations bill; or, in the case of substantive legislation, propose wholesale revisions that legislative sponsors must either accept or muster a three-fifths majority to override.

The net effect has been that final appropriations from the state's general funds—the accounts that pay for most education and human services programs and make up more than half of the budget—have almost every year been within 1 percent to 2 percent of the level proposed by Thompson at the start of the budget process.

"If we give [Thompson] a budget that's way out of line, he can use that [veto] authority to rewrite it any way he wants, and we're stuck. Of course that enhances Mandeville's power," says Representative Woods Bowman, a Democrat from Evanston who chairs the House Appropriations II Committee. (In Illinois, the House and Senate each have two appropriations committees.)

"Mandeville appears to have unique influence on levels of spending," says Democratic Senator Howard W. Carroll of Chicago, chairman of the Senate Appropriations I Committee and perhaps the most influential budget writer in the General Assembly. "He is the one who puts the ink in the veto pen."

Mandeville is also the sole gatekeeper for appropriations requests from state agencies under the control of the governor. Any agency spending request not accompanied by what is known as a "Dr. Bob letter" dies a quick death in the offices of the legislative appropriations staff.

But beyond the authority he wields for the governor, Mandeville has developed a reputation in state government for fiscal wizardry—some would prefer "sleight of hand"—such that one might almost expect him to enter a budget hearing decked out with a top hat, black cape and magic wand, rather than a simple felt-tipped marker and an oversized pad of graph paper. Mandeville's admirers attribute it to his unsurpassed knowledge of the details of state government and the techniques of public finance, plus an open, pull-no-punches attitude toward sharing information. "There are some people in government who we don't trust," says Senator John W. Maitland Jr., ranking Republican on the Senate Appropriations II Committee. "In the appropriations process, when we sit down and go over all the agency budgets every year before the bills ever get to committee, sometimes we get the feeling that the agency fiscal officers aren't telling us everything we ought to be told. I don't have that feeling with Bob Mandeville. I think he has been able to generate a spirit of trust."

His critics don't question his technical expertise, but they also portray Mandeville as a master of blue smoke and mirrors, someone who can argue that a $200 million balance in the general funds is evidence of sound fiscal management, then contend with equal force weeks or months later that a $200 million balance is a standing invitation to budget disaster. "One of Mandeville's characteristics is his ability to over-simplify a very complex issue, often with a disarming result," says a statehouse insider. "The only way you can counter Mandeville is to come up with a more technical, complex explanation. You're always put on the defensive. It works . . . because people are too lazy to figure out what it means."

Nonetheless, Mandeville offers "telling the truth" as the secret to good relations with lawmakers, and insists that in his shop, spin isn't supposed to get in the way of facts. "You present things differently in different climates," he says. "Basically, what I try to do is present things as they are. If, for example, the loyal opposition makes a statement, I may respond in a way that counteracts that statement. That may be perceived by some as shading the truth, but I think you can look at numbers and have more than one interpretation of their meaning.". . .

Many believe Mandeville's longevity in his job has left him with less room to maneuver. "There's not quite as much awe or surprise or prestige as there was in earlier years, when it was just Mandeville on one level and everyone else scrambling to keep up," Whitley says. "It's much more of a professional head-to-head relationship now. He's been with us long enough that he's taught the rest of us a lot about the budget."

Mandeville says he's occasionally tempted by offers to do the same thing in the private sector for considerably more money. He says he turned down a $200,000-a-year offer last year from a "major financial institution." "One of the reasons is that I'm not sure there's a more interesting job than a high-level job in government. Even as a deputy budget director I was making decisions that affected programs and the lives of people. I've talked to people who've left government and were at a fairly high level, and they say they're fairly bored.". . .

TOMORROW'S BILL
COMES DUE TODAY

Carlos Monteriva left the bank with a frown on his face. His meeting with two of the bank officers had not turned out the way he had hoped it would. They had been polite—even concerned—but not very helpful. Carlos had hoped that they would give him some ideas for resolving the latest financial crisis in Desert Rock. Ten years ago, when Carlos had become the chief financial officer of Desert Rock, he had looked forward to a relatively easy finish to his twenty-eight-year career in public service. Desert Rock's population had been growing at a steady rate of about 17 percent a year. The dry climate and spectacular scenery of the Southwest high desert was attracting a steady stream of retired couples to the area. The tax base was expanding, as new retirement communities with moderately expensive homes were built within the city limits.

Planning the expansion of city services to meet the growth curve had been exciting. New sewers, streets, parks, and a civic center had all been financed with very modest tax increases every other year. Carlos chuckled as he remembered how carefully those increases had been scheduled in the off-election year to spare the councilman the embarrassment of running for reelection right after increasing taxes. The bond issue to build the civic center had been more difficult to pass, but an aggressive publicity campaign stressing the future benefits had convinced the voters that the construction was an investment in the future of the community.

The first sign of any problem came just two years ago. The Economy League at the state level decided to do a study of employer pension plans in the state. The league was interested in the topic because so much of the net income of residents in the state depended on pension payments. The debate at the national level over Social Security had alerted them to a potential problem. Carlos had been eager to see the results because Desert Rock was one of those communities in which pension payments were a primary source of income. When the study was released, Carlos and his counterparts in other cities in the state were shocked.

The study pointed out that the private employers in the state were doing a good job of ensuring that money was being put aside to support the projected pensions of their employees. The public sector, however, was in serious trouble—at least from the point of view of the league. Unlike the private employers, most of the local governments were paying pensions out of current revenues. With a very small number of employees currently on retirement, this was not a significant percentage of the annual budget. The study raised a concern, however, about the future. As the size of the local government work force rose to meet the demands for more and better services from a growing population, the number of people scheduled to retire over the next twenty years would grow exponentially. By the year 2010, the study predicted, more than 30 percent of local budgets would be devoted to pension payments.

Last year, the state legislature had responded to the study and to the pressure of the Economy League and the Public Employees Advocacy lobby. The Public Pension Act of 1989 mandated that local governments were required to reduce their unfunded pension liability to zero over the next thirty years. As Carlos walked back to his office overlooking the piazza, he mentally reviewed the provisions of the act:

1. All municipalities were required to set up a trust fund into which payments were to be made to cover pensions.
2. All municipalities were required to submit biannual actuarial studies indicating the "normal cost" of fully funding pension liabilities.
3. During the first ten years, the municipalities were required to phase in their payments, beginning with 10 percent in the first year and rising by an additional 10 percent each year to 100 percent in the tenth year.
4. Failure to make the proper payments would result in the subtraction of state money of the same amount in the Local Government Assistance account.

Carlos had gone to the bank earlier to discuss setting up a pension trust fund. The First National Bank of Desert City had regretfully indicated that it did not engage in that kind of business. Moreover, it knew of only one bank in the state that did. When Carlos pointed out that the bank might wish to consider starting such a fund, the president of the bank, John Rodgers, looked over his reading glasses and commented: "We've tried to stay out of local politics because someone always gets angry. We don't intend to lose any of our customers over this issue."

Later in the week, Carlos received a reply to his letter of inquiry from the Setting Sun Bank in the state capital. They would be happy to set up the trust fund under their normal arrangements, which they had included. Skimming over the agreement, Carlos discovered that Setting Sun Bank was going to make a tidy little profit by investing Desert Rock's pension money. Worse yet, the penalty clauses for failure to deposit the required amounts were very severe. The final insult was a requirement that Desert Rock transfer its payroll deposits to Setting Sun as part of the agreement.

Carlos pulled the phone toward him and dialed the number for Naomi Winterwind. Naomi had joined his staff four years ago after working for her tribal investment company. She was an expert in budgetary systems with an emphasis on computerized systems. Naomi arrived with a stack of printouts and a puzzled look on her face. "We've already done the initial run on next year's budget for the council. Any changes now would have to be hand written in the margins." As Carlos explained the problem, Naomi began to smile. "I don't see anything to smile about in all of this," snorted Carlos. "Oh but I do," beamed Naomi. "I've been after you and the council to install a two-year budget process ever since I started here. This is the perfect opportunity."

The council room was practically deserted when the meeting began. Carlos gave his standard report and then asked for permission to address the council on the pension fund issue. Richard Cowper, mayor of Desert Rock, nodded for Carlos to proceed. Quickly Carlos outlined what he had discovered and the various steps that he thought should be taken. When he finished, he asked if there were any questions. "I'll start," said Percy Whitworth, one of the council members. "Does this mean that we can't hire more people in the future? It seems the more people you hire, the larger the required payments." "Maybe we should start hiring more part-time people," said Mayor Cowper. "They don't have the same pension liability, do they?"

"My solution," piped up Alonzo Chiesa, the city attorney, "is to renegotiate the contracts with the employees. We could change to a private pension plan, where all we do is pay the premium and the private company worries about funding." "But how do we control the cost of that?" shot back Mayor Cowper. "You know what is happening to insurance premiums." City Manager Jim Carson held up both hands, leaned forward in his chair and spoke softly: "Before we rearrange everything over just one issue, let's look at the whole picture. I suggest that we ask Carlos to bring us a proposed revision of next year's budget to the next meeting." Jim looked down the table with a twinkle in his eye. "I'll bet someone on your staff could even come up with some figures for the year after next."

DISCUSSION QUESTIONS

1. Do you think that the state legislature was wise in requiring the local governments to fully fund their pension plans?
2. What advantages *and disadvantages* would a two-year budget process have for the city?
3. What other effects would you expect this state requirement to have on personnel policies, aside from the ones mentioned in the council meeting?

WHERE DO WE PARK
ALL THOSE CARS?

The fifth time around the block, Bert Harborstone began to get angry. To begin with, it was raining. Second, he was late for the meeting, and third, the meeting was about this very problem. Bert had just been appointed to the Municipal Parking Authority by city council. An owner of three hardware stores in the city, he had been showing up at city council meetings to complain about the lack of parking places on the streets around his stores. At the Chamber of Commerce, he was jokingly known as "Meter Mad Bert." Bert didn't think it was very funny. The parking meters in front of his stores were always full and people usually put enough money in the meter for the full two-hour maximum.

Bert had wanted council to reduce the maximum time to 30 minutes. He thought that this would increase the turnover in the spaces and make it more likely that people would come into his stores to shop. At the meetings, however, he also usually heard objections from the owner of the movie theater just down the street from one of his stores. Movies ran for about two hours, he argued, and if the spaces were restricted to 30 minutes, his customers wouldn't be able to park near the theater. The owner of a nearby restaurant had agreed. "People need more than half an hour to eat a meal," he had said. "Besides, we better be careful about this parking business; lots of people comment that the parking at the mall is plentiful and free. If we make it too inconvenient or too expensive, they'll simply stop coming downtown."

The city council had gotten tired of hearing the same arguments month after month. They voted to establish a parking authority and to charge it with the responsibility for solving the problem. When Bert was appointed, he was determined to convince them to solve the problem once and for all. The answer was to increase the number of available spaces rather than change the usage time or the fees. What Crestwood needed was a parking garage, thought Bert, as he finally slipped into a space just being vacated. Bert shrugged his shoulders when he discovered that the space was in front of a fire hydrant. "Typical," he muttered as he hurried into the building.

A young man was speaking as Bert took his seat at the table in the front of the room. Leaning over to Matty Pilsnor on his right, Bert whispered, "Who's that?" Matty brushed back her hair and hissed back, "Doug Walters from the Department of Transportation." Bert settled back to listen. "In conclusion, the Department of Transportation predicts that, with the completion of the limited access highway next September, Crestwood can expect the average number of vehicles transiting the city to increase by approximately 800 per day. This increase will begin slowly but rise rapidly as commuters relocate to Crestwood from the north side of the metropolitan area." Doug looked around the room and said, "I'd be happy to answer questions, but I should warn you that the department does not make recommendations."

Farther down the table Mike Fischer, chairman of the authority, thanked Doug and turned to the other members. "Now that Bert is here, I think we ought to get started on the agenda. We've heard Mr. Walters' projections of even more traffic in the city, and you have a report in front of you that details the current parking availability. I must say that we can't study this issue too much longer. The first item on the agenda is yours, Stewart."

Stewart Pinehurst cleared his throat and began in a dry voice: "When I was appointed to this board, most of you thought that I would be the last person to suggest this, but I propose that we build a parking garage on the site of the abandoned railroad station. I know that I have been pushing for expansion of public transportation and wanted that site for a bus terminal, but at this point, we can't wait for five to seven years to set up a brand new bus system." "I second the motion," blurted Bert. Mike Fischer smiled. "It isn't a motion yet Bert, but your comment in favor is noted." "Since I knew about this idea last week when I set up the agenda, I've invited Joshua Jones from the city manager's office to join us. Joshua put together the bond issue for the city when they built the new city building, and I thought he might tell us about how difficult it might be for us to do the same thing for the parking garage."

The board members turned to a middle-aged black man who was sitting quietly to one side of the room. Joshua got to his feet and looked directly at the assembled board members. "You're going to be disappointed in my comments," he began. "Six years ago when we built the city building, the municipal bond process was a lot different than it is today." Joshua passed out sheets of paper that listed the changes in the last few years. Bert looked down at his copy, which read:

Tax Reform Act of 1986

Set limits to the total amount of bonds any state may issue, including those issued by local government, with the state controlling the division;

Eliminated the arbitrage advantage of tax exempt bonds by prohibiting reinvestment of bond revenues;

Lowered the percentage of allowable private participation to 10 percent from 25 percent to qualify for tax-exempt status.

"Let me explain," said Joshua. "The first item isn't a problem for you yet, but it might be. Our state is still under the total amount allowed, but the law allocating the total amount between the state government and the local governments is being discussed in the capital. The state is reaching its limit and may take the remaining amount away from the local governments."

Joshua paused for comments and then went on. "The second item refers to a practice that really helped us with the city building. We issued the bonds at a face value of five million dollars, paying 6.25 percent interest over fifteen years. After the bonds were sold, we took the five million and invested in high-grade corporate bonds paying 10.5 percent. In the two years it took us to build the building, we gained about twenty thousand dollars, which paid for the cost overruns in construction. That's not possible anymore." Several board members looked dismayed.

"The real problem for you," sighed Joshua, "is the third item." "Why's that?" interrupted Bert. "Because," continued Joshua, "typically a parking garage is not operated by the authority that builds it. Usually, the authority enters into an agreement with a private company to operate the facility and repay part of the bond issue as revenue becomes available. In the past, the private company could have paid 25 percent of the bond issue as part of the deal. Now that's reduced to 10 percent if you want to sell the bonds as tax-exempt. That means you will have to set the parking rates pretty high to make sure that you generate enough revenue to pay the interest and retire the bonds on schedule. In fact, it may turn out to be more expensive to park in the garage than to park at a meter."

As Joshua sat down there was silence around the table in the front of the room. After the years of wrangling about the parking problem and the hours of informal discussion about how to solve it, the board members were astonished that the federal government had apparently taken away the best option. "It's not over yet," stated Bert. "While it may not be as easy or as inexpensive, I still think that we should do it. The parking problem isn't going to get better, only worse, and the longer we delay, the more expensive its going to be to find the land and build the building. Besides, tax reform isn't forever, and things may change in the future."

DISCUSSION QUESTIONS

1. Why did the federal government change the law concerning tax-exempt bonds?
2. What advantages would the Municipal Parking Authority gain if it operated the facility with its own employees?
3. What arguments would you use to convince the state legislature to allow local governments to use all of the remaining bond authorizations?

CONTRACTING FOR MANDATORY RECYCLING SERVICES

"That tears it," said Loretta, as she slammed down the phone. Turning to her assistant borough manager, Carson Smith, she ran her fingers through her hair and propped her head up with her hands. "The legislature just passed the Recycling Act, and our lobbyist says that the governor will sign it as soon as he gets it." "Is that all that bad?" responded Carson. "The good part is that we do need to recycle; the bad part is that the legislature wants the law to go into effect in six months," moaned Loretta. "We'd better get cracking on that recycling plan we started several weeks ago," Carson said. "More importantly," replied Loretta, "we need to call the mayor and tell him that the option to do it ourselves isn't available anymore."

Loretta Mihn had been aware of the problem since her last meeting of the Borough Manager's Association. She had listened carefully to the explanations by the experts from the Department of Environmental Services about the decisions facing the boroughs. The easy ones were what to recycle. The boroughs had to choose five of seven possible substances: glass, newsprint, plastic, aluminum, tin, cardboard, and organic yard waste. The hard decision was whether to use the borough garbage equipment to collect and recycle the items to industry, or whether to contract with a private firm.

Soon after she had returned to her office from the meeting, Loretta had asked Carson to start collecting information about the desirability of each of the seven products. At the next borough council meeting, she had presented the options and the likely profit from each item. Council had quickly picked aluminum, tin, newsprint, cardboard, and glass. The question of whether to contract out or do it with borough equipment and workers, however, split the council into three groups. One group wanted to use the borough equipment because it believed that it was possible to make some income from the service. A second group wanted to contract out because it believed that the profits would disappear because, as the new law made tons of materials available, the purchasers of those items would quickly be oversupplied. The third group indicated that it wanted more information about the choice and could see arguments in favor of both options.

The day after the meeting, the mayor stopped by to see Loretta. Mayor Althouse was up for reelection in the fall and was particularly conscious of the reaction of the voters to any new programs. He had agreed with the third group and was determined that he would be able to explain his vote during the campaign. Loretta called in Carson, and the three of them spent the afternoon going over the options in some detail. At the end of the session, the mayor indicated that he thought using the borough equipment was the cheapest route because the only additional expense at first would be the additional hours of labors and the fuel and maintenance on the trucks. "Besides," he said, "we can always contract out later if we don't come out ahead."

When the mayor left, Loretta asked Carson what he thought. "Well," said Carson thoughtfully, "it might be hard to contract out after the law goes into effect. If we can't sell at a profit, it will be pretty obvious to the bidders. Since all this will be public information, I don't see how we will convince anyone to take over our program at a loss." "Maybe we should go ahead and look at both options for the time being," sighed Loretta. "You look into doing it with our trucks, and I'll see about having the borough lawyer draw up a request for bids."

Two weeks later, Loretta and Carson went to lunch to compare notes on the two options. Carson seemed uneasy as he started to outline his findings. "To begin with, we don't have enough trucks, and we haven't really got a place to hold the stuff until we can collect enough to make it feasible to transport to the buyer. Second, the union isn't too happy about the overtime needed to collect it. They say that one extra shift per week is all they think we can ask for under the current contract. The only way I can see it working is if we buy two additional trucks and hire four more people."

"What about the buyers?" asked Loretta. "Will they come and pick up the stuff for us, and what kind of price are they offering?" "Well, three of the buyers said that they don't own any trucks to pick it up, and the other two said that if they come to get it, the price they are willing to pay goes way down," replied Carson. "One company said that they would come and get it all—meaning all five types—at a fixed price, but only if we can guarantee a certain volume. If we don't have the volume, then they get the stuff free."

"My option is even worse," said Loretta. "The solicitor drew up the request for bids and I called several of the major companies likely to bid. All of them said that they were willing to bid only if we allowed them to charge the customers directly. More importantly, they said that they would only agree to a charge rate for six months at a time." Loretta looked down at the figures on a sheet of paper and frowned. "According to some of the numbers suggested, it will cost about five dollars a month for a pickup once a week."

"What happens after six months?" asked Carson. "They would be able to raise the rate up to 50 percent for the second six months. And if the contract is for more than one year, they would have that option in each six-month period." "Would the council be able to do anything about it if they raised the rate to the maximum each time?" Carson asked. "Not without voiding the contract and having to pay severe penalties," Loretta responded. "But that wouldn't solve the problem, since the state still requires us to maintain the program."

The day after the phone call from the state capital indicating that the legislature had passed the Recycling Act, the mayor showed up in Loretta's office. "Are we ready to go with our recycling plan?" he asked. Loretta indicated that he should pull up a chair and prepare for some bad news. "To put our program into effect within ninety days with our own equipment is just not possible. We don't have the money in the budget to buy two new trucks or to hire four new workers. The collective bargaining agreement with the borough workers still has two more years to run, so we can't even start with the trucks and people we have." "So where does that leave us?" asked the mayor.

"Our only option now is to publish the request for bids and hope that we get something reasonable," sighed Loretta. "I want to look more closely at how to protect our residents from being exploited," grumbled the mayor. "I'm not going to let some outfit come in here and rip everybody off just because the governor wants to take credit for getting this program in place immediately."

DISCUSSION QUESTIONS

1. What provisions would you put into the contract to protect the residents?
2. What other courses of action might the borough take?
3. Explain how "privatization" might provide an advantage for the borough after the initial period of adjustment.

PERSONNEL AND
HUMAN RESOURCES

—

Obviously, the people who staff public and nonprofit agencies are essential to the effective and responsible accomplishment of the organization's goals. For this reason, your effectiveness in managing human resources will be one of the most important topics facing you as a public manager. How can you recruit, train, and motivate the most talented people to work in public organizations? How can you increase the productivity of your agency? These concerns are central to public personnel management. But you will also need to understand issues in public personnel in order to deal with some even more complex political concerns. How can you help assure a public bureaucracy that is neither unresponsive to political leadership nor overly politicized? How can you help assure a public bureaucracy that is responsive to the needs of its employees, especially women and minorities? And how can you help protect both the rights of employees and the citizens with whom they interact?

These broad questions relating to the shape of public service have been the subject of much thought and legislation over the years. Early politicians in this country appointed their friends and supporters to positions in public agencies, a system know as the "spoils system" (from the phrase "To the victor belong the spoils"). By the late nineteenth century, however, abuses of the spoils system had become so widespread that reformers began to seek establishment of a "merit system," through which appointments would be made on the basis of merit—the ability to perform the job. Such a system was first instituted at the federal level with the passage of the Pendleton Act in 1883 and was emulated by state and local governments over the next several decades.

Although the federal merit system initially covered a relatively small number of employees, it has been extended over time to the point that today it covers nine out of every ten federal employees. (State and local governments have also extended merit employment to larger numbers of employees and have dramatically improved the degree of professionalism in government.) Assuring that the substantial number of federal employees under the merit system were treated fairly and protected from political interference was, for many years, the responsibility of the U.S. Civil Service Commission. However, a landmark piece of legislation passed during the Carter administration divided responsibility between the Office of Personnel Management (OPM), responsible for personnel policy, and the Merit System Protection Board, responsible for investigations and appeals. In addition, the Civil Service Reform Act of 1978 sought to streamline the personnel system and to increase the flexibility of managers with respect to personnel issues.

Another aspect of recent efforts at civil service reform has been increased attention to equal employment opportunity and affirmative action. Generally, "equal employment opportunity" refers to efforts to eliminate discrimination, whereas "affirmative action" refers to positive efforts to increase the representation of underrepresented groups in the public work force. Unfortunately, a great deal of confusion has arisen in connection with the implementation of affirmative action programs; for example, charges of "reverse discrimination" have often been raised and have become the basis for a series of important Supreme Court decisions in this area.

In this chapter, we will focus on several broad questions that you may face in the area of personnel administration. But, before getting into the discussion, you should be aware of two important concerns. First, whereas we focus here on general issues in personnel policy, there are many specific issues ranging from classification policy to performance evaluation to unionization that you need to be familiar with. Each of these issues, however, should be informed by the broad concerns we will address here. Second, we will give particular attention to personnel policy at the federal level. It is here that the most intense discussions of the shape of the public service have occurred over the past decade or two. Most of the lessons we learn from the federal experience, however, can be quite helpful at the state, local, and nonprofit levels as well.

Consider, for example, the different perspectives on public personnel policy outlined by Larry M. Lane—the merit system model, the political management model, and the public service model. Lane suggests that neither the traditional merit approach nor more recent efforts to increase the control of political managers is sufficient for the public service of the future. An alternative public service model, Lane argues, would require an approach to public management that emphasizes commitment on the part of the work force rather than control of the work force. You should especially note the attributes of the merit system, political management, and public service models as they are outlined in the two tables that Lane presents.

Following Lane's conceptual article, we present two articles written by recent directors of the federal Office of Personnel Management: Alan K. Campbell, who held the position during the Carter administration, and Constance Horner, who held the position during the Reagan administration. Although the ideological positions of the two writers differ, their opinions about the way to constitute and maintain a high-quality federal work force bear some interesting similarities. You might especially note the concern that both Campbell and Horner have for increasing managerial flexibility. Again, although this discussion focuses on the federal personnel system, you should be able to apply the lessons learned here at the state and local levels as well.

As we have mentioned, governments at all levels have struggled with questions of equal opportunity and affirmative action over the past couple of decades. John Nalbandian presents a review of recent Supreme Court decisions in the area of affirmative action and analyzes the values on which the Court seems to be basing its decisions. As Nalbandian points out, in affirmative action cases—as in many other areas of public administration—some balance between efficiency and social equity must occur. But compare Nalbandian's treatment of these values with that of H. George Fredrickson's, presented in chapter 4.

In an appropriate follow-up to our discussion of efficiency, John M. Greiner discusses ways in which those who staff public agencies might be motivated toward higher-quality work. Concerns for improving the quality and productivity of work in the public sector have been widely expressed, and many new programs have been implemented at the federal, state, and local levels. Greiner's discussion especially well emphasizes the way in which such efforts can be integrated into the larger system of personnel management within a particular jurisdiction. Be sure to note the specific approaches that are being tried, and try to identify local cases in which these are being used.

As the final article in this chapter, we present the report of the National Commission on the Public Service, better known as the Volcker Commission. This group, brought together to consider ways to reinvigorate the federal service, provides an interesting set of recommendations for recruiting "the best and the brightest" to government service and for creating circumstances under which public service would once more be considered a valuable and indeed honorable endeavor. Again, many of the specific recommendations are suitable for use in state and local systems. And, certainly, recommendations about restoring a greater sense of dignity and worth to the public service are applicable at all levels. We should all acknowledge more often the rewards of public service.

In this chapter, we profile Edward J. Perkins, director general and director of personnel in the U.S. Foreign Service. Perkins, whose career has taken him to some extremely interesting places, is now trying to deal with some thorny personnel issues facing the Foreign Service. You should, of course, take note of the five personnel issues that are now on Perkins' agenda, but you should also get once more a sense of the excitement of public service. (Just imagine the experiences Perkins has had!)

The first case in this chapter presents the collision of two typical problems in public personnel systems. First, the decline of revenues has made it difficult to simply hire more people. Second, at the same time, the often elaborate system of classification makes it difficult to adjust to changing circumstances. "A Working Manager: Classification as If People Mattered" will show you some of the difficulties of coping with these two problems, and you will be asked to help provide some of the answers.

"Affirmative Action for Leadership?" poses the question of whether affirmative action should be carried beyond the initial hiring and promotion decisions to the more delicate question of who leads. As you follow the difficulties of the main actor, you will see the next generation of questions that must be addressed for women and minorities in the public service. Although the passage of time may remedy some of the problems of the past, this case will alert you to the new problems in our future.

Personnel systems are often treated as a systemic question. "An Opportunity to Get Motivated" shows you the attitudes and values involved in trying to install productivity improvement programs in the public sector. As you listen to the internal debate about whether to join a new personnel system, you will hear the pros and cons of changing from a safe and secure system with modest rewards to a more risk-oriented system with the potential for higher and different rewards. Solving these problems will be one of the hardest challenges for personnel management in the coming decades.

PUBLIC SERVICE: FROM TRANSITION TO REGENERATION

Larry M. Lane

The decade of the 1980s is a transition period which offers opportunities for the reshaping of the federal work force. Out of this transition, the nation will determine either to follow its recent trends toward political management, to return to the older merit system concept, or to find some new solution to the problems of the public service. Clearly, it is critical that some conclusion be reached on the model of the public service that is to be adopted and supported.

The development of future public service policy requires completion of three tasks:

- exploration and development of appropriate models for the public service;
- creation and utilization of a democratic policy process to arrive at political consensus about the appropriate model to be implemented; and
- development of technical methodologies to achieve the consensus model.

Currently, public service policymakers are running to technical solutions without fully understanding the model sought and without using an adequate political policy process.

EMERGING AND RETREATING MODELS

Herbert Kaufman has provided a useful value framework for helping to understand the evolution of public personnel policies.[1] He postulates a history of shifting emphasis among representativeness, neutral competence, and executive leadership. The traditional merit system model featured a joining of neutral competence to executive leadership. In that combination, representativeness

and political responsiveness suffered. In the past two decades, the emphasis has shifted toward a joining of political responsiveness to executive leadership, and competence has suffered.

Recent policy objectives of management control by the executive branch have moved in the direction of the creation of a political management model as a replacement for the merit system model of the public service. The characteristics of the new model are brought into clear relief by Edie Goldenberg's analysis of four possible models for the public service.[2] Goldenberg identifies the four models as:

- passive extension of the presidency;
- active supporter of the presidency;
- broker of conflicting interests; and
- protector of the public interest.

Clearly, the policies of recent administrations have moved in the direction of a combination of the first two models in a political management approach to public personnel administration. Goldenberg's other models are more representative of the merit system which developed for almost one hundred years after the Pendleton Act in 1883.

Undoubtedly, part of the current problem in defining public personnel policy has been an intensification of disagreement regarding which model should be achieved. Recent definers of administration personnel policy (Alan Campbell, Donald Devine, Constance Horner) have pursued the political management model. Although the Congress agreed with Campbell in passing the Civil Service Reform Act in 1978, it has seemed to have second thoughts more recently as it has defended the remnants of the merit system model.

Now, in a period of confusion and system breakdown, the retreating merit system and the emerging political management model both need to be contested by a third possibility—a public service model which is based on current theories and practices of effective human resource utilization. Salient aspects of the policy agenda for each model are discussed below.

POLITICAL MANAGEMENT POLICY AGENDA

The political management model of the public service has emerged in recent years as the model of choice of administrations in power. The shift toward this model began in the Nixon administration and was formalized with the passage of the Civil Service Reform Act of 1978. Although the act is couched in merit system terms, it has clearly opened the door to the development of the political management model.

This model has not emerged in any specific, articulated, consistent way. Part of the confusion and uncertainty which currently afflict the public service is due to the undefined nature of the emergent model in a time of system transition. This transition is particularly difficult for the large numbers of employees who entered the public service and developed their career and value orientations in line with the concepts of the merit system.

WORK FORCE REDUCTION

A leading premise of the emerging political management model appears to be that the older cohorts of the existing federal work force should be motivated to leave the service. . . . This approach ignores questions of program effectiveness, continuity, and retention of needed expertise.

In the political management model, the hastened retirement of older workers is not intended to create significant opportunities for new entry-level hiring. For example, a bill introduced by Senator Roth would specifically prevent agencies from routinely filling positions that were vacated by individuals taking advantage of early retirement. The objective is to foster reduction of the size of the permanent work force, particularly in the domestic agencies, and to create additional opportunity and rationale for contracting out of public work. This policy position of privatization would avoid the difficulty of recruiting in a tightening labor market as the supply of available entry-level candidates is reduced by the baby-bust factor.

POLITICAL AND
TEMPORARY APPOINTMENTS

In the political management model, recruitment for long-term careers is minimized, and emphasis is placed on political appointments and hiring for temporary periods. . . .

The intent of the political management model is to continue to diminish the influence of employee groups, unions, professional associations, and their representation in Congress. The civil service personnel system, founded in law and regulation, also continues to be attacked by the Office of Personnel Management. Policy initiatives concentrate on short-term behavioral and performance control mechanisms such as pay for performance and drug testing.

SHORT-TERM PERSPECTIVE

In this model, it is simply unnecessary to build long-term effectiveness through career enhancement and development. Pay and benefits must be sufficient only for the attraction of candidates for immediate job requirements, and position classification grade levels are more influenced by political or market demands than by analysis of duties or responsibilities.

Concepts of comparable worth are resisted. Retention of the work force is not significant, thereby limiting the required investments in pay, benefits, and training. The retirement systems which are advocated are those which stress portability of benefits and which are not required to contribute to long-term retention. Performance concerns stress immediate responsiveness to political leadership. In this model, there is little need for human resource planning or long-term institutional commitment. Reliance is on local labor markets to meet demands of the moment. . . .

DEVELOPING A PUBLIC
SERVICE MODEL

Creative and professional solutions to the demographic, political, and managerial problems which are so manifest in current public administration require the creation of a new model for the federal service. In this spirit, Patricia Ingraham and Carolyn Ban have proposed a start toward the resolution of fundamental public sector issues with the development of the idea of a public service model.

This model features a renewed emphasis on career programs and technical expertise, a bridging of the gulf between political and career managers, a "new commitment by political executives to informed management competencies," and a "move away from the insularity of both neutral competence and partisan responsiveness to a common ground where goals and priorities are informed by systematic consideration of the public good and the public interest."[3] . . .

RETENTION POLICY

Specifically, in the public service model, personnel management policy would answer the aging work force condition with measures to motivate retention for additional years of service. A policy of retention would have significant long-term cost savings implications and would be compatible with a larger societal need to discourage early retirement and to retain older workers in the active labor force.

The approach to the problem is more complex than merely extending the age for retirement eligibility. Additional financial incentives for longer service are needed. Correction of compensation imbalances would also be required in order to provide continuing incentives for professional and technical personnel to remain in the service.

A policy decision to retain older workers would reach to issues of retention of baby-boom generation employees. Maintaining job satisfaction would require attention to questions of motivation, training and development, participation in the decision process, amelioration of arbitrary authority, and campaigns to restore the image of the public service. Additional emphasis would be required on career planning and counseling, work place and schedule flexibility, day care facilities, and other work place amenities and benefits.

These measures would need to be supported by a return to personnel management professionalism and a restoration of federal personnel management institutions as a vital partner in the management process.

RECRUITMENT AND PAY

In the public service model, the problems of recruitment in tightening labor markets would be addressed by fundamental pay reform which would restore credibility, if not comparability, to federal entrance salaries. Additionally, there would be a recreation of the symbolism and mechanisms of competitive examinations; aggressive recruitment campaigns; emphasis on entry-level hiring for long-term careers;

careful control on the numbers of allowable non-career appointments; and maintenance of in-house capability in professional, administrative, and support occupations. The challenge of the changing nature of federal work would be met by definition of new, critical occupations and the creation of carefully planned recruitment, development, and retraining agendas for new kinds of work.

LEADERSHIP

There is no dearth of relevant ideas. The principal problem is the creation of a political, managerial, and organizational climate that will permit trust and employee participation, as well as the development of innovative public personnel processes. Policies, pronouncements, and mechanisms are not sufficient for the creation and maintenance of a productive work force. The key ingredient is management behavior throughout the organization, and particularly at the leadership levels.

The environment that has been created by the political management of the last two decades has been characterized by secretiveness, subjectivity, ideological certainty, arbitrariness, and adversarial relationships. The employee reaction has been flight, hostility, passivity, and at best a mechanical response to political program imperatives.

The real challenge for a public service model will be to establish political protection for sound human resource management. Such a protection is possible only in the framework of professionally competent leadership for federal personnel management.

SUMMARY OF COMPETING MODELS

It may be useful to offer a schematic comparison of the three competing models. Because personnel management is sharply conditioned by the overall management environment, it is necessary to look at the models at two different levels. [Table] 1 summarizes a comparison of management system characteristics. [Table] 2 represents a comparison of the different approaches to specific personnel management policies and programs. These summary comparisons are preliminary and indicative rather than definitive. The intention is to capture the essential ingredients of the policy agendas and to provide a framework for further consideration.

Table 1—Management System Characteristics

Policy Area	Model		
	Merit System	Political Management	Public Service Model
Management theory	Scientific management	Theory X	Theory Z
Management style	Bureaucratic	Authoritarian	Participative
Decision process	Formalistic	Top down	Dialogue/discourse
Required expertise	System	Task	Professional
Time perspective	Static	Short-term	Long-term
Political influence	Neutrality	Partisanship	Protected competency
System stability	Continuity	Discontinuity	Org. culture maintenance
Limits on discretion	Rules/regulations	Political imperatives	Ethical/professional standards
Responsiveness	Mechanistic, by the book	Immediate, unquestioning	Participative process
Motivation	Careerism	Money/power	Public interest/service
Orientation to change	Resistance	Coercion	Employee involvement
Communications	Channeled	One way	Multidirectional
Personnel institutions	Legalistic	Weak	Influential

Table 2—Personnel System Characteristics

Policy Area	Model		
	Merit System	Political Management	Public Service Model
Recruitment	Centralized	Decentralized	Competitive career system for central corps of administrators; decentralized flexible system for support and project personnel; contracting on as-needed basis.
Appointment/tenure	Long-term/career	Temporary/job	
Selection	Competitive	Non-competitive; patronage	
Classification system	Rank in position	Rank in person	Job/person synthesis
Basic compensation	Equity system	Labor market	Modified prevailing rates
Pay adjustment	Longevity	Pay for performance (political)	Pay for performance (prof./tech.)
Benefits	Moderate	Private sector average	Model employer
Retirement	Defined benefit	Defined contribution	Combination system
Incentives	Career progression	Monetary	Self-actualization
Training	Career development	Job skill training	Human resource development
Performance evaluation	Pro forma	Quantitative	Contractual
Discipline	Procedural	Punitive	Preventive/corrective
Labor relations	Paternalism	Unilateralism	Consultative
Human resource planning	Extrapolation	Action/reaction	Strategic
Employment security	Seniority/vet. pref.	At management discretion	Guaranteed security
Equal emp. opportunity	Color blind	Politically determined	Race/gender sensitive
Conflict of interest	Legalistic	Deemphasized	Ethical emphasis
Employee rights	Legally established	At managerial discretion	By managerial guarantee

DEMOCRATIC POLICY PROCESS

Obviously, the public service model is not yet adequately developed, and the merit system model is in disorderly retreat. At the same time, the emergence of the political management model of the public service is occurring on an ad hoc basis without full public policy debate. Typically, in a period of lack of consensus, there has been heated political controversy but no well-informed discussion that should be at the heart of the policy process.

In a representative democracy, it is essential that significant policy issues be resolved through the working of a democratic policy process. Such a process requires that substantive issues be openly considered and informed by the input of a broader cross-section of interests than just the president and his political administration.

The recent history of public personnel management policy formulation has been one of arbitrary executive action. The result has been a high degree of work force demoralization. The continuing result will be loss of capacity. Expertise will be lost and not replaced; accountability will decline; employee motivation will disappear. . . .

NEED FOR EXECUTIVE LEADERSHIP

Any full airing of the issues will be very difficult without the support or at least tolerance of the president and his administration. Nonetheless, if consensus is not achieved soon on the proper direction of public personnel management policy, the nation will risk serious and perhaps irreversible decline in the capacity of its government. Absent presidential leadership, other policy actors—Congress, professional associations, employee groups, interest groups, the public administration community, the media, and the public—are beginning to focus on the implications of current policy confusion and on the opportunities for redefinition of the public service.

The convening of the National Commission on the Public Service, under the leadership of Paul Volcker, is a particularly hopeful sign. Broad public support is necessary for whatever model is adopted. This support can only be developed if the issues are broadly debated, if professional personnel expertise is brought into the policy process, and if issues can be publicly clarified before solutions are imposed.

CONCLUSION

There is need for haste in devising solutions to the major problems of the public service. The quality, capability, and responsiveness of the public work force are of vital importance to the ongoing question of whether a republic of the magnitude and scope of the United States can successfully govern itself without falling prey to authoritarianism on one hand or chaos on the other. Patchwork solutions will not suffice. The system is deteriorating so rapidly that prospects for continuing governmental effectiveness are becoming problematic.

In the nineteenth century, when the public personnel system last collapsed, America had the time and the geographic insulation to permit a long evolutionary approach to solutions. Now, there is no margin for muddling through. The competent workers required by the complexity and sophistication of the economic, social, and technical tasks of government are departing, and replacements are not readily at hand. The challenge is to develop a consistent and effective approach to assuring an adequate supply of people to perform the public business responsively and competently. This can only be done if policies are based on data, analysis, and a clear idea of objectives of the policy system.

COMMITMENT INSTEAD OF CONTROL

The policy imperatives for the creation of work force excellence, creativity, and productivity have been clearly identified in theories of social and organizational psychology. The appropriate lessons are being drawn by almost all the current management literature on excellence, organizational culture, creativity, and the state of the American work ethic. In the private sector context, the basic message is that organizational effectiveness requires a shift from a strategy of work force control to one of work force commitment.[4] Seemingly, these lessons have been lost on recent federal personnel policymakers.

VALUE OF THE WORKER

In specific reference to public policy and administration, the people who comprise the public service require and deserve something more than facile economic and behavioral assumptions, something better than political contempt, denigration, and manipulation. The people of the public service are essential to American democratic government. A hundred and fifty years ago, Alexis de Tocqueville caught sight of the key problem of people in organizations when he said:

> It would seem as if the rulers of our time sought only to use men in order to make things great; I wish that they would try a little more to make great men; that they would set less value on the work, and more on the workman; . . . [5]

The workers of democratic government require an enlightened and creative public service system. The design of such a system only requires a comprehensive effort, within the context of democratic politics, toward the creation of a new and meaningful public service system.

NOTES

1. Kaufman, Herbert, "Administrative Decentralization and Political Power," *Public Administration Review*, Vol. 24, January/February 1969, pp. 3–15.
2. Goldenberg, Edie N., "The Permanent Government in an Era of Retrenchment and Redirection," in Lester M. Salamon and Michael S. Lund, eds., *The Reagan Presidency and the Governing of America*, Washington, The Urban Institute Press, 1984, pp. 381–404.
3. Ingraham, Patricia W., and Carolyn R. Ban, "Models of Public Management: Are They Useful to Federal Managers in the 1980's?" *Public Administration Review*, Vol. 46, March/April 1986, pp. 152–160.
4. Walton, Richard E., "From Control to Commitment in the Workplace," *Harvard Business Review*, Vol. 64, March–April 1985, pp. 77–84.
5. Quoted in Kaplan, Abraham, *American Ethics and Public Policy*, New York, Oxford University Press, 1963, p. 90.

REFLECTIONS ON CSRA'S FIRST DECADE

Alan K. Campbell

More than ten years have passed since the Congress enacted the Civil Service Reform Act of 1978 (CSRA). As one who helped craft the legislation and secure its passage, I am often asked what I think of its accomplishments. Has it succeeded in doing what we hoped it would do? My feeling is that, insofar as the act put the means in place to improve the federal personnel system, it worked. But whether CSRA's various provisions will be employed to the system's fullest advantage still remains to be seen.

This has been a turbulent decade for federal employees. While the overall size of government—as measured by the number of employees—has not decreased, the mix of government activities, and therefore the distribution of employment among the various agencies, has undergone substantial change, with the major shift being from domestic to defense agencies. These factors, in themselves, have made for upheaval in the system. But more disruptive to the civil service have been the continuing effects of bureaucrat-bashing, which created an atmosphere that could hardly have been less conducive to civil service reform.

Antigovernment rhetoric, of course, did not come out of nowhere. It was a spin-off of the disillusionment that took hold in the wake of the Great Society. In the 1960s and early 1970s, the federal government accepted the challenge of confronting a number of vast social problems for which solutions were unknown, and many of its efforts to solve these problems absorbed a lot of money, expanded the bureaucracy, and then did not work as well as was predicted. Eventually the public bought the notion that government—and by extension, those who worked for it—were not the solution, but the problem. The Louis

Harris organization polled Americans in 1964 and asked, "Does the government waste a lot of money?" Forty-seven percent said yes. When the question was asked again in 1978, many more respondents—78 percent—said yes.

Also contributing to the deteriorating attitude toward government was the slowdown in the growth of the nation's economy. Slower economic growth meant that any significant expansion in government programs would have to be paid for, not out of new income, but out of people's pockets. They resisted. Antitax initiatives such as California's Proposition 13 spread across the country. It seemed unfair, many argued, for taxpayers to pick up the tab for programs they did not believe were working. Americans generally believed in what their government was trying to do: 88 percent, according to the 1978 Harris Poll, supported Social Security; 76 percent supported health programs; 70 percent supported education programs; 68 percent supported law enforcement programs; 65 percent supported job programs for the unemployed. The problem was that far fewer people believed the government could make these programs succeed.

This was the climate in which President Jimmy Carter put the 1977 Personnel Management Project members to work studying and drafting legislation to reshape the civil service. President Carter said that "there is no inherent conflict between careful planning, tight management, and constant reassessment on the one hand and compassionate concern for the plight of the deprived and the afflicted on the other. Waste and inefficiency never fed a hungry child, provided a job for a hungry worker, or educated a deserving student." Here was recognition that the personnel function—involving a range of dry, if not altogether boring, issues such as classification, job analysis, productivity improvement, and training and development—has a great bearing on how well the government does its job.

TWO LARGE PROBLEMS

Those of us engaged in the project discerned two overriding personnel problems in the civil service. First, we found that the federal government's personnel system had developed into a web of restraints designed primarily to prevent patronage, favoritism, and other abuses. In this sense it worked against itself: The same measures intended to prevent people from doing bad things can just as easily prevent them from doing good things. Second, we found that the layering of political appointees at the upper levels of federal agencies—assistant secretaries, deputy assistant secretaries, etc.—unduly limited the potential for career civil servants to fill high-level positions, and created serious tensions between career and noncareer personnel.

These two developments contributed to an environment in which no one felt a responsibility to make the system work: No one had a sense of *ownership*. Political appointees, serving for brief periods, sought to make their mark in some high-profile area, improve their resumes, and move on with their careers. Meanwhile, career federal employees, serving under a succession of political appointees, felt an obligation only to their jobs, not to the system of which they were a part. All this, it seemed to us, helped create a system that failed to emphasize either top-flight performance or the management tools necessary to ensure it. The primary purpose of personnel policies and practices is to encourage quality performance among all employees. Every policy and practice should be measured against this standard and performance should be measured against preestablished individual and organizational goals.

REORGANIZING FOR CHANGE

One of our first recommendations was to bring responsiveness and flexibility to the personnel system by eliminating the Civil Service Commission. We felt the Commission had accumulated a set of mutually exclusive functions, and consequently was fulfilling none of them well. Although bipartisan in make-up, it was expected to work for the President, establishing personnel policies and advising and assisting executive branch agencies in achieving effective personnel management. At the same time, it was expected to stand aside from the fray and oversee the integrity of the merit system, protect employee rights, decide employee appeals, and perform a variety of other adjudicatory functions. The Commission's conflicting duties undermined both its performance and its credibility. So we split the agency and its roles. Under Reorganization Plan No. 2 of 1978, the Office of Personnel Management (OPM) became the President's personnel arm. The Merit Systems Protection Board became the merit system watchdog.

The creation of OPM was designed, in part, to put a more responsive personnel structure in place and thereby open the personnel system to change. One such change was in authority. The Civil Service Reform Act authorized OPM to delegate personnel authority to the departments and agencies; in fact, when I was OPM Director we delegated some 64 authorities. Why do so? Because when personnel authority is exercised from a distance, it serves merely as a control. When it is delegated to the department or agency —or even better, down to the manager of each operating unit—it becomes a tool for improving the performance of operations. I felt then—and continue to feel now—that day-to-day personnel decisions belong in the hands of the people charged with accomplishing the goals of the agency. The personnel staff should assist line managers, but authority must reside with the managers.

THE SENIOR EXECUTIVE SERVICE

Another major provision of CSRA was the creation of the Senior Executive Service (SES). The SES was intended to make it more feasible for career federal managers to fill high-level positions and to make the career-noncareer relationship more rational. In the SES, the designation "career" or "noncareer" became affixed to positions rather than individuals; it meant that a qualified career SES member could be called upon to fill a high-level "noncareer" post, yet retain his or her career status upon completion of the assignment. At the same time, we abolished the idea that rank—that is, pay and position in the hierarchy—was inherently a part of the position description, and established the principle of SES rank-in-person, so that an executive could be paid at a level commensurate with the personal rank he or she had earned.

In addition, we set at 10 percent the maximum proportion of SES members who could be political appointees—the percentage that existed at the time CSRA was passed. (Despite a common perception that the number of political appointments to upper-level positions has increased in the 1980s, the 10 percent limit has not been violated. But it is also true, regrettably, that the number of career SES members moving into the upper-level positions does not seem to have risen.)

Better performance was our goal in arguing for the SES, as well as for other features of CSRA such as merit pay for middle managers. We hoped to get the most out of federal managers by establishing bonuses and merit pay, by making it somewhat easier to deal with inadequate performance, and by encouraging the adoption of performance appraisal systems.

Establishing workable measures of performance is a difficult task in government—more so than in the private sector. The obvious difference between a private company and a government agency is that the agency has no bottom line by which to measure its success. But, even in business, bottom-line considerations are not the only ones. In my own corporation, about 60 percent of each employee's bonus is based on the financial performance of his or her unit; the other 40 percent is based on nonfinancial measures, such as client satisfaction and retention, preparation of employees for new roles, and use of training programs. So it is possible to develop nonfinancial goals against which performance can be measured. I remain convinced that, even in government, there is no program in which managers who are assigned a set of responsibilities and goals cannot develop a means of determining how well these responsibilities and goals are being accomplished. Private-sector enterprises set up appraisal measures because they have to in order to survive. Federal employees face less risk of losing their jobs, but like all workers, they need a reliable measure of their performance to give them a sense of accomplishment and ownership of the organization of which they are a part.

Some agencies have done a very good job of developing measures of accomplishment, but I do not know of any governmentwide effort to try to understand what's working well, and where. Some still contend that OPM or the Office of Management and Budget should develop performance measures and impose them on the agencies. I believe, however, that the agencies would resist such a move—and they should. And if such a system were imposed, the blame for its failures would fall on those who devised it, rather than on the managers responsible for making it work. I worry over the tendency in government, when there is a broad management problem, to assign the solution to a central agency rather than to the operating agencies. Even the role of oversight or coordination can very quickly become an authority role. The more useful function for a central agency is to offer technical assistance, review, and record keeping, and to help give visibility to innovative approaches and success stories from the agencies.

PUBLIC- VERSUS PRIVATE-SECTOR TECHNIQUES

There has been much talk about how the federal government ought to adopt private-sector management techniques. But one has to recognize that private-sector approaches have changed over time. Years ago, the organization of the federal government—its internal structure, its allocation of personnel—looked a lot like the private sector. Just as in government, the biggest firms had as many as 15 layers of management. And just as in government, there was a tremendous reliance on staff—personnel people, finance people, management types—versus line. American business has since learned that this sort of management approach, along with the accompanying staff overhead, makes it uncompetitive with its restructured domestic and international rivals. The government, though, with no direct competition to deal with—only a slowly building public resentment—has been less quick to learn the lesson and adopt the appropriate management and organizational changes. But that is why I think the CSRA laid the groundwork for eventual success: It allows agencies to innovate if and when they decide to do so.

The act did not prescribe solutions to the government's personnel problems. Instead, it enabled the federal personnel system to explore and implement its own solutions. Some argued at its passage, and continue to argue, that increased discretion at the agency level will create the potential for abuse of the system. This may well be true, but the old, more restrictive system is not the answer. I do not think, for example, that the sort of personnel abuses that took place early in this decade at the Environmental Protection Agency would have been prevented under the old system.

In a personnel system as enormous as the federal government's, there is no legislative solution to the eternal conflict between central control and autonomy. Eventually, it comes down to the luck of the draw—having leaders who make the most of the opportunities afforded them, and enjoying times in which the opportunities are there. Certainly, the administration that took office in 1981 had its own agenda, which to a considerable extent worked against the greater autonomy encouraged by CSRA. The delegation of personnel authorities by OPM came to a halt; in fact, many of the 64 delegations made by the previous administration were rescinded. But other factors also inhibited innovation: The kinds of experimental personnel projects encouraged by CSRA would probably have been more widespread if the times had not been marked by growing deficits and antigovernment sentiment.

So, in the sense that this has been an unruly decade for government, there is no way of knowing just how successful the reforms of CSRA can be. The act *allows* things to happen; it does not require them. In the last 18 months or so of the Reagan administration, for example, OPM began to reverse itself in many areas. And even where progress has not been what we might have hoped, some progress has been made. For instance, complaints are heard concerning the SES. The number of career SES personnel in high positions does not seem to have gone up. Training programs for SES members and opportunities for movement across agency lines have not met expectations. Yet

the bonus system—a matter of great controversy during enactment of CSRA and in the days thereafter—seems well accepted now. And the fact that SES members carry rank-in-person rather than rank-in-position allows for easier movement of managers, if not from agency to agency, at least within agencies themselves. And regarding the degree to which talented career SES people are chosen for high posts, the fact that they have not been of late does not mean that they will not be in the future.

For federal employees, the tone has to be set by the President. This one has gotten off to an encouraging start. But the government's personnel system exists in a larger environment that is not just political but economic and social. It will take a while to see whether the best use is made of CSRA.

One additional note: An issue that civil service reform does not address is that of adequate pay for federal managers. The recent inability of the Congress to address this issue raises a serious challenge to the ability of the federal government to attract and retain its share of the nation's most talented managers. The public debate about pay focused almost exclusively on appropriate compensation for Members of Congress, when the greatest threat to effective government comes from inadequate pay for executive branch managers and members of the judiciary. Civil service reform, or, perhaps better said, effective personnel leadership, is invariably dependent on executive leadership. Without competitive pay—competitive with state and local governments, nonprofit organizations, and business—there is no way such leadership, either career or noncareer, can be retained or attracted. In the long run, effective implementation of civil service reform and, similarly, the overall quality of executive branch management rely on fairness in pay. Current executive pay does not meet this test.

BEYOND MR. GRADGRIND: THE CASE FOR DEREGULATING THE PUBLIC SECTOR

Constance Horner

Some conservatives look at federal bureaucrats in much the same way that Charles Dickens' character Thomas Gradgrind viewed his factory employees in *Hard Times*—as "a bad lot altogether, gentlemen; that, do what you would for them they were never thankful for it, gentlemen; that they never knew what they wanted; that they lived upon the best and bought fresh butter; and insisted on mocha coffee, and rejected all but prime parts of meat, and yet were eternally dissatisfied and unmanageable." The practical consequence of this "Gradgrindism" is that conservatives have been much less enthusiastic about removing paperwork and regulatory burdens from the civil service than they have been about deregulating the private sector. Some have even supported highly centralized new controls on the bureaucracy, despite their opposition to *dirigisme* everywhere else.

But deregulation of the public sector is as important as deregulation of the private sector, and for precisely the same reason: to liberate the entrepreneurial energies of Americans at work. Nearly a quarter of the income of this nation is spent by or through the federal government. It matters a great deal how well or poorly that income is spent. A crisp, decisive, lean, productive civil service, able to decide and act, rather than wait and see, would lead to smaller, more accountable government, allow more resources to remain in the private sector, and also improve the quality of government services.

The government takes in about $2.5 billion a day and spends about $2.9 billion. The federal payroll alone is $84 billion a year, with over $25 billion more in retirement benefit outlays, and almost $9 billion in health and life insurance. No doubt, much of what the federal government does might be better done by the private sector, or in some cases not done at all. But some services are so important that conservatives and liberals alike can agree that they should be provided as effectively as possible, no matter who does the providing.

Consider this short list of civil service positions:

- Nurses caring for patients in experimental cancer research at the National Institutes of Health hospitals;
- SDI research scientists and engineers;
- Customs service agents who intercept drugs at our borders;
- USDA food inspectors insuring the purity of meat and poultry;
- Justice Department criminal investigators probing organized crime;
- EPA employees directing the cleanup of a toxic waste site;
- Social Security clerks processing almost 5 million claims a year;
- Statisticians at the Bureau of Labor Statistics who tell us if employment is going up or down;
- FAA air traffic controllers;
- Park Service rangers who fight fires in our national parks;
- SEC attorneys and auditors monitoring securities transactions to prevent fraud;
- Transportation and nuclear power plant safety inspectors.

The senior bureaucrats charged with these responsibilities, though perhaps somewhat more risk-averse than some private sector managers, are as competent, hardworking, creative, and motivated toward superior performance as any American executives. The problem is that they are trapped in systems that make it unusually difficult for them to perform well. Many struggle heroically for a lifetime against the constraints that prohibit superior accomplishment and keep trying to serve the public, even without recognition. Others give up and become passive processors of paper. But all of them deserve a full-faith effort from political leadership to liberate their energies by removing the barriers to full performance. That means a serious effort to deregulate, simplify, and decentralize public management. . . .

The size of the government work force could be substantially reduced if public managers had more flexibility in making basic personnel and purchasing decisions, and if lower paperwork requirements freed them to focus more on the services they are supposed to provide. Let's look at what federal managers can't do because of the tens of thousands of pages of regulations restricting their every move.

Federal managers have little discretion to use pay to reward and retain good employees. As a rule, superior performance goes unrewarded with better pay. Nor does promotion come more swiftly to workers who show superior commitment and talent. Status on the basis of seniority is the dominant ethos of civil service administration.

Federal managers are not allowed to use compensation to attract talent. The starting salaries they offer to outstanding graduates of superior colleges and universities cannot be any higher than those to weaker students from lesser institutions. Managers can't decide how many people to hire, for what jobs, at what salary levels. Except for the Department of Defense, which has been exempted from personnel ceilings by Congress, the Office of Management and Budget (OMB) decides how many people an agency needs (and sometimes where to put them). Sometimes, OMB sets a maximum and Congress a minimum. It would be much better if senior managers could get their appropriated budgets and decide how many people to hire, at what pay levels, to get the job done.

Federal managers consume hours negotiating with agency personnel specialists over the proper placement of jobs and employees in a system that has more than 700 occupations, 18 grades, and 10 steps a grade. There are 74 pages of rules on how much to pay a secretary. Taking disciplinary action means coping with protracted and complex appeals procedures, including agency appeals, union-negotiated arbitration, EEOC determinations, and the federal courts. There is ceaseless disputation.

In one typical case, for example, a postal employee was removed for inability to perform the job. With all the panoply of staff and contending lawyers, the appeal went in sequence for hearings, review, and adjudication to the Merit Systems

Protection Board (MSPB), the Equal Employment Opportunity Commission, back to the MSPB, and then to a so-called special panel. The process took more than five years. The employee had worked for the government three years and nine months. And this case didn't include a union-negotiated grievance procedure or a trip to the Federal Appeals Court, which would have added months or years to the process.

Procurement contracts for work and equipment take so long to execute and require so many levels of "clearance" that technology is frequently out of date by the time it arrives or else it doesn't match equipment in other units. Outstanding contractors are lost because they can't wait or don't meet often unreasonable requirements.

The General Services Administration (GSA) has been trying for some time to replace the government's crotchety 25-year-old telephone system. The idea is to save the government about $100 million a year, improve the quality of service, and add much-needed capacity for data-transmission. Attempts to win a preliminary contract for the new system have been thwarted by: (1) the insistence by an influential congressman that the contract be split into parts, (2) investigations into allegations of conflict of interest and criminal misconduct by GSA officials, and (3) a bidding process that was just too complicated to hold the attention of more than a handful of the 70 companies initially expressing interest. The contract may now not even be awarded until the next administration. In the meantime OPM can't get in a phone system able to handle its 8,000 or so inquiries each week about employee retirement benefits.

Federal managers usually have no idea what their budgets are until the fiscal year is almost over. Agency leadership, uncertain over money cutbacks, potential freezes, and so on, must withhold spending until the last minute, or move it around in a kind of agency-wide shell game or check-kiting scheme. And even when agencies know their budgets, managers cannot allocate funds according to their judgment about priorities. Instead, central office-imposed personnel limitations and congressional micro-management join together to govern their decisions in ways that are counterproductive to good administration. . . .

Each of the rules, regulations, and requirements of the U.S. Civil Service is well intentioned and designed to preclude unfairness or error. Together they have led to an administratively moribund system that disallows the exercise of human judgment and discretion. (The personnel rules alone amount to 6,000 pages—more than the Bible, the Rand McNally World Atlas, the Manhattan Yellow Pages, Robert's Rules of Order, and *A Tale of Two Cities* combined.) Remember the Greek goddess Medusa and her snaky locks—anyone who looked at her would freeze, permanently, into inaction? The systems with which we've surrounded federal line managers are just as convoluted and ugly as those snaky locks, and have much the same effect—one good look at them and government managers lose heart, energy, and will. They lose, thereby, some of their capacity to serve the public well.

Henry David Thoreau once said: "Any fool can make a rule!" It's much harder to *deregulate*. To be effective, public sector managers, like their private sector counterparts, need the power to make key decisions over personnel and budget. They have to be able to move employees from jobs they can't do to ones they can, to award a contract for two weeks' work in less than three months' time, to expend budget on another secretary or another electronic engineer, whichever is more needed, without subjection to endless petty harassment by rules and "clearances.". . .

[An] experiment began in 1980 at two California naval weapons labs, one at the Naval Ocean Systems Center in San Diego and the other at the Naval Weapons Center at China Lake in the Mojave Desert. (It is commonly referred to as the "China Lake" experiment.) The labs were engaged in crucial research and development efforts (development of the Sidewinder and Skipper missiles, as well as research into undersea surveillance and weapons systems and Arctic submarine warfare), yet they were unable to get and keep personnel of the highest quality. Working with OPM, the Navy put in place a new and radically simplified system for defining jobs and hiring, promoting, and paying personnel. The new system put managers more in charge of the work they're accountable for. It is a simple, performance-based, and market-oriented system.

The new system grouped 120 occupational series into a few broad career paths.

It abolished the complex, 180-step general schedule and replaced it with four to six broad pay bands. Managers move strong performers up within these bands or into different jobs without regard to rigid seniority or classification rules.

It replaced complicated, multi-paged position descriptions produced by the personnel office with a short, computerized list of job elements *managers* could use.

It introduced an element of market-based pay at the entry level so managers could compete with the private sector for quality recruits.

It based all pay increases on performance. Performance-related pay is still available in only a limited way elsewhere in the federal government.

These are common, everyday practices in the private sector, but they are revolutionary for the public sector. They are based on two principles historically anathema to government operations but necessary to sound management—relying on human judgment rather than overregulated systems to make decisions; and making clear performance distinctions among workers, with rewards for better work. These are profoundly conservative principles. They recognize that the use of discretion and judgment, the exercise of intelligence and character enlarge human capacities. They recognize that material incentives spur effort and increase productivity. . . .

How has the China Lake experiment worked? Evaluations show resounding success. Management and employee morale are up, recruits have much higher college grade-point averages, managers spend *less* time on personnel matters (although they are making *more* of the decisions), and, most significantly, in increasing numbers strong performers are staying on the job and weak ones are leaving. This is as close to nirvana as a federal manager can get. . . .

There are other promising experiments in personnel reform. Last fall, OPM approved an experiment in "productivity gain-sharing" at McClellan Air Force Base in Sacramento. Under this experiment developed jointly by management and labor, rigid job classifications are simplified, allowing workers to move where they are needed, and employee groups are rewarded with bonuses when they save taxpayer money by increasing productivity. The National Bureau of Standards is studying whether a China Lake-type system can attract the scientists and engineers it needs in a time when they are in short supply nationally. The Navy, which is exempted from arbitrary personnel ceilings, is now trying the concept of "managing to payroll," that is, allowing line managers to decide the number and mix of staff needed to get the job done within the budget.

While we cannot put "China Lake" into effect government-wide without legislation, OPM is engaged in major administrative simplifcations and delegations that place responsibility in the hands of senior civil servants, decentralize decision-making (with central management agencies assuming more of an oversight role), and allow greater latitude for the exercise of judgment in decision-making. OPM has recently increased the delegation of hiring authority from itself to the agencies; it has allowed agencies to waive rigid qualification rules when they want to move employees from one job to another, and it is experimenting with broad, generic job standards that allow line managers, rather than central personnel staffs, to classify positions. Literally hundreds of restrictions and requirements have been waived, simplified, or delegated.

How can we characterize the impact of these changes? They save an extraordinary amount of time. Through better technology and decentralization (optical scanners for tests and direct hire authority for agencies), OPM has cut the hiring process for a secretary, for example, from eight weeks to one day. These broad changes prevent all the warping of common sense that occurs when rules override judgment, or when decisions are made by distant regulatory overseers rather than by those who are affected by the results. . . .

What remains is a potentially far more serious threat than ideology—incompetence. This threat is now only a cloud on the horizon. But unless we change the government's ways of doing business, it will eventually attract only the less able among the American work force. Good managers and professionals will not remain at jobs that give them only a passive role. They want to work where their strongest talents can be used, their efforts rewarded and their intelligence and judgment allowed to influence decisions regarding production, service, and quality.

We know from the private sector that trimming corporate staffs and giving line managers more decision-making flexibility can increase performance and accountability. All the great management books—from Peter Drucker to Tom Peters—say procedures should be simple, paperwork should be kept at a minimum, and line managers should have the tools they need to get their jobs done.

Political and intellectual circles often emphasize the importance to democratic government of institutions such as the presidency, the political parties, and the Congress. Little, if any, attention is paid to the Civil Service. Yet, like political parties or the judiciary, it is a basic component of democratic government. If the Civil Service performs competently and is amenable to political leadership, democratic governance is strengthened. Labor and socialist governments, such as Australia's and Spain's, look to our civil service as a model for overcoming paralysis of will and purpose in their public sectors. New or fragile democracies look to us for reassurance that they, too, can have a civil service that is responsive and incorruptible and that serves the public interest with honor and pride. But without change in the way we manage our civil service, time is not on the side of democracy, for them—or for us.

THE U.S. SUPREME COURT'S "CONSENSUS" ON AFFIRMATIVE ACTION

John Nalbandian

Twenty-five years ago Congress passed the Civil Rights Act of 1964, and 18 years ago the U.S. Supreme Court provided its first significant review in *Griggs* v. *Duke Power Company.*[1] Since *Griggs*, the Court has considered several employment discrimination cases, and it finally appears possible to identify the conditions under which a public employer can consider race in personnel actions.

This article delineates those conditions by examining the analytical approach employed by the Court in deliberating employment discrimination cases. It then discusses the conflicting values debated in these cases, and in the last part it speculates on the future of affirmative action.

FACTORS IMPEDING CONSENSUS

For a number of years, the Court has confronted different issues which complicated an early answer to the question, "Under what conditions can a public employer take race into consideration in employment decisions?" On the statutory side, unanticipated issues and ambiguities resulting from legislative compromise dictated evolutionary development of the law.[2] These complicating factors are outlined before describing the Court's approach to employment discrimination cases.

First, varied statutory and constitutional issues suggest different standards of judicial review. The analysis in this article focuses on Title VII of the Civil Rights Act of 1964 as amended by the Equal Employment Act of 1972 and the Equal Protection Clause of the 14th Amendment to the United States Constitution. Cases involving claims against *private employers* have been litigated under Title VII which prohibits discrimination in employment based on race, color, religion, gender, or national origin. A case may be filed against a *public employer* under Title VII and/or as a constitutional claim under the Equal Protection Clause of the 14th Amendment. That clause says that no state shall "deny to any person within its jurisdiction the equal protection of the laws." Over the years, the Court has narrowed the differences in its approach to statutory versus constitutional issues.

Second, while administrators commonly use the term "affirmative action," the Court has struggled to sort out the legal distinctions between "color blind" personnel practices, consideration of race as one among several factors in personnel decisions, and focus on race as the major factor in employment decisions. Further confounding these distinctions are the legal differences between the vehicles of affirmative action: voluntary plans, provisions included in consent decrees, and court orders.

A third factor obscuring clear cut conclusions about the use of race consciousness in personnel actions arises from differences between the assumptions about discrimination contained in Title VII and litigation subsequently confronted. When amending Title VII in 1972, Congress acknowledged its prior naivete: "In 1964, employment discrimination tended to be viewed as a series of isolated and distinguishable events, for the most part due to ill-will on the part of some identifiable individual or organization. . . . Experience has shown this view to be false."[3] Unfortunately, the Court has had to confront cases involving systemic, yet, in some cases, unintentional discrimination where individual victims are not easily identifiable.

Growing out of these assumptions about discrimination is a fourth factor—the essentially remedial nature of Title VII and the challenge of voluntary affirmative action. The law was designed to compensate individuals who had suffered discrimination. The letter of the law did not envision the possibility of employers taking voluntary steps to overcome racial imbalances in their work force without formally having been found guilty of discrimination. Yet, starting with *Steelworkers* v. *Weber*,[4] the Court observed that precluding voluntary affirmative action would run contrary to the spirit of the law.

Finally, an appeal to legislative intent to answer questions of law frequently justifies conflicting positions. This is notably true with regard to Section 706(g) of Title VII, which some justices argue was intended to permit court ordered relief only for identifiable victims of discrimination. While Chief Justice Rehnquist, a strong supporter of this interpretation, claims that the language itself is clear in 706(g), he acknowledges that the legislative history "may be fairly apportioned among both sides."[5]

Each of these factors has challenged the Court's ability definitively to interpret employment discrimination law. Further, legal debate will continue over unresolved points of law like the difference in the meaning of "strict scrutiny," standards of review in Title VII versus 14th Amendment cases, and constitutional standards of review in gender versus race-based affirmative action. Nevertheless, case law has developed since 1971, and it is possible now to generalize at least about the *reasoning* employed by the Court when analyzing employment discrimination cases.

THE COURT'S TWO-PART ANALYTICAL APPROACH

Something like a working consensus appears present within the Court that review of race-conscious affirmative action requires a two-part analysis. The first part examines the justification for taking race into consideration. The second focuses on the content of the affirmative action with particular attention to the consequences for nonminority employees.

JUSTIFICATION FOR RACE-CONSCIOUSNESS

Justification for taking affirmative action ranges from overcoming imbalances in "traditionally segregated job categories"[6] to remediating the effects of intentional discrimination.[7] While the Court has not yet agreed fully on what constitutes sufficient justification, *the more impact the affirmative action has on nonminorities, the more justification is required.* For example, the Court determined that "societal discrimination" did not

constitute justification for a race-conscious layoff provision—even though contained in a collective bargaining agreement. According to the Court, an inference of *employer* discrimination would have been required.[8]

The most stringent requirement for a public employer is demonstrating a "compelling government purpose" for the use of racial classifications in employment decisions. A lesser standard would be an "important government purpose." But in many ways the Court's argument over standards of justification are rendered moot with Justice O'Connor's observation that "The Court is in agreement that, whatever the formulation [of a level of scrutiny like 'compelling' versus 'important'] employed, remedying past or present racial discrimination by a state actor is a sufficiently weighty state interest to warrant the remedial use of a carefully constructed affirmative action program."[9]

Many administrators do not realize that an inference of employer discrimination may be drawn from a conspicuous racial imbalance in segments of the employer's work force compared to segments of a relevant labor market.[10] Wherever a strong *inference* of employment discrimination can be found, at least a "firm" basis exists for affirmative action.[11]

MEANS-ENDS ANAYLSIS

The second half of the Court's reasoning concentrates on the substance of the race-conscious plan or relief. The Court is concerned with limiting affirmative action tightly within the scope of the problem that it is supposed to solve. Regardless of whether a Title VII or 14th Amendment claim, the Court's primary concern in evaluating the scope of affirmative action is with the burden placed on innocent nonminorities.[12]

While the Court has approved benefits to nonvictim minorities,[13] it prefers remedies which provide "make-whole relief" to identifiable victims. With make-whole relief, victims receive what they would have gotten had they not been discriminated against, and nonvictim minorities do not benefit from a racial preference. But even in cases involving make-whole relief, the Court is inclined to review the impact on nonminorities. For example, in *Teamsters* the Court granted make-whole relief but remanded the case to the District Court to determine the actual victims of discrimination. The Supreme Court said: "The District Court will again be faced with the delicate task of adjusting the remedial interests of the discriminatees and the legitimate expectations of other employees innocent of any wrongdoing."[14]

While the Court has acknowledged that innocent third parties may have to bear some of the burden in race-conscious relief,[15] it is more likely to approve where the burden is diffuse and not borne by particular individuals. In *United States v. Paradise*, Justice Powell expressed his standard for judging the impact on third parties. He wrote: "Unlike layoff requirements, the promotion requirement at issue in this case does not 'impose the entire burden of achieving racial equality on particular individuals,' and it does not disrupt seriously the lives of innocent individuals."[16]

In addition to this guidance, in *Paradise* Justice Powell succinctly summarized four additional criteria used by the Court to assess whether or not race-conscious relief is narrowly tailored to the problem it is supposed to solve. They are: "(i) the efficacy of alternative remedies; (ii) the planned duration of the remedy; (iii) the relationship between the percentage of minority workers to be employed and the percentage of minority group members in the relevant population or work force; and (iv) the availability of waiver provisions if the hiring plan could not be met."[17]

Paradise illustrates the applicability of Justice Powell's five criteria. The District Court had found the Alabama Department of Public Safety guilty of intentional discrimination and recalcitrant in complying with the terms of subsequent decrees, including development of a valid promotion testing procedure. Frustrated with the delays, the District Court ordered a one-for-one promotion quota which the United States, supporting the Department of Public Safety, claimed violated the Equal Protection Clause of the 14th Amendment.

With the exception of Justice Stevens, who concurred in the judgment supporting the quota but who would have granted broader discretion to the District Court because the case involved intentional discrimination by a governmental body, the Court utilized its two-pronged analysis. The Court unanimously agreed that the District Court had rightly based its enforcement order on a compelling interest in eradicating the Department of Public Safety's "pervasive, systematic, and obstinate discriminatory" exclusion of blacks.[18] The Court's disagreement centered on the nature of the remedy, with Justices Brennan, Blackmun, Marshall, and Powell concluding that it was narrowly tailored and Justices O'Connor, Scalia, and White and Chief Justice Rehnquist finding the opposite.

Justice Brennan writing for a plurality reasoned that (1) no alternatives to the quota were brought to the District Court; (2) the one-for-one requirement was flexible in several ways including: a waiver provision if no qualified minorities were available; promotion only when the Department determined the need for additional supervisory personnel; duration contingent upon the Department's development of a valid promotion procedure; and anticipation of the quota as a one-time occurrence by the District Court; (3) while the one-for-one rate failed to correspond to the 1 to 3 ratio of blacks to whites in the relevant work force, it was appropriate considering the Department's past discrimination and delays in implementing the necessary promotion procedure; and (4) the requirement did not impose an unacceptable burden on innocent nonminorities.

Justice O'Connor's dissenting opinion, joined by Chief Justice Rehnquist and Justices Scalia and White, reiterated the view she expressed in *Sheet Metal Workers* where she argued strongly against quotas—and reluctantly endorsed goals—in court-ordered remedies because of their impact on innocent nonminorities.[19] In *Paradise* she reiterated that conclusion, focusing on what she called the Court's "standardless" view of a "narrowly tailored" remedy for the discrimination which had occurred. She fundamentally objected to the District Court's failure to entertain alternative remedies more specifically targeted at the goal of inducing the Department of Public Safety to develop a valid promotion procedure. She argued that consideration of alternatives is the least action required by the "narrowly tailored" standard.[20] Second, she objected to the one-for-one ratio arguing that it far exceeded the 25 percent minority trooper force eligible for promotion and, therefore, was arbitrary.

The two-part analysis is illustrated as well in *Johnson* v. *Transportation Agency*,[21] the other case coming before the Court in 1987. The parallel analyses in contrasting cases like *Paradise* and *Johnson* underscore the Court's growing consensus on its analytical approach to employment discrimination cases. *Paradise* came to the Court involving constitutional issues stemming from a court order in response to intentional racial discrimination. The Court reviewed *Johnson* as a Title VII case involving voluntary affirmative action to overcome gender imbalances in "traditionally segregated job categories."

Paul Johnson applied for promotion to the position of road dispatcher with the Transportation Agency in Santa Clara County, California. Diane Joyce also applied for the job in which women were obviously underrepresented. The hiring authority determined both applicants to be qualified and eligible for the promotion. Under the county's affirmative action plan, Joyce was hired over Johnson who had received two more points than Joyce on the basis of an interview. Thus, the Court was faced with determining if an affirmative action plan which led to the hiring of a woman over a male violated Title VII.[22]

In a 6-3 judgment, the Court upheld the plan. Justice Brennan delivered the Court's opinion. The majority found the County's actions consistent with the provisions that the Court established in *Weber*. The County's plan was designed to break down traditionally segregated job categories. The plan established short-term goals which did not unnecessarily trammel the interests of nonminorities (males), did not require discharge of nonminorities (males) in favor of minorities (females), did not create an absolute bar to advancement of nonminorities (males), and were temporary in nature and not designed to maintain a racial (gender) balance but to eliminate an imbalance.[23]

In sum, while it is not always possible to predict the Court's decision, one can be increasingly confident that both majority and minority opinions will follow the same points of reasoning. In other words, the framework of analysis has become increasingly clear with the development of case law. The framework focuses on the justification for affirmation action and an examination to determine whether the means narrowly fit the scope of the problem. In assessing the consequences of affirmative action, the Court pays significant attention to the impact on nonminorities.

THE VALUE DEBATE WITHIN THE COURT

So far, this article has attempted to summarize the legal reasoning which underpins the Court's analysis in employment discrimination cases. But to understand more clearly the Court's direction, one must identify and examine the values debated within this analytical framework.

For 18 years the Court has debated the appropriate balance in employment discrimination cases between the competing values of individual rights, social equity, and efficiency in its effort to clarify the meaning of the law. This section views the Court's affirmative action decisions in terms of these values.

As a value, *individual rights* includes the expectations that employees and job applicants have of fair treatment and protection from arbitrary decisions, particularly in actions affecting job security and seniority. The Court's emphasis on "make-whole relief" to identifiable victims of discrimination reflects the value of individual rights. Similarly, its emphasis on protecting the interests of nonminorities grows out of its respect for individual rights. Thus, the key task of balancing the interests of minority victims and innocent nonminorities fundamentally revolves around questions of individual rights.

While the Court does not use the term *social equity*, its opinions nevertheless reflect this value which cannot be ignored in understanding human resources policy and administration. Another term for social equity might be "distributive justice." Adherence to the value of social equity results in fair treatment of people as members of a class rather than as individuals. Preference on the basis of race, gender, age, religion, or national origin reflects the value of social equity. Social equity is frequently expressed in compensatory terms where an action is taken to overcome some classwide past injustice or hardship. Social equity results in race-conscious affirmative action to nonvictim minorities as opposed to make-whole relief to identifiable victims of discrimination. One of the most common expressions of social equity, predating affirmative action by a century, is veterans preference awarded to individuals who have served in the armed forces and who may have lost a competitive position in the labor market.

Because the Court analyzes percentages of minorities to nonminorities in a work force to make inferences about underutilization and to assess progress in overcoming the effects of past discrimination, the value of social equity frequently is confused with a similar value, "representation." Clearly, moving towards a work force that is representative of the racial balance in a relevant labor pool demonstrates affirmative action progress. However, representativeness is used as a measure or instrument of this progress, not as an end value. The goal of eradicating past discrimination expresses the end value of social equity.[24]

Frequently people look upon social equity with suspicion. Among the reasons are: a preference in this culture to make awards based on variation in individual merit rather than either/or distinctions which erase individual differences. The value of social equity necessarily highlights differences due to race, gender, and national origin in a culture which largely seeks to downplay these differences.

Efficiency in the provision of public services is commonly measured with various input/output ratios. In personnel administration efficiency is advanced generally when personnel actions are taken on the basis of merit. Thus, efficiency is reflected in affirmative action with the concern for the qualifications (knowledge, skills, and abilities) of applicants.

The history of employment discrimination cases first focused on the values of individual rights and efficiency consistent with the assumption that violations of anti-discrimination law would consist of discreet incidents involving a victim and a person who had committed a discriminatory act. Victims would receive make-whole relief which would be balanced against the rights and interests of other victims and innocent nonminorities. The Court's unanimous opinion in *Griggs* emphasized that *individuals* should be subject to color blind criteria in employment decisions. Individual rights are expressed in the view that race-conscious relief should be confined to the identifiable victims of discrimination. This view is seen clearly in *Albemarle Paper Company* v. *Moody*[25] where the Court went to great lengths to specify how an employee could create the inference that he or she was a victim of discrimination, and in *Firefighters* v. *Stotts*,[26] where the Court implied a general

policy limiting relief only to identifiable victims of discrimination.

Finally, a major expression of individual rights is the Court's concern that the burden that innocent nonminorities are called upon to bear in race-conscious relief will not cause them undue harm. This concern is expressed in all Court opinions where minority nonvictims benefit from race-conscious relief. It is even expressed where make-whole relief is involved, particularly when the job security of nonminorities might be affected. According to Justice Stewart, writing for the Court in *Teamsters*, "Especially when immediate implementation of an equitable remedy threatens to impinge upon the expectations of innocent parties, the courts must 'look to the practical realities and necessities inescapably involved in reconciling competing interests,' in order to determine the 'special blend of what is necessary, what is fair, and what is workable.' "[27]

In Justice Rehnquist's minority opinion in *Weber*, he expressed the unequivocal viewpoint that employment discrimination boils down to questions of individual rights: "I find a prohibition on all preferential treatment based on race as elementary and fundamental as the principle that 'two wrongs do not make a right.' "[28]

The problem with approaching employment discrimination from the perspective of individual rights alone is found in situations where systemic discrimination has created insidious barriers to fair treatment. For example, where blacks know it is a waste of time to apply for a job or a promotion, make-whole relief is very difficult to assign.[29] Further, to the extent that the Court has endorsed affirmative action to overcome race and gender imbalances in traditionally segregated job categories, as it did in *Weber* and *Johnson*, trying to limit relief to identifiable victims of discrimination is impractical.

Thus, in addition to individual rights, social equity has influenced the Court's decisions. These decisions invoke preferential treatment to minorities who may not have been victims of discrimination, with preference to them stemming from their minority status as opposed to characteristics which differentiate minority members one from the other or from nonminority employees or applicants. *Weber, Sheet Metal Workers, Firefighters, Paradise,* and *Johnson* (gender) all provide some kind of goal or quota with preference to minorities. Of course, in each of these cases, the Court makes a special effort to assess the impact of the goal or quota on the rights of nonminorities, recognizing that social equity can impinge upon individual rights and that the values require some balancing.

The strongest expressions of social equity go beyond establishment of goals and quotas to remedy employer discrimination. Justice Stevens has led the argument. In *Wygant*, he wrote in a dissenting opinion that the Court "should consider whether the public interest, and the manner in which it is pursued, justifies any adverse effects on the disadvantaged groups."[30] This "public interest" standard is distinguished from the stricter standards of "compelling" or even "important" government purposes, and it would open the door to broader justification for race-conscious personnel actions. More recently, in a concurring opinion in *Johnson*, where the Court supported the use of gender classification, Justice Stevens emphasized that "the opinion does not establish the permissible outer limits of voluntary programs undertaken by employers to benefit disadvantaged groups."[31] Further, he wrote: "Instead of retroactively scrutinizing his own or society's possible exclusions of minorities in the past to determine the outer limits of a valid affirmative-action program—or indeed, any particular affirmative-action decision—in many cases the employer will find it more appropriate to consider *other legitimate reasons to give preferences to members of underrepresented groups*" [emphasis added].[32] These other reasons might include, "simply to eliminate from their operations all de facto embodiment of a system of racial caste."[33]

The sharper the emphasis on any particular value in a Justice's opinion, the more likely it is to be isolated and countered. Efficiency is one such counter concern, especially to social equity arguments. But the efficiency argument itself has become muted over the years; in reality it moved to the background as social equity advanced. As an example, in 1971 in *Griggs*, Chief Justice Burger delivered the Court's unanimous opinion endorsing a color blind interpretation of the law where job qualifications are the controlling factor in personnel decisions: "Congress has not commanded that the less qualified be preferred over the better

qualified simply because of minority orgins. Far from disparaging job qualifications as such, Congress has made such qualifications the controlling factor, so that race, religion, nationality, and sex become irrelevant."[34]

Sixteen years later in *Paradise*, the Court drew no distinction between "more or less qualified." The emphasis was solely on the "qualified," implying a dichotomy between "qualified" and "not qualified." In addition, instead of qualifications being the centerpiece as in *Griggs*, in *Paradise* they were used merely as one of several factors ameliorating the impact of a promotion quota— an expression of social equity. Delivering a plurality opinion for a 5-4 Court, Justice Brennan wrote that the promotion quota "may be waived if no qualified black candidates are available."[35]

Presently, the Court is attempting to balance the three values. This can be seen in the two most recent cases, *Paradise* and *Johnson*. In *Paradise*, a 5-4 Court supported an order for a promotion quota. But in justifying the remedy, which emphasized social equity, the Court acknowledged several qualifying conditions. Among those, in deference to the efficiency value it waived the quota in the absence of qualified minorities. In addition, the Court held that the quota would not trammel the individual rights of particular nonminorities because its impact was diffuse.

One finds similar compromises in *Johnson*. The hiring authority considered gender as a factor in the promotion decision, suggesting sensitivity to the social equity value. With respect to Johnson's individual rights, the Court argued that he was not due a promotion, and denial in this particular case would not preclude a promotion in the future. As to the efficiency value, with both candidates being certified as well-qualified in an initial assessment, both the hiring authority and the Court— with a lively dissent—found negligible the two-point difference separating Johnson from Joyce on the basis of a subsequent interview.

In sum, it is clear that those who favor class-conscious affirmative action place higher priority on social equity than those who favor individual rights. Practically speaking, while acknowledging the Court's rhetoric on efficiency, one may question the influence of this value in the Court's calculations. But regardless of the relative priorities, no decision of the Court in an employment discrimination case involving nonvictim beneficiaries is likely to occur in the near future without reflecting all three of these values.

NOTES

1. *Griggs* v. *Duke Power Company*, 401 U.S. 424 (1971).
2. In their dissent in *Teamsters* v. *United States*, 431 U.S. 324, p. 392 (1977), Justices Brennan and Marshall quoted the Congressional Record on this point, "in any areas where a specific contrary intention is not indicated, it was assumed that the present case law would continue to govern the applicability and construction of Title VII."
3. *Ibid.*, p. 383, fn 7.
4. *Steelworkers* v. *Weber*, 443 U.S. 193 (1979).
5. *Firefighters* v. *Cleveland*, 92 L Ed 2d 405, 437 (1986).
6. *Johnson* v. *Transportation Agency*, 94 L Ed 615 (1987).
7. *United States* v. *Paradise*, 94 L Ed 203 (1987).
8. *Wygant* v. *Jackson Board of Education*, 90 L Ed 2d 260, p. 269 (1986).
9. *Ibid.*, p. 276.
10. *Teamsters, supra.*, pp. 339, 358.
11. Consistent with *Teamsters*, a Title VII case, the various opinions in *Wygant, supra.*, pp. 270, 278, and 289, support this assertion with regard to constitutional review. More specifically, whenever a person or group can demonstrate inference of employer discrimination—usually through a labor market demographic analysis—the burden shifts to the employer to show that the underutilization of minorities results from job related personnel practices or bona fide occupational qualifications.
12. See *Sheet Metal Workers* v. *EEOC*, 92 L Ed 2d 344 (1986) for the Court's parallel analysis of Title VII and Equal Protection Clause claims.
13. A variety of cases have reinforced this point since *Weber, supra.* Included most recently are: *Johnson, supra.*; *Paradise, supra.*; *Sheet Metal Workers, supra.*; and *Firefighters, supra.*
14. *Teamsters, supra.*, p. 372.
15. *Wygant, supra.*, pp. 272–275.
16. *Paradise, supra.*

17. *Ibid.*, p. 233.
18. *Ibid.*, p. 221.
19. *Sheet Metal Workers, supra.*
20. *Paradise, supra.*, p. 242.
21. *Johnson, supra.*
22. The hiring authority did not regard the difference in the interview scores between Joyce and Johnson as significant (*Ibid.*, p. 626). In their dissent, pp. 650–651, Justices Scalia and White and Chief Justice Rehnquist took issue with this claim.
23. *Ibid.*, p. 629.
24. Correspondence (June 1988) with David Rosenbloom assisted my exploration of the relationship between social equity and representativeness.
25. *Albemarle Paper Company* v. *Moody*, 422 U.S. 405 (1975).
26. *Firefighters* v. *Stotts*, 467 U.S. 561, pp. 579–580, 582–583 (1984).
27. *Teamsters, supra.*, p. 375.
28. *Weber, supra.*, p. 228, fn 10.
29. See *Teamsters, supra.*, pp. 365–368, and Justices Brennan, Blackmun, and Marshall's dissenting opinion in *Stotts, supra.*, pp. 612–613.
30. *Wygant, supra.*, pp. 293–294.
31. *Johnson, supra.*, p. 637.
32. *Ibid.*, p. 640.
33. *Idem.* Justice Stevens' advocacy of race consciousness extended to the value of effectiveness as well as social equity. In *Johnson, supra.*, p. 640, and in *Wygant, supra.*, pp. 294–295, Stevens cited examples where taking race into account in personnel actions can increase the effectiveness of a work force. One example was where a police force sought to integrate itself to enhance community relations. Thus, racially balancing a work force—that is, making it representative of a relevant labor pool or community— can impact effectiveness as well as social equity. However, the two goals may be pursued independently, and, in my observation, when the Court endorses racial preference, it does so primarily in pursuit of social equity—to eradicate the effects of past discrimination—not effectiveness.
34. *Griggs, supra.*
35. *Paradise, supra.*, p. 227.

MOTIVATIONAL PROGRAMS AND PRODUCTIVITY IMPROVEMENT IN TIMES OF LIMITED RESOURCES

John M. Greiner

For many state and local governments, these are times of shrinking resources and rising demands. The litany of conflicting pressures is all too familiar by now. On the one hand, the public continues to demand more and better services—more help for the increasing numbers of homeless and hungry, better police and fire protection, greater excellence in education. On the other hand, the cost of providing these services continues to rise steeply; state and local governments have faced an average annual inflation rate of 7.5 percent over the past four years, a total increase of nearly 34 percent since 1980 in the cost of doing business.[1] Meanwhile, intergovernmental transfer payments—especially Federal aid—have decreased sharply while taxpayer resistance to higher levies has continued. The upshot, as Levine has observed, is that problems of perennial resource *scarcity* have been converted into problems of resource *shrinkage* for many state and local governments.[2]

Productivity improvement—the production of more and/or better services for each tax dollar and staff hour invested—has been an especially attractive strategy for many governments facing tight or shrinking resources. A 1983 survey of local governments found that 67 percent of the 460 responding cities had undertaken formal productivity efforts,[3] and a recent telephone survey revealed that productivity improvement activities were under way in virtually all state governments.[4] Productivity improvement has been particularly attractive to local governments under serious financial stress. In a recent study of responses by seventeen Massachusetts local governments to the funding cuts that accompanied Proposition 2½ (a property tax initiative similar to California's Proposition 13), productivity improvement was found to be the second most common response (after cost cutting and reductions in service levels) for police and fire departments; it was also popular among libraries and public works departments.[5]

A variety of productivity improvement strategies are available to state and local governments. Most of them fall into five broad categories: (1) introduction of new or improved technology, (2) improvement of operational procedures, (3) revision of organizational structures, (4) enhancement of the skills of management and line employees, and (5) improvement of employee motivation. Each of these strategies requires the acquiescence and cooperation of government employees—management as well as labor—to succeed. From accepting new technologies to responding to employee incentives, public employees represent a critical element in the productivity improvement equation.

Of all the major approaches to productivity improvement, motivational strategies are probably affected the most by employee concerns and values. For purposes of this article, a motivational strategy is any effort to induce employees to initiate and sustain activities that can directly or indirectly improve service productivity. This definition is quite broad, encompassing everything from monetary incentives to quality circles, suggestion awards to career ladders.[6]

The potential productivity benefits from the introduction of motivational programs are considerable: 42 percent of the operating expenditures of state governments in fiscal year 1983 and 56 percent of those for local governments that year involved salaries and wages.[7] For some services (for example, police and fire), personnel costs account for 70 to 80 percent of operating expenditures. Thus, there are likely to be opportunities for significant savings through better utilization of human resources in state and local governments.

The need for incentives and other programs to improve employee motivation appears to be especially strong in an environment of tight resources and cutback management. During such periods, governments tend to reduce and/or delay the investments needed to maintain their human capital.[8] The subsequent erosion of the government's human capital is manifested in numerous ways—less training; deterioration of salary levels and other reward systems; fewer opportunities for career growth, and so forth. This often triggers what Levine terms employee "disinvestment": Employees attempt to cut their losses by reducing their contributions to the organization. The result is all too often "a decrease in the skill levels of public workforces, a decline in their energy and responsiveness, a concommitant decline in their performance, and worst of all, a further decline in the confidence and support of the public for government in general."[9]

In the wake of Proposition 2½, many of these symptoms were evident in Massachusetts cities and towns, including increased employee stress, poor morale, loss of skilled staff, curtailment of prior employee incentives, and concern that increasing numbers of employees would suffer occupational burnout.[10] These symptoms often persisted well after the initial shock of Proposition 2½ had begun to abate and funding levels had once again begun to rise.[11] By not turning their attention to renewal of their human resources through the use of motivational and other such strategies, these governments risk future personnel problems that can seriously damage long-range service delivery and productivity.

THREE IMPORTANT MOTIVATIONAL APPROACHES

To provide an indication of the scope and variety of the motivational programs available to governments, as well as of the potential tradeoffs and conflicts that must be faced in implementing such programs, the remainder of this chapter will focus on three popular motivational approaches: performance targeting (in particular, the use of management by objectives); monetary incentives; and job enrichment (specifically, the use of quality circles).

PERFORMANCE TARGETING

Performance targeting is the process of (l) making explicit to employees, either individually or as a group, the level and type of work performance expected and (2) providing subsequent feedback on and discussions of performance achievements. While several types of performance targeting can be found in state and local governments, probably the most important variant is management by objectives (MBO). According to the MBO paradigm, superior and subordinate managers jointly identify common goals and objectives, areas of responsibility, and expected results for the coming performance period. In some cases, these expectations and targets are formalized as a performance contract between a manager and his or her superior. Such contracts typically include a work plan for achieving the given objectives and indicate mutual responsibilities in support of that work plan. After the objectives and the corresponding performance targets have been agreed upon, there are periodic assessments and reviews of the manager's performance in meeting the specified targets.

Performance targeting in the form of MBO is common in state and local governments. In a 1976 ICMA survey, 42 percent of the 377 responding local governments reported using MBO.[12] A 1983 survey of municipal police departments found that 47 percent of the 300 respondents utilized MBO.[13]

Information on the effectiveness of such programs in improving productivity is, however, much more difficult to come by. A review of the (limited) "hard" evidence available on the impacts of state and local MBO efforts suggests that target setting per se, for example, exclusive of any linkage to monetary rewards) has led to documentable but modest improvements in service productivity.[14] There have sometimes been other benefits as well, including improved communication, better understanding by employees of what is expected of them, more effective management, and better documentation for the public of agency achievements.

Nevertheless, a review of public sector MBO findings suggests that the effectiveness of state and local government MBO efforts is greatly influenced by the manner in which programs are designed, implemented, and administered. The achievement of productivity improvements appears to depend in large part on the use of performance targets that either are clearly focused on service outcomes (rather than processes) or emphasize the identification and completion of productivity improvements projects (for example, "Identify at least one project per quarter that will reduce costs or improve services without sacrificing service quality, and implement at least half of them"). Other factors that appear necessary for an effective MBO effort include the specification of work plans for target achievement; provision of interim targets; central review and oversight of all performance objectives and targets to ensure that they are fair, challenging, and realistic; regular, timely feedback to employees on their performance; and one-to-one meetings between managers and their superiors to review overall target achievements.[15]

There are indications that the motivational potential of MBO efforts is often overlooked.[16] To take advantage of this potential, governments need to fully utilize the participative features of MBO (for example, by involving line employees in the specification and review of performance targets).[17] Governments also need to ensure that the MBO program is taken seriously—for example, by stressing regular, one-to-one (and perhaps group) reviews of target achievements; by not making it too easy to revise (loosen) targets if they are not met; and by establishing individual accountability for target achievement, through sanctions and counseling when targets are not met and through praise and (nonmonetary) rewards when targets are exceeded.

MONETARY INCENTIVES

Monetary incentives are cash awards used to induce desired behavior or results. The awards can be contingent on the performance of an individual or of a group. In the public sector, such incentives can take many forms—performance bonuses, merit and other performance-based wage increases, shared savings plans, suggestion awards, safety and attendance incentives, and so forth.[18]

While it may seem at first inappropriate to consider the introduction of monetary incentives in periods of tight or shrinking resources, such programs should not be dismissed out of hand. When properly designed, such incentives appear to be among the most effective of the various motivational approaches available. Moreover, some types of monetary incentives—in particular, shared savings plans—may not require additional financial resources.[19] Furthermore, it has been suggested that the introduction of monetary incentives and other special employee rewards may

be especially important during a period of tight resources, when such recognition can serve as a means for combatting employee disinvestment.[20]

Except for merit increases, monetary incentives have not been especially common in the public sector. Of the respondents to a 1978 member survey by the International Personnel Management Association, 42 percent reported the use of merit increases based on performance.[21] Suggestion awards and performance bonuses were reported by only 16 percent and 12 percent, respectively, of the responding jurisdictions, and shared savings plans were even less common.

While "hard" information on the effectiveness of public sector monetary incentives plans is scarce, a few useful findings have emerged.[22] Merit pay, as usually handled in the public sector, is not generally very effective at stimulating improved productivity, but performance bonuses, shared savings plans, and performance-based wage increases for line personnel have given evidence of significantly improving service productivity if they are based on clearly defined, objective, outcome-oriented performance criteria. While group incentives (with monetary awards contingent upon the performance of an entire group) are motivationally less effective than individual incentives (which focus on the performance of individual employees), group plans appear to be considerably more acceptable (and, therefore, feasible) for public employees.

Still, public sector pay-for-performance plans have not given consistent evidence of being effective in stimulating professional and management personnel. In particular, linking target achievement to monetary rewards for managers within the context of an MBO system led to no additional improvements in performance in three cities where such systems were studied.[23] Similarly, in a recent test of incentive bonuses for local offices of the Employment Service in the states of Kansas and New Jersey, cash awards did not serve as a major productivity stimulus for management and professional personnel, although lower-level, nonprofessional staff were often motivated by such awards.[24] Indeed, in many of the foregoing examples, the establishment of a linkage between pay and performance provoked considerable dissension and job dissatisfaction among management personnel.

As in performance targeting, the effectiveness of a monetary incentive plan depends critically on careful, sensitive design and implementation of the program. Great care must be taken to ensure that the performance assessment procedure is objective and equitable and that the linkage between rewards and performance is direct, timely, and understandable. The awards themselves should be large enough to serve as meaningful stimuli (preferably at least $1,000 and, ideally, 10 percent of an employee's salary)[25] and abundant enough for all deserving individuals or groups to receive them (artificial limits on the number of persons who can receive awards in any given incentive period should be avoided). Finally, there should be plenty of timely feedback on employee (or group) performance during the incentive period, and again when the awards are announced. It is important to ensure that all persons clearly understand just how the winners earned their rewards.

Overall, successful implementation of monetary incentives in the public sector is usually very difficult, requiring the investment of considerable time, effort, and patience while demanding exceptional care and sensitivity on the part of those responsible for implementation. Governments contemplating the introduction of monetary incentives must be willing to assume the risks, tolerate the criticisms, and provide significant top management and staff support over the long haul. Indeed, private sector monetary incentive plans often require four to five years before the "bugs" are worked out; it would be unrealistic to expect the process to proceed much faster in the public sector.

QUALITY CIRCLES AND INCREASED PARTICIPATION

Quality circles are small groups of mostly nonsupervisory personnel who meet voluntarily on a regular basis to identify, analyze, and solve problems they experience in their own work.[26] Quality circles represent a form of increased participation, a class of formal programs designed to give nonsupervisory personnel greater opportunities to contribute to decision making and problem solving concerning their own work

units. Other public sector examples of increased participation include joint labor-management committees, councils composed of elected employee representatives, and various forms of participative management (for example, the inclusion of a line employee on a city's management team). Increased participation, in turn, is one aspect of job enrichment, a large class of motivational programs that includes the use of teams, task forces, job rotation, and job redesign.[27]

Quality circles are attracting increasing interest among state and local governments. Such programs have recently been reported in nineteen states, and in a 1984 ICMA survey, 8 percent of the 1,238 responding municipalities reported the use of quality circles.[28] In a similar survey of municipal police departments, 16 percent of the 300 respondents indicated that they were using quality circles.[29]

Systematic assessments of public sector quality circles have been quite rare, although some evaluative information is now available on programs in Orlando, Florida; Dallas, Texas; and Los Angeles and Hayward, California.[30] To date, however, there appears to be little evidence that quality circles involving government employees produce major improvements in service delivery or productivity.[31] Such circles have usually focused on improving working conditions and in solving relatively small-scale operating problems. Only infrequently has any attention been directed to significant issues of service delivery with the potential for major productivity improvements.

As with performance targets and monetary incentives, quality circles' effectiveness appears to depend critically on proper design and implementation. Inadequate attention to fundamentals—ensuring that participation is voluntary; alleviating potential attendance problems due to shift conflicts; providing the circle with direct access to top management in presenting recommendations; giving adequate recognition to participants—has apparently limited the effectiveness of a number of quality circles in the public sector.[32] However, public sector use of quality circles is currently at an embryonic stage. With more experience, the above problems can be alleviated, and perhaps productivity impacts can be increased.

TRADEOFFS AND CONFLICTS IN IMPLEMENTING MOTIVATIONAL PROGRAMS

In selecting and implementing motivational strategies for government employees, administrators must overcome a number of potentially serious obstacles. In a 1978 ICMA survey of municipal use of employee incentives, 38 percent of the 1,661 responding municipalities reported encountering one or more obstacles in trying to implement such programs.[33] Fiscal constraints constituted the most common barrier (they were reported by 69 percent of the 546 cities reporting at least some implementation obstacles). Other common problems included political obstacles (36 percent), restrictive labor agreements (29 percent), management opposition (21 percent), employee opposition (20 percent), legal barriers (20 percent), and civil service rules and policies (18 percent).[34]

In the following paragraphs, we will review some of the major tradeoffs and conflicts that must be faced in using motivational techniques to improve productivity. For the purpose of this discussion, attention will be focused on the three types of motivational programs already described.

EFFECTIVENESS

Many have expressed concern regarding the effectiveness of motivational techniques for improving the productivity of public employees. For instance, Klingner recently reported that many local public managers were "quite unenthusiastic about the potential of improved human resource management for increasing productivity."[35] Given the scarcity of objective, systematic information on the impacts of such programs, these views are not surprising.

As a group, motivational approaches have not given much evidence of being able to produce major, across-the-board improvements in public sector productivity. To be sure, a few highly successful programs have been undertaken in such cities as Flint (Michigan) and Philadelphia,[36] but, in general, savings have been modest.

In a synthesis of private sector and academic research on the effectiveness of various types of motivational programs, the median change in performance after the introduction of monetary incentives was +30 percent; the median change after implementation of target setting was +16 percent; and the median performance change for programs to increase participation was +0.5 percent.[37] Combined approaches—for example, target setting combined with monetary incentives—were even more effective, with a median performance change of +40 percent. Private sector research has also shown that the effectiveness of a monetary incentive program in stimulating improved performance decreases with the size of the incentive group.[38] Thus, individual incentives are the most effective variant, followed by group incentives and, in last place, organizationwide incentives (for example, a Scanlong plan, whose group of interest is the entire organization). While the above findings are based on private sector and laboratory results, the data available from the public sector seem to support these relationships and orderings.

The foregoing results pose some dilemmas for state and local use of motivational techniques. The most effective programs—monetary incentives—are the most difficult to implement and have been of questionable value for management and professional employees, at least for the magnitudes of incentive awards likely to be feasible in most governments. In addition, the most effective type of monetary incentive program—individual incentives—has been especially controversial (and often ineffective) in the public sector. Therefore, it is likely that public administrators will often have to compromise on effectiveness in order to facilitate implementation—for example, by focusing on target setting and monetary incentive plans involving group rather than individual bonuses.

The effectiveness of public sector motivational plans is also, however, strongly affected by design and implementation considerations. Inadequate attention to such factors can compromise the effectiveness of even the most carefully selected incentive approach.

RESOURCE NEEDS

Implementation and operation of motivational programs for public employees can generate a requirement for several different kinds of resources, including dollars, time, expertise and support from management and the general public.

Of course, any such resource needs must be viewed within the contexts of (1) the fiscal stress and scarcity that characterize many of the governments most in need of motivational initiatives and (2) the uncertainty concerning the magnitude of the savings and productivity improvements expected from the use of a given motivational technique.

Costs. Out-of-pocket expenditures are generally highest for monetary incentive programs, although well-designed shared savings plans and suggestion awards have frequently recovered their costs from the savings they generate. A major expenditure in connection with monetary incentives is the cost of the awards. Indeed, some of the guidelines noted previously for designing effective monetary incentives tend to drive the cost of the awards even higher (for example, rewards that are at least $1,000 and, ideally, 10 percent of salary, and no limits or quotas on the number of persons who can earn awards in any given performance period). Other likely expenses in connection with monetary incentives include the extensive amount of staff time needed to develop and properly implement such a program; expenses for training, recordkeeping, data collection, and data processing; and, in some cases, the cost of auditing the performance data.[39] Expenditures of these magnitudes (often in the tens and hundreds of thousands of dollars) may be hard to sell to employees at a time when wages are being frozen and staff are being laid off.

Out-of-pocket costs for quality circles and MBO programs are usually much more modest, typically several thousand dollars. The primary expenses will be for consultants to help with program initiation and training and—in the case of quality circles—training materials for use by the jurisdiction after the consultants are gone. Another important cost in connection with these two programs is the time spent by program participants in training activities, quality circle meetings, negotiation, documentation, review of MBO targets, and so forth. In the case of MBO, however, such costs are often viewed as a necessary element of agency management, rather than as special program expenses.

Training. Adequate training is a vital input for each of the three types of motivational programs. Too often, training in connection with public

sector motivational efforts has been inadequate. When training materials from private sector programs are available (for example, for MBO and quality circles), such materials should be carefully adapted to the needs of public sector employees and environments. (For instance, police officers in Orlando, Florida, complained that their training materials, which came from the private sector, seemed almost childish; they moved too slowly for police tastes, oversimplified analytic procedures most officers already knew or were capable of grasping quickly, and utilized industrial examples that were far removed from the kinds of problems typically addressed by a police department.)

Adequate training is essential in connection with monetary incentives. Employees must clearly understand how a program works—the precise connection between pay and performance—if such incentives are to be effective. Unfortunately, these connections are sometimes rather complex (for instance, regression techniques may be used to establish performance standards or to adjust for external factors). Such sophisticated features are likely to be useless and perhaps even counterproductive if there is not adequate training to explain how they work, so that employees can accept them as valid.

Continuing efforts to train new employees—new members of monetary incentive groups, newly appointed managers coming under MBO programs, new members of quality circles—is also important, especially in view of high turnover in some government agencies. Periodic "refresher" training for all employees involved with motivational programs is also needed; without it, one is likely to find that employee enthusiasm is waning, program procedures are increasingly being misapplied, and the overall effort is being taken for granted.

Specialized Expertise and Advice. Governments are unlikely to have all the in-house expertise necessary for implementing motivational plans. Outside consultants are usually necessary in connection with MBO and quality circle efforts to help with program design and startup, provide training and advice to the initial program participants, and train the trainers—a process necessary for institutionalization of the program. Although the design and implementation of monetary incentives can often be completed without out-side help, external expertise may be needed in connection with the more complex incentive efforts (for example, when sophisticated analytic techniques are employed to adjust for potential inequities and changing external factors).

Time and Energy Needed to Implement and Operate the Program. All three types of motivational programs require considerable expen-ditures of energy, time, and patience if they are to be implemented properly. This is especially true for monetary incentives, which are usually the most difficult programs to implement. Program administrators must take the time to ensure that the necessary groundwork is done and done prop-erly. This groundwork includes meaningful, early involvement of employees; careful and thorough design and testing of program mechanisms and procedures (monetary incentive formulas, central-ized review and oversight mechanisms for MBO, overtime or comp time for employees participating in quality circles, and so forth); establishment of data collection and performance feedback mechan-isms that are accurate, valid, and timely enough to support the intended motivational effort; and adequate training of supervisory and nonsuper-visory personnel. Hurriedly implemented motiva-tional programs have rarely succeeded in the public sector. A government must be ready to move slowly but deliberately, perhaps using a phased approach that includes pilot efforts, and it must be ready to invest its energies and commitment over a long enough period (at least several years) for the in-evitable "bugs" to be identified and worked out.

Management Time and Support. One of the most critical resources needed for a successful motivational program is a commitment of top management's support and involvement. If a monetary incentive plan, MBO system, or quality circle is to be taken seriously by government employees, top management must demonstrate the seriousness of its own commitment to the long-range success of the effort. This means investing management time and prestige in the program. Anything less will be a signal to employees that "this too shall pass."

Public and Political Support. Political and public opposition has rarely been a problem in

connection with public sector MBO and quality circle efforts. Indeed, the implementation of such programs has often stimulated support from these quarters. Thus, introduction of these techniques is often perceived as indicative of effective, in-novative public administrators who are ready to adopt the latest methods. Several public officials have noted that an important side benefit of MBO programs is the ability to clearly demonstrate the accomplishments of an agency, using target achievement data.

Public and political support for monetary incentives has, however, been less consistent. While some have praised such approaches for bringing business techniques to the public sector, others have been quick to complain about "paying public employees a bonus to do what they are already being paid to do." Administrators must plan carefully and avoid giving critics any basis for such concerns—for example, by actively involving line employees in the design of incen-tive plans, by relying on objective performance data and precisely specified formulas for making any rewards, by establishing challenging perfor-mance targets, and by providing for audits of performance data and other checks that may be needed to ensure the accuracy and credibility of the information.[40]

In summary, although motivational programs place demands on the availability of a variety of critical resources, most of those resources are internal and likely to be available to a committed government, even in a time of fiscal stress. When resources—for instance, financial resources and specialized expertise—must come from outside, the needs of MBO and quality circles are likely to be modest. Only monetary incentives are likely to require costly external resources that may be difficult for an agency to afford. In such instances, outside "seed" money may be needed, although in the case of shared savings programs, such investments may ultimately be repaid from savings generated by the program.

CONCLUSION

This chapter has examined two interrelated issues: (1) the need for and use of motivational strategies for improving productivity, especially in a period of tight or shrinking resources; and (2) the tradeoffs, concerns, and conflicts that must be addressed in implementing such efforts. The following important points have emerged:

1. Motivational approaches constitute a potentially attractive means of improving productivity, especially during (or immediately after) a period of fiscal stress.

2. Although management by objectives (MBO) is relatively common, state and local governments rarely take full advantage of the motivational potential of MBO systems.

3. "Hard" information on the effectiveness of public sector motivational efforts is scarce. However, as a group, motivational approaches generally have provided modest improvements in productivity, at most.

4. Monetary incentives are potentially the most effective motivational approach from the standpoint of improving productivity (although group monetary incentives tend to be more practical than individual incentives in the public sector). MBO and other target-setting approaches have also given evidence of modest productivity improvements. Quality circles, while promising, have not yet demonstrated a capacity to generate major productivity increases in the public sector.

5. Shared savings plans and MBO systems seem to be among the most attractive motivational approaches from the standpoints of cost, effectiveness, and ease of implementation.

6. In general, effectiveness depends critically on the manner in which the motivational plans are designed and implemented. Careful, sensitive design and implementation of such programs is imperative (and very difficult, especially in the case of monetary incentives).

7. Important elements of any effort to introduce employee motivational programs should be the use of a carefully planned and unhurried design and implementation period, as well as early meaningful involvement of employees at all levels (and of their unions) in designing and planning the motivational effort.

8. Other important issues and concerns that must be addressed include acquisition of adequate resources; alleviation of constraints imposed by existing laws, personnel rules, organizational structures, and contractual agreements; and resolution of potential incompatibilities between the motivational program selected and the employees' (as well as management's) needs and values.

9. The key to effective, satisfying motivational programs is sustained, visible commitment and support from top management, and early institutionalization of the effort to ensure that it will survive long enough (four to five years) for the inevitable "bugs" to be worked out.

Motivational programs represent a fragile, management initiative. Without adequate nurturing and support from management, such efforts will die, but with care in their selection, design, and execution, many such programs offer considerable promise for improving productivity and renewing a government's human capital.

NOTES

1. The average annual inflation rate was computed from quarterly data on the implicit price deflator for state and local government purchases of goods and services. *Survey of Current Business*, 63 (July 1983): 87, and 64 (July 1984): 87.

2. Charles H. Levine, "Retrenchment, Human Resource Erosion, and the Role of the Personnel Manager," *Public Personnel Management Journal*, 13 (Fall 1984): 249–263.

3. Theodore H. Poister and Robert P. McGowan, "The Contribution of Local Productivity Improvement Efforts in a Period of Fiscal Stress," *Public Productivity Review*, in press.

4. Theodore H. Poister, Harry P. Hatry, Donald M. Fisk, and John M. Greiner, *Centralized Productivity Improvement Efforts in State Government* (Washington, D.C.: The Urban Institute, 1984).

5. John M. Greiner and Harry P. Hatry, *Coping with Cutbacks: Initial Agency-Level Responses in 17 Local Governments to Massachusetts' Proposition 2½* (Washington, D.C.: The Urban Institute, 1982); reprinted in Lawrence E. Susskind and Jane F. Serio, eds., *Proposition 2½: Its Impact on Massachusetts* (Cambridge, Mass.: Oelgeschlager, Gunn, and Hain, 1983).

6. For reviews of state and local government usage of various types of motivational programs, see John M. Greiner, Harry P. Hatry, Margo P. Koss, Annie P. Millar, and James P. Woodward, *Productivity and Motivation: A Review of State and Local Government Initiatives* (Washington, D.C.: The Urban Institute, 1981); John M. Greiner, Lynn Bell, and Harry P. Hatry, *Employee Incentives to Improve State and Local*

Government Productivity (Washington, D.C.: National Commission on Productivity and Work Quality, 1975); and John M. Greiner, "Incentives for Municipal Employees: An Update," *Urban Data Service Reports*, 11, 8 (August 1979).

7. *Government Finances in 1982–83*, Series GF83 no. 5, U.S. Department of Commerce, Bureau of the Census (Washington, D.C.: U.S. Government Printing Office, 1984), p. 17.

8. Levine, "Retrenchment," pp. 252–253.

9. Levine, "Retrenchment," p. 255.

10. Greiner and Hatry, *Coping with Cutbacks*, pp. 130–131.

11. John M. Greiner, *The Impacts of Massachusetts' Proposition 2½ on the Delivery and Quality of Municipal Services* (Washington, D.C.: The Urban Institute, 1984), pp. 55–56.

12. *The Status of Local Government Productivity* (Washington, D.C.: International City Management Association, 1977).

13. Harry P. Hatry and John M. Greiner, *How Can Police Departments Better Apply Management-by-Objectives and Quality Circle Programs?* (Washington, D.C.: The Urban Institute, 1984), p. 7.

14. See, for instance, Greiner and others, *Productivity and Motivation*, chapter 10; Harry P. Hatry, John M. Greiner, and Richard J. Gollub, *An Assessment of Local Government Management Motivational Programs: Performance Targeting With and Without Monetary Incentives* (Washington, D.C.: The Urban Institute, 1984); and Hatry and Greiner, *How Can Police Departments Better Apply Management-by-Objectives . . . ?*

15. See the references cited above.

16. See, for instance, Harry P. Hatry and John M. Greiner, *Issues and Case Studies in Teacher Incentive Plans* (Washington, D.C.: The Urban Institute, forthcoming), chapter 7; and Hatry and Greiner, *How Can Police Departments Better Apply Management-by-Objectives . . . ?*

17. See, for instance, John P. Mohr, "MBO: The Horse to Pull Your Quality Circle Cart," *The Quality Circle Journal*, 5 (November 1982): 4.

18. For a review of these and other monetary incentives used in the public sector, see Greiner and others, *Productivity and Motivation*, part one (especially chapter 3).

19. Shared savings plans involve monetary rewards for groups of workers. Under such plans, a specific portion of the cost savings achieved by a group within a given period is distributed—often as a bonus—among the employees in the group.

20. Levine, "Retrenchment," p. 257.

21. Greiner, "Incentives for Municipal Employees," p. 3.

22. See, for instance, Greiner and others, *Productivity and Motivation*, chapters 4 and 5.

23. Hatry, Greiner, and Gollub, *An Assessment of Local Government Management Motivational Programs*.

24. John M. Greiner and Annie P. Millar, *Employee Productivity Incentives for Local Offices of the Employment Service: The Experiences of Kansas and New Jersey*, vols. 1 and 2 (Washington, D.C.: The Urban Institute, 1984).

25. Charles Peck, *Pay and Performance: The Interaction of Compensation and Performance Appraisal* (New York: The Conference Board, 1984), p. 16.

26. For more details on quality circles, see James L. Mercer, "Quality Circles: Productivity Improvement Processes," *Management Information Service Report*, 14, 3 (March 1982); Joyce L. Roll and David L. Roll, "The Potential for Application of Quality Circles in the American Public Sector," *Public Productivity Review*, VII (June 1983): 122–142; Robert Wood, Frank Hall, and Koya Azumi, "Evaluating Quality Circles: The American Application," *California Management Review*, XXVI (Fall 1983): 37–53; and *The Police Chief*, 51 (November 1984): 46–56 (a series of four articles on police applications of quality circles).

27. These approaches are described in Greiner and others, *Productivity and Motivation*, chapters 20, 22, and 23.

28. Poister and others, *Centralized Productivity Improvement Efforts*, p. 13; and unpublished data from ICMA's survey, "Employee Incentives—1984."

29. Hatry and Greiner, *How Can Police Departments Better Apply Management-by-Objectives . . . ?*, p. 7.

30. Hatry and Greiner, above. See also Quality Circle Steering Committee, *Pilot Quality Circle Program Evaluation* (City of Hayward, California, 1983); and Susan Page Hocevar and Susan A. Mohrman, *Quality Circles in a Metropolitan Police Department*, Report G84-12(60) (University of Southern California, Center for Effective Organizations, 1984).

31. Hatry and Greiner, *How Can Police Departments Better Apply Management-by-Objectives . . . ?*, p. 122.

32. Hatry and Greiner, above.

33. Greiner, "Incentives for Municipal Employees," p. 17.

34. Greiner, "Incentives for Municipal Employees," p. 16.

35. Donald E. Klingner, "Personnel, Politics and Productivity," *Public Personnel Management Journal*, 11 (Fall 1982): 277–281.

36. John M. Greiner, Roger E. Dahl, Harry P. Hatry, and Annie P. Millar, *Monetary Incentives and Work Standards in Five Cities: Impacts and Implications for Management and Labor* (Washington, D.C.: The Urban Institute, 1977), chapters 4 and 5.

37. Edwin A. Locke, Dena B. Feren, Vickie McCaleb, Karyll N. Shaw, and Anne T. Denny, "The Relative Effectiveness of Four Methods of Motivating Employee Performance," paper presented to the American Psychological Association, (New York, September 1979).

38. Raymond A. Katzell and Daniel Yankelovich, *Work, Productivity, and Job Satisfaction: An Evaluation of Policy-Related Research* (New York: The Psychological Corporation, 1975), pp. 318–321.

39. For instance, the need to follow up and verify a sample of reported job placements in connection with productivity incentives for local offices of the Employment Service in Kansas and New Jersey added $72,000–$80,000 to the cost of each plan over the eighteen-month trial period. See Greiner and Millar, *Employee Productivity Incentives for Local Offices of the Employment Service*, vol. 2, p. 147.

40. For instance, to ensure that data on reported placements were above reproach in connection with a trial of productivity incentives for local offices of the Employment Service in Kansas and New Jersey, a monthly sample of the placements reported by *each* office was followed up with employers to check the validity of those placements. On one occasion, the presence of the follow-up effort convinced an investigative reporter that it would not be worth his time to look for possible irregularities in the distribution of the incentive rewards. See Greiner and Millar, *Employee Productivity Incentives for Local Offices of the Employment Service*, vol. 2, p. 231.

LEADERSHIP FOR AMERICA: SUMMARY AND MAIN CONCLUSIONS

The Volcker Commission

The central message of this report of the Commission on the Public Service is both simple and profound, both urgent and timeless. In essence, we call for a renewed sense of commitment by all Americans to the highest traditions of the public service—to a public service responsive to the political will of the people and also protective of our constitutional values; to a public service able to cope with complexity and conflict and also able to maintain the highest ethical standards; to a public service attractive to the young and talented from all parts of our society and also capable of earning the respect of all our citizens.

A great nation must demand no less. The multiple challenges thrust upon the Government of the United States as we approach the 21st Century can only reinforce the point. Yet, there is evidence on all sides of an erosion of performance and morale across government in America. Too many of our most talented public servants—those with the skills and dedication that are the hallmarks of an effective career service—are ready to leave. Too few of our brightest young people—those with the imagination and energy that are essential for the future—are willing to join.

Meanwhile, the need for a strong public service is growing, not lessening. Americans have always expected their national government to guarantee their basic freedoms and provide for the common defense. We continue to expect our government to keep the peace with other nations, resolve differences among our own people, pay the bills for needed services, and honor the people's trust by providing the highest levels of integrity and performance.

At the same time, Americans now live in a stronger, more populous nation, a nation with unprecedented opportunity. But they also live in a world of enormous complexity and awesome risks. Our economy is infinitely more open to international competition, our currency floats in a worldwide market, and we live with complex technologies beyond the understanding of any single human mind. Our diplomacy is much more complicated, and the wise use of our unparalleled military power more difficult. And for all our scientific achievements, we are assaulted daily by new social, environmental, and health issues almost incomprehensible in scope and impact—issues like drugs, AIDS, and global warming.

Faced with these challenges, the simple idea that Americans must draw upon talented and dedicated individuals to serve us in government is uncontestable. America must have a public service that can both value the lessons of experience and appreciate the requirements for change; a public service that both responds to political leadership and respects the law; a public service with the professional skills and the ethical sensitivity America deserves.

Surely, there can be no doubt that moral challenge and personal excitement are inherent in the great enterprise of democratic government. There is work to be done of enormous importance. Individuals can make a difference.

But unfortunately there is growing evidence that these basic truths have been clouded by a sense of frustration inside government and a lack of public trust outside. The resulting erosion in the quality of America's public service is difficult to measure; there are still many examples of excellence among those who carry out the nation's business at home and abroad. Nevertheless, it is evident that public service is neither as attractive as it once was nor as effective in meeting perceived needs. No doubt, opposition to specific policies of government has contributed to a lack of respect for the public servants who struggle to make the policies work. This drives away much of our best talent which can only make the situation worse.

One need not search far to see grounds for concern. Crippled nuclear weapons plants, defense procurement scandals, leaking hazardous waste dumps, near-misses in air traffic control, and the costly collapse of so many savings and loans have multiple causes. But each such story carries some similar refrains about government's inability to recruit and retain a talented work force: the Department of Defense is losing its top procurement specialists to contractors who can pay much more; the Federal Aviation Administration is unable to hold skilled traffic controllers because of stress and working conditions; the Environmental Protection Agency is unable to fill key engineering jobs because the brightest students simply are not interested; the Federal Savings and Loan Insurance Corporation (FSLIC) simply cannot hire and pay able executives.

This erosion has been gradual, almost imperceptible, year by year. But it has occurred nonetheless. Consider the following evidence compiled by the Commission's five task forces on the growing recruitment problem:

- Only 13 percent of the senior executives recently interviewed by the General Accounting Office would recommend that young people start their careers in government, while several recent surveys show that less than half the senior career civil servants would recommend a job in government to their own children.
- Of the 610 engineering students who received bachelors, masters, and doctoral degrees at the Massachusetts Institute of Technology and Stanford University in 1986, and the 600 who graduated from Rensselaer Polytechnic Institute in 1987, only 29 took jobs in government at any level.
- Half the respondents to a recent survey of federal personnel officers said recruitment of quality personnel had become more difficult over the past five years.
- Three-quarters of the respondents to the Commission's survey of recent Presidential Management Interns—a prestigious program for recruiting the top graduates of America's schools of public affairs— said they would leave government within 10 years.

If these trends continue, America will soon be left with a government of the mediocre, locked into careers of last resort or waiting for a chance to move on to other jobs.

But this need not and should not be. By the choices we make today, we can enter the 21st century with a public service fully equipped to meet the challenges of intense competition abroad and growing complexity at home. The strongest wish of the Commission is that this report can be a step in that process, pointing toward necessary changes, while serving as a catalyst for national debate and further efforts at all levels of government.

America should and can act now to restore the leadership, talent, and performance essential to the strong public service the future demands. To those ends, the Commission believes:

- First, the President and Congress must provide the essential environment for effective leadership and public support.
- Second, educational institutions and the agencies of government must work to enlarge the base of talent available for, and committed to, public service.
- Third, the American people should demand first-class performance and the highest ethical standards, and, by the same token, must be willing to provide what is necessary to attract and retain needed talent.

These three themes—*leadership, talent* and *performance*—shape this report. They are both wide-ranging and interrelated. They also provide a framework for a concrete agenda for action, directed toward a series of basic goals discussed in further detail in the report that follows. Specifically, to strengthen executive *leadership*, we call upon the President and Congress to:

- Take action now by word and deed to rebuild public trust in government;
- Clear away obstacles to the ability of the President to attract talented appointees from all parts of society;
- Make more room at senior levels of departments and agencies for career executives;
- Provide a framework within which those federal departments and agencies can exercise greater flexibility in managing programs and personnel; and
- Encourage a stronger partnership between presidential appointees and career executives.

To broaden the government's *talent base*, we call upon educational institutions and government to:

- Develop more student awareness of, and educational training for, the challenges of government and public service;
- Develop new channels for spreading the word about government jobs and the rewards of public service;
- Enhance the efforts to recruit top college graduates and those with specific professional skills for government jobs;
- Simplify the hiring process; and
- Increase the representation of minorities in public careers.

To place a greater emphasis on quality and *performance* throughout government, we ask for the public and its leaders to:

- Build a pay system that is both fair and competitive;
- Rebuild the government's chief personnel agency to give it the strength and mandate it needs;
- Set higher goals for government performance and productivity;
- Provide more effective training and executive development; and
- Improve government working conditions.

To further these basic goals, the Commission makes a series of specific recommendations throughout the report. . . . Twelve key proposals deserve mention here:

First, Presidents, their chief lieutenants, and Congress must articulate early and often the necessary and honorable role that public servants play in the democratic process, at the same time making clear they will demand the highest standards of ethics and performance possible from those who hold the public trust. Members of Congress and their staffs should be covered by similar standards. Codes of conduct to convey such standards should be simple and straightforward, and should focus on the affirmative values that must guide public servants in the exercise of their responsibilities.

Second, within program guidelines from the President, cabinet officers and agency heads should be given greater flexibility to administer their organizations, including greater

freedom to hire and fire personnel, provided there are appropriate review procedures within the Administration and oversight from Congress.

Third, the President should highlight the important role of the Office of Personnel Management (OPM) by establishing and maintaining contact with its Director and by ensuring participation by the Director in cabinet level discussions on human resource management issues. The Commission further recommends decentralization of a portion of OPM's operating responsibilities to maximize its role of personnel policy guidance to federal departments and agencies.

Fourth, the growth in recent years in the number of presidential appointees, whether those subject to Senate confirmation, non-career senior executives, or personal and confidential assistants, should be curtailed. Although a reduction in the total number of presidential appointees must be based on a position-by-position assessment, the Commission is confident that a substantial cut is possible, and believes a cut from the current 3,000 to no more than 2,000 is a reasonable target. Every President must have politically and philosophically compatible officials to implement his Administration's program. At the same time, however, experience suggests that excessive numbers of political appointees serving relatively brief periods may undermine the President's ability to govern, insulating the Administration from needed dispassionate advice and institutional memory. The mere size of the political turnover almost guarantees management gaps and discontinuities, while the best of the career professionals will leave government if they do not have challenging opportunities at the sub-cabinet level.

Fifth, the President and Congress must ensure that federal managers receive the added training they will need to perform effectively. The education of public servants must not end upon appointment to the civil service. Government must invest more in its executive development programs and develop stronger partnerships with America's colleges and universities.

Sixth, the nation should recognize the importance of civic education as a part of social studies and history in the nation's primary and secondary school curricula. Starting with a comprehensive review of current programs, the nation's educators and parents should work toward new curricula and livelier textbooks designed to enhance student understanding of America's civic institutions, relate formal learning about those institutions to the problems students care about, and link classroom learning to extracurricular practice.

Seventh, America should take advantage of the natural idealism of its youth by expanding and encouraging national volunteer service, whether through existing programs like ACTION, the Peace Corps, and VISTA, or experiments with initiatives like President Bush's Youth Engaged in Service (YES), and some of the ideas contained in the Democratic Leadership Council's citizen corps proposal.

Eighth, the President and Congress should establish a Presidential Public Service Scholarship Program targeted to 1,000 college or college-bound students each year, with careful attention to the recruitment of minority students. Admission to the program might be modeled on appointment to the military service academies—that is, through nomination by members of Congress—and should include tuition and other costs, in return for a commitment to a determined number of years of government service.

Ninth, the President should work with Congress to give high priority to restoring the depleted purchasing power of executive, judicial, and legislative salaries by the beginning of a new Congress in 1991, starting with an immediate increase of 25 percent. At the same time, the Commission recommends that Congress enact legislation eliminating speaking honoraria and other income related to their public responsibilities.

Tenth, if Congress is unable to act on its own salaries, the Commission recommends that the President make separate recommendations for judges and top level executives and that the Congress promptly act upon them.

Needed pay raises for presidential appointees, senior career executives, and judges should no longer be dependent on the ability of Congress to raise its own pay.

Eleventh, the President and Congress should give a higher budget priority to civil service pay in the General Schedule pay system. In determining the appropriate increase, the Commission concludes that the current goal of national comparability between public and private pay is simplistic and unworkable, and is neither fair to the civil service nor to the public it serves. The Commission therefore recommends a new civil service pay-setting process that recognizes the objective fact that pay differs by occupation and by localities characterized by widely different living costs and labor market pressures.

Twelfth, the President and Congress should establish a permanent independent advisory council, composed of members from the public and private sector, both to monitor the ongoing state of the public service and to make such recommendations for improvements as they think desirable. The Commission applauds President Bush's pledge of leadership of the public service. Indeed, his recent statements reflect the spirit and concerns that led to the creation of the Commission. However, the problems that make up this "quiet crisis" are many and complex, and have been long in the making. Corrective action will not only require presidential leadership and congressional support, but must be part of a coherent and sustained long term strategy. The proposed independent advisory council is designed to ensure that the state of the public service remains high on the national agenda.

This report speaks directly to a number of audiences: to the *American people* about the importance to their civic institutions of talented men and women; to *young people* about the challenges and satisfactions they can find in serving their government; to *candidates for elective office* about the long-term costs of "bureaucrat bashing"; to the *media* about the need not only to hold public servants to high standards but also to recognize those who serve successfully; to *university schools of public affairs* about developing curricula for the training of a new generation of government managers; and to *business leaders* about the importance of quality government support to the private sector.

Finally, the report speaks to the *civil service* about its obligations to the highest standards of performance. The Commission fully supports the need for better pay and working conditions in much of government. But the Commission also recognizes that public support for those improvements is dependent on a commitment by the civil servants themselves to efficiency, responsiveness, and integrity.

EDWARD J. PERKINS:
ON TOP AT FOGGY BOTTOM

Nancy M. Davis

Last September, ambassador Edward J. Perkins left his post in South Africa to become the highest-ranking official in the U.S. Foreign Service. He is now director general and director of personnel for the State Department.

Now, the weighty burden of apartheid on South African blacks has nothing in common with the travail of transient life borne by U.S. diplomats. Nevertheless, both groups are benefiting from Perkins' leadership at seminal times.

Perkins, 61, was appointed the United States' first black ambassador to South Africa in 1986, just after Congress passed economic sanctions against that country. His tenure was marked by an adversarial relationship with South Africa's ruling National Party. "I was challenging the government to be more human by showing support of those who dared challenge apartheid," he says, adding, "I did not take this job to represent black America. I wanted to represent the American people. All of us in the mission were trying to create conditions for change."

This dignified man sheltered protesters in the embassy and often appeared in tumultuous courtrooms to sit silently through blacks' trials. "I tried to show that the U.S. was against arbitrary arrests," he says, recalling one poignant treason case involving five members of the United Democratic Front. The trial was moved to a small border town to keep people away, but the people went, and Perkins went.

Perkins met the men after they were acquitted. He calls them "politicians, the best and the brightest, and surprisingly moderate." In them, the world can see what South Africa can be after apartheid, Perkins says. Five months after he left South Africa, the ambassador began to see his aspirations realized as black leader Nelson Mandela was released from prison. Perkins is predicting that South Africa will have a black president within 10 years.

Now the foreign service may also be on the cusp of change, albeit a less dramatic turning point than South Africa's. For even Perkins, who is not one to complain, confesses, "Morale in the foreign service is pretty low right now." He adds that Secretary James A. Baker III "has made it plain he wants to improve the atmosphere between himself and the career service." Perkins is referring to charges that the Administration has packed U.S. embassies with political appointees . . . and that the Secretary has insulated himself in a small coterie.

But it isn't only politics that's transforming the hidebound diplomatic corps. There are at least five other issues involved—and they're all on Perkins' agenda.

First, the courts are pressing for changes in the way women and minorities are hired and promoted. Since the mid-1970s, the number of women foreign service officers has increased from 10 percent to about 25 percent of the 4,000 total. Minorities now comprise roughly 12 percent. "But you can't just put up recruiting posters and expect to get a representative sample," Perkins says. So, he's planning to develop a network of college professors and community leaders to identify and prepare qualified youth—of both sexes—for service. The entrance exam, struck down because of cultural bias, is being revised.

Second, Perkins must find a way to cope with the needs of officers whose spouses work outside the service, causing the officers to refuse some overseas assignments.

Third, budget cuts are forcing senior managers to conserve training dollars. Perkins must implement a new policy that requires coursework to be closely related to current or future assignments.

Fourth, recent studies have found that the foreign language skills of many officers need to be improved.

Finally, two task forces—composed of foreign service officers—are recommending changes in the traditional "up-or-out" career track. In the future, for example, officers may be required to serve a minimum of three years in any grade before promotion. As a result, most officers would have 27-year careers before they peak.

"We also have to have a different kind of foreign service," Perkins says. Today's officers have to understand how diverse institutions operate, he insists. Officers who were formerly asked to select a specialty—such as economics, for instance—at the beginning of their careers will now wait five years before having to make a choice. They will thus have the opportunity to consider a variety of roles. And, for the first time, some will become "multifunctional" managers rather than specialists. "It is these people who will be our future leaders," Perkins states.

Perkins' own career followed a traditional route and featured stints in Thailand, Ghana and Liberia, with a doctorate in public administration along the way. He looks back upon Thailand as his favorite post. Ironically, the least favorite was a tour of duty in Washington, where he served as a personnel officer. It was "a frustrating time because I was [moving] from [jobs that required] learning a culture to learning how to get along in the foreign service with an esoteric and strange culture of its own. I also thought [senior officials] could have promoted me earlier than they did," he says, exhibiting some of the raw ambition that landed him in this top spot.

Perkins' drive to excel in foreign affairs began in a Portland, Ore., high school, where he was a member of an international club that sponsored lectures by foreign service officers. He also worked as a part-time laborer on the docks of the port city. It's no wonder he caught the wanderlust, watching ships unload cargo from "strange and esoteric" cultures around the world.

A WORKING MANAGER: CLASSIFICATION AS IF PEOPLE MATTERED

Morning found the usual smells and sounds in Rockwall State Penitentiary. Just as in the previous endless mornings, the smell of too many bodies mingled with the sounds of too many loud voices. Joel Haskins looked up from his empty coffee cup and squinted through the bars that confined his observation room. Just beyond his line of sight, he could sense the day shift assembling in the ready room. They were laughing and exchanging crude jokes as they lined up for inspection. Joel checked the status board and grimaced. Four red lights winked on and off among the forty or so steady green ones. "Another below strength watch," he thought. "That's the third one this week, and the tenth this month."

Pulling the duty rooster down from the rack, Joel began to make notes in the margin. As he reassigned people from one group to the other to balance the work crews, he wondered for the hundredth time why he had agreed to take the experimental position of lead guard. As the most experienced member of the forty-five member guard unit, he had felt that maybe his experience could help straighten out an increasingly chaotic situation. Over the past five years, Joel had watched as the inmate population doubled and the guard strength increased by only six men. To make matters worse, the new warden had decided that all new officers had to have a college degree in some relevant subject. The final blow had come with the opening of new positions in the federal prison system for experienced corrections officers. Three of the officers at Rockwall had immediately applied for and been accepted into the federal system, leaving only two regular officers to supervise the entire force at Rockwall.

As Joel was briefing the new watch in the duty room, Alicia Eggers was driving through the front gates. Two months ago, Alicia had transferred from the central office in the state capital to Rockwall. She still felt funny as she stopped at the gates for identification and a search of her car. "Big day for you today?" inquired the guard, as he handed back her ID. "Does it show that much?" Alicia gulped. "Naw, just a little. You're all dressed up and the look on your face reminds me of my daughter on her wedding day—excited and nervous." Alicia smiled and relaxed. "Well, its not quite that important, but I have to make a presentation to the prison Board of Visitors this afternoon about my special project." "Good luck to you," the guard mumbled as he turned away to the next car in line.

Alicia parked her car in the area marked "staff" and walked slowly up the steps to the main administration building. She knew that she had to make a decision that morning and then sell it to the Board of Visitors that afternoon. Three years ago, when she had graduated from the Master of Public Administration Program at the state university, she hadn't anticipated feeling this nervous. Then she had been sure that hard work and careful preparation would allow her to make the right decisions and prepare her to justify them to anybody. Now she knew better. As she walked to her office, she mentally reviewed her special project.

Immediately after graduation, she had taken a position with the State Department of Corrections as a classification specialist. She had done very well in her personnel courses and had quickly caught on to the elaborate job descriptions, union contracts, and legal definitions in the state personnel system. Her first project, the reclassification of positions in the central records office, had been a success. She had managed to reduce the work force and still make progress on the backlog of records waiting to be processed. That success had brought her to the attention of the executive director of the State Prison Board.

He had called her to his office and explained that the commissioner wanted someone to investigate the possibility of creating a middle ground between the rank-and-file guards and the officers in the prison system. The problem, he explained to her, was that a recent manpower study indicated that the system needed to hire some 180 new guards over the next several years to keep up with the growth of the inmate population. Normally, that would have meant promoting about eighteen people to officer level. Unfortunately, the system was experiencing a decline in the number of officers, as some retired and others left for better jobs in the federal government. Because, by law, officers had to have five years of experience or a degree in criminal justice, the system couldn't simply promote more guards to the rank of officer. What he wanted Alicia to do was to define a new level between the rank and file and the officers so that expansion could take place without overtaxing the remaining officers.

Summoning her courage, Alicia had agreed on one condition. She didn't want this to be a long-distance, on-paper project. She wanted to be able to run a pilot project at one of the prisons to see how the new position would work before she proposed it as a permanent classification. The executive director had agreed, and Alicia had chosen Rockwall as the best trial situation. From the central office, it had seemed like a straightforward exercise. She had carefully reviewed the various responsibilities, authorities, and training requirements of the guard positions and of the officer positions. On paper, it appeared to be a matter of shifting a few duties from the officers to a guard. After two months at Rockwall, she knew it wasn't that simple.

When Alicia reached her desk, she make a quick decision. Picking up her phone, she called the main guard station and asked the duty officer to send Joel Haskins down to her office at his earliest convenience. Replacing the phone, she pulled out her latest file on the project and began to reread her report. Originally, she had divided the responsibilities into three categories: managerial, supervisory, and technical. Her list now looked like this:

Managerial
Responsible for preparation of monthly budget requests, including routine equipment replacement

Responsible for scheduling vacations, personal days, sick leave and other leave days as specified in the contract

Responsible for recommending policy changes concerning the movement and confinement of inmates

Supervisory

Responsible for biweekly fitness reports on each member of the guard force on the shift

Responsible for twice daily head counts of inmates within the assigned unit

Responsible for changes in the daily duty roster according to required duties and prevailing policies.

Technical

Visit each observation station at least twice each day to ensure that proper procedures were being followed

Check all "pass through" areas for proper mechanical functioning at least once each shift

Brief the shift as it reported for duty and debrief as it reported off duty, and transfer information to the new watch officer before signing out

Alicia frowned as she studied all of the comments she had written on the sheet over the past weeks. She and Joel had met weekly to discuss the way things were working. Joel had convinced her to drop several of the original technical assignments because there wasn't enough time in the eight-hour shift. She wasn't sure that he was very happy about all the paperwork that remained, but this would be the last chance to revise the list before she made her presentation.

DISCUSSION QUESTIONS

1. If you were Alicia, what questions would you ask Joel when he came to your office?
2. If you were Joel, what aspects of the new position would you try to change?
3. If you were a member of the Board of Visitors, what questions would you have for Alicia after she finished her presentation?

AFFIRMATIVE ACTION FOR LEADERSHIP?

Captain William Folker looked out at the twenty people sitting in the auditorium. Since early this morning, they had been processed, examined, interviewed, oriented, and tested. Now he had to convey to them the utter seriousness of the remainder of the training they were about to undergo. "The fun part is over, folks," he began. "From now on until we finish this training, I expect you to remember that my life literally depends on you. It won't surprise you to hear that I have grown very attached to my life, just as I expect that you have grown attached to yours. Lest you think that I am exaggerating, let me tell you that the two previous directors of training at the Hazardous Fire Training Academy did not make it to retirement."

The group shifted uneasily in their seats. Several of the older members exchanged glances and looked away toward the extreme left front of the room. Sitting together in the first row were four people who looked straight ahead. They seemed to sense the attention from the other members and held themselves perfectly still. The captain followed the gazes and glanced down from the podium and scowled. "Lest we forget that this is an historic occasion, I'll remind the group that we have our first female candidates for specialist training. The most important thing we must all remember is that at the fire site, each person must perform as expected—no less and no more. It doesn't matter who that person is, only that the other team members can depend on him—or her."

Jessica Martray gave a mental sigh. "It never changes," she thought. "Just when you think it might be possible not to have the issue brought up, some clown goes out of his way to make a big deal." Jessica had worked hard over the past five years to get this nomination from her local fire department. The initial battle to get her job as a fire fighter had been fairly easy. Her scores on the exams were the highest in her test group. When she graduated from the state fire training program in the top ten of her class, the city council had been suitably impressed. Only one member of the council had made any comment at all when she was appointed to the department; the other fire fighters had accepted her with only a few reservations.

Her application for specialist training had been a different story. The week after she submitted the request, her chief had stopped her after a shift. "Look," he said, "I don't want a hassle about this. Your request is going to be denied because you don't have enough seniority to go to specialist training." Jessica had looked surprised. "There wasn't any requirement of years in rank in the notice of availability posted last week. Besides, as far as I know, there aren't any other applications from this department." "That doesn't matter," the Chief retorted. "The nominations are made by the chief and I'm not approving yours."

As Jessica drove home from the station she puzzled over the chief's behavior. He had always been fair with her and had even complimented her at a couple of the fires over the past years. She decided to stop at Donny Bookman's house on her way home. Donny had retired from the force a few years ago, but he still had a lot of contact with the members. When she rang the bell, Donny yelled from the backyard, "Come around the side if you want to talk, I'm doing steaks on the grill." Jessica walked around to the back and sat in a lawn chair. She explained the problem and asked Donny what he thought.

"That's easy," said Donny. "The problem is that the chief thinks you'll get certified and then they'll have a real problem." "How's that?" Jessica asked. Donny put down his barbecue fork and turned to her. "You really don't get it, do you? If you get the certification and come back to the department, that puts you in a potential command rank. Some of the members would think that was a bit much."

Jessica was stunned. She hadn't thought much about that part of the training. Fire fighters with specialist certification in hazardous techniques were automatically made temporary shift commander if the fire being fought were declared hazardous. Because specialists were trained in using equipment and techniques for containing hazardous materials fires, the policy was to have the specialist direct the efforts rather than serve in the line. That meant that she would be directing the efforts of people with many more years of experience and in some pretty dangerous situations.

Donny broke into her thoughts. "Why not go to the union? They were pretty strong in support of your joining the force; maybe they'll help now." Jessica thought that was unlikely. The union had been a strong supporter, but she had the feeling that the union leadership was going to be careful with something that might make the chief angry. Besides, if the chief was right, the union couldn't do very much about it anyway. When she joined the force, the national union had been pushing affirmative action as a way to get more fire fighters onto the local forces. One of the best arguments for increasing the "manpower" of local fire departments had been to demand that female fire fighters be added. This was a different issue, with no court cases that she knew of to force the issue.

In her locker one day the next week, Jessica had found a folded note that had been stuffed through the air vents. The note was from the president of the local union and simply said "Wait your turn." Jessica slammed the door of the locker in exasperation. "What turn?" she thought. "Nobody else wants to do the training because it takes six weeks away from their families and only part of the cost is paid by the department. They just don't want to risk a fight with some of the guys over taking orders from a woman."

Jessica was unusually quiet during her shift, and nobody said anything to her about the issue. On her way out, she stuck her head into the lieutenant's station. "I'm taking a personal day tomorrow so call in the standby." "Right," said Lt. Stokes. "Um, don't take this personally, but I think you're pushing it too fast." "What's that mean?" asked Jessica. "The mayor had the chief up on the carpet this morning about your request. Seems that one of the local chemical companies had agreed to pick up the cost of training a hazardous specialist and your request is getting a second look by council."

The chief called her at home the next afternoon. "You're going to the Specialist Training Academy starting two weeks from Friday. The council made the decision last night, over my objections, but I know that you'll do just fine and represent the force to the best of your ability. While you're there, please try to figure out how to solve the problem you're going to create when you get back."

As Jessica got up from her seat in the front row and began filing out of the auditorium at the Hazardous Fire Training Academy, she wondered if the three other women had the same problem. How was she supposed to concentrate on the training techniques and the new equipment with the problem of what to do about the resistance from the men in the force at home weighing on her mind? Captain Folker stepped in front of the women just before they reached the door. Jerking his head toward the other trainees, he said: "Don't worry about them. When you have all the gear on, it's hard to tell who's human, let alone who's female. Besides, they'll be just as scared of the responsibility for issuing orders as you will."

DISCUSSION QUESTIONS

1. Was the Chief right to be concerned about how well the men in his force would respond to a female taking charge at the scene of a hazardous fire?
2. What would you do, if you were in Jessica's position, to help the situation when you returned to the local fire house?
3. Does affirmative action extend to selecting people for leadership positions, or is it only applicable for the general hiring process?

AN OPPORTUNITY
TO GET MOTIVATED

The bulky interoffice memo sat on Larry Standish's desk for two days. It was a three-page document with a spiral-bound booklet attached. As he was clearing his desk late on Friday afternoon, he noticed that the packet had a routing slip attached. The previous name had been signed three days ago and Larry felt a little guilty that he hadn't gotten around even to looking at it. "Well, I'll make this the last item for the week," he muttered to himself as he settled back into his chair. Two hours later, Larry noticed that he was the only person left in the office. The rest of the cubicles were dark, and the late afternoon sun had almost set. Larry tore off the two pages of notes he had made on a yellow pad and tossed the package back onto his desk.

On the Metro going home, Larry thought about the risks and opportunities he had discovered in that memo. The memo had announced a new personnel system being established in his agency. The program was strictly voluntary—for the moment at least. The new director of the agency was a true believer in the value of motivational programs for public employees. Larry remembered the speech the director had given when she assumed her post. "My job is not to motivate you—my job is to provide enough incentives so that you motivate yourselves." She had gone on to describe some of the incentives she intended to provide. Larry had trouble remembering any of them at the moment, but he was sure that she had mentioned the new personnel system.

Pulling out the notes he had made, Larry began to organize each item as either a plus or a minus. On the plus side was the possibility of receiving substantial merit increases in pay if he joined the new system. On the negative side, the merit increases would be granted based on the performance of a "task group" composed of seven to twelve people. Larry wasn't sure that he wanted his pay to depend on the work of other people. In the new system, people would be assigned to the task groups based on their operational responsibilities. The memo had stated quite clearly that assignment to the group was to be on a "mutual agreement basis" between the employee and his or her supervisor. Because Larry had a good working relationship with his supervisor, that would be no problem for the moment. "But," thought Larry, "what if my next supervisor and I don't see eye to eye? Could I be reassigned to another group involuntarily?" Larry made a note to ask someone about that.

The next item on the plus side was the institution of "quality work circles" in the new system. Larry had several friends in the private sector who participated in similar groups. All of them said the meetings were useful and that sometimes ideas proposed by the group actually were adopted by the managers. Larry thought that would be unlikely in his agency, but stranger things had happened. On the minus side was the training requirement. The new system required each participant to attend one training session per month on a Saturday morning. The sessions were free, but Larry was reluctant to surrender any more of his private life to his job. Still, Larry mused, he would be home in time to see the games on television, and it might be nice to get into the city without having to fight weekday commuting crowds.

The item that had the biggest plus on Larry's list was the chance for promotion. During the past two years, Larry had given up hope of getting to the next level in the agency. His evaluations were always good, but rarely excellent. Each cycle seemed to find some crucial area in which he was only average. Larry frowned as he remembered his last evaluation, which had rated him as average on initiative. His job didn't allow very much discretion and he wondered how he could show initiative without breaking at least one of the many, many rules governing his small part of the agency's operations. The new system included a chance for new responsibilities. The "job enrichment" part of the system wasn't clearly spelled out in the package, but Larry had carefully noted the part where it said "responsibilities assumed by participants may result in the reclassification of the position to a higher level."

As Larry left the Metro and headed for his car in the parking lot, he worried about the final item on his list. He hadn't decided whether to put it in the plus or minus category. The final item was the "target productivity goals," which he and his supervisor were to agree to before he entered the program. Before Larry had joined the public service, he had had a bad experience with a piece-rate job in the private sector. His quotas had been raised so many times that he suspected that the business was adjusting the system to prevent workers from gaining any advantage from the increased rate of work. In his present position, it would be much harder to decide exactly how to define increased productivity.

The problem, Larry knew, was that productivity was almost always measured quantitatively. There were aspects of what Larry did that could be counted. For example, the number of documents Larry examined and signed each day could be used as a measure. The problem was that the documents required careful scrutiny. How would Larry and his supervisor agree on a qualitative measure of Larry's work? For example, Larry reflected, sometimes he found a problem that took him an entire morning to resolve; other documents had only minor errors that could be cleared up with one phone call. If the system merely wanted him to work faster, he decided he wasn't interested.

The other parts of Larry's work could more easily be measured on a productivity basis. Larry was proud of his skills on the computer system at the office. He rarely made any errors when he entered data, and his proficiency at information retrieval was the envy of his co-workers. "That part will be easy to measure, and I have some ideas about how to speed up that process already. Maybe I can show some initiative in this new program that will help the entire group," Larry thought with a wry smile.

At the red light, Larry tried to pull all of the pluses and minuses together. He really was curious about the new system, and his spirit of adventure urged him to jump in just for a change. On the other hand, his family was growing, and this wasn't the time in his life to risk more problems on the job. As Larry turned into the driveway, he decided to sit down and hold a family discussion about his choice. "I'll tell them this is a quality circle for the family," he chuckled.

DISCUSSION QUESTIONS

1. Given what you have read about Larry and his job, would you recommend that he join the new program?
2. Do you agree that it is the responsibility of managers to provide motivation for employees, or is that an individual's own responsibility?
3. To what extent is the type of work done by public servants more or less difficult to measure on a productivity basis?

MANAGEMENT SKILLS FOR PUBLIC ADMINISTRATORS

If you want to be an effective and responsible administrator, you will need a good understanding of the context of modern public administration and a good grasp of the technical areas, such as budgeting or personnel. But your ultimate success or failure will depend as much or more not on "what you know" but on "what you can do." Your ability to act will be based on a variety of personal and interpersonal skills, such as your capabilities as a leader, your effectiveness in oral and written communications, and your effectiveness in working under conditions of stress and ambiguity. If you are able to improve your skills in these areas, you will be far more effective.

The need to develop these skills, especially the skills associated with successful leadership, has been a topic of considerable recent discussion. Many commentators have decried a failure of leadership in our society, by that, meaning not only a disenchantment with those who lead major social institutions but also a vacuum of leadership throughout organizations. Unless people throughout public and private organizations can assume leadership within their areas of responsibility, we will likely be denied the most creative and imaginative solutions to the problems we face as a society. Knowing how to "read" a group, to articulate a vision for the group, and "energize" people to act will be an increasingly important set of skills.

In addition to the personal and interpersonal skills you will need to develop, there are a variety of tools and techniques that are available to help in your managerial work. Among those that have received the greatest attention recently are strategic planning and strategic management, productivity improvement programs, organization development, technological innovation (including computerization), and total quality management. Knowing something about each of these areas will enable you to assess their potential use in your organization and also to apply more generally some of the insights the approach provides. For example, although the term *organization development* (or OD) typically refers to programs of planned change aided by an outside facilitator, you can use many of the techniques and recommendations that are associated with OD in the day-to-day management of your organization.

We begin the readings with a discussion on leadership by one of the most popular writers on leadership today, Warren Bennis. Bennis notes that more and more decisions are being made in public forums and that more and more people are wanting to be a part of the decision process. Under these circumstances, traditional uses of power may be insufficient to move organizations in the directions they need to move. As an alternative, Bennis describes "transformative leadership" as a genuinely participative and noncoercive approach. In addition to understanding Bennis' concept of transformative leadership, you should pay special attention to the distinction that Bennis (and others) makes between management and leadership.

Effective communication is obviously essential to effective public management. But communications can be distorted in many different ways. Edgar H. Schein approaches this topic through a consideration of nine elements of "face-to-face relationships," elements that can either clarify or confuse communications between individuals. Especially take note of Schein's emphasis on personal growth through self-reflection and self-critique as an aid to improving our understanding of others and our ability to communicate effectively with them.

Robert T. Golembiewski moves the discussion further along by indicating some of the "cultural" features associated with high-performance public organizations. Although the focus is on incentive plans, this article actually says more about the organizational conditions under which improved performance is likely. You should pay special attention to the contrasting cultures illustrated in Table 1 and to the characteristics of high-performing systems listed in Table 2. Note how these characteristics are consistent with Bennis' and Schein's views of organizational life.

In the next article, we return to the theme of improving quality and productivity, but this time we approach the topic from a management perspective. Barry Bozeman underlines the need for managers to take a strategic rather than a tactical approach to their work. In part, Bozeman's recommendation is that managers will increasingly need to be capable of and ready for change. You should pay special attention to the skills the individual manager needs to manage strategically—information processing skills, political skills, analytical skills, and human relations skills.

One important development affecting the management of public organizations today is the rapid computerization of many different functions. Kenneth L. Kraemer and John Leslie King point out that computing in public organizations today is not limited to the traditional areas of financial management but extends to a large number of other applications. In doing so, computing raises not only technical questions but human and organizational questions as well. Among these is the question of how organizations might be restructured based on new information-processing capabilities, a question that Kraemer and King answer by saying that computing applications reflect existing perspectives within public organizations. (We will discover a far different answer to this question in the article by Harlan Cleveland in chapter 8.)

The final selection in this chapter is a statement prepared by the federal Office of Management and Budget outlining an approach to management improvement known as Total Quality Management (TQM). Based on the approach to quality control of such authors as W. Edwards Deming, Joseph Juran, and Philip Crosby, TQM is a comprehensive effort to place quality issues at the top of the organization's agenda and seeks to improve quality through a variety of techniques, ranging from strategic planning to training and development to quality assurance. TQM has been adopted in many private firms and is now being required in all federal agencies. In addition, state and local governments are just beginning to experiment with TQM concepts. Despite the listing of specific techniques here, you should understand the general cultural or philosophical commitment that organizations interested in TQM must make.

The profile in this chapter describes the work of Ann McKernan Robinson, head of the Office of Consumer Affairs in the U.S. Postal Service. Robinson's work typifies the new interest in quality and service that is central to TQM. As you will see, she is concerned with listening and responding to the comments and complaints of citizens, something she considers essential to maintaining a high-quality organization. You should also notice the comments on Robinson's own leadership style.

The cases for this chapter illustrate some of the day-to-day skills required of managers. In "Relocation of the Midburg Housing Project," you will confront the issue of strategic planning.

Most managers are expected to see into the future and anticipate problems before they occur. In this case, you will discover that actions in the present have long-term consequences. Even when you see the problems coming, it is often difficult to decide what strategy will turn out to be successful. This case will also alert you to the dangers of allowing planning to be driven by facts and figures rather than by people and ideas.

The role of political executives is often overlooked in the literature on management. "Solving One Problem Creates Another" offers an interesting example of the kind of situations that sometimes face political executives. As you read the case, you will understand the need for toughness as well as intelligence in the successful manager. This case brings together several larger themes, including ethics and privatization.

"The Mess in Somewhere City" will help you to understand the ambiguous nature of scientific research, and the need for leaders to use it wisely. In addition to having some expertise in research procedures, leaders need to be sensitive to the uses to which research can be put. The case will offer you an opportunity to see how this process works.

From a very different perspective, "Siding with Superanalyst" presents you with a clear look at an age-old problem. Most of us assume that our actions are justified and that other people may just not understand our motivations. Part of a manager's responsibility is to see the world through the eyes of others. This case will help you to understand how our actions may be based on simple—and therefore quite likely, deficient—assumptions about how organizations (and people in general) work. The case provides you with an opportunity to watch a problem develop without you having to suffer the consequences in "real life."

THE ARTFORM OF LEADERSHIP

Warren Bennis

To understand the artform of leadership the following question must be addressed: What are the components of an organization that can translate intention into reality and sustain it? The question itself contains a complexity and depth as well as a chronic elusiveness. The question, probably because of just those characteristics, tends to be avoided—although it addresses the essence of organizational leadership. And even when it is obliquely touched on, writers tend to avoid the orchestral richness that inheres in the question for the doctrinal, predictable, and prosaic clichés. Between the blur produced by trying to say too much at once and the banality produced by dismissing mysteries, there remains the possibility of articulating just what it is that enables some organizations to translate an intention into reality and sustain it. This is the starting point for an examination of what I am calling transformative power.

THE ENVIRONMENT OF LEADERSHIP IN THE 1980s

This much can be said about leadership for the 1980s: Those responsible for governing the enterprise will be spending more and more of their time managing external relations. All organizations are surrounded by an increasingly active, incessant environment, one that is becoming more and more influential—the senior partner, as it were—in all kinds of decisions that affect the institution.

Leadership (and its companion, decision making) will become an increasingly intricate process of multilateral brokerage, including constituencies both within and without the organization. More and more decisions made will be public decisions; that is, the people they affect will insist on being heard. Leaders will have to reckon with the growing role of the media as a "fourth branch" of government available for use by the people who oppose or support a particular decision. The idea of a relatively small group of "movers and shakers" who get things done is obsolete. Increasing numbers of citizens and stakeholders, and even those who are only indirectly involved in an issue, have interested themselves in its outcome—and when the decision goes the "wrong way," very noisily so. This state of affairs has led one writer to describe the organization of today as a "jungle of closed decisions, openly arrived at."

The bigger the problem to be tackled, the more power is diffused and the greater the number of people who have to be involved. Thus, decisions become more and more complex, more ill defined, affecting more and more different (and sometimes conflicting) constituencies.

Inevitably there will be frustration, not only among leaders but among followers who ask, "Who's in charge here?" as more and more people/groups have to be consulted. Leaders ask, "How do you get everybody in the act and still get some action?"

Ambiguity and surprise are ubiquitous. Leaders have to lead under uncertain, risky conditions in which it is virtually impossible to get ready for *something* when you have to get ready for *anything*. Just as effective leaders know about, and are becoming more competent at coping with, the politicization of our institutions—by which I mean that institutions are becoming the focus for a new kind of politics, that is, mobilizing public opinion and working more closely with state and federal legislative bodies and with other key constituencies— they are also learning more about an enlarged concept of the "management team."

No longer can "managing external relations" be left in the hands of the public relations department. Top leadership must be involved—directly. In short, the political role of the organization leadership's responsibility must be reconceived. These trends, these changing characteristics of the organizational/managerial environment that we are now living with, will become even more pronounced and problematic over the next ten or so years.

The Three Components of Transformative Power

Leader. Some important clues about the nature of effective leadership have come out of my recently completed study of eighty chief executive officers (CEOs) plus ten in-depth interviews conducted over the past few months with ten successful, "innovative" leaders. These studies provide a basis for making some generalizations about those leaders who successfully achieved mastery over the noisy, incessant environment—rather than simply reacting, throwing up their hands, and living in a perpetual state of "present shock." In short, the study I am about to summarize was able to illuminate some of the darkness around the question earlier posed: How do organizations translate intention into reality and sustain it? Leadership is the first component, although, as we shall see later, leadership must be held within a context of other interacting factors.

What all these effective CEOs shared and embodied was directly related to how they construed their role. To use a popular distinction, they viewed themselves as *leaders*, not *managers*, which is to say that they were concerned with their organization's basic purposes, why it exists, its general direction. They did not spend their time on the "how to," the proverbial "nuts and bolts," but on purpose, on paradigms of action. In short, they were concerned not with "doing things right" (the overriding concern of managers) but with "doing the right thing." They were capable of transforming doubts into the psychological grounds of common purpose.

The question that guided my study was what common set of characteristics, if any, those leaders possessed who were capable of translating intention into reality. The answer clarifies the role of the effective leader. In varying degrees, it seemed that all the CEOs possessed the following competencies:

1. *Vision:* The capacity to create and communicate a compelling vision of a desired state of affairs—to impart clarity to this vision (or paradigm, context, frame—all those words serve) and induce commitment to it.
2. *Communication and alignment:* The capacity to communicate their vision in order to gain the support of their multiple constituencies.
3. *Persistence, consistency, focus:* The capacity to maintain the organization's direction, especially when the going gets rough.
4. *Empowerment:* The capacity to create environments—the appropriate social architecture—that can tap and harness the energies and abilities necessary to bring about the desired results.
5. *Organizational learning:* The capacity to find ways for the organization to monitor its own performance, compare results with established objectives, have access to a continuously evolving data base on which to review past actions and base future ones, and decide how, if necessary, the organizational structure and key personnel must be abandoned or rearranged when faced with new conditions.

In short, nothing serves an organization better—especially during these times of agonizing doubts and paralyzing ambiguities—than leadership that knows what it wants, communicates those intentions successfully, empowers others, and knows when and how to stay on course and when to change.

Intention. The second element is the "compelling vision" mentioned earlier, what will now be called "the intention." The expression of an intention is the capacity to take an organization to a place it has never been before, the unknown. The characteristics of the intentions that successful leaders use include the following:

- *Simplicity.* This characteristic is akin to Occam's razor, the law of parsimony. It implies that each assumption or element is independent. The word *simple* derives from the notion of one or unity.
- *Completeness.* This criterion requires that all the available facts be included. In most organizations the bulk of the major tasks to be accomplished are easily and readily incorporated within almost any kind of organizational structure. It is those few remaining tasks that test or prove the adequacy of the organization. Not only should the organization be capable of incorporating tasks that need to be performed at the time it is set up, it should also be capable of adjusting to and assimilating new tasks as they arise.
- *Workability.* Does the intention deliver the goods? Does the context achieve the organizational

goals or contribute to them? William James, as usual, says it well: "By their fruits ye shall know them, not by their roots."

- *Communicability.* The last criterion for judging intentions, communicability, contains two components. The more obvious one is the ease with which the context is understood by the organization. The robustness of the organization, in terms of its empowerment, depends to a large extent on the degree to which the context is clear and understood. The other meaning I give to this criterion is what in *est* terms, I believe, would be called "alignment"— not alignment of organizational members, though, but alignment with other contexts indigenous to the particular organization. In other words, the effectiveness of organizational structure depends partly on the mutual relatedness of its various contexts.

The problem with the foregoing characteristics is betrayed by application of one of them, "completeness." The list is not complete. Originality, muting of ego, subtlety, and an esthetic are all important, but space limitations preclude anything but their mention now. The one exception is "an esthetic," an exception based both on its significance and on its neglect. Indeed, I believe that the esthetic of the intention plays an important— perhaps the key—role in understanding how intention can lead to implementation. That is, after all, the whole point of leadership (more about that later).

Organization. Transformative power implies a transaction between the leader and the led, between the leadership and some sort of participative response. If the leadership expresses the characteristics noted earlier and if the vehicle of this expression, the intention(s), is effectively expressed, the organization becomes a blending of each individual's uniqueness into collective action.

Such an organization is similar to something observed in healthy individuals; in fact, it is isomorphic with a healthy identity in an individual. More technically, we can assume that an organization possesses a healthy identity—organizational integrity—when it has a clear sense of who it is and what it is to do; and that is a way of defining *organizational integrity.*

Achieving organizational integrity is easier said than done. Part of the problem is the lack of understanding of the various substructures that all organizations, no matter how small, contain. One block to our understanding is perpetuated by the myth of organization-as-monolith, a myth reinforced almost daily by the media and the temptation of simplicity. The myth is not only grossly inaccurate but dangerous as well. When the evening paper, for example, announces that the Defense Department or the University of California or IBM (or any corporate body, for that matter) will pursue this or that course of action, the said action is typically ascribed to a single, composite body, *the* administration. This "administration," whose parts vibrate in harmony and whose acts, because we are denied a look at the human drama that leads up to them, take on an air of superhuman detachment, is as mythical as the griffin. Into every step taken by "*the* administration" goes a complicated pattern of meetings, disagreements, conversations, personalities, emotions, and missed connections. This very human process is bureaucratic politics. Parallel processes are responsible for our foreign policy, the quality of our public schools, and the scope and treatment of the news that the media choose to deliver to us each day.

Our perceptions of organizational decision making, based on such reports and other sources of information, tend to emphasize the *product* of decision making, never (or rarely) the *process*. The result, of course, is false—at times, destructively so. The elements of chance, ignorance, stupidity, recklessness, and amiable confusion are simply not reckoned with; they are selectively ignored, it seems. Thus, the public rarely sees the hundreds of small tableaux, the little dramas, that result in a policy statement or a bit of strategy. It sees only the move or hears only the statement, and it not unreasonably assumes that such an action is the result of a dispassionate, mechanistic process in which problems are perceived, alternative solutions weighed, and rational decisions made. Given human nature, that is almost never so.

For an organization to have integrity, it must have an identity—that is, a sense of who it is and what it is to do. In personality theory, analogously, every person is a summation of various "selves." If those units of the person are not in communication, then the person cannot maintain valid communications with others. The problem of integrity, which is central to much of the contemporary literature in the mental health field, can in organizations be examined by understanding the various "organizational selves" or structures that exist.

Every organization incorporates four concepts of organization, often at odds with one another or existing in some strained coherence: (1) the *manifest* organization, or the one seen on the organization chart and formally displayed. (2) The *assumed* organization, or the one that individuals perceive as the organization (what they would produce were they asked to draw their view of the way things work, much like the legendary New Yorker's view of the United States in which the Hudson River abuts Los Angeles). (3) The *extant* organization, or the organization as revealed through systematic investigation—say, by an outside consultant. (4) The *requisite* organization, or the organization as it would be if it were in accord with the reality of the situation within which it exists.

The ideal, but never realized, situation is that in which the manifest, the assumed, the extant, and the requisite are aligned as closely as possible. Wherever these four organizational concepts are in contradiction, the organizational climate is such that the organization's identity is confused and its integrity difficult to achieve.

Another useful analogy with mental health can be drawn here. Many, if not all, psychotherapeutic schools base their notions of mental health on the degree to which the individual brings into harmony the various "selves" that make up his or her personality. The healthy person will be much the same person as he or she is known to others.

Virtually the same criterion can be used to establish organizational integrity—that is, the degree to which the organization maintains harmony among, and knowledge about, the manifest, assumed, extant, and requisite concepts. All four concepts need not be identical. Rather, all four types should be recognized and allowance made for all the tensions created by imbalances. It is doubtful that an organization can (or even should) achieve total congruence. The important factor is recognition, a heightened consciousness of the confusions and contradictions.

To achieve organizational openness and, through it, integrity, each individual within the organization—particularly the leader—must strive to be open. From its embodiment in the individual, openness moves to the group level and, through individual and group interaction, infuses the organizational culture that sustains openness. The process is as slow as the building of a pyramid, and far more complex.

THE ARTFORM OF LEADERSHIP

We have gone only partway in understanding leadership (and transformative power) by decomposing the three key elements at the political center of a complexly organized aggregate—that is, an organization—into (1) a leader or governing elite or strategic core, (2) a set of symbolic forms expressing a tapestry of intentions, and (3) those constituent groups and individuals who make up the membership of the organization. The intention and its expression—crowns and coronations, limousines and conferences—give what goes on in organizations its aura of being not merely important but in some odd fashion connected with the way the world is built. The gravity of organizational leadership and the solemnity of high worship spring from impulses more alike than might first appear.

The extent to which leadership is truly effective is based on the extent to which individuals place symbolic value on the intentions and their expression—the esthetic I mentioned earlier. What makes the difference between transformative power and other forms is the relationship of the governed to the active centers of the social order. Such centers have nothing to do with geometry and little with geography. They have nothing to do with "humanizing the workplace," Theory X or Theory Y, with "quality of worklife" or "participative management." What is important is that the organization and its members are essentially concentrated on what appear to be *serious acts*. Active centers consist in the point or points in a society where its leading ideas come together with its leading institutions to create an arena in which the events that most vitally affect members' lives take place. The artform of leadership means involvement, even oppositional involvement, with such arenas and with the momentous events that occur in them that translates intention into reality and sustains it. I have in mind a sign not of popular appeal or inventive craziness, but of being near the heart of things.

It is crucial, necessary, that leaders use a set of symbolic forms expressing the fact that they are, in truth, *leading*. Whether the symbolic expression of context, its symbolization, takes the form of stories, ceremonies, insignia, formalities, and appurtenances that have been inherited or, in more revolutionary times, invented makes no difference. Whatever the expression, the crowns and coronations, limousines and conferences serve to mark the center and give what goes on there its aura of being not merely important but in some fashion connected with the way the world is built.

It is not, after all, standing outside the social order in some excited state of self-regard that makes a leader numinous. It is not a "System 4" or a "Theory Y" or a grid score of "9,9" that makes a leader effective. It is a deep, intimate involvement near or at the heart of things that motivates and empowers.

Where the vision/intention is esthetically and compellingly presented, the space within can be ambiguous and oblique. When I began to realize that the relationship between the expression of the intention, the context, is clear and the space within as ambiguous and roomy, I then began to see how *the dialectic of the oblique to the specific is the artform of leadership*. The precise tension between them is the difference between *proceeding*, which is what the "compelling vision" propels, and *deciding*, which goes on within the space generated by the vision.

Without spelling out the details, the relationship between the vision and the space it generates and holds reveals why transformative leadership, which is what I have been talking about, is genuinely participative and noncoercive. This relationship also provides some clues to why Japanese managers have surpassed their earlier masters.

IMPROVING FACE-TO-FACE RELATIONSHIPS

Edgar H. Schein

The challenges of management in the 1980s are enormous, but they are fairly easy to identify. The great difficulties that we face lie not in deciding *what* our goals should be, but in determining *how* to achieve them. Our problems in this area are problems of *implementation*: how can we reach goals that are often perfectly clear but seemingly impossible to attain.

Several explanations of these problems readily come to mind:

- Large systems have become too complex to be understood.
- "Bureaucracy" makes it impossible to get anything done.
- Intergroup hostility paralyzes all constructive effort.
- Power politics undermine and subvert rational action.
- Irrationality and human resistance to change defeat even the wisest programs.

All of these explanations are true, but they are also incomplete. Sometimes they are used only as excuses for failure rather than as constructive analyses of our management problems. On the other hand, we *have* learned something about implementation in the last forty years or so, and what we have learned takes us back to one fundamental principle: societies, organizations, and families are *human* groups, and the face-to-face relationships among the members of these groups are a basic element of any social action. Whatever else we need in the way of systems, procedures, and mechanisms, the process of social action always starts with face-to-face relationships among people.

Face-to-face relationships can be thought of as the glue that holds organizations together, and such relationships are the links in the implementation chain. Therefore, we should take a fresh look at these relationships to see if we can articulate some of the skills which can make them more constructive, and thus enable us to move toward solving some of the pressing problems of the 1980s.

THE ELEMENTS OF FACE-TO-FACE RELATIONSHIPS

What does it take to build, maintain, improve, and, if need be, repair face-to-face relationships? I would like to discuss nine different elements, which are all closely interrelated yet distinct in important ways. These elements reflect motives and values, perceptual skills, and behavioral skills:

1. Self-insight and a sense of one's own identity;
2. Cross-cultural sensitivity—the ability to decipher other people's values;
3. Cultural/moral humility—the ability to see one's own values as not necessarily better or worse than another's values;
4. A proactive problem-solving orientation—the conviction that interpersonal and cross-cultural problems can be solved;
5. Personal flexibility—the ability to adopt different responses and approaches as needed by situational contingencies;
6. Negotiation skills—the ability to explore differences creatively, to locate some common ground, and to solve the problem;
7. Interpersonal and cross-cultural tact—the ability to solve problems with people without insulting them, demeaning them, or destroying their "face";
8. Repair strategies and skills—the ability to resurrect, to revitalize, and to rebuild damaged or broken face-to-face relationships;
9. Patience.

I would like to discuss each of these elements in turn, putting most of the attention on those which have been insufficiently attended to in prior analyses and on those which are especially relevant to repair strategies.

SELF-INSIGHT

One can hardly work out common goals with others if one does not know where one's own values and goals lie. Leaders and managers especially must know where they are going, and they must be able to articulate their own goals. Parents and spouses must make a valiant effort to lift to the surface what is often left implicit—their own life goals and targets—so that there can be genuine negotiation among family members in the different life stages.

Self-insight is a *competence*—the ability to see oneself accurately and to evaluate oneself fairly. Through feedback from others and through systematic self-study, we can improve our ability to see ourselves. As we increase in self-insight, we lay the foundations for self-acceptance, which is to some extent, a prerequisite for some of the other skills to be discussed.

CROSS-CULTURAL SENSITIVITY

It goes without saying that we cannot offer leadership if we do not have perspective on ourselves and on others, and we cannot gain such perspective if we continue to be ethnocentric—to notice and appreciate only our own culture and values. Cross-cultural issues are not limited to the dramatic differences which can be identified in how different countries operate. Many of the most harmful cases of cultural misunderstanding occur right under our noses—with our spouses, friends, children, and subordinates—because norms, values, and behavioral codes vary widely within any country. American managers often tell tales of woe of trying to transfer people from the deep South to Manhattan, or from an urban center to a rural plant site.

A costly misunderstanding occurred in the small town where we used to spend our summers. The local wood-turning mill employed both men and women from the community, and the pay scales had developed historically around the status system in the town. A new manager who had experience in a progressive urban mill noticed that some of the skilled women operators were grossly underpaid in relation to their male counterparts. He set about to rationalize the pay structure to reflect actual skill levels. This action led to wives bringing home bigger paychecks, which neither they nor their husbands could accept in terms of the status system in the town. The dissatisfaction and turmoil that resulted from upsetting the social order was completely unanticipated by this manager.

Deciphering values, motives, aspirations, and basic assumptions across *occupational* and *social class lines* is particularly difficult. It is hard for the son of a successful middle-class businessman to understand the values and career aspirations of the son of an immigrant or an unskilled worker. It is hard for the general manager to understand the values and career aspirations of the technically oriented person and vice versa. It is hard for people in the different functional areas of a business to decipher each other's values and aspirations.[1]

CULTURAL DIFFERENCES BETWEEN COUNTRIES

When we go to countries where a different language is being spoken and where the culture is obviously different, we do wake up to the need to sharpen our deciphering skills. But even then we have a strong tendency to look for similarities and to rationalize that "people are people" and "business is business" no matter where it is conducted. My own tendency to ignore differences was brought home to me during a visit to Australia, which is superficially and historically similar to the U.S. It took me quite a while to discover that while Australians (like Americans) are achievement oriented, they also have the "tall poppy syndrome": one must not stand out above the crowd; one must accomplish things without seeming to work too hard at them; and one must not take too much personal credit for one's accomplishments. The son of a friend of mine told us how, after waiting all day for the perfect wave, he had finally succeeded in having a brilliant ride on his surfboard. When he hit the beach, he told his watching friends—as he knew he had to—"Boy that was a *lucky* one."

I kept hearing how complacent and security oriented the Australians were even when I was dealing with what seemed to be some pretty tough, aggressive managers. What one's true motives are and what is culturally acceptable as a legitimate explanation of one's motives are, of course, not necessarily the same. In comparing America and

Australia, one sees a paradoxical reversal. In Australia, people claim to be mostly security oriented, though companies admitted they had many aggressive, ambitious, power-seeking managers working for them. In the U.S., the popular image is that most people are ambitious and want to climb right to the top of the organization—though I encounter a growing number of allegedly ambitious managers who admit in private that they are not motivated to continue the "rat race," that they would like early retirement, or that they are considering another career altogether. Both public images reflect cultural norms, yet both are to some degree a misrepresentation of the actual state of affairs. The public selves we wear—the way we are supposed to present ourselves to others—is a strongly ingrained set of cultural values in its own right, and tact prevents us from puncturing the illusions which cultures teach us to project.

"FACE WORK"

Erving Goffman has written articulately about what he calls "face work"—the behavior of people in a social situation which is designed to help everyone maintain the self which they choose to project in that particular situation.[2] Selves are forever constructed, and the audience for any given performance is culturally bound to uphold as much as possible the identities which the actors claim. At the minimum, we nod and say "uh huh" when someone is talking to us, or we try to laugh politely at a joke that is not really funny, or we ignore embarrassing incidents. If our boss tells us through his actions or demeanor that he believes himself to be very competent in handling a given meeting, we rarely challenge this claim even though we may privately believe that he will totally mismanage it. The skill in this situation is our ability to compensate for his incompetence or to repair what damage may have been done. But we do not destroy his face.

THE RECIPROCITY OF RELATIONSHIPS

One of the most interesting features of the cultural norms of face-to-face interactions is their symmetric, reciprocal, exchange nature. We sometimes get into difficulty because we do not know how to complete an interaction. When someone in a strange country offers you an object in his house because you have admired it, are you supposed to take it and reciprocate at some future time when the visitor is in your home, or is it appropriate to refuse? The whole question of when and how to say yes or no is fraught with difficulty if we are talking across cultures or subcultures. And, as many businessmen have found out, how to interpret a yes or a no is even more difficult.

The ability to detect the subtleties of how others perceive situations and of what the values of others are requires both formal training and practical experience. Learning a new language would seem to be a prerequisite since so much of every culture is encoded into the language. Many people pride themselves on their extensive travel, even making lists of how many countries they have been in, without ever encountering or deciphering any of the cultures of those countries; they do not learn the languages and therefore miss the important nuances of what is going on. On the other hand, I have heard repeatedly from multinational companies that one of the best prescriptions for success in an overseas assignment is to take time to learn the local language.

CULTURAL/MORAL HUMILITY

Beyond self-insight and the ability to understand others, we need something which we might call cultural/moral *humility*. Can we not only sense the values of other people but, more importantly, positively appreciate them? Can we see our own culture and values only as *different*, not necessarily as *better*? Our tendency to think of things as "funny" or "odd" is a good diagnostic here. I have often been shown or told about funny things people do in other countries. An American visitor to the mainland of China found it very amusing that some Chinese farmers were so proud of owning tractors which were, in fact, useless; the tractors could not turn on the tight terraces and they did not have attachable plows to pull. The fact that a Chinese farmer did not even know the function of the pin to which the plow attaches struck this American as very funny and weird. It never occurred to him that his own utilitarian, pragmatic values might not be the only relevant ones in this situation.

A few years ago, a group of American students teased one of their German peers about his heel-clicking, head-nodding, hand-shaking formality. After some months of being teased, he stopped them one day with the statement: "When I go to work in the morning, I go to my boss's office, click my heels, bow my head, shake his hand, and then tell him the truth." The teasing stopped.

Many American managers lack cultural humility. We are more pragmatic than other people, and if we encounter people less pragmatic, we view *them* as odd rather than wonder about the oddity of our being so pragmatic. We don't consider our own culture as funny, odd, and in need of explanation, yet *it is our culture which is probably in a statistical sense the most different from all other cultures. . . .* My point is not to dissect the value system of the U.S. but rather to identify a strong tendency I have seen in managers all over the world (Americans and non-Americans alike) to be ethnocentric—to assume that one's own values are the best, and that one is excused from having to know what others think and value, or at least from having to take very seriously what others think and value. Such an absence of cultural humility can be a dangerous weakness when we are attempting face-to-face negotiations or problem solving. This point is important whenever we deal with people whose values are different from our own, whether these people are within our society or are from other countries.

PROACTIVE PROBLEM-SOLVING ORIENTATION

Solving face-to-face problems, especially where difficult cross-cultural understanding and humility are required, presupposes a faith that problems *can* be solved if one works at them and an assumption that active problem solving will produce positive results. Communication and understanding are difficult to achieve, but if one does not even try, then there is no possibility for achievement.

A proactive orientation is itself to some degree a cultural characteristic. When Americans take the "can do" attitude, how do we determine when we

are coming on too strongly, or when we are actually intruding in private lifespace in our eagerness to establish constructive face-to-face relationships in order to solve problems. The anthropologist Edward Hall has given us many excellent examples of how conducting business in different cultural contexts must be delicately handled, lest we invade people's territory and unwittingly destroy the possibility of better relationships.[3]

What I mean by a "proactive orientation" is a *motivation* to work on problems, not necessarily a high level of overt *activity*. We must base our actual course of action on genuine cultural understanding and not simply on a desire to act. As in the case of international diplomacy, we should always be ready to negotiate. No matter how bad the situation is between management and employees in a company or industry, each party should always be ready to sit down and try again to talk face-to-face.

PERSONAL FLEXIBILITY

It does us little good to sense situations accurately if we cannot take advantage of what we perceive. I know people who can tell you exactly what is going on but who cannot alter their own behavior to adjust to what they know to be the realities. One of the reasons why experiential learning methods—such as sensitivity training or transactional analysis workshops—have been so successful is that they allow experimentation on the part of participants, thus permitting the participants to enlarge their repertory of face-to-face behavior. Role playing is perhaps the prototype of such behavioral training and is clearly a necessary component of face-to-face skill development.[4]

NEGOTIATION SKILLS

Much has been written about the process of negotiation and the skills needed to be an effective negotiator. To a considerable degree, what has been said reflects the same themes that I am focusing on here. Negotiation requires great sensitivity, humility, self-insight, motivation to solve the problem, and behavioral flexibility. Part of the sensitivity required is the ability to decipher others' values. Another part is the ability to elicit information from others and to judge the validity of that information. Face-to-face relationships are not always benign, not always comfortable, not always safe, and not always open, yet they are always crucial to problem solving. Especially in situations where there initially is conflict, we need the ability to maintain relationships so that negotiations can continue, to decipher messages when deliberate concealment is attempted, to convince and to persuade, to bluff when necessary, and to figure out what the other will do in response to our own moves.

As we know, negotiations can become so dangerous and threatening to one's face that we have to resort to neutral third parties as catalysts, go-betweens, message carriers, and the like. Often what is most needed is to explain the values and goals of each principal to the other. Principals often lack the skills to reveal themselves to each other without making themselves seem either too vulnerable or too threatening.[5]

One of my Australian manager friends speculated that a lack of verbal articulation skills seriously hampers negotiation in his country. He noticed that in many labor-management confrontations in Australia each side would blurt out bluntly, and with some pride at their own ability to be so open, exactly what their *final* demands were. When these demands proved to be incompatible, an impasse occurred. The situation then deteriorated to name calling and to seeing the other side as being stubborn and exploitative. This manager speculated that the educational system was partly responsible for this situation in that written English is heavily emphasized in school while spoken English is hardly attended to at all. He thought of Australians as being quite inarticulate, on the average, and therefore at a real disadvantage in face-to-face negotiations.

The important point is to recognize that openness is not an absolute value in face-to-face relationships. For some purposes, it is better not to reveal exactly where one stands. One of the ways that relationships become more intimate is through successive minimal self-revelations which constitute interpersonal tests of acceptance: if you accept this much of me, then perhaps I can run the risk of revealing a bit more of myself. Total openness may be safe and charming when total acceptance is guaranteed, but it can become highly

dangerous when goals are not compatible, and acceptance is therefore not guaranteed at all.[6]

INTERPERSONAL AND CROSS-CULTURAL TACT

Negotiation requires great tact. The tactfulness I refer to here is the *behavioral* manifestation of the cultural humility discussed above. If we don't feel humble in the face of others' values, we will certainly offend them. On the other hand, if we feel that there is genuinely room for different values in this world, then we have the basis for showing in our speech and behavior an adequate level of respect for others.

REPAIR STRATEGIES AND SKILLS

The repair strategies and repair skills needed to fix broken or spoiled relationships, careers, lives, negotiations, and other interpersonal or intergroup situations are probably the most important yet least understood of face-to-face skills. As the world becomes more complex and more intercultural, there will be more communication breakdowns, diplomatic disasters, losses of confidence and trust, hurt feelings between individuals and groups, hostilities, wars, and other forms of social pathology and disorder. It will not help us to resign ourselves to such situations, to lament our cruel fate, or to merely explain why something happened; what *will* be helpful is our attempting to repair these situations.

The concept of "repair strategies" was brought to my attention by Jacqueline Goodnow, a cognitive social psychologist who now teaches in Australia. She has been struck by the Australian tendency to "knock" things rather than to solve problems. I often heard the phrase in Australia that "we are a nation of knockers," which means that when things go wrong there is a tendency to blame government, unions, management, multinationals, OPEC, or any other handy group rather than to figure out how to repair the situation.

THE PERCEPTION OF NEW ELEMENTS

Repair strategies presume and require not only constructive motivation but also *the ability to see new elements in the situation which one may not have noticed before*. The new elements may be in *oneself*; one may discover that one has been unfair or selfish, or lacking insight concerning the consequences of one's own behavior or concerning one's true motives. In this instance repair may begin with apology.

One may also discover new things in the *other people* in the situation; *they may have changed in significant ways*. One of the most damaging things we do in our face-to-face relationships is to freeze our assumptions about ourselves and others. Our stereotype of the other person can become a straight jacket or a self-fulfilling prophecy. McGregor gave us the best example of this years ago in noting that if we assume people are lazy we will begin to treat them as if they *are* lazy, which will eventually train them to *be* lazy.[7] The energy and creativity which they might have applied to their jobs then gets channeled either into other situations or into angry attempts to defeat the organization.

We want and need predictability in our relationships, but that very need often prevents us from repairing damaged relationships. It may be psychologically easier to see the worker as lazy and hostile because we can then predict his or her behavior and can know exactly how to respond. To renegotiate the relationship, to permit some participation, or to admit that we may have been wrong in our assessment is to make ourselves psychologically vulnerable. We then enter a period in the relationship that may be less predictable.

As in the case of negotiation, we may need the help of third parties—counselors, therapists, consultants, or other helpers—to get through the period of vulnerability and instability. Often the motivation to repair is there but the skill is not—in the sense that neither party has self-insight, the capacity to hear the values or goals of the other, the articulateness to negotiate without further destruction of face, or the emotional strength or self-confidence to make concessions to reach at least a common ground of understanding.

TAKING THE OTHER'S PERSPECTIVE

Sociologists taught us long ago that in childhood the very process of becoming social is a process of learning to take the role of the other. We could

not really understand each other at all—even though we live in the same culture and speak the same language—without the ability to put ourselves in the other person's shoes. We could not develop judgments, standards, and morals without the ability to see our own behavior from the standpoint of others, which gradually becomes abstracted into what sociologists call the "generalized other," or what we sometimes label as our "reference group." Guilt and shame, the products of one's internalized conscience, can be thought of as the accumulated empathy of a decade of growing up. As adults we have the capacity to see ourselves from others' perspectives and this capacity should help us to develop repair strategies. Why is it, then, that so often we end up in complete disagreement, convinced that the only thing the other party really wants is to gain a selfish advantage at our expense?

One factor certainly is our need to maintain our position and our pride. Having suffered an affront, a loss of face, or a loss of advantage sometime in the past, we feel the only safe thing to do is to protect ourselves from any repetition of such an unpleasant event. We may, in addition, recognize that our own interest and that of the other party are genuinely in conflict. If we are in a zero-sum game, we may not be able to afford too much sympathy for our opponent. In such an instance, a repair strategy would call for the ability to locate some superordinate goals, where goal conflict is not intrinsic, and to build a new set of interactions around such superordinate goals. Skillful diplomats, negotiators, and statesmen build their entire careers around the development of such repair strategies. They create one repair strategy after another as the people they deal with destroy one relationship after another.

Ordinary day-to-day relations within families, between managers and subordinates, and between groups in organizations are forever in danger of breaking down. We must be prepared to diagnose the situation when breakdown occurs and to have the skills to repair it, if repair is needed. . . .

THE INTERPLAY OF FACE-TO-FACE SKILLS

Each party in the relationship must first achieve some self-insight, some sense of one's own commitments so that defensiveness and denial can be reduced. We cannot hear others if we cannot accept ourselves. Next we need the kind of cross-cultural sensitivity I have been talking about, the relaxed, open ability to hear others' values with empathy and perspective. Once we can hear each other, we can begin to seek the common ground, the goals or aspirations around which some common activities can be designed; we can begin to renegotiate the relationships to make it possible for the desirable activities to happen. If, in hearing each other, we find a genuine lack of common ground, we can negotiate a reduced level of intimacy in the relationship yet maintain a high degree of mutual acceptance of what each cares about; this can lead to nondestructive separations, more limited interactions with children, or both.

LABOR-MANAGEMENT RELATIONS

My second example has to do with face-to-face skills and repair strategies in labor-management situations. I am struck by the degree to which these situations seem to turn into intergroup struggles—struggles among unions, managements, and government bodies or political parties. Once the conflicts have escalated to the intergroup level, it is easy to give up one's proactive problem solving orientation and to resign oneself to the idea that the problem is essentially unsolvable. Yet when one looks at successful enterprises—those which have managed to maintain harmony between management and employees—one realizes that the key to this harmony is a high degree of mutual trust, active listening, appropriate levels of participation, and consistently constructive face-to-face communications.

An example will highlight what I mean. A plant manager told me that he had spent many years developing a constructive relationship with his employees, in spite of the fact that they belong to a strong national union which periodically calls for national strikes. One year his employees refused to strike. They were told by the national union that it would get all the suppliers of the plant to refuse to deliver, thus effectively shutting the plant down. Under these conditions, the manager and the employees got together and

agreed that the employees should go out on strike, but everyone knew that it was not over local issues. The manager did not hold it against his subordinates that they had gone out on strike.

Intergroup trust, reinforced by open face-to-face communications on relevant issues, was strong enough to keep this plant functioning well even in a larger context that made periodic strikes inevitable. What we can learn from this is that constructive face-to-face relationships are necessary even though they may not be sufficient. Solving a problem at the national level will probably be useless if there continue to be destructive low-trust relationships within the enterprise.

DISENGAGING THE CRITICAL MIND

Achieving trust in a labor-management situation that has developed into a hostile intergroup conflict over a period of decades seems like a tall order. One prerequisite to working out the problem at the group level will be, as I have argued, the reestablishment of constructive face-to-face relationships. This will only be possible if both managers and workers find a way to see each other in less stereotypic ways. There is a need here to introduce in the interpersonal arena what Zen, gestalt training, encounter groups, and other training programs have emphasized—relaxing the active critical mind enough to let our eyes and ears see and hear what is really out there rather than what we *expect* to see and hear. Just as the person who is learning to draw must suspend what he or she knows intellectually about what things should look like, and, instead, must learn to see what is really out there, so the person concerned about repairing human relationships must first see not what he or she expects or knows should be there, but what is actually there.[8]

I don't think it is accidental that Americans are so preoccupied with sensitivity training, Zen meditation, inner tennis, and, most recently, right-side brain functions.[9] What all of these programs and approaches have in common is a focus on learning how to perceive oneself, others, and the environment realistically, which apparently requires a certain relaxation of our active critical functions and a deliberate disengaging of our analytical selves. We cannot improve face-to-face relationships if we cannot perceive accurately. And accurate seeing and hearing is for many of us a lost skill that we must somehow regain. The place to begin practicing this skill is in our families and in our immediate superior-subordinate and peer relations.

If we cannot see ourselves and others in this relaxed, uncritical way, then we cannot develop perspective, humility, or tact, and we run the danger of acting on incorrect data. On the other hand, if we can really learn to see each other, and if we can combine more accurate perception with the ninth element in my list—patience—then we have some chance of improving and repairing face-to-face relationships. . . .

NOTES

1. See P.R. Lawrence and J.W. Lorsch, *Organization and Environment* (Boston: Division of Research, Harvard Business School, 1967).

2. See E. Goffman, *Interaction Ritual* (Chicago: Aldine, 1967).

3. See E. Hall, *Beyond Culture* (Garden City, NY: Anchor, 1977).

4. See: E.H. Schein, *Organizational Psychology*, 3rd ed. (Englewood Cliffs, NJ: Prentice-Hall, 1980), chs. 9 and 13; T.A. Harris, *I'm OK—You're OK* (New York: Avon, 1967); E. Polster and M. Polster, *Gestalt Therapy Integrated* (New York: Bruner/Mazel, 1973).

5. See R.E. Walton, *Interpersonal Peacemaking: Confrontations and Third-Party Consultation* (Reading, MA: Addison-Wesley, 1969).

6. See W. Bennis, J. Van Maanen, E.H. Schein, and F.I. Steele, *Essays in Interpersonal Dynamics* (Homewood, IL: Dorsey, 1979).

7. See D. McGregor, *The Human Side of Enterprise* (New York: McGraw-Hill, 1960).

8. See B. Edwards, *Drawing on the Right Side of the Brain* (Los Angeles: J.P. Tarcher, 1979); F. Frank, *The Zen of Seeing* (New York: Vintage, 1973).

9. See R.E. Ornstein, *The Psychology of Consciousness* (San Francisco: W.H. Freeman, 1972).

OD PERSPECTIVES ON HIGH PERFORMANCE

Robert T. Golembiewski

. . . What do we reasonably know about how to induce superior performance in organizations, with special reference to merit pay plans? My orientation will be consistent with what is called Organization Development, or OD. I have written elsewhere at length about various aspects of OD as they apply in the public sector (e.g., Golembiewski, 1978; 1979; 1985). Here note only that the OD success rates—both in business and government—are quite high (e.g., Golembiewski et al., 1981). This suggests that the theory and experience underlying OD are tolerably useful, given that major theoretical and practical lacunae exist. I emphasize these success rates because their underlying theory and experience will be reflected in the summary below of OD perspectives on superior performance.

In general, this review of OD perspectives reflects much good news, but also some that is very bad.

As for the good news, we have a tolerably precise view of how to induce superior performance in an OD mode. Major aspects of such an approach will be reviewed below, with an emphasis on how they relate to intrinsic features of work as well as to extrinsic rewards such as merit pay. This good news is tempered by a crucial requirement: even the very best medicine cannot do you any good if you spit it out. Hence involvement in, and ownership of, changes in an OD mode are always required. There are no quick-fixes of policy, structure, or procedure, nor any imposition downward from the tops of hierarchies.

Now for the basic bad news. Most of concern with compensation has a Band Aid quality, with compensation plans used as patches intended to remedy weak points of the bureaucratic structure

and spirit that dominate both public and business organizations. Moreover, until recently (e.g., Lawler, 1981), few installations of compensation plans have been guided by OD orientations, given signal exceptions such as firms like TRW. Oppositely, indeed, most traditional management systems rest on values that flatly contradict OD values, and that is as true for compensation plans as for other sets of policies/procedures (e.g., Golembiewski, 1963).

A bit of history will be helpful here. OD intervenors did not replace bureaucratic biases by developing compensation plans compatible with OD values. Rather, OD intervenors focused on interaction—early through the emphasis on T-Groups, and more lately via the great attention given to team building or development. The goal: to build an appropriate culture first, which infrastructure would guide the subsequent development of policies, procedures, and structures. This often proved awkward. Evidence indicates that simultaneous emphasis on both interaction and policies/procedures/structures is ideal (e.g., Marrow et al., 1967). Moreover, despite evidence that the traditional primary focus on "process" can and does "work" (e.g., Golembiewski and Carrigan, 1970a; 1970b), failure to apply such planned cultures to the reconstruction of formal systems promptly can be counterproductive. Seductively, the very success of interaction-first approaches in inducing an "era of good feelings"—interpersonal openness and even warmth—can have the paradoxical effect of assigning too low a priority to such reconstructive work on systems. Consequently, the last 5–10 years have seen more explicit OD attention to policies, procedures, and structures generally, and specifically to compensation plans (e.g., Lawler, 1981).

These caveats aside, what does OD theory and practice tell us about installing compensation plans likely to generate high-level performance? Four themes will get attention, in turn. Each will contribute powerfully to the success of various technical applications such as merit pay programs.

- sufficient "cultural preparedness," or development of a set of values and associated skills to guide interaction and search

- overarching goals to guide decision-making, a full "culture" with norms, myths, and so on
- a structural model that encourages integrative effort
- a compatible set of organizational sub-systems

Major behavioral findings relevant to the success or failure of compensation plans such as merit pay are highlighted below.

USEFUL GUIDES FOR INTERACTION

Formal systems like compensation plans have the most impact when they rest on patterns of interaction that facilitate the formation and maintenance of agreement. Without such guides, formal systems may prove counterproductive.

In OD parlance, this prescription urges up-front attention to what might be called the "cultural preparedness" of the host for a formal system. Figure 1 provides one convenient way of illustrating this central point. Most organizations are characterized by degenerative interaction, of which the common consequences often excite native cunning if not paranoid suspicion by employees even about formal plans that are definitely in the individual's self-interest. The "probable consequences" illustrated in Figure 1 suggest the multiple forms in which degenerative interaction can burden or overwhelm the development and application of formal systems.

Hence the OD prescription for regenerative interaction as pre-work for installation of merit pay plans. Patently, such plans often will involve some kind of performance measurement and appraisal, and high trust (among other factors) will help make the best of what typically is a difficult process fraught with opportunities to point accusing fingers.

This OD prescription is not for "pie-in-the-sky, bye-and-bye." Appropriate designs are available to induce such change, and their theoretical bases have attained a tolerable specificity over two and more decades of experience (e.g., Golembiewski, 1979, Vol. 1). Moreover, the success rates in multiple evaluation studies range from 50 to 90 percent, depending on the population and the specific measures of "success" (e.g., Nicholas, 1982; Golembiewski, 1985). Relevantly, success rates differ little in public vs. business settings; and public applications are proportionately as common as those in other sectors (Golembiewski, et al., 1981). Both facts contradict the usual stereotypes, but so much the worse for those stereotypes.

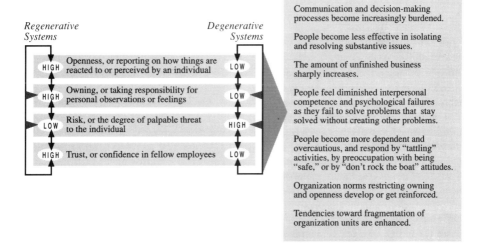

FIGURE 1
A Contrast of Two Idealized Patterns of Interaction

In general, the dilemma/invention model underlies transitions toward regenerative interaction. Different presenting conditions—a new work group, a "crisis of agreement" or a "crisis of disagreement," etc. (e.g., Dyer, 1977; Golembiewski, 1979, Vol. 2: 152–161)—will require different learning designs. Commonly, however, individuals prefer moving toward regenerative interaction; the values underlying them, and the actual state typically differs more or less radically from this ideal. That is the "dilemma." Greater clarity about the ideal and the actual state highlights the discrepancy, which usually induces motivational energies to reduce the discrepancy and thus to diminish the sense of psychological failure. These energies often get effectively directed at "invention."

Note that individual groups often will differ widely in the details of both their dilemmas and inventions, even when in the same organization and doing identical tasks. By hypothesis, this provides an explanation of an apparent paradox. Success rates for applications to single teams or groups approximate 75–90 percent, *for cases of disagreement or conflict* (Golembiewski, 1979, Vol. 1: 336–344), a conclusion about which I am so confident that I contract not to accept a consultant's fee if evaluation does not support my expectations. But the experience with *a single design* applied to a collection of work units is quite mixed (e.g., Porras and Wilkins, 1980; Eden, 1985). Credibly, in short, diagnosis of specific loci of application should precede the choice of design. Moreover, not only does a crisis of agreement—e.g., Janis' (1972) "groupthink"—require a different design, but I estimate success rates are very low for this presenting condition.

For various reasons, and particularly because public compensation and benefits specialists have been little influenced by OD philosophy and practice, public efforts typically give precious little up-front attention to the induction of regenerative interaction. Little or no resources, for example, were so earmarked in the 1978 federal effort to inaugurate merit compensation for senior officials. Indeed, if anything, the development and application of the pay policies of the Civil Service Reform Act heightened degenerative interaction. The failures to gain appropriate supporting legislation and appropriations are well-known (e.g., Gaertner

and Gaertner, 1985). Moreover, the uneven processes of selecting merit pay recipients often bred distrust, if not resentful mockery, in the absence of suitable interaction such as that described by the regenerative model. To illustrate this conclusion, I am reliably informed that one agency used a curious way of selecting that 20 percent of its executives who by law could get bonuses in a particular year. All executives were listed alphabetically and—you guessed it—the first-fifth of the roster was ticketed for awards in Year 1. The turn for the second-fifth would come in Year 2, and so on.

Tragic.

Such gross curiosities no doubt are untypical, but the general point holds. Merit plans require a substantial up-front trust and confidence, especially given that differences in judgement always will exist, errors will occur, and personnel atrocities will be rumored, at least. Regenerative interaction proposes to provide a socio-emotional infrastructure to cushion these probabilities or inevitabilities.

Regenerative interaction seems to meet individual needs, it should be patent. Interested readers can develop the analysis easily enough—e.g., by showing how openness can meet such Argyrian dimensions for self-actualization as a long time perspective, interdependence vs. dependence, and self-discipline vs. control by others.

AN APPROPRIATE CULTURE

Incentive systems generally, and merit plans particularly, need to be nested in supportive "cultures." Appropriate-culture creation should be viewed as conceptually related to the development and application of formal systems like merit pay, and often as requiring prior attention.

The significance of "tight cultures" is much with us nowadays, of course (e.g., Peters and Waterman, 1982; Deal and Kennedy, 1982). Indeed, good reasons support this current version of *the* managerial schemes being advertised everywhere and sold to many organizations. Cultures are value-filled, that is to say, and they permit self-discipline while they also define definite parameters for the exercise of bounded-freedom.

That is, people know what things are important; decisions are likely to "fit" because their broad parameters have been pre-programmed; and individuals can experience the sense of personal transcendence that comes from being part of a morally-consequential and value-bounded enterprise. Such factors provide an uplifting context for the banality and repetition that are an inevitable part of every collective enterprise.

"Culture" or "character" may be thought of as a substantially-integrated statement of general agreements about ideals involving several major domains. For example, one may reasonably view "culture" as specifying content for these three aspects of organizations:

- niche, which relates to the portfolio of goods and services provided
- standing, which relates to the intended rank-of-performance within a niche, compared to other organizations providing similar goods and services, or compared to some ideal standards where no counterparts exist
- style, or the specific ways in which an organization's members are to go about acting on niche and standing.

Substantial variability in organization "cultures" exists in the natural state. As is well-known (e.g., Thompson, 1956; Goodsell, 1985), sub-units of even highly-bureaucratized agencies in the same niche not only can have different standings but may also reflect profoundly-contrasting styles. Legislation may go a substantial distance toward circumscribing or even determining niche, but the complex value-infusing processes underlying standing and style derive from more diverse sources—from personalities, the times, managerial philosophies, the vagaries of chance (Kaufman, 1985), and so on.

Over the past two decades, especially, conscious attention has been devoted to inducing organizational "cultures" or "styles" or "characters" with quite specific properties. Both businesses (e.g., Golembiewski and Carrigan, 1970a, 1970b) and public agencies (Golembiewski and Kiepper, 1976; 1983a; 1983b) have been hosts of such cultural transformations. No doubt the most frequent efforts of this kind have occurred at the plant level in American industry (e.g., Perkins, Nieva, and Lawler, 1983). In the public sector, perhaps the most extensive cases involved the U.S. Department of State (e.g., Warrick, 1975) and the early NASA (Sayles and Chandler, 1971). Although the former effort "failed" in a public sense and the latter "succeeded," both share basic cultural commonalities. Table 1 details some of the commonalities, relying on a NASA label—self-forcing, self-enforcing system. For contrast, the culture common in bureaucratic organizations is also sketched in Table 1.

TABLE 1
Sketches of Two Opposing "Cultures" or "Characters"

Components of Traditional Cultures	Components of Self-Forcing, Self-Enforcing Cultures
1. one-to-one bias in relationships	1. multiple relationships: e.g., one-to-one, one-to-many, many-to-many
2. norms against the sharing of data, especially with superiors about negative evaluations of peers	2. norms support the sharing of all data positive and negative, at all levels
3. interaction characterized by closedness or severely-hedged openness	3. interaction characterized by trust, at least as a presumption until explicitly violated
4. focus on the "part"—on jurisdictions and roles	4. focus on the "whole"—on integrated flows of work
5. practices and norms oriented toward avoiding blame and seeking credit	5. toward "automatic responsibility" and toward seeking solutions

See Golembiewski (1979), Vol. II: 61–69.

The contrasting implications of the two organizational cultures or styles should be apparent, in general. Regenerative interaction poorly suits the bureaucratic model, for example. There, trust, owning, and openness will be low, while risk will be high. Moreover, the social balkanization in the bureaucratic style will in several ways inhibit the development and application of broadly-accepted merit plans, almost by definition.

Let us go a bit beyond generalities, with the knowledge that even this "bit" is well beyond most public-sector experience but with the conviction that practical expressions do exist of the two thrusts sketched above. What do compensation systems look like, what products does their philosophy generate, when regenerative interaction and non-traditional cultures exist? Illustratively:

- system *knowledge* about compensation will be deep and detailed and available to all employees—in programs like "open job-posting," in such details as the size of "bonus pots," and especially in an understanding acceptance of the local principles underlying compensation decisions
- system *features* will be dominated by an orientation toward meeting employee needs and by implied trust in employees, as in "cafeteria benefit programs" that increase employee influence over the character and form of compensation and that are responsive to changing conditions of employees
- system *administration* will provide multiple opportunities for employee involvement and participation, as in peer appraisal of performance and in awarding merit pay, bonuses, and promotions
- system *design* will reflect involvement *and* impact of broad ranges of employees, ideally at start-up but also in periodic reviews and updates

Different organizations will reflect different mixes of these four perspectives—on system knowledge, features, administration, and design—depending on where they start from, and how long they have been working at building regenerative interaction and a culture supporting pay-for-performance. The most fulsome experience has been in businesses, to be sure (e.g., Lawler, 1981). . . .

COMPATIBLE ORGANIZATION SUB-SYSTEMS

. . . Experience of the last decade or so permits a comprehensive view of the kind and character of managerial sub-systems that will evolve in response to efforts to integrate those emphases. Table 2 "puts it all together," as it were, building mainly on experience in the business sector inspired by the *quality of workinglife* movement focused largely on the plant level (e.g., Perkins, et al., 1983; Zager and Rosow, 1982). Generally, this experience rests on a basic exchange: high involvement and performance require that work be need-satisfying across a broad range. Competitive pressures have encouraged such system-building, as has the pace of change. Value commitments also undergird such approaches to "industrial humanism" (e.g., Bernstein, 1980; Nightingale, 1982; Golembiewski, 1985).

Table 2 is largely self-explanatory. . . . Detail is available elsewhere (e.g., Golembiewski, 1986a, and 1986b) but, in general, the point is that merit plans should not be thought of in isolation from other managerial sub-systems. Pay plans can either reinforce the thrust of other sub-systems, or subvert their thrust. More specifically, the Table 2 work setting contrasts pointedly, and point-by-point, with traditional . . . worksettings. In general, Table 2 systems are oriented toward problem-solving rather than hierarchy-serving, and the several sub-systems ideally reinforce this orientation. Table 2 distinguishes 10 sub-systems of a high-performing organization and, although more could be distinguished, the ten provide a reasonably comprehensive view of the sub-systems compatible with merit pay and other policies for gain-sharing or cost-saving.

Consider a mundane example of the Table 2 philosophy—employee parking. Given traditional thoughtways, the guideline for designing and locating parking spaces is simple and sovereign: "them what has, gets." High-status individuals get prime locations, typically reserved and perhaps even covered. Others scramble for what is left over, and often will have the opportunity—given executive travel—to reflect on the paradoxes of organizational life as they rush past unoccupied spaces to avoid a sudden shower or other inclemencies. In the system intending high

TABLE 2
Characteristics of High-Performing Settings

I. Organization Structure
- Designed around teams handling a flow of work vs. departmentation around separate tasks
- Oriented toward low-cost performance on a flow of work ("lean") vs. gaining authorization of large cadres of separate functional/processual specialists ("fat")
- Few hierarchical levels and supervisors
- Little reliance on conventions such as "line" and "staff"
- Uses participative council or other similar decision-making bodies at plant as well as lower levels

II. Job Design
- Emphasis is on challenging and motivating jobs
- Jobs are enriched
- Autonomous teams are utilized
- Oriented around increasing employee/team control over work

III. Information System
- Has open, multi-lateral, and multi-channel features
- Carries broad range of data on many topics related to jobs
- Deliberately seeks to stimulate upward as well as downward communication

IV. Career System
- Provides several tracks for employee growth and development, with counseling available
- Rests on mobility-enhancing features, e.g., open job posting and active training efforts

V. Selection
- Based on realistic preview of job responsibilities, with an emphasis on helping potential employees to ascertain the degree of "fit" between organization and personal skills/preferences
- Strong team input, as in interviewing as well as in decision to hire
- Emphasis on potential for learning and inter-personal process skills
- Heavy commitment of resources

VI. Training
- Involves peers and intact teams
- Emphasizes economic education and interpersonal skills
- Heavy commitment of resources

VII. Reward System
- Has strong egalitarian features, as in having all salaried employees as opposed to white-collar vs. blue-collar
- Based on skills possessed, rather than specific tasks actually performed
- Encourages skill development, even far beyond tasks currently performed
- Includes gain-sharing, ownership, or other features to enhance motivation by tying rewards to performance

VIII. Authority System
- Has major participative features, in cases extending to substantial employee control over production processes and other central aspects of work
- Reflects strong bias toward "law of the situation" rather than toward hierarchy, toward who has the skills or information rather than who has the rank
- Relies on clear and shared measures of performance and goals, which change the quality of management and supervision from monitoring to facilitating performance, from ordering to coaching, from exerting influence to respecting a common discipline

(continued)

TABLE 2 *(continued)*
Characteristics of High-Performing Settings

IX. Personnel Policies
- Emphasize stability of employment
- Focus on performance rather than hierarchy
- Established on basis of strong participative input

X. Physical Lay-Out
- Reduces or eliminates invidious status distinctions
- Is safe and pleasant
- Is defined in accordance with flow of work and organization structure, e.g., decision-making rooms near several worksites

---

Nine of the 10 categories come from Perkins *et al.*, 1983: 14. The several characteristics are conflated from personal observation and several sources: Perkins *et al.*, 1983: 5–15; Golembiewski, 1965; Walton, 1977: 422–433; and Zager and Roscow, 1982.

---

involvement, the focus is far more on encouraging and rewarding superior performance, which means avoiding the sending of mixed messages as much as sending intended ones. Witness this resolution of parking priorities congenial to Table 2. How to use decisions about who-parks-where to contribute to enhanced performance, or at least to avoid reducing performance? Some organizations reserve only a few prestige locations which get assigned, irrespective of job-level, to the high-performers of the past week or month. *Everyone else* takes a space on a first-come, first-served basis.

The details of Table 2 will not necessarily apply in all work settings, even as that visual summarizes the experience at the plant level in industry. That is, "office work" may not be easily adapted to some of the exhibit's features. But Table 2 is intended as a general rather than as a specific template for designing all work settings. Table 2 reflects one set of ways in which a consistent philosophy can influence the development of the major sub-systems whose combination we normally label "organization."

REFERENCES

ARGYRIS, C. (1957). *Personality and Organization.* New York: Harper & Row.

BERNSTEIN, P. (1980). *Workplace Democratization.* New Brunswick, N.J.: Transaction Books.

DEAL, T. E. and A. A. KENNEDY (1982). *Corporate Cultures.* Reading, Mass.: Addison-Wesley.

DYER, W. (1977). *Team Building.* Reading, Mass.: Addison-Wesley.

EDEN, D. (1985). "Team Development." *Journal of Applied Psychology* 70: 94–100.

FORD, R. (1969). *Motivation in the Work Itself.* New York: American Management Association.

GAERTNER, K. N. and G. H. GAERTNER (1985). "Performance-Contingent Pay for Federal Mangers." *Administration and Society* 17: 7–20.

GOLEMBIEWSKI, R. T. (1963). "A Behavioral Approach to Wage Administration." *Academy of Management Journal* 6: 366–377.

——— (1965). *Men, Management, and Morality.* New York: McGraw-Hill.

——— (1979). *Approaches to Planned Change,* Vols. I and II. New York: Marcel Dekker.

——— (1984). "Organizing Public Work, Round Three," pp. 237–270 in R. T. Golembiewski and A. Wildavsky (eds.) *The Costs of Federalism.* New Brunswick, N.J.: Transaction.

——— (1985). *Humanizing Public Organizations.* Mt. Airy, Md.: Lomond.

——— (1986a). "Public-Sector Organization: Why Theory and Practice Should Emphasize Purpose, and How to Do So," in R. C. Walker (ed.) *A Centennial History of the American Administrative State.* New York: Macmillan.

——— (1986b). "Linking Interaction and Techno-Structural Emphases: A Synthesis for High-Performing Organizations." *Journal of Health and Human Resources Administration* (in press).

——— (1987). "Why Theory and Practice Should Empha- size Purpose, and How to Do So," in R. C. Walker (ed.), *A Centennial History of the American Administrative State.* New York: Macmillan, in press.

GOLEMBIEWSKI, R. T. and S. B. CARRIGAN (1970a). "Planned Change in Organization Style Based on Laboratory Approach." *Administrative Science Quarterly* 15: 330–340.

———, (1970b). "The Persistence of Laboratory-Induced Changes in Organization Styles." *Administrative Science Quarterly* 15: 330–340.

GOLEMBIEWSKI, R. T. and W. EDDY (1978). *Organization Development in Public Administration.* New York: Marcel Dekker.

GOLEMBIEWSKI, R. T. and A. KIEPPER (1976). "MARTA: Toward an Effective Open Giant." *Public Administration Review* 36: 46-60.

———, (1983a). "Organizational Transition in a Fast-Paced Public Project." *Public Administration Review* 43: 247–254.

———, (1983b). "Lessons from a Fast-Paced Public Project." *Public Administration Review* 43: 547–556.

GOLEMBIEWSKI, R. T., C. W. PROEHL, JR., and D. SINK (1981). "Success of OD Applications in the Public Sector." *Public Administration Review* 41: 679–682.

GOODSELL, C. T. (1985). *The Case for Bureaucracy.* Chatham, N.J.: Chatham House.

HERZBERG, F., B. MAUSNER, and B. B. SNYDERMAN (1959). *The Motivation to Work.* New York: Wiley.

JANIS, I. (1972). *Groupthink.* Boston: Houghton-Mifflin.

KAUFMAN, H. (1985). *Time, Chance, and Organizations.* Chatham, N.J.: Chatham House.

LAWLER, E. E., III. (1981). *Pay and Organization Development.* Reading, Mass.: Addison-Wesley.

MARROW, A. D., S. SEASHORE, and D. G. BOWERS (1967). *Management by Participation.* New York: Harper & Row.

NICHOLAS, J. M. (1982). "The Comparative Impact of Organization Development Interventions on Hard Criteria Measures." *Academy of Management Journal* 7: 151–173.

NIGHTINGALE, D. V. (1982). *Workplace Democracy.* Toronto: University of Toronto Press.

PERKINS, D. T., V. F. NIEVA, and E. E. LAWLER, III. (1983). *Managing Creation.* New York: Wiley.

PETERS, T. J. and R. H. WATERMAN, JR. (1982). *In Search of Excellence.* New York: Harper & Row.

PORRAS, J. I., and A. WILKINS (1980). "Organization Development in a Large System." *Journal of Applied Behavioral Science* 16: 506–534.

SAYLES, L. R. and M. CHANDLER (1971). *Managing Large Systems.* New York: Harper & Row.

THOMPSON, J. D. (1956). "Authority and Power in Two 'Identical' Organizations." *American Journal of Sociology* 62: 290–301.

WALTON, R. (1977). "Work Innovations at Topeka." *Journal of Applied Behavioral Science* 13: 23–47.

WARRICK, D. P. (1975). *A Theory of Public Bureaucracy.* Cambridge, Mass.: Harvard University Press.

ZAGER, R. and M. P. ROSOW (eds.) (1982). *The Innovative Organization.* New York: Pergamon Press.

STRATEGIC PUBLIC MANAGEMENT AND PRODUCTIVITY: A "FIREHOUSE THEORY"

Barry Bozeman

The fundamental challenge for contemporary managers is no mystery: how to do more (or almost as much) with less. Thus far, the watchword of the 1980s has been "productivity." Productivity is a concern that knows no boundaries: the private sector has productivity problems of its own. The rate of productivity growth in the United States has been steadily falling since the mid-1960s. In the manufacturing sector the average annual rate of growth in labor productivity was a robust 3.13 percent between 1948 and 1965, but it declined to an average of 2.47 percent between 1965 and 1973 and 1.7 percent between 1973 and 1980.[1]

Problems of productivity and competitiveness crop up all over the board. As a result of a failure to retool and revitalize plants many steel companies are in danger. An inability to compete with low-wage foreign labor has virtually demolished the shoe industry. Even the U.S. General Services Administration is purchasing thousands of Japanese typewriters because they are less expensive and just as durable as those provided by domestic manufacturers. Speaking of the Japanese, seminars are springing up everywhere so we can learn about Japanese management techniques. And, of course, one of the first things the Japanese tell is that their management techniques are closely modeled on those developed, but underutilized, in the U.S.

Explanations for the declining rate of U.S. productivity abound. Some point to declining research and development expenditures,[2] others speak of the costs of complying with government regulations,[3] and still others offer pop sociology and tell us of the decline in the work ethic. But one of the most popular themes is the failure of management. Among the more important management problems are the rapidity of executive succession, the predominance of short-range perspectives, the distortion of incentives, and separation of ownership from the production process. In contrast to the widely documented organizational commitment of Japanese managers, American managers seem chiefly interested in climbing the career ladder as quickly as possible by achieving short-run results for superiors that have as little long-run stake in the organization as they. Managers then quickly move to another organization so that the same experience can be replicated at a higher level of the organizational pyramid.

My contention is that one of the most important obstacles to productivity in both business and government is the ascendancy of tactical management over strategic management. This is a problem that is not confined to any particular sector. Certainly many of the barriers to government productivity are different than those facing business but both are plagued by myopic management.

Productivity problems can't be solved by alchemy, wizardry or the quick fix. The key to doing more with less lies in how it is done. More effective management can do much to enhance productivity in government and business.

THE CHALLENGE OF STRATEGIC MANAGEMENT

There is no single prescription for management success. Effective management is, in part, the matching of strategy, resources, tasks and structure—and a match that works well in one context may not in another. Nevertheless, there are some management styles that are more often effective than others. I argue for a style of management that is more difficult to achieve under conditions of resource scarcity but, by the same token, is especially valuable during periods of retrenchment. I use the term strategic management to describe this style, but I am less concerned about nomenclature than the behavior that is required.

Simply stated, strategic management involves the development of contingent managerial strategies that can effectively respond to changeable policies and priorities. It encourages stability and a commitment to longer time horizons but, at the same time, allows for adaptability to change. Strategic management makes severe demands and requires uncommon talents. Not every manager, not even every gifted manager, will possess the innate abilities required for strategic management. But if strategic managers are almost always in short supply, they are also a tremendous resource. If strategic managers were just a little more plentiful and if organizational systems could exploit rather than frustrate their talents, many managerial problems might be greatly diminished. Before further describing strategic management let us contrast its general assumptions with those of other more common management styles including reactive management, responsive management and long-range planning. In contrasting styles of management, I refer to a typology that I've termed the "Firehouse Theory of Management Styles."

THE FIREHOUSE THEORY OF MANAGEMENT STYLES

We find four basic managerial styles in our firehouse, each embodying a different approach to fire-fighting. The reactive manager has developed a coherent approach to management and gives little thought to the relation of management to policy objectives. The reactive manager responds to emergent crises in an habitual and routine manner. The manager is not highly activated during periods when there is no crisis, but this is not usually a problem since there is almost always a crisis. When there is no real crisis the reactive manager can invent or imagine one. The reactive manager is an intrepid fire-fighter but is not much on fire prevention. Usually this is because he perceives himself as relatively powerless and if the fires he fights are not acts of God, they might as well be.

Resource scarcity reinforces reactive management even among those who are not by disposition reactive managers. With resource scarcity more of the crises are real rather than imagined and the problems are less tractable. Routine and habitual managerial responses may seem the only hedge

against the utter chaos that occurs as fires break out on every block.

The responsive manager, unlike the reactive manager, capably meets most managerial challenges and is generally viewed as effective. Indeed, the vast majority of good, productive managers are responsive managers. The responsive manager does not react in a routine or habitual fashion but has developed a repertoire of responses and attempts to match the problem or objective to some component of his repertoire. And the responsive manager does not indiscriminantly chase fires. He responds to a crisis but he also manages to achieve longer range objectives and carefully evaluates crises before allowing them to interrupt his normal work flow. The responsive manager is usually effective, but he is victim to a shortcoming that limits his range of effectiveness. His chief weakness is that he does little to anticipate change (reasoning that he has little control over broad policy matters and political events). He is satisfied to focus on attacking problems after they have been clearly established. He has skill and a repertoire of responses but not a managerial strategy. He adapts to his environment but his adaptation is limited.

The long-range planner, now a vanishing breed, is the polar opposite of the reactive manager. The long-range planner has the future mapped out and steadfastly refuses to let reality get in his way. His life, unlike the reactive manager, is not dominated by crisis. He is not a fire-fighter—in most instances he is inured to crises. In fact, he sets more fires than he puts out. As small unattended fires become raging infernos, the long-range planner and his plans are likely candidates for incineration.

The strategic manager, like the much maligned long-range planner, has a vision of management as something more than fire fighting and something more even than the matching of the appropriate response to a set policy problem. Unlike the long-range planner, the strategic manager's vision is clouded by the fine mist of reality. The strategic manager recognizes the limits on his freedom to set objectives and constraints on his ability to achieve objectives set by others. But whereas the less aggressive responsive manager seeks only to develop a broader range of responses so as to be prepared to meet unknown future demands, the strategic manager seeks to anticipate change. He is concerned with predicting fires, understanding fire hazards, and preventing fires.

Sometimes the strategic manager even seeks to manage change. He is no more prescient than the rest of us. The strategic manager's objective is not to tell the future but to minimize surprise. Accordingly, the strategic manager is sold on the value of hypothetical thinking. His goal is not simply to match his repertoire of responses to the demands of the moment, but to anticipate demands so that he may respond with greater care or so that he may develop new responses that might be required for a new set of circumstances. The strategic manager not only has objectives and strategies; he has multiple objectives and multiple strategies for meeting those objectives.

A strategic management style is no insurance of success. The requirements for effective strategic management are diverse. Among the most important is information management skills. An important element of strategic management is anticipation. Anticipation requires information, an ability to use information, and the imagination to fit together the pieces of a puzzle. The costs of information and certainty of uncertainty assure that some pieces of the puzzle will be missing. This makes management strategy even more important.

THE SKILLS OF THE STRATEGIC MANAGER

Strategic management requires a number of skills and it matters little whether the manager is located in a government office building or in the headquarters of a private corporation.

Space does not permit a full elaboration of the skills needed for strategic management. But I would like to identify a few and say a bit about each. I think effective strategic management requires skills in three related activities: information processing, politics, and analytical reasoning.

Information Processing Skills. The single feature that most distinguishes strategic managers from others is exceptional information processing ability. I do not mean that the strategic manager need be a computer jockey or even an avid reader. Nor does the strategic manager necessarily gather more information than others. Instead, he is concerned about information efficiency (gathering as much information as needed and no more), information balance (having the right kinds of information), information validity (having the correct information), and information synthesis (putting it all together in timely fashion).

Strategic management is not possible without considerable information processing ability. The chief distinguishing feature of the strategic manager is an ability to anticipate and understand change. This requires attention not only to the immediate environment of his organization but also to developments in technology and society that might impinge on managerial strategies and objectives. This requires receptivity to a variety of kinds of information as well as skills in making sense of the information.

One common mistake that managers make is seeking too much information, especially too much information of the wrong kind. Sometimes this is in the belief that if enough information is gathered, especially enough technical information, problems will solve themselves. This kind of reasoning in part flows from a misunderstanding of the types and uses of information. Most managers have need for three broad types of information: simple information, political information, and expository information. We can use the term "simple information" to refer to information that is uncomplicated and descriptive: information that is easily collected, coded, and can be stored in archives or computer files. It is readily available and is usually cheap, especially if economies of scale are involved and computer technology is available. Information about such matters as client-social worker ratios, units of goods and services provided, or number of vehicles registered are examples of simple information. This is "data" in the strictest sense: coded, discrete observations.

Another broad category of information can be referred to as "political information." Political information tells us about the preferences, self-interest, and power resources of others. Political information is sometimes scarce because it is highly changeable, easily misinterpreted and disclosure may be against the interest of relevant parties.

A third category, "expository information," provides an explanation. The explanation may be exact or approximate, true or false, rooted in evidence or intuition. Expository information can vary from scientific and technical information that seeks to explain events from information derived from scientific research, to organizational mythologies that seek to explain some event in relation to previous occurrences in the history of the organization.

The key point is that no single type of information is sufficient and one of the most important skills required of the strategic manager is determining the types of information needed and then fitting together a sometimes odd mixture that may include data from organizational records, findings reported in technical journals, an experienced employee's recollections of a previous program, and information about clients' reactions to a program. The magic is in the mix.

This general point implies another: the strategic manager must develop an information system (and here I use the term broadly), that is expansive but at the same time efficient. The strategic manager develops respect for a variety of sources of information and develops an ability to work with everything from (if available) interactive computer terminals to so-called "invisible colleges" comprised of individuals working on similar problems and informally sharing needed information.

And what about computers? The strategic manager is neither techniphobe nor technophile. He realizes that computers can be quite useful for certain narrow-gauged problem-solving activities but he also knows their limits. He is concerned about hardware and software, but he is just as concerned about "humanware": that is, the need to develop effective informal communications among people.

Political Skills. Every manager needs some minimal political skills to survive even the most benign political environment. One of the most important skills in "the art of the possible" (as politics is sometimes called) is knowing what is not possible. The aim of the strategic manager is to shape existing resources, opportunities and constraints so as to produce the best possible outcome. Sometimes the best possible outcome will be satisfactory, sometimes it will be virtually ideal, and sometimes it will be rotten. By having a good notion of the feasibility of various levels of accomplishment the strategic manager efficiently exercises power.

Power is a scarce resource, especially for middle managers, and must be used with care. Whatever the source of power—coercion, persuasion, blackmail, charisma—power is quickly consumed once its potential energy is converted to kinetic. The strategic manager is particularly adept at the conservation of power. He is not a fighter of lost causes; instead he accepts lost causes as constraints and modifies his managerial strategies accordingly. By the same token, he does not shy away from using available power resources when it is clear that the issue is important and its outcome hangs in the balance. And since he is also skilled in information processing and analytical reasoning, he is better able than most to make such computations.

Another political skill that is more important for strategic managers than others is a skill that has been called "constituency analysis." The strategic manager must be able to understand the interests and values of others, especially as they might pertain to an anticipated problem. This is particularly difficult because the other parties to the anticipated problem may not have yet taken a position because they may not have yet recognized the problem. Remember, the strategic manager anticipates problems and opportunities that others might overlook. By correctly gauging the interests, values and actions of constituencies, the strategic manager can formulate a managerial strategy, refine it and, if necessary, make modifications, before others have even become aware of the problem. Such is the value of information.

Analytical Skills. Strategic managers must have superior analytical skills but this does not mean that they need be well versed in statistics, mathematics or such tools as linear programming or accounting (though such skills are often helpful). The analytical skills required of the strategic manager are especially demanding because they cannot easily be obtained from formal training. The most important analytical skill is the ability to abstract one's self from the immediate environment and look for patterns and common events. In many cases managers become so inextricably tied to the immediate environment that every problem seems unique, site-specific, and ultimately, impenetrable.

Management consultants are often struck by the fact that problems that they've encountered dozens of times in a wide variety of organizations are perceived as absolutely unique by those persons directly affected by the problem. This is, of course, understandable. In a basic philosophical sense every problem and every set of events is unique. But the strategic manager cannot afford to see just the unique features of problems, he must also be vigilant in searching out points of commonality, patterns and generalizations. Otherwise there can be no learning, one can draw no lessons from experience, and any attempt to develop a coherent management strategy is thwarted.

But in seeking patterns the strategic manager must have enough analytical ability to look for something more than broad generalities. He must also look for, in the social scientist's terms, intervening variables. That is to say, he must be aware of the contingencies that are involved in various problems. Some of these contingencies come with known values and some with unknown values, some with high degrees of risk, others with little risk. The strategic manager is a "natural social scientist," seeking to determine patterns of causation, contingencies, constraining variables, and leverage points. The strategic manager is devoted to hypotheticals and is never too quick to accept explanations.

The strategic manager may be the last to say that he works with abstract models, and he may never commit them to paper, but, like any good analytical thinker, he is by necessity a model builder. Models, being nothing more than abstract simplifications of reality, are essential for anyone hoping to view the world as something more than a hopelessly confusing swirl of unique and unrelated events. The strategic manager's models, whether they be highly formalized and mathematical depictions or simple half-conscious assumptions about relationships among variables and outcomes, are of vital importance in developing managerial strategies.

A final skill required of the strategic manager is human relations ability. I haven't focused on this critial prerequisite of effective managment. This apparent neglect is not to diminish the importance of human relations skills; quite the contrary. I have said little about human relations skills because this is a prerequisite for any minimally effective approach to management. The skills the strategic manager cultivates are not developed in a social vacuum. Ultimately all management requires cooperative activity and human relations skills are vital to any managerial task.

CONCLUSION

In conclusion we might consider the prospects for strategic management. Certainly there are great barriers to the emergence of this approach to management: Overly rigid bureaucracies that constrain managerial freedom; reward systems that sometimes not only fail to reward creative management but act as a deterrent; fear of managerial innovation; high degrees of political turnover and executive succession.

Nevertheless I am cautiously optimistic. We have already borne witness to the grim challenges of austerity management. But scarcity only highlights the need for good management. Moreover, scarcity sometimes encourages creative response. Researchers tell us that innovative and risk-taking behavior are most likely under two quite different conditions: safe and resource-rich environments and unstable environments dominated by scarcity.

To put it another way, it looks like a great many fires are going to break out in the next decade. Maybe we will be exhausted from all the fire fighting and maybe we will be scorched by some of the fires, but we might also learn a lot more about fire fighting techniques.

NOTES

1. G. M. Kuper, Testimony in *Special Study on Economic Change*, U.S. Congress Joint Economic Committee (Washington, 1980).
2. National Science Foundation, *Research and Development in Industry* (Washington, 1979).
3. G. Christainsen, F. Gallop and R. Haveman, "Environmental and Health Safety Regulations, Productivity Growth and Economic Performance," U.S. Congress Joint Economic Committee (Washington, 1980).

COMPUTING AND PUBLIC ORGANIZATIONS

Kenneth L. Kraemer and John Leslie King

Use of computing has steadily permeated organizations in the past three decades, occasionally experienced dramatic expansions, and currently shows no signs of abating. The number of interactive users of computing increased fivefold from 1974 to 1984.[1] The increasing power and sophistication of computer systems as a function of price has had dramatic effects in expanding the availability and utility of computing, as illustrated by the introduction of microcomputers in 1980. At the same time, these changes raise questions about the long-term impacts of computing. A technology with such appeal and power undoubtedly affects the individuals and organizations that use it.

Most computing use takes place by individuals in organizations. Even with the growing use of personal computers in homes, formal organizations remain the dominant locus of computing activity and are expected to remain so until at least the year 2000. This article, therefore, focuses on computing in organizations, exploring the kinds of changes that have been observed and can be expected. In particular, it addresses the dynamics of computing use with respect to organizational structure, employment, quality of work life, decision making, organizational politics, and the management of computing in organizations.

The findings reported here are based on empirical research conducted into computing use in complex organizations over the past 15 years.[2] Most of the research has been conducted by the URBIS Group at the University of California, Irvine,[3] and has focused on computing in government, particularly local governments, both within the United States and in other developed countries. While important differences exist between local

governments and other public organizations, significant benefits are derived from selecting them as "laboratory animal" for study.[4] Moreover, comparison of findings from these studies across organizational contexts indicates that they are applicable to most public organizations and to private organizations in the service sector as well.

Great speculation exists about the effects which computerization *will have* on organizations, but considerably less empirical research exists about the effects which computing *does have* on organizations. Kling provides an overview of the larger organizational and social issues in computing.[5] Attewell and Rule provide a very useful summary of what we know and what we do not know about computing in *private* organizations, based on empirical research.[6] Both studies observed that there were few clear-cut answers to the key questions of how computers affect organizations.

The objective of this article is to draw together the findings from earlier research and to extend that knowledge through its integration with recent research on computing in organizations. The following sections therefore summarize the results of prior research and very recent research related to six topics: (1) computing and organization structure, (2) computing and employment, (3) computing and work life, (4) computing and decision making, (5) computing and organizational politics, and (6) the management of computing.

COMPUTING AND ORGANIZATIONAL STRUCTURE

Most of the debate about computing and organizational structure focuses on whether computing results in centralizing or decentralizing decision making in the organization. Centralization in this context refers to the distance between where a decision problem emerges and where in the organization's hierarchy decisions about that problem are made. Generally, a centralized organization is one in which most decisions are made at the top by a single individual or small group.

Those who claim a centralizing influence from computing cite one of two factors as relevant in this process. Leavitt and Whisler[7] predicted that computing systems would execute routine decisions and pass the remainder to top management along with monitoring and exception reporting systems that would signal needs for top management action. Thus, computing would centralize most organizational decision making by replacing human decision makers with machines and increasing top-management control. An alternative view of the centralizing influence of computing was based on the traditional tendency of organizations to centralize computing operations due to the economies of scale inherent in consolidation.[8] By centralizing the processing and storage of important information that could be used for decision making, the process of centralizing decision making would be easier to accomplish. Centralization of decision making would only occur, of course, when some individual or group exploited this potential.

Those who predict a decentralizing influence from computing have been less numerous than have those proclaiming centralization, but their numbers have increased with the advent of mini- and microcomputers.[9] They predict that through decentralized access to central information (provided through time-sharing systems, departmental minicomputers, distributed personal computers, and distribution of computer-based reports) many decisions formerly handled by top management would be handled by middle management and operatives, either because the decision authority would be delegated downward as information became more widely available or because middle managers and operatives would exploit the opportunity provided by the technology.

The empirical research suggests that computing *per se* is neither a centralizing nor a decentralizing influence. Most early studies of computing, and a few later ones, indicated that computing had a centralizing effect on organizational decision making.[10] Other studies concluded that computing had led to decentralization.[11] More recent systematic and empirical studies indicate that computing has resulted in centralization of some decisions and decentralization of others.[12]

Careful examination of these studies reveals that a simple characterization of computing as leading to greater centralization or decentralization of organizations is problematic. The context in which computing is used is a much stronger influence on whether organizations centralize or decentralize than is the technology. The technology supports either arrangement; which arrangement is followed in any particular instance is a function of organizational history, management, and politics. Often, as more recent studies show, computing involves elements of both centralization and decentralization, with central managers and staff obtaining greater oversight across decision areas (e.g., budget, staffing, performance) and operating managers and staff obtaining greater latitude within them.[13] In general, computing tends to reinforce the prevailing tendencies in organizations. Those that are inclined to centralize will tend to utilize computing to do so and vice versa.

These findings reveal a critical fact about computing and organizational structure: generally speaking, computing by itself is insufficient to affect organization structure in significant ways. An organization will not centralize or decentralize merely because computing begins. This does not mean, however, that computing plays no role in the structure of organizations. Computing can be a powerful tool for facilitating structural changes determined for other reasons.[14] For example, centralization of fiscal control is facilitated by centralized financial accounting, which in turn is greatly facilitated by use of computerized accounting systems that provide access to financial information to departments through terminals, but retain control over financial transactions at the center. Alternatively, use of local computers can permit effective departmental accounting under a decentralized fiscal authority structure. The important point is that computing can be used as an instrument to facilitate structural changes or to reinforce existing structures, but it cannot bring these about in the first instance.

Overall, the question remains whether, after computing is in place across many organizations, the resulting structures are more centralized or decentralized. Robey's research suggests that centralization more commonly follows computing implementation than does decentralization.[15] But since computing facilitates either structural arrangement, it is likely that Robey's finding is as much a result of the historical tendency of organizations towards centralization as it is a result of the greater facilitation of centralization by computing. While organizational use of computing has been increasingly coincidental with an increase in organizational centralization, to conclude that computing has caused the centralization is an error. Rather, computing has probably facilitated centralization at most, and these two forces have been interactive. The desire of managers to centralize has been facilitated by computing which, in turn, has reinforced their desire to centralize. However, the desire to centralize existed first in the minds of the managers.

COMPUTING AND EMPLOYMENT

Computing's effect on employment has been hotly debated over the years but rarely studied systematically. The first empirical studies of the effects of computers on employment were conducted by the Department of Labor 25 years ago to determine whether administrative computing would result in massive displacement of clerical workers in organizations.[16] The concern about displacement arose naturally because a central "benefit" of computing was the computer's ability to perform certain tasks much more rapidly and accurately than people. Computing was seen by some critics as allowing wholesale replacement of people by machines. This view was reinforced by an often explicit, and always implicit, feature of ads for computing systems—the claim that such systems would save money and reduce costs by allowing organizations to cut personnel. The response in defense of computing has maintained that even if computing does result in reduction of need for people in some jobs, it also can create new jobs through expansion of output. The debate, in short, has centered on the *net effect*: Would there be more jobs or less jobs in the economy after computing?

The answer to this question is extremely difficult to assess because many interacting factors contribute to employment effects in addition to the technology. Computer automation has resulted in the elimination of jobs in the service sector, of which government is a part. For example, the number of telephone operators declined sharply over the past 15 years as the telephone system has been automated. The same can be said of newspaper printers and bank tellers over the

past ten years.[17] But such clear-cut cases are uncommon. Most jobs that can be automated are not as discrete as those of telephone operators, newspaper printers, or bank tellers. Clerical workers, for example, do a wide variety of tasks both within a job and across clerical jobs, some of which can be automated and some of which cannot.

While job displacement among clerical workers is expected to be large because of office automation, its effects will vary across employment sectors and specific job titles. Indeed, although computerization clearly displaced clerical workers between 1960 and 1980, the total number of clerical workers in the United States actually increased overall because of normal growth in the volume of work and the extension of the scope of activities made possible by computers.[18] Therefore, to determine the effect of automation on employment for individual job categories is difficult. Determining the automation effects across organizational sectors and the economy as a whole is nearly impossible due to interactive effects and the large number of possible causes for unemployment. The statistical measures used to determine employment conditions simply are not precise enough to definitively answer the question of what effect computing has had on employment overall. At a crude level, however, we know that major advances in computer technology have been implemented over the last 25 years, and these advances have not been directly associated with a decline in employment overall.[19]

The primary conclusion about computing and employment in the service sector, therefore, is that *no one knows definitively the net effects*. But the judgment of experts is that the job displacement effects have so far been offset by job expansion and new job creation, especially with rapid diffusion of the technology.

COMPUTING AND WORK LIFE

The impact of computing on the work life of employees in computer-using organizations has revolved around the question of whether jobs become "better" or "worse" as a result of automation. On the downside has been the concern that computing would result in the "deskilling" of jobs by stripping skilled jobs of their conceptual content.[20] On the upside has been the prospect that computing would upgrade the jobs of workers by taking over mundane tasks and freeing workers to perform interesting and creative tasks.[21]

Unlike the situation with computing and employment, considerable empirical evidence exists about computing's effect on work life. Computing is generally seen by employees as having positive effects on their quality of work life.[22] Specifically, in various studies by the URBIS Group and others, computing is seen by employees as having (1) improved job performance, (2) improved the work environment, and (3) presented few problems in their day-to-day work. With respect to the work environment in particular, computing has either been benign or marginal. In their study of 2,400 end users, Danziger and Kraemer[23] report:

> Three-fourths of the end users indicate that computing has provided them with a greater sense of accomplishment in their work. Few report any impacts on the level of supervision, and the majority report no change in their capacity to influence others. The only negative work environment effect reported by a plurality of end users is increased time pressure for staff professionals and desk-top workers—roles with pervasive data handling responsibilities. But decreases in time pressure due to computing are more common than increases among managers and street-level bureaucrats.

Elsewhere they state that "We have identified many cases where the context of computing use does have a significant effect on the differential impacts of computing on people at work." And the ". . . sociotechnical interface, is the element in the context of use that is most consistently related to computing impacts across all role-types."

These findings are significant because they refute predictions about deskilling and job degradation effects of computerization. They also point to the significance of the organizational and social environment of computing. Moreover, they result from systematic, detailed studies performed in the government sector, and their results are confirmed by studies in the private sector as well. One important qualification about the studies, however, is that, by their nature, they exclude those who were displaced by computing; they

include only those who remained after computerization. This is an acceptable limitation since the interest here is in computing impacts on work life.

COMPUTING AND DECISION MAKING

Decision making generally refers to situations where a person or group must define the parameters of a "decision problem," acquire factual information about the problem, adopt (or invent) an analytical framework in which to evaluate the factual data in light of "goals," and arrive, through a logical process, at some determination of what to do. Computing's contribution to decision making is said to come from two features. First is enhancement of the ability to organize and maintain the base of factual information that must be used to understand the situation. This includes collection and storage of information, but more importantly, it includes the ability to retrieve the right information at the right time. Second is provision of greater power to analyze information, particularly quantitative information. This power is derived from the modeling capabilities of computing, in which very large amounts of information can be reduced to key indicators that are comprehendable by decision makers. Most characterizations of the decision-making assistance offered by computers have focused on these two capabilities. The ultimate vision of computer-aided decision making is the decision support system (DSS), in which the high-level decision makers have on-line access to powerful models and all the data necessary to run the models under different assumptions.

In reality, the impact of computing on decision making thus far has been much more impressive at the operational level of decision making than at the management and planning level envisioned by DSS proponents. Most computer-aided decisions relate to narrow choices affecting circumscribed events: for example, whether to buy personal computers so departmental analysts can run spreadsheet programs. Such decisions typically are resolved through analysis of information that is not on any local computer system (e.g., "Shouldn't we really wait for new, more powerful PCs?" or "Shouldn't the department head get one before the analysts do?" and "Do we have the money?"). Computing has made it possible to answer questions of an "enabling" nature, such as whether there will be sufficient funds to afford any computing equipment. Thus, computer-based information is used to set the stage for decisions, which is an important but often overlooked contribution to decision making.

Similarly, computing contributes to the process of determining whether decisions need to be made. An example is provided by the exception-reporting capabilities in most financial systems. A decision about what to do with a department that is overspending its budget is only worth considering when a department is overspending. Computing has made it possible to build such exception reporting into most financial and personnel management systems, and these capabilities have become critical to effective organizational control. Computing makes it easier to monitor for situations in which decisions need to be made. Thus, computing has made a major contribution to decision making by helping decision makers determine when they need to decide certain matters.

These contributions to decision making do not carry the excitement that surrounds the DSS vision. They pale in comparison to potential developments in expert systems and other emerging fields of computer science. Yet they are important in practical terms because they reflect the daily realities of organizational decision making.

Computing has been applied to much more complex decision situations than those noted above, and the results of these applications are worth noting for the ways in which they reinforce the need to focus on the context of decision-making. The most notable examples of computing application to complex decision making in government are the use of large-scale computerized models for setting policy. Briefly, large modeling systems do not result in "answers" to the larger question of what should be done. Rather, these modeling systems have important effects on the process of decision making which in turn affect the outcomes of the process. Studies of model use in both the federal government and local governments show that computing contributes to the decision making process in several ways. First, computer-based models provide a framework for defining what is part of the decision problem and

what is not thereby facilitating discussion and debate. Second, computer-based models impose discipline on the analytical process. This is particularly important in controversial decision situations where the different parties at interest have access to the models. Models require their users to specify precisely the assumptions they are making and the basic facts of the decision situation. Omissions and changes are easy for the opposition to spot. This discipline helps make the factual bases of different positions clear to all and contributes to more rapid assessment of the factual versus ideological bases of different positions.[24]

Third, computer-based models help the different parties in a decision situation to agree on what is important and what is not. This is partially an artifact of the discipline imposed by modeling, but it is also due to the fact that models can focus attention on areas of disagreement that require compromise. In some cases, major progress toward a decision is made by using the model to clarify which alternatives will and will not be considered, what criteria will be used for evaluating the alternatives, and how various criteria will be weighted.[25]

Finally, it appears that use of models in decision making can serve, over time, to help educate and improve the skills of decision makers and analysts. This again is due in part to the discipline enforced by modeling. But it also comes about as decision makers and analysts gain familiarity with the processes involved in considering various factors in a methodical way. Of particular importance is the tendency of modeling to force the user to learn to discriminate between those factors that are critical to decision outcomes and those that are not and to focus on the critical factors. In a related way, modeling helps to clarify for decision makers when facts are insufficient to yield a clear preference among alternatives. This is the case in a large number of decision situations, and it helps to identify where judgment is required.

COMPUTING AND ORGANIZATIONAL POLITICS

Characterizing computing as an instrument by which different goals might be accomplished can lead to the incorrect conclusion that computing is simply a neutral tool in organizational life to be used as best fits the organization. In fact, the potency of computing in decision making, if not in other areas, makes it politically very important. The political significance of computing arises from three features of computing use.

First is the political significance of the information processed by computers. Information *per se* is not power, but those with the best information are often successful at accomplishing their objectives. Depending on how computing and information systems are organized and provided, different individuals and factions in organizations can gain or lose power relative to others. This is especially true in the context of the contributions of computing to decision making mentioned above.

Second is the "resource politics" of computing, arising from the fact that those who control computing govern a large investment of organizational resources. Control over these resources brings power, both through building a base for further increases in demands on resources and through control over capabilities that others in the organization or its clients need.

Finally, computing brings "affective power" due to its inherent attractiveness as an activity. Those who are engaged in computing are perceived by many as advanced, sophisticated, and professional. Also, since many people are intimidated by technical jargon and computer printouts, these can be used effectively to obfuscate the underlying issues in disputes and to weaken opposition.

The fundamental question about computing and organizational politics is who gains and who loses from computing. Some have predicted that computing will alter the political profile of organizations by shifting power to technocrats.[26] Others have suggested that computing can strengthen pluralistic features of organizations by providing different interest groups with the ability to respond to their opposition with the tools of technology.[27] Still others maintain that computing reinforces the status quo, by providing the existing power elite with the tools to perpetuate and strengthen their power.[28] Recent empirical research suggests that the latter is the most common outcome of computing.[29]

This "reinforcement" of political influence is in some ways an extension to observations made above about computing's impacts. Computing is not in itself a powerful and influential force in organizations. But it does provide the opportunity to reinforce prevailing policy and attitudes toward larger organizational issues. These policies and attitudes are typically shaped by those already in powerful positions, and computing naturally is absorbed as a tool by this elite. The elite decides what resources will be invested in computing, what control structures will govern when and how computing is used, and what priorities will be honored in system development and implementation. This power results in the singular opportunity to decide who will benefit from computing and who will not.[30] It is important to note that this power does not require that the elite be technically skilled in computing. It requires only that the elite control the acquisition and application of technical skill. This finding is significant because it challenges assumptions about the potential "democratizing" effects of computing. Instead of democratizing organizations, computing has been empirically determined to be a powerful tool of the status quo.

THE MANAGEMENT OF COMPUTING

The management of computing has become increasingly complex as new technologies continue to be introduced and become more widely diffused among organizations. A considerable portion of the research on the management of computing has focused on the question of which policies are most effective at controlling computer use. Much of this work has proceeded from the premise that preferred policies (i.e., those that work) could easily be identified from those that do not work well. In the absence of empirical data on the actual effects of policies, most prescriptions for management of computing have been rational characterizations of how computing "ought to" take place. This is particularly true in the extensive literature on business information systems, but it has shown up repeatedly in public administration literature as well. Unfortunately, the realities of computing management do not support these rationalistic assumptions, and there is tremendous variability in the effectiveness of computing across organizations.

The most comprehensive empirical study of the management of computing in government was the

URBIS research on local government computing.[31] This research sought to identify the management policies most closely associated with reduced costs and improved benefits of computing use. Among the policies considered were: centralized versus decentralized arrangements for computing service provision; user involvement in design of systems; use of charge-out policies to recover costs and allocate computer resources; and use of steering committees and policy boards to govern computing policy. Surprisingly, the most important variable correlating with overall success of computing implementation proved to be the organization's commitment to advanced technology. Those governments with higher levels of automation, more sophisticated applications, more sophisticated personnel, higher levels of computer utilization, and greater routinization of computing, consistently had the highest payoffs from computer use. These payoffs included better information for decision making, greater administrative control, and improved operational performance. The other management policies were clearly of secondary importance in comparison with the state of the technology.

Subsequent research by King and Kraemer revealed further surprises about the relationship between policy for management of computing and outcomes of computing use. The four policies of charge out, user involvement in system design, extensive user training, and use of steering committees proved to be highly associated with major problems in computing as identified by users.[32] Thus, the policies presumably adopted in response to computing problems were only marginally effective at alleviating them. There are two possible explanations for failure of management policies to control computing problems. The first is that simply adopting a policy does not mean that the policy is well implemented. Many policies exist in name only; they are not implemented effectively. This hypothesis restores faith in the policies by assigning the failure of policy to the implementers, but it begs the question. Recommendation of policies which people do not follow is not sensible. Alternatively, computing could be so difficult to manage successfully that the best intentions of well-meaning people simply are not up to the challenge. If the purpose of broad policy prescriptions is to provide guidance for dealing with the common problems organizations face, the prescriptions themselves must be based on correct diagnosis, an understanding of the etiology of the problem, and knowledge of effective treatment and prevention. Such understanding and knowledge is currently lacking.

Many popular policy recommendations are based on sound assumptions that should be borne in mind in any case. For example, the maxim of involving users in the design of systems is based on the belief that systems designed to aid or perform organizational tasks are likely to benefit from input by those who currently do the tasks. Similarly, charge-out policies are based on the belief that people make more cost-effective use of resources when they have to pay for them. But the distance between intentions and what can actually be accomplished is often great, and this is where the more intractable management problems arise. Policies often backfire. For example, the laudatory goal of improved training of users in computing enables them to use the systems, but it also makes them more demanding and expectant of service than they were before. If service does not improve commensurately with expectations, users can end up even more dissatisfied. This is a particularly serious problem from a research standpoint, since much of the information systems literature is built on the assumption that measurement of user satisfaction is an adequate surrogate for measurement of system quality.[33]

Some research suggests that the most successfully run computing enterprises have a relative absence of formal policy.[34] They are run by service-oriented, visionary, technically skilled, and managerially competent people who maintain tight control over computing activities and enjoy backing by top government officials. In a sense, this is simply a repeat of Plato's observation that the best government is that of the benevolent philosopher-king. But if computing can be successfully managed without use of many of the policies espoused in the academic and professional journals, what good are the policies? Very recent research suggests that the applicability of particular policies depends on local conditions and that few policies are applicable to all government organizations. To determine which circumstances fit with which policies, one must identify the causal forces that shape the evolution of computing in organizations.

Several models of computing evolution exist in organizations. Most are tied to private sector research, but the issues being considered are sufficiently broad to make them applicable to all sectors. These models are fraught with problems: they focus too much on simplistic notions about organizational behavior and overrate the power of the technology to cause organizational change. They suggest that the growth and evolution of computing in organizations is primarily driven by technological change, the adoption of which is mediated by organizational concerns for maintaining control and stability. They postulate either a progressive direction of change or a theoretical end state of computing maturity or stability toward which organizations proceed through a series of developmental steps.[35]

King and Kraemer propose an alternative view in which the most powerful forces shaping computing use are those of organizational demand.[36] "Supply" is seen as the available computing technology and expertise to apply it, while "demand" is the existing and perceived need of an organization to apply computing to given tasks. The most important feature of their model is its focus on the context in which computing is used and decisions about computing are made. It uses a framework embodying the relationship between organizational context and technical infrastructure, factored along both intraorganizational and extraorganizational lines. Key factors outside the organization, such as changes in economic conditions, organizational mandates, clientele, and available technology, influence the internal organizational context in which decisions about computing take place. It is the interplay of these external forces and the internal organizational context that shape the nature of computing in the organization.

In this view, computing is a complex social enterprise that involves the continuing mobilization of social forces internal and external to the user organization for its initiation, development, and maintenance. Generally, data processing leadership is the pivotal force, but it requires the support of top management and of literally hundreds of others who are managers and endusers in the operating departments of the organization. Husbanding that support involves: socializing each new wave of top management, department management, and department users;

reinforcing that socialization by creating a positive culture complete with rituals, stories, and heroes; operating near capacity so that resources are adequate for current tasks and demonstrate technical efficiency, but obviously inadequate for new tasks without data processing growth; and planning for and justifying data processing growth in terms of organizational performance (e.g., "service to clients," "market share").

The ability of data processing leadership to create and sustain that support, however, is dependent upon several external forces as well. Chief among these are political, economic, and technological conditions in the environment which shape the organization's ability to invest in computing. A managerial ideology positively influences the receptiveness of top management to computing investments. Fiscal strength positively influences the ability and motivation to make computing investments in order to achieve productivity and effectiveness gains. While fiscal weakness might also motivate top management to make such investments, the capacity to realize the motivation may be lacking. Technological innovation, in the form of cost/performance improvements or new technical capabilities, positively influences data processing leadership's ability to show performance payoffs from current investments that reinforce both the managerial ideology and fiscal strength and maintain the support of operating departments and end users.

The empirical research strongly suggests that computing can only be understood by understanding the forces that shape organizational decision makers' ideas about what computing should be applied to, how it should be applied, and how it should be managed. Further study is required to establish the basic linkages between external events and internal actors' perceptions of what is possible and what is reasonable for their own organizations. This will permit the identification and assessment of the forces that shape organizational opportunities and constraints in computing and produce a more general model of the evolution of computing in organizations than has been available heretofore.

CONCLUSION

Computing has had important effects on public organizations. In some cases, public organizations are performing tasks that simply could not have been done without computing capability; in others, the use of computers has changed governmental processes and outcomes. But overall computing has not had the dramatic effects periodically predicted. Despite its attractiveness as a new and interesting technology, it is not the *deus ex machina* that transforms government organizations.[37] Rather, computing fits within existing organizational life and exerts subtle influences. This does not mean, however, that computing is an activity that is easily managed. Even when managers have a clear idea of the objectives they hope to accomplish with computerization, they discover that actual experiences with the technology are driven by many forces in addition to the dispositions of organizational leaders and organizational factions. The challenge for public administration researchers and educators, as well as practicing managers, is to focus on the actual experiences with computing technology as guides for how best to channel its use. In part this is accomplished by the systematic testing of theories about computing management arising from the private and public sectors. Concepts that have proven utility will stand out in time. But a more serious challenge is to conduct focused, empirical research on the causes behind the problems in the management of computing technology.

NOTES

1. Gabriel Goren, "Economic Dimensions of the Growth of the Computing Industry in the Last Three Decades," Working paper (Irvine. Public Policy Research Organization, University of California, 1984).
2. The findings reported here are drawn from three principal sources. First is the body of published research on computing in public organizations and, to a lesser extent, in private organizations conducted over the past 15 years. Second, are case studies of computing in local governments. These include cross-sectional studies of 56 local governments in ten countries conducted in 1976, case studies of computer models in federal agencies and local governments conducted in 1980, and longitudinal case studies in seven local governments conducted in 1984. Third are national surveys of computing use in local governments. The major surveys are those conducted of 700 U.S. local governments in 1975

and replicated again in 1985 and of 2,400 end users of computing conducted in 1976. This research was supported by grants from the National Science Foundation and by a research agreement with the IBM Corporation.
3. Members of the URBIS Group and the major works resulting from their research include: James L. Perry and Kenneth L. Kraemer, *Technological Innovation in American Local Governments* (New York: Pergamon, 1979); Kenneth L. Kraemer, William H. Dutton, and Alana Northrop, *The Management of Information Systems* (New York: Columbia University Press, 1981); Kling, *op. cit.*, 1980; Kraemer, Dutton, and Northrop, *op. cit.*, 1981; Kenneth L. Kraemer and James N. Danziger, "Computers and Control in the Work Environment," L. Kraemer, *The Dynamics of Computing* (New York: Columbia University Press, 1985); William H. Dutton and Kenneth L. Kraemer, *Modeling as Negotiating* (Norwood, NJ: Ablex, 1985); James N. Danziger and Kenneth L. Kraemer, *People and Computers* (New York: Columbia University Press, 1986); Kenneth L. Kraemer, Sigfried Dickhoven, Susan Fallows Tierney, and John Leslie King, *DataWars* (New York: Columbia University Press, forthcoming); Kenneth L. Kraemer, John Leslie King, Debra Dunkle, Joseph P. Lane, and Joey George, "Computing Change in Organizations" (Irvine: Public Policy Research Organization, University of California, 1986).
4. A few of these benefits are worth mentioning. Local governments are generally stable organizations. They rarely go out of business; they are buffered from the radical effects of the business cycle that affect most private organizations and that tend to swamp the measurable effects of computing use. Local governments also are numerous, generally autonomous with respect to one another, and perform similar functions. Unlike the national or state governments, local governments provide a broad array of different approaches to computing use for study. Local governments are by nature accessible for study. There is little concern for proprietary information or organizational secrecy common to many other organizations. This makes it possible to explore the important relationships between organizational goals, decision-making practices, structure, resources, and personalities as they relate to computing. Finally, local governments are service organizations and findings from their study are generalizable to other service organizations in government and industry.
5. Rob Kling, "Social Analyses of Computing: Theoretical Perspectives in Recent Empirical Research," *Computing Surveys*, vol. 12 (March 1980), pp. 132–146.

6. Paul Attewell and James Rule, "Computing and Organizations: What We Know and What We Don't Know," *Communications of the ACM*, vol. 27 (December 1984), pp. 1184–1192.

7. Harold Leavitt and Thomas Whisler, "Management in the 1980's," *Harvard Business Review*, vol. 36 (November/December 1958), pp. 41–48.

8. John Leslie King, "Centralization vs. Decentralization of Computing: Organizational Considerations and Management Options," *ACM Computing Surveys*, vol. 15 (December 1983), pp. 319–349.

9. Anthony Oettinger, "Communications in the National Decision Making Process," in Martin Greenberger (ed.), *Computers, Communications and the Public Interest* (Baltimore: The Johns Hopkins University Press, 1971), pp. 74–114; and Richard Bingham, "Wired City," *Urban Affairs Quarterly*, vol. 20 (December 1984), pp. 265–272.

10. Christopher Argyris, "The Challenge to Rationality and Emotionality," *Management Science*, vol. 17 (February 1971), pp. 275–292; Kenneth C. Laudon, *Computers and Bureaucratic Reform* (New York: John Wiley and Sons, 1974); Enid Mumford and Olive Banks, *The Computer and the Clerk* (London: Routledge and Kegan Paul, 1967); Charles Myers, *The Impact of Computers on Management* (Cambridge: MIT Press, 1967); Nicole Leduc, "Communicating Through Computers," *Telecommunications Policy*, vol. 3 (September 1979), pp. 235–244.

11. Peter Blau, C. M. Falbe, W. McKinley, and P. Tracy, "Technology and Organization in Manufacturing," *Administrative Science Quarterly*, vol. 21 (March 1976), pp. 20–40; Peter Blau and Richard Schoenherr, *The Structure of Organizations* (New York: Basic Books, 1971); S. R. Klatzky, "Automation, Size and Locus of Decisionmaking," *Journal of Business*, vol. 43 (April 1970), pp. 141–151; Jeffrey Peffer, *Power in Organizations* (Marshfield, MA: Pitman Publishing, 1981); Fredrick Withington, *The Real Computer: Its Influences, Uses and Effects* (Reading, MA: Addison-Wesley, 1969).

12. Nels Bjorn-Anderson and P. Pederson, "Computer-Facilitated Changes and Management Power Structures," *Accounting, Organizations, and Society*, vol. 5 (March/April 1977), pp. 203–216; Nels Bjorn-Anderson, "The Impact of Electronic Digital Technology on Traditional Job Profiles," in Organization for Economic Cooperation and Development (OECD), *Microelectronics, Productivity, and Employment* (Paris: OECD, 1981); Kling, *op. cit.*, 1980; Kraemer, Dutton, and Northrop, *op. cit.*, 1981; Kenneth L. Kraemer and James N. Danziger, "Computers and Control in the Work Environment," *Public Administration Review*, vol. 44 (January/February 1984), pp. 32–42; Daniel Robey, "Computer Information Systems and Organization Structure," *Communications of the ACM*, vol. 24 (October 1981), pp. 679–686; Daniel Robey, "Computers and Management Structure: Some Empirical Findings Re-Examined," *Human Relations*, vol. 30 (November 1977), pp. 963–976; Daniel Robey, "Information Systems and Organizational Change: A Comparative Case Study," *Systems, Objectives, Solutions*, vol. 3 (August 1983), pp. 143–154.

13. Kraemer, Dutton, and Northrop, *op. cit.*, Chapter 7; M. Lynn E. Markus, "Implementation Politics: Top Management Support and Involvement," *Systems, Objectives, Solutions*, vol. 1 (November 1981), pp. 203–205.

14. Rob Kling, "Automated Welfare Client Tracking and Service Integration," *Communications of the ACM*, vol. 21 (June 1978), pp. 484–493; Kenneth L. Kraemer and William H. Dutton, "The Interests Served by Technological Reform," *Administration and Society*, vol. 11 (May 1979), pp. 80–106; Kraemer, Dutton, and Northrop, *op. cit.*, 1981; King, *op. cit.*, 1983.

15. Robey, *op. cit.*, 1981.

16. See for example: U.S. Department of Labor, Bureau of Labor Statistics, *Adjustments to the Introduction of Office Automation: A Study of Some Implications of the Installation of Electronic Data Processing in 20 Offices in Private Industry with Special Reference to Older Workers* (Washington: U.S. Government Printing Office, 1960); *Impact of Office Automation in the Internal Revenue Service* (1963); *Impact of Office Automation in the Insurance Industry* (1966).

17. Organization for Economic Cooperation and Development (OECD), *Microelectronics, Robotics and Jobs*, ICCP No. 7 (Paris: OECD, 1982), pp. 38–40. Excellent treatment of the employment impacts question and the problems of research in this area is contained in: J. Rada, *The Impact of Microelectronics* (Geneva: International Labour Office, 1980); and Z. P. Zeman, "The Impacts of Computer/Communications on Employment in Canada: An Overview of Current OECD Debates" (Ottawa: Institute for Research on Public Policy, 1979); and OECD, *Microelectronics, Productivity and Employment*, ICCP No. 5 (Paris: OECD, 1981).

18. R. W. Riche, "Impact of Technological Change," OECD Conference Paper (Paris: OECD, 1981).

19. OECD, *op. cit.*, 1981, 1982.

20. Harry Braverman, *Labor and Monopoly Capital: The Degradation of Work in the Twentieth Century* (New York: Monthly Review, 1974); James Driscoll, "Office Automation: The Dynamics of a Technological Boondoggle," in Robert Landau and James Blair (eds.), *Emerging Office Systems* (Norwood, NJ: Ablex Publishers, 1982), pp. 259–277.

21. Charles Myers, *The Impact of Computers on Management* (Cambridge: MIT Press, 1967); Daniel Bell, *The Coming of the Post-Industrial Society* (New York: Basic Books, 1973); Vincent Giuliano, "The Mechanization of Office Work," *Scientific American*, vol. 247 (September 1982), pp. 148–165.

22. A. J. Jaffe and Joseph Froomkin, *Technology and Jobs: Automation in Perspective* (New York: Praeger, 1966); Steven Dubnoff, "Interoccupational Shifts and Changes in the Quality of Working Life in the American Economy, 1900–1970," paper presented at the Society for the Study of Social Problems, San Francisco (1978); Russell Rumberger, "The Changing Skill Requirements of Jobs in the U.S. Economy," *Industrial and Labor Relations Review*, vol. 34 (July 1981), pp. 578–590; Rob Kling, "The Impacts of Computing on the Work of Managers, Data Analysts, and Clerks" (Irvine: Public Policy Research Organization, University of California, 1978); Kenneth L. Kraemer and James N. Danziger, "Computers and Control in the Work Environment," *Public Administration Review*, vol. 44 (January/February 1984), pp. 32–42; Jon Shepard, *Automation and Alienation: A Study of Office and Factory* (Cambridge: MIT Press, 1971).

23. Danziger and Kraemer, *People and Computers*, Chapter 11.

24. John Leslie King, "Successful Implementation of Large Scale Decision Support Systems: Computerized Models in U.S. Economic Policy Making," *Systems, Objectives, Solutions*, vol. 3 (November 1983), pp. 183–205; John Leslie King, "Ideology and Use of Large-Scale Decision Support Systems in National Policymaking," *Systems, Objectives, Solutions*, vol. 4 (April 1984), pp. 81–104; Kraemer, Dickhoven, Tierney, and King, *DataWars* (1986); and Dutton and Kraemer, *Modeling as Negotiating* (1985).

25. Clarifying the issues can also make compromise more difficult. Pack and Pack report that use of urban land use models sometimes make political decision making more difficult because the models help clarify who wins and who loses under difficult land use patterns. In contrast, ambiguity sometimes speeds up decision making, although there is considerable question about whether the resulting decisions are as good as they might have been without the ambiguity. Howard Pack and Janet Pack, "The Resurrection of the Urban Development Model," *Policy Analysis*, vol. 3 (Summer 1977), pp. 407–427.

26. Anthony Downs, "A Realistic Look at the Payoffs from Urban Data Systems," *Public Administration Review*, vol. 27 (September 1967), pp. 204–210; Theodore J. Lowi, "Government and Politics: Blurring of Sector Lines," in *Information Technology: Some Critical Implications for Decision Makers* (New York: The Conference Board, 1972), pp. 131–181; Don Price, *The Scientific Estate* (Cambridge: Harvard University Press, 1965); Langdon Winner, *Autonomous Technology* (Cambridge: MIT Press, 1977).

27. Oettinger, *op. cit.*; Edward Blum, "Municipal Services," in Harold Sackman and Barry W. Boehm (eds.), *Planning Community Information Utilities* (Montvale, NJ: AFIPS Press, 1972), pp. 45–68.

28. Eric P. Hoffman. "Soviet Metapolicy: Information Processing in the Soviet Union," *Administration and Society*, vol. 5 (August 1973), pp. 200–232; Hoffman, "Technology Values, and Political Power in the Soviet Union," in F. Fleron, Jr. (ed.), *Technology and Communist Culture* (New York: Holt, Rinehart and Winston, 1977), pp. 397–436.

29. William H. Dutton and Kenneth L. Kraemer, "Technology and Urban Management: The Power Payoffs of Computing," *Administration and Society*, vol. 9 (November 1977), pp. 304–340; Kenneth L. Kraemer, "Computers, Information, and Power in Local Governments," in Abbe Mowshowitz (ed.), *Human Choice and Computers* (Amsterdam: North Holland, 1980), pp. 213–215; Kenneth L. Kraemer and William H. Dutton, "The Interests Served by Technological Reform," *Administration and Society*, vol. 11 (May 1979), pp. 80–106; Danziger, Dutton, Kling, and Kraemer, *Computers and Politics, op. cit.*

30. The need to absorb complexity into systems has been termed the "law of the conservation of complexity" by Louis Robinson, speech at the 1983 IBM University Studies Conference, Raleigh, NC (October 1983).

31. Kraemer, Dutton, and Northrop, *The Management of Information Systems, op. cit.*

32. King and Kraemer, *The Dynamics of Computing, op. cit.*

33. John Leslie King, "Local Government Use of Information Technology: The Next Decade," *Public Administration Review*, vol. 42 (January/February 1982), pp. 25–36.

34. Richard I. Nolan, "Managing the Computer Resource: A Stage Hypothesis," *Communications of the ACM*, vol. 16 (July 1973), pp. 399–405; *ibid.*, *Management Accounting and Control of Data Processing* (New York: National Association of Acountants, 1977); *ibid.*, "Managing the Crisis in Data Processing," *Harvard Business Review*, vol. 57 (March/April 1979), pp. 399–405; Cyrus F. Gibson and Richard I. Nolan, "Managing the Four Stages of EDP Growth," *Harvard Business Review*, vol. 52 (January/February 1974), pp. 76–88; John Leslie King and Kenneth L. Kraemer, "Evolution and Organizational Information Systems: An Assessment of Nolan's Stage Model," *Communications of the ACM*, vol. 27 (May 1984), pp. 466–475; John

Leslie King and Kenneth L. Kraemer, "The Dynamics and Evolution of Computing," *Computers Environment and Urban Systems*, vol. 11 (Fall 1986).

35. King and Kraemer, *op. cit.*, 1985.

36. King and Kraemer, *op. cit.*, 1984, 1985; Kenneth L. Kraemer, John Leslie King, Debra Dunkle, Joseph P. Lane, and Joey George, "Computing Change in Organizations" (Irvine: Public Policy Research Organization, University of California, 1986).

37. King and Kraemer, *op. cit.*, 1985.

DESCRIPTION OF TOTAL QUALITY MANAGEMENT (TQM)

Office of Management and Budget

Total Quality Management is a total, integrated organizational approach for meeting customer needs and expectations that involves all managers and employees, and uses quantitative methods and employee involvement to improve continuously the organization's processes, products and services. TQM is based on the principles taught by W. Edwards Deming, Joseph Juran, and Philip Crosby (among the most well-known authorities on quality) and the practical experience over the past 10 years of numerous private and public sector organizations which have implemented quality improvement. This collective body of knowledge and experience has been integrated into a total management approach that is best described under seven headings. The description provided below presents TQM as it would exist in an advanced phase in an organization.

Top Management Leadership and Support. Top managers are directly and actively involved in the TQM process. They take the lead in establishing an environment and culture that encourage change, innovation, risk-taking, pride in work, and continuous improvement on behalf of all customers. They exhibit a highly visible, personal leadership and communicate the organization's quality vision, goals, and values to all members. Managers provide the resources, time, and training necessary for the organization to improve quality and productivity. They show by example that open communication (vertically and horizontally) and information sharing are the organizational norm. They understand that quality improvement is a long-term process, not to be compromised by short-term considerations. Managers remove barriers to improvement; e.g.,

they delegate authority to the lowest feasible level, deregulate work, and discourage the "quick-fix" mentality that seeks short-term results at the expense of long-term goals. Managers establish trust, encourage cooperation among organizational units to achieve better service, and reward behavior that reflects the organization's TQM goals. They establish an organization structure that fosters effective implementation of the quality improvement process.

Strategic Planning. Strategic planning drives the organization's improvement efforts. Short and long-term goals for quality improvement are established across the organization and are integrated into the strategic plan. Customer needs and expectations as well as issues relating to improved supplier relationships are considered and incorporated into the strategic plan. Resources are allocated to support the quality improvement objectives the organization wants to achieve. Periodically-revised business plans at sub-organizational levels provide the who-what-when details for the strategic plans. Business plans include quality improvement projects with measurable goals for each organizational unit and managers are held accountable for their achievement. A dynamic organizational plan is in place to assure that structural changes and people capabilities are able to accommodate changes in the organization's environment.

Focus on the Customer. Management actively seeks ways to make all employees aware of customers and their needs. Employees can identify both the internal and external customers of all their products and services. They understand that their primary task is to satisfy customer requirements and expectations. Communication with customers, as with suppliers, is open, continual and two-way to ensure that clear definitions of needs and expectations are received and problems and concerns are understood. Customer perceptions of performance are continually measured, evaluated, and reported to responsible managers and employees. Feedback data are used to improve processes and services and provide input for strategic planning. Access by customers to information about the organization's products or services is easy and trouble-free. Complaints about aspects of the organization's services are solicited and corrected. Trends in customer satisfaction indicators are positive. The validity and objectivity of monitoring methods is ensured. Where expectations, desires and perceptions of different customer groups are in conflict with each other, the organization strives to achieve a balance among them that best fulfills the organization's mission.

Satisfying public service customers is constrained by the public policy process and the need to base many decisions on law rather than on individual desires. However, the organization uses several ways to reconcile the differences between what customers want and what the system allows. First, laws often recognize differences among groups of people and different circumstances within those groups. These differences are recognized and respected in dealing with people. Second, there are well established standards for informing people about services and providing due process for their grievances. The organization uses every opportunity to volunteer information and let people voice their concerns. Third, the organization pays attention over time to what customers identify as important. This becomes an important data base of information for the organization to use in modifying or changing the law. Finally, public employees are people dealing with other people. The organization provides responsive, courteous behavior which is always within the bounds of law.

Commitment to Training and Recognition.
Managers and employees receive ongoing training to enable them to keep abreast of changing job requirements and prepare for greater responsibilities. A key element of training for all managers and employees is quality awareness and the use of tools, technologies, and techniques to support continuous improvement. The scope, intensity, and timing of training depends on organization level, the nature of work, and specific processes under review for improvement. Training is tailored to support the vision and goals of the organization; it is objectively assessed and documented, and periodically updated. Training plans are fully integrated into overall strategic planning. Training investment shows clear evidence of the priority placed on human resource development.

Employees are motivated to achieve total quality through trust, respect and recognition.

Managers believe that employees want to do a good job; they personally, regularly, and fairly recognize individuals and teams for measurable contributions to quality improvement. Rewards and recognition are broad-based and innovative, encompass all levels of the organization, are centered on team quality and productivity improvement, and include peer recognition as a part of the reward structure. Celebration of small successes is common. Performance plans for managers include measurable quality improvement objectives. Evaluations focus on the degree to which the objectives are met.

Employee Empowerment and Teamwork.
Management provides an environment that supports employee involvement, contribution, and teamwork. Where unions exist, union leaders are involved in high-level policy and decision-making groups, such as Quality Councils or Policy Boards. Teamwork is the vehicle for cooperation and communication among managers, supervisors, unions, and employees in addressing quality improvement issues. The demands of quality, cost, schedule, and mission that cross organizational units are met through cross-functional team cooperation. Employees have clear avenues for participation and involvement; e.g., as members of self-regulating work teams responsible for an entire process or group of customers, contributors to developing and implementing improvement plans, suggestors of ideas for improvement, participators in establishing work unit performance measures and goals, evaluators of processes, and decision-makers in many aspects of their work and work environment. Hierarchies are reduced in favor of cooperative teams and networks. Employees have a strong feeling of empowerment and team ownership of work processes because sufficient power, rewards, information and knowledge are moved to the lowest levels of the organization to enable everyone to accomplish their work with excellence. As a result, everyone feels "ownership" of quality improvement and exhibits personal pride in the quality of their work.

Measurement and Analysis of Processes and Outputs.
All information required to support total quality of processes and products/services is complete, timely, accurate, useful, and clearly communicated to those who need it. The scope of the

data includes: customers and suppliers (both internal and external), internal operations, products/services, employees, comparisons or benchmarks of other organizations, and safety/environmental considerations (if appropriate). This information is the basis for developing quality measures that cover all aspects of work processes and all products and services provided a customer. Customer satisfaction measures are used extensively. These measures are used by employees to identify problems, determine root causes, identify solutions and verify that proposed remedies produce the expected results. Structures methodologies that employ quantitative methods and statistical techniques are used to improve processes. The emphasis on prevention, measurement and analysis applies equally to all the organization's processes—administrative, research, accounting, human resource, legal, policy development, or service-based. Measurement and analysis supports continuous improvement.

Quality Assurance. Products, services, and processes are designed and verified to meet customer needs and expectations. Processes which produce the organization's products and services are controlled, optimized and maintained. There is sufficient standardization within the organization to ensure compatibility. Comprehensive assessments of the quality assurance system as well as of products/services are performed at appropriate intervals. An approach exists for translating assessment findings into quality documentation supporting quality assurance. Quality assurance systems are updated to keep pace with changes in technology, practice and quality improvement. Product and service performance standards are set for internal support functions such as finance and accounting, personnel and administrative support. There is an established method to verify that the organization's quality requirements are being met by suppliers and other providers of goods and services. The organization compares (benchmarks) its products, services and internal operations with the "best" in the private or public sectors (e.g., other Federal agencies, state and local governments, and the governments of other countries).

Source: Office of Management and Budget, Draft Circular A-132, 1990.

ANN McKERNAN ROBINSON: THE WINDOW IS ALWAYS OPEN

Pepper Smith

When Ann Robinson's friends used to complain to her about their mail—Robinson has worked for the U.S. Postal Service since 1966—she used to say, "The window is closed." Then, in 1985, she became consumer advocate for the Postal Service, and the window has never shut since.

As head of the Office of Consumer Affairs, Robinson leads the Postal Service's effort to respond to consumer feedback and take corrective action. "We are basically ombudsmen for the general public," she says.

The office also informs consumers about postal services and products and educates postal employees about consumer expectations.

With a 19 percent proposed postal rate increase on the horizon, the window is becoming crowded. "Our volume of complaints is already beginning to rise," Robinson said shortly after the proposal was announced in March. She knows there will be outcries at first, but she feels consumers will be more tolerant of higher rates than of poorer service. "We try to remind people that the cost of everything is rising in their lives, and that the Postal Service does not receive any tax dollars. I think as long as service is good, it will be OK. We want the public to feel they're getting their money's worth."

To combat potential consumer outrage, Robinson has been taking the initiative. "In the past we would have waited to see what happened. Now, in the first month after the postmaster general's announcement, we began sending our officers on whirl-wind speaking tours in every city, and all of us have tried to be available to the media."

Robinson has learned the usefulness of hearing complaints. "When you understand what people are dissatisfied about, you can solve the problem," she says. "It's what they don't tell you that becomes negative advertising."

To listen to postal customers and improve postal service, Robinson has instituted programs such as the National Consumer Service Card. Postal customers can write requests or problems on the card, available at any post office, and the Postal Service will respond within 10 working days. A copy is sent to the local post office and another copy is sent to the U.S. Postal Data Center in St. Louis, where complaints are analyzed for national trends.

Her department's efforts have helped to make the Postal Service a leader in customer service programs in both the public and private sectors. At last year's Society of

Consumer Affairs Professionals awards, the Postal Service won first place for customer service training. "We're proud of that award, because we were competing with a lot of Fortune 500 companies," Robinson says.

"This year, we're going to have a dynamite entry with our Postal Answer Line," she adds. This telephone service provides pre-recorded messages in 62 sites, explaining a plethora of postal services, from certified mail to passport applications.

Postmaster General Anthony M. Frank expanded Robinson's duties in 1988 to include oversight of all service measurement systems. Under her leadership, the Postal Service will conduct its first external service audit. "This is a major corporate cultural change for this organization," explains Robinson, "but you cannot be in a service industry and keep your own report card." Price Waterhouse, an accounting firm, will test mail deliveries in the fourth quarter of this year. Robinson says plans are in the works for an external audit of customer satisfaction and another on third-class mail delivery.

Robinson joined the Postal Service as a management intern in 1966. Since then she has managed the Employment and Placement, Distribution Procedures and International Mail Classification divisions at postal headquarters. From 1983 to 1985 she was executive assistant to the postmaster general.

She earned a master's degree in management from the Massachusetts Institute of Technology as the Postal Service's Sloan Fellow. She also has a bachelor's in education from Temple University and has done post-graduate study at the University of Virginia and at the University of Pennsylvania's Wharton School of Business.

Born in Norristown, Pa., she now lives in Washington with her husband, Armand, an attorney and publisher. She enjoys stamp collecting—what did you expect, baseball cards?—and running.

Annette Dresseler, a consumer services projects specialist, has seen tremendous growth in her specialty under Robinson's leadership. "Before Ann Robinson came, this was just a letter response center," Dresseler says. "She has expanded the whole concept of consumer affairs, brought it to the forefront and proved that in order for the Postal Service to succeed, we must listen to our customers."

Robinson has enjoyed the Postal Service's unique position of being in both public and private arenas. "Working for the Postal Service is exciting because your feet are in two worlds: One is in the private sector, and the other is in the public sector. I enjoy the public service aspect of the job; I'd also love to eat Federal [Federal Express Corp.] for lunch tomorrow."

She hopes the Postal Service will adopt the same competitive attitude. "To paraphrase Florida Power and Light," says Robinson: "We have to behave as if we have competition, so if the day ever comes when we do, customers will choose us because we've been giving good service."

For Robinson, that kind of service means "treating each and every customer as if they count, for they do. You ought to expect to be treated courteously and get the service that you want.

"We have a slogan around here, 'Every customer counts, every single one,' and we really mean it."

RELOCATION OF THE MIDBURG HOUSING OFFICE

Ten years ago, the municipal Department of Public Housing decided to consolidate all of the managers into a central unit located in the new public office building in the city's center. Since then, the city has grown and the majority of public housing units are now being constructed several miles away from the downtown area. As the director of public housing, Donald Houston and his unit managers have been spending increasing amounts of time going from the sites of the public housing complexes and back to the central office. The introduction of computers into Donald's operations has made it less necessary for all managers to be located in the same building. He decided that it is time to look at the option of moving the central management location to another site.

At the same time, the prevailing philosophy in the public housing field has gone from advocating massive complexes to endorsing scatter sites and is now moving back to focusing on high-density rehabilitation of deteriorating structures. This means that Donald's planning variables are more complex than merely following the public housing projects and moving toward the periphery of the city. There are several other options he should consider.

Donald's best estimate of the costs of moving the central office depends on three assumptions: first, that he would be able to rent office space in the periphery at 50 percent less than the prevailing rate in the central city; second, that he would need a 20 percent increase in office space to accommodate expansion of his staff; and third, that his travel expenses will be reduced by 60 percent if he does relocate. Because he will be able to use city trucks and employees, he has decided not to include in his plans the costs of the actual physical move.

One of Donald's staff had suggested that he consider establishing two or more satellite centers on opposite sides of the city and reduce the central office staff proportionately. Another of Donald's staff had pointed out that he might be able to bring the new units closer to the existing central office by redirecting the future development efforts at rehabilitating existing central city sites. Unfortunately, rehabilitating existing structures is 1.75 times more expensive than building new units. Estimating that he would need 8,200 new units over the next five years, Donald decided that this strategy may not be very cost effective.

Using the following data on current operations, Donald set about constructing a plan for the future location of the central office over the next five years:

Staff size: 26
Rental: $183,000/yr
Office size: 4,685 sq. feet
Travel expenses: $38,912/yr

By the time Donald had completed his plan, six weeks had passed and he knew that his decision had to be put into action. Donald called his staff together and passed out copies of his analysis. Most of the staff calmly took the news that they could expect to be relocated over the next year or so; they had heard rumors about the move. One member asked Donald if his decision was final. "All plans are final, subject to instant revision if someone comes up with a better idea," quipped Donald.

"That's not very funny," grumbled one of the older members of the group. "You haven't told us why we need to move or how it will improve the services we deliver to the residents." Donald had a sheepish look on his face. "You're right; I haven't involved very many of you in this process because I thought the decision needed to be made on the basis of cost and convenience." As Donald looked around the room he saw the sardonic smiles on the faces of several other people. "Let's start with the plan that I developed and use that as a working document. Next week we'll discuss any changes or other options anyone can present."

Donald took the next forty-five minutes to go over his proposal. Rather than concentrating on the data, Donald emphasized the need to spend less time traveling and more time solving problems in the projects. He shared his misgivings about the shift toward rehabilitation of existing units and emphasized the long-term implications of this move. At the end of the meeting, Donald confessed that he thought the offices should be closer to the projects, if only to symbolize the commitment of the agency to its clientele: "You won't find that in the plan, but that's the way I feel."

The next week's staff meeting was a lively session with several arguments aired about the merits of moving closer to the housing projects. At the end of the meeting, the group agreed that Donald's original plan was probably the best option anyone could identify. Donald overheard a conversation between two staff members as they left the room: "Well, we didn't make many changes but at least now we understand why we are doing this and what is likely to go wrong."

Over the next several months, Donald tried to remember the experience of his initial miscalculation. Increasingly he took problems to his staff for discussion before any plans were committed to paper. When the offices were finally relocated, Donald sent individual letters to all of the staff thanking them for sharing their ideas and commitment. He received several replies, one of which he really appreciated. The reply read, "Thanks for the note—it's nice to have a leader who looks to the future by asking the followers about the present."

DISCUSSION QUESTIONS

1. Why did Donald belive the decision was a technical one, and what framework of analysis was he using when he first discussed the decision with his staff?
2. Should leaders always involve their staff, or are there some decisions that should be based on facts alone?
3. Using the information in the case, present your own proposal for relocating the office.

SOLVING ONE PROBLEM
CREATES ANOTHER

Thomas Winker had been hired by the mayor to work on a project for New York City. Thomas, formerly a free-lance consultant, liked the idea of working when he wanted to work, but he had mixed feelings about coming in "at the top" as a political executive. Nevertheless, his last project had been overseas, and he was glad to be back in New York, his original home town. The mayor had hired Thomas to analyze the advisability of either "contracting out" garbage collection, expanding city garbage collection capacity, or going to a twenty-four-hour collection system. Thomas saw evidence of the problem that morning as he drove over the bridge to Manhattan. At that very moment, he could look out the window of his car and see the garbage barges being towed down the East River; they weren't a pretty sight.

As Thomas watched the traffic inch forward over the bridge, he thought over the initial briefing he had received by fax two weeks ago in Paris. The city currently operates a sanitation department of 2,538 people using 781 garbage trucks. The cost of one day for each truck is $720 in wages for three people (eight-hour shift) and $200 for maintenance. The collective bargaining contract calls for a "shift differential" of 15 percent above the standard $30 per hour for the truck crews if the crews work other than 6:00 A.M. to 3:00 P.M. or any other nonstandard eight-hour shift. The contract has three years to go before it expires.

A recent study indicated that there is a 60 percent chance that the amount of garbage to be collected in the city will increase by 14 percent the next year and by 18 percent the following year. The briefing also indicated that many of the larger firms in the city are contemplating using a private garbage service (WE-HAUL, Inc.), which had recently begun competing with the city. The briefing concluded that whereas the amount of garbage to be collected would rise, there was a 40 percent chance that the amount the city would be required to collect might either fall slightly or remain steady.

As the traffic sped up after the bridge, Thomas reviewed the list of the information he still needed that he had made the night before. First, he needed to know what it would cost to maintain the current fleet of trucks if the city collected garbage twenty-four hours a day. Second, he needed some information about what new trucks would cost. If he recommended that the city expand its garbage pickup, he was sure that the mayor's office would want cost estimates. When he reached his office, Thomas went right to work. A quick check of the maintenance records for the large trucks indicated that he could expect a 20 percent increase in maintenance costs if he recommended that the city operate the trucks twenty-four hours a day. Thomas called the TIDY-TRUCK manufacturer and got a quote of $82,000 for a new truck if the city ordered that year. They also told him that they expect a 6 percent price increase next year.

Just after Thomas put down the phone, his liaison with the city, Rachael Swiniki, called to tell him that the private contractor (WE-HAUL) had offered to collect the additional garbage at a "special rate" for the city of $18 per ton for the first year and $20 per ton for the second year. Rachael ended the conversation by casually adding, "Just so that you know, since you're relatively new in town, WE-HAUL is a non-union company. " Thomas thoughtfully replaced the phone in its holder. He swiveled his chair around to his computer and called up his appointments for the next few days. The day after next, he was scheduled to meet with the president of the local sanitation workers' union. When the union heard about the offer from WE-HAUL, they were going to be quite concerned about the possibility of the city contracting to a nonunion operator.

Antonio Piace was not what Thomas had expected as the president of the sanitation workers' union. When Antonio entered the office, his most prominent feature was the very expensive suit he wore—or perhaps it was the Harvard Law School tie. Thomas had the feeling that Antonio knew more about him than he did about Antonio when Antonio began the conversation by asking Thomas how it felt to be back in New York after all these years. "It's nice to see a home-town boy get some of the work from the city, " Antonio purred. Thomas leaned back in his chair and regarded Antonio through half-shuttered eyes. "Why don't we save the 'good old boy' routine for later?" Thomas said softly. "By the way, your Bronx accent certainly doesn't show at all."

Antonio relaxed and grinned. "So you've done your homework, too. Good, that will save me the trouble of establishing my tough-guy side." Thomas returned the smile and suggested that they get right to the point. Antonio arranged some papers in his lap and began what was obviously a carefully prepared statement. "The union signed an agreement four years ago that included a clause prohibiting the contracting of bargaining union work to outside organizations. In addition, the contract contains a clause that requires union approval of any change in hours or working conditions beyond those necessitated by emergency situations. Finally, the contract provides for an expedited grievance process for policy grievances." Antonio looked directly at Thomas. "We intend to make sure that the contract is either enforced or renegotiated entirely."

Thomas allowed the silence to stretch out to a full minute. Then he slowly leaned over the desk toward Antonio. "First of all, the city legal department's interpretation of the no-contracting clause is that it applies only to 'current bargaining unit work.' They are quite confident that new garbage collection can be contracted out by calling it a 'special service.' Second, emergency conditions may include a public health hazard, which persists when garbage is not collected promptly. Such a condition might last for several years. Finally, the grievance process you refer to requires the city to appoint a neutral arbitrator who is mutually acceptable. I'm sure you can appreciate just how long that might take if one side or the other were very hard to please." The two men looked at each other with measured stares.

Antonio rose to leave. As he put his papers back into his briefcase he paused, shrugged his shoulders, and slipped one across the desk to Thomas. "Before you make your final recommendation to the city, I suggest that you look into this issue." On the paper Thomas saw three names and a rather large figure with a dollar sign in front of it. "Should I recognize these names?" said Thomas in a puzzled tone. "You would if you knew who owned WE-HAUL," said Antonio. At the door he turned and said, "The money represents the total campaign contributions made to the mayor by those people. Have a nice day."

Thomas picked up the piece of paper and looked at it with distaste. He had wondered why the city had created a new position to make the recommendation when the Sanitation Department had people who were almost as well qualified. He had wondered even more why the mayor had called him back from Europe to do the report. Some of the reasons were becoming clear. The numbers made contracting out the most prudent financial option, but it was sure to cause labor trouble. Now the suggestion that the outside contractor had exercised some political pull to get the inside track made it even more obvious why Thomas had been asked to do the study. If a newly appointed "expert" recommended that the city contract out, it would look better than if the city simply decided to award the contract to a well-connected firm. Thomas closed his eyes and rubbed his forehead. He had left Paris for this?

DISCUSSION QUESTIONS

1. Do you think that the union is right when it insists that garbage collection has to be done by members of the union?
2. Should it have any effect at all on Thomas's recommendation that the owners of WE-HAUL were heavy contributors to the mayor's campaign?
3. In making his recommendation, what compromise could Thomas advise the city to offer the union?

THE MESS IN SOMEWHERE CITY

The outgoing mayor had shaken all the hands of both friends and enemies and departed from city hall, creating a general feeling of relief among those who were staying on. Her four years as mayor had been filled with new initiatives and a great deal of turmoil. One of the programs that had begun immediately after she was first elected was a job training program for those on welfare in Somewhere City. The mayor had deftly combined federal, state, and city funds to make it possible for almost all of the welfare recipients to enroll in some form of job training. Ira Barrish, a program analyst for the city, was hoping that the new mayor would do a little stock-taking before plunging into additional initiatives.

Norman Worton, head of the transition team of the new mayor, asked Ira to look into the results of all this job training. Norman told Ira that he wants an answer to two questions: did the programs result in fewer people on welfare? and did the people find employment in the type of job for which they were trained? As an experienced program analyst, Ira knew that getting the information was only the beginning of the problem.

Ira thought back to the way the program was set up. As each welfare applicant was enrolled, the caseworker filled out a form that indicated the education and work experience of each applicant. Then each client took a rudimentary skills test, which indicated what type of skills he or she might need to develop before being enrolled in the program. Finally, each client took a preference test, which indicated the type of work each found interesting. Using those three scores, the caseworker referred the client to one of five job-training programs: clerical, mechanical, janitorial, retail sales, or bookkeeping.

The training programs were run by the local community college, which provided a ten-week program of three hours a night, two nights a week. Over 80 percent of those enrolled finished the program. The former mayor had been very proud of that figure. The community college tried to keep track of the graduates of the training by sending out surveys every three months to determine what each student was doing. As a result, it should be possible to get a current address for about 75 percent of all of the people who have gone through the program.

"It will be harder to determine whether each person who found employment is actually using the skills learned in the training," thought Ira. He needed to design a survey instrument that will help determine this. Clearly, the most difficult task is how to figure out a way to determine whether the number of people on welfare has declined. Because the welfare records are confidential, Ira will not be able simply to ask the Welfare Department to match the names on the Welfare Department lists. Although the total number of cases is available and the number of new cases opened and old cases closed each month can be determined, Ira will still have to figure out what is a reasonable way to estimate the impact of the program.

With a sigh, Ira returned to the office to draft a preliminary plan to answer the two questions posed by the transition team leader. Ira knew his own tenure with the city may in fact be partly determined by how well this study was designed. Within a few days, Ira had constructed three surveys: one to be sent to the clients who had finished the program, one to be sent to the employers who had hired the clients, and one to welfare workers who had initially screened the clients.

Norman Worton had worked at a variety of jobs over the past ten years. His appointment to head the transition team for the new mayor was a big break, and he intended to make the most of it. Norman called Ira late one afternoon just before the offices closed. "How is the study of the job training programs going?" Norman inquired. "Fine," said Ira. "The responses are still trickling in, but it looks like we will have about a 70 percent response." "Is that good or bad?" Norman asked. "That's pretty good for this type of research," Ira replied. "So, was the program a success or not?" Norman asked eagerly.

"That depends on how you define success," Ira hedged. "The vast majority of the respondents are employed—almost 80 percent in fact. The problem is that they aren't necessarily employed in the fields for which they were trained. To tell the truth, only about 20 percent of those who are employed found jobs in their field of training. Most of the others are working in the personal services industry." "What is the personal services industry?" Norman said in a puzzled voice. "Well, personal services include working at the fast food outlets," Ira responded.

"What about the welfare caseload? Has there been any decrease?" Norman asked uneasily. "The total number of cases is about the same as it was before the program began," Ira said firmly, "but I think that is a kind of success. With unemployment rising in the city, we should have experienced an increase instead of a level rate." "How are you going to write this up for the mayor?" Norman asked. "I think I'll put together some charts showing the data and let the mayor decide whether the program ought to continue," said Ira. "Good idea," Norman said. "The mayor will probably have his own ideas about what constitutes success or failure."

DISCUSSION QUESTIONS

1. What do you think explains the overall high rate of employment but the low rate of employment in the field of training?
2. Do you think that Ira should have set up criteria for judging the program before the research was begun?
3. What other factors could Ira have considered in studying the impact of the training program?

SIDING WITH SUPERANALYST

Ken Welch was a summer intern in the management services division of a large federal installation. During his three-month assignment, Ken was to undertake a variety of projects related to the management concerns in the various laboratories at the center. The management services division was a part of the Department of Personnel but, since personnel in the division often acted as troubleshooters for top management, the unit enjoyed considerable prestige within the department and, correspondingly, received special attention from its director.

After a period of about two weeks, in which Ken was given a general introduction to the work of the division, the department, and the center, Rick Arnold, one of the permanent analysts, asked Ken to help him with a study of the recruitment process in one of the computer laboratories. Because this was exactly the kind of project Ken had hoped would grow out of his summer experience, he jumped at the opportunity to become involved. He was especially pleased that Rick, who was clearly one of the favorites of the division's chief and who was jokingly but respectfully known as "Superanalyst," had asked for his help. In addition to gaining some experience himself, Ken would have the opportunity to watch a high-powered management analyst at work. Moreover, since it was clear that Rick had the ear of the division's chief, there were possibilities for at least observing some of the interactions at that level, perhaps even participating in meetings at the highest levels of the center's management. All in all, it was an attractive assignment, one on which Ken immediately began to work.

As it turned out, however, Ken could not do all that much. Because Rick was the principal analyst, he clearly wanted to take the lead in this project, something that seemed perfectly appropriate to Ken. But, as Rick had several other ongoing projects, there were considerable periods in which Ken found himself with little to do on the recruitment project. He was therefore more than happy to help out when Eddie Barth, one of the older members of the staff, asked if Ken would help him put together some organizational charts requested by top management. Eddie was one of a small group of technicians who had formed one of the two units brought together several years before to form the management services division. Ken soon discovered that the construction of an organizational chart, especially in the hands of these technicians, became a highly specialized process, involving not only endless approvals but also complicated problems of graphic design and reproduction far beyond what might be imagined. Ken was certainly less interested in this work than in the more human problems he encountered in the recruitment project, but Eddie had always been cordial and seemed to be happy to have some help. So Ken drew charts.

After a couple of weeks of working on the two projects, Ken began to receive signals that all was not well with his work. Another intern in the office overheard a conversation in the halls about the overly energetic interns that had been hired. One of the secretaries commented that she hoped Ken could "stand the heat." As Ken felt neither overly energetic nor under any heat, these comments were curious. Maybe they were talking about someone else, he thought.

A few days later, however, Ken was asked to come to Jim Pierson's office. Jim, another of the older members of the staff, who, Ken thought, had even headed the technical unit, had remained rather distant, though not unpleasant, during Ken's first weeks at the center. While others had been quite friendly, inviting Ken to parties and asking him to join the personnel department's softball team, Jim had seemed somewhat aloof. But then Ken and Jim had very little contact on the job, so maybe, Ken reasoned, it was not so strange after all. Ken saw the meeting as a friendly gesture on Jim's part and looked forward to getting better acquainted. Any hopes of a friendly conversation, however, were immediately dispelled: as soon as Ken arrived, Jim began a lecture on how to manage one's time, specifically pointing out that taking on too many projects meant that none would be well done. Although there were no specifics, Jim was clearly referring to the two projects on which Ken had been working.

Ken was stunned by the meeting. No one had in any way questioned the quality of his work; there were no time conflicts between the two projects, and, even if there had been, Ken wondered, why would Jim take it on himself to deliver such a reprimand? Later that afternoon, Ken shared his conversation with the other intern, who commented that Jim had always felt angered that, when the two units were brought together, he was not made director. Ken hinted at the controversy the next day in a conversation with Rick but received only a casual remark about the "out-of-date" members of the division. Ken began to feel that he was a pawn in some sort of office power struggle and immediately resolved to try to get out of the middle. As soon as he had an opportunity to see the division chief, he explained the whole situation, including his feeling that no real problems existed and that he was being used. The chief listened carefully but offered no real suggestions. He said he would keep an eye on the situation.

Later in the week, at a beer-drinking session after a softball game, the director of the department of personnel asked how the internship was going. In the ensuing conversation, Ken told him what had happened. The director launched into a long discourse on the difficulties he had experienced in reorganizing units within his department. But he also pointed out how the combination of the two units into the division had decreased his span of control and made the operation of the department considerably easier. It was clear that he preferred the more analytical approach to management services represented by the chief and by Superanalyst. In part, he said that the reorganization had buried one of his main problems, or, Ken thought later, maybe he said it would do so soon.

DISCUSSION QUESTIONS

1. What do think accounted for the confusion Ken Welch experienced?

2. What underlying assumptions about human behavior provide the basis for Ken's actions?
3. What assumptions seem to underlie the actions of others?
4. How would you suggest that communications in the organization be improved to prevent misunderstandings of this sort?

PUBLIC ADMINISTRATION
AND THE FUTURE

—

Where do we go from here? What does the future hold for administrators in public organizations at the federal, state, and local levels, as well as for those in nonprofit organizations? First, you will likely find the institutions of government undergoing tremendous change over the coming years. Traditional hierarchical structures and the rigid management practices that have sustained them are being challenged in both the public and private sectors. The search for more democratic processes in the administration of government will very likely continue, potentially aided by technological developments that make a wider sharing of information and control possible. In this process, we are likely to experience less concern for rules and structures than for the needs, interests, and values of the individual.

Beyond these institutional shifts, there is no question that public administrators in the coming decades will be involved in trying to solve some of the most difficult and intractable problems facing the planet—problems ranging from energy and the environment to global stability. In facing such problems, you will need exceptional skill, insight, and creativity. Equally important, you will need the personal and interpersonal skills to make things happen, even in circumstances marked by complexity, ambiguity, and turbulence. The successful manager will be the manager who can make things happen, in spite of all the difficulties the "real world" presents. Finally, as a public manager, you will need to be even more sensitive to the ethical issues facing public organizations in a democratic society. There will be opportunities for public administrators in the future to open their organizations to greater involvement and, in turn, to build a greater sense of commitment and responsibility on the part of both citizens and public employees. Nothing will be more important in this effort than to restore a sense of dignity and worth to the public service.

These sentiments are echoed in the four articles in this chapter. We begin with Harlan Cleveland's characterization of the "twilight of hierarchy." Cleveland sees the growth of an information society as having profound implications for the structure of future organizations. Arguing that the management of information is different from the management of things, Cleveland suggests that the old ways of managing (using concepts such as secrecy, control, and hierarchy) are no longer appropriate. Consequently, older pyramids of influence are giving way to new approaches to shared information and shared organization. (You'll find plenty to debate in reading this article!)

Next, Ken Hunter, a futurist working in the General Accounting Office at the federal level, suggests some ways in which federal managers may participate in resolving some extremely difficult political and economic concerns that are now emerging. Hunter recommends that we develop a new way of thinking and acting on problems, one that is global, long-term, and cross-cutting. You might note that one of Hunter's hopes for the future lies in developing more effective leaders—leaders who can deal with change and complexity.

The article that follows is a review of the implications of future trends for state and local government prepared by Henry H. Hitchcock and Joseph F. Coates. Hitchcock and Coates outline a number of major areas of concern that will likely occupy those at the state and local levels for several decades. You should note the wide variety of topics that are on the agenda of those in state and local governments. No longer are governments at these levels unidimensional; now they are both busy and complex. Correspondingly, the need for highly trained professionals to work in these areas will be great.

Finally, similar forecasts with respect to nonprofit organizations are offered by Forrest P. Chisman. Central to his analysis is a lesson that will apply to many public organizations—that the future depends in part on our nation's capacity to draw on a wide range of public and private resources in the solution of public problems. Chisman underscores a positive role for government complemented by the work of voluntary and nonprofit organizations.

Our final profile features Robert L. Bendick, Jr., Director of Rhode Island's Department of Environmental Management. This profile shows how an individual with an interest in an important topic—in this case, environmental quality—can make a difference through involvement in public service. The article also shows that it's not necessarily easy. Both the political and the managerial challenges are significant. Especially note the examples of Bendick's relationship with the legislature and with the governor's office, but also the excitement and significance of Bendick's work.

The two cases in this chapter are purely speculative. In the first case, "A Room with a View— At a Price," you will see one possible expansion of the information-gathering ability of the government. The case poses questions about what is an appropriate role for government in the leisure activities of citizens. The case also indicates how computers might be used to monitor the performance of future public administrators on behalf of citizens' rights.

"Volunteers in Service to the World" looks at the possibilities of a dramatic expansion of volunteerism. You may not be happy about some of the features of this type of organization, but the case explores the process by which many people will escape the confines of contemporary bureaucracies. The role of technology in both of these cases is assumed to be benign; this may be more a wish than a certainty. By creating the visions of our future now, we increase slightly the chances that our actions will produce a future we desire.

THE TWILIGHT OF HIERARCHY: SPECULATIONS ON THE GLOBAL INFORMATION SOCIETY

Harlan Cleveland

THE INFORMATIZATION OF SOCIETY

It is still shocking, 40 years later, to remember that the Manhattan Project, the huge secret organization which produced the atom bomb during World War II, did not employ on its staff a single person whose full-time assignment was to think hard about the policy implications of the project if it should succeed. Thus no one was working on nuclear arms control—though I. I. Rabi says he and Robert Oppenheimer used to discuss it earnestly over lunch. We have been playing catch-up, not too successfully, ever since.

The Manhattan Project was not an exception; it was the rule. For 300 years until the 1970s, science and technology were quite generally regarded as having a life of their own, an "inner logic," an autonomous sense of direction. Their self-justifying ethic was change and "growth." But in the 1970s, society started to take charge—not of scientific discovery but of its technological fallout. The decision not to build the SST or deploy an ABM system even though we knew how to make them, the dramatic change in national environmental policy, and the souring of the nuclear power industry, bear witness.

The most prominent and pervasive consequence of the people's concern about the impacts and implications of new technologies is what the French call "l'informatization de la société." The made-up word, which we will Americanize to "informatization," will serve as well as any to describe what is happening to some of our key concepts and conceptions as information becomes the dominant resource in "post-industrial society." (The new word is certainly better than "post-industrial," which describes the future by saying it comes after the past.)

The revolutions that began with Charles Babbage's "analytical engine" (less than 150 years ago) and Guglielmo Marconi's wireless telegraphy (not yet a century old) started on quite different tracks. But a quarter of a century past, computers and telecommunications began to converge to produce a combined complexity, one interlocked industry that is transforming our personal lives, our national politics, and our international relations.

The industrial era was characterized by the influence of humankind over things, including nature as well as the artifacts of man. The information era features a sudden increase in humanity's power to think and therefore to organize.

The "information society" does not replace, it overlaps, the growing and extracting and processing and manufacturing and recycling and distribution and consumption of tangible things. Agriculture and industry continue to progress by doing more with less through better knowledge, leaving plenty of room for a knowledge economy that, in statistics now widely accepted, accounts for more than half of our work force, our national product and our global reach.

A DOMINANT RESOURCE, A DIFFERENT RESOURCE

The size and scope of "the information society" are now familiar even in the popular literature. We can take it as read that information is the dominant resource in the United States, and coming to be so in other "advanced" or "developed" countries. To take only one cross-section of this startling shift, the actual production, extraction and growing of things now soaks up a good deal less than a quarter of our human resources. Of all the rest, which used to be lumped together as "services," more than two-thirds are information workers. By the end of the century, something like two-thirds of all work will be information work. . . .

It is not only in the United States that the informatization of society has proceeded so far so fast. A study by the Organization for Economic Cooperation and Development (the club of richer nations, with headquarters in Paris) puts the average information labor force of several of its member countries at more than one-third of the total during the early- to mid-1970s, and rising: the information component of labor increased its share of the total by 2.8 percent for each five-year period since World War II.

Farming, which in some people's vocabularies is the most primitive of pursuits, is probably farther ahead than most industries in the embedding of information in physical processes. Says agricultural economist G. Edward Schuh: "All of the increase in agricultural output from the mid-1920s through the mid-1970s (a fifty-year period!) came about with no increase in the capital stock of physical resources. It was all due to new knowledge or information. That makes clear the extent to which knowledge is an output or resource."

If information (organized data, refined into knowledge and combined into wisdom) is now our "crucial resource," as Peter Drucker describes it, what does that portend for the future? Thinking about the inherent characteristics of information provides some clues to the vigorous rethinking that lies ahead for all of us:

1. *Information is expandable.* In 1972, the same year *The Limits to Growth* was published, John McHale came out with a book called *The Changing Information Environment* which argued that information expands as it is used. Whole industries have grown up to exploit this characteristic of information: scientific research, technology transfer, computer software (which already makes a contribution to the U.S. economy that is three times the contribution of computer hardware), and agencies for publishing, advertising, public relations, and government propaganda to spread the word (and thus to enhance the word's value).

The ultimate "limits to growth" of knowledge and wisdom are time (time available to human minds for reflecting, analyzing, and integrating the information that will be "brought to life" by being used) and the capacity of people—individually and in groups—to analyze and think integratively. There are obvious limits to the time each of us can devote to the production and refinement of knowledge and wisdom. But the capacity of humanity to integrate its collective experience through relevant individual thinking is certainly expandable—not without limits, to be sure, but within limits we cannot now measure or imagine.

2. *Information is not resource-hungry.* Compared to the processes of the steel-and-automobile economy, the production and distribution of information are remarkably sparing in their requirements for energy and other physical and biological resources.

Investments, price policies and power relationships which assume that the more developed countries will gobble up disproportionate shares of "real" resources are overdue for wholesale revision.

3. *Information is substitutable.* It can and increasingly does replace capital, labor, and physical materials. Robotics and automation in factories and offices are displacing workers and thus requiring a transformation of the labor force. Any machine that can be accessed by computerized telecommunications doesn't have to be in your own inventory. And Dieter Altenpohl, an executive of Alusuisse, has calculations and charts to prove that, as he says, "The smarter the metal, the less it weighs."

4. *Information is transportable*—at close to the speed of light. As a result, remoteness is now more choice than geography. You can sit in Auckland, New Zealand, and play the New York stock markets in real time—if you don't mind keeping slightly peculiar hours. And the same is true, without the big gap in time-zones, of people in any rural hamlet in the United States. In the world of information-richness, you will be able to be remote if you want to, but you'll have to work at it.

5. *Information is diffusive.* It tends to leak—and the more it leaks the more we have. It is not the inherent tendency of natural resources to leak. Jewels may be stolen; a lump or two of coal may fall off the coal car on its way from Montana; there is an occasional spillage of oil in the ocean. But the leakage of information is wholesale, pervasive, and continuous. In the era of the institutionalized leak, monopolizing information is very nearly

a contradiction in terms; that can be done only in more and more specialized fields, for shorter and shorter periods of time.

6. *Information is shareable.* Shortly before his death, Colin Cherry wrote that information by nature cannot give rise to exchange transactions, only to sharing transactions. Things are exchanged: if I give you a flower or sell you my automobile, you have it and I don't. But if I sell you an idea or give you a fact, we both have it. An information-rich environment is thus a sharing environment. That needn't mean an environment without standards, rules, conventions and ethical codes. It does mean the standards, rules, conventions and codes are going to be different from those created to manage the zero-sum bargains of market trading and traditional international relations.

THE EROSION OF HIERARCHIES

I am not a scholar of information/communication theory, but in my listening and reading as a practicing generalist I am struck with three seminal ideas as containing the most nourishment for our purpose, which is to think about how the new information environment is likely to modify our inherited assumptions about rule, power and authority.

One is that information (in its generic sense) is not like other resources, nor, as some would have it, merely another form of energy. It is not subject to the laws of thermodynamics, and efforts to explain the new information environment by using metaphors from physics will just get in our way.

A second idea I find nourishing is that the ultimate purpose of all knowledge is to organize things or people, arrange them in ways that make them different from the way they were before. This is true of rearranging the genes in a chromosome, and it is equally true of rearranging people's ideas to create a movement. There is no such thing as useless knowledge, only people who haven't yet learned how to use it. This was the powerful message carried in a 1979 article in *Science* by Lewis Branscomb, chief scientist of IBM. He wrote that information is so far from being scarce that

it is in "chronic surplus." There is still plenty for scientists to find out, but "the yawning chasm is between what is already known by some but not yet put to use by others."

A third insight, from the late British communications theorist Colin Cherry, is the distinction between the information ("message") itself and the service of delivering it. You may own the journal you hold in your hand, but you don't own its contents, the facts and ideas in the journal. Neither, now that I have written them down and you and I are sharing them, do I.

The historically sudden dominance of the information resource has, it seems to me, produced a kind of theory crisis, a sudden sense of having run out of basic assumptions. This is not only the product of information and communication technologies (and their fusion in the new systems that are sprouting daily in the deregulated environment created when the U.S. government by deciding to stop suing IBM and settle with AT&T said in effect that information and telecommunications were all really one industry—for which again the French have a name, *l'informatique*). Other dramatic extensions of scientific rationalism and engineering genius such as nuclear fission and gene-splicing—all with an indispensable assist from the new information technologies—have also made their contribution to the *bouleversement* of long-held social and political convictions.

But somewhere near the center of the confusion is the trouble we make for ourselves by carrying over into our thinking about information (which is to say symbols) concepts developed for the management of things—concepts such as property, depletion, depreciation, monopoly, "inevitable" unfairness, geopolitics, the class struggle, and top-down leadership.

The assumptions we have inherited are not producing satisfactory growth with acceptable equity either in the capitalistic West or in the socialist East. As Simon Nora and Alain Minc wrote in their landmark report to the President of France: "The liberal and Marxist approaches, contemporaries of the production-based society, are rendered questionable by its demise."

The most troublesome concepts are those which were created to deal with the main problems presented by the management of things—problems such as their scarcity, their bulk, their limited substitutability for each other, the expense and trouble in transporting them, the paucity of information about them (which made them comparatively easy to hide) and the fact that, being tangible, they could be hoarded. It was "in the nature of things" that the few had access to resources and the many did not.

Thus, the inherent characteristics of physical resources ("natural" and man-made) made possible the development of hierarchies of power based on control (of new weapons, of energy sources, of trade routes, of markets, and especially of knowledge), hierarchies of influence based on secrecy, hierarchies of class based on ownership, hierarchies of privilege based on early access to valuable resources, and hierarchies of politics based on geography.

Each of these five bases for discrimination and unfairness is crumbling today—because the old means of control are of dwindling efficacy, secrets are harder and harder to keep, and ownership, early arrival, and geography are of dwindling significance in getting access to the knowledge and wisdom which are the really valuable legal tender of our time.

Out of dozens of assumptions requiring a newly skeptical stare in the new knowledge environment, these five seem to me to bear most directly on leadership and management, because they are likely to affect most profoundly the ways in which, and the purposes for which, people will in future come together in organizations to make something different happen.

POWER AND PARTICIPATION

Knowledge is power, as Francis Bacon wrote in 1597. So the wider the spread of knowledge, the more power gets diffused. For the most part individuals and corporations and governments don't have a choice about this; it is the ineluctable consequence of creating—through education—societies with millions of knowledgeable people.

We see the results all around us, and around the world. More and more work gets done by horizontal process—or it doesn't get done. More and more decisions are made with wider and wider consultation—or they don't "stick." If the Census Bureau counted each year the number of committees per thousand population, we would have a rough quantitative measure of the bundle of changes called "the information society." A revolution in the technology of organization—the twilight of hierarchy—is already well under way.

Once information can be spread fast and wide—rapidly collected and analyzed, instantly communicated, readily understood by millions—the power monopolies that closely-held knowledge used to make possible were subject to accelerating erosion.

In the old days when only a few people were well educated and "in the know," leadership of the uninformed was likely to be organized in vertical structures of command and control. Leadership of the informed is different: it results in the necessary action only if exercised mainly by persuasion, bringing into consultation those who are going to have to do something to make the decision a decision. Where people are educated and are not treated this way, they either balk at the decisions made or have to be dragooned by organized misinformation backed by brute force. Recent examples of both results have been on display in Poland.

This is the rationale for Chester Barnard's durable theory of the executive function: that authority is delegated upward. As "director" of an organization, you have no power that is not granted to you by your "subordinates." Eliciting their continuous (and if possible cheerful) cooperation is your main job as director; without it, you cannot get the most routine tasks (for which others are holding you, not your staff, responsible) accomplished. Indeed, nowadays in many offices orders that used to be routinely accepted are now resisted or refused. In the modern American office, if you want a cup of coffee you don't take that co-worker, your secretary, off her (or his) own work to get it for you.

In an information-rich polity, the very definition of "control" changes. Very large numbers of people empowered by knowledge—coming together in parties, unions, factions, lobbies, interest-groups, neighborhoods, families, and hundreds of other structures—assert the right or feel the obligation to "make policy."

Decision making proceeds not by "recommendations up, orders down," but by development of a shared sense of direction among those who must form the parade if there is going to be a parade.

Collegial not command structures become the more natural basis for organization. Not "command and control," but conferring and "networking," become the mandatory modes for getting things done.

"Planning" cannot be done by a few leaders, or by even the brightest whiz-kids immured in a systems analysis unit or a planning staff. Real-life "planning" is the dynamic improvisation by the many on a general sense of direction—announced by the few, but only after genuine consultation with those who will have to improvise on it.

More participatory decision making implies a need for much information, widely spread, and much feedback, seriously attended—as in biological processes. Participation and public feedback become conditions precedent to decisions that stick.

That means more openness, less secrecy—not as an ideological preference but as a technological imperative. Secrecy goes out of fashion anyway, because secrets are so hard to keep.

Most of the history we learn in school is so narrowly focused on visible leaders that it may give us the wrong impression about leadership processes even in earlier times. We learn that Genghis Khan or Louis XIV or Ibn Saud or the emperor of Japan or George Washington said this and did that—as though he thought it up by himself, consulted with nobody and wrote it without the help of a ghostwriter. But even in ancient, "traditional" societies I suspect that effective leadership consisted in being closely in touch with where the relevant publics were ready to be told to go.

Consensus is a prominent feature of many cultures now dismissed as "primitive." The Polynesians in the Pacific Islands with their circular village councils and the American Indians around their campfires made (and in some degree still make) decisions by fluid procedures which may induce more genuine participation than a "modern" meeting run by parliamentary procedure. In the agora of Athens and the Roman "Senate and public" (the SPQR), there seems to have been lively participation by those (well-born male citizens) qualified to take part.

The difference in the current scene is the sheer scale of the relevant publics. In "democratic" Athens slaves, women, tradesmen and other noncitizens didn't presume to play in the decision games. The notion that "all Men," let alone whole peoples, had inalienable rights came in only with the Enlightenment, a scant three centuries ago—and has been made effective, still in a minority of the world's nations, only in the 20th century. (In Switzerland, women still can't vote.)

Participatory fever is contagious. "Public policy" used to mean "what the government does." Now it includes corporate policies, collective bargaining agreements, the cost of health care, the recruitment of university presidents, lobbying practices, equal employment opportunity, environmental protection, tax shelters, waste disposal, private contributions to political candidates, the sex habits of employees, or just about any other "insider" activities that outsiders think are important enough to engage their time and attention.

The biggest issues so far have to do with the quality of public responsibility that shows forth in the actions of corporations, universities, hospitals, and the thousands of other structures in which executives make the decisions that serve people, cost them, anger or please them.

The rising tide of participation is reflected in dramatic organizational changes. Big corporations now usually have a vice president for keeping the corporation out of trouble with nosy outsiders, or even with their own stockholders and employees, who raise questions about what the company ought to produce, who it ought to employ, and how it ought to invest its money.

Should "my" company, or any American company, make and market nerve gas, even if the government does want to buy some? Should "my" company, or any American company, promote nuclear proliferation by selling to developing countries nuclear power plants that make plutonium, the fuel for nuclear weapons, as a byproduct of generating electricity? Shouldn't "my" company have more women, and blacks, and American Indians in its employ—and especially in its board and top management? Should a company whose stock I own invest my money in South Africa? Should "my" company, or any American company, pass the "social costs" of its profit-seeking—overcrowding, the paving of green space, radioactive risk, dirt, noise, toxic waste, acid rain, or whatever—to the general public? Should our community hospital perform abortions, splice genes, change people's sex, invest in expensive equipment that can help only a few affluent patients? Should our state university do secret work for the Defense Department? Should the CIA recruit our students for who-knows-what clandestine wars in other people's countries?

Such questions cannot be brushed aside without raising their decibel level. There are ways to deal with all of them: shifts of policy or consultative processes or diversionary moves or public explanations—in descending order of probable effectiveness. But the visibly responsible leaders increasingly have to build into their organizations, not as a public relations frill but as an essential ingredient in "bottom line" budgeting, staff members competent to help develop strategy on such issues as these. And the visible executive now has to be personally competent to defend the organization's public posture in public debate.

These "public responsibility" issues can make or break companies, products, and executive reputations. If you don't believe that, take a Nestle executive to lunch and ask him about marketing baby formula in the Third World.

DILEMMAS OF OPENNESS

The push for participation by all kinds of people, and the inherent leakiness of the information resource, combine to produce the modern executive's most puzzling dilemma. The dilemma must have been familiar to the first cave people who tried to bring other cave people together to get something done. But for us moderns, the scale of the perplexity is without precedent. The dilemma can be summarized in one question: How do you get everybody in on the act and still get some action? . . .

NAVIGATING THE NINETIES

Ken Hunter

Each day as I scan news reports of world events, I see a hurricane of change washing the world, with the United States in the eye of this hurricane, simply drifting. And I wonder: How long can this country continue to drift? When will the storm hit us? What will we do then?

Signs of this storm of change are everywhere. Japan, whose exports were once ridiculed as cheap and shoddy, is gaining major market share in industry after industry with its quality goods and services. The countries of Western Europe have chosen to create a single integrated market and have taken actions that seem likely to bring them to that goal within the decade. China is attempting economic reform without political reform—an unbalanced approach that is creating problems for Beijing and that leaves expectations for change in the 1990s fairly modest. The Soviet Union and Eastern Europe, on the other hand, are pursuing a more integrated strategy of economic *and* political reforms, including new political institutions and major arms reductions; these reforms now have enough momentum to guarantee major and enduring changes, although no one, including the Eastern Bloc countries themselves, seems certain of what the final outcome will be.

Throughout the rest of the world, decentralization and regionalism are in style. Problems that central governments have not been able to solve in the past few decades are being dealt with either on a smaller scale, by local governments and private industry, or on a broader scale, by regional organizations such as the Organization of American States or the Association of Southeast Asian Nations. Moreover, international organizations, such as those under the umbrella of the United Nations, are beginning to be used more extensively for their originally intended purposes—peacekeeping, world development financing, and settling of disputes—rather than just as rhetorical platforms. People all over the world are struggling toward new conceptions of democracy, economic health, and national security. Their leaders are searching for workable strategies to deal with current problems and for the powerful ideas, such as regional economic integration and sustainable development, that can guide the future actions of individuals and nations.

World history is at a turning point. Is the United States making the necessary adjustments? The gauges on the ship of state indicate that, on average, the country is economically and socially stable, with its internal systems functioning adequately. But these gauges only measure broad trends; they obscure the wide disparities that exist among different geographic regions and economic sectors. Furthermore, they don't register the problems that may—perhaps soon—emerge as full-blown crises.

So where does the United States go from here? Can we ride out the 1990s in the eye of the hurricane? Or must we pass through the storm? Is our post-World-War-II-vintage craft sturdy enough to make it? And, assuming we do get through, what lies beyond the storm that we need to be ready to deal with?

Only one thing is certain: The world we face in the future will be vastly different from the one we know now. The forces of change will see to that. There is no going back.

HOW WE GOT WHERE WE ARE

World War II left the United States with a storehouse of technology ready for use, an underemployed labor force, a huge pent-up economic demand, and no economic competitors in the global marketplace. Under these conditions, the United States was launched forward on a massive wave of economic growth that didn't begin to lose its force until the 1970s—a casualty of major changes in this country and abroad that had begun in the late 1960s. The events that signaled this turning point are all familiar: Vietnam, Watergate, the end of the Bretton Woods agreement, Roe vs. Wade, Nixon's opening to China, the entry of Japan Inc. into the global marketplace, and the rise of OPEC.

These events, it seems to me, have put Americans into a state of shock and denial. U.S. leaders and citizens alike have been denying that these changes are significant and that they require changes in our own behavior. Only in the past few months have events forced us to examine the nature of the major shifts taking place in the world, and so far that examination is very superficial. The majority of Americans remain focused on their own needs and desires, continuing the high-consumption life-style that we can now maintain only through credit and sales of assets. Little or no attention is paid to the future.

What's been going on in Washington all the while? Not much. The electorate is denying that serious problems exist, and the political consensus basically favors the policies that were created between the 1930s and the 1960s. So the nation's elected representatives have a mandate only to oversee the administration of government operations and to maintain the status quo by making the marginal changes required by external forces. Lacking any big assignments, they have taken on many little assignments, mostly on behalf of individual constituents and special interest groups. Through all this, these elected leaders have been able (with the help of the media) to make the annual endeavor to provide routine government funding and to implement needed marginal changes in policy seem like a really big event. Such a spectacle helps assure the markets that these marginal changes are all that's really needed and that business can continue as usual.

FROM ISSUES TO BIG MESSES

As the decades of denial have rolled on, the imbalances and conflicts we generally call "issues" have grown into "big messes." They are all long-term—it took years of neglect to create the messes we have in the environment, in drug addiction and the illegal industry that supports it, in the nation's financial institutions, in our education system, in infrastructure, and in housing. Again and again it turns out that technical analysts and auditors have reported internally on these deteriorating conditions but that policy officials have remained unconvinced and failed to take action at a time when the corrections would have

been easier and cheaper to make than they are now or will be in the future.

This pattern appeared in both the savings-and-loan industry and the weapons production industry; in both cases, GAO was the independent agent that gradually discovered the extent of the mess and painted a picture of it for the public. The thrift industry began deteriorating after the laws regulating it were changed in the early 1980s. By 1985, GAO had assessed the industry's condition and alerted Congress that the industry had problems with the quality of its assets as well as with interest rates. Unfortunately, it took four more years for the situation to get bad enough that any action was taken.

In the case of the nuclear weapons production industry, by the early 1980s GAO had reported that the federal government's nuclear facilities had safety and health problems and that the Department of Energy's oversight was inadequate. GAO discovered more and more problems as the 1980s progressed; it continued to report on them and to increase its estimates of the clean-up costs. As these estimates passed the $100-billion mark—nearly a decade after GAO began examining the problems—the issue finally got onto the nation's policy agenda. The search for solutions is now under way.

I expect the same pattern of events to emerge in other areas during the 1990s. Major water supply systems will continue to deteriorate and may collapse. The existing system of financial markets will be increasingly unable to effectively handle the global, continuous flow of transactions in stocks and commodities while at the same time serving as the primary source of capital financing. Health care in inner cities and rural communities will keep deteriorating, and there will be increased conflict among those who provide services, those who finance services, consumers, and regulators, with no real mechanism for resolving these disputes. Environmental damage will continue, and it may become clear that some of this damage is not reversible and that we must adapt to permanently deteriorated living conditions. In addition, there will be the wild cards—problems that we cannot foresee today.

One characteristic these really big messes share is longevity: It takes years for these major problems to brew. They also tend to be global in scope, since political borders have proven almost irrelevant to the flow of pollution, communications, money and credit, technology, weapons, and migration. Furthermore, these issues are cross-cutting. Such problems as the trade deficit, the underclass, and the deterioration of the nation's infrastructure don't fit into the prescribed domains of existing legislative committees, executive departments, academic disciplines, industry associations, and long-established interest groups, so they are automatically kicked upstairs and become the responsibility of the leadership.

Unfortunately, America's political institutions have great difficulty dealing with issues that are long-term, global, or cross-cutting. Americans generally have a natural "Pollyanna" factor—a basic optimism, a penchant for highlighting good news and denying indications of problems. Americans also tend to be shortsighted, favoring actions that have short-term benefits and long-term costs and opposing actions whose initial costs are clearly defined but whose benefits are unclear or off in the future. For example, the compromise strategy to address the savings-and-loan industry crisis was crafted to fit the industry's needs and the government's immediate budgetary constraints; it will be up to future generations to pay off the long-term debts that are now being incurred to cover payments to individuals who had money in the failed institutions.

Similarly, a natural protectionist bias emerges in any issue that involves international relationships. Jobs for American workers automatically become a major factor to be considered. If the issue is aid to developing countries, the question is, "How much of it will be used to buy goods and services from U.S. suppliers?" If the issue is intellectual property rights, the question is, "How can we protect the rights of Americans who hold patents, trademarks, or copyrights?" If the issue is the structure of regional trade arrangements, such as those emerging in Europe and Asia, the question is, "How can U.S. companies be guaranteed access to these markets?"

Compounding these problems is the fact that issues that are cross-cutting—as many of these are—bring out the worst bureaucratic instincts of even the most well-meaning people. All these issues tend to be forced onto top leaders, who must deal with petty bickering as well as substantive problems. For instance, to address the nation's drug abuse problem it became necessary to install a new White House official with a strong personality who could coordinate the wide array of actions under way in law enforcement, the military, foreign diplomacy, and health and social services. Each sector has its own view of the problem and its own approach—a situation that, if not handled skillfully, can become totally chaotic.

Because the really big messes are long-term, *and* global, *and* cross-cutting, our attempts to manage them have been less than adequate. Environmental policies, for example, include plenty of short-term fixes and lots of "further study of the problems and the alternatives"; lots of protection of U.S. industry, so that it can remain competitive and not have to absorb the costs of the environmental damage it creates; and plenty of bureaucratic conflict at all levels—international, national, state, and local.

Despite these impediments to real progress on major problems, people continue to seek elected office in this country. But they have learned to keep their campaigns free of any real examination of the big messes, which cannot be discussed in 20-second sound bites and which people really don't want to hear about, anyway. Not having campaigned for any substantive policy changes, elected officials have no mandate for advocating such changes or for even raising fundamental questions. Their only mandate is to seek marginal changes that will make the problems go away for now. So that's basically what Washington has been up to.

LOOKING TO THE 1990s

How long can the United States continue to avoid these unresolved issues while other countries have accepted the need for change and begun the process of reform? How might the dynamics of public policy in the United States change in the 1990s? What might trigger such a change?

It appears that America can maintain its addiction to high consumption and low investment as long as the Japanese and West Germans are willing to accept this country's credit and to defer their own consumption. Right now, they seem content to do so. Certainly some change in America's relationships with those two countries seems inevitable: Sooner or later the World-War-II residue of fear and suspicion must be confronted, and the next decade seems likely to see some restructuring of global military relationships. But it's difficult to say whether such a restructuring would result in a major reduction of the U.S. share of the defense bill in the Far East and Europe, or in Japan and Germany increasing their militaries beyond narrowly defined defensive forces. Neither Japan nor Germany seems likely to force these issues anytime soon, since they are sensitive and could create a great deal of conflict.

So one must look elsewhere for forces that might drive the United States to change its behavior and its policies. What about the American people? In general, their civic literacy is very poor; there seems to be little interest in how the government operates or in the processes of change. The individuals who will have to pay the bills for the country's current excesses, and whose standard of living will as a result be lower than that of their counterparts in West Germany and Japan, are now too young to vote or else don't vote in large numbers. Therefore, they are not likely to force change through the electoral process—but they would be quick to take their protests into the streets if some event pushed them beyond their threshold of tolerance.

Who else might trigger change? Existing businesses and interest groups have invested so much time and energy in gaining influence in the current system that they are among the strongest advocates of maintaining the status quo. Entrepreneurs are too few and too detached from the policy process to have much impact on it. And the majority of people in political leadership positions developed their values and approaches to public policy during the boom years. The President and most of the congressional leaders and committee chairs started their work in public office well before the major changes of the late 1960s and early 1970s. Back then, during the boom years, problems could be addressed one at a time, the international aspects of domestic issues were not significant enough to influence policy decisions, and innovation and analysis of options were worth doing since there were resources available to launch major new programs. Leading and legislating—designing and implementing new programs—were fun.

The major world changes that began more than 20 years ago removed the fun. Managing cutbacks and fighting to keep programs alive isn't much of a treat—policymaking just isn't what it used to be. Today's leaders still remember the good old days and seem to resent the politics of limits and survival. They seem to be having as much trouble as the public in accepting that changes need to be made.

Major changes can always be triggered by crises. But what kind of crisis might do it in the 1990s? Military threats and conflicts? Less and less likely, with the cold war thawing and the conflicts that endure being shifted to the agendas of international organizations. A stock market crash? The stock markets seem to have become detached from the real world of investment and the economy: The market can drop substantially without affecting the economy in any major way. A severe recession? It seems to me that a recession as severe as that of 1982 could be rationalized as inevitable after so many years of growth. How about the collapse of a major system—such as a communications system, air traffic control, the water supply to a major city, or an energy supply—that would cause serious economic and social disruption? These systems are so decentralized that they would deteriorate rather than collapse completely. Therefore the impact of a system's deterioration would be local and varied. Furthermore, the incident would be treated as a natural disaster rather than as the result of human neglect and so would not cause any demand for major change.

If there is no triggering event to make us examine our behavior and its consequences, we will have great difficulty cleaning up the big messes and we will miss some big opportunities. We can then expect to continue our slide downward relative to other nations that are conserving, saving and investing, and strengthening their long-term economic capabilities. Because the U.S. economy is large compared to the economies of other nations, we can be inefficient for a long time without losing overall economic leadership. But we can expect to lose leadership in a few more individual industries. For example, the U.S. software industry will probably remain a craft in which very talented people apply their skill to producing ever more sophisticated products for smaller and smaller markets, while another nation's industry will implement an approach to developing bread-and-butter-type software for huge markets in schools, offices, and homes.

In addition, the consequences of our long-term neglect of crucial problems will begin to mount up. Employers will continue to encounter new entrants into the labor market who lack the skills to become effective workers, let alone high performers. Environmental damage will continue to lower living conditions in this country. Homeless, drug-addicted, mentally ill, and unskilled individuals will continue to live below the safety net; some of them will continue to resort to drugs and crime as escapes, however temporary, from their hopeless lives.

As the decade drifts on, the American people's threshold of tolerance for relative discomfort may be approached or even passed. Parents will become troubled that they cannot be sure their children's living standard will be higher than theirs was; many will conclude that it will be lower. It will become more apparent that the entry of women into the labor market since the early 1970s was not just a matter of choice but was in many cases the only way for families to make ends meet. People will become aware that the Japanese and the Europeans are living better than Americans are—and they'll wonder how that could have happened. There will be growing concern with the quality of all types of products and services, especially public goods such as the roads on which people drive their (expensive) imported cars. Americans will also feel more uneasy and uncertain about the reliability of the water and power delivery systems. This country has demonstrated a high tolerance for ineffectiveness and inefficiency, but one has to believe that at some point there's a limit.

The mounting level of concern will probably translate into a shift in voter attitudes and expectations. The campaigns for the 1992 or 1996 elections may begin to address questions about the future and about the changes that need to be implemented now to make that future better for ourselves and our children. Interestingly, most of today's leaders who got their starts in the good old boom days will be out of active politics. The debates will be among candidates who entered politics during the last turning point— the 1968-73 period—when they ran for office as environmentalists, anti-Vietnam-War advocates, and post-Watergate political reformers. They gained office because, for that very brief period, voters were hungry for real reforms. Some of these representatives fought for those reforms, but as their constituents' hunger for change has dissipated, they have settled for marginal adjustments, quick fixes, and numbers games year after year. How these politicians handle shifts in voter attitudes and shape them into mandates for real change will be one of the critical variables in the next decade's political landscape. My hunch is that enough of them will take advantage of the opportunity to launch a real reform effort.

Such a grass-roots-driven modernization movement would include an array of policy changes. It could be directed at creating a government that is not just smaller, as the budget deficit dictates, but that is also *smarter*. In other words: A sharp reduction in subsidies to obsolete and inefficient producers. A big investment in education and training, in infrastructure, science, and technology— but with a focus on modernization. Revisions in accounting and financial practices that would force current producers and consumers to pay for the costs of environmental clean-up and protection rather than passing them on to future generations. Restructuring of organizations, simplification of computer software, and widespread training so that there will finally be some real benefits from the massive investments that have been made to bring computer technology into the workplace. Creating information services that cut through the information glut (which makes managing more difficult than ever) and enable people to see and deal with problems effectively. A new social contract that reflects the realities of the two-earner family. A shift in the formal and continuing education of the nation's leaders that emphasizes global, long-term, and cross-cutting ways of thinking rather than the currently prevalent short-term, narrow, discipline-based approaches. An acceptance of the constant need to monitor changes occurring in the world so that normal problems can be dealt with before they become big messes that can be fixed only through herculean efforts.

Unfortunately, to anticipate that such a transformation could take place quickly and directly is just wishful thinking. I do not believe that this country can sail through the 1990s without being affected by the storm of change occurring around us. How would we respond if the Japanese and West Germans really acted like our bankers (which they are) and began dictating the terms of U.S. fiscal, monetary, and industrial policies? How would we respond to a major upheaval in Mexico? How would we respond to widespread wars throughout Africa and the Middle East that included the use of tactical nuclear and biological weapons? How would we respond to the accidental detonation of a single nuclear weapon? How would we respond if the AIDS virus threatened to spread broadly among the white, heterosexual, non-intravenous-drug-using population of this country? How would we respond to evidence that environmental damage in some parts of the world might take hundreds of years to reverse and that millions of people should be relocated? How would we respond to a really big earthquake—much bigger than the one that hit San Francisco last year? How would we respond to a movement to restructure the United Nations, to strengthen its authority over international affairs, and to transform such places as Berlin and Hong Kong into "world cities" under U.N. sovereignty?

In my opinion, we have not prepared ourselves well for such contingencies. So far, however, we have been exceptionally lucky; and we have become fairly good at managing crises—at least one at a time. Therefore, it seems likely that the 1990s will not see a cataclysm but rather a long, drawn-out process of gradual change. Our bankers in Tokyo and Frankfurt will continue to support us, and over the course of the decade we will face several discrete and reasonably manageable crises.

This is about as optimistic as I can be. Of course, there is always the threat that our luck could fail and that several crises could converge upon us at once, overwhelming our leaders and political institutions and forcing major changes under adverse conditions, as in the 1930s. I'm reminded of the qualification that Herman Kahn attached to his forecasts: "assuming good luck and good management." Getting through the 1990s with a healthy polity, society, economy, and environment is going to require a considerable amount of both.

ACTIONS TODAY

The United States should follow a basic strategy of keeping the current big messes from getting totally out of hand *and* of acting on opportunities whenever possible. As we make policy decisions in pursuit of this strategy, three simple, over-arching ideas can serve as guides. First, we need to adopt a way of thinking about and acting on problems that is global, long-term, and cross-cutting. Second, we ought to keep in mind that education and training are the keys to success; so when in doubt, we should invest more in learning. Third, we should expect our elected leaders to manage change in our society and we should hold them personally accountable for the results not only of their actions but also of their decisions *not* to take action.

The need to develop new ways of thinking is critical. The solutions to problems do not lie in the traditional, narrowly defined boxes such as academic disciplines, but in the gaps between them. We need the flexibility, capacity, and know-how to take the ideas from one box and merge them with those from another. We need information systems and reporting procedures that highlight problems *before* they become big messes. We learn by trial and error—a risky and time-consuming process that requires a long-term perspective and a lot of patience.

Consider, for example, the restructuring of European political, military, and economic relationships that is now going on. This appears to be one of the most complex sets of social changes ever undertaken. One of its remarkable features is that the leaders who are guiding the reform process seem to be attempting to respond in moderation to each other and to each new phase of the situation. This contrasts sharply with the traditional process of change through war or revolution, with whoever wins getting to redesign the social and political institutions. Most individuals involved in Europe's current transition seem to understand that they have made a major shift to a new set of rules and that they are now at the very frontiers of social change, where each day's events must be evaluated before the next day's actions can be planned. In other words, Europeans are now fully engaged in creating their own future.

Another illustration of the need for new ways of thinking—a less positive example, unfortunately—is the current necessity of shifting from a strategy of all-out economic development without consideration of environmental costs to a global strategy of sustainable development. Such a shift requires new approaches in energy, agriculture, transportation, and housing, as well as in the way industry functions. But this shift is occurring slowly, which means that both the old and the new strategies are currently being used. This can lead to unwise choices.

A good example is energy. The search for an inexpensive, renewable energy source is a major focus of scientific research. Fusion researchers keep saying that they can deliver in another 20 years for a few more billion dollars (a promise we've heard every year for more than 20 years now). Modest research also continues on other alternatives. At the same time, the oil industry constantly explores for and discovers new sources, thereby increasing the quantity of proven reserves of oil and gas. And in most of the world, only half-hearted efforts are being made at conservation. In other words, we seem to be *counting* on a big energy breakthrough in the 21st century. I have great respect for our scientists' capabilities, but I think that to count on a breakthrough is irresponsible. It would be far wiser to assume that we will only have the technology that now exists and then be pleasantly surprised when and if the scientists come through.

The second of my guiding principles for the 1990s—that education is of paramount importance—touches on all areas of this country's life. Why is learning so important? For the individual, it creates more choices about what kind of work one does and who one works for, about how one spends one's leisure time, and about how one deals with the growing complexities of everyday life. For employers and for the economy, learning determines the quality of the work force and the company's—or the nation's—relative competitiveness in the marketplace. For society, learning affects the diversity and quality of the organizations, products, and services that are available. For the polity, it sets the electorate's intellectual level and degree of participation, the quality of the candidates, and the richness of the policy choices that are laid out. My approach would be to build into all education programs not only a core of basic knowledge but also a set of skills that would enable people to keep learning new material and solving new problems throughout their lives.

The third of my guiding principles—that the leader of any type of organization needs to know how to manage change—is likely to become more and more important as the major transitions occurring in the world continue to unfold. Leaders tend to spend most of their time juggling the many current issues—the problems and opportunities—that must be dealt with if their organizations are to operate smoothly and perform a societal function effectively. A leader's job is to understand the forces that are driving the need for change; to sort out those issues that require fundamental change from those that call for only marginal adjustments; to have a sense of his or her organization's capacity to tolerate shocks and stress and to respond to crises and challenges; to jettison the formula approaches, such as Gramm-Rudman, individual and business entitlements, and indexing to inflation, that have substituted for decision-making in the past few decades; and to manage both fundamental and marginal changes in such a way that the short-term and long-term strategies are consistent and mutually reinforcing and comprise a clear and coherent vision of the organization's future. All in a day's work for the average superstar statesperson.

In other words, back to basics. The basics for the 1990s: a more generalist way of thinking; education and training focused on the learning and application of skills; and leadership aimed at effectively performing societal functions over the long term.

INTO THE 21st CENTURY

Although I'm frustrated sometimes by the slow pace at which we deal with the big messes and potential opportunities, each day I read about people and organizations that are taking outstanding and innovative actions along the lines I've advocated here. I am encouraged that, in some places at least, new strategies and techniques are being implemented. I have to hope that these developments will spread, and that from the ranks of doers and thinkers will emerge a group of statespersons who can provide the leadership we need if we are to navigate safely into the 21st century.

THE FUTURE OF STATE AND LOCAL GOVERNMENT AS SEEN IN THE FUTURES LITERATURE

Henry H. Hitchcock and Joseph F. Coates

Thousands of people in over 30 state and local futures studies and more than 150 journal articles, documents, and books agree that the future of state and local government will be shaped by trends and issues reflecting national and international demographic, economic, political, and environmental changes. For example, the movement of people to the South and West will create a boom in the Colorado Front Range, Arizona, and Texas while Delaware, New York, and Massachusetts come to grips with declining urban population. The movement to a service economy creates jobs in Florida and North Carolina while displacing workers in Michigan and Pennsylvania. International integration of agriculture means states such as Iowa and Minnesota are looking for ways to help their displaced farmers.

This summary draws out recurring trends and issues to provide an integrated perspective on the future of state and local government as seen in the futures literature. . . . The summary covers three things: the recurrent issues, the common emerging issues, important trends and issues which get little or no attention in the literature.

TRENDS

The trends relating to the 17 topics are listed in Exhibit S-1 [p. 382]. Most are variations of one of the following ten trends. By recognizing the commonalities among the diverse trends, their implications become easier to understand. . . . The following gives brief descriptions and examples of each of these ten recurring trends:

1. *Steadily rising costs*: The costs of housing, energy, administration, materials, health care, and almost all social services are going up. This puts pressure on state and local governments to cut back or become more efficient.

2. *More aggressive demands for resources*: Despite rising costs, most people see growing demands for natural and physical resources—land, energy, minerals, water, housing, infrastructure, recreational facilities, and forests. The development, management, and protection of these resources will be a growing concern of state and local governments.

3. *Citizens' growing demands for services*: People also want more services such as day care, welfare, Medicaid, health care, adult education, arts, recreational programs, police, and fire protection. Since many of these are public services, the demands will be strongly felt in many city halls, county seats, and state capitals.

4. *Declining and vacillating federal support*: Since the Depression, the national government has become involved in many aspects of state and local life. With pressures to reduce the federal deficit and strengthen defense, that long-term trend is ending. Federal support is declining across the board from arts to transportation. This change means state and local governments will have to be increasingly self-reliant in terms of revenue generation and program development and implementation.

5. *More state and local innovation*: In response to growing physical, natural, and human resources demands, state and local governments have been enhancing their abilities to manage many different types of activities including energy research and development, revenue diversification, auditing and budgeting, planning, and the use of information technologies. This trend will continue as more people demand more services from these governments.

6. *An aging, growing, more diverse population*: The growing numbers of elderly and minorities will add to the concerns of state and local governments in terms of housing, health

care, transportation, education, and social services. These problems will be most acute in the nation's cities. Some areas such as Northeastern central cities and Midwestern rural farm counties may lose population. But, the general trend is growth. This will bring demands for new services and facilities.

7. *The rise of the South and West and the decline of the North and East*: Population growth, economic development, immigration, natural resource consumption, transportation demand, housing demand, and environmental contamination will grow fastest in the states of the South and West, especially Florida, Texas, Arizona, California, Colorado, and Nevada.

8. *A cascade of infrastructure and environmental problems*: The physical plant and the environment of the states and localities of the U.S. will continue to deteriorate. Money for repairing bridges, water systems, railroad tracks, and mass transit will be hard to find. Economic development will work against efforts to keep open spaces, protect groundwater, or improve air quality. People will still want a better environment and infrastructure.

9. *Change and disruption from the introduction of new technologies*: Information technologies—computers, telecommunications, robotics, and the like—will further the shift to a service-based economy. Materials and biological technologies will alter the way farming and construction are done. These technologies hold the promise of improving the efficiency and effectiveness of many aspects of state and local government.

10. *Integration of the global and U.S. economy*: In several areas such as energy and agriculture the integration of local economies into the international can create severe dislocations—such as lost jobs and declining wages. This global integration also means that more of the decisions which affect the economic health of state and localities are out of their control.

ISSUES

The issues facing the state and local governments in the future are listed in Exhibit S-2 [p. 383]. Out of these issues come eight recurring conflicts or issues which although state and local in origin may

take on national prominence in the future. The eight recurring issues are:

1. Development versus environmental protection
2. Federal versus state and local responsibilities
3. The elderly, poor, and minorities versus other priorities
4. Who pays versus who gains
5. Efficiency versus expanding needs
6. Integration versus local control
7. Regulation versus deregulation
8. New problems versus continuing problems

The following section describes each of these recurring issues:

1. *Development versus environmental protection*: Perhaps the most commonly cited and most troublesome issue for state and local governments is balancing the effects of growth such as traffic congestion, farmland conversions, and water pollution with the jobs, small business opportunities, and increased tax bases such growth brings.

2. *Federal versus state and local responsibilities*: With declining federal support, there is increased questioning of the role of the federal government in the management of many state and local problems such as energy, agriculture, transportation, social services, infrastructure, and housing.

3. *The elderly, poor, and minorities versus other priorities*: One of the ironies of the future is that as the number of elderly and minorities grows, the resources to meet their needs will decline. In areas such as transportation, housing, health care, social services, urbanization, and economic development there will be recurrent issues over the role of state and local governments in meeting the needs of the less fortunate.

4. *Who pays versus who gains*: The issue of who gains and who loses will rise in importance as states and localities are forced to make difficult choices between the competing needs of different groups. Issues such as comparable worth, taxation, the effects of industrialization of agriculture, and access to health care will plague state and local governments for the next decade.

5. *Efficiency versus expanding demands*: Declining budgets and increasing demands will drive increased attention to the efficiency of government operations, health care delivery, social

service delivery, and repair and maintenance of infrastructure.

6. *Integration versus local control*: Part of the drive for efficiency will be growing interest in integrating the functions of government to achieve economies of scale. In some cases this may mean proposals for regional governments. However, attempts to integrate transportation, the arts, social services, and other aspects of government organizations will run up against increased demands for local control and citizen access to decisions that affect them.

7. *Regulation versus deregulation*: Despite the apparent trend toward deregulation, the state and local governments will continue to face demands for and conflicts around regulation of activities such as day care, automobile use, resource exploitation, land use, electric utilities, and overall growth.

8. *Continuing problems versus new problems*: The states and local governments will continue to face difficult issues such as reducing crime, improving the quality of education, housing abandonment in central cities, conflicts over land use, and finding enough funds to pay for the services and facilities the citizens want.

NEGLECTED TRENDS AND ISSUES IN THE FUTURES LITERATURE

The literature on the future of state and local governments tends to overlook several important areas for the future of state and local governments. The five categories of neglected trends and issues are:

1. National systems in a local setting
2. Newly emerging environmental problems
3. Opportunities for innovation
4. The needs of the elderly, poor, and minorities
5. The implications of new technologies

The following are brief synopses of the types of trends and issues that receive little or no attention in the literature.

1. *National systems in a local setting*: Growing air traffic, international freight traffic, and the future of nuclear power are examples of national techno-economic systems whose operations have significant effects on local economies and societies. These should be important parts of state and local perspectives on the future.

2. *Newly emerging environmental problems*: There are a set of new environmental problems emerging including declining rangeland quality, wildlife protection, wetlands degradation, fisheries management, and indoor air pollution. These will become important concerns in many states and local areas.

3. *Opportunities for innovation*: There are many opportunities for innovation in the future of state and local government. Lotteries, alternative work schedules, vocational education, and new housing arrangements are a few examples of innovations that could be used to manage some of the more troublesome issues facing the states and localities.

4. *The needs of the elderly, poor, and minorities*: The problems of the elderly, minorities, and poor go beyond the few issues noted in the literature to include minority unemployment, the problems of migrant workers, the need for programs to deal with hunger and homelessness, and the continuing need for public housing.

5. *Implications of technology*: Technologies such as biotechnology, computers, manufactured housing, and health care technologies can and will have pervasive effects on many issues of concern to state and local governments from internal management to environmental protection.

WHAT NEXT?

As these trends and issues shape the world of state and local governments, administrators, planners, and associations will need to have a better understanding of the underlying causes of change. This review of the futures literature is an early step in that process of understanding. Additional steps include:

- selecting areas of greatest potential importance to state and local governments,
- doing more detailed assessments on the future of selected areas,
- analyzing options for state and local governments and those that support them,
- taking action at national, state, and local levels.

EXHIBIT S-1
Trends Shaping State and Local Government

ENERGY
1. Rising energy costs
2. Shift from oil and gas to alternative sources
3. Increased use of conservation
4. Growing energy demand (South/West)
5. Continued integration into global energy markets
6. Evolving state and local management capability

ENVIRONMENT
1. Continued concern for environmental protection
2. More groundwater contamination
3. Increased hazardous wastes concerns
4. More solid wastes
5. Continued pollution of surface waters
6. Declining air quality

NATURAL RESOURCES
1. Increased consumption of natural resources
2. Growing demand for water resources
3. More mineral exploitation
4. Growing demand for forest products

AGRICULTURE
1. Integration into the global economy
2. Industrialization of agriculture
3. Concentration of farms
4. Loss of cropland
5. Loss of topsoil

HOUSING
1. Growing demand for housing—owner and rental
2. Rising costs of housing
3. Demand exceeds supply of affordable housing
4. Movement to rehabilitation
5. Rising number of planned communities
6. Introduction of new technologies into old and new buildings

LAND USE AND PLANNING
1. Continued urbanization
2. Expanding metropolitan areas
3. Changing role of center cities
4. Continued movement to rural areas
5. Growing demand for recreation facilities

TRANSPORTATION
1. Continued dominance of the automobile
2. Growing public transportation ridership (South/West)
3. No significant change in transportation technology
4. Growing public transportation deficits
5. Increasing congestion in growth areas

INFRASTRUCTURE
1. More bridge and road repairs
2. More railroad track abandonment
3. Need to upgrade water systems
4. Emerging demand for information infrastructure
5. More state and local financing innovations

(continued)

HEALTH	1. Rising health care costs
	2. Increasing demand for health care, especially among the elderly
HUMAN RESOURCES POPULATION	1. Slower, uneven population growth
	2. Aging of the population
	3. More Hispanics
	4. Continued concentration of minorities in cities
HUMAN RESOURCES SERVICES	1. Decline in federal support for social programs
	2. Increased demand for day care
	3. More crime
	4. Growing importance of voluntarism
GENERAL GOVERNMENT AND ORGANIZATION	1. Increased state and local responsibility
	2. More citizen involvement
	3. Growing tension among state and local governments
	4. Cooperation and competition among public and private sector
GOVERNMENT MANAGEMENT	1. Increased importance of planning
	2. Greater demand of accountability
	3. Slowing rate of growth of governments
	4. Growing role of information technology
EDUCATION AND TRAINING	1. Changing enrollment patterns
	2. More adult education
	3. Declining federal funding
	4. More alternative educational methods
	5. Increasing job retraining efforts
	6. More teachers' unions
ARTS	1. Increasing interest in the arts
	2. Declining federal government funding
TAX AND FINANCE	1. Increasing service demands
	2. Decreasing federal aid
	3. Continued borrowing difficulties
	4. Increased state and local financial burden
	5. More revenue diversification
ECONOMIC DEVELOPMENT	1. Economic growth primarily in the South and West
	2. More jobs but continued unemployment
	3. Growing tourism industry
	4. Movement to a service economy

EXHIBIT S-2
Emerging Issues for State and Local Governments

ENERGY	1. Balanced energy development
	2. The role of the federal government
	3. Need for multistate regulation
	4. Meeting the energy needs of the poor

(continued)

ENVIRONMENT	1. Increasing environmental protection 2. Conflict between development and protection 3. Fairly meeting the needs of small and rural communities
NATURAL RESOURCES	1. Conflict among uses of natural resources 2. Public management and regulation of resources
AGRICULTURE	1. Impacts of industrialization 2. State initiatives to protect farmers 3. Federal agricultural policy
HOUSING	1. Growing disparity in housing quality between rich and poor 2. Emerging conflicts over tenants' rights 3. Public vs. private responsibilities for housing supply 4. Housing abandonment in central cities
PLANNING AND LAND USE	1. Conflict over land uses 2. Controlling growth 3. Providing services for the poor
TRANSPORTATION	1. Federal subsidies for public transportation 2. Intersuburban public transportation 3. Intermodal coordination 4. Restrictions on automobile use
INFRASTRUCTURE	1. Effects of federal policies 2. Allocation of financial resources
HEALTH	1. Limited access to health care services 2. Health care efficiency
HUMAN RESOURCES— POPULATION	1. Managing the effects of growth 2. Meeting the needs of the elderly 3. Language
HUMAN RESOURCES—SERVICES	1. Reducing fragmentation in social services administration 2. Regulating day care 3. Reducing crime
GENERAL GOVERNMENT AND ORGANIZATION	1. Reducing fragmentation of government 2. Improving citizen access 3. Enhancing state and local capacities
GOVERNMENT MANAGEMENT	1. Comparable worth 2. Need for efficiency
EDUCATION AND TRAINING	1. Educational deficiencies 2. Insufficient funding
ARTS	1. Adequate financial support 2. Effective coordination of support
TAX AND FINANCE	1. Implications for economic development 2. Equity
ECONOMIC DEVELOPMENT	1. Balancing economic growth with environmenal protection 2. Displaced workers and distressed communities 3. Fostering small businesses

ALTERNATIVE FUTURES FOR THE [NONPROFIT] SECTOR

Forrest P. Chisman

This chapter describes three alternative futures for the relationship between the independent sector and two other major centers of institutional power in the United States, business and government. The first two alternatives are projections based on the way in which these institutions have influenced each other in recent years. The third is a proposal for changing the role that the independent sector has played. In making these sorts of projections, it is hard to avoid merely embroidering on the obvious. And the obvious is that, in the normal course of affairs, the future of nonprofit organizations and activities will depend largely on whether the American economy achieves solid and sustained real growth in productivity and profits and whether government, particularly at the federal level, revives the spirit of activism that in the past has enabled it to come to grips with the nation's major social and economic problems.

There is nothing novel about this forecast. In this century, at least, the independent sector has prospered largely through partnerships with business and government. Business has been crucial as a donor, creator of endowed organizations, and customer for nonprofit services. In addition, the general state of the economy, as reflected in business conditions, directly or indirectly, determines how much real income Americans have available as well as its distribution and, hence, the willingness of individuals to make charitable contributions. The role of government is critical for many of the same reasons. Lester Salamon (1985) and others have documented how dependent most independent-sector organizations are on government grants and contracts for service delivery. And, of course, the areas of the sector

that Salamon did not study—many health care services and traditional forms of education—are the most dependent of all.

Finally, the linkage among government, business, and the nonprofit world comes full circle when one considers that a major goal of government at all levels is maintaining economic prosperity. And the rate of economic growth often determines how much Americans are willing to invest in government services, as the influence of economic worries on both the Carter and Reagan administrations most recently has shown.

In short, when government and business grow, the independent sector grows too. When they slow down, it falls on hard times. Given this perennial linkage, three possible scenarios should be of particular interest to those who are concerned about future relationships among the sectors.

AN OPTIMISTIC SCENARIO

The first scenario assumes a rosy future. If we can work the present kinks out of our economy, the United States could well experience a period of healthy economic growth well into the next century—at least until the burden of dealing with the retirement of the baby boom generation falls on us, and possibly beyond if we make adequate provision for that pivotal development. If this rosy scenario unfolds, businesses will reinvigorate their programs of corporate philanthropy and public service. Some of their contributions obviously will go to the traditional beneficiaries of corporate largesse: educational, research, cultural, and local improvement efforts in the communities where particular companies have their operations or in areas of endeavor where they perceive at least some indirect self-interest.

But new twists in business support can also be expected. Many large companies are now coming to realize that it is very much in their self-interest to help their employees deal with a wide range of personal problems that have not previously been of concern to corporate America. For example, we are likely to see more corporate investment in day care, long-term care facilities, continuing education, innovative health care experiments, and possibly even affordable rental housing. Most companies know that they are not very good at running enterprises of this sort: it literally is not any of their business. Thus, many are likely to turn to the people who do have a track record: independent-sector organizations. This is already happening in the day-care field, where most of the (admittedly small) corporate investment takes the form of either contracts with nonprofit providers or payments to employees that allow them to buy services on their own, again usually from non-profits (U.S. Bureau of Labor Statistics, 1988).

So, if the economic future is rosy, independent-sector organizations should gear up for a flood of demand to help corporations with human service projects, and they should begin planning the most effective ways to do so now. One way to proceed is to seek out a few companies that are willing to serve as testing grounds for the development of model programs. "The company store" or early-twentieth-century "welfare capitalism" may well be replaced by the company grant or contract of welfare capitalism in a new form, and if it is, nonprofits would do well to be ready.

To imagine a rosy future on the governmental side, it is necessary only to recall the statements of the large field of presidential candidates during the 1988 election campaign, particularly the Democrats. Most of the candidates appeared to believe that the nation should develop a more adequate system of health insurance: a system that would protect the thirty-seven million people now without coverage, pay the costs of catastrophic illness for the elderly, and lighten the burden of long-term care. Most also believed that we need to improve the quality of our educational system at all levels, convert welfare programs into jobs programs, help poor children get a better start in life, solve the problems of the homeless, do a better job of protecting the environment, and stabilize our shaky financial markets. And opinion polls have repeatedly shown that a majority of voters both share these goals and say that they are willing to pay substantially more in taxes to achieve them. Cognizant of these sentiments, the 100th Congress passed legislation implementing welfare reform, catastrophic health care insurance for the elderly, and other activist measures, and the 101st Congress is attempting to grapple with other issues on the human services agenda.

If Washington gets back into the business of doing these sorts of things, it is obviously going to need partners, as it has in the past. In the first instance, the partners are likely to be state and local governments. But when it actually comes to service delivery, they in turn will work through independent-sector organizations, as they always have. Or at least it should be hoped that they will. It is frightening to imagine most public welfare departments, on their own, trying to develop individualized evaluation, training, placement, and day-care packages for welfare mothers, as the 1988 Family Support Act (welfare reform) calls on them to do. While there are many able people in state and local agencies who understand what is involved in this sort of undertaking, the constraints under which they work will make it very difficult for them to gear up quickly to deliver comprehensive "work-welfare" services on a large scale, as they are required to do, without a great deal of outside help. Likewise, it appears that most government efforts to shelter the homeless have been less effective than more modest voluntary-sector initiatives.

In short, if there is a revival of federal activism, the independent sector should get ready for a truly enormous surge of demand, because the likely directions of new activism will be heavily weighted in the areas of improved human services in which most of the sector specializes. And, importantly, much of that demand will be to deliver services that nobody today fully understands how to provide. Mainstreaming welfare mothers and caring for the homeless have already been mentioned. We can add to that list developing cost-effective, noninstitutional systems of long-term care, establishing more abundant high-quality child nutrition and day-care services, finding mechanisms to provide universal, affordable health care services, and working with government to fight drug abuse, reduce dropout rates, upgrade elementary and secondary education, and develop better environmental strategies.

In all probability, there is no one best way to do any of these things, no "cookie cutter" model for the nation as a whole. Different approaches will be effective in different locales. And that is why the independent sector is particularly important in a rosy future. The sector is everywhere, it takes many different forms, and it often has strong community ties. It should use these advantages to do its homework: to look for ways to accomplish the things that we presently do not know how to accomplish, before the demands of a revived federal government arrive. Otherwise, nonprofits will be caught unprepared and once more face the charge "voluntary-sector failure." More importantly, they will be letting the nation down.

What must the sector do? Make up-front investments. Experiment now with progressive states and communities (and there are a lot of them) to find models for the future. And do not look only at service technology. Look too at new management and financial structures, such as chartering nonprofit corporations in the areas of day care, long-term care, health insurance, and so forth. Finally, develop improved systems of recruitment, so that the very best people will be attracted to newly expanded efforts.

A PESSIMISTIC SCENARIO

So much for optimism. The independent sector must also face up to another possibility.

Anyone who is paying attention must have very grave doubts about whether this country's economy will, in fact, take off again in the near future and whether the federal government will continue to adopt progressive measures. With regard to the former, the reasons for doubt can be found on the business pages of any major newspaper: the recovery of the mid-1980s was always artificial in a great many ways, productivity has lagged, many sectors are besotted with wasteful speculative activity, foreign competition is stiff, financial markets suffer from borderline schizophrenia, and so forth.

On the political front, we have faced a cruel paradox epitomized by the fate of the candidates who entered the 1988 presidential primaries. Although most of the candidates promised a new wave of activism, and although overwhelming majorities of the public supported their agendas, nobody seemed to believe what they said. The presidential contenders appeared to be suffering from a credibility gap that could well destroy the prospect that the president and Congress we elected will pursue a progressive course. And, strangely, that gap had little to do with either the candidates or their proposals.

The same polls that showed widespread public support for those proposals also showed that the public is highly skeptical about the ability of government to deliver on its promises. In other words, ordinary Americans would like to enjoy the benefits of all the new initiatives discussed, but they have a hard time believing that any of those measures can be implemented, at the federal level, anyway. They apparently find it difficult to imagine an America in which they can count on national government to solve national problems. During the 1988 campaign, this public skepticism meant that the candidates who advocated progressive reforms appeared to be the more unrealistic in the field. The public assumed that the more outspoken candidates could not possibly be serious about the bold ideas they set forth: in their innermost thoughts, they must have been contemplating some diminished version of what they described. As a result, there was a temptation for many of the "smart" people on the campaign trail to pull their punches, to lapse into a rhetoric of half measures and vaguely stated good intentions. There was a lot of talk about "first steps," "trade-offs," and "goals" that would be achieved only at some time in the indefinite future.

But the credibility gap that separated candidates from voters was more than a cruel twist of fate for those who aspired to be president. It was a gutting of the American political process. What should be the essence of politics in this country—responding to public needs and aspirations—became impolitic in much of the presidential campaign. The result was an election without meaning: an election that signified nothing, ratified nothing, sent no message that would guide or constrain either the president or Congress. And the person who can take most credit for these turn of events is none other than Ronald Reagan.

The greatest success of the Reagan presidency was to focus public attention on concerns about the size and scope of government, rather than on questions about its effectiveness in meeting national needs (see Chisman and Pifer, 1987, pp. 85–118). The president who began his term by declaring that "government is the problem" and then ran up a massive federal deficit to prove his point propagated two great myths: that big government is inherently a bad thing and that even if it were not bad, we cannot afford it anyway.

This is old stuff from conservatives, and every few decades the nation rediscovers that it simply is not true. In an increasingly complex and inter-dependent society, national government must play a large role in securing the general welfare. And big government in the United States has a long string of successes to its credit: greatly reducing poverty among the elderly and other groups, advancing civil rights, making home ownership and higher education possible for tens of millions of people, building and maintaining our national transportation system, promoting science and technology, subsidizing virtually every sector of our economy, and much more. Everyone in the United States benefits enormously from big government, and few Americans would be willing to live without the benefits it confers. Moreover, no one can realistically believe that America will be able to meet the challenges of the future in areas such as health, education, and the environment without the national leadership and resources that only the federal government can provide.

So much for the issue of size. The issue of cost is also illusory. The United States devotes a far smaller portion of its gross national product to social programs than most other developed countries do, and there are few economists who believe that devoting somewhat more would harm our national prosperity. Social spending does not destroy national wealth; it reroutes it to building a stronger society and economy. Federal deficits *are* a problem, but most economists believe that we can afford to pay for the government we have and to buy somewhat more if we need it to solve our national problems. But despite the transparent falsehood of Reaganism's two great myths, most politicians and "experts" these days feel obliged to pay homage to the idea that we live in "an era of limited resources." And the same people portray the federal deficit as a stopper to any serious discussion of large new initiatives.

In short, shrouded in a cloud of misunder-standing and distrust, candidates and voters appear to have spent a great deal of time "faking each other out" in 1988 and since. And there is a very good chance that the result will be a continuation of the do-nothing politics of the Reagan years. That would be a very great national

tragedy. The problems that face us today are not just temporary aberrations. They are the results of enormous social and economic changes that are profoundly transforming the lives of each and every one of us (see Chisman and Pifer, 1987, pp. 169–218). Changes in the structure of our economy are creating widespread anxiety about job security, skills, and incomes. Social changes such as the entry of women into the work force are sending families in search of more adequate systems of day care for their children and long-term care for their elderly parents. America has developed an underclass of several million people, and children raised in that environment will make up a large proportion of the workers and citizens of tomorrow. And American society is aging: in the future we will have fewer active workers and more dependent retirees, whose cost to society, particularly in the area of health care, is soaring out of sight (see Pifer and Bronte, 1986).

In sum, in virtually every area of our social and economic life, this country is on a collision course with the future. But because of the political confusion created by eight years of Reaganism, there is a good chance that we will not act to avert that collision very soon. What happens to the independent sector then? What happens to it if a pessimistic scenario on both the economic and political fronts comes true? If past history is any guide, the sector will suffer, diminish, muddle through, try to fill gaps, speak out, and hope, as it has in recent years. And, as in recent years, it will seek partnerships with progressive industries and state and local governments that are trying to fill the void left by federal inaction. That is not a wholly gloomy prognosis, but it is certainly not as attractive as the rosy scenario outlined above. And in light of the national tragedy that would result from continued federal inaction and economic decline, people who care as much about the future of the nation as most people working in the independent sector do can hardly be expected to find it acceptable. They have already seen their numbers dwindle and their influence diminish. They cannot relish more of the same.

THE SECTOR AS MOVEMENT

If the pessimistic scenario unfolds, and if people working in the independent sector find it unacceptable, there is another approach to the future they should consider adopting. The sector might be mobilized to put the shoe on the other foot: rather than responding to political and economic events, it might take the leadership in bringing about progressive change. This would require more than leadership in small ways. Independent-sector organizations already support progressive institutions and contribute to meeting neglected needs on a case-by-case basis. These efforts are eminently worthwhile, and they should certainly be continued. But leaders of the independent sector should also consider the possibility of using their resources to raise national consciousness and force action on a larger scale.

For example, looking back over the history of voluntary activities in the United States, we see that there is obviously a great difference between the grange movement, the settlement-house movement, the cooperative movement, and the trade-union movement of the late nineteenth and early twentieth centuries and more recent independent-sector activities. They were *movements*. They were everywhere; they mobilized enormous numbers of people; they tried to *solve* problems by voluntary action, not just "make a contribution"; and inevitably they were breeding grounds for reform politics. Of course, they failed to solve the problems entirely, but their large efforts at the very least forced government to get involved. And they created institutions that continue to be of importance to our national life. Their reform culture also nurtured future activists, and the approaches they developed through trial and error often proved to be critically important experiments for future state-building developments.

If these examples seem too remote from the experience of today, there is a type of movement with which most people in the independent sector are intimately familiar. One of Andrew Carnegie's concerns was for the future of college teachers. In particular, he believed that they deserved a decent income in their retirement years. So he set up the Carnegie Foundation (now the Carnegie Foundation for the Advancement of Teaching) for the purpose of providing pensions to all retired professors. That was truly an ambitious effort to solve a problem by voluntary effort. And it was a failure in its initial form. Carnegie and his advisers soon realized that no endowed foundation could

possibly muster the resources required. So they set up the insurance plan now called TIAA-CREF—the Teachers Insurance and Annuity Association and the College Retirement Equities Fund—on which many people in the independent sector now depend for a great part of their retirement income.

Like the grangers, the co-ops, the settlement houses, and the unions, TIAA was also a movement, in the sense that it entailed the active involvement of large numbers of people banding together for their mutual benefit. And, like those other efforts, it was a *self-help* movement: it asked something of its members as well as of its sponsors or the public at large. That was at a time when few companies had private pension plans and long before Social Security. TIAA met a real need. And together with social insurance ideas that another nonprofit institution, the University of Wisconsin, developed in working with state government, it served as a model, experiment, and forcing activity for developments in both the public and private sectors (see Stevens, 1988).

If the economy falters and the Bush administration proves to be a fizzle in terms of social reform, it is at least worth considering whether independent-sector organizations should band together in large-scale efforts of this sort. There are some very hopeful recent precedents. Two of the most noteworthy were initially developed by the Ford Foundation. They are Michael Sviridoff's Local Initiatives Support Corporation (LISC), dealing with low-income housing problems, and the Manpower Demonstration Research Corporation (MDRC), originally headed by Barbara Blum and now ably led by Judith Gueron. It is impossible to exaggerate the importance of MDRC in changing the conventional wisdom in the political world about how welfare programs should be structured and in bringing about welfare reform. And it is impossible to exaggerate the influence of LISC in the area of housing policy, let alone the enormous good it has done for thousands of low-income people and their communities. Although sponsored by foundations, various levels of government, and industry, they, like earlier movements, are based on the idea of self-help: tenant-managed housing in the case of LISC and helping people to become self-supporting in the case of MDRC. They deserve the encouragement of everyone in the independent sector in their continuing efforts to grow and influence thinking.

There is no danger that the success of such groups will create the impression that government action is unnecessary. Unlike earlier movements, they acknowledged at the outset that the problems they are trying to solve are too vast: they are simply trying to do as much as they can. But the more they do, the more pressure they exert on government and business to act by showing skeptical politicians and businesspeople that complex problems really *can* be solved. Government and business come to believe that all they have to do is to replicate what such groups are doing on a larger scale. Even if this is not true, their example at least creates a constituency in government, business, and the general public for a reform agenda.

So, if the worst-case economic and political scenarios come true, independent-sector organizations should consider banding together to launch other large-scale, coordinated movements in areas where they can hope to have some impact. The plight of the homeless is an example of the type of problem that commends itself. This is because of the enormous public concern it has generated, because it is almost everywhere, and because, in any particular location, fairly small numbers of people are affected. To take just one case, it is estimated that there are 5,000 to 6,000 homeless people in the nation's capital, Washington, D.C. It seems criminal that so small a number of distressed people cannot be helped and helped very well. If the cost of providing shelter, food, counseling, treatment, training, and outplacement assistance, as appropriate, for each one of these people is estimated at what would have to be a very high number, poverty-level income, $25 million to $30 million would be required. Given the fact that local government already makes a substantial contribution, the cost of a government–voluntary-sector partnership that would do a first-rate job of coming to grips with the problem in Washington would be far less than that. It would be well within the capacity of a consortium of large and small nonprofits, particularly with a special fund-raising effort. And, of course, the cost would be reduced if there was more emphasis on self-help, rather than just custodial care: if the more able among the

homeless were involved in running the shelters and if the major goal of the effort was to help homeless people either return to their families or find better ways to care for themselves.

Admittedly, voluntary organizations already do a lot for the homeless. But they might consider submerging their institutional identities long enough to make this or some other problem *the* priority for a coalition of groups. And the priority should be not just to help but to solve the problem to the greatest extent possible, with involvement by both the general public and the beneficiaries of voluntary-sector action. Of course, the voluntary sector should not take permanent responsibility for caring for the homeless or similar problems. But if it takes up this or some similar challenge and succeeds, or even makes a good showing, there is a good likelihood that government at every level would feel compelled to mount an adequate response. The plight of the homeless is only an example of a great many worthy causes around which the independent sector might organize a movement. It does not matter which is selected. The important thing is to create a strong and visible impression on the public mind and on the minds of politicians that social problems can and must be solved: forcing action by example.

This view of how the sector might function as a movement implies that the conservative theory of the independent sector is just wrong. Independent-sector activism will not and should not replace government and business activism. It never has. The more any one sector leads in addressing major problems, the more likely it is that the others will follow. And government and business are the greatest copy-cats of all when it comes to human service issues. Conservatives should know this better than anyone else. The development of the conservative "movement" as an intellectual force in the United States over the last few decades was to a significant extent funded by donations from wealthy individuals and conservative foundations. And that funding entailed not only support for research and writing but also the development of intellectual networks and the dissemination of ideas. Independent-sector activism on the right fostered a movement that eventually contributed to a major change of direction by government at the national level.

Independent-sector organizations that are on the progressive side and primarily committed to supporting ideas rather than activism can profit from the example of conservatives. Why do progressive foundations do so little to disseminate progressive ideas? Too often they are content to fund research and writing without taking into account the fact that those products must be aggressively sold in the marketplace of ideas. Most people who have developed intellectual products—books, reports, and so forth—that set forth progressive ideas find that there is practically no place they can turn to to get the type of high-powered assistance required to bring those ideas to public attention, even if they have the money to pay for it. There is practically nobody in that business. One way that organizations devoted to ideas and concerned about the lack of social progress could help to stage a "movement" would be to establish a full-service public relations agency capable of providing a complete menu of assistance at reasonable cost to their members and grantees.

But this is only one way to instigate a movement. There are many other ways, and they are all valid undertakings at all points on the political spectrum. In fact, many causes, such as the condition of the homeless, should provide fertile common ground for independent-sector organizations with widely different perspectives. The conclusion of this chapter is simply the following: if political and economic clouds blot out a bright future for the independent sector, leaders of the sector should consider combining their efforts to change the climate within which they operate. They should consider forcing action by example: showing that major public problems can and must be solved by mounting large-scale efforts to solve them. And if they do, they should make a special effort to involve as many members of the public as they possibly can.

REFERENCES

CHISMAN, F., and PIFER, A. *Government for the People: The Federal Social Role: What It Is, What It Should Be.* New York: Norton, 1987.

PIFER, A., and BRONTE, D. L. (eds.). *Our Aging Society: Promise and Paradox.* New York: Norton, 1986.

SALAMON, L. M. *Partners in Public Service: Toward a Theory of Government-Nonprofit Relations.* Washington, D.C.: Urban Institute Press, 1985.

STEVENS, B. "Blurring the Boundaries: How Federal Social Policy Shaped Private Sector Welfare Benefits." In M. Weir, A. S. Orloff, and T. Skocpol (eds.), *The Politics of Social Policy in the United States.* Princeton, N.J.: Princeton University Press, 1988.

U.S. BUREAU OF LABOR STATISTICS. *Recent Trends in Daycare: A Survey of Corporate Provision.* Washington, D.C.: U.S. Government Printing Office, 1988.

ROBERT L. BENDICK, JR.: AN ENVIRONMENTAL CHIEF TRIES TO PROTECT RHODE ISLAND FROM ITS ECONOMIC SUCCESS

Peter Lord

When Robert L. Bendick, Jr., stepped up to the microphones in the rotunda of the Rhode Island statehouse, he said he was a little nervous. He was about to do something he had never done before, and he hoped it wouldn't create a stink.

Oh, but it did.

The brief comments Bendick made that day in April last year were immediately labeled by some of the state's top lawmakers as inappropriate, unprofessional and irresponsible. The kindest complaint was that his remarks were premature. All this because Bendick, director of the state's Department of Environmental Management, suggested that the General Assembly was sitting on some key environmental bills proposed by his boss, Republican Governor Edward D. DiPrete.

"Maybe they're going to get to them," Bendick said during the press conference, "but we only have three or four weeks left, and frankly I don't sleep at nights thinking about the fact that we're in the greatest period of environmental change in the state's history, and these things don't seem to be a high priority on the agenda of the General Assembly."

Department heads just don't take on the legislature in Rhode Island. But Bendick did. And after the first rush of criticism, he got away with it. He was praised in an editorial in the state's largest newspaper. And the General Assembly went on to approve so many new environmental initiatives—from a $65 million open space program to $46 million to protect drinking water supplies—that many leaders called it a historic year for Rhode Island's environment.

Bendick laughed recently at the image of himself taking on the legislature and said, "I sometimes marvel that I did that. It's not something you can do often. But it had results because people believed I felt strongly, and that's why I did it."

That's how it's gone for Bendick, who directs a department of nearly 700 full-time and 500 part-time employees, with a budget of $42 million and control over grants and aid programs running into tens of millions of dollars. He has cajoled, surprised and argued with political leaders on behalf of Rhode Island's environment for so long and so successfully that one of the few things people agree on in this politically contentious state is that Bob Bendick is doing a pretty good job.

There are still plenty of critics. Environmental groups complain that Bendick hasn't done enough to increase his staff and budget. They say that he's not tough enough on polluters, and that he gives in perhaps too frequently to DiPrete on development and budget issues. Real estate interests complain that his department is too slow in reviewing their development proposals.

But there's also plenty of evidence of Bendick's success. For instance, in the Northeast, where the average term of a state environmental director is about a year, Bendick has held office more than six years. A Democrat, Bendick has kept his job through Democratic and Republican administrations.

And although he works in the country's smallest and one of its most densely populated states, he has made a name for himself as a savior of open space and scenic lands. He's raised money to upgrade most of the state's older parks. He pushed successfully for the creation of a joint Massachusetts-Rhode Island park system running 40 miles along the Blackstone River, which flows through both states, and for another park covering 3,000 acres on seven islands in Narragansett Bay. He's also helped set aside hundreds of acres on Block Island, two major beaches and thousands of acres of woodlands.

He won passage of legislation previously unheard of in this region, which imposes a surcharge on water bills to raise tens of millions of dollars to buy and protect the watersheds and aquifers used by Rhode Islanders.

Finally, he has begun tough regulatory programs. They include the nation's first mandatory statewide effort to recycle paper, cans and glass; strict rules to prevent the leaking of underground gasoline storage tanks; and a special investigative unit for environmental crimes—primarily illegal transportation and dumping of hazardous wastes—that in three and a half years has brought 1,300 charges against 53 individuals and companies, so far resulting in fines totaling more than $1 million.

"He gets things done," said Michael A. Mantell, general counsel for the World Wildlife Fund and the Conservation Foundation. "He has a vision that's rare. And then he goes about doing it, in a sort of quiet, behind-the-scenes manner. I've dealt with a lot of state environmental leaders. He's one of the best."

Far and away, Bendick has made his name saving open space. And to outsiders, that may seem a contradiction considering Rhode Island's close borders. Just 48 miles from north to south and 37 miles wide, with a big thumbprint in the middle covered by Narragansett Bay, the state is best known for congested cities that birthed the American factory system. The state is second only to New Jersey in population density.

But there's a secret in those figures. As recently as 1980, as much as 87 percent of the state's population lived in the cities, leaving miles of open beaches and rolling countryside disturbed by only an occasional village or farm.

That has begun to change. An economic boom has swept New England, pushing real estate prices as high as the White Mountains and spurring a surge in construction that has covered rural villages with executive homes and coastal harbors with condominiums. The *Hartford Courant* in neighboring Connecticut, in a series of articles last summer, said the boom had left throughout New England a residue of sadness and "a longing for the social and physical landscape that is being swept away."

Bendick's goal has been to save some of Rhode Island's landscape from all this economic success. Not only has he led the state's efforts to upgrade its parks and set aside great new swaths of land, but he also has overseen tremendous expansion of the offices that review permits for septic systems and wetlands development.

Some of the recognition he's received for his efforts can be seen in his office a block from the statehouse. In a small outer conference room, books overflow the shelves and prop up plaques marking national honors he has received. On one wall is a photograph of a red silo. One of Bendick's hobbies is photography, and his subjects are often pastoral scenes or ocean vistas.

Bendick has something of a professorial look about him as he comes out of his office to greet a visitor. A bald spot is covered with a sweep of black hair. He wears wire-rimmed glasses, a blue oxford-cloth shirt and khaki pants. The knot of his tie is pulled loose. He's of average height and thinner than most men of 42 can hope to be.

Bendick was born in Manhattan and grew up in the suburbs of New York City and Los Angeles. He received his bachelor's degree in history from Williams College. At that time, in the late 1960s, the big issues were urban: poverty, housing and the like. "I was one of those people Bobby Kennedy inspired to get involved, and urban issues were at the forefront at the time."

But "my true love has always been the outdoors," Bendick said, and even while studying for a master's degree in urban planning at New York University, he took courses in ecology, botany and biology. One summer, he worked for the U. S. Forest Service in Idaho.

His first job after graduating from NYU was in the economically depressed mill city of Woonsocket in northern Rhode Island, where he worked for eight years as city planner. (He and his wife, Jill, have remained in Woonsocket, raising their three children, ages 16, 11 and 8.) During the years he worked there, he served on a commission that led to the creation of the state's new environmental agency. Finally, Bendick said, "I came to the conclusion I wanted to combine my love of the outdoors and the environment in what I did for a living."

Bendick joined the new agency as assistant director for administration and planning in 1978, and began work on the state's park systems. "He hit the ground running when he joined DEM," recalled Sean O. Coffey, a Democratic state senator from Providence who was then the agency's counsel. "He learned the issues. He spent the time. He had all kinds of ideas about park development. That's what he loves. He hikes. He camps." . . .

When the neighbors of a chemical company were up in arms over odor problems, [Stephen G.] Morin [a one-time department representative who now heads its wetlands division] recalled that Bendick visited them and sat on one citizen's washing machine while he listened to complaints. More recently, a neighborhood was furious when PCB-contaminated wastes from a nearby dump blew through the residents' yards. Bendick faced them at a meeting and admitted that because of staff shortages, the dump hadn't been inspected in two years.

Bendick acknowledged that it's difficult to face angry citizens. "But if you always do the right thing, people at least start to trust your motives. Also, as director, you've got to do your best to be an advocate for the environment, not just a processor of regulations. That's why I've had good support from the environmental groups."

Little Rhode Island is home to the Northeast's largest environmental group, Save the Bay Inc. It started with a few people trying to keep an oil refinery out of Narragansett Bay and now has 10,000 members in the state.

Save the Bay has complained for years that the state doesn't spend enough to clean up the environment. Spokesman Chip Young said sometimes the group felt it was doing all the lobbying, and Bendick wasn't doing enough to back them up. "He has never had adequate staff or financial resources, and that's made his job much more difficult," said Young, "but for a person who has often had a lot of political heat put on him, this past year he still spoke out strongly on getting environmental bills moving. . . . Over the years, he's bent on some issues more than he should have, but his management style of giving and taking has helped him last in a cross fire of environmental issues. Now there's no way anyone is going to take on Bob Bendick without incurring the wrath of the environmental community."

One of the best-known incidents in Bendick's career occurred soon after DiPrete was elected governor. Bendick acknowledged that he gave the owners of a controversial dump who were major DiPrete campaign contributors an extra month beyond a state-imposed deadline to close down. He did so, he said, after one of the governor's top aides asked him "to be reasonable."

The decision caused a furor. Trudy Coxe, Save the Bay's executive director, called the postponement "wishy-washy behavior" that "makes it very difficult for DEM to be taken seriously." Days later, Bendick moved the deadline back to within days of the original date.

Asked recently about the incident, Bendick said, "When I was asked about it at the time, I said [the call from the governor's office] happened. I don't know if that hurts my credibility, or his, or both." But he quickly pointed out that his investigators recently obtained a 715-count indictment against the same dump owners. The charge: operating a landfill without a license.

There was another flap recently when Bendick conceded to a reporter that he was made "uncomfortable" when another of DiPrete's aides asked people in his department to speed approvals for a housing complex in which the governor's son was involved as an engineer. . . .

For a planner, Bendick doesn't have much insight into his own future. "Five years from now? I don't know, maybe I'll be hanging in a hammock. I doubt I'll be at DEM. It's also unlikely I'll be a consultant, as most other [former] directors do. Why? I guess because the environment is a cause for me—I would find a lot of difficulty working for power companies. Maybe I'll join an environmental advocacy group."

One thing he can count on, at least in his current job, is support from DiPrete, as long as he is governor.

Said DiPrete in a recent interview, "The funniest thing I can say about him is he's a Democrat, and this year the Democratic candidate for governor [businessman Bruce Sundlun, who says Bendick hasn't done enough to clean up the bay] went up to his home town and announced he'll fire him if he wins the election. And me, a Republican governor . . . I come out and defend him. What more can you say?"

A ROOM WITH A VIEW—AT A PRICE

The national Fair Accommodations Act had only been in force for a few months when the first serious problems began to arise. The Congress had debated the issue of discrimination in hotel, motel, and resort reservations for more than five years. The statute that emerged was hailed as a victory for the consumer. All businesses providing overnight accommodations for more than fifty people were required to participate in the World Reservations System. Each business was required to input their reservations into a computer network based in Denver. Included in that information was the name, address, race, religion, and national origin of each customer. The Bureau of Fair Accommodations ran an analysis of the composition of each business on a quarterly basis to determine whether discriminatory patterns were present.

The technology to run the system was superb. None of the predicted snags and glitches had occurred. The expense to most businesses was very modest. Many of the large hotel and motel chains were already connected to computerized reservations, and only the smaller businesses had to buy new equipment. At first the customers had balked at providing the information, but a combination of discounts on room rates and refusal to confirm guaranteed reservations by the large chains had overcome the resistance.

The first problem surfaced in the electronic mailbox of Sharif Untermeyer. Sharif was the information and analysis officer for the Bureau of Fair Accommodations. On his screen one morning was a request from Collections International for a listing of reservations at Mountain Hideout Resorts over the next two months. Sharif keyed in a set of instructions, and the screen indicated that there were two thousand or so reservations in the system. Several more instructions made the request make sense. In three of the categories used by the bureau, there was only one reservation listed. Sharif blanked his screen and typed a quick query to his supervisor.

Months before, the bureau had promulgated rules concerning the release of information from the system. Essentially, the rules stated that specific names, addresses, or other unique information identifying individuals could not be released. The rules did allow for release of analytic reports on individual businesses. There had been some grumbling about "competitive trade secrets" being jeopardized, but generally the accommodations industry had gone along with the system. What Sharif now suspected was that certain debt-collection agencies were using the system to try to locate people who had peculiar backgrounds. For example, in the reservation system for the coming month, Mountain Hideout Resorts listed only one Caucasian, Buddhist of Irish descent.

Under the much strengthened Freedom of Information Act, the electronic mail message that requested the data had automatically triggered a similar message in the Department of Justice information system. If, within ten days, Sharif did not release the information or file a statement identifying the rule that precluded its release, the Department of Justice system would alert Collections International and automatically file a petition with the federal district court for a court order requiring the release of the information.

Ben Carrado, Sharif's supervisor, muttered a mild oath in Spanish when he read the query. He had only forty-eight hours to respond to Sharif. The new Public Productivity Monitoring Program had logged the query and would deduct points from his base monthly rating if he took longer to respond. Last month, he had lost points because his monthly review of employee morale had been twelve hours late. "These damn machines have no mercy," he sighed. Quickly he phoned the legal department.

When Jeb Disque's face appeared on the visaphone, Carrado knew he had called at a bad moment. Jeb's normally composed features were twisted into a scowl. "I'll bet you called about the Collections International request," Jeb growled. Startled, Ben stammered, "Well, yes, um, I was." Jeb rubbed his face with his hands, "Those turkeys have been driving me nuts all day. I've called a teleconference with the Justice Department for tomorrow morning. Collections International's legal department faxed me a copy of the suit they intend to file if we don't comply. To top it all off, my friend from Barney, Biddle, and Brown tipped me off that they intend to file daily requests as soon as we start releasing the information."

Ben Carrado turned away from his desk and looked out the window. If we give the information to one collection agency, all the others will want it too, he thought. On the other hand, someone is sure to sue us for invasion of privacy if they get served with legal papers while on vacation. Worse yet, the only people whom the collection agencies will be able to find will be minority group members who will stick out in our reports. Information is always a two-edged sword, Ben concluded; it allows us to monitor conditions to prevent one wrong while it makes it possible for other wrongs to take place.

DISCUSSION QUESTIONS

1. What should Ben recommend that Sharif do—release the information or deny the request, and why?
2. What new rules should the agency establish to protect the identity of the people staying at the travel lodges and resorts?
3. Does the "right to privacy" mean that a person should be able to travel without anyone knowing where he or she is staying?
4. Should the government help private businesses locate people who haven't paid their debts?
5. Does the increasing amount of information collected by the government and the increasingly sophisticated technology for retrieving this information threaten basic rights of citizens?

VOLUNTEERS IN SERVICE
TO THE WORLD

Connie and Winslow Webster listened to the wind as it whistled through the trees at the edge of Lake Varese. They had come to this part of northern Italy for their anniversary. Ten years ago, they had given up positions with their respective governments and joined Volunteers International. Neither of them regretted the choice one bit. At first, they had struggled to adjust to the lack of any permanent assignment. Connie had never been outside of her native Italy before joining the VI. The constant travel and relocations had been exciting at first, then very wearing. Eventually, she had come to accept the idea that she wouldn't be staying in any one place for more than a year or two. Winslow, on the other hand, had always traveled a great deal. His skills as a labor mediator had taken him all over the world on behalf of his government.

Volunteers International (VI) was started in the 1990s by a small group of experts who had become convinced that national governments were simply too big and too cumbersome to solve the important problems of the world. Using the burgeoning telecommunications network, some forty or so people began to offer their expertise to any organization they deemed worthy—at no cost beyond operating expenses. At first, the idea seemed too romantic to be practical. Gradually, the number of members increased to the hundreds and a system of assignments began to emerge.

The system worked well, even twenty years after its beginnings. Organizations posted a concise description of the problem they needed help with on an electronic bulletin board, along with a description of their goals and purposes; members of Volunteers International were free to indicate their willingness to help through the same bulletin board. What made the system unique was that an artificial intelligence program monitored the bulletin board and indicated to all parties when enough people with the appropriate skills had indicated an interest. Through the same system, a conference session to discuss the project was arranged between the organization representatives and the members of VI. If agreement was reached, a project team was put together to work on the problem.

About half the time, the teams needed to travel to the site of the project to investigate or to deliver specific services. VI provided transportation as part of the agreement. The organization being helped was responsible for food, lodging, and incidental expenses. What had amazed everyone initially was the number of times the solution—or at least a good start on a solution—could be accomplished simply by combining the right kind of expertise. The ability to work interactively through the telecommunications network without the need to travel to face-to-face meetings helped immensely.

Connie's specialty was biotechnology. At first, she worried that not having regular access to a modern laboratory would mean that her skills would deteriorate quite rapidly. She soon discovered that many of the most modern labs were only too happy to have her volunteer to work on a problem for a fraction of what it would have cost to recruit a permanent employee. Winslow had never doubted that his services would be in demand. The negotiation of labor contracts and the resolution of labor disputes required two ingredients: an ability to fashion compromises and a reputation for fairness. Winslow was a welcome member of many of the teams put together by Volunteers International.

By the turn of the century, Volunteers International had more than a thousand members and several hundred projects under way at any given time. Gradually, members began to give up their regular jobs to devote themselves to full-time volunteer work. Major corporations, foundations, and eventually governments began to fund the organization on a regular basis. There was some grumbling about a "brain drain" when recent graduates from the major technical universities chose to work with Volunteers International immediately after graduation. One international organization charged that Volunteers International was actually a front for one of the former superpowers, but because no one was forced to join, the charge drew more laughter than credence.

The only serious crisis for Volunteers International had come when several governments had tried to impose taxes on the services rendered. For a year or two, the membership declined sharply as people simply stopped participating. Because the tax revenues collected were far smaller than the costs of determining who owed what, most of the governments dropped their attempts. One reason may have been the publication of a study done by a Volunteers International group, indicating that the primary beneficiaries of the "at-cost services" had been units of government all over the world.

Connie and Winslow had often remarked that the most obvious difference between their old jobs and their work with Volunteers International was the absence of the traditional "organization overburden." Without layers of superiors to report to, the team members spent very little time writing progress reports. Because the sponsoring organization provided the funding, team members had only a minimal number of financial forms and expense vouchers to complete. They both agreed that the lack of the semimandatory social events that used to consume a fair amount of their leisure time was not missed at all. Most of all, they didn't miss the office politics, with egos rubbing against other egos over who got the biggest office or the nicest view.

Once they had adjusted to the constant uncertainty of changing locations and not knowing what they would be doing several years from the present, they were content to enjoy their freedom. Volunteers International was not the answer to all of the problems of the world, but it was one answer to many of the barriers that had prevented people with problems from getting in touch with people with answers.

As they turned away from the lake and began to walk down the path toward the hotel, Connie wondered what the next ten years would bring. She still wanted to start a family and maybe settle down in one place to raise her children, but there were still lots of problems to be solved. Maybe the example of Volunteers International had finally awakened the world in general to the twilight of hierarchy and the dawning of the age of voluntary commitment rather than organizational loyalty.

DISCUSSION QUESTIONS

1. What problems beyond those discussed in the case do you see for this type of organization?
2. Do you think people are basically happier if they volunteer to help, or do they really need to be told what to do?
3. Do you see a trend away from large organizations to smaller, more flexible groups, or do you think that the problems of the future will require even bigger organizations?

CREDITS

Pages 4–13: D. H. Rosenbloom, "Public Administrative Theory and the Separation of Powers," *Public Administration Review,* May–June, 1983, pp. 219–227. © by the American Society for Public Administration (ASPA), 1120 G. Street NW, Suite 500, Washington DC 20005. All rights reserved. Reprinted with permission.

Pages 13–23: D. F. Kettl, "The Perils and Prospects of Public Administration," *Public Administration Review,* July–August, 1990, pp. 411–419. © by the American Society for Public Administration (ASPA), 1120 G Street NW, Suite 500, Washington DC 20005. All rights reserved. Reprinted with permission.

Pages 24–35: R. B. Denhardt, "Five Great Issues in Organization Theory," in *The Handbook of Public Administration,* Jack Rabin et al. (Eds.). Copyright © 1990. Reprinted by courtesy of Marcel Dekker, Inc.

Pages 36–39: T. Arrandale, "Time Is Running Out For One of the Last of the Great Water Buffalos," *Governing,* June, 1989, pp. 46–50. Reprinted by permission of Congressional Quarterly, Inc.

Pages 49–57: M. M. Harmon, "Administrative Policy Formation and the Public Interest," *Public Administration Review,* September–October, 1969, pp. 483–491. © by the American Society for Public Administration (ASPA), 1120 G Street NW, Suite 500, Washington DC 20005. All rights reserved. Reprinted with permission.

Pages 58–67: J. F. Springer, "Policy Analysis and Organizational Decisions," *Administration and Society,* February, 1985, pp. 475–508. Copyright 1985 by Sage Publications, Inc. Reprinted by permission.

Pages 68–75: P. W. Ingraham, "Policy Implementation and the Public Service," in *The Revitalization of the Public Service,* R. Denhardt and E. Jennings (Eds.) University of Missouri, 1987, pp. 145–155. Reprinted with permission.

Pages 76–83: L. M. Salamon, "Rise of Third-Party Government," *The Bureaucrat,* Summer, 1987, pp. 27–31; Fall, 1987, pp. 25–27. Reprinted with permission.

Pages 84–85: N. M. Davis, "Anthony R. Kane: Behind National Transportation Policy," *Government Executive,* March, 1990, p. 54. Reprinted with permission.

Pages 97–104: R. C. Moe, "Traditional Organizational Principles and the Managerial Presidency: From Phoenix to Ashes," *Public Administration Review,* March–April, 1990, pp. 129–140. © by the American Society for Public Administration (ASPA), 1120 G Street NW, Suite 500, Washington DC 20005. All rights reserved. Reprinted with permission.

Pages 105–112: F. M. Kaiser, "Congressional Oversight of the Presidency," *Annals of the American Academy of Political and Social Sciences,* September, 1988, pp. 75–89. Copyright 1988 by Sage Publications, Inc. Reprinted by permission.

Pages 113–125: P. J. Cooper, "Conflict or Constructive Tension: The Changing Relationship of Judges and Administrators," *Public Administration Review,* November, 1985, pp. 643–652. © by the American Society for Public Administration (ASPA), 1120 G Street NW, Suite 500, Washington DC 20005. All rights reserved. Reprinted with permission.

Pages 126–135: D. S. Wright, "Federalism, Intergovernmental Relations, Intergovernmental Management: Historical Reflections and Conceptual Comparisons," *Public Administration Review,* March–April, 1990, pp. 168–178. © by the American Society for Public Administration (ASPA), 1120 G Street NW, Suite 500, Washington DC 20005. All rights reserved. Reprinted with permission.

Pages 136–139: H. G. Rainey and H. B. Milward, "Public Organizations: Policy Networks and Environments," in R. H. Hall and R. E. Quinn (Eds.) *Organization Theory and Public Policy,* 1983, pp. 133–146. Copyright 1983 by Sage Publications, Inc. Reprinted by permission.

Pages 140–143: A. Ehrenhalt, "The New City Manager: 1) Invisible, 2) Anonymous, 3) Non-Political, 4) None of the Above," *Governing,* September, 1990, pp. 41–46. Reprinted by permission of Congressional Quarterly, Inc.

Pages 156–162: D. W. Stewart, "Professionalism vs. Democracy: Freidrich vs. Finer Revisited," *Public Administration Quarterly,* Spring, 1985, pp. 13–25. Reprinted with permission.

Pages 163–173: J. C. Thomas, "Citizen Involvement in Public Management," *The Revitalization of the Public Service,* R. Denhardt and E. Jennings (Eds.), University of Missouri, 1987, pp. 39–53.

Pages 174–182: H. G. Fredrickson, "Public Administration and Social Equity," *Public Administration Review,* March–April, 1990, pp. 228–237. © by the American Society for Public Administration (ASPA), 1120 G Street NW, Suite 500, Washington DC 20005. All rights reserved. Reprinted with permission.

Pages 183–189: J. S. Bowman, "Administrative Dissent: Whistle-Blowing," in *Handbook of Organization Management,* William B. Eddy (Ed.) New York: Marcel Dekker, Inc., 1983, pp. 89–102. Copyright © 1983. Reprinted by courtesy of Marcel Dekker, Inc.

TO THE OWNER OF THIS BOOK:

We hope that you have found *Public Administration in Action*, by Robert B. Denhardt and Barry R. Hammond, useful. So that this book can be improved in a future edition, would you take the time to complete this sheet and return it? Thank you.

Instructor's name: _____

Department: _____

School and address: _____

_____

1. The name of the course in which I used this book is: _____

_____

2. My general reaction to this book is: _____

_____

_____

3. What I like most about this book is: _____

_____

_____

4. What I like least about this book is: _____

_____

_____

5. Were all of the chapters of the book assigned for you to read?   Yes   No

    If not, which ones weren't? _____

6. Do you plan to keep this book after you finish the course?   Yes   No

    Why or why not? _____

_____

7. On a separate sheet of paper, please write specific suggestions for improving this book and anything else you'd care to share about your experience in using the book.

Optional:

Your name: _____ Date: _____

May Brooks/Cole quote you, either in promotion for *Public Administration in Action* or in future publishing ventures?

Yes: _____ No: _____

Sincerely,

Robert B. Denhardt
Barry R. Hammond

FOLD HERE

FOLD HERE